Conceptual and Theoretical Approaches to Corporate Social Responsibility, Entrepreneurial Orientation, and Financial Performance

Inna Sousa Paiva
Business Research Unit, Instituto Universitário de Lisboa, Portugal

Luísa Cagica Carvalho
Polytechnic Institute of Setubal, Portugal & CEFAGE, University of Évora, Portugal

IGI Global
DISSEMINATOR OF KNOWLEDGE

A volume in the Advances in Business Strategy and Competitive Advantage (ABSCA) Book Series

Published in the United States of America by
IGI Global
Business Science Reference (an imprint of IGI Global)
701 E. Chocolate Avenue
Hershey PA, USA 17033
Tel: 717-533-8845
Fax: 717-533-8661
E-mail: cust@igi-global.com
Web site: http://www.igi-global.com

Library of Congress Cataloging-in-Publication Data

Names: Paiva, Inna Sousa, editor. | Carvalho, Luísa Cagica, 1970- editor.
Title: Conceptual and theoretical approaches to corporate social responsibility, entrepreneurial orientation, and financial performance / Inna Sousa Paiva, Luísa Cagica Carvalho, editors.
Description: Hershey, PA : Business Science Reference, [2020] | Includes bibliographical references and index. | Summary: “”This book explores new trends in corporate social responsibility, entrepreneurial orientation, and financial performance”--Provided by publisher”--Provided by publisher.
Identifiers: LCCN 2019036938 (print) | LCCN 2019036939 (ebook) | ISBN 9781799821281 (hardcover) | ISBN 9781799821298 (paperback) | ISBN 9781799821304 (ebook)
Subjects: LCSH: Social responsibility of business.
Classification: LCC HD60 .C6225 2020 (print) | LCC HD60 (ebook) | DDC 658.4/08--dc23
LC record available at https://lccn.loc.gov/2019036938
LC ebook record available at https://lccn.loc.gov/2019036939

This book is published in the IGI Global book series Advances in Business Strategy and Competitive Advantage (ABSCA) (ISSN: 2327-3429; eISSN: 2327-3437)

British Cataloguing in Publication Data
A Cataloguing in Publication record for this book is available from the British Library.

All work contributed to this book is new, previously-unpublished material. The views expressed in this book are those of the authors, but not necessarily of the publisher.

For electronic access to this publication, please contact: eresources@igi-global.com.

Advances in Business Strategy and Competitive Advantage (ABSCA) Book Series

Patricia Ordóñez de Pablos
Universidad de Oviedo, Spain

ISSN:2327-3429
EISSN:2327-3437

MISSION

Business entities are constantly seeking new ways through which to gain advantage over their competitors and strengthen their position within the business environment. With competition at an all-time high due to technological advancements allowing for competition on a global scale, firms continue to seek new ways through which to improve and strengthen their business processes, procedures, and profitability.

The **Advances in Business Strategy and Competitive Advantage (ABSCA) Book Series** is a timely series responding to the high demand for state-of-the-art research on how business strategies are created, implemented and re-designed to meet the demands of globalized competitive markets. With a focus on local and global challenges, business opportunities and the needs of society, the **ABSCA** encourages scientific discourse on doing business and managing information technologies for the creation of sustainable competitive advantage.

COVERAGE

- Globalization
- Ethics and Business Strategy
- Small and Medium Enterprises
- Strategic Management
- Balanced Scorecard
- Adaptive Enterprise
- Value Chain
- Business Models
- Innovation Strategy
- Competitive Strategy

IGI Global is currently accepting manuscripts for publication within this series. To submit a proposal for a volume in this series, please contact our Acquisition Editors at Acquisitions@igi-global.com or visit: http://www.igi-global.com/publish/.

The Advances in Business Strategy and Competitive Advantage (ABSCA) Book Series (ISSN 2327-3429) is published by IGI Global, 701 E. Chocolate Avenue, Hershey, PA 17033-1240, USA, www.igi-global.com. This series is composed of titles available for purchase individually; each title is edited to be contextually exclusive from any other title within the series. For pricing and ordering information please visit http://www.igi-global.com/book-series/advances-business-strategy-competitive-advantage/73672. Postmaster: Send all address changes to above address.

Titles in this Series

For a list of additional titles in this series, please visit: www.igi-global.com/book-series

Implementing Knowledge in Organizations for Improved Performance Outcomes Emerging Research and Opportunities
Michael J. Gravier (Bryant University, USA) and Ted Farris (University of North Texas, USA)
Business Science Reference • © 2020 • 260pp • H/C (ISBN: 9781799824879) • US $195.00

CSR and Socially Responsible Investing Strategies in Transitioning and Emerging Economies
Anetta Kuna-Marszałek (University of Łódź, Poland) and Agnieszka Kłysik-Uryszek (University of Łódź, Poland)
Business Science Reference • © 2020 • 346pp • H/C (ISBN: 9781799821939) • US $235.00

Handbook of Research on the Strategic Management of Family Businesses
Jesús Manuel Palma-Ruiz (Universidad Autónoma de Chihuahua, Mexico) Ismael Barros-Contreras (Universidad Austral de Chile, Chile) and Luca Gnan (Università degli Studi di Roma "Tor Vergata", Italy)
Business Science Reference • © 2020 • 350pp • H/C (ISBN: 9781799822691) • US $275.00

Utilizing Gamification in Servicescapes for Improved Consumer Engagement
Miralem Helmefalk (Linnaeus University, Sweden) and Leif Marcusson (Linnaeus University, Sweden)
Business Science Reference • © 2020 • 300pp • H/C (ISBN: 9781799819707) • US $225.00

Cases on Strategic Management Issues in Contemporary Organizations
Mona Rashidirad (University of Brighton, UK)
Business Science Reference • © 2020 • 300pp • H/C (ISBN: 9781799816300) • US $195.00

Competitive Drivers for Improving Future Business Performance
Carlos Martins (Lusiada University - North, Portugal) and Paula Rodrigues (Lusiada University - North, Portugal)
Business Science Reference • © 2020 • 360pp • H/C (ISBN: 9781799818434) • US $225.00

Handbook of Research on Approaches to Alternative Entrepreneurship Opportunities
José Guilherme Leitão Dantas (CARME, School of Technology and Management, Polytechnic of Leiria, Portugal) and Luísa Cagica Carvalho (Institute Polytechnic of Setúbal, Portugal & CEFAGE, University of Évora, Portugal)
Business Science Reference • © 2020 • 450pp • H/C (ISBN: 9781799819813) • US $295.00

Challenges and Opportunities of Corporate Governance Transformation in the Digital Era
Mikhail Yevgenievich Kuznetsov (Moscow State University, Russia) and Maria Igorevna Nikishova (Financial University Under the Government of the Russian Federation, Russia)
Business Science Reference • © 2020 • 230pp • H/C (ISBN: 9781799820116) • US $235.00

IGI Global
DISSEMINATOR OF KNOWLEDGE

701 East Chocolate Avenue, Hershey, PA 17033, USA
Tel: 717-533-8845 x100 • Fax: 717-533-8661
E-Mail: cust@igi-global.com • www.igi-global.com

Editorial Advisory Board

Table of Contents

Detailed Table of Contents

Corporate social responsibility is conceptualized as a voluntary activity of organizations, which evidence the inclusion of environmental and social objectives in the interactions with stakeholders, as well as in their operational activities. Thus, the general objective was to analyze the characteristics of the publications related to the topic corporate social responsibility in the last three decades, in the Web of Science and in Scopus databases. There was an increase in the number of articles published per year with the "boom" in the years 2013 to 2018, in both databases. The authors at the Copenhagen Business School (79; 129) and York University (92; 104) were where the most scientific articles published on the subject on both databases. Regarding the main research areas in publications on corporate social responsibility, there seems to be a convergence in the main research areas of most published articles.

This chapter analyzes research in social responsibility (SR) reporting in higher education institutions (HEI), addressing different aspects: a longitudinal assessment, the theoretical approaches, the adopted methodologies, and its main results. A systematic literature review is undertaken. To do so, the ISI Web of Knowledge and Scopus databases were used to retrieve the articles for analysis. The articles were limited to business and management research area. Findings show that literature on SR reporting in HEIs is still in its infancy and it is very heterogeneous, with only 24 articles addressing this theme. Most articles resorted to qualitative methodologies, emphasizing the case study. Findings also show a lack of normalization regarding reporting. Stakeholders' theory and the seek for legitimacy are crucial in SR disclosing in HEIs. Several contributions emerge, namely the provision of a comprehensive review of the current state of research on SR reporting in HEIs and, consequently, a call for increasing the awareness of such organizations towards the importance of this theme.

Cause-related marketing (CRM) is currently considered one of the main initiatives of corporate social responsibility (CSR). CRM programs offer numerous advantages for all the parties involved: companies,

they perform, and in the future these studies will serve to reflect the deficiencies observed in order to improve the information offered.

This article gives an overview of corporate governance in Mozambique. The mandatory disclosure of sustainability information leads to an increase in the social responsibility of managers. In this sense, the measure can possibly improve the ethical behaviour of the companies, while at the same time allowing for the reduction of the levels of corruption. The reputation in the business world creates a good image and can be transmitted in a reduction of risks to shareholders, and attraction of investments. This work contributes to the literature, and a greater understanding of sustainability in developing countries, particularly in Mozambique.

Two divergent theories emerge from the literature on CEO duality. The agency theory advocates that a dual CEO negatively affects corporate performance, because it compromises the monitoring and control of the CEO, whilst the stewardship theory suggests the contrary effect due to the unity of command it presents. For a sample of 26 non-financial listed Portuguese firms from 2002 to 2016, this study draws on agency and stewardship theories to evaluate the relationship between CEO duality and firm performance, proxied by Tobin's Q. Using ordinary least square (OLS) and two stage least squares (2SLS) techniques to control potential problems simultaneity between CEO duality and firm performance, the author finds a negative relationship between CEO duality and Tobin's Q. This suggests that investors perceive no value in having a concentration of power with a dual leadership structure. Therefore, this study recommends that the positions of chairman and CEO should be separated for listed Portuguese firms.

The world´s population is growing, day by day, and the latest trends in pertinent magazines show people preferring cities more and more than the countryside. This brings us to take a closer look on the effects brought with this urban sprawl. Cities grow in a dimension; city planners have to excogitate more and more innovative city concepts and solutions in order to cope with this increase of population and with maintain the cities infrastructure and systems. This has led to the term, Smart City, which was coined to reflect or at least promote innovative and smart solutions not only for today but for coming generations. This chapter reflects on a case study of an Asian city that developed a plan to become a smart city. This research focused essentially on the sustainable perspective of a smart city and present some results and best practices that could be implemented by other cities that aim to become smart.

Based on the behavioral aspect of the governance theory, this chapter explores the effect of the firm performance and corporate governance (CG) on corporate social responsibility (CSR) engagement by investigating their causal effects. Using annual reports of a large and extensive sample of French firms for the year 2014-2016, we find that firm performance significantly improves that firm's social responsibility, but it has a significant and negative impact when we consider corporate government as a contingency factor. The results show that the existence of institutional administrator is in favor of CSR while it is the inverse effect when we consider the other independent administrators. However, we fail to find any significant impact of administrator's expertise. Our results suggest that pressures exerted by outsiders and corporate governance mechanisms influence CSR practices. Overall, our study implies that corporate governance attributes play a vital role in ensuring organizational legitimacy through CSR. The study findings should be of interest to regulators and policy makers.

Research has been conducted to extend our understanding of CSR by revealing CG mechanism antecedent effects on firm social engagements. In spite of this, few studies aimed to understand the impact of the performance of those mechanisms on CSR. To our knowledge, our study is the first to measure CG performance and its role in the expansion of CSR in an emerging country. We also analyze some component of firm performance that could potentially affect a firm's social commitment. Using a data survey questionnaire consisting of 37 items assessing CSR engagement measured by a self- constructed index and firm level data of 76 listed Moroccan firms, empirical results underline the impact of corporate governance performance and firm's performance on CSR. These results suggest that governance mechanism performance and firm performance are principal drivers of CSR particularly for big business. Debts have shown a reducing effect. Thus, our study of CSR commitment index allows for a clearer and more robust assessment of CG on Moroccan firm CSR activities.

Preface

Over the past few years, we have witnessed the enormous success of corporate social responsibility in businesses all over the world. In particular, we have seen an international scenario in which governments foster both growth through entrepreneurship and achievement of sustainable development, by creating tools such as UN Global Compact for worldwide impact in order to reconcile business interests with the demands of communities. The impact of corporate social responsibility at national and international level has been unequivocal in the creation of jobs and wealth, and new solutions for development have been enabled.

While not ignoring these important developments in corporate social responsibility, our main goal is to fully unleash the broad potential of corporate social responsibility, entrepreneurship, and firm's performance activity, exploring and highlighting new trends in this area. There is currently an extensive literature addressing the main topics on corporate social responsibility; however, the extant research has a focus which is too limited compared to the wide diversity of corporate social responsibility in business.

Corporate social responsibility and entrepreneurship is a new sub-area of entrepreneurship profiled as one of the concepts that, in conjunction with business strategy, can redirect organizational performance research in new directions. In addition, with the same goal of improving performance, some authors point out the suitability of adopting this type of multiple strategic orientation. This book focuses on new trends of corporate social responsibility from the entrepreneurial point of view and on firm performance. Specifically, in this area, we are called to change our approach towards a long-term growth, replacing the short-term vision which had come to be adopted in recent times.

Moreover, by focusing on a particular kind of corporate social responsibility and entrepreneurship, whatever its relevance, instead of contributing to the scientific progress of this field we will be preventing researchers from observe the multifaceted issue and, therefore, from developing theory which offers insight and value. The aim of this book is to make a significant contribution by presenting work with new knowledge in the field of corporate social responsibility and entrepreneurship.

With this publication, therefore, the editors intend to expand the concept of corporate social responsibility, entrepreneurial orientation and financial performance research in order to exploit conceptual and theoretical approaches as a relevant and current subject for our collective development.

The book consists of twenty chapters which the editors decided to organize in two sections: Section 1: Conceptual and Theoretical Perspectives and Section 2: Applied Perspectives: The Context of Countries, Regions and Cities. It may be said that the boundaries between these sections are somewhat obscure as the chapters are more or less related. It is believed, however, that this structure will make consulting the book more effective as the first section focuses primarily on activities upstream of the theoretical perspectives of corporate social responsibility, while the second section deals with the practical application of corporate social responsibility in the context of different countries, regions and cities.

Section 1 incorporates six chapters which are more concerned with the conceptual and theoretical developments of corporate social responsibility. In the first chapter, "Corporate Social Responsibility and Financial Information: Theoretical Approaches and Recent Developments," Irina Gavancha and Inna Paiva start by referring to the evolution of the concept of corporate social responsibility, highlighting the theories associated with financial information, namely signaling theory, capital need theory, agency theory, and legitimacy theory. In this context, the authors argue that corporate social responsibility and the disclosure of financial information is important not only because the theory of information asymmetry is one of the most important modern developments in accounting, economics, finance, management, and other business studies, but also because the association between corporate social responsibility and the disclosure of financial information could have broad implications for financial markets.

In the next chapter, entitled "Corporate Social Responsibility: Benefits and Costs of its Implementation," Dolores Vazquez, Luis Valdez Juárez and Juan Sánchez Domínguez present corporate social responsibility as a current important strategy in organizations and then focus their chapter on economic, social and environmental concerns under the perspective of the triple bottom line. In this context, they discuss a set of the numerous benefits derived from the implementation of socially responsible actions in companies.

In the third chapter, "Corporate Social Responsibility the Comparation Scientific Production in Web of Science and in Scopus: The last three decades," Luciana Rosa, Maria Martins-Rodrigues, Tais Godoy, Waleska Campos, Clandia Gomes, and Larissa Barbieri start the chapter by presenting the broad definitions and approaches regarding the historical roots of corporate social responsibility. Then, the authors make an extensive literature review, focusing on bibliometric research into characteristics of national and international scientific production related to the theme of corporate social responsibility, obtaining 12330 publications in the Web of Science and 14262 publications in Scopus, related to themes, found mainly in the following areas: business, management and accounting, social sciences, economics, econometrics and finance, and environmental science.

The following chapter entitled "Social Responsibility Reporting in Higher Education Institutions - The Systematic Literature Review," by José Vale, Rui Bertuzi, and Albertina Monteiro, is dedicated to a systematic literature review in the education sector, addressing two different aspects: longitudinal assessment and theoretical approaches. This study provides a descriptive summing-up of how literature on social responsibility in higher education institutions evolved over time: what are the main theoretical approaches adopted, the main methodologies used and the results from all the articles that passed into the final sample. It provides a comprehensive review of the current state of research in social responsibility reporting in higher education institutions. Also, this chapter gives methodological details of how a literature review on this theme should be conducted and contributes to an increased awareness in higher education institutions towards the importance of this theme.

The fifth chapter is entitled "Anything Goes in Cause-Related Marketing? The Case of the 'Solidarity' Traffic Radar," in which M. Mercedes Ladero and Clementina Galley Casquet introduce cause-related marketing as one of the main initiatives of corporate social responsibility. Their chapter reveals that although most cause-related marketing campaigns succeeded, several of them were involved in scandals, such as, the controversy caused by cause-related marketing campaigns which resurfaced with the installation of the so-called 'solidarity traffic radar'. In spite of this, the research indicates that analysis of controversial campaigns can help organizations to be more aware of the opportunities and threats that cause-related marketing can offer in "difficult" situations.

Section 1 closes with the chapter "Corporate Social Responsibility and Disclosure of Socio-environmental Risks by Credit Unions," by Rodrigo Almeida, Marguit Neumann, Simone Leticia Sanches, and Valéria Bressan. It connects corporate social responsibility and socio-environmental risk, themes that have gained importance in the realm of Brazilian credit unions. Their research focuses on the groups of stakeholders included in Sicredi's socio-environmental risk disclosure, which were: members, employees, government, communities, and the media. As theoretical contributions, this study provides discussions around corporate social responsibility and socio-environmental risk in credit unions and aids the literature on mechanisms to identify socio-environmental risks such as the use of checklists, a portfolio risk map, and georeferencing.

Section 2 incorporates nine chapters which are more concerned with the applied perspectives of corporate social responsibility. It includes chapters on the context of individual countries, such as Portugal, Spain, Mozambique, France, and Morocco, as well as chapters with a multinational perspective. Thus, the seventh chapter "Linking Corporate Social Responsibility reporting with the UN Sustainable Development Goals: Evidence from the Portuguese stock market," by Sónia Monteiro, Verónica Ribeiro, and Kátia Lemos, focuses on the question of how listed companies' sustainability reporting includes their contributions towards the sustainable development goals on the 2030 United Nations Agenda. In fact, an increasing number of organizations are aligning their corporate purpose with the execution of sustainable strategies and sustainable development goals. The authors provide initial evidence of reporting on sustainable development goals in the Portuguese stock market context and demonstrate that, from a sample of 46 listed companies, none published integrated reports and only 12 published sustainability reports or non-financial statements. To conclude, the chapter highlights that the major challenges placed on organizations and professionals involve identifying priority sustainable development goals for their activities and stakeholders, incorporating them into their strategy, setting goals for their success and measuring and reporting on their progress.

The subsequent chapter, "Integrated Reports and Board's Diversity: An international perspective," by Ana Isabel Lopes and Maria João Braz, explores the influence of the diversity characteristics some boards - board size, board independence, gender diversity, role duality and board experience - on the recognition of leading practices of integrated reports, distinguishing between reference reports and regular reports and based on a sample of international reports. The authors conclude that larger boards have a higher likelihood of producing an integrated report that is highlighted as a reference and is thus of higher quality. This is a contribution to the literature on integrated reporting, a new concept that has been growing over the years, demanding new studies to be added to the existing literature.

In turn, the ninth chapter, "Corporate Social Responsibility Reporting and climate change: Carbon emissions disclosures by Portuguese companies," undertaken by Ana Florindo, Kátia Lemos, Sónia Monteiro, and Verónica Ribeiro, focuses on the study of that extent of disclosures of carbon emissions in Portuguese companies which operate in environmentally sensitive industries and explores the factors that explain this extent. The chapter concludes that social pressure, pressure from shareholders and market pressure influence the disclosure of CO2 emission permits in Portuguese companies.

Following this is the chapter entitled "Which Local Governments Provide Suitable Promotion of Entrepreneurship?," in which Teresa Nevado-Gil, Maria Pache-Durán, Inna Paiva and Luisa Carvalho use the content analysis technique to analyze the information that the city councils of the capitals of Spanish provinces offer to entrepreneurs through their institutional pages. The results of this chapter should help municipalities reflect on the important work they perform and, in the future, these studies will serve to reflect the deficiencies observed in order to improve information offered and performance.

In the eleventh chapter, "An Exploratory Study on Corporate Governance and Integrated Reporting in the Mozambican context: What Mozambique have been done in Corporate Governance," Angelica Violeta Chiau addresses issues in corporate governance and integrated undeveloping setting. It is a study that draws attention to the fact that, despite the good examples of the adoption of integrated reports, as noted in South Africa and Brazil, these reports are not yet mandatory in Mozambique. The study concludes that reputation in the business world creates a good image and can be transmitted as a reduction of risks to shareholders, and as an attraction for investment.

In the next chapter, entitled "CEO Duality and Firm Performance," Sandra Alves focus on CEO duality and the impact on business performance in Portuguese listed companies, based on two theories: agency theory advocates that a dual CEO negatively affects corporate performance, and stewardship theory suggests a contrary effect due to the unity of command it presents. The author concludes that investors perceive no value in having a concentration of power with a dual leadership structure. These results also suggest that firms which changed their leadership structure from duality to non-duality show an improvement in performance after the change.

Jannis Elm and Luisa Carvalho are the authors of the 13th chapter, "Best Practices to Become a Sustainable Smart City: The case of Singapore". The authors reflect broadly on a case study of the Asian city that developed a plan to become a smart city. This research focused essentially on the sustainable perspective of a smart city and presents some results and best practices that could be implemented by other cities whose aim is to become smarter. Throughout the chapter, the authors discuss the factors of a smart cities which try hard to be totally sustainable.

The subsequent chapter, "The Impact of Firm Performance and Corporate Governance on Corporate Social Responsibility: Evidence from France," by Souhaila Kammoun, Sahar Loukil, and Youssra Loukil, explores the main determinants of corporate social responsibility strategy among corporate governance mechanisms and firm performance. To conclude, the chapter highlights that firm performance emerged as a vital determinant of corporate social responsibility.

The publication ends with the fifteenth chapter, "The relationship between CSR, Corporate Governance and Firm Performance: Evidence from Moroccan listed firms" in which Souhaila Kammoun, Sahar Loukil, Youssra Loukil, and Abdelmajid Ibenrissoul also deal with the advances in knowledge about implementing corporate social responsibility practices in Morocco, examining whether governance mechanisms and firm performance underlie corporate social responsibility performance. Throughout the chapter, the authors provide theoretical and practical guidelines for researchers and decision makers to help them determine what strategies are necessary to fulfil social commitments and improve social welfare.

In short, the book starts by covering a set of activities upstream of corporate social responsibility, and then addresses a significant, though not exhaustive, set of different types of entrepreneurial orientation and financial performance, often paving the way for more in-depth investigations which will allow us to continue expanding this as a relevant theme for our collective future.

To conclude, we would like to thank the authors whose collaboration has made this project possible and express our hope that readers will find this publication inspiring and useful.

Inna Sousa Paiva
Business Research Unit, Instituto Universitário de Lisboa, Portugal

Preface

Luísa Cagica Carvalho
Polytechnic Institute of Setubal, Portugal & CEFAGE, University of Évora, Portugal

Section 1

Conceptual and Theoretical Perspectives

Chapter 1
Corporate Social Responsibility and Financial Information:
Theoretical Approaches and Recent Developments

Irina Filipa Gavancha
Instituto Universitário de Lisboa, Portugal

Inna Sousa Paiva
https://orcid.org/0000-0002-9980-7503
Business Research Unit, Instituto Universitário de Lisboa, Portugal

ABSTRACT

The importance of corporate social responsibility (CSR) has been increasing especially in the last decade, due to the positive pressure exerted by society in general. This chapter analyses the relevance of CSR, associated theories and studies carried out in the last decade related to financial information and consequently accounting quality. The strong link between CSR and financial information that is directed towards knowledge of mitigation of asymmetry information is evident. We aim to contribute to the development of sustainability accounting, presenting assumptions that mitigate the blocks of practice of CRS acts that make the return of positive elements possible, namely the image of entities and their financial economic improvement.

INTRODUCTION

Social and environmental concerns have been increasing in recent years and have a significant impact on the daily lives of companies that have been adapting to the demands made by society, forcing the various players to adapt efficiently. For this reason, the rise of these concerns leads to a new stage of business which arouses our interest in analysing the non-financial information disclosure that underlies corporate social responsibility (CSR) practices and the disclosure of financial information.

DOI: 10.4018/978-1-7998-2128-1.ch001

As the business world is encouraged to work actively towards CSR in addition to providing a business opportunity in today's world, it frequently reflects the expectations of firms' customers, human resources, society and stakeholders (Mark-Herbert & Von Schantz, 2007). Previous studies on the relationship between accounting and sustainability argue that the concept of sustainability and the associated use of accounting have been deliberately simplified and oriented towards supporting the business interests of firms. Firms only adopt a sustainability approach if it can generate economic returns. In this regard, Milne, Tregidga, and Walton (2009) claim that sustainability issues are managed exclusively for the purposes of maintaining control over natural resources and technologies and boosting economic efficiency. Schaltegger, Bennett, and Burrit (2006) emphasize that the basis of financial reporting is the accounting information which transmits an organization's financial performance to its stockholders. Later it became necessary to make new changes that would allow a different accounting approach, that of management, and later, in a strategic way, the use of the term sustainability report, which began to have an impact on issues such as the ecology, economy and social issues.

As a consequence, this study becomes extremely important in improving a continuous understanding of theories associated with CSR because it is a relevant and recent topic for accounting researchers (Martin & Moser, 2012). It raises accounting issues that have not yet been fully investigated, such as the importance of asymmetry information and the forms of disclosure of mandatory and voluntary information which should be taken into account, in which we can frame CSR. It is further noted that there are various definitions of CSR and many studies suggest that it generally refers to serving people, communities and the environment in ways that go above and beyond what is legally required of a firm (Ioannou & Serafeim, 2014). Overall, CSR is an extension of a firm's efforts to foster sustainability by sound business practices (Cui, Jo, & Na, 2018).

Furthermore, the theoretical reflection of CSR and the disclosure of financial information is important not only because the theory of information asymmetry is one of the most important modern developments in accounting, economics, finance, management and other business studies, but also because the association between CSR and the disclosure of financial information could have broad implications for financial markets.

For this purpose, we will address the theories associated with CSR practices as well as some studies conducted in the area since 2010 related to financial information and consequently accounting quality. This new but not recent relationship between accounting and sustainability due to the growth of communication has generated rapid growth in the area, and these reports for the transmission of information related to management and accounting methods had a new foundation: sustainability (Schaltegger, Bennett, & Burrit, 2006).

According to Schaltegger and Wagner (2006), the performance of sustainability can also be analysed from two perspectives, the first related to an inside-out strategy since the strategy is the accounting-driver for sustainability reporting and the second from an outsider-in perspective, through reporting-driven sustainability accounting. This provides for future investigations to analyse the correlation between the impact of asymmetry information, CSR practices and financial information provided through accounting.

This chapter is structured as follows: after the introduction, section 2 offers the theoretical background of corporate social responsibility, its concept, approaches and requirements. Section 3 reviews the literature on disclosure of financial information and the most used theories in these fields. The final section presents a discussion of our findings and summarizes our conclusions.

CORPORATE SOCIAL RESPONSIBILITY

Concept and Approaches

Corporate social responsibility is a concept which has become prevalent in business reporting. Most corporations have a policy concerning corporate social responsibility and produce a report detailing these activities. The term that is often used to report good practices by corporate entities is corporate social responsibility. There are several definitions underlying this theme which is used as the driver of the transmission of information between a corporate entity and its stakeholders. The broad definition of corporate social responsibility is concerned with global corporations, governments and the local society in which it resides or operates.

Davis (1973, p. 312) defines CSR as the firm's considerations of, and response to, issues beyond the narrowly economic, technical, and legal requirements of the firm to accomplish social benefits along with the traditional economic gains which the firm seeks. The International Organization for Standardization (2010) established CSR as the purpose of companies to incorporate socially responsible behaviours into their decisions. The European Commission (2011) defines CSR as a concept whereby companies integrate social and environmental concerns into their business operations and their interaction with their stakeholders on a voluntary basis.

Corporate sustainability is a common term used in association with CSR. The activities of corporate sustainability are very similar to those of CSR but somewhat broader in scope. Corporate sustainability focuses on long-term shareholder value by incorporating best practices in the following areas: ethics, governance, transparency, business relationships, financial return, product value, employment practice and environmental protection (Epstein, 2008). The relationship between organizations and the practice of socially responsible acts should not be dissociated, since CSR is concerned with the internal and external stakeholders of the organization being treated ethically and in a socially responsible way, allowing stakeholders' human development (Hopkins, 2003).

Empirical studies establish that CSR is not a recent issue but dates back to the 1950s, when Howard Bowen explained why companies tend to show an interest in becoming socially and environmentally responsible. It gained more explicit exposure in the 20th century, when environmental concerns intensified and consumers became eager to be aware of the practices adopted by companies; it was from this point on that the consumer became an individual with demands regarding corporate social responsibility.

The significant concern about CSR practices and the need to address socio-environmental issues have created various needs over the years, involving many stakeholders, such as: sovereign entities, through the creation of mandatory legislation on social responsibility practices; entities directly addressed with such normative practices and guidelines related to CSR practices; or entities that have created assumptions enabling them to effectively apply best practices through the implementation of the International Organization for Standardization (ISO) and the assumptions of the Global Reporting Initiative (GRI).

Any actions which an organization undertakes will have an effect on the external environment within which that organization resides. It must be recognized that this environment includes both the business environment in which the firm operates, the local societal environment and the global environment. This effect of the organization can take the following forms:

- Exploitation of natural resources as a part of its industrial processes;
- Competition between itself and other firms in the same market;

- Development of a local community through the creation of employment opportunities;
- Modification of the landscape due to raw material extraction or waste product storage.
- The distribution of wealth created within the firm to the owners of that firm and the workers;
- Influence on climate change and the way in which the emission of greenhouse gases are exacerbating this.

Organizations can have a very significant effect upon their external environment and can change the environment through their activities. There are innumerable propositions which we can identify related to the development theme. Lantos (2001) considers that there are three different types of CSR (ethical, altruistic and strategic); Bowen's (1953) new knowledge is related to the creation of an obligation for top managers and managers regarding society so that they can act in a concerted way to reach their objectives (Rahman, 2011).

Requirements Around CSR

Previous literature highlights the following CSR basics: (i) sustainability, (ii) accountability and (iii) transparency (Ramdhony, 2018; Ioannou & Serafeim, 2017). Sustainability is concerned with the effect which an action taken in the present has upon the options available in the future. Sustainability implies that society must use no more of a resource than can be regenerated. This can be defined in terms of the carrying capacity of the ecosystem and described with models of resource consumption (Hawken, 1993).

Accountability is concerned with how an organization's actions affect the external environment, and therefore how it assumes responsibility for the effects of actions taken. More specifically, the concept implies reporting those circumstances to all parties affected by those actions. Accountability therefore necessitates the development of appropriate measures of environmental performance and reporting the actions of the firm.

Finally, transparency, as a principle, means that the external impact of the actions of the organizations can be ascertained from that organization's reporting and pertinent facts are not disguised within that reporting. Transparency is of particular importance to external users of such information as these users lack the background details and knowledge available to internal users. CSR practices have become a norm rather than an exception because of the diffusion of multinational companies through export, and shareholders expect to increase their wealth, taking into account the high expectations created by society (Ramdhony, 2018).

Despite being a theme that is much in trend, the lack of transparency of some companies has led to necessary regulation being created for this matter, making voluntary practices mandatory (Ramdhony, 2018; Ioannou & Serafeim, 2017). Ioannou and Serafeim (2017) indicate that the first attempts at sustainability reports in both Europe and the United States date back to 1967. However, at the time there was no contribution by governmental organizations, a situation that was reversed in the following decade, when Austria, Germany, the Netherlands and Switzerland implemented an investment approach that excluded non-socially responsible companies; the analysis was based on their social and ethical performance.

These incentives, based on the evident need for regulation, highlighted the moment when legislators decided to create regulations related to this matter. This was the necessary step for members of the non-profit organization Coalition for Environmentally Responsible Economies (CERES) and the Tellus Institute to set up the Global Reporting Initiative (GRI) in 1997.

In the information content provided by the Global Reporting Initiative (2019), there was a noticeable evolution with the creation of guidelines underlying sustainability reporting. The first was launched in 2000 and was generalized to the financial sector in 2008, providing software tools for the effect and associating its assumptions with practices related to assumptions of the International Organization for Standardization. The structure of a corporate social responsibility report accompanied by GRI information must take several assumptions into account, since this report is intended to serve all organizations regardless of their nature, location or size (GRI, 2006).

A report with GRI indicators is divided into categories: the first is related to aspects of economic performance, presence in the market and indirect economic impacts; the second is directed towards the material aspects – energy, water, biodiversity, emissions and waste, products and services, product conformity and transportation; the third presents labour aspects, the relationship between employees and their respective hierarchies, health and hygiene at work, training and education; the fourth concerns human rights directives and addresses discrimination, security practices, indigenous rights and freedom of association and negotiation; the fifth regards society, where corruption, community, public policies and unfair competition are addressed; and finally, the indicators related to product liability point to customer health and safety, product labelling, communication and marketing and compliance (GRI, 2006).

In addition to the aforementioned assumptions, the ISO standards applicable to CSR should be considered, such as: ISO 14001, which is associated with family standards and provides practical tools for companies and organizations of all types that seek to manage their environmental responsibilities; ISO 26000, which provides guidance on whether or not companies can operate in a socially responsible manner, contributing to the well-being and health of society; and ISO 50001, on energy-efficient use to save money and help conserve and combat climate change.

The assumptions previously presented demonstrate the importance of the dissemination of non-financial information, which is directed at organizations' CSR practices. Investors have a greater appetite for these reports since they have become a medium- and long-term objective which defines the structure of the business, enables the increase of certifications and meets the demands of investors (Anderson, 2015).

The drafting of these reports has a positive impact as companies demonstrate the transparency and rigour of their practices to their stockholders as well as rooting a new business culture and competitive advantage vis-à-vis their peers (Ernst & Young, 2013). However, all information disclosed depends on an issuer, which may not intend to disclose the variants practised by its organization. In addition, Brunsael (2009) argued that activities associated with CSR have grown in importance as they can be analysed as a competitive advantage for companies. In spite of a historical evolution of CSR-SME dichotomies, we can identify that public companies have a structure that allows them to prepare practices with greater emphasis on their sustainable character.

Finally, CSR activities in the field of the protection of the environment focus on designing environmentally friendly products or production processes, efficient use of resources and reduction of waste and pollution and applying ecological assessment to suppliers concerning their environmental standards.

FINANCIAL INFORMATION AND CORPORATE SOCIAL RESPONSABILITY

Disclosure of Financial Information

Financial information may be referred to as the best way to interpret a company's financial data, which includes financial elements and is congruently linked to accounting. From a global perspective, associated with the disclosure of financial information, there are gaps that have implications for finance, management and other areas, such as information asymmetry (Kagan, 2018), whereby asymmetry of information is one of the areas of greatest relevance in the development between finance and accounting.

This theme must be related to transparency and disclosure of information since these are among the representative pillars of governance, which can be described in two categories: mandatory requirements and voluntary information (Sheata, 2014). More complex information tends to show a greater distance in financial areas because the difficulty in obtaining this data can be great (Kagan, 2018). This situation extends to all non-financial information, in particular that related to CSR, since managers are more aware of both the plans and the programmes of the companies that they manage than the stakeholders.

As mentioned, companies tend to designate all CSR practices to the manager assigned to the position, making it necessary to mitigate one of the key problems related to asymmetry of information: the transparency of information provided by the company to its shareholders. This is because these companies are demonstrating that the voluntary disclosure of this information is an added advantage for them to consistently seek to improve their financial information and reduce the asymmetry of information between parties (Kim et al., 2014; Kim et al., 2012; Clarkson et al., 2008).

There is a link that extends to non-financial information, which underlies the disclosure of sustainability reports, and it is important to mention that in empirical studies associated with CSR, they demonstrate their relationship with various theories, such as: (i) agency theory, which is commonly linked to CSR practices where the objective is to analyse the conflicts that arise in companies and that differ from the interests of the agents involved (Martins, 2016); (ii) stakeholder theory, associated with an individual or group that can affect or be affected by the achievement of a company's objectives (Freeman, 1984); (iii) legitimacy theory, which can be assessed from a sustainability point of view by its implication in the dissemination of environmental information (Dias and Pinheiro, 2014); and (iv) capital need theory, associated with the companies' needs to raise capital at a low cost and voluntary disclosure.

Recently, researches have examined various outcomes of corporate social responsibility engagements and disclosure of financial information, in particular analyst forecast (Adhikari, 2016; Myring & Shortridge, 2010), stock returns, investments and insider trading (Becchetti et al., 2015; Borghesi et al., 2014; Boubakri et al., 2016; Grifo et al., 2015; Gao, 2014), tax avoidance (Hoi, 2013; Huseyno and Clamm, 2012) political connections (Lin et al., 2014), and firm performance, information asymmetry and earnings quality (Lys et al., 2015; Kim et al., 2012: Cho et al., 2013; Sheata, 2014).

To analyse our study, we conducted a literature search where there is evidence of studies that focus on the analysis of financial information and its correlation with non-financial disclosure, that is, the use of CSR practices. Our research covers various methodologies applied by different authors and different conclusions and shows that financial information has been expanded in recent years and that it has underlying CSR practices, as we can see in Table 1:

Regarding corporate social responsibility and analyst forecasts, Myring and Shortridge (2010), indicate that analysts use two types of information to make their observations. The first is related to commonly disclosed information, mandatory and voluntary financial information, and information obtained through

Table 1. Studies on Financial Information and Corporate Social Responsibility

Author (s)	Objective (s)	Methodology	Conclusions
Adhikari (2016)	To ascertain the influence of financial analysts, the relationship between sales and CSR and the impact of the existence of analysts in the practice of CSR activities.	Data from 2001 to 2011; Databases of MSCI ESG Research and Institutional Brokers Estimate Systems; Econometric model.	Financial analysts have an influential role in companies and those with greater coverage by analysts present a lower score in CSR practices. The agency problem is approached.
Arvidsson (2011)	To analyse management teams' views regarding different aspects related to the disclosure of non-financial information in the annual report.	Questionnaire survey addressed to investor-relation managers (IRMs) at the largest companies listed on the Stockholm Stock Exchange.	The focus of disclosure of non-financial information may be mandated to be driven by consumers, and company managers have recognized the importance of providing additional information, including non-financial indicators beyond mandatory requirements.
Becchetti, Ciciretti and Hasan (2015)	To ascertain the correlation between idiosyncratic volatility and social responsibility.	Data: Companies listed between 1992 and 2010; Databases: Institutional Brokers Estimate System and Risk Metrics´ KLD; Econometric method.	CSR reduces the response to productive shocks and, in turn, the welfare of the interested parties. There is a combined effect of less predictable profits, reducing the risk of conflicts between the parties in turn.
Borghesi, Houston and Naranjo (2014)	To identify factors that lead companies to invest in CSR practices.	Database: KLD Research & Analytics allowed the CSR scores to be obtained in six categories: Community, Diversity, Employees, Environment, Humanitarian and Product; Econometric model	Larger companies with a higher level of investment in advertising tend to be more socially responsible and those with greater ownership are those that invest the least in CSR.
Boubakri, Ghoul, Wang, Guedhami (2016)	To analyse cross-listing and CSR dynamics in the USA.	Data: 2002 to 2011 Databases: Thomson Reuters and Compustat Global; Linear regression model.	CSR levels are higher in listed companies than in non-listed companies. The companies that have the best results in the applicability of socially responsible activities tend to present these results to third parties and on a voluntary basis.
Cheung (2016)	To identify CSR channels and mechanisms that can affect the liquidity of companies.	Data: 1991 and 2011. Econometric model.	There is a positive and significant correlation between CSR and the cash resources of the companies, evidencing the link between the cash participations and highlighting the systematic risk channel, which is the most relevant for CSR.
Cho, Lee and Pfeiffer (2013)	To investigate the relationship between CSR performance and asymmetry information and what the effects of investors are on this relationship.	Use of performance punctuation provided by KLD STAT.	CSR performance has a positive effect on investors, reducing information asymmetry, and regulatory action is appropriate to mitigate information selection.
Crifo, Forget and Teyssier (2015)	To analyse the impact and disclosure of CSR practices in the financing of capital.	Data: 330 observations Econometric model	Irresponsible corporate policies can prevent financing and increase its cost. Disclosure of ESG may be considered as a defensive strategy to protect company value and access to capital.
Cui and Jo (2018)	To make an empirical analysis between CSR and information asymmetry.	Through a mathematical model, with a sample of U.S. companies and several characteristics that explain the model.	The relationship between information asymmetry and CSR is increased when companies increase efforts to build a good reputation and are positively related to smaller measures of information asymmetry.
Gao, Lising, Zhang (2014)	To analyse companies that promote investment in CSR and profits or not.	Data: 650 European Union companies, between 1991 and 2000 Econometric model.	There is a negative connotation between CSR and insider trading, which is associated with the level of awareness of CSR practices; It is recognized that executives who perform CSR practices have lower profits than those who do not.
Huseyno and Klamm (2012)	To ascertain the effect of three measures of corporate social responsibility on corporate governance, community and diversity in tax evasion in companies that use tax services audits.	Data: S & P 500 companies; Databases: Compustat and Audit Analytics; the KLD Stats data was used for the financial companies; Econometric analysis.	Firms with strong CSR outline strategies to reduce costs not only for the benefit of shareholders, but also for the benefit of society. Profitable businesses are in a better position to participate in donations and in some cases it may be socially acceptable to reduce tax payments.
Kim, Park and Wier (2012)	This study analyses socially responsible companies and the impact on the transparency and reliability of financial information transmitted to investors, compared to those that do not use the same criterion for the practice of CSR.	Database: Compustat Sample: observations from 1991 to 2009; Econometric analysis.	Companies that conduct CSR activities have an incentive to be honest, trustworthy and ethical, so they prepare financial reports in a transparent way, as companies become more cautious in their designs and tend to have a long-term vision.
Lin, Tan, Zhao and Karim (2014)	To analyse corporate social responsibility practices for building business.	Data: municipal rotation events of mayors using a sample consisting of companies listed on the Shenzhen or Shanghai stock market Period: between 2005 and 2009. Econometric analysis.	When a representative of the municipal government is replaced, the level and activity of CSR are systematically increased in the listed companies that work in this city as their core policies, that is, NSOEs, small companies and companies that operate in cities with more corrupt governments.
Lys, Naugton and Wang (2015)	To analyse the linked association between CSR with expenses and the future financial performance of the companies.	Databases: Thomson Reuters ASSET4 database, Compustat's financials and I/B/E/S. Sustainability reports were also used where the use of Global Reporting Index (GRI) practices was evident. Econometric methods.	There is no association between CSR, cost and financial performance of companies, and sustainability reporting is one of the channels through which stockholders may interfere with the future of these companies and financial perspectives.
Myring and Shortridge (2010)	To demonstrate that the quality of information in accounting disclosure is underpinned by the measures adopted by governance.	Data: the Corporate Library, Compustat, and the Institutional Brokers Estimate Systems (I/B/E/S). Mathematical model	The results indicate that the corporate governance evaluated by the Corporate Library does not seem to influence the environment faced by the analysts, that is, the disclosure of information has no impact on the question analysed.

continued on following page

Table 1 continued

Author (s)	Objective (s)	Methodology	Conclusions
Sheata (2014)	To address the theoretical aspects of voluntary disclosure in economics.	Analysis of the theories used to explain voluntary disclosure, determinants and sources of voluntary information.	Theories of agency, signalling, need for capital and legitimacy are theories related to the dissemination of voluntary information. There is no consensus on some aspects of voluntary disclosure and its relation to the cost of capital.

Source: Own Elaboration

other methods, which are not available to all. These authors argue that stronger corporate governance presents higher quality financial information, enabling analysts to make reliable forecasts.

On the other hand, analysts give more importance to information not disclosed by companies with low levels of disclosure due to the poor quality of the information contained in the reports presented. They tested two hypotheses: the first is that poor corporate governance results in a possible lower consensus among analysts; the second that analysts' forecasts will be more accurate than the higher margin forecasts when governance is weak, leading to the results presented in Table 2:

Adhikari (2014) concluded that financial analysts have an influential role in companies and that those that have greater coverage by analysts present lower scores in CSR practices. The agency problem is approached in this study. With respect to corporate social responsibility and stock returns, Becchetti et al. (2015) concluded that CSR reduces the response to productive shocks and, in turn, the welfare of the interested parties. There is a combined effect of less predictable profits, reducing the risk of conflicts between the parties in turn. Identification of CSR channels and mechanisms that can affect the liquidity of companies was studied by Cheung (2016). This study found that there is a positive and significant correlation between CSR and the cash resources of the companies, evidencing the link between cash participations and highlighting the systematic risk channel, which is the most relevant for CSR.

Regarding identification of factors that lead companies to invest in CSR practices, Borghesi et al. (2014) concluded that larger companies with higher levels of investment in advertising tend to be more socially responsible and those with greater ownership are those that invest the least in CSR. Additionally, this study also found that younger CEOs tend to invest more in CSR practices and that these practices are part of a strategy for maintaining political relationships and a high level of media scrutiny. This is no surprise, given that recent studies demonstrated a strong link between observable board characteristics and better firm reputation (Brammer et al., 2009).

In the cross-country comparative study, Boubakri et al. (2016) found higher CSR levels in listed companies than in non-listed companies. The companies that have the best results in the applicability of socially responsible activities tend to present these results to third parties on a voluntary basis. Huseyno and Klamm (2012) studied the effect of three measures of corporate social responsibility on corporate governance, community and diversity in tax evasion in companies that use tax services audits. These authors concluded that firms with strong CSR outline strategies to reduce costs not only for the benefit of shareholders, but also for the benefit of society. Profitable businesses are in a better position to participate in donations and in some cases, it may be socially acceptable to reduce tax payments. This study is important for an understanding of the link between CSR and tax avoidance.

Although there is no universally agreement behind the association between CSR and firm performance, information asymmetry and earnings quality, most previous literature points out a stakeholder theory-based CSR-information asymmetry nexus. There is evidence that efforts by managers who voluntarily disclosure additional information help to reduce the practice of earnings management and improve the

Table 2. Results of Myring and Shortridge's study (2010)

Results
The dispersion in analysts' forecasts is positively related to the number of elements accompanying the company and the change in net profit.
If board size increases, the dispersion of forecasts made by analysts reduces, so the accuracy of analysts' forecasts has no impact with variation in governance structures.
The size of the company is not related to the consensus of the analysts; the results showed that the relationship between the quality of corporate governance and the characteristics of the forecasts has limitations.
The individual mechanisms of corporate governance are related to dispersion and consensus in analysts.
Source: Myring, M. and Shortridge, R. (2010)

quality of financial information. In particular, Lys et al. (2015) found that high-performing firms want to signal their quality by highlighting their good performance.

Firms with high levels of CSR are expected to disclosure more non-financial information. Ki et al. (2012) indicate that improved corporate transparency through frequent voluntary disclosures reduces information asymmetry between insiders and outsiders. The study by Sheata (2014) presents six motivations and four restrictions with regard to the determinants of voluntary disclosure. The motivations are information asymmetry, corporate control contest, stock compensation, increased analyst coverage, management talent signalling and limitations of mandatory disclosure and these are corroborated by Healy and Palepu (2001) and Graham et al. (2005). The restrictions are disclosure precedent, proprietary costs, agency costs and political costs, explained as follows in Table 3.

Cho et al. (2013) argue that CSR performance reduces asymmetry problems, but this result is not visible in high-ownership companies. The study by these authors identifies the fact that investors explore private information about CSR performance which brings about an influence between their performance and information asymmetry, and it is even indicated that CSR practices contribute positively to the reduction of this issue. CSR practices are positively related to the financial and non-financial information provided by company managers and the latest studies converge on the complex asymmetry of information.

To summarise, previous studies document that shareholders have reasons to care about CSR disclosure because of its association with lower levels of errors in analyst forecasts and reduced earnings management. These are important findings about what drives firms' CSR activities and disclosures, and these results have natural ties to archival research issues in traditional financial accounting. Additionally, the literature demonstrates that theories associated with information asymmetry are signalling theory, capital need theory, agency theory and legitimacy theory (Sheata, 2014), discussed in the next section. Thus theory corroborates the interconnection between asymmetry information and CSR, since two of the theories related to CSR are agency and legitimacy, as previously addressed and indicated by other studies (Reverte, 2009).

Table 3. Motivations and Restrictions observed by Sheata (2014)

Motivations	
Information asymmetry	In the issue of capital by means of shares or debts, the asymmetry between managers and external investors is reduced, as is the cost of financing. Thus, voluntary disclosure of information may occur when voluntary disclosure is increased for external investors.
Corporate control contest	The disclosure of information may be greater when there is a need to undervalue the company, that is, the managers increase the disclosure of information, explaining the poor performance and reducing the possibility of devaluation of the company's shares.
Stock compensation	The reward of managers with share-based compensation motivates the voluntary disclosure of information which encourages these managers to meet the interests of the shareholders and previously to correct some perception of devaluation before the purchase of a share.
Increased analyst coverage	Analysts have lower costs in acquiring voluntary information if it is disclosed, translating into a larger number of analysts following that company.
Management talent signaling	One of the determinants of a company's market value is investors' perception of the ability to forecast change, so managers prefer to disclose voluntary financial and non-financial information to demonstrate their level of ability. However, some managers consider that this threshold could be negative and be used against them by their regulators.
Limitations of mandatory disclosure	Voluntary disclosure can be used to fill gaps in mandatory disclosure.
Restrictions	
Disclosure precedent	The market expects the company to commit to continuing voluntary disclosures, which may lead to reduced disclosure of such information.
Proprietary costs	Managers prefer non-disclosure of voluntary information to avoid affecting the competitive position of the company, even if it increases the cost of capital and is considered to be a competitive disadvantage vis-à-vis its peers.
Agency costs	Some managers prefer to stay away from possible foci, away from career and external reputation concerns, avoiding the maximum disclosure of voluntary information.
Political costs	In order for voluntary information not to be used by regulators against managers, they prefer not to disclose it. Although the political costs depend on the size of the company, in order to avoid threats and reduce expected attention, managers do not proceed to a higher level of disclosure.

Source: Sheata (2014)

THEORIES AROUND CORPORATE SOCIAL RESPONSABILITY

Agency Theory

Agency theory helps predict the behaviour of an individual, the principal, who delegates the work to another, the agent, with the expectation that the agent will make decisions that are in the best interest of the director (Jensen and Meckling, 1976) by providing a structure that allows the understanding of incentive alignment and information asymmetry, which influences managers' decisions. We can able understand the flow of this theory in Figure 1.

The type I agency problem consists of the separation between ownership and control, which leads to a divergence between management and owner interests (Jensen & Meckling, 1976). These agency problems arise when asymmetric information coexists with divergent objectives between managers and shareholders. Managers with little ownership may have incentives to manage accounting figures so as to increase earnings-based compensation, relax contractual constraints or avoid debt covenants (Healy, 1985; Holthausen et al., 1995), thus giving rise to high agency costs for owners.

Figure 1. Flow of Theory Agency
Source: *Adapted from Williams (2019)*

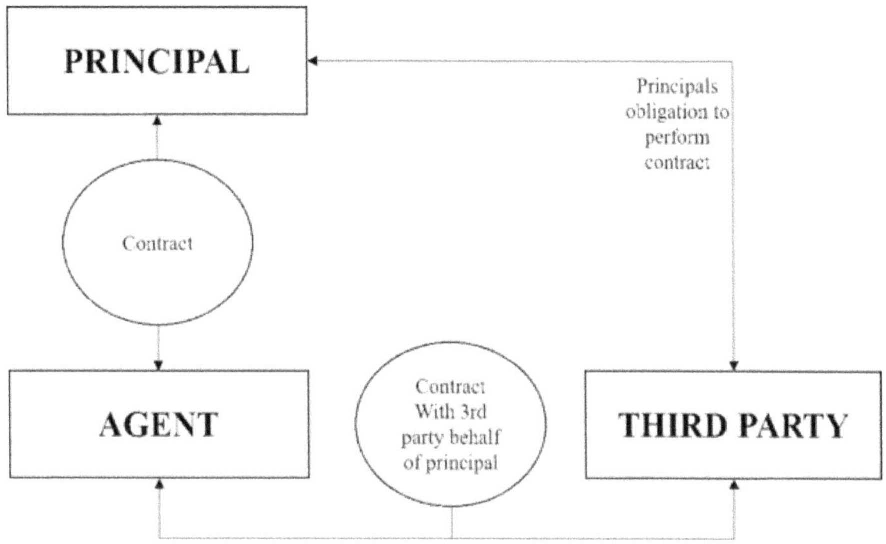

The type II agency problem arises from conflicts between controlling and non-controlling shareholders, which can result in executive entrenchment and large incentives to report a weak financial position (Fama & Jensen, 1983). However, social performance expenditures reduce net income. Therefore, firms that prefer to conduct and disclose social performance are more likely to have lower contracting and monitoring costs, and to have high political costs.

Belkaoui and Karpik (1989) suggested that the decision to disclose social performance is positively correlated with social performance, economic performance and political visibility, and negatively with hiring and monitoring costs. A feature of a manager's work environment is that it serves to alleviate the agency problem if a company has an express commitment to corporate social responsibility. Corporate social responsibility is stated as a strategic company response to inconsistencies that occur between corporate profitability goals and social goals (Heal 2004). It also represents a subset of an organization's values and culture (Aguilera et al., 2004).

Being socially responsible at the organizational level involves actions such as allocating resources for proper enforcement (for example, those that protect workers' health and safety or provide equal treatment for all employees).

Stakeholder Theory

The concept of stakeholders was defined by Freeman (1984) as an individual or group that can affect or be affected by the achievement of a company's objectives (Freeman, 1984). This theory is based on the consideration that maximizing wealth for shareholders fails to maximize wealth for society and all its members and that only a concern with managing all stakeholder interests achieves this. It further states that all stakeholders must be considered in the decision-making process of the organization.

The first criterion, therefore, is power. It is a necessary condition to the extent that the strategy adopted towards the stakeholders is linked to the resources they control and to their degree of interdependence

Figure 2. Principal Stakeholders of the Firms
Source*: Adapted from Freeman et al. (2007)*

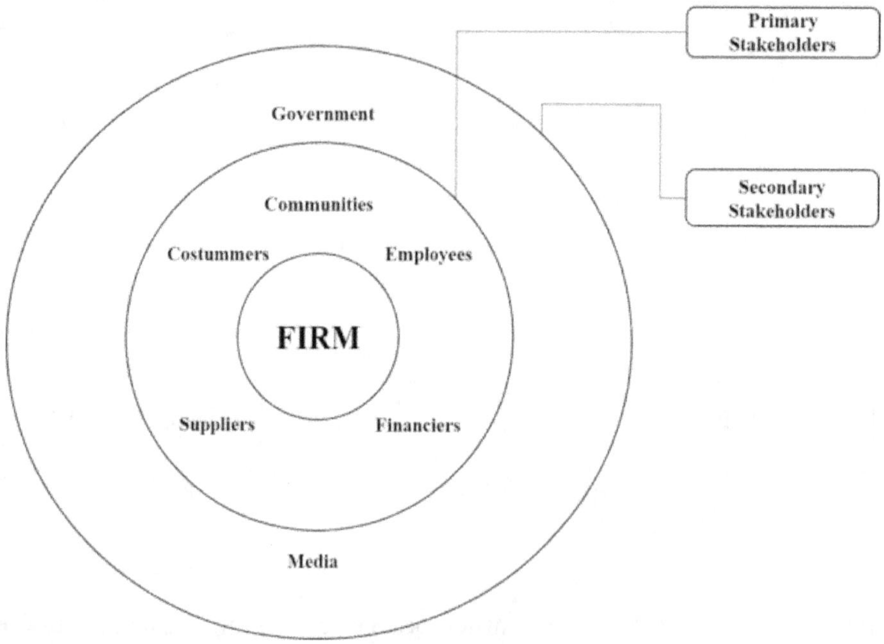

with the company. This dimension comes from Pfeffer and Salancik's analysis (1978) but was also taken up by Frooman (1999), Gioia (1999) and Trevino and Weaver, (1999). According to these authors, all companies need resources possessed by external groups. In exchange, the groups demand that certain expectations be met, which is part of the power they exercise over the company in terms of dependence. The second criterion is the legitimacy of these stakeholders, which is their moral right, over and above the legal context, to intervene in the life of the company.

This theory demonstrated that stakeholder management, or corporate social responsibility, is not an end in itself but is simply seen as a means for improving economic performance. Clarkson (1995) suggests that a stakeholder is relevant if they have invested something in the organization and are therefore subject to some risk from organization activities. This author separates these into two groups: voluntary and involuntary stakeholders. The first group includes shareholders, investors, employees, managers, customers and suppliers and they will require some value added otherwise they may choose not to invest in that organization. The second group includes individuals, communities, ecological environments and other specific interest groups for certain industries which do not choose to deal with the organization and therefore may need some form of protection, possibly through government legislation or regulation.

Stakeholder management has significant information needs. It is extremely difficult to manage for a variety of stakeholders if there is no measurement of how the organization has performed for those stakeholders. Therefore, non-financial measures will be of great importance and recently there have been a number of multi-dimensional performance measurement frameworks that can be argued to have some level of stakeholder orientation.

This approach on the part of the stakeholders leads to an interpretation of the theory as an extension of agency theory, by placing these groups as principals. They include shareholders, creditors, employees, customers, suppliers, local communities and the public. The behaviour of these groups is therefore perceived as a constraint on corporate strategy. They are not intrinsically hostile to the firm but may become so if their interests do not converge. Freeman (1984) and Roberts (1992) for example, reveal that the role of the directors is to evaluate the demands of the different groups and to make them coincide with the company's objectives. The directors are thereby their agents contracting for the firm (Hill & Jones, 1992; Jones & Wicks, 1999; Gioia, 1999; Bowen, Ducharme & Shores, 1995).

Stakeholder theory is used in empirical and analytical analyses of the firm and of the environment in which it operates. The difficulty in defining the pressures of these stakeholders means, however, that the studies carried out in this field identify the pressure groups but do not measure the strength of their expectations (Lerner and Fryell, 1994; Marx, 1992; Soutar, McNeil and Molster, 1995).

Legitimacy Theory

Guthrie, Cuganesan, and Ward, (2006), use a theory of legitimacy derived from the concept of organizational legitimacy defined by Downling and Pfeffer which verifies whether a threat of legitimacy occurs when there is a divergence between the system of values of a company and the social system of which company is part (Downling & Pfeffer, 1975). According to O'Donovan (2000), this theory originated in 1975 through the empirical studies that related this theory to sociology and philosophy (Weber, 1966).

This theory can be evaluated from a standpoint related to accounting, since the agent (accountant) can direct the information to be provided by the companies to its stakeholders. However, this information is controlled by the company given the social pressures, the demand of consumers, suppliers and others (Dias, 2009). The same authors indicate that from another perspective, we can relate this theory to another paradigm, which is related to sustainability by its implication in the dissemination of environmental information.

According to legitimacy theory, companies disclose social responsibility information to present a socially responsible image so that they can legitimize their behaviours to their stakeholder groups. Legitimacy theory is based on the idea that a social contract exists between business and society (Branco & Rodrigues, 2006). Society is considered to allow companies to exist and have rights, and in return expects them to fulfil their expectations about how their operations should be conducted. Therefore, in order to survive, a company must ensure that the activities it undertakes are actually in accordance with the values and norms of society or are perceived as such. When society's expectations are not fulfilled, that is, the company's current or perceived behaviour is not in accordance with social values and norms, a breach of contract exists, and a legitimacy gap may develop.

The previous opinion is corroborated by other authors, indicating that this theory is implicit in the push for companies to continue with successively new certifications related to the values of society as a whole (Deegan, 2003). Thus, contextualizing this theory, we can relate that the associated accounting information of socioeconomic indicators covers society and is seen as a whole, and that a company that provides information disclosure in these two areas is clearly involved with society.

Signalling Theory

Developed by Michael Spence, this economic theory is used to describe behaviour between two parties, both individually and organizationally. In general, there is an element that wants to pass certain information to a third party, who must choose how the signal is interpreted (Connelly, et al., 2010).

According to Porter (1980), signalling theory is associated with companies that indicate their intentions, purposes and objectives and is used as a tool that tends to reduce information asymmetry between the parties (Hetze, 2016). Guthrie, Cuganesan and Ward (2006), state that this theory is also associated with the social contract which was indicated by Shoker and Sheti (1973) that all business, with no exception, operates in socially and represents society's expectations. These authors also claim that this contract is hard to define because the expectations are not permanent and the terms of this contract are precise or that company managers might have a different perspective.

Previous literature indicates that this theory is directly and indirectly associated with CSR practices (Guthrie et al., 2006) and this type of information, whether mandatory or voluntary, is provided to all its stakeholders, allowing companies to disseminate good practices used in the area of corporate social responsibility, as well as results that may lead to potential investors, as their reputation as an organization is being improved (Campbell et al., 2001; Verrecchia, 1983).

We also observing the following elements that Simaens and Koster (2013) outlined, such as: (i) the sender is the organization that has privileged information that is not known to the receiver; (ii) communication is deliberate and demonstrates an effort to convey organizational attributes; and (iii) stakeholders do not have information about the organization and would like to receive it.

Capital Need Theory

Choi (1973) states that capital need theory is associated with companies' needs to raise capital at a low cost and with voluntary disclosure. Although Botosan (2006) indicates the opposite, the Financial Accounting Standards Board (FASB) (2001) indicates a positive relation between voluntary disclosure and the cost of capital.

This theory is also commonly associated with corporate reporting, even if there is an increase in non-voluntary disclosure as estimates of capital increase (FASB, 2001). Other studies also point out that this theory is associated with non-voluntary relationship information as there may be incentives for disclosure (Gray et al., 1995), demonstrating that disclosing sales excellence information can bring new investors, who push a positive entity option as well as pushing up the company's economic value and increasing the value of its accessories (Cooke, 1989; Stanga, 1976).

Despite the negative correlations identified by some authors as described above, it can be concluded that information asymmetry can be reduced through the practice of voluntary information disclosure. This theory has two underlying points, the first being that the cost of capital can be negatively influenced by the excessive dissemination of information by the company and the second that it allows the asymmetry problem to be attenuated, as mentioned by Collett and Hrasky (2005).

CONCLUSION

In spite of the important roles of corporate social responsibility and disclosure of financial information in recent years, there is only limited empirical evidence of these issues. Previous literature allowed a clear relationship between the CSR and asymmetry of information to be ascertained, having as there was a need to find ways to mitigate the possibility of information asymmetry with CSR activities.

We found that previous studies document that shareholders have reasons to care about CSR disclosure because of its association with lower levels of errors in analyst forecasts and reduced earnings management. These are important findings about what drives firms' CSR activities and disclosures, and these results have natural ties to archival research issues in traditional financial accounting. Additionally, the literature demonstrates that the theories associated with information asymmetry are signalling theory, capital need theory, agency theory and legitimacy theory (Sheata, 2014), discussed in the next section. Thus, theory corroborates the interconnection between asymmetry information and CSR, since two of the theories related to CSR are agency and legitimacy, as previously addressed and indicated by other studies (Reverte, 2009).

We intend to contribute to the development of sustainability accounting, presenting assumptions that mitigate blocks to practices of CSR acts which enable the return of elements which are positive for the image of the entities and for their financial economic improvement make.

As the evolution of CSR in corporations continues, we expect that a future study that examines CSR and disclosure of financial information will significantly contribute to our understanding of the relations between earnings management, information asymmetry and management behaviours and aggregate firm-level data. Further work also needs to take into account the impact of disclosure of financial information and CSR on long-term financial horizons across countries. Research on why and how firms' engagement in CSR differs across countries may provide additional understanding regarding the complex relations between CSR, earnings management, information asymmetry and market effect and firm value. Future research should also examine the impact of reputation of firms and ethical decision-making on the quality of financial information across countries and their cultures.

REFERENCES

Belkaoui, A., & Karpik, P. (1989). Determinants of Corporate Social Decision to Disclose Social Information. *Accounting, Auditing & Accountability Journal*, *2*(1), 09513578910132240. doi:10.1108/09513578910132240

Bennet, M., Burrit, R., & Schaltegger, S. (2006). Sustainability Accounting and Reporting. Eco-Efficient. In *Industry and Science*. Springer.

Boston College Center & EY. (2013). Value of Sustainability Reporting. Retrieved from http://www.ey.com/Publication/vwLUAssets/EY__Value_of_sustainability_reporting/$FILE/EY-Value-of-Sustainability-Reporting.pdf

Brunsael, P. (2009). Corporate Social Responsibility as Competitive Advantage and Strategic Necessity [Dissertação]. University of Agder.

Choi, F. D. S. (1973). Financial disclosure and entry to the European capital market. *Journal of Accounting Research*, *11*(2), 159–175. doi:10.2307/2490187

Clarkson, P. M., Li, Y., Richardson, G. D., & Vasvari, F. P. (2008). Revisiting the relation between environmental performance and environmental disclosure: An empirical analysis. *Accounting, Organizations and Society*, *33*(4), 303–327. doi:10.1016/j.aos.2007.05.003

Collett, P., & Hrasky, S. (•••). Voluntary Disclosure of Corporate Governance Practices by Listed Australian Companies. *Corporate Governance*, *13*(2), 188–196.

Commission of the European Communities. (2001). Green Paper. Promoting a European Framework for Corporate Social Responsibility. Retrieved from http://eur-lex.europa.eu

Commission of the European Communities. (2011). *A renewed EU strategy 2011-14 for corporate social responsibility*. Brussels: European Commission.

Connely, B., Hoskisson, R., & Certo, S. (2010). Ownership as a Form of Corporate Governance. *Journal of Management Studies*, *47*(8), 1561–1589. doi:10.1111/j.1467-6486.2010.00929.x

Cooke, T. E. (1989). Disclosure in the corporate annual reports of Swedish companies. *Accounting and Business Research*, *19*(74), 113–124. doi:10.1080/00014788.1989.9728841

Dahlsrud, A. (2008). How corporate social responsibility is defined: an analysis of 37 definitions. *Corporate Social Responsibility and Environmental Management*, *15*, 1-13. doi:10.1002/csr/132

Davis, K. (1973). The case for and against business assumption of social responsibilities. *Academy of Management Journal*, *16*(2), 312–323.

Deegan, C. (2003). *Environmental management accounting: An introduction and case studies for Australia (EMAP)*. Sydney: Institute of Chartered Accountants in Australia.

Dias, A. (2009). O Relato da Sustentabilidade Empresarial: práticas em Portugal [Dissertação]. Universidade Aberta, Lisboa.

Dowling, J., & Pfeffer, J. (1975). Organizational Legitimacy: Social Values and Organizational Behavior. *Pacific Sociological Review*, *18*(1), 122–136. doi:10.2307/1388226

Drucker, P. (1984). The New Meaning of Corporate Social Responsibility. *California Management Review*, *26*(2), 53–63. doi:10.2307/41165066

Epstein, M. J. (2008). *Making sustainability work: Best practices in managing and measuring corporate, social, environmental, and economic impacts*. San Francisco, CA: Berret-Koehler Publishers, Inc.

Fama, E., & Jensen, M. (1983). Separation of ownership and control. *The Journal of Law & Economics*, *26*(2), 301–325. doi:10.1086/467037

Freeman, R. (1984). *Strategic management: A stakeholder approach*. Cambridge University Press.

Frooman, J. (1999). Stakeholder Influence Strategies. *Academy of Management Review*, *24*(2), 191–205. doi:10.5465/amr.1999.1893928

Gietzman, M., & Irelan, J. (2005). Cost of Capital, Strategic Disclosures and Accounting Choice. *Journal of Business Finance & Accounting*, *32*(3-4), 599–634. doi:10.1111/j.0306-686X.2005.00606.x

Global Reporting Index – GRI. (2006). Diretrizes para o Relatório de Sustentabilidade. Retrieved from http://www.ipai.pt/

Global Reporting Index – GRI. (2019). GRI's History. Retrieved from https://www.globalreporting.org/information

Guthrie, J., Cuganesan, S., & Ward, L. (2008). Disclosure Media for Social and Environmental Matters within the Australian Food and Beverage Industry. *Social and Environmental Accountability Journal, 28*(1), 33–44. doi:10.1080/0969160X.2008.9651789

Healy, P. M. (1985). The effect of bonus schemes on accounting decisions. *Journal of Accounting and Economics, 7*(1-3), 85–107. doi:10.1016/0165-4101(85)90029-1

Hetze, K., & Winistörfer, H. (2016). CSR communication on corporate websites compared across continents. *International Journal of Bank Marketing, 34*(4), 501–528. doi:10.1108/IJBM-02-2015-0022

Hopkins, M. (2003). The Planetary Bargain: Corporate Responsibility Matters (1st ed.). Academic Press. Doi:10.4324/9781849773201

International Organization for Standardization. (2010). ISO 26000: Social Responsibility. Retrieved from: https://www.iso.org/iso-26000-social-responsibility.html

International Organization for Standardization – ISO. (2019). Guidance on Social Responsibility. Retrieved from https://www.iso.org/standard/42546.html

Ioannou, I., & Serafeim, G. (2014). The impact of corporate social responsibility on investment recommendations: Analysts' perceptions and shifting institutional logics. *Strategic Management Journal, 36*(7), 1053–1081. doi:10.1002mj.2268

Jensen, M., & Meckling, W. (1976). Theory of firm: Managerial behaviour, agency costs and ownership structure. *Journal of Financial Economics, 3*(4), 305–360. doi:10.1016/0304-405X(76)90026-X

Kagan, J. (2018). Asymmetric information. Investopedia. Markets & Economy. Investopedia. Retrieved from https://www.investopedia.com/terms/a/asymmetricinformation.asp

Kim, Y., Li, H., & Li, S. (2014). Corporate social responsibility and stock price crash risk. *Journal of Banking & Finance, 43*, 1–13. doi:10.1016/j.jbankfin.2014.02.013

Kim, Y., Park, M., & Wier, B. (2012). Is earnings quality associated with corporate social responsibility? *The Accounting Review, 87*(3), 761–796. doi:10.2308/accr-10209

Lantos, G. (2001). The boundaries of strategic corporate social responsibility. *Journal of Consumer Marketing, 18*(7), 595–632. doi:10.1108/07363760110410281

Mark-Herbert, C., & Von Schantz, C. (2007). *Communicating corporate social responsibility–brand management.* EJBO-Electronic Journal of Business Ethics and Organization Studies.

Milne, M., Tregidga, H., & Walton, S. (2009). Words not actions! The ideological role of sustainable development reporting. *Accounting, Auditing & Accountability Journal, 22*(8), 1211–1257. doi:10.1108/09513570910999292

Mitchell, R., Agle, B., & Wood, J. (1997). Toward a Theory of Stakeholders Identification and Salience: Defining the Principle of Who and What Really Counts. *Academy of Management Review, 22*(4), 853–886. doi:10.5465/amr.1997.9711022105

Moser, D. V., & Martin, P. R. (2012, May). A Broader Perspective on Corporate Social Responsibility Research in Accounting. *The Accounting Review, 87*(3), 797–806. doi:10.2308/accr-10257

Myring, M., & Shortride, R. (2010). Corporate Governance and the Quality Of Financial Disclosures. Journal of Business Ethics. *International Business & Economics Research Journal.*, *9*(6), 103–110. doi:10.19030/iber.v9i6.589

Perrini, F., & Russo, A. (2010). Investigating Stakeholder Theory and Social Capital: CSR in Large Firms and SMEs. *Journal of Business Ethics*, *91*, 201–221. doi:10.100710551-009-0079-z

Pfeffer, J., & Salancik, G. (1978). The External Control Of Organizations: A Resource Dependency Perspective. *Economic Journal (London)*, *23*, 2. doi:10.2307/2231527

Rahman, S. (2011). Evaluation of Definitions: Ten Dimensions of Corporate Social Responsibility. *World Review of Business Research*, *1*(1), 166-176.

Ramdhony, D. (2018). The Implications of Mandatory Corporate Social Responsibility—A Literature Review Perspective. *Theoretical Economics Letters*, *8*(3), 432–447. doi:10.4236/tel.2018.83031

Reverte, C. (2009). Determinants of Corporate Social Responsibility Disclosure Ratings by Spanish Listed Firms. *Journal of Business Ethics*, *88*(2), 351–366. doi:10.100710551-008-9968-9

Reverte, C. (2012). The Impact of Better Corporate Social Responsibility Disclosure on the Cost of Equity Capital. *Corporate Social Responsibility and Environmental Management*, *19*(5), 253–272. doi:10.1002/csr.273

Schaltegger, S., & Wagner, M. (2006). Integrative Management of Sustainability Performance, Measurement and Reporting. International Journal of Accounting. *Auditing and Performance Evaluation*, *3*(1), 1–19. doi:10.1504/IJAAPE.2006.010098

Shehata, N. (2014). Theories and Determinants of Voluntary Disclosure. *Accounting and Finance Research.*, *3*(1), 18–26. doi:10.5430/afr.v3n1p18

Stanga, K. G. (1976). Disclosure in published annual reports. *Financial Management*, *5*(4), 42–52. doi:10.2307/3665456

ADDITIONAL READING

Ballou, B., Casey, R., Grenier, J., & Heitger, D. (2012). Exploring the strategic integration of sustainability initiatives: Opportunities for accounting research. *Accounting Horizons*, *26*(2), 265–288. doi:10.2308/acch-50088

Burritt, R., Schaltegger, S., & Zvezdov, D. (2011). Carbon management accounting: Explaining practice in leading German companies. *Australian Accounting Review*, *21*(1), 80–98. doi:10.1111/j.1835-2561.20 doi:10.00121.x

Burritt, R., & Tingey-Holioyak, J. (2012). Forging cleaner production: The importance of academic practitioner links for successful sustainability embedded carbon accounting. *Journal of Cleaner Production*, *36*(1), 39–47. doi:10.1016/j.jclepro.2012.02.001

Commission of the European Communities. (2001). Green paper Promoting a European Framework for Corporate Social Responsibility. Retrieved from http://eur-lex.europa.eu

Spence, C., Husillos, J., & Correa-Ruiz, C. (2010). Cult position science and the death of politics: A critical review of social and environmental accounting research. *Critical Perspectives on Accounting*, *21*(1), 76–89. doi:10.1016/j.cpa.2008.09.008

KEY TERMS AND DEFINITIONS

Agency Theory: An agency relationship is described as a situation in which one party (the principal) delegates work to another party (the agent). Agency theory attempts to explain two problems. The type I agency problem consists of the separation between ownership and control, which leads to a divergence between management and owner interests. The type II agency problem arises from conflicts between controlling and non-controlling shareholders, which can result in executive entrenchment.

Corporate Social Responsibility: A number of corporate activities that focus on the welfare of stakeholder groups other than investors, such as customers, employees, suppliers and society.

Legitimacy theory: According to legitimacy theory, companies disclose social responsibility information to present a socially responsible image so that they can legitimize their behaviours to their stakeholder groups. Legitimacy theory is based on the idea that a social contract exists between business and society.

Stakeholder theory: This theory is based upon that maximizing wealth for shareholders fails to maximize wealth for society and all its members and that only a concern with managing all stakeholder interests achieves this. It states that all stakeholders must be considered in the decision-making process of the organization.

Chapter 2
Corporate Social Responsibility: Benefits and Costs of Its Implementation

Dolores Gallardo Vazquez
University of Extremadura, Spain

Luis Enrique Valdez Juárez
Technological Institute of Sonora, Mexico

Juan de la Cruz Sánchez Domínguez
https://orcid.org/0000-0003-4830-193X
University of Extremadura, Spain

ABSTRACT

Corporate social responsibility (CSR) is a current important strategy in organizations today. Numerous factors that affect the global functioning of organizations have determined the need to incorporate a look towards sustainable development. This implies considering the integration of not only economic, but also social and environmental concerns in the day-to-day of the companies. We move, therefore, under the perspective of the Triple Bottom Line. In addition, the exercise of CSR will motivate the achievement of competitive advantages for organizations. Given this, this article seeks to analyze the numerous benefits derived from the implementation of socially responsible actions in companies. These are structured from different organizational approaches: personal sphere, organizational field, personal and organizational fields and financial area. Together with them, the implementation of the CSR may entail the need to incur certain costs, which are also referred to in the study. Finally, we propose some future lines of research

INTRODUCTION

The study of ethics and CSR is of recent interest due to the rising amount of corporate scandals, such as the Volkswagen emission scandal that happened in 2015. Owing to the digital age, consumers are now more and best informed and require companies to behave ethically and more responsibly (Low, Ong, & Tan, 2017). Generally, there is some confusion between the concepts of ethics and social responsibility;

DOI: 10.4018/978-1-7998-2128-1.ch002

new definitions arose in the 1980s, based on most advanced empirical research. The variation includes business ethics, corporate, stakeholder theory and management and corporate performance, which got into scene in the 1970s (Carroll, 1999). Ethics is defined as the fundamental principle that produces actions to prevent harm to others, when an individual or group has the chance to do it for its own benefit (Boddy, 2011). Business ethics is an attempt to set out a standard by which all the employees of an organization know what is expected from them (Sullivan, 2009); however, businesspeople are often very affected by their superiors and colleagues when making decisions.

CSR is a business philosophy which reinforces the need for corporations to behave ethically as good corporate citizens, not only by obeying laws, but also by conducting their activities in a way which avoids causing environmental pollution or exhausting world scarce resources. Businesses have begun to behave in a more socially responsible manner, which is argued that can pay off in the long term, even when it implies some short-term financial sacrifices. Thus, the discussion of corporate behaviour and social responsibility has taken more relevance within a new perspective of competitiveness and sustainable development (Low et al., 2017).

We are entering a new era of working, in which organizations had got to change their ways of making business towards a new organization model, different of the one they had been using before, oriented towards a bigger group of stakeholders and with a new work vision. Companies are working using the *Triple Bottom Line* perspective (Elkington, 2000), and at the same time they're taking into account the *Stakeholder Theory*.

When we write about the *Triple Bottom Line* perspective, we are talking about the three dimensions (economic, social and environmental) that form the basic pillars of Corporate Social Responsibility (CSR). The European Union, in its *Green Paper: Promoting an European Framework for Corporate Social Responsibility* (Commission of the European Communities, 2001, p. 8) defines CSR as "a concept whereby companies integrate social and environmental concerns in their business operations and in their interaction with their stakeholders on a voluntary basis". In more recent times, the Commission of the European Communities (2011) remarked the responsibility companies have because of their impact in society, and referred clearly to the need of cooperation between the interested parts "to integrate social, environmental, ethical, human rights and consumer concerns into their business operations and core strategy" (Commission of European Communities, 2011, p. 6).

Another theoretical explanation of why companies are applying CSR practices, apart from the *Triple Bottom Line*, is the stakeholder theory, which defines stakeholders as individuals, groups and organizations that have an interest in the processes and outcomes of the firm and upon whom the firm depends for the achievement of its goals (Freeman, 1984). It promotes a practical, efficient, effective and ethical way to manage organizations in a turbulent and complex environment (Freeman, Harrison, & Wicks, 2007). Harrison, Freeman and Abreu (2015) explain why: the stakeholder theory is practical because all firms have to manage stakeholders. It is efficient because stakeholders that are treated well tend to reciprocate with positive attitudes and behaviours towards the organization. And it is effective because it collects the energy of stakeholders and uses it for the accomplishment of the organization's objectives. Another interesting point is, as Harrison, Bosse, and Phillips (2010, p. 58) put it, that "a company that manages for stakeholders allocates more resources to satisfying the needs and demands of its legitimate stakeholders than what is necessary to simply retain their willful participation in the productive activities of the company."

Doing socially responsible actions brings companies some benefits. Literature summarises them in CSR's three dimensions. The social dimension is concerned with the wellbeing of people and communities (Choi & Ng, 2011). In this dimension, CSR, specially oriented to the human capital that works for the organization, is a very powerful management tool which makes employees assess the meaning of the activities they're making, increasing their motivation and retention (e.g., Bidwell, 2011; Campbell, Coff, & Kryscynski, 2012; Burbano, Mamer, & Snyder, 2018). Some authors also state that moral or prosocial motivations are the explanation of the employees' positive answers to CSR (e.g., Rupp, Ganapathi, Aguilera, & Williams, 2006; Rupp, Shao, Thornton, & Skarlicki, 2013; Gond, Akremi, Swaen, & Babu, 2017; Kim, Kim, Han, Jackson, & Ployhart, 2017). The need of improving organizations gets reviewed at the same time the innovation based in the creativity of the employees, who adopt a positive attitude towards their jobs (Gharleghi, Jahanshahi & Nawaser, 2018). Starting from this, employees adhere to the objectives and values of the company (Song, 2009), and the intentions of leaving the company lowers (Avey, Luthans, & Youssef, 2010). Some companies stand out for their actions towards the communities. The literature highlights the positive relationship between corporative philanthropy and the organization's visibility (Brammer & Millington, 2006; Hao, Farooq, & Zhang, 2018), and it is observed that the organizations make a positive contribution to the communities by integrating their social initiatives with community compromise.

The environmental dimension has become increasingly important to the consumers, observing high interest on this topic since the 1980s (Choi & Ng, 2011), with various approaches such as climate change, acid rain, energy efficiency, among others. In this dimension, the adoption of measures based in new technologies and processes that is important for the betterment of the functioning by creating less residues are important, as is the proactive behaviour of the employee in this direction (Jabbour & de Sousa Jabbour, 2016; Yuriev, Boiral, Francoeur, & Paillé, 2018). The literature analyses the good use of energy and raw materials and the cycle of life assessment, in order to lessen the environmental impacts (de Beer & Friend, 2006; Browne, O'Regan & Moles, 2012). Recently the eco-controls and eco-audits have become more common in organizations, and the effect of applying this type of measures that tend to diminish the environmental impacts and increase the performance is an increase of efficiency, thus requiring their study and application to continue (Henri & Journeault, 2010; Daddi, Magistrelli, Frey, & Iraldo, 2011; Nishitani, Kaneko, Fujii, & Komatsu, 2012). From marketing's point of view, the idea of green marketing is gaining momentum, and it's being used in "green" applications to traditional topics, such as advertising and promotion, consumer behaviour, and purchase intention (Choi & Ng, 2011). The topic of the carbon emissions disclosure, within the environmental disclosure perspective, is a hot topic nowadays, and it will cause the companies to have more legitimacy (Berthelot & Robert, 2011; dan Basuki, 2016). The companies of this industry tend to reveal their information about carbon dioxide emissions, to show that they are responsible and to reduce the threat to their legitimacy (Borghei, Leung & Guthrie, 2016). At the same time, this disclosure can bring a better economic future for the companies, because the potential investors will end up investing (Healy & Palepu, 2001). In more recent times, Liu, Zhou, Yang, and Hoepner (2016) stated that carbon dioxide emissions can have little negative impacts, but they are significative for the economic performance of the organization. At the same time, the diminishing of carbon dioxide emissions has more additional benefits, like the reduction of operating costs, a better reputation and an increase of the loyalty of stakeholders.

The economical dimension is crucial, because every company needs some positive performance in order to continue existing, to comply with their obligations with their stakeholders, and to undertake more CSR activities. A good economic performance will determine the continuity of the company and it will help to avoid the loss of jobs, insecurity and financial risks (Choi & Ng, 2011). In this dimension two linked items can be identified: On one hand, the usual financial performance, that wants to diminish costs, and on the other hand, the will to fulfill the external stakeholders' (such as employees, customers, and suppliers) economic interests, on a quest to increase their wellbeing and standard of living (Sheth, Sethia, & Srinivas, 2011).

Starting to undertake CSR actions implies assuming some kind of costs. The formation of employees, the attention to customer chains, the commitment with the suppliers, etc., are costs that the company will only be able to recover in the medium or long term (McWilliams & Siegel, 2001; Carrol & Shabana, 2010). The social exposure of the organizations is also submitted to assessment processes which, sometimes, make the companies to incur in some associated costs (Morsing & Schultz, 2006; Thorne, Mahoney, Gregory, & Convery, 2017).

Finally, CSR means that organizations obtain competitive advantage, so it seems plausible to establish a link between CSR and competitiveness. In the short term, it's not possible to establish a link between CSR and the improvement of competitiveness, CSR could even harm it. But in the long term, CSR can favour the competitiveness of organizations in the market (Commission for the European Communities, 2008).

The voluntary integration of actions by the enterprises allows them to help sustainable development reach further (Gallardo-Vázquez, Sánchez-Hernández, & Corchuelo, 2013), and at the same time give them multiple benefits. In order to organise the benefits the academic literature have explained, we're going to establish four different groups: A) Personal sphere; B) Organizational field; C) Personal and organizational fields; and D) Financial area. We're going to explain them briefly in the next section.

The academic literature is very clear in that numerous benefits and costs exist that are associated to CSR activities. Nevertheless, they are dispersed, so it was not possible to find a research that showed a wide and structured compilation of them. So, the goal of this study is to make a theoretically structured description of the benefits and costs associated with the implementation of CSR in the organizations. The contributions of this study are diverse, and it is focused both to the academia and to business managers.

To this end, this chapter is organized as follows. After this introduction, the benefits of CSR are explained in the second section, divided in four paragraphs: benefits in the personal sphere, in the organizational field, in both the personal and organizational fields at the same time and in the financial field. Then the costs of implementing CSR are explained in the third section. The chapter ends with the discussion and conclusion in the last section, as well as with the explanation of some key concepts.

BENEFITS OF APPLYING CSR PRACTICES IN THE ORGANIZATIONS

As the literature says, applying CSR practices is advantageous for the organizations, and a lot of benefits and advantages are observed, which we are going to comment in the next pages. We have grouped them in various groups, taking their traits in common into account.

Benefits of CSR in the Personal Sphere

This first group of benefits of CSR takes us to the internal sphere of CSR, the so-called Internal Corporate Social Responsibility (ICSR). The internal character is determined by the attention being paid to the stakeholders of internal nature, the internal stakeholders. Among them we fundamentally include the owners of the organizations and the employees. Hao, Farooq and Zhang (2018) consider that the employees are the true internal resources of companies. The benefits we'll comment now are oriented mainly to them. They are a very important internal stakeholder in CSR matters (Aguilera, Rupp, Williams, & Ganapathi, 2007; Farooq, Rupp, & Farooq, 2017), because they are able to carry on with initiatives and at the same time to commit with socially responsible organizations (Stites & Michael, 2011).

1. CSR promotes social conscience culture, increasing the involvement and commitment with the organization. The employee involved in CSR practices deepens the knowledge of his or her internal states of mind, and analyses his or her contribution to the social conscience generated, so the employee feels committed with the organization he or she is working for. The organizational commitment is interpreted as the psychological attachment that an individual feels for his or her organization (O'Reilly & Chatman, 1986; Allen & Meyer, 1996). On that sense, we can quote Turker's (2009a, 2009b) approach of six dimensions about internal practices of CSR, oriented to the participation of employees in voluntary activities, career opportunities, desires and needs of employees, balance between family life and work, organizational justice and equality and training and education. As a consequence, and a result of CSR, the previous practices lead to work-related satisfaction, defined by Locke and Latham (1990) as a pleasant and positive mental attitude which is the result of work appraisal or experience. This work-related satisfaction is the result of the perception of the employees of how good their work gives the elements considered important. The addition of ICSR practices to an organization implies activities strongly linked with the physical and psychological working environment of the employees, promoting the conscience of social culture and the commitment to the organization needed to generate work-related satisfaction. Other studies support the fact that CS practices on an organization would have a positive and significant influence on their employees' commitment (Brammer, Millington, & Rayton, 2007). Later, Jones (2010) argues that employees who receive support from their company when carrying out social activities are more likely to feel strongly attached to the organization, showing a strong commitment with it. Caligiuri, Mencin, and Jiang (2013) and Hao et al. (2018) show that corporate volunteer programs could be an important source of employee engagement and commitment, promoting benefits for the organization.

2. Encouragement of employees' motivation and pride of being part of the company. We find ourselves in the generation of the so-called emotional commitment of the employee with the organization he or she works for. This emotional commitment is related to the understanding and accepting by the employees of the objectives and values of the organization, and their personal emotional linking with it (Meyer & Allen, 1991; Avolio & Gardner, 2005), creating a feeling of being part of the organization. Motivation determines what employees do, how they do it and how hard they work (Meyer, Becker, & Vandenberghe, 2004). Researchers have started to take into account the role of motivation in the obtaining of results by the employees (Graves, Sarkis & Zhu, 2013; Pelletier & Aitken, 2014), making a difference between external and internal motivation. In external motivation, the employees undertake socially responsible actions because of factors external to themselves; they are looking for rewards or approval (Graves & Sarkis, 2012; Graves et al., 2013; Koestner & Losier, 2002). Internal motivation, on the other hand, comes from the employee, the so-called inherent motivation (Graves & Sarkis, 2012; Graves et al., 2013; Koestner & Losier, 2002), by which the employees undertake actions to comply with their own values, completely embracing the importance of sustainability. Nevertheless, there is a time when both types of motivations unite and create a whole, so the employee gets 100% integrated into the organization. According to the Social Identity Theory framework, when an organization attempts to engage in corporate social activities, its business professionals can be proud of being members of the organization, thus committing them affectively (Brammer et al., 2007; Turker, 2009b).

3. Employee social abilities get better. The enrichment that CSR actions contribute to an employee by means of his or her work, have a significance that goes beyond his or her own motivation and personal

Figure 1. Benefits caused by CSR oriented in the personal sphere
Source: The authors

and work-related satisfaction. It reaches aspects such as the achieved autonomy (Hackman & Oldham, 1976). Adler (1991) found that the organizations in which employees express higher perceptions in abilities, autonomy and feedback report higher levels of satisfaction and motivation, which leads to expressing higher levels of CSR benefits. RSC can cause more proactivity in the employees of an organization, as well as more personal initiative, more collaboration with their colleagues and more commitment to organizational excellence (Salanova & Schaufeli, 2004). Following Luthans and Youssef (2004), a series of psychological characteristics of employees which are crucial to the development of the organization must be optimized, such as: self-efficacy, hope or willpower, realistic optimism, and resilience.

4. Employees' empathy levels get reinforced. Firstly, we must say, to focus the topic, that from the 90s onwards the study of empathy is done from the perspective of Emotional Intelligence (EI). One approach to the EI study was done by Bar-On (1997, 2000) in his emotional-social intelligence model. For this author, empathy is a component of the factor called interpersonal abilities, defined as the capacity of being conscious of and understanding the emotions, feelings and ideas of others, being considered a cognitive component (Fernández-Pinto, López-Pérez, & Márquez, 2008). CSR literature says that socially responsible actions are able to allow workers to acquire that ability to internalize the thoughts and desires of the other.

In Figure 1 we show a diagram that summarises the benefits that we have spoken about on the last paragraphs.

Benefits of CSR in the Organizational Field

The second group of CSR benefits shows how the organization, also from an internal point of view, can reach positive behaviours once it starts to undertake some socially responsible processes and strategies. Among these advantages that can be observed internally in the organizations, we are going to emphasize reputation, the impact on the public image, loyalty, the increase of productivity and profits, etc.

1. Better organizational reputation and social visibility. Reputation is the perception that the public has about a company or brand (Lai, Chiu, Yang, & Pai, 2010), which is a public and subjective attribute, and a consensus exists about the perceived impression of the corporate image of the company. Organizational reputation is the whole of attributes, both economical and non-economical, that are joined to the organization and generated by its past actions, which determine the status of the organization within the industry. Reputation is a valuable and all-embracing resource, which is strongly linked to the execution of socially responsible activities on the organizations (Castilla-Polo & Ruíz-Rodríguez, 2017; González-Ramos, Manzanares-Donate, & Gómez-Guadamillas, 2014). CSR programmes in organizations contribute to the increase of organizational reputation (Baldarelli & Gigli, 2014; Jo, Kim, & Park, 2015). Authors like Roberts and Dowling (2002) and Baldarelli and Gigli (2014) add that a good reputation is an asset that will allow the organization to make additional benefits, like better social visibility, more profitability and sustained performance. Other recent studies say that CSR increases organizational reputation (Cegarra-Navarro, Reverte, Gómez-Melero, & Wensley, 2016; Li, Xin, Chen, & Ren, 2017; Maldonado-Guzmán, Pinzón-Castro, & Leana-Morales, 2017).

2. It has a positive impact on the public image of the organization, reinforcing brand loyalty. The most important asset of any organization is the value its clients give it, and the image it transmits. Image has a value that goes way beyond symbolic. Corporative image is the first impression that buyers have of a company and is a personal and subjective attribute (Villafañe, 2001). It's very important for the companies to preserve its public image and to be socially responsible in all its operations (Chen, Patten, & Roberts, 2008; Pérez-Ruiz & Rodríguez del Bosque, 2012). Jones, Willness and Madey (2014) found that companies engaged in social responsible activities with the community got a positive image and are better able to attract suitable employees. Later, Cegarra-Navarro et al. (2016) said that the Small and Medium Enterprises (SMEs) are adding CSR practices to their processes, and increasing their image. Also, Hameed, Riaz, Arain, and Farooq (2016) stated that employees will develop a positive social image of their organization in case the last one was able to be involved with social corporate responsible activities with the community. So, community development also enhances the outsider's perception of the firm (Farooq et al., 2017). Other studies say that CSR improves the image of the company and strengthens the brand (Cegarra-Navarro et al., 2016; Li et al., 2017; Maldonado-Guzmán et al., 2017).

3. It increases productivity, sales and profits. Barney, Ketchen, Wright, McWilliams, and Siegel (2011) said that when an organization reaches a certain level of competitive success by means of its resources and capabilities, due to, for example, its CSR actions, as a consequence its productivity and profitability improve. Following the same line of thought, the literature remarks that CSR practices on organizations help to achieve better performances and economical results, positively affecting productivity and organizational competitiveness (Tang, Hull, & Rothenberg, 2012; Valenzuela, Jara-Bertin, & Villegas, 2015). Rupp et al. (2006) say that if an employee feels that his or her organization is acting in a socially irresponsible way, it's possible for them to show negative behaviours at work. On the other hand, if they feel that their organization is acting responsibly, then it's possible for them to show positive attitudes towards the company and that they work in a more productive way. At the same time, organizations are conscious that employees are their closest contact with clients and suppliers, being able to develop lasting links and relationships on the long term. Literature shows that implementing CSR strategies increases the incomes of an organization, because they turn it into a model that is attractive for consumers (Wheeler, Colbert & Freeman, 2003). Also, happy employees lead to more sales and profit for the organization.

4. It increases internal motivation. Motivating employees has always been one of the greatest worries inside organizations, that is, satisfying the needs of the people that employ their talent in the organiza-

tion, so they don't work out of habit. Today that worry is one of the main worries of executives, because apart from the mentioned habit, a general feeling of resignation, sadness and uncertainty with which a lot of people start their day everyday must be added. Organizations try to find innovative formulas to strengthen a motivation that is very difficult to find via salary incentives, career plans, formative plans or new projects to develop. This motivation comes from CSR actions (Wheeler et al., 2003). Murray (2007) said that increased employee motivation is a key driver, observing that people are seeking meaning at work and, it has become clear that staff motivation is a powerful bottom-line benefit of corporate responsibility. Sprinkle and Maines (2010) think the same, saying that CSR may increase employee motivation and reduce the need for costly performance evaluation. Hur, Moon, and Ko (2018) found that in the intrinsic motivation of the employees the positive relationship between CSR perceptions and their creativity mediated, another benefit we will comment later.

5. It improves the working environment inside the company. Using socially responsible human resources management programmes the working environment can improve, both individually and as an organization, which will have better organizational performance as a result (Wheeler et al., 2003).

6. CSR promotes innovation. There is a significant and positive relationship between CSR and innovation (Carroll & Shabana, 2010; Wagner, 2010; Padgett & Galán, 2010; Gallardo-Vázquez & Sánchez Hernández, 2013; Oh, Chang, & Martynov, 2011). Authors as De Miguel (2011) state that SMEs that implement CSR are more innovative, creating benefits for everyone implied, both businesspeople and stakeholders. R&D intensity positively influences CSR (Padgett & Galán, 2010). CSR-oriented innovation leads to high social profits (Wagner, 2010). Literature says the socially responsible actions allow organizations to hire more innovative people, which influences positively in the organization's level of innovation (Williamson, Lynch-Wood & Ramsay, 2006). Proactive organizations in CSR tend to be technological leaders in their industries, and are generally better that the companies which have reactive positions relating to the innovation strategy when developing socially responsible actions (McGregor & Fontrodona, 2008). Recent studies are stating that big, medium and small enterprises are adopting more innovative business models with a sustainable and responsible approach, and are including them in their processes, products and services, which lead them to an increase in innovation activities (Adams, Jeanrenaud, Bessant, Denyer & Overy, 2016; Martínez-Conesa, Soto-Acosta & Palacios-Manzano, 2017). It is possible to talk of a mediating role of innovation in the relationship between performance and CSR too (Reverte, Gómez & Cegarra, 2016).

7. Improvement of energy efficiency. Socially responsible activities, such as recycling and other activities to reduce the consumption of natural resources, apart from minimizing their negative impacts on environment, will achieve significant economical savings. This benefit impacts the economical dimension of the organization in a positive way. Energy efficiency tries to protect the environment, reducing the intensity and creating a habit on the user of consuming just the strict necessary. Due to the increase of CO_2 emissions to the atmosphere, the energy efficiency has become a way of taking care of the planet and of favouring sustainable development (Escribano, 2012). Given the awareness of organizations about social responsibility and climate change, they are giving more and more boost to actions and measures that regulate energy use to avoid waste, achieving a very significant yearly effect which, at the same time, favours turnover.

8. Achieving legitimacy in the industry. Organizations' CSR of an industry, when added, represent the CSR of the industry and justify their bigger or smaller legitimacy on the economic system in which they operate. Schuman (1995, p. 574) defines legitimacy as "the general assumption that the activities of an organization are desirable, correct or appropriate when done as part of a socially constructed system

of rules, values, beliefs and definitions". Legitimacy of organizations require the fulfilment of a "social contract", by which organizations agree to satisfy social demands, receiving the approval of their objectives, as well as some type of reward that guarantees their existence (Deegan, 2002). A CSR strategy determines the legitimacy of the organization against others, as it is wanted and accepted by others. That, at the same time, will help to assure the existence of the organization on the long term (Williamson & Lynch-Wood, 2008). The acquisition of legitimacy for an organization is closely linked to the execution of its External Corporate Social Responsibility (ECSR), which is closer to the public perception of the organization's reputation, because the ECSR efforts give recognisable and externally visible symbols of the attractiveness and differentiation of the organization (Farooq et al., 2017).

9. It makes bargaining easier. CSR makes the management of an organization easier establishing channels so that the interests of all the interlocutors can be taken into account when decisions are made (Wheeler et al., 2003). From an internal point of view, the organizations that manages to enter their employees and associates with the philosophy and organizational culture based on CSR get a big variety of benefits, such as the increase of productivity, both individual and organizational, motivation gets better, a bigger resource-saving conscience is generated, and the relationship with customers and suppliers gets better (Server Izquierdo & Capó i Vicedo, 2011). From an external point of view, socially responsible organizations have experimented better practices and results with their clients, suppliers and with society, which helps improve their sales, utility and reputation (Waldman et al., 2006; McWilliams, Siegel, & Wright, 2006). This bargaining and communication actions, both internal and external, have allowed organizations to tighten the continued relationships with their stakeholders; relationships which can also help organizations to generate new ideas, make their products better, establish competitive prices, make their processes better and to have bigger focus on the weaknesses of the organization, in order to ease them by means of a strategic decision making process (Barba-Sánchez & Atienza-Sahuquillo, 2010; Smith & Williams, 2011).

10. More competitive success and performance. Some authors point out that the organizations that carry socially responsible actions out will have more competitive success (Fombrun & Van Riel, 2004; Kechiche & Soparnot, 2012; Kramer & Porter, 2006; Gallardo-Vázquez & Sánchez-Hernández, 2014; Boulouta & Pitelis, 2014). Morata, Vilà, and Suárez (2010) show that CSR can be an opportunity for the organization to differentiate itself from the closest competitors. At the same time, socially responsible organizations have a better performance (Erhemjamts, Li & Venkateswaran, 2013; Inoue & Lee, 2011). Literature has lengthily shown the relationship existing between CSR and performance in organizations (Herrera, Larrán, Martínez, & Martínez-Martínez, 2016; Mason & Simmons 2011; Rodrigo, Durán & Arenas 2016). Jones (2010) showed that employees engaged in social activities in their companies should get a better performance. Jones et al. (2014) found that companies engaged in socially responsible activities would obtain a good performance. Hameed et al. (2016) said that CSR actions could generate performance and value.

Figure 2 shows a diagram of the benefits explained in the second group.

Benefits of CSR in the Personal and Organizational Fields

On the third group we are going to introduce some benefits derived from socially responsible actions with incidence in the personal field and organizational sphere at the same time. There is no doubt whatsoever that individual and organization form a whole, the actions of one and the other mutually reinforce. We

Figure 2. Benefits caused by CSR oriented in the organizational field
Source: The authors

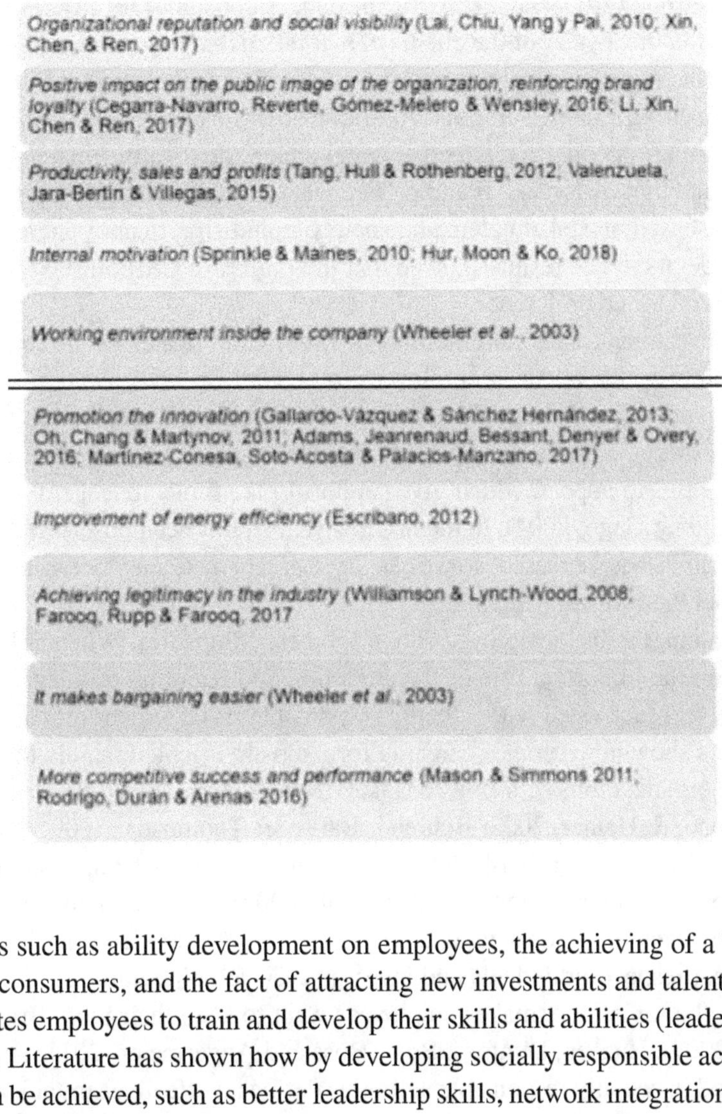

observe advantages such as ability development on employees, the achieving of a bigger loyalty to the organization from consumers, and the fact of attracting new investments and talent to the organization.

1. CSR stimulates employees to train and develop their skills and abilities (leadership, initiative, creativity, teamwork). Literature has shown how by developing socially responsible actions, better abilities and knowledge can be achieved, such as better leadership skills, network integration and strategic vision (Colbert & Kurucz, 2007; Needleman, 2008). A paper by Hur et al. (2018) suggests that perceptions of CSR by the employees are positively related to their creativity. At the same time, Abdelmotaleb, Metwally, and Saha (2018) found a positive association between CSR perceptions and employee creative behaviors. The authors confirm that these CSR perceptions have influenced positive affect at work, leading employees to greater level of engagement in the creative process. A paper by Gond, Igalens, Swaen, and El Akremi (2011) suggests that the organization of the Human Resources-CSR interface can improve or hinder the contribution of HR to responsible leadership. Supanti, Butcher, and Fredline (2015) found some beneficial effects for employees who engage a socially responsible activity in hotels. The authors identified: fun, pride, developing skills and building teamwork.

2. It improves the relationship with consumers, and gets better loyalty. Consumers admire organizations that value their employees, develop social projects, care about the environment and put effort into making

positive actions for society (Bhattacharya & Sen, 2004; Pivato, Misani, & Tencati, 2008). Finally, CSR is a factor that guarantees a better relationship with consumers and determines their fidelity. Martínez and Rodríguez Del Bosque (2013) say that CSR influences consumer loyalty. These authors present a CSR influence model in the loyalty of the clients of a hotel, including simultaneously the identification of the customer with the organization, trust, and the satisfaction as mediators, showing the direct effects of the constructs defined. Martínez, Pérez and Rodríguez del Bosque (2014) confirmed the role of CSR as a tool to generate both functional and affective brand image and loyalty. Finally, Liu, Wong, Rongwei, and Tseng (2014) found that customers' brand preference can be enhanced by their perceptions on CSR. Two CSR initiatives, based on stakeholders and society, could significantly increase loyalty intention, although to varying degrees. The results showed that the impact of CSR on stakeholders has a stronger influence on customers' brand preference.

3. CSR attracts investment. Literature points out those CSR strategies attract socially responsible investment funds, allowing the talent of employees to be kept, so CSR has become an asset for companies, increasing brand value. During the last decade, the offer of venture funds comprising shares selected using CSR criteria, and the rise of the demand of a socially responsible investment has made CSR specialized agencies to appear, which give support to the funds management, audit and evaluate the companies (Antolín & Gago, 2004). In the last few years it has been observed that the investment in socially responsible funds has increased, so we can say that when organizations undertake CSR actions, they are able to attract the investors' attention.

4. CSR attracts talent, the best employees go to the best companies. When talking about CSR it is mandatory to mention the important role of the attraction and retention of talent in organizations. It's clear that employees feel motivated with socially responsible management practices which are clearly defined. Some studies show how people searching for a job are oriented mainly to socially responsible companies instead of organizations with either an insufficient CSR or bad reputation (Greening & Turban, 2000; Backhaus, Stone, & Heiner, 2002; Behrend, Baker, & Thompson, 2009; Alniacik, Alniacik, & Genc, 2011; Tsai, Joe, Lin, & Wang, 2014). It has also been observed that employees react not only to the way they're treated by their organization (Aguilera et al., 2007), but also to how others are treated both in and outside the organization (Cropanzano, Byrne, Bobocel, & Rupp, 2001). They feel good forming part of companies that respect individuals and invest in their learning abilities. CSR attracts talent for the company and, at the same time, makes employees want to keep their jobs (Bruch & Walter, 2005; Colbert & Kurucz, 2007). Hansen, Dunford, Boss, Boss and Angermeier (2011) suggest that the managers that get involved in socially responsible activities define an effective strategy not only as a tool to proclaim shared values to the stakeholders of the organization, but also as a tool to gain the hearts and minds of employees to retain talent during more time inside the organization.

5. It strengthens communication and credibility. CSR programmes are generating a positioning of organizations toward communications. At the same time, the interest of the media for CSR translates as an improvement of the public image of the organizations, a differentiating element from their rivals and an element of credibility (Colbert & Kurucz, 2007). Hur, Kim, and Woo (2014) state that CSR has a positive and direct effect on the credibility of the corporate brand. In a sample of 867 people in South Korea, they also observed that the credibility of the corporate brand mediates in the relationship between CSR and corporative reputation, another benefit we also mentioned earlier. The results of Haigh and Brubaker (2010) showed that the reduction of the offensive strategy led to higher perceptions of the relationship organization-public and CSR. The strategy of image recovery used has an impact on the perceptions of the stakeholders about the credibility of the source.

Figure 3. Benefits caused by CSR oriented in the personal and organizational fields
Source: The authors

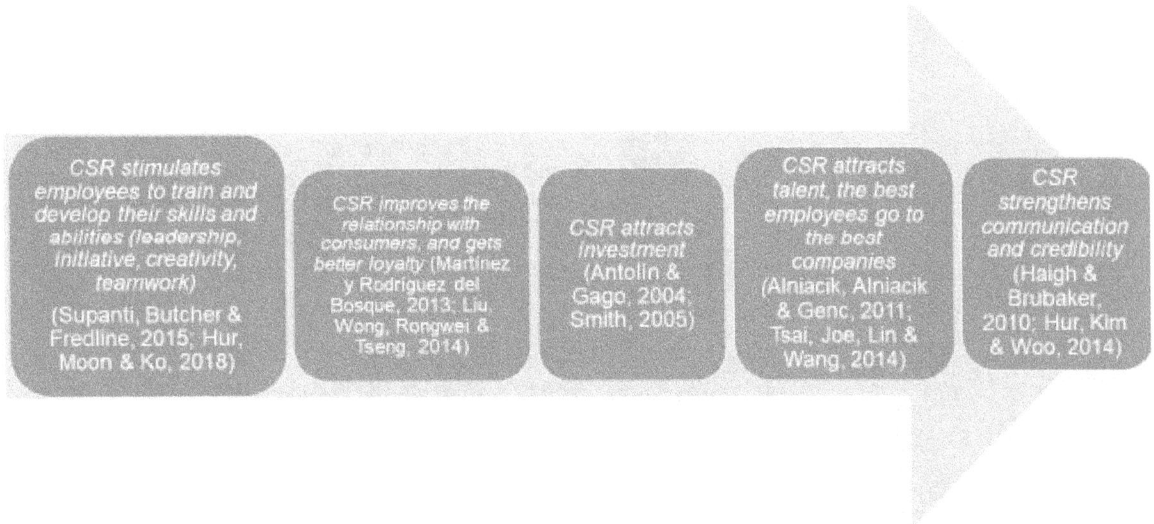

Figure 3 shows a diagram which summarises the benefits mentioned on block C.

Benefits of CSR in the Financial Area

In this fourth section we are going to comment some benefits derived from socially responsible actions that have an impact in the financial area of the organization. They are, without any doubt whatsoever, important benefits, because if the organization didn't have them, it wouldn't undertake CSR activities. We have observed advantages such as the increase of profitability and also costs and organizational risks reduction.

1. Increase of profitability or financial performance. As we stated previously, the positive attitude of employees will have a positive impact on organizations, which will also translate in a direct and positive effect in organizational performance (Colbert & Kurucz, 2007; Wong & Laschinger, 2013). Bolanle (2012) analysed the relationship between corporate social responsibility and profitability in the Nigerian banking industry. The study concluded that there is a positive relationship between banks CSR activities and profitability. At the same time, Mahbuba and Farzana (2013) found a significant and positive relationship between CSR and profitability in the case of Dutch Bangla Bank Ltd. Silva and Lopes (2019) found a positive relationship between the participation of companies in the Corporate Sustainability Index and their ROA. This result is atractive for companies to stimulate the participation in the index in order to improve its performance. Yoon and Chung (2018) investigated the restaurant firm's financial performance in order to know the firm's profitability. The results showed that internal CSR generate an increase of the firm's operational profitability, that is, the direct and positive link between CSR and profitability observed by other authors. Platonova, Asutay, Dixon, and Mohammad (2018) analyzed the relationship between CSR and financial performance for Islamic bank in the Gulf Cooperation Council region over the period 2000-2014. The results reveal a significant and positive relationship between the variables under study.

Figure 4. Benefits caused by CSR oriented in the financial area
Source: The authors

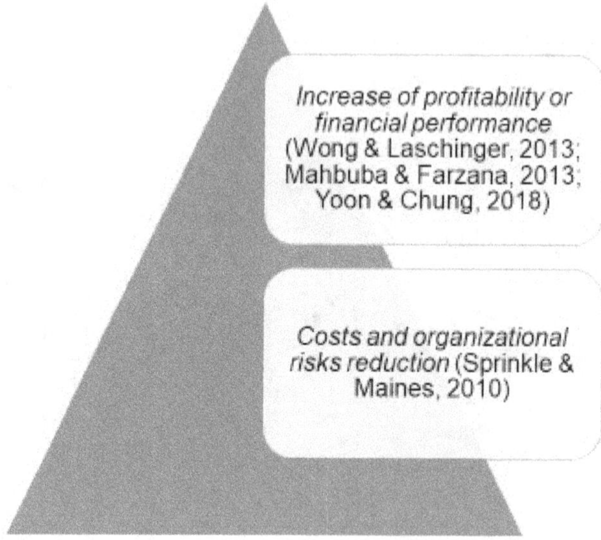

2. Costs and organizational risks reduction. As we know, CSR is related to energetic efficiency. Socially responsible organizations will analyse where resources are spent, in order to be able to apply cost-reducing practices and improve environmental policies. These practices include: installing water fountains to avoid the use of plastic bottles, avoid discharging the toilet twice, changing the light bulbs for low consumption, implement a switching off lights policy, recycling printer and copiers consumables, changing paper-based support for online support, using hybrid or electric vehicles and changing machinery for more energy efficient machinery. Sprinkle and Maines (2010) refer the costs reduction of Wal Mart company in 2006, by reducing transport costs with an initiative of the way toys were packed. The company also saved tons of corrugated materials, oil barrels, trees and containers. On the other hand, the same authors remark that the conservation of energy is an area about which the companies give information about their significant savings in operating costs. Ecology and Environment, Inc. (2008) informed about an 80% reduction of the annual emissions of carbon dioxide of its headquarters. That meant an important saving for the company in economic terms.

Figure 4 shows a diagram of the benefits we have commented in paragraphs 1 and 2 above.

COSTS OF IMPLEMENTING CSR PRACTICES IN COMPANIES

Apart from the multiple benefits that CSR has, we cannot ignore the existence of some risks that implementing CSR implies. Among all of them, we can emphasise the following ones:

1. The initial cost of implementing CSR, and the cost of maintaining it. Generally bigger organizations have bigger benefits when adopting and implementing CSR strategies, owing to their organizational, financial and economic power. Nevertheless, some experts have stated that in some occasions those multinational companies face bigger costs than SMEs in the medium and long term, mainly owing to

the big deployment of human (education of the employees and the department responsible of those actions), financial (philanthropy actions, social campaigns, investment on certifications, etc.), technical and ethical resources in their processes (machinery and ecological products), and those bigger costs are also caused by the neglect of the supervising of the social, economic and environmental actions (Merminod, & Paché, 2011; Høgevold et al., 2014). It is also worth noting that CSR costs depends mainly on the model one is wishing to adopt, and on which model the organization is able to sustain. Some of the initial costs increase when the company grows; in the management of the supply chain, the so-called bullwhip effect is one of the factors that can cause a big disruption in its operations, owing to the scarce supervision of the tasks, which has an impact on the satisfaction degree of the stakeholders (Asgary & Li, 2016). In order to see CSR costs as an investment in the medium and long term, expert authors like McWilliams and Siegel (2001) and Carrol and Shabana (2010) have stated that, the bigger the investment and expenditure applied on CSR actions, the bigger the tendency of the profitability of the company rising.

2. Media pressure that some socially responsible organizations have to endure, because their actions are more observed. In this sense, Fombrun and Shanley (1990), Brammer and Millington (2005) and Brammer, He and Mellahi (2015) have said that CSR is strongly associated with social evaluations of the esteem within society. CSR affects company evaluation (Lichtenstein, Drumwright & Braig, 2004). We have said that socially responsible firms are more attractive to prospective employees (Greening & Turban, 2000). This is good, but it means being in the crosshairs of many people.

3. The fact that the publication of a CSR report means being more scrutinized by clients and competitors. It is known that nowadays CSR is very important for SMEs and bigger organizations; but some unresolved topics remain, like the communication or diffusion of CSR results derived from the strategies and actions they undertake during a certain period of time. In regions with a high economic, social and cultural development, like North America and Europe, the spreading of results via formal reports, validated by local and international institutions, has become a determinant practice for all the involved parts: investors, employees, clients, suppliers and community (Morsing & Schultz, 2006; Thorne et al., 2017). Nevertheless, in regions with economies in development, this matter is still a challenge (Dawkins, 2005). Reports with which companies communicate with their stakeholders are aligned to the sustainable development goals established by the World Pact of the United Nations. Some companies of different industries have been spreading this type of information via traditional media, like the press, radio, television, forums or mouth to mouth, while another ones use more modern media like social networks, websites and some more linked with new technologies (Sweeney & Coughlan, 2008; Bals & Tate, 2017).

FUTURE RESEARCH DIRECTIONS

The contributions of this study are diverse, both to academia and to managers. The study, made by revising theoretical and empirical literature, has allowed us to discover new paths for future analysis. Firstly, it's important to say that this study is a compilation of existing literature, and that in some cases, in spite of the vast quantity of information analysed, some relevant studies on the CSR field could have been omitted during the selection, revision and development process of this document. Our contribution ends offering a very wide and complete research, to which any researcher can resort to know about the majority of benefits and costs present in literature. This can lead to subsequent bibliometric studies, and to studies of structured literature review. Secondly, from an epistemological point of view, the different theoretical currents for and against CSR are a crucial element when defining the topics to develop, owing to the wide and complex existing literature. Thirdly, the study offers managers a decision-making tool, and reading it could help them to value the positives and negatives of implementing socially responsable actions, and by taking that into account, making the right decisions and the way to undertake.

Finally, to improve and to face these limitations, it's convenient to combine this type of studies with empirical analyses, in order to strengthen results and conclusions of the document. Owing to the topic being so relevant in the organizational context, it is necessary to continue analysing the effects CSR has on the different sized organizations, not only to investigate what happens both in and outside it, but also to make strategic decisions that help strengthen its development and economic growth. For that, it's convenient to add some crucial aspects of organizational competitiveness like reputation, circular economy and eco-innovation.

CONCLUSION

The topic explained in this chapter forces us to reflect about some important questions linked amongst them. On one hand, the main topic, Corporate social responsibility, the group of voluntary actions that companies add to their strategy, in its economic, social and environmental dimensions, hoping to achieve different results and at the same time the satisfaction of the different stakeholders with which it interacts. We can't deny that it is a very novel and wide strategy, which wants to achieve a lot with very little: it starts undertaking voluntary activities, which a relatively low cost and a lot of results and the satisfaction of the involved parts are going to be obtained.

As it has become evident during the chapter, from the internal sphere of CSR it has been observed how employees consider themselves the true internal resources of the organizations (Hao et al., 2018), and they are considered a very important internal stakeholder (Aguilera et al., 2007; Farooq et al., 2017). On that group of benefits, we have remarked how the employee feels committed with the organization he or she is a part of, which generates work-related satisfaction, concluding that CSR determines employee commitment (Brammer et al., 2007). But at the same time, the role of motivation in the employees obtaining results is remarked (Graves et al., 2013; Pelletier & Aitken, 2014), generating the so-called emotional commitment of the employees with the organization they are part of. CSR also allows the development of higher levels of abilities, autonomy, personal initiative and proactivity by the employees.

In the organizational field, also from an internal point of view, the organization is able to get more reputation, an intangible asset that will also allow it to achieve more related advantages, such as a sustained performance (Cegarra-Navarro et al., 2016; Li et al., 2017; Maldonado-Guzmán et al., 2017). Also, worth noting is the improvement of corporate image, and also the increase of sales and productivity, which is an important benefit stated by authors like Barney et al. (2011) and Valenzuela et al. (2015). On that same area, the increase of internal motivation is remarked; an important benefit that every employer has tried to achieve in his or her organization while trying to maintain the good development of business in difficult times (Murray, 2007). Also promoting innovation as a necessary strategy in organizations if they want to survive on the market, observing the interest of adopting models which link innovation with sustainability (Adams et al., 2016; Martínez-Conesa et al., 2017). The improvement of energetic efficiency, necessary for taking care of the planet and the achievement of sustainable development, and also the wish to obtain legitimacy in the industry, observing that CSR gives elements that legitimate the organization in the market (Farooq et al., 2017). And finally, organizations are able to achieve more competitive success (Kramer & Porter, 2006; Gallardo-Vázquez & Sánchez-Hernández, 2014).

In the personal and organizational fields, CSR generates bigger abilities and knowledge, such as improved leadership abilities, network integration and strategic vision (Colbert & Kurucz, 2007; Needleman, 2008). Moreover, CSR influences the consumers' loyalty (Martínez & Rodríguez del Bosque, 2013). At the same time, CSR strategies attract socially responsible investment funds. CSR attracts talent into the organizations (Tsai et al., 2014). And, finally, CSR has a positive effect on the credibility of the corporate brand (Hur et al., 2014).

In the financial area, the literature shows that the undertaking of socially responsible actions will determine an increase of profitability (Yoon & Chung, 2018; Silva & Lopes, 2019), as well as costs and organizational risks reduction (Sprinkle & Maines, 2010).

In relation with the costs of implementing CSR actions, the initial and maintenance costs are highlighted, remarking that CSR costs mainly depends of the model one wishes to adopt and of what the company can maintain. Big companies have greater costs than SMEs in the medium and long term because of the deployment of resources they make and the scarce supervision they have. Another type of cost is related to the pressure of the media that some socially responsible organizations have to withstand, due to their actions being continually monitored, which makes them feel like what they do is being evaluated (Brammer et al., 2015). Finally, publishing CSR information is a difficult task for the organizations, and when it finally happens, the fact of publishing CSR reports leads to a more intense scrutiny by the stakeholders.

Finally, it is important to say that nowadays CSR is being questioned and has lit some controversy because of factors going from real commitment to the lack of ethics in the internal practices of organizations with their stakeholders (Freeman, Wicks, & Parmar, 2004). Though it is true that a lot of organizations adopt and use CSR as a business strategy focused on the integral benefit of their stakeholders, there is another group of organizations that has been taking advantage of the trend and adopting these practices as a marketing strategy (Di Benedetto, 2017) trying to attract more customers and to increase their sales, but with relatively short termed results, which differs a lot from the theories focused in generating real value for stakeholders, which generate sustained results (Lee, 2008; McWilliams, 2015).

REFERENCES

Abdelmotaleb, M., Metwally, A.B., E.M., & Saha, S. K. (2018). Exploring the impact of being perceived as a socially responsible organization on employee creativity. *Management Decision*, *56*(11), 2325–2340. doi:10.1108/MD-06-2017-0552

Adams, R., Jeanrenaud, S., Bessant, J., Denyer, D., & Overy, P. (2016). Sustainability-oriented innovation: A systematic review. *International Journal of Management Reviews*, *18*(2), 180–205. doi:10.1111/ijmr.12068

Adler, N. J. (1991). *International Dimensions of Organizational Behavior*. Boston: PWS-Kent.

Aguilera, R. V., Rupp, D. E., Williams, C. A., & Ganapathi, J. (2007). Putting the S back in corporate social responsibility: A multilevel theory of social change in organizations. *Academy of Management Review*, *32*(3), 836–863. doi:10.5465/amr.2007.25275678

Allen, N. J., & Meyer, J. P. (1996). Affective, continuance, and normative commitment to the organization: An examination of construct validity. *Journal of Vocational Behavior*, *49*(3), 252–276. doi:10.1006/jvbe.1996.0043 PMID:8980084

Alniacik, U., Alniacik, E., & Genc, N. (2011). How corporate social responsibility information influences stakeholders' intentions. *Corporate Social Responsibility and Environmental Management*, *18*(4), 234–245. doi:10.1002/csr.245

Antolín, M., & Gago, R. (2004). Responsabilidad Social Corporativa: La última innovación en management. *Universia Business Review*, *1*, 28–39.

Asgary, N., & Li, G. (2016). Corporate social responsibility: Its economic impact and link to the bullwhip effect. *Journal of Business Ethics*, *135*(4), 665–681. doi:10.100710551-014-2492-1

Avey, J. B., Luthans, F., & Youssef, C. M. (2010). The Additive Value of Positive Psychological Capital in Predicting Work Attitudes and Behaviors. *Journal of Management*, *36*(2), 430–452. doi:10.1177/0149206308329961

Avolio, B. J., & Gardner, W. L. (2005). Authentic leadership development: Getting to the root of positive forms of leadership. *The Leadership Quarterly*, *16*(3), 315–338. doi:10.1016/j.leaqua.2005.03.001

Backhaus, K., Stone, B., & Heiner, K. (2002). Exploring the relationship between corporate social performance and employer attractiveness. *Business & Society*, *41*(3), 292–318. doi:10.1177/0007650302041003003

Baldarelli, M. G., & Gigli, S. (2014). Exploring the drivers of corporate reputation integrated with a corporate responsibility perspective: Some reflections in theory and in praxis. *The Journal of Management and Governance*, *18*(2), 589–613. doi:10.100710997-011-9192-3

Bals, L., & Tate, W. (2017). Transparency. In *Implementing Triple Bottom Line Sustainability into Global Supply Chains* (pp. 90–155). Routledge. doi:10.4324/9781351285124

Bar-On, R. (1997). *The Emotional Quotient Inventory (EQ-i): a test of emotional intelligence*. Toronto: Multi-Health Systems.

Bar-On, R. (2000). Emotional and social intelligence: insights from the emotional quotient inventory. In R. Bar-On & J. D. A. Parker (Eds.), *Handbook of emotional intelligence* (pp. 363–388). San Francisco, CA: Jossey-Bass.

Barba-Sánchez, V., & Atienza-Sahuquillo, C. (2010). Integration of the environment in managerial strategy: Application of the resource-based theory of competitive advantage, dynamic capabilities and corporate social responsibilities. *African Journal of Business Management*, *4*(6), 1155.

Barney, J. B., Ketchen, D. J. Jr, Wright, M., McWilliams, A., & Siegel, D. S. (2011). Creating and capturing value: Strategic corporate social responsibility, resource-based theory, and sustainable competitive advantage. *Journal of Management*, *37*(5), 1480–1495. doi:10.1177/0149206310385696

Behrend, T., Baker, B., & Thompson, L. (2009). Effects of pro-environmental recruiting messages: The role of organizational reputation. *Journal of Business and Psychology*, *24*(3), 341–350. doi:10.100710869-009-9112-6

Berthelot, S., & Robert, A. M. (2011). Climate change disclosures: An examination of Canadian oil and gas firms. *Issues in Social and Environmental Accounting*, *5*(1/2), 106–123. doi:10.22164/isea.v5i2.61

Bhattacharya, C. B., & Sen, S. (2004). Doing better at doing good: When. why, and how consumers respond to corporate social initiatives. *California Management Review*, *47*(1), 9–24. doi:10.2307/41166284

Bidwell, M. (2011). Paying more to get less: The effects of external hiring versus internal mobility. *Administrative Science Quarterly*, *56*(3), 369–407. doi:10.1177/0001839211433562

Boddy, C. (2011). *Corporate psychopaths* (1st ed.). Basingstoke: Palgrave Macmillan. Retrieved from http://www.loc.gov/catdir/enhancements/fy1114/2011003111-d.html

Bolanle, A. B. (2012). Corporate Social Responsibility and Profitability of Nigeria Banks. A Causal Relationship. *Research Journal of Finance and Accounting*, *3*(1), 6–18.

Borghei, Z., Leung, P., & Guthrie, J. (2016). The Nature Of Voluntary Greenhouse Gas Disclosure - An Explanation Of The Changing Rationale: Australian Evidence. *Meditari Accountability in Research*, *24*(1), 111–133.

Boulouta, I., & Pitelis, C. N. (2014). Who needs CSR? The impact of corporate social responsibility on national competitiveness. *Journal of Business Ethics*, *119*(3), 349–364. doi:10.100710551-013-1633-2

Brammer, S., He, H., & Mellahi, K. (2015). Corporate social responsibility, employee organizational identification, and creative effort: The moderating impact of corporate ability. *Group & Organization Management*, *40*(3), 323–352. doi:10.1177/1059601114562246

Brammer, S., & Millington, A. (2005). Corporate reputation and philanthropy: An empirical analysis. *Journal of Business Ethics*, *61*(1), 29–44. doi:10.100710551-005-7443-4

Brammer, S., & Millington, A. (2006). Firm size, organizational visibility and corporate philanthropy: An empirical analysis. *Business Ethics a European Review*, *15*(1), 6–18. doi:10.1111/j.1467-8608.2006.00424.x

Brammer, S., Millington, A., & Rayton, B. (2007). The contribution of corporate social responsibility to organization commitment. *International Journal of Human Resource Management*, *18*(10), 1701–1719. doi:10.1080/09585190701570866

Browne, D., O'Regan, B., & Moles, R. (2012). Comparison of energy flow accounting, energy flow metabolism ratio analysis and ecological footprinting as tools for measuring urban sustainability: A case-study of an Irish city–region. *Ecological Economics*, *83*, 97–107. doi:10.1016/j.ecolecon.2012.08.006

Bruch, H., & Walter, F. (2005). The keys to rethinking corporate philanthropy. *MIT Sloan Management Review*, *47*, 48–56.

Burbano, V. C., Mamer, J., & Snyder, J. (2018). Pro bono as a human capital learning and screening mechanism: Evidence from law firms. *Strategic Management Journal*, *39*(11), 2899–2920. doi:10.1002mj.2947

Caligiuri, P., Mencin, A., & Jiang, K. (2013). Win–win–win: The influence of company-sponsored volunteerism programs on employees, NGOs, and business units. *Personnel Psychology*, *66*(4), 825–860. doi:10.1111/peps.12019

Campbell, B. A., Coff, R., & Kryscynski, D. (2012). Rethinking sustained competitive advantage from human capital. *Academy of Management Review*, *37*(3), 376–395. doi:10.5465/amr.2010.0276

Carroll, A. B. (1999). Corporate social responsibility: Evolution of a definitional construct. *Business & Society*, *38*(3), 268–295. doi:10.1177/000765039903800303

Carroll, A. B., & Shabana, K. M. (2010). The business case for corporate social responsibility: A review of concepts, research and practice. *International Journal of Management Reviews*, *12*(1), 85–105. doi:10.1111/j.1468-2370.2009.00275.x

Carroll, A. B., & Shabana, K. M. (2010). The business case for corporate social responsibility: A review of concepts, research and practice. *International Journal of Management Reviews*, *12*(1), 85–105. doi:10.1111/j.1468-2370.2009.00275.x

Castilla-Polo, F., & Ruiz-Rodríguez, M. C. (2017). Usefulness of the Information on Intangible Assets Derived From Corporate Social Responsibility. *Paper presented at the European Conference on Intellectual Capital*. Academic Press.

Cegarra-Navarro, J. G., Reverte, C., Gómez-Melero, E., & Wensley, A. K. P. (2016). Linking social and economic responsibilities with financial performance: The role of innovation. *European Management Journal*, *34*(5), 530–539. doi:10.1016/j.emj.2016.02.006

Chen, J. C., Patten, D. M., & Roberts, R. (2008). Corporate charitable contributions: A corporate social performance or legitimacy strategy? *Journal of Business Ethics*, *82*, 131–144. doi:10.100710551-007-9567-1

Choi, S., & Ng, A. (2011). Environmental and economic dimensions of sustainability and Price effects on consumer responses. *Journal of Business Ethics*, *104*(2), 269–282. doi:10.100710551-011-0908-8

Colbert, B. A., & Kurucz, E. (2007). Three conceptions of Triple Bottom Line Business Sustainability and the Role for HRM. *HR. Human Resource Planning*, *30*(1), 21–29.

Comisión de las Comunidades Europeas. (2001). *Libro Verde. Fomentar un Marco Europeo para la Responsabilidad Social de las Empresas*.

Comisión de las Comunidades Europeas. (2011). *Comunicación de la comisión al Parlamento Europeo, al consejo, al comité económico y social europeo y al comité de las regiones. Estrategia renovada de la UE para 2011-2014 sobre la responsabilidad social de las empresas*. Comisión Europea, Bruselas.

Commission of the European Communities. (2008). Communication from the commission to the council, the European parliament, the European economic and social committee, and the committee of the regions: A mid-term assessment of implementing the EC biodiversity action plan. *Journal of International Wildlife Law and Policy*, *12*(3), 216–228. doi:10.1080/13880290903199425

Cropanzano, R., Byrne, Z. S., Bobocel, D. R., & Rupp, D. E. (2001). Moral virtues, fairness heuristics, social entities, and other denizens of organizational justice. *Journal of Vocational Behavior*, *58*(2), 164–209. doi:10.1006/jvbe.2001.1791

Daddi, T., Magistrelli, M., Frey, M., & Iraldo, F. (2011). Do environmental management systems improve environmental performance? Empirical evidence from Italian companies. *Environment, Development and Sustainability, 13*(5), 845–862. doi:10.100710668-011-9294-8

Dan Basuki, I. (2016). Carbon Emission Disclosure: Studi Pada Perusahaan Manufaktur Indonesia. *Jurnal Akuntansi dan Keuangan, 18*(2), 92-104. doi:10.9744/jak.18.2.92-104

Dawkins, J. (2005). Corporate responsibility: The communication challenge. *Journal of Communication Management, 9*(2), 108–119. doi:10.1108/13632540510621362

De Beer, P., & Friend, F. (2006). Environmental accounting. A management tool for enhancing corporate environmental and economic performance. *Ecological Economics, 58*(3), 548–560. doi:10.1016/j.ecolecon.2005.07.026

De Miguel, M. L. (2011). *La Responsabilidad Social Empresarial en la pequeña y mediana empresa: Guía de buenas prácticas. Proyecto Impulsa-RSE Pyme financiado por el Ministerio de Industria Turismo y Comercio.*

Deegan, C. (2002). The Legitimising Effect of Social and Environmental Disclosures – A Theoretical Foundation. *Accounting, Auditing & Accountability Journal, 15*(3), 282–311. doi:10.1108/09513570210435852

Di Benedetto, C. A. (2017). Corporate social responsibility as an emerging business model in fashion marketing. *Journal of Global Fashion Marketing, 8*(4), 251–265. doi:10.1080/20932685.2017.1329023

Elkington, J. (2000). Cannibals with forks: The triple bottom line of 21st century business. *Journal of Business Ethics, 23*(2), 229–231. doi:10.1023/A:1006129603978

Erhemjamts, O., Li, Q., & Venkateswaran, A. (2013). Corporate social responsibility and its impact on firms' investment policy, organizational structure, and performance. *Journal of Business Ethics, 118*(2), 395–412. doi:10.100710551-012-1594-x

Escribano Francés, G. (2012). Desarrollo energético sostenible y energías renovables. *Cuadernos Económicos de ICE, 864*, 73–83.

Farooq, O., Rupp, D. E., & Farooq, M. (2017). The multiple pathways through which internal and external corporate social responsibility influence organizational identification and multifoci outcomes: The moderating role of cultural and social orientations. *Academy of Management Journal, 60*(3), 954–985. doi:10.5465/amj.2014.0849

Fernández-Pinto, I., López-Pérez, B., & Márquez, M. (2008). Empatía: Medidas, teorías y aplicaciones en revisión. *Anales de Psicología, 24*, 284–298.

Fombrun, C., & Shanley, M. (1990). What's in a name? Reputation building and corporate strategy. *Academy of Management Journal, 33*(2), 233–258.

Fombrun, Ch. J., & Van Riel, C. B. M. (2004). *Fame & fortune: How successful companies build winning reputations*. FT Press.

Freeman, R. E. (1984). *Strategic Management: A Stakeholder Approach.* Boston: Pitman Publishing.

Freeman, R. E., Harrison, J. S., & Wicks, A. C. (2007). *Managing for stakeholders: survival, reputation and success*. Yale University Press.

Freeman, R. E., Wicks, A. C., & Parmar, B. (2004). Stakeholder theory and "the corporate objective revisited". *Organization Science*, *15*(3), 364–369. doi:10.1287/orsc.1040.0066

Gallardo-Vázquez, D., & Sánchez-Hernández, M.I. (2013). Análisis de la incidencia de la responsabilidad social empresarial en el éxito competitivo de las microempresas y el papel de la innovación. *Universia Business Review*, *38*, 14-31.

Gallardo-Vázquez, D., & Sánchez-Hernandez, M. I. (2014). Measuring Corporate Social Responsibility for competitive success at a regional level. *Journal of Cleaner Production*, *72*, 14–22. doi:10.1016/j.jclepro.2014.02.051

Gallardo-Vázquez, D., Sánchez-Hernández, M. I., & Corchuelo-Martínez-Azúa, M. B. (2013). Validación de un instrumento de medida para la relación entre la orientación a la responsabilidad social corporativa y otras variables estratégicas de la empresa. *Revista de Contabilidad*, *16*(1), 11–23. doi:10.1016/S1138-4891(13)70002-5

Gharleghi, B., Jahanshahi, A. A., & Nawaser, K. (2018). The outcomes of Corporate Social Responsibility to employees: Empirical evidence from a developing country. *Sustainability*, *10*(3), 698. doi:10.3390u10030698

Gond, J. P., Akremi, A. E., Swaen, V., & Babu, N. (2017). The psychological microfoundations of corporate social responsibility: A person-centric systematic review. *Journal of Organizational Behavior*, *38*(2), 225–246. doi:10.1002/job.2170

Gond, J. P., Igalens, J., Swaen, V., & El Akremi, A. (2011). The Human Resources Contribution to Responsible Leadership: An Exploration of the CSR–HR Interface. In N. M. Pless & T. Maak (Eds.), *Responsible Leadership*. Dordrecht: Springer. doi:10.1007/978-94-007-3995-6_10

González-Ramos, M. I., Manzanares-Donate, M. J., & Gómez-Guadamillas, F. (2014). Propuesta de una escala para la medición de la responsabilidad social corporativa. *Pecvnia*, *18*(18), 1–18. doi:10.18002/pec.v0i18.1641

Graves, L. M., & Sarkis, J. (2012). Fostering employee proenvironmental behavior: the role of leadership and motivation. In D. R. Gallagher (Ed.), *Environmental Leadership: a Reference Handbook* (pp. 161–171). Thousand Oaks, CA: Sage. doi:10.4135/9781452218601.n18

Graves, L. M., Sarkis, J., & Zhu, Q. (2013). How transformational leadership and employee motivation combine to predict employee proenvironmental behaviors in China. *Journal of Environmental Psychology*, *35*, 81–91. doi:10.1016/j.jenvp.2013.05.002

Greening, D. W., & Turban, D. B. (2000). Corporate social performance as a competitive advantage in attracting a quality workforce. *Business & Society*, *39*(3), 254–280. doi:10.1177/000765030003900302

Hackman, J. R., & Oldham, R. G. (1976). Motivation through the design of work: Test of a theory. *Organizational Behavior and Human Performance*, *16*(2), 250–279. doi:10.1016/0030-5073(76)90016-7

Haigh, M. M., & Brubaker, P. (2010). Examining how image restoration strategy impacts perceptions of corporate social responsibility, organization-public relationships, and source credibility. *Corporate Communications, 15*(4), 453–468. doi:10.1108/13563281011085538

Hameed, I., Riaz, Z., Arain, G. A., & Farooq, O. (2016). How do internal and external CSR affect employees' organizational identification? A perspective from the group engagement model. *Frontiers in Psychology, 7*, 1–13. doi:10.3389/fpsyg.2016.00788 PMID:27303345

Hansen, S., Dunford, B., Boss, A., Boss, R., & Angermeier, I. (2011). Corporate Social Responsibility and the Benefits of Employee Trust: A Cross-Disciplinary Perspective. *Journal of Business Ethics, 102*(1), 29–45. doi:10.100710551-011-0903-0

Hao, Y., Farooq, Q., & Zhang, Y. (2018). Unattended social wants and corporate social responsibility of leading firms: Relationship of intrinsic motivation of volunteering in proposed welfare programs and employee attributes. *Corporate Social Responsibility and Environmental Management, 25*(6), 1029–1038. doi:10.1002/csr.1681

Harrison, J. S., Bosse, D. A., & Phillips, R. A. (2010). Managing for stakeholders, stakeholder utility functions, and competitive advantage. *Strategic Management Journal, 31*(1), 58–74. doi:10.1002mj.801

Harrison, J. S., Freeman, R. E., & Abreu, M. (2015). Stakeholder theory as an ethical approach to effective management: Applying the theory to multiple contexts. *Revista Brasileira de Gestão de Negócios, 17*(55), 858–869. doi:10.7819/rbgn.v17i55.2647

Healy, P. M., & Palepu, K. G. (2001). Information Asymmetry, Corporate Disclosure, and the Capital Markets: A Review of the Empirical Disclosure Literature. *Journal of Accounting and Economics, 31*(1-3), 405–440. doi:10.1016/S0165-4101(01)00018-0

Henri, J.-F., & Journeault, M. (2010). Eco-control: The influence of management control systems on environmental and economic performance. *Accounting, Organizations and Society, 35*(1), 63–80. doi:10.1016/j.aos.2009.02.001

Herrera, J., Larrán, M., Martínez, I., & Martínez-Martínez, D. (2016). Relationship between corporate social responsibility and competitive performance in Spanish SMEs: Empirical evidence from a stakeholders' perspective. *Business Research Quarterly, 19*(1), 55–72. doi:10.1016/j.brq.2015.06.002

Høgevold, M., Svensson, N., Wagner, G., Petzer, B. J., Klopper, D., Carlos Sosa Varela, H. B., ... Ferro, C. (2014). Sustainable business models: Corporate reasons, economic effects, social boundaries, environmental actions and organizational challenges in sustainable business practices. *Baltic Journal of Management, 9*(3), 357–380. doi:10.1108/BJM-09-2013-0147

Hur, W. M., Kim, H., & Woo, J. (2014). How CSR leads to corporate brand equity: Mediating mechanisms of corporate brand credibility and reputation. *Journal of Business Ethics, 125*(1), 1–12. doi:10.100710551-013-1910-0

Hur, W. M., Moon, T. W., & Ko, S. H. (2018). How employees' perceptions of CSR increase employee creativity: Mediating mechanisms of compassion at work and intrinsic motivation. *Journal of Business Ethics, 153*(3), 629–644. doi:10.100710551-016-3321-5

Inoue, Y., & Lee, S. (2011). Effects of different dimensions of corporate social responsibility on corporate financial performance in tourism-related industries. *Tourism Management*, *32*(4), 790–804. doi:10.1016/j.tourman.2010.06.019

Jabbour, C. K. C., & de Sousa Jabbour, A. B. L. (2016). Green human resource management and green supply chain management: Linking two emerging agendas. *Journal of Cleaner Production*, *112*, 1824–1833. doi:10.1016/j.jclepro.2015.01.052

Jo, H., Kim, H., & Park, K. (2015). Corporate environmental responsibility and firm performance in the financial services sector. *Journal of Business Ethics*, *131*(2), 257–284. doi:10.100710551-014-2276-7

Jones, D. A. (2010). Does serving the community also serve the company? Using organizational identification and social exchange theories to understand employee responses to a volunteerism programme. *Journal of Occupational and Organizational Psychology*, *83*(4), 857–878. doi:10.1348/096317909X477495

Jones, D. A., Willness, C. R., & Madey, S. (2014). Why are job seekers attracted by corporate social performance? Experimental and filed tests of three signal-based mechanisms. *Academy of Management Journal*, *57*(2), 383–404. doi:10.5465/amj.2011.0848

Kechiche, A., & Soparnot, R. (2012). CSR within SMEs: Literature review. *International Business Research*, *5*(7), 97. doi:10.5539/ibr.v5n7p97

Kim, A., Kim, Y., Han, K., Jackson, S. E., & Ployhart, R. E. (2017). Multilevel influences on voluntary workplace green behavior: Individual differences, leader behavior, and coworker advocacy. *Journal of Management*, *43*(5), 1335–1358. doi:10.1177/0149206314547386

Koestner, R., & Losier, G. F. (2002). Distinguishing three ways of being internally motivated: a closer look at introjection, identification, and intrinsic motivation. In E. L. Deci & R. M. Ryan (Eds.), *Handbook of Self-determination Research* (pp. 101–122). Rochester, NY: University of Rochester.

Kramer, M. R., & Porter, M. E. (2006). Estrategia y sociedad: El vínculo entre ventaja competitiva y responsabilidad social corporativa. *Harvard Business Review*, *84*(12), 42–56.

Lai, C. S., Chiu, C. J., Yang, C. F., & Pai, D. C. (2010). The effects of Corporate Social Responsibility on Brand performance: The mediating effect of industrial Brand equity and corporate reputation. *Journal of Business Ethics*, *95*(3), 457–469. doi:10.100710551-010-0433-1

Lee, M. D. P. (2008). A review of the theories of corporate social responsibility: Its evolutionary path and the road ahead. *International Journal of Management Reviews*, *10*(1), 53–73. doi:10.1111/j.1468-2370.2007.00226.x

Li, D., Xin, L., Chen, X., & Ren, S. (2017). Corporate social responsibility, media attention and firm value: Empirical research on Chinese manufacturing firms. *Quality & Quantity*, *51*(4), 1563–1577. doi:10.100711135-016-0352-z

Lichtenstein, D. R., Drumwright, M., & Braig, B. M. (2004). The effect of corporate social responsibility on customer donations to corporate-supported nonprofits. *Journal of Marketing*, *68*(4), 16–32. doi:10.1509/jmkg.68.4.16.42726

Liu, M. T., Wong, I. A., Rongwei, C., & Tseng, T. H. (2014). Do perceived CSR initiatives enhance customer preference and loyalty in casinos? *International Journal of Contemporary Hospitality Management, 26*(7), 1024–1045. doi:10.1108/IJCHM-05-2013-0222

Liu, Y. S., Zhou, X., Yang, J. H., & Hoepner, A. G. F. (2016). Corporate Carbon Emission and Financial Performance: Does Carbon Disclosure Mediate the Relationship in the UK?

Locke, E. A., & Latham, G. P. (1990). *A theory of goal setting and task performance*. Englewood Cliffs, NJ: Prentice Hall.

Low, M. P., Ong, S. F., & Tan, P. M. (2017). Positioning ethics and social responsibility as a strategic tool in employees' affective commitment. Evidence from Malaysian small medium-sized enterprises (SMEs). *Annals in Social Responsibility, 3*(1), 2–22. doi:10.1108/ASR-12-2016-0013

Luthans, F., & Youssef, C. M. (2004). Human, social and now positive psychological capital management: Investing in people for competitive advantage. *Organizational Dynamics, 33*(2), 143–160. doi:10.1016/j.orgdyn.2004.01.003

MacGregor, S. P., & Fontrodona, J. (2008). *Exploring the fit between CSR and Innovation*. Working Paper. IESE Business School University of Navarra.

Mahbuba, S., & Farzana, N. (2013). Corporate Social Responsibility and Profitability: A Case Study on Dutch Bangla Bank Ltd. *International Journal of Business and Social Research, 3*(4), 139–145.

Maldonado-Guzmán, G., Pinzón-Castro, S. Y., & Leana Morales, C. (2017). Corporate Social Responsibility and Firm Reputation in Mexican Small Business. *Advances in Management and Applied Economics, 7*(5), 29.

Martínez, P., Pérez, A., & Rodríguez del Bosque, I. (2014). CSR influence on hotel brand image and loyalty. *Academia (Caracas), 27*(2), 267–283. doi:10.1108/ARLA-12-2013-0190

Martínez, P., & Rodríguez del Bosque, I. (2013). CSR and customer loyalty: The roles of trust, customer identification with the Company and satisfaction. *International Journal of Hospitality Management, 35*, 89–99. doi:10.1016/j.ijhm.2013.05.009

Martinez-Conesa, I., Soto-Acosta, P., & Palacios-Manzano, M. (2017). Corporate social responsibility and its effect on innovation and firm performance: An empirical research in SMEs. *Journal of Cleaner Production, 142*, 2374–2383. doi:10.1016/j.jclepro.2016.11.038

Mason, C., & Simmons, J. (2011). Forward looking or looking unaffordable? Utilising academic perspectives on corporate social responsibility to assess the factors influencing its adoption by business. *Business Ethics (Oxford, England), 20*(2), 159–176. doi:10.1111/j.1467-8608.2011.01614.x

McWilliams, A. (2015). Corporate social responsibility. In Wiley Encyclopedia of Management. Wiley.

McWilliams, A., & Siegel, D. (2001). Corporate social responsibility: A theory of the firm perspective. *Academy of Management Review, 26*(1), 117–127. doi:10.5465/amr.2001.4011987

McWilliams, A., Siegel, D. S., & Wright, P. M. (2006). Corporate social responsibility: Strategic implications. *Journal of Management Studies, 43*(1), 1–18. doi:10.1111/j.1467-6486.2006.00580.x

Merminod, N., & Paché, G. (2011). Supply management and corporate social responsibility: The challenge of global chain traceability. *Journal on Chain and Network Science*, *11*(3), 213–222. doi:10.3920/JCNS2011.x201

Meyer, J. P., & Allen, N. J. (1991). A three-component conceptualization of organizational commitment. *Human Resource Management Review*, *1*(1), 61–89. doi:10.1016/1053-4822(91)90011-Z

Meyer, J. P., Becker, T. E., & Vandenberghe, C. (2004). Employee commitment and motivation: A conceptual analysis and integrative model. *The Journal of Applied Psychology*, *89*(6), 991–1007. doi:10.1037/0021-9010.89.6.991 PMID:15584837

Morata, F., Vilà, B., & Suárez, C. (2010). *La responsabilidad social de la empresa a debate. Lecciones de la crisis*. Barcelona: IUEE.

Morsing, M., & Schultz, M. (2006). Corporate social responsibility communication: Stakeholder information, response and involvement strategies. *Business Ethics (Oxford, England)*, *15*(4), 323–338. doi:10.1111/j.1467-8608.2006.00460.x

Murray, S. (2007). Bottom-line benefits special award corporate responsibility: Ethical concerns are a growing factor in staff motivation. *Financial Times*, 11.

Needleman, S. E. (2008). The latest office perk: Getting paid to volunteer — more companies subsidize donations of time and talent; bait for millennial generation. *The Wall Street Journal Online*. Retrieved from http://online.wsj.com/article/SB120940853880850351.html

Nishitani, K., Kaneko, S., Fujii, H., & Komatsu, S. (2012). Are firms' voluntary environmental management activities beneficial for the environment and business? An empirical study focusing on Japanese manufacturing firms. *Journal of Environmental Management*, *105*, 121–130. doi:10.1016/j.jenvman.2012.03.054 PMID:22542980

O'Reilly, C. A., & Chatman, J. (1986). Organizational commitment and psychological attachment: The effects of compliance, identification, and internalization on prosocial behaviour. *The Journal of Applied Psychology*, *71*(3), 492–499. doi:10.1037/0021-9010.71.3.492

Oh, W. Y., Chang, Y. K., & Martynov, A. (2011). The effect of ownership structure on corporate social responsibility: Empirical evidence from Korea. *Journal of Business Ethics*, *104*(2), 283–297. doi:10.100710551-011-0912-z

Padgett, R., & Galán, J. (2010). The effect of R&D Intensity on Corporate Social Responsibility. *Journal of Business Ethics*, *93*(3), 407–418. doi:10.100710551-009-0230-x

Pelletier, L. G., & Aitken, N. M. (2014). Encouraging environmental actions in employees and in the working environment: a self-determination theory perspective. In E. M. Gagn (Ed.), *The Oxford Handbook of Work Engagement, Motivation, and Self-determination Theory* (pp. 314–334). Oxford: Oxford University Press.

Pérez-Ruíz, A., & Rodríguez del Bosque, I. (2012). La imagen de la Responsabilidad Social Corporativa en un contexto de crisis económica: El caso del sector financiero en España. *Universia Business Review*, *33*, 14-29.

Pivato, S., Misani, N., & Tencati, A. (2008). The impact of corporate social responsibility on consumer trust: The case of organic food. *Business Ethics (Oxford, England)*, *17*(1), 3–12. doi:10.1111/j.1467-8608.2008.00515.x

Platonova, E., Asutay, M., Dixon, R., & Mohammad, S. (2018). The impact of Corporate Social Responsibility Disclosure on Financial Performance: Evidence from the GCC Islamic Banking Sector. *Journal of Business Ethics*, *151*(2), 451–471. doi:10.100710551-016-3229-0

Reverte, C., Gómez, E., & Cegarra, J. (2016). The influence of corporate social responsibility practices on organizational performance: Evidence from Eco-Responsible Spanish firms. *Journal of Cleaner Production*, *112*, 2870–2884. doi:10.1016/j.jclepro.2015.09.128

Roberts, P. W., & Dowling, G. R. (2002). Corporate reputation and sustained superior financial performance. *Strategic Management Journal*, *23*(12), 1077–1093. doi:10.1002mj.274

Rodrigo, P., Durán, I. J., & Arenas, D. (2016). Does it really pay to be good, everywhere? A first step to understand the corporate social and financial performance link in Latin American controversial industries. *Business Ethics (Oxford, England)*, *25*(3), 286–309. doi:10.1111/beer.12119

Rupp, D. E., Ganapathi, J., Aguilera, R. V., & Williams, C. A. (2006). Employee reactions to corporate social responsibility: An organizational justice framework. *Journal of Organizational Behavior*, *27*(4), 537–543. doi:10.1002/job.380

Rupp, D. E., Shao, R., Thornton, M. A., & Skarlicki, D. P. (2013). Applicants' and employees' reactions to corporate social responsibility: The moderating effects of first-party justice perceptions and moral identity. *Personnel Psychology*, *66*(4), 895–933. doi:10.1111/peps.12030

Salanova, M., & Schaufeli, W. B. (2004). El engagement de los empleados: Un reto emergente para la dirección de los recursos humanos. *Estudios Financieros*, *261*, 109–138.

Server Izquierdo, R. J., & Capó i Vicedo, J. (2011). The interrelationship between the demands of Corporate Social Responsibility and co-operative principles and values. *CIRIEC-España. C.I.R.I.E.C. España*, *73*, 213–232.

Sheth, J. N., Sethia, N. K., & Srinivas, S. (2011). Mindful consumption: A customer-centric approach to sustainability. *Journal of the Academy of Marketing Science*, *39*(1), 21–39. doi:10.100711747-010-0216-3

Silva, V., & Lopes, W. G. (2019). Environmental accounting: Analysis of the participation in the business sustainability index (ise) and the profitability of the companies listed in in Brazil. *Revista Gestao & Tecnologia [Journal of Management and Technology]*, *19*(2), 109–125. doi:10.20397/2177-6652/2019.v19i2.1563

Smith, N. C., & Williams, E. (2011). Responsible consumers and stakeholder marketing: Building a virtuous circle of social responsibility. *Universia Business Review*, *30*, 68–79.

Song, S.-H. (2006). Workplace Friendship and Employees' Productivity: LMX Theory and the Case of the Seoul City Government. *International Review of Public Administraton*, *11*(1), 47–58. doi:10.1080/12294659.2006.10805077

Sprinkle, G. B., & Maines, L. A. (2010). The benefits and costs of corporate social responsibility. *Business Horizons*, *53*(5), 445–453. doi:10.1016/j.bushor.2010.05.006

Stites, J. P., & Michael, J. H. (2011). Organizational commitment in manufacturing employees: Relationships with corporate social performance. *Business & Society*, *50*(1), 50–70. doi:10.1177/0007650310394311

Suchman, M. C. (1995). Managing legitimacy: Strategic and institutional approaches. *Academy of Management Review*, *20*(3), 571–610. doi:10.5465/amr.1995.9508080331

Sullivan, J. D. (2009). *The moral compass of companies: Business ethics and corporate governance as anti-corruption tools. (No. 7)*. Washington, DC: International Finance Corporation. Retrieved from http://hdl.handle.net/10986/23980

Supanti, D., Butcher, K., & Fredline, L. (2015). Enhancing the employer-employee relationship through corporate social responsibility (CSR) engagement. *International Journal of Contemporary Hospitality Management*, *27*(7), 1479–1498. doi:10.1108/IJCHM-07-2014-0319

Sweeney, L., & Coughlan, J. (2008). Do different industries report corporate social responsibility differently? An investigation through the lens of stakeholder theory. *Journal of Marketing Communications*, *14*(2), 113–124. doi:10.1080/13527260701856657

Tang, Z., Hull, C. E., & Rothenberg, S. (2012). How corporate social responsibility engagement strategy moderates the CSR–financial performance relationship. *Journal of Management Studies*, *49*(7), 1274–1303. doi:10.1111/j.1467-6486.2012.01068.x

Thorne, L., Mahoney, L. S., Gregory, K., & Convery, S. (2017). A comparison of Canadian and US CSR strategic alliances, CSR reporting, and CSR performance: Insights into implicit–explicit CSR. *Journal of Business Ethics*, *143*(1), 85–98. doi:10.100710551-015-2799-6

Tsai, Y. H., Joe, S. W., Lin, C. P., & Wang, R. T. (2014). Modeling job pursuit intention: Moderating mechanisms of socio-environmental consciousness. *Journal of Business Ethics*, *125*(2), 287–298. doi:10.100710551-013-1919-4

Turker, D. (2009a). Measuring corporate social responsibility: A scale development study. *Journal of Business Ethics*, *85*(4), 411–427. doi:10.100710551-008-9780-6

Turker, D. (2009b). How corporate social responsibility influences organizational commitment. *Journal of Business Ethics*, *89*(2), 189–204. doi:10.100710551-008-9993-8

Valenzuela Fernández, L., Jara Bertín, M., & Villegas Pineaur, F. (2015). Prácticas de Responsabilidad Social, reputación corporativa y desempeño financiero. *RAE-Revista de Administração de Empresas*, *55*(3), 329–344. doi:10.1590/S0034-759020150308

Villafañe, J. (2001). La reputación corporativa como factor de liderazgo. *Área Abierta*, (1), 4.

Wagner, M. (2010). Corporate Social Performance and Innovation with High Social Benefits: A Quantitative Analysis. *Journal of Business Ethics*, *94*(4), 581–594. doi:10.100710551-009-0339-y

Waldman, D. A., De Luque, M. S., Washburn, N., House, R. J., Adetoun, B., Barrasa, A., ... Dorfman, P. (2006). Cultural and leadership predictors of corporate social responsibility values of top management: A GLOBE study of 15 countries. *Journal of International Business Studies*, *37*(6), 823–837. doi:10.1057/palgrave.jibs.8400230

Wheeler, C., Colbert, B., & Freeman, R. E. (2003). Focusing on value: Reconciling corporate social responsibility, sustainability and a stakeholder approach in a network world. *Journal of General Management*, *28*(3), 1–28. doi:10.1177/030630700302800301

Williamson, D., & Lynch-Wood, G. (2008). Social and environmental reporting in UK company law and the issue of legitimacy. *Corporate Governance: The International Journal of Business in Society*, *8*(2), 128–140. doi:10.1108/14720700810863760

Williamson, D., Lynch-Wood, G., & Ramsay, J. (2006). Drivers of Environmental Behavior in Manufacturing SME and the Implications for CSR. *Journal of Business Ethics*, *67*(3), 317–330. doi:10.100710551-006-9187-1

Wong, C. A., & Laschinger, H. K. S. (2013). Authentic leadership, performance, and job satisfaction: The mediating role of empowerment. *Journal of Advanced Nursing*, *69*(4), 947–959. doi:10.1111/j.1365-2648.2012.06089.x PMID:22764828

Yoon, B., & Chung, Y. S. (2018). The effects of corporate social responsibility on firm performance: A stakeholder approach. *Journal of Hospitality and Tourism Management*, *37*, 89–96. doi:10.1016/j.jhtm.2018.10.005

Yuriev, A., Boiral, O., Francoeur, V., & Paillé, P. (2018). Overcoming the barriers to proenvironmental behaviors in the workplace: A systematic review. *Journal of Cleaner Production*, *182*, 379–394. doi:10.1016/j.jclepro.2018.02.041

ADDITIONAL READING

Chong, W. N., & Tan, G. (2010). Obtaining intangible and tangible benefits from Corporate Social Responsibility. *International Review of Business Research Papers*, *6*(4), 360–371.

González Ramos, M. I., Donate Manzanares, M. J., & Guadamillas Gómez, F. (2014). El efecto del papel mediador de la reputación corporative en la relación entre la RSC y los resultados económicos. *Revista de Estudios Empresariales*, *1*, 67–89.

Hodinková, M., & Sadovský, Z. (2016). The benefits of corporate social responsibility introduction in small and medium-sized enterprises: A systematic review of the literature. *Business: Theory and Practice*, *17*(4), 345–352.

Jelic, M. C. (2016). Responsabilidad Social Corporativa y rendimiento económico: Los costos económicos y los beneficios de la RSC. *Revista Cultura Económica*, *92*, 41–55.

Túñez López, J. M., & Valarezo González, K. (2012). RSC: Reputación, Sostenibilidad, Compromiso. *Chasqui. Revista Latinoamericana de Comunicación*, *117*, 61–66.

KEY TERMS AND DEFINITIONS

Benefits of CSR: positive results derived from the undertaking of socially responsable actions in organizations. They are very numerous and have very diverse orientations, for the company and also for employees and society as a whole.

Competitive Advantage: a better position on the market related to the competitors.

Corporate Social Responsibility: voluntary integration by the organizations of social and environmental concerns in its business operations and the relationships with their interlocutors.

Legitimidad Organizacional: social acceptance of organizations, which means that they should develop a collection of actions that are appropriate for communities because they are adjusted to a set of regulations, values and beliefs that determine their behaviour and legitimate them in their market, sector and with the society they are set into.

Stakeholders: people, individuals and groups of people that affect, can affect and can be affected by the activities of an organization. They are considered to be an essential element on the strategic planning of the organizations.

Sustainable Development: development that satisfies present needs without compromising the capacity of future generations, guaranteeing the balance between economic development, taking care of the environment and social wellbeing.

Triple Bottom Line Perspective: accounting framework with three parts (social, environmental and financial). Some organizations have adopted this framework in order to evaluate their performance in a broader perspective to create greater business value.

Chapter 3
Corporate Social Responsibility:
The Comparison of Scientific Production in Web of Science and in Scopus Over the Last Three Decades (1988-2018)

Luciana Aparecida Barbieri da Rosa
https://orcid.org/0000-0001-9240-0236
Universidade Federal de Santa Maria, Brazil

Maria Carolina Martins-Rodrigues
https://orcid.org/0000-0003-2575-8611
CIEO, Universidade do Algarve, Portugal

Tais Pentiado Godoy
https://orcid.org/0000-0001-5021-5315
Universidade Federal de Santa Maria, Brazil

Waleska Yone Yamakawa Zavatti Campos
Pontifícia Universidade Católica do Rio de Janeiro, Brazil

Clandia Maffini Gomes
Universidade Federal de Santa Maria, Brazil

Larissa Cristina Barbieri
Faculdade de Educação São Luis, Brazil

ABSTRACT

Corporate social responsibility is conceptualized as a voluntary activity of organizations, which evidence the inclusion of environmental and social objectives in the interactions with stakeholders, as well as in their operational activities. Thus, the general objective was to analyze the characteristics of the publications related to the topic corporate social responsibility in the last three decades, in the Web of Science and in Scopus databases. There was an increase in the number of articles published per year with the

DOI: 10.4018/978-1-7998-2128-1.ch003

"boom" in the years 2013 to 2018, in both databases. The authors at the Copenhagen Business School (79; 129) and York University (92; 104) were where the most scientific articles published on the subject on both databases. Regarding the main research areas in publications on corporate social responsibility, there seems to be a convergence in the main research areas of most published articles.

INTRODUCTION

The concern to provide the necessities of the present generations guaranteeing that the future generations the satisfaction of their primordial characterizes the definition of sustainable development. The attribution of the companies as intermediaries that enjoy the assets, play a fundamental role what we call Corporate Social Responsibility. The theme Corporate Social Responsibility (CSR) has been researched since the beginning of the 20th century, but began to have importance in the 1950s (Bowen, 1957).

For Melo Neto and Froes (2001, p. 217) "social responsibility is more than a concept. It is a personal and institutional value that is reflected in the attitudes of companies, entrepreneurs, and all their employees and partners."

In Brazil, the studies intensified in the 70's, the first insights in the academic environment began with some random researches, however in the companies the practical inexistence was notorious. Only in 1980 did the organizations intensify community-oriented actions and thus started the Brazilian studies on the subject (Ashley et al., 2000; Landrum & Ohsowski, 2018). This situation was maintained until the mid-1990s, when the subject regained social responsibility forces and practices, and began to be adopted by some companies.

In this scenario, Ribeiro et al. (2001) and El Akremi et al. (2018) emphasizes that in the 1990s, the intensification and importance of Social Responsibility in Brazil began, and an alliance between government, companies, and society began to be developed worldwide; thus, promoting the third sector whose objective was to reduce inequalities between the individuals. Thus, organizations that are aware of their role began to share with the State the responsibility to reduce social problems, such as the creation of foundations, institutes, and partnerships with public and private institutions.

Since then there is a growing interest in the subject, both by the entrepreneur and by the academic community (Fischer, & Mendonça, 2002; Aznar-Sánchez et al., 2019). The rise of the theme shows that the adhered nomenclature thrived from social responsibility to corporate social responsibility, spreading to corporate citizenship (Carroll, 1999). Borger (2001): complements that:

"CSR can be seen as a moral obligation of business management or as a result of the pressure of society organized by policies and legislation that protect human rights, promote better working conditions and preserve the environment for present and future generations" (p. 7).

In this perspective, Albuquerque (2009), Landrum and Ohsowski (2018), and Wang et al. (2018), complement that Corporate Social Responsibility is an instrument that helps identify Social Responsibility methods in relation to the elements that cover them, such as: investment, conflicts, representation and sustainability.

Given this situation, Tachizawa (2011) emphasizes that CSR is being considered as a criterion and a reference to excellence for the business environment, being a way of solving social and environmental problems, with the purpose of guaranteeing sustainability for business. Argenti (2014), complements that:

"While corporate social responsibility is assuming a central role thanks to a business environment that is facing increasing risks, adopting a socially responsible strategy can offer a compelling advantage for large companies. Responsible business practices do not necessarily undermine a company's profits" (p. 145).

Based on these inferences and knowing the importance of Corporate Social Responsibility in the business sphere, the research problem was elaborated: "What are the contributions of international publications on Corporate Social Responsibility in Elsevier's Scopus multidisciplinary databases and Web of Science Institute for Scientific Information (ISI), later maintained by Clarivate Analytics (formerly owned by Intellectual Property and Science of Thomson Reuters), from 1988 to 2018. Therefore, the present study has as general objective: To analyze the characteristics of the publications related to the topic Corporate Social Responsibility in the last three decades, in the databases.

This study, after presenting a brief introduction, aims to present brief definitions and approaches regarding the historical roots of Corporate Social Responsibility (CSR), concept and definitions of Corporate Social Responsibility (CSR) and the state of the art about CSR.). Next, the methodological approach (3) used is presented and, to follow up the study, the presentation and discussion of the results (4), then the final considerations and suggestions for future studies are presented (5).

THEORETICAL REFERENCE

Historical Roots of Corporate Social Responsibility (CSR).

The competition between organizations is growing, and to ensure competitive advantage, organizations begin to adopt strategies based on moral and ethical thinking related to the development of society. In this way, discussions about corporate social responsibility are present in corporate environments, academia and civil society.

Corporate social responsibility (CSR) has its roots in old debates (Kreitlon, 2004), and in the last decades, they have been discussed in organizations, with their characteristics based on ethical issues, both internally and externally, employees, suppliers, customers, community, society and the environment as a whole (Soares, 2004). The first steps on CSR were made in the United States, and consequently in Europe until its arrival in Brazil in the year 2000.

However, since the 1950s, the RGC has developed significantly (Farcane & Bureana, 2015). This evolution can be observed through different organizational terms, such as corporate social sensitivity and corporate social performance (Farcane & Bureana, 2015). In the year 1953, the book Social Responsibilities of the Businessman and Howard R. Bowen was published, this being pointed out as the forerunner of the CSR theory, in this book the author discusses the role that organizations in society, emphasizing that actions of organizations affect people's lives in many ways (Carroll, 1999; Windsor, 2001). Bowen, in his work, advises that entrepreneurs have an obligation to take actions and make decisions that are considered to be coveted by society (Carroll, 2015).

In the following decade, there was an intensification in the discussions on CSR. Until the early 1960s, in the view of organizations, they must account for a single public: shareholders, who according to Friedman (1962), organizations should use their resources in the activities that develop their profits, are honestly profiting in the market their priority is the investors. But at the end of the 1960s, the debates on the subject were the concerns that organizations had not only limited themselves to profit maximization but rather to understanding thoughts about better use of society's resources for social purposes (Silva et al., 2018). In this way, CSR was incorporated into the public debate on social problems related to diversity, poverty, pollution and income distribution. In addition, this promoted a greater involvement of the organizations in environmental movements, governmental regulations and the emergence of the preoccupation with the security in work (Bertoncello, & Chang, 2007).

Despite the growing discussion about the relationship between society and organization, a clear definition of CSR has not yet been developed (Lee, 2008). However, at the end of the year 1970, organizations realize that they need to be aware of a significant decrease in their practices in the impact of society since an organization's CSR encompasses legal, philanthropic, ethical and economic perspectives. Community at a given time (Carroll, 1979). As a result, based on the proposal of a conceptual model of corporate social performance published in 1979, Carroll was the first to attribute a broader meaning to corporate social responsibility (Bertoncello & Chang, 2007).

Up to that point, CSR had gained several conceptualization's and definitions. Therefore, all these concepts could be incorporated into distinct groups, which reflected the responsibilities that organizations should take before society (Silva et al., 2018). Carroll (1979) developed a conceptual model that, according to him, reflected on the essential aspects present in corporate social performance. It has, therefore been possible to observe that organizations have not only legal and economic but also ethical obligations.

In the 1980s, fewer definitions emerged than previously, but with more empirical studies and applications. As one of the main arguments put forward, it is pointed out that responsibility and profitability were complementary elements, as well as the idea that it is desirable for businesses to convert social responsibility into business opportunities (Drucker, 1986).

According to Madrakhimova (2013), in the 1990s, CSR thinking became globally accepted, increasingly being driven to the expectations of consumers, investors, citizens and public authorities (Katsoulakos et al., 2004). Therefore, until the 2000s, organizations did not know how to take advantage of CSR practices and thus did not link the concept to the business model.

In this way, the concerns regarding the social performance of the companies, are more pronounced from the years 2000 (Leandro, & Rebelo, 2011). In the 2000s and onwards, CSR was a strategic issue, a kind of global phenomenon, with a clear interest and growth of this concept in the European community (Carroll, 2008). The organizations were aware that they could benefit from CSR practices and added in their planning a more significant concern with the environment (GRI, 2012).

In 2001, the Commission of the European Communities issued the strategy for sustainable development in CSR, the proposal for this document highlights the creation of a multi-stakeholder forum, whose objective is to discuss corporate social responsibility, identifying tools and instruments of use convergent and common. In the same year, in the revision of Agenda 21, the United Nations issues the Millennium Declaration, which identifies the eight major goals to be achieved by 2015, in terms of improving environmental and social conditions.

Since then, some actions have reinforced the important role that corporate social responsibility represents in business and competitiveness, indicating its relevance to overcome the embryonic idea that CSR would only be a fad (Almeida, 2007; Keinert, 2008). More recently, some scholars argue that organizations can jointly integrate the market and the community, thus reinforcing concerns inherent to CSR (Gallardo-Vázquez & Sanchez-Hernandez, 2014). Therefore, organizations have sought to create value for the market and also for society, adopting responsibility for social duty (Pereira & Gonçalves, 2019).

Therefore, the Ethos Institute (2013) describes that CSR is about a transparent, ethical and supportive positioning of the company in relation to all the publics with which it relates, as well as establishing business goals according to the sustainable development of the company. Society, with the aim of preserving natural resources, respecting diversity and reducing inequalities (Silva et al., 2018, Custodio & Moya, 2013).

Concept and Definitions of Corporate Social Responsibility (CSR)

The concept of corporate social responsibility is associated with values of the post-industrial society. From this, CSR starts to gather the aspirations of social agents in the business plan of corporate institutions, thus creating new concepts. Thus, the activities of the organizations directly involved the community and the social agents where it is inserted, making it necessary to incorporate social objectives into the business plan (Tenório, 2015).

However, according to Carroll (1991), RSC is composed of four dimensions that can be presented in a pyramid form. Therefore, at the base of the pyramid is the economic responsibility, made up of organizations whose main objective is to be profitable, and to remain competitive and efficient. Above is the legal responsibility, since all organizations must follow the existing external and internal legislation. By the third scope, the whole organization has the duty to be morally ethical and respect the moral of the society to which it is inserted. And at the top of the pyramid, one has the philanthropic responsibility that is focused on the importance of organizations in collaborating to improve the quality of life of the community, with charitable actions and social development Carroll (1991).

For the World Business Council for Sustainable Development (WBCSD), CSR is an ethical behaviour of the organization with society. It concerns responsible management that does not serve the interests of shareholders, but also of all stakeholders, hence it is associated with human rights, environmental protection, employee rights, supplier relationships, community involvement, and stakeholder law (WBCSD, 1999). It is observed that, in both cases, CSR is the relationship between the organization and the community to which it is inserted.

The Commission of the European Communities (2001) divides CSR into two dimensions, internal and external. Internal, social responsibility practices was direct at employees, with concern for investments in human capital, safety and health of workers, and being guided to environmentally responsible practices, based on efficient management of natural resources. Since in the external dimension, it is aimed at the local community, with the involvement of other stakeholders, such as suppliers, business partners, public authorities, clients and ONG`s. Thus, organizations were expected to act ethically with all their partners respecting human rights, obey established laws and contribute to the sustainable development of the planet (Nodari et al., 2017). As a result, there is a better integration between organization and community, with the promotion of environmental issues, the development of cultural actions and charitable donations (Commission of the European Communities, 2001).

Despite the varied definitions that CSR has, according to its social and historical context, according to Farley and Voinov (2016), there is a consensus for organizations to be called socially responsible. For an organization to be CSR, it must at least recognize the impacts caused by its activities on society, manage the economic, environmental and social impacts originating from its activities, at local and global levels; and accomplish these purposes through constant dialogue with stakeholders (Brzeszczynski & Mcintosh, 2014).

To this end, investments with CSR are considered as strategic means for organizations to understand stakeholder information needs, with the objective of minimizing the negative implications of the activity at the national level and automatically maximizing employee satisfaction (Attig et al., 2016). Authors such as Arthaud-Day (2005) and Detomasi (2008), describe CSR as a voluntary activity of organizations, which highlight the inclusion of environmental and social objectives in interactions with stakeholders, as well as in their operational activities. Farley and Voinov (2016), on the other hand, broaden this concept by describing that the relationship between CSR and stakeholders is a set of actions of the organization that positively interferes with current stakeholder interests and will not violate the requirements of future stakeholders.

It should be noted that there is no universal definition or concept of Corporate Social Responsibility, although its concept basically consists of organizations promoting social, environmental and economic development. For the authors Machado et al. (2010), the volume of social and environmental investments performed by organizations varies according to the sector they belong to, respecting the characteristics and the different demands of society.

As for Baumann-Pauly et al. (2013), the concept of CSR is associated with the management of the relationship between internal Stakeholders, the coordination of the relationship with the State and other interstate Institutions, corporate responsibility and performance as a member of a global community. Thus, a study was conducted by the Corporate Reputation Business Monitor - Merco (2014), of the first six companies that stand out for their reputation for social responsibility, two of which belong to the banking sector. It is noteworthy that the study on corporate social responsibility practices is relevant in the Brazilian banking sector (Feitosa et al., 2014).

Although the concept of CSR encompasses a number of advantages through investors and stakeholders, six characteristics of CSR can be mentioned: voluntary, focused on external effects management, classifying the various stakeholder groups, the need to integrate social, environmental and economic responsibility in business operations and day-to-day decision-making must be implanted in the practice and values of an organization and goes beyond philanthropy, focusing on operational considerations (Witchkonska, 2016).

Thus, Irigaray et al. (2017) describe the main aspects of CSR as ethical and agreed commitments, local communities' development, sustainability, environmental recovery projects, and risk mitigation and preservation. Thus, the managers of the 100 largest national companies linked to the São Paulo Stock Exchange Index (Ibovespa) were asked about practices related to CSR, and it was verified that only a quarter understood the *lato sensu* principles. If large companies find it difficult to define CSR practices, micro, small and medium-sized enterprises, it is likely that CSR will continue to be an informal and intuitive process (Gallardo-Vázquez & Sanchez-Hernandez, 2014).

In some studies, carried out on CSR, they describe the level of involvement that the socially responsible practices have about the organization and its employees, which is of positive influence and of extreme comprehensiveness (Duarte et al., 2014). For Brazilian Association of Technical Standards (ABNT), through National Standard ABNT NBR 16001, it defines CSR based on the impacts that organizations generate in the environment and in society. By default, organizations must adopt ethical and transparent conduct, thus contributing to sustainable development. It must try to reach out to all stakeholder perspectives and act according to the current legislation (ABNT, 2017).

Therefore, the concept of CSR has taken multidimensional, interdisciplinary and systemic proportions, with a focus on the relationships between stakeholders linked directly or indirectly to the business (Ashley et al., 2000). In this sense, CSR is no longer just related to the philanthropic side, with actions directed to the community and admits a vision of relationship networks, which provides behavioral patterns for all activities intrinsic to the organization's business (Aligleri et al., 2002). Consequently, the obligation of an organization to be socially responsible ceases to be only the manufacturer and has a range of the entire productive chain of which the organization is a part.

The State of the Art on Corporate Social Responsibility: A Longitudinal Study

Studies of CSR have engendered fruitful debates over the past decade on policy agendas for the area, where CSR is viewed as having intentional or unintended political impacts, or even in situations where there are political impacts on CSR. The companies by offering services such as health and education, exercises a political role previously reserved to the state, so that political ideology within the organization also impacts CSR. (Scherer et al., 2016)

Already researches on corporate social micro-responsibility seek to highlight psychological aspects of the impacts of corporate social responsibility on individuals, especially in the field of industrial psychology studies. The researches in the area of micro-RSC propose the approach between organizational psychology and CSR, in favour of studying the effects of CSR on individuals and stakeholders, focusing on the individual level of analysis, not organizational or institutional. (Gond et al., 2017, Jain & Jamali, 2016; Rupp & Mallory, 2015)

The process of image making about CSR by clients has also been the subject of numerous studies that seek to analyse the perceptions of consumers about the credibility and image of the company in CSR initiatives. Thus, the renewal of the CSR strategy may increase or customer loyalty in strong brands or the maintenance of the CSR strategy seems to be the most important scenario (Han et al., 2019; Pérez & Del Bosque, 2015). Favourable for less established brands (Li et al., 2019).

There are also studies that relate the positive impacts of CSR on consumer perception, satisfaction, and brand loyalty. In particular, products of companies involved in activities of social goodwill are perceived by the clients as having a better performance (Bolton, & Mattila, 2015; Martínez, & Del Bosque, 2013; Rivera et al. 2016).

CSR is also capable of influencing employees' perceptions and behaviour, motivating and engaging them. A study by Flammer and Luo (2017) has shown that firms can react to adverse employee behavior by strategically increasing their CSR investments tied to benefits such as health and safety policies and the balance between professional routine and family life. Thus, CSR can be an instrument of employee governance.

In this same sense, Zhou et al. (2018) and John et al. (2019) have shown that CSR perceived by employees stimulates organizational pride. Organizational pride, on the other hand, has a direct and positive impact on satisfaction with work performance and affective commitment. Management implications come from such a finding, as organizations must envisage enabling the environment and develop a sustainable policy as a means to foster competitive advantage because perceived CSR engenders intangible rewards to the organization. Finally, CSR can bring benefits to various stakeholders, i.e. employees, through better welfare, to the company, through greater participation and engagement, and to the relationship between employees and confidence and sense of identification between the parties (Su & Swanson, 2019).

The financial performance and market value of a company can be affected by the company's CSR strategy. This is because of the company's innovation capacity and product quality impact on customer satisfaction, increasing market value. Thus, the positive effect of CSR on organizational performance stems from improved competitive advantage, reputation and customer satisfaction engendered through CSR (Baker et al., 2006).

Similarly, Kang et al. (2016) show that companies with CSR will probably benefit financially from the investments made in the area. Wang et al. (2016) demonstrate that the relationship between CSR and financial performance is positive and significant. This endorses the argument that prior CSR expands and increases the company's future financial performance, even in times of crisis (Lins et al., 2017). However, in publicly traded companies, when CSR is conceived as an agency cost, initial pessimistic recommendations can be generated for shareholders. Over time, companies with high CSR rates are being evaluated in a more optimistic way to shareholders, a fact that should be taken into consideration by publicly traded companies (Ioannou & Serafeim, 2015).

The cost of capital of companies becomes cheaper, as the level of company involvement with CSR increases. Thus, the better relationship with employees, the increase of environmental policies and new product strategies contributes significantly to the reduction of the cost of capital of the companies (El Ghoul et al., 2011; Silva, & Santos, 2011).

Studies related to gender diversity, stability and expertise in the boards of companies with CSR reveal that the diversity of boards is positively associated with the better performance achieved in CSR, as the diverse board can better meet the needs stakeholders (Bear et al., 2010; Harjoto et al., 2015, Rao & Tilt, 2016).

The next topic will be explained about the methodological procedures of the study.

METODOLOGY

Description of Research

In the present article, the technique of bibliometric, quantitative and statistical type was used, it has a fundamental role in the analysis of the behavior and performance of the production of scientific knowledge and exposure of relevant literature in the various research areas (Pimenta et al., 2017) and Garousi (2015) define bibliometric as a set of mathematical and statistical techniques and procedures that allow among others to measure the diffusion of the production and dissemination of scientific knowledge in a certain subject to evaluate the growth of this production, in books, articles, documents, newspapers.

According to Café and Bräscher (2008), it is fundamental to standardize the physical description and content of these documents, mentioning the relevant items and the dispersion concepts of the researched literature, in order, to scientific research papers with similar properties,

Data from this bibliometric analysis were collected in March 2019 by using Boolean operators to expand the research so that we can have a better comparison with reality in the two large multidisciplinary databases, Thomson Reuters's Web of Science (WOS) and Elsevier's Scopus.

In order to reduce the risk of lack of documents due to different coverage of publication and research, the two databases were used. The researched terms were "Corporate Social Responsibility", in all areas of research without differentiation. The period of research, from publications, was from 1988 to 2018, once the year 2019 is in progress.

Thus, in order to compare the articles collected in the Web of Science and in Scopus, we identified the main authors who wrote on the subject, the growth of the researches in the terms during the period in question, the main newspapers, main institutions, main countries and languages, areas of knowledge

Graph 1. Distribution of articles by type of publication

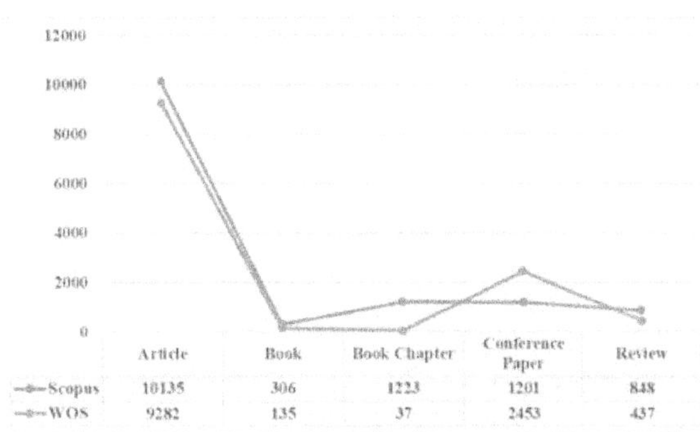

and the relationship between authors with more publications and those most cited. In Excel spreadsheet, comparison tables were created to analyze the data.

It is verified the existence of an index with citations in both the Web of Science and in Scopus, where each title, authors, year, number of citations, type of documents and year of publication are mentioned for each article.

Stages of Research

This research was divided into two stages. Initially, the terms "Corporate Social Responsibility" in the search field of WOS and Scopus, if delimiting the period between 1988 and 2018. They then proceeded to the survey of the general characteristics of the publications.

In the second stage, the most cited publications were compared with the authors who published the most in the same period. Figure 1 shows the steps of the research.

Therefore, according to the steps described in Figure 1, the bibliometric analysis of the aforementioned study was performed, presented below.

Figure 1. Stages of research

Table 1. Search Terms

Terms	Web of Science	Scopus
Corporate Social Responsibility	12330	14262

RESULTS

The results of the research, which was carried out based on the appropriate Boolean operators for refinement, are presented in order to broaden the scope of research to include the greatest possible number of results in the years 1988 to 2018. We found 12330 articles scientific in Web of Science and 14262 in Scopus, when it comes to "Corporate Social Responsibility", as shown in Table 1.

General Characteristics of the Publications

The general characteristics of publications related to "Corporate Social Responsibility": are as follows: 1. Main authors, 2. Title of sources, 3. Main institutions, 4. Year of publications, 5. Main countries, 6. Languages, 7. Research areas, 8. Keywords, and 9. Finance Agencies. Then, the number of publications per author and the number of citations will be presented.

Main Authors

The first analysis was in relation to the authors. Graph 2 shows the author and the number of published articles on the topic in the analysed period.

As for the representativeness of the articles by the author, it is observed that there are sixteen authors common in both bases: Amran, A.; Bhattacharya, C.B.; García-Sánchez, I.M.; Gond, J.P.; Husted, B.W.; Jamali, D.; Jo, H.; Kolk, A.; Lee, S.; Lindgreen, A.; Lund-Thomsen, P.; Martínez-Ferrero, J.; Moon, J.; Palazzo, G.; Pérez, A.; Scholtens, B.

The author who most published in Scopus was Jamali, D. with 42 publications and in WOS there was García-Sánchez, I.M. also with 42 publications.

Jamali, D is the author most cited works in the Scopus database deal with the important relationship between theory and practice in the context of corporate social responsibility, with more than 368 citations each (Jamali, 2008; Jamali, & Mirshak, 2007). In this sense, researchers are concerned about the interlocution of academic theory with social reality, so that corporate governance is positively impacted by sustainability processes in the triple bottom line perspective (Jamali, Safieddine, & Rabbath, 2008; Zhang, Oo, & Lim, 2019).

With regard to author García-Sánchez, Isabel-Maria, in the Web of Science database, the most cited articles deal with the role of corporate social responsibility reporting in stakeholder engagement, understood as entities or individuals interested in the sustainable conduct of society. company (Frias-Aceituno et al., 2013; Prado-Lorenzo et al., 2009). In line with García-Sánchez et al. (2019), Prado-Lorenzo et al. (2009) and Wang and Gao (2016), corporate social responsibility reports act as a mechanism for disclosing the sustainable strategic actions taken by companies that seek to increase their reputation with impact on competitiveness, financing, stakeholder engagement and monitoring.

Graph 2. Distribution of articles by authors

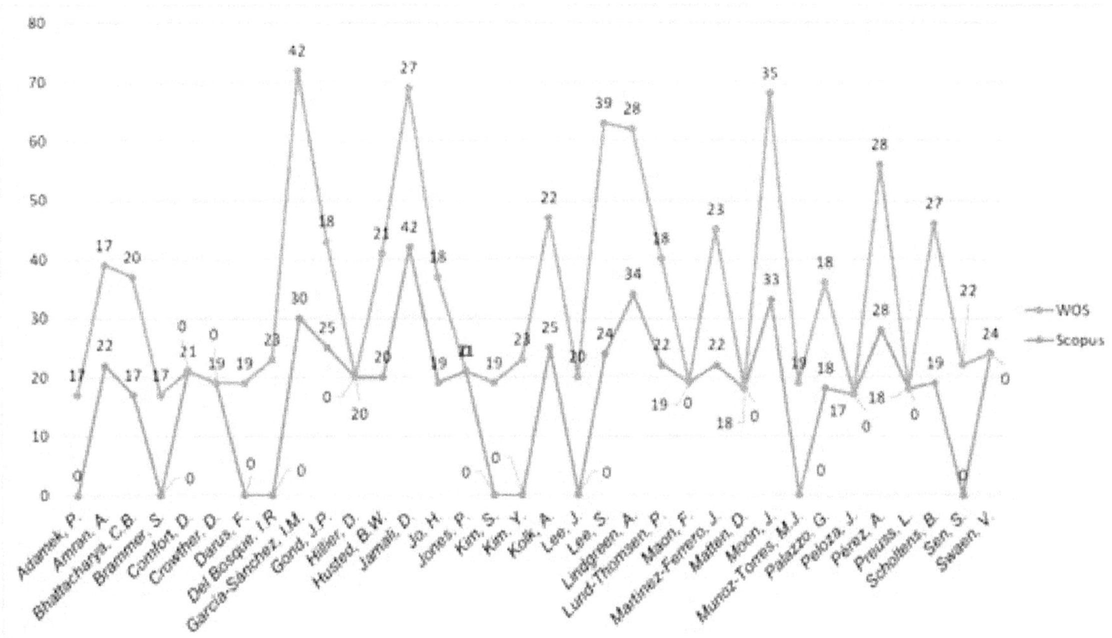

Title of Sources

The most impact papers with most scientific articles published on the topic in Web of Science and Scopus: Business and Society; Business Strategy and the Environment; Corporate Social Responsibility and Environmental; Management; Journal of Business Ethics; Journal of Business Research; Journal of Cleaner Production; Social Responsibility Journal; Sustainability (Graph 3).

Most of the publications have been found in the area's newspapers, which show that they will be a reference for the articles on these subjects, and there are also publications of articles in multidisciplinary journals.

The journal "Journal of Business Ethics" contains an article with an initial discussion on ethical foundations of corporate social responsibility in Corlett (1988). In the same journal, there is also an important study by Garriga, & Melé (2004), with 1224 citations in Scopus, where the authors map the theoretical field about corporate social responsibility in order to clarify theoretical controversies, or, in other words, map the territory on the topic.

Main Institutions

In Graph 4 are presented the institutions that most published works related to the theme "Corporate Social Responsibility."

The authors at the Copenhagen Business School (79;129) and York University (92;104) were the most scientific articles published on the subject on both bases, Web of Science e Scopus.

Graph 3. Distribution of articles by Title of sources

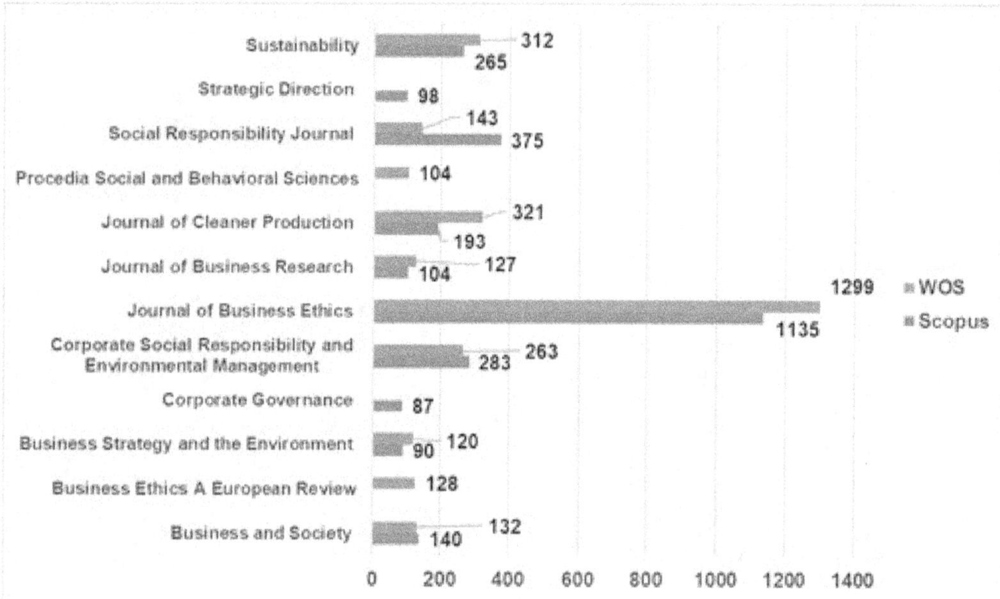

Graph 4. Distribution of articles by main institutions

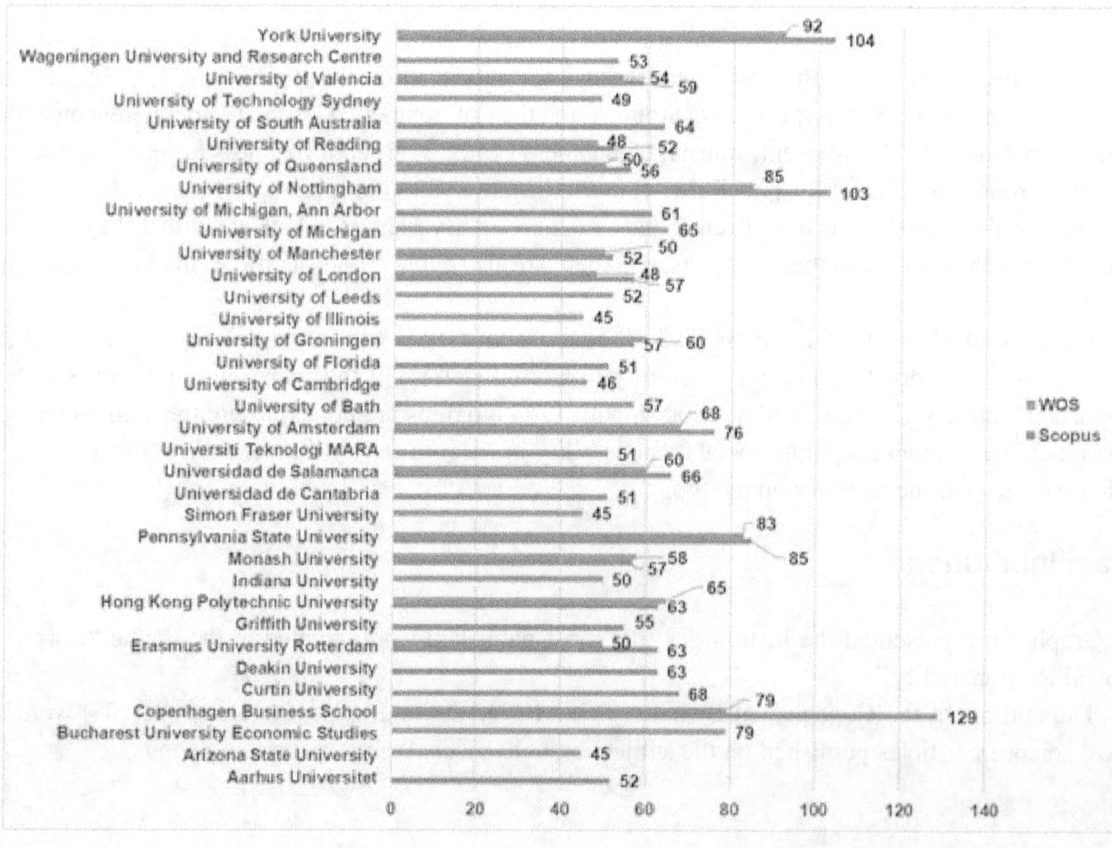

As stated by Silinske et al. (2014), it is possible to state that institutions that have more publications in the area are more devoted to sustainability issues considering the triple bottom line perspective, which in turn involves aspects economic, social and environmental (Elkington, 1994), subject related to corporate social responsibility.

Annually Published Articles

At this point, we will follow the growth of the publications in the two databases, in the period under study. The total of scientific production in the period under analysis were 26592, with 14262 publications in Scopus and 12330 articles in the Web of Science (Table 2).

In the period between 1988 and 2018, There was an increase in the number of articles published per year with a “boom” in the years 2013 to 2018, in both bases.

The review made it clear that issues widely discussed during this period (2013-2018) largely involve sustainable supply chain management practices (Ahi, & Searcy, 2013; Beske et al., 2014; Dubey et al., 2017), corporate social responsibility reports (Landrum, & Ohsowski, 2018; Wang et al., 2018), CSR impacts on financial performance (Platonova et al., 2018; Wang, & Sarkis, 2017), Relationship between CSR and Marketing (Boccia, & Sarnacchiaro, 2018; Hildebrand et al., 2017), and finally, stakeholder perception and pressure on CSR (Boiral et al., 2017; El Akremi et al., 2018)

In this sense, in addition to the growth in the number of publications, researchers can look for topics recently discussed to favor the development of the research field in corporate social responsibility.

Table 2. Total publications between 1988 and 2018 distributed per year

ANO	Scopus	WOS	ANO	Scopus	WOS
1988	3	0	2004	147	76
1989	7	0	2005	281	98
1990	6	0	2006	283	124
1991	12	0	2007	387	221
1992	8	0	2008	522	359
1993	7	0	2009	776	516
1994	9	9	2010	798	566
1995	8	5	2011	966	667
1996	12	12	2012	922	675
1997	11	13	2013	1129	806
1998	12	10	2014	1216	921
1999	15	12	2015	1342	1537
2000	18	20	2016	1503	1761
2001	39	27	2017	1655	1839
2002	45	21	2018	1998	1988
2003	125	47			
		Total...................		14262	12330

Graph 5. Distribution of articles by country

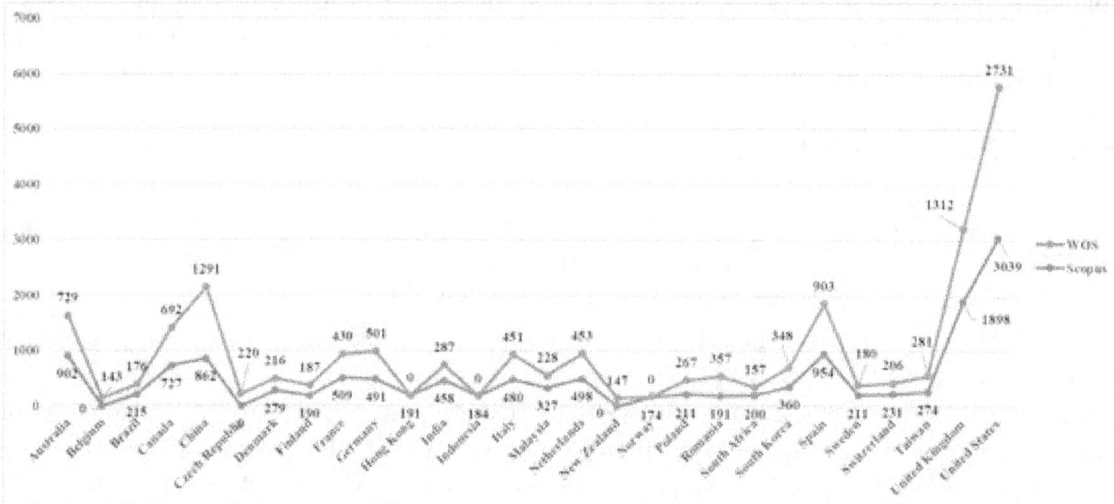

Main Countries

The bibliometric analysis identified, at this point, the number of articles distributed by the countries of origin and database such as: USA (2731; 3039), United Kingdom (1312; 1898), China (1291; 862), Portugal (0;124) and Brazil (215; 176) (Graph 5).

From graph 5, and in line with that found by Aznar-Sánchez et al. (2019) and Feng, et al. (2017) in studies of corporate social responsibility and sustainability. It can be said that research on corporate social responsibility has grown in breadth and interest around the world. It is noticed that researchers from all continents published on the subject, which highlights the global importance of the subject.

Graph 6. Distribution of articles by language

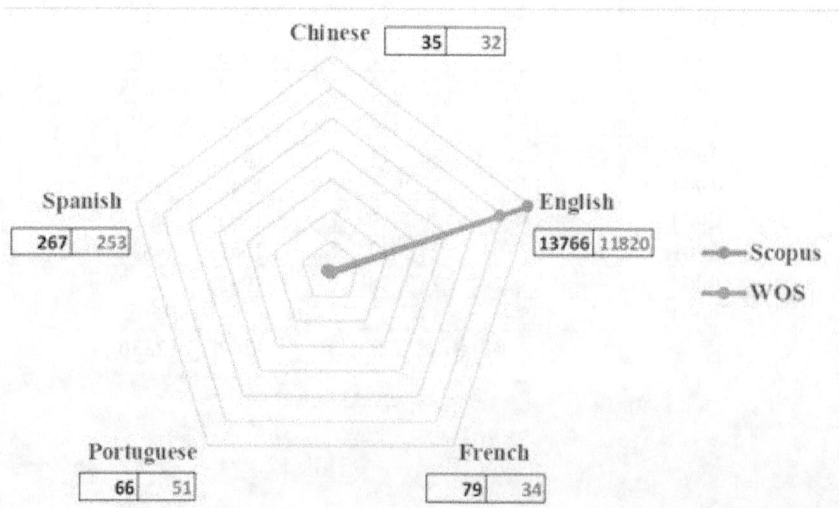

Main Languages

With regard to the languages of the works published in the study area, 25,586 are published in English, 11,820 in the Web of Science and 13766 in Scopus, as shown in Graph 6.

The high number of publications in the English language may be due to the fact that works published in English have a higher number of citations than those published in different languages, in statically controlled situations, according to a study by Di Bitetti and Ferreras (2017).), where the authors suggest that this is a result of the increased global accessibility afforded by the English language.

Research Areas

Regarding the main Research Areas in publications on "Corporate Social Responsibility", there seems to be a convergence in the main research areas of most published articles: Business, Management and Accounting, Social Sciences, Environmental Science (Figure 2).

The research areas related to studies of corporate social responsibility highlight the interdisciplinary characteristic of the theme, addressing studies of management, engineering, environment, health,

Figure 2. Research areas

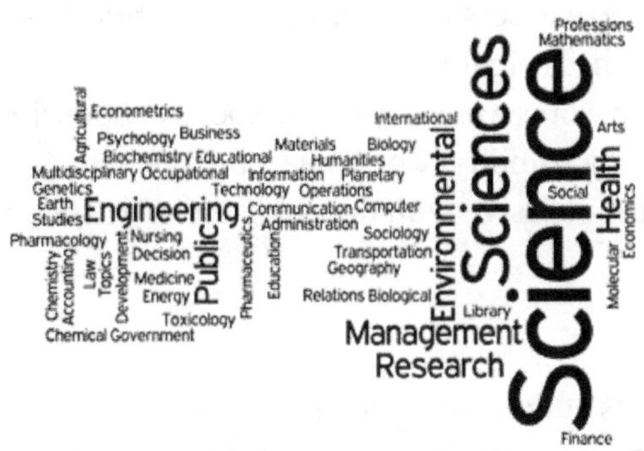

Figure 3. Keywords of the research articles

Figure 3 shows some keywords similar to those found in the study by Feng et al. (2017) which dealt with corporate social responsibility in the supply chain, among which stand out sustainability, sustainable development, economic and social effects, corporate strategy and social aspects. This highlights the centrality of such keywords in CSR studies, regardless of the areas and subareas to which the studies apply.

Figure 4. Study Finance Agencies

economics, public sector, technology, psychology, among others. The interdisciplinary characteristic of corporate social responsibility has already been highlighted by Akin and Yilmaz (2016) and Breitbarth et al. (2015).

In the next section, the keywords in the articles will be analyzed.

Most Used Keywords

The keywords represent a source of access to scientific articles, briefly show the content, research methods and/or tools used in the studies (Figure 3).

The most commonly used keywords were: Corporate Social Responsibility, Sustainable Development, CSR, Sustainability, Social Responsibility, Corporate Strategy, which strengthens the selection of the bibliographical portfolio, as it is cohesive with the objective of the research (Figure 4).

Funding Agencies

We present the funding agencies at this point (Figure 4)

In relation to the funding agencies of the work including the theme in research, it was found those with the highest number of publications: National Natural Science Foundation of China, Social Sciences and Humanities Research Council of Canada, Economic and Social Research Council (ESRC). These data evidence the importance of financing in the development of research worldwide.

A study by Auranen and Nieminen (2010) indicates that, as financial agents, they play an important role in the development and development of research around the world, however, a matter of scientific study that involves more complex aspects of what funding is. Thus, policy makers should consider political, systemic and cultural issues for the development of science in each nation.

Most Cited Articles from 1988 and 2018

Among the data from the Web of Science and Scopus survey on "Corporate Social Responsibility", from 1988 to 2018, it is important to highlight Table 3 which presents the foremost publications in the number of citations, shows a slight juxtaposition between the two bases.

Table 3. List of the most cited publications in the period 1988 to 2018

Scopus	WOS	Title	Authors	Source Title	Year
2999		Strategy & society: The link between competitive advantage and corporate social responsibility	Porter, M.E., Kramer, M.R.	Harvard Business Review	2006
2289		Corporate social responsibility: A theory of the firm perspective	McWilliams, A., Siegel, D	Academy of Management Review	2001
2165		The pyramid of corporate social responsibility: Toward the moral management of organizational stakeholders	Carroll, A.B.	Business Horizons	1991
2047		Corporate social responsibility: Evolution of a definitional construct	Carroll, A.B.	Business and Society	1999
1664		Does doing good always lead to doing better? Consumer reactions to corporate social responsibility	Sen, S., Bhattacharya, C.B.	Journal of Marketing Research	2001
1645		The company and the product: Corporate associations and consumer product responses	Brown, T.J., Dacin, P.A.	Journal of Marketing	1997
1393	1277	"Implicit" and "explicit" CSR: A conceptual framework for a comparative understanding of corporate social responsibility	Matten, D., Moon, J.	Academy of Management Review	2008
1381		Why would corporations behave in socially responsible ways? An institutional theory of corporate social responsibility	Campbell, J.L.	Academy of Management Review	2007
1230		Corporate social responsibility and financial performance: Correlation or misspecification?	McWilliams, A., Siegel, D	Strategic Management Journal	2000
1224		Corporate social responsibility theories: Mapping the territory	Garriga, E., Melé, D.	Journal of Business Ethics	2004
1040		Corporate social responsibility, customer Satisfaction, and market value	Luo, X., Bhattacharya, C.B	Journal of Marketing	2006
1039		Corporate social responsibility: Strategic implications	McWilliams, A., Siegel, D.S., Wright, P.M.	Journal of Management Studies	2006
1026		Putting the s back in corporate social responsibility: A multilevel theory of social change in organizations	Aguilera, R.V., Rupp, D.E., Williams, C.A., Ganapathi, J.	Academy of Management Review	2007
1012	866	How corporate social responsibility is defined: An analysis of 37 definitions	Dahlsrud, A.	Corporate Social Responsibility and Environmental Management	2008
951	856	The business case for corporate social responsibility: A review of concepts, research and practice	Carroll, A.B., Shabana, K.M	International Journal of Management Reviews	2010
877	803	What We Know and Don't Know About Corporate Social Responsibility: A Review and Research Agenda	Aguinis, H., Glavas, A	Journal of Management	2012
	1626	From a literature review to a conceptual framework for sustainable supply chain management	Seuring, Stefan; Mueller, Martin	Journal of Cleaner Production	2008
	574	An organizational theoretic review of green supply chain management literature	Sarkis, Joseph; Zhu, Qinghua; Lai, Kee-hung	International Journal of Production Economics	2011
	558	The New Political Role of Business in a Globalized World: A Review of a New Perspective on CSR and its Implications for the Firm, Governance, and Democracy	Scherer, Andreas Georg; Palazzo, Guido	Journal of Management Studies	2011
	543	Maximizing Business Returns to Corporate Social Responsibility (CSR): The Role of CSR Communication	Du, Shuili; Bhattacharya, C. B.; Sen, Sankar	International Journal of Management Reviews	2010
	536	The Relationship Between Corporate Social Responsibility and Shareholder Value: an Empirical Test of The Risk Management Hypothesis	Godfrey, Paul C.; Merrill, Craig B.; Hansen, Jared M.	Strategic Management Journal	2009
	514	Voluntary Nonfinancial Disclosure and the Cost of Equity Capital: The Initiation of Corporate Social Responsibility Reporting	Dhaliwal, Dan S.; Li, Oliver Zhen; Tsang, Albert; Yang, Yong George	Accounting Review	2011
	457	A literature and practice review to develop sustainable business model archetypes	Bocken, N. M. P.; Short, S. W.; Rana, P.; Evans, S.	Journal of Cleaner Production	2014
	453	Corporate social responsibility: A process model of sensemaking	Basu, Kunal; Palazzo, Guido	Academy of Management Review	2008
	432	Sustainable supply chain management: evolution and future directions	Carter, Craig R.; Easton, P. Liane	International Journal of Physical Distribution & Logistics Management	2011
	334	Does it Pay to be Different? An Analysis of the Relationship Between Corporate Social and Financial Performance	Brammer, Stephen; Millington, Andrew	Strategic Management Journal	2008

It should be noted that, in between the most cited articles we have "Strategy & society: The link between competitive advantage and corporate social responsibility" by Porter and Kramer published in Harvard Business Review, in 2006, with 2999 citations, in Scopus. And, in WOS, "From a literature review to a conceptual framework for sustainable supply chain management" de Seuring and Mueller, with 1626 citations, published in the Journal of Cleaner Production, in 2008.

Through the analysis of citations, it is evident that corporate social responsibility is a topic of academic and social relevance, as it attracts the attention of researchers in the study of theory and empirical reality. It is assumed that the citations are eloquent indications of the academic influence of researchers and themes.

The presence of electronic scientific articles favors the analysis of citations and improves the accuracy of the measurement performed, impacting the mode and quality of studies on the scientific structure of citations (Boyack et al., 2018).

CONCLUSION

The present study aimed to verify the characteristics of the national and international scientific production that relate the theme of "Corporate Social Responsibility". In order to reach the goal, a bibliometric research was carried out in the two databases, obtaining 12330 publications in the Web of Science and 14262 publications in Scopus, related to these themes, mainly in the following areas: Business, Management and Accounting, Social Sciences, Economics, Econometrics and Finance and Environmental Science.

Subsequently, the distribution of publications on the subject was analysed, and it was verified that of the 15 articles most cited in each database, four appear in the two databases. We have as an example the article: "What We Know and Don't Know About Corporate Social Responsibility: A Review and Research Agenda", by Aguinis and Glavas, published in the Journal of Management, in 2012, cited 1680 times, 877 in Scopus and 803 in WOS.

The authors, Porter, M.E., Kramer, M.R., of the most cited article in Scopus "Strategy & society: The link between competitive advantage and corporate social responsibility" are not among the twenty-five authors who published more on the subject, during the study period.

It should be noted that, the authors Moon, Matten, Palazzo, Bhattacharya, Moon, Sen, Bhattacharya, Palazzo, Brammer, Jamali, and Lindgreen, who are among those who wrote the most, are among the most cited.

The authors Matten and Moon, wrote "Implicit and explicit CSR: A conceptual framework for a comparative understanding of corporate social responsibility", with 1277 citations, published in Academy of Management Review, in 2008; Palazzo wrote "The New Political Role of Business in a Globalized World: A Review of a New Perspective on CSR and its Implications for the Firm, Governance, and Democracy" coauthors Scherer with 558 citations, published in Journal of Management Studies, in 2011; Bhattacharya and Sen wrote "Maximizing Business Returns to Corporate Social Responsibility (CSR): The Role of CSR Communication" and Du with 543 citations, published in International Journal of Management Reviews, in 2010; Palazzo, coauthor of "Corporate social responsibility: A process model of sensemaking" with Basu with 453 citations, published in Academy of Management Review, in 2008; Brammer, coauthor of the article "Does it Pay to be Different? An Analysis of the Relationship Between Corporate Social and Financial Performance" with Sutherland, cited 344 times, published in Strategic Management Journal, in 2008.

In this way, it is possible to verify that there is the same relation between the publications with the largest publications in "Corporate Social Responsibility," in both databases. It was found that most of the publications found in both databases are articles, which in the period between 1988 and 2018; there was an increase in the number of articles published per year with a "boom" in the years 2013 to 2018, in both bases. Most of the studies were published in the journals Corporate Social Responsibility and Environmental Management, Journal of Business Ethics and Social Responsibility Journal, which stand out with the largest number of publications.

It has been found that the United Kingdom, United States e China lead the ranking of the countries that published the most on the subject, and the English language predominates in publications with a total of 25586, being 13766 in Scopus and 11820 in the Web of Science.

It is worth noting that, in Brazil (215;176) in Scopus and the Web of Science have been published on the subject researched, while in Portugal was published 124 papers, in Scopus, which indicates that this theme should be further elaborated by researchers, mainly Portuguese and Brazilians who seek originality in their work.

The contribution of this article to the studies in Management is due to the resulting indicators regarding the research institutions and the newspapers that stand out most in the production of the knowledge on the subject at the international level.

The present study found the following limitations: 1) the main limitation of this study refers to the fact that only the terms "Corporate Social Responsibility" were used; 2) the information presented is limited to articles selected only in Web of Science and Scopus; 3) the bibliometric analysis limited to authors, articles, sources, institutions, countries, language and period.

Thus, it is suggested that for future research it is necessary to use other research terms; perform other bibliometric analyses, such as the formation of networks of authors and institutions; to carry out a systemic analysis with the aim of analysing other contents different from those analysed in the present study, such as: what theories have been worked together in which countries, what themes emerged in Corporate Social Responsibility.

RERERENCES

Ahi, P., & Searcy, C. (2013). A comparative literature analysis of definitions for green and sustainable supply chain management. *Journal of Cleaner Production, 52*, 329–341. doi:10.1016/j.jclepro.2013.02.018

Akin, A., & Yilmaz, İ. (2016). Drivers of Corporate Social Responsibility Disclosures: Evidence from Turkish Banking Sector. *Procedia Economics and Finance, 38*, 2–7.

Albuquerque, J. L. (2009). *Gestão ambiental e responsabilidade social: conceitos, ferramentas e aplicações*. São Paulo: Atlas.

Aligleri, L. M., Aligleri, L. A., & Câmara, M. R. G. (2002). Responsabilidade Social na Cadeia Logística: uma Visão Integrada para o Incremento da Competitividade. In Proceedings of the II Encontro de Estudos Organizacionais, Recife. Academic Press.

Almeida, F., & Sobral, F. (2007). Influência dos valores culturais na Responsabilidade Social das Empresas. *Revista Portuguesa e Brasileira de Gestão, 6*(3), 52–61.

Argenti, P. (2014). *A comunicação empresarial: a construção da identidade, imagem e reputação*. São Paulo: Campus.

Arthaud-Day, M. L. (2005). Transnational corporate social responsibility: A tri-dimensional approach to international CSR research. *Business Ethics Quarterly*, *15*(1), 1–22. doi:10.5840/beq20051515

Ashley, P. A., Coutinho, R. B. G., & Tomei, P. A. (2000). Responsabilidade social corporativa e cidadania empresarial: uma análise conceitual comparativa. In Proceedings of the *XXIV Encontro da ANPAD, Florianópolis, 2000*. Florianópolis: Anais.

Attig, N., Boubakri, N., El Ghoul, S., & Guedhami, O. (2016). Firm internationalization and corporate social responsibility. *Journal of Business Ethics*, *134*(2), 171–197. doi:10.100710551-014-2410-6

Auranen, O., & Nieminen, M. (2010). University research funding and publication performance-An international comparison. *Research Policy*, *39*(6), 822–834. doi:10.1016/j.respol.2010.03.003

Aznar-Sánchez, J. A., Velasco-Muñoz, J. F., Belmonte-Ureña, L. J., & Manzano-Agugliaro, F. (2019). Innovation and technology for sustainable mining activity: A worldwide research assessment. *Journal of Cleaner Production*, *221*, 38–54. doi:10.1016/j.jclepro.2019.02.243

Baumann-Pauly, D., Wickert, C., Spence, L. J., & Scherer, A. G. (2013). Organizing Corporate Social Responsibility in Small and Large Firms: Size Matters. *Journal of Business Ethics*, *115*(4), 693–705. doi:10.100710551-013-1827-7

Bear, S., Rahman, N., & Post, C. (2010). The Impact of Board Diversity and Gender Composition on Corporate Social Responsibility and Firm Reputation. *Journal of Business Ethics*, *97*(2), 207–221. doi:10.100710551-010-0505-2

Bertoncello, S. L. T., & Chang JR, J. (2007). A importância da responsabilidade social corporativa como fator de diferenciação. *FACOM–Revista da Faculdade de comunicação da FAAP*, *17*, 70-76.

Beske, P., Land, A., & Seuring, S. (2014). Sustainable supply chain management practices and dynamic capabilities in the food industry: A critical analysis of the literature. *International Journal of Production Economics*, *152*, 131–143. doi:10.1016/j.ijpe.2013.12.026

Boccia, F., & Sarnacchiaro, P. (2018). The Impact of Corporate Social Responsibility on Consumer Preference: A Structural Equation Analysis. *Corporate Social Responsibility and Environmental Management*, *25*(2), 151–163. doi:10.1002/csr.1446

Boiral, O., Heras-Saizarbitoria, I., & Testa, F. (2017). SA8000 as CSR-Washing? The Role of Stakeholder Pressures. *Corporate Social Responsibility and Environmental Management*, *24*(1), 57–70. doi:10.1002/csr.1391

Bolton, L. E., & Mattila, A. S. (2015). How does corporate social responsibility affect consumer response to service failure in buyer-seller relationships? *Journal of Retailing*, *91*(1), 140–153. doi:10.1016/j.jretai.2014.10.001

Borger, F. G. (2001). *Responsabilidade Social: efeitos da atuação social na dinâmica empresarial* [Tese de Doutoramento]. Universidade de São Paulo, Faculdade de Economia e Administração.

Bowen, H. R. (1957). *Responsabilidades sociais do homem de negócios*. Rio de Janeiro: Civilização Brasileira.

Boyack, K. W., van Eck, N. J., Colavizza, G., & Waltman, L. (2018). Characterizing in-text citations in scientific articles: A large-scale analysis. *Journal of Informetrics*, *12*(1), 59–73. doi:10.1016/j.joi.2017.11.005

Breitbarth, T., Walzel, S., Anagnostopoulos, C., & Van Eekeren, F. (2015). Corporate social responsibility and governance in sport: "Oh, the things you can find, if you don't stay behind! *Corporate Governance (Bingley)*, *15*(2), 254–273. doi:10.1108/CG-02-2015-0025

Brzeszczynski, J., & McIntosh, G. (2014). Performance of portfolios composed of British SRI stocks. *Journal of Business Ethics*, *120*(3), 335–362. doi:10.100710551-012-1541-x

Café, L., & Bräscher, M. (2008). *Organização da informação e bibliometria. In Encontros Bibli: Revista Eletrônica de Biblioteconomia e Ciência da Informação* (pp. 54–75). Especial.

Carroll, A. B. (1979). A three-dimensional conceptual model of corporate performance. *Academy of Management Review*, *4*(4), 497–505. doi:10.5465/amr.1979.4498296

Carroll, A. B. (1991). The pyramid of corporate social responsibility: Toward the moral management of organizational stakeholders. *Business Horizons*, *34*(4), 39–48. doi:10.1016/0007-6813(91)90005-G

Carroll, A. B. (1999). Corporate social responsibility evolution of a definitional construct. *Business & Society*, *38*(3), 268–295. doi:10.1177/000765039903800303

Carroll, A. B. (2008). A History of Corporate Social Responsibility: Concepts and Practices. In A. Crane, A. McWilliams, D. Matten, J. Moon, & D. Siegel (Eds.), *The Oxford Handbook of Corporate Social Responsibility* (pp. 19–46). Oxford: Oxford University Press.

Carroll, A. B. (2015). Corporate social responsibility: The centerpiece of competing and complementary frameworks. *Organizational Dynamics*, *44*(2), 87–96. doi:10.1016/j.orgdyn.2015.02.002

Comissão Das Comunidades Europeias. (2001). Livro Verde: Promover um quadro europeu para a responsabilidade social das empresas.

Corlett, J. (1988). Schefflerian ethics and corporate social-responsibility. *Journal of Business Ethics*, *7*(8), 631–638. doi:10.1007/BF00382797

Custodio, A. L. M., & Moya, R. (2013). *Indicadores Ethos de Responsabilidade Social Empresarial*. São Paulo: Instituto Ethos.

Detomasi, D. A. (2008). The Political Roots of Corporate Social Responsibility. *Journal of Business Ethics*, *82*(4), 807–819. doi:10.100710551-007-9594-y

Di Bitetti, M. S., & Ferreras, J. A. (2017). Publish (in English) or perish: The effect on citation rate of using languages other than English in scientific publications. *Ambio*, *46*(1), 121–127. doi:10.100713280-016-0820-7 PMID:27686730

Drucker, P. (1986). Management: Tasks, Responsibilities, Practices (Truman Tal ed.). Academic Press.

Duarte, A. P., Gomes, D. R., & Neves, J. G. (2014). Finding the jigsaw piece for our jigsaw puzzle with corporate social responsibility. *Management Research: The journal of the iberoamerican Academy of Management Journal*, *12*(3), 240–258.

Dubey, R., Gunasekaran, A., Papadopoulos, T., Childe, S. J., Shibin, K. T., & Wamba, S. F. (2017). Sustainable supply chain management: Framework and further research directions. *Journal of Cleaner Production*, *142*, 1119–1130. doi:10.1016/j.jclepro.2016.03.117

El Akremi, A., Gond, J. P., Swaen, V., De Roeck, K., & Igalens, J. (2018). How Do Employees Perceive Corporate Responsibility? Development and Validation of a Multidimensional Corporate Stakeholder Responsibility Scale. *Journal of Management*, *44*(2), 619–657. doi:10.1177/0149206315569311

El Ghoul, S., Guedhami, O., Kwok, C. Y., & Mishra, D. (2011). Does corporate social responsibility affect the cost of capital? *Journal of Banking & Finance*, *35*(9), 2388–2406. doi:10.1016/j.jbankfin.2011.02.007

Elkington, J. (1994). Towards the Sustainable Corporation: Win-Win-Win Business Strategies for Sustainable Development. *California Management Review*, *36*(2), 90–100. doi:10.2307/41165746

Farcane, N., & Bureana, E. (2015). History of Corporate Social Responsibility Concept. *Annales Universitatis Apulensis Series Oeconomica*, *2*(17), 31–48.

Farley, J., & Voinov, A. (2016). Economics, socio-ecological resilience and ecosystem services. *Journal of Environmental Management*, *183*, 389–398. doi:10.1016/j.jenvman.2016.07.065 PMID:27480914

Feitosa, M. J. S., Souza, N. M. O., Santos, R. S., & Firmo, L. A. (2014). Estágio de desenvolvimento da responsabilidade social empresarial no setor bancário: Um estudo em uma agência do Banco do Brasil. *Revista Metropolitana de Sustentabilidade*, *4*(3), 15.

Feng, Y., Zhu, Q., & Lai, K. H. (2017). Corporate social responsibility for supply chain management: A literature review and bibliometric analysis. *Journal of Cleaner Production*, *158*, 296–307. doi:10.1016/j.jclepro.2017.05.018

Fischer, R. M., & Mendonça, L. R. (2002). Terceiro Setor: Inventário da Produção Brasileira. In *ISTR – Fifth International Conference: Transforming Civil Society, Citizenship And Governance: The Third Sector in an Era of Global (Dis)Order*. Academic Press.

Flammer, C., & Luo, J. (2017). Corporate social responsibility as an employee governance tool: Evidence from a quasi-experiment. *Strategic Management Journal*, *38*(1), 163–183. doi:10.1002mj.2492

Frias-Aceituno, J. V., Rodriguez-Ariza, L., & Garcia-Sanchez, I. M. (2013). The role of the board in the dissemination of integrated corporate social reporting. *Corporate Social Responsibility and Environmental Management*, *20*(4), 219–233. doi:10.1002/csr.1294

Friedman, M. (1962). *Capitalismo e liberdade*. São Paulo: Nova Cultura.

Frynas, J. G., & Stephens, S. (2015). Political Corporate Social Responsibility: Reviewing Theories and Setting New Agendas. *International Journal of Management Reviews*, *17*(4), 483–509. doi:10.1111/ijmr.12049

Gallardo-Vázquez, D., & Sanchez-Hernandez, M. I. (2014). Measuring Corporate Social Responsability for competitive success at a regional level. *Journal of Cleaner Production*, *72*(1), 14–22. doi:10.1016/j.jclepro.2014.02.051

García-Sánchez, I. M., Hussain, N., Martínez-Ferrero, J., & Ruiz-Barbadillo, E. (2019). Impact of disclosure and assurance quality of corporate sustainability reports on access to finance. *Corporate Social Responsibility and Environmental Management*, *26*(4), 832–848. doi:10.1002/csr.1724

Garousi, V. (2015). A bibliometric analysis of the Turkish software engineering research community. *Scientometrics*, *105*(1), 23–49. doi:10.100711192-015-1663-x

Garriga, E., & Melé, D. (2004). Corporate Social Responsibility Theories: Mapping the Territory Social Responsibility Corporate Theories. *Journal of Business Ethics*, *53*(1/2), 51–71. doi:10.1023/B:BUSI.0000039399.90587.34

Global Reporting Initiative. (2012). Relatórios de sustentabilidade da GRI: quanto vale essa jornada?

Gond, J. P., El Akremi, A., Swaen, V., & Babu, N. (2017). The psychological microfoundations of corporate social responsibility: A person-centric systematic review. *Journal of Organizational Behavior*, *38*(2), 225–246. doi:10.1002/job.2170

Han, H., Yu, J., & Kim, W. (2019). Environmental corporate social responsibility and the strategy to boost the airline's image and customer loyalty intentions. *Journal of Travel & Tourism Marketing*, *36*(3), 371–383. doi:10.1080/10548408.2018.1557580

Harjoto, M., Laksmana, I., & Lee, R. (2015). Board Diversity and Corporate Social Responsibility. *Journal of Business Ethics*, *132*(4), 641–660. doi:10.100710551-014-2343-0

Hildebrand, D., Demotta, Y., Sen, S., & Valenzuela, A. (2017). Consumer responses to corporate social responsibility (CSR) contribution type. *The Journal of Consumer Research*, *44*(4), 738–758. doi:10.1093/jcr/ucx063

Husted, B. W., & Allen, D. B. (2009). Strategic Corporate Social Responsibility and Value Creation. *Management International Review*, *49*(6), 781–799. doi:10.100711575-009-0016-5

Instituto Ethos. (2013). Responsabilidade social empresarial e sustentabilidade para a gestão empresarial. Fernanda Gabriela Borger. Retrieved from http://www3.ethos.org.br/cedoc/responsabilidade-social-empresarial-e-sustentabilidade-para-a-gestao-empresarial/#.WP0fjf9v9cv

Ioannou, I., & Serafeim, G. (2015). The impact of corporate social responsibility on investment recommendations: Analysts' perceptions and shifting institutional logics. *Strategic Management Journal*, *36*(7), 1053–1081. doi:10.1002mj.2268

Irigaray, H. A. R., Vergara, S. C., & Araújo, R. G. (2017). Responsabilidade Social Corporativa: O que revelam os Relatórios Sociais das Empresas. *Organizações & Sociedade*, *24*(80), 73–80. doi:10.1590/1984-9230804

Jain, T., & Jamali, D. (2016). Looking Inside the Black Box: The Effect of Corporate Governance on Corporate Social Responsibility. *Corporate Governance*, *24*(3), 253–273. doi:10.1111/corg.12154

Jamali, D. (2008). A stakeholder approach to corporate social responsibility: A fresh perspective into theory and practice. *Journal of Business Ethics*, *82*(1), 213–231. doi:10.100710551-007-9572-4

Jamali, D., & Mirshak, R. (2007). Corporate Social Responsibility (CSR): Theory and practice in a developing country context. *Journal of Business Ethics*, *72*(3), 243–262. doi:10.100710551-006-9168-4

Jamali, D., Safieddine, A. M., & Rabbath, M. (2008). Corporate governance and corporate social responsibility synergies and interrelationships. *Corporate Governance*, *16*(5), 443–459. doi:10.1111/j.1467-8683.2008.00702.x

John, A., Qadeer, F., Shahzadi, G., & Jia, F. (2019). Getting paid to be good: How and when employees respond to corporate social responsibility? *Journal of Cleaner Production*, *215*, 784–795. doi:10.1016/j.jclepro.2019.01.074

Kang, C., Germann, F., & Grewal, R. (2016). Washing Away Your Sins? Corporate Social Responsibility, Corporate Social Irresponsibility, and Firm Performance. *Journal of Marketing*, *80*(2), 59–79. doi:10.1509/jm.15.0324

Katsoulakos, P., Koutsodimou, M., Matraga, A., & Williams, L. (2004). A historic perspective of the CSR movement. CSRQuest Sustainability Framework. Retrieved from www.csrquest.net/uploadfiles/1D.pdf

Keinert, C. (2008). *Corporate Social Responsibility as an International Strategy*. Leipzig, Germany: Physica-Verlag A Springer Company.

Kreitlon, M. P. (2004). A ética nas relações entre empresas e sociedade: fundamentos teóricos da responsabilidade social empresarial. In Proceedings of the XXVIII Encontro Anual da Anpad, Curitiba, 2004. Academic Press.

Landrum, N. E., & Ohsowski, B. (2018). Identifying Worldviews on Corporate Sustainability: A Content Analysis of Corporate Sustainability Reports. *Business Strategy and the Environment*, *27*(1), 128–151. doi:10.1002/bse.1989

Leandro, A., & Rebelo, T. (2011). A responsabilidade social das empresas: Incursão ao conceito e suas relações com a cultura organizacional. *Revista Exedra*, 11-40.

Lee, M. D. P. (2008). A review of the theories of corporate social responsibility: Its evolutionary path and the road ahead. *International Journal of Management Reviews*, *10*(1), 53–73. doi:10.1111/j.1468-2370.2007.00226.x

Li, Y., Liu, B., & Huan, T. C. (2019). Renewal or not? Consumer response to a renewed corporate social responsibility strategy: Evidence from the coffee shop industry. *Tourism Management*, *72*, 170–179. doi:10.1016/j.tourman.2018.10.031

Lins, K. V., Servaes, H., & Tamayo, A. (2017). Social Capital, Trust, and Firm Performance: The Value of Corporate Social Responsibility during the Financial Crisis. *The Journal of Finance*, *72*(4), 1785–1824. doi:10.1111/jofi.12505

Luo, X., & Bhattacharya, C. (2006). Corporate Social Responsibility, Customer Satisfaction, and Market Value. *Journal of Marketing*, *70*(4), 1–18. doi:10.1509/jmkg.70.4.001

Machado, M. R., Machado, M. A. V., & Santos, A. (2010). A relação entre setor econômico e investimentos sociais e ambientais. *Contabilidade, Gestão E Governança, 13*(3), 102–115.

Madrakhimova, F. S. (2013). Evolution of the concept and definition of corporate social responsibility. In *Proceedings of the Global Conference on Business & Finance Proceedings* (pp. 113-118). Academic Press.

Martínez, P., & Del Bosque, I. R. (2013). CSR and customer loyalty: The roles of trust, customer identification with the company and satisfaction. *International Journal of Hospitality Management, 35*, 89–99. doi:10.1016/j.ijhm.2013.05.009

Melo Neto, F. P., & Fróes, E. S. C. (2001). Gestão da responsabilidade social corporativa: o caso brasileiro – da filantropia tradicional à filantropia de alto rendimento e ao empreendedorismo social. Rio de Janeiro: Qualitymark Ed.

Merco. (2014). Merco responsabilidad y gobierno corporativo. Retrieved from http://www.merco.info/br/ranking-merco-responsabilidad-gobierno-corporativo

Nodari, P. C., Calgaro, C., & Síveres, L. (2017). *Ética, direitos humanos e meio ambiente: reflexões e pistas para uma educação cidadã responsável e pacífica.* EDUCS – Editora da Universidade de Caxias do Sul.

Pereira, T. H. M., & Gonçalves, C. A. (2019). Responsabilidade social corporativa: práticas e percepções. *Revista observatorio de la economía latinoamericana*, (Enero), 01-07.

Pérez, A., & Del Bosque, I. R. (2015). How customers construct corporate social responsibility images: Testing the moderating role of demographic characteristics. *BRQ Business Research Quarterly, 18*(2), 127–141. doi:10.1016/j.brq.2014.04.003

Pimenta, A. A., Portela, A. R. M. R., Oliveira, C. B., & Ribeiro, R. M. (2017). A bibliometria nas pesquisas acadêmicas, SCIENTIA: Revista de Ensino. *Pesquisa e Extensão, 4*(7), 1–13.

Platonova, E., Asutay, M., Dixon, R., & Mohammad, S. (2018). The Impact of Corporate Social Responsibility Disclosure on Financial Performance: Evidence from the GCC Islamic Banking Sector. *Journal of Business Ethics, 151*(2), 451–471. doi:10.100710551-016-3229-0

Prado-Lorenzo, J. M., Gallego-Alvarez, I., & Garcia-Sanchez, I. M. (2009). Stakeholder engagement and corporate social responsibility reporting: The ownership structure effect. *Corporate Social Responsibility and Environmental Management, 16*(2), 94–107. doi:10.1002/csr.189

Rao, K., & Tilt, C. (2016). Board Composition and Corporate Social Responsibility: The Role of Diversity, Gender, Strategy and Decision Making. *Journal of Business Ethics, 138*(2), 327–347. doi:10.100710551-015-2613-5

Ribeiro, C. T. L. (2001). *Responsabilidade social empresarial. Apoio às comunidades carentes. 2001.* Salvador: Universidade Federal da Bahia.

Rivera, J. J., Bigne, E., & Curras-Perez, R. (2016). Effects of Corporate Social Responsibility perception on consumer satisfaction with the brand. *Spanish Journal of Marketing, 20*(2), 104-114.

Rupp, D. E., & Mallory, D. B. (2015). Corporate Social Responsibility: Psychological, Person-Centric, and Progressing. *Annual Review of Organizational Psychology and Organizational Behavior*, *2*(2), 11–36.

Scherer, A. G., Rasche, A., Palazzo, G., & Spicer, A. (2016). Managing for Political Corporate Social Responsibility: New Challenges and Directions for PCSR 2.0. *Journal of Management Studies*, *53*(3), 273–298. doi:10.1111/joms.12203

Silinske, J., Marquetto, M. F., Grohmann, M. Z., Battistella, L. F., & Madruga, L. R. da R. G. (2014). Bibliometric study about sustainability in the field of entrepreneurial economy. *Organizations and Sustainability*, *3*(2), 101–120.

Silva, E. C., Azevedo, A. S., Barros, M., & Reis, N. D. (2018). Responsabilidade social corporativa na produção de cacau: Análise das ações da indústria de chocolate. *Novo Hamburgo*, *15*(1), 183–204.

Silva, R. R., & Santos, M. J. N. (2011). A importância da responsabilidade social corporativa para a potenciação do capital social em pequenas e médias empresas. *Revista de Ciências da Administração*, *12*(27), 190–207.

Soares, G. M. P. (2004). Responsabilidade social corporativa: Por uma boa causa!? *RAE Eletrônica*, *3*(2), 1–15. doi:10.1590/S1676-56482004000200007

Su, L., & Swanson, S. R. (2019). Perceived corporate social responsibility's impact on the well-being and supportive green behaviors of hotel employees: The mediating role of the employee-corporate relationship. *Tourism Management*, *72*, 437–450. doi:10.1016/j.tourman.2019.01.009

Tachizawa, T. (2011). *Gestão ambiental e responsabilidade social corporativa: estratégias de negócios focadas na realidade brasileira*. São Paulo: Atlas.

Tenório, F. G. (Ed.). (2015). *Responsabilidade social empresarial: teoria e prática*. Rio de Janeiro: Editora FGV.

Wang, Q., Dou, J., & Jia, S. (2016). A Meta-Analytic Review of Corporate Social Responsibility and Corporate Financial Performance. *Business & Society*, *55*(8), 1083–1121. doi:10.1177/0007650315584317

Wang, S., & Gao, Y. (2016). What do we know about corporate social responsibility research? a content analysis. *Irish Journal of Management*, *35*(1), 1–16. doi:10.1515/ijm-2016-0001

Wang, Z., Hsieh, T. S., & Sarkis, J. (2018). CSR Performance and the Readability of CSR Reports: Too Good to be True? *Corporate Social Responsibility and Environmental Management*, *25*(1), 66–79. doi:10.1002/csr.1440

Wang, Z., & Sarkis, J. (2017). Corporate social responsibility governance, outcomes, and financial performance. *Journal of Cleaner Production*, *162*, 1607–1616. doi:10.1016/j.jclepro.2017.06.142

Windsor, D. (2001). The future of corporate social responsibility. *The International Journal of Organizational Analysis*, *9*(3), 225–256. doi:10.1108/eb028934

Witchkonska, J. (2016). Corporate Social Responsibility: Selected Theoretical and Empirical Aspects. *Comparative Economic Research*, *19*(1), 28–43.

World Business Council for Sustainable Development. Corporate Social Responsibility: meeting changing expectations. WBCSD Publications, 2001. Retrieved from http://old.wbcsd.org/pages/edocument/edocumentdetails.aspx?id=82&nosearchcontextkey=true

Zhang, Q., Oo, B. L., & Lim, B. T. H. (2019). Drivers, motivations, and barriers to the implementation of corporate social responsibility practices by construction enterprises: A review. *Journal of Cleaner Production*, *210*, 563–584. doi:10.1016/j.jclepro.2018.11.050

Zhou, Z., Luo, B. N., & Tang, T. L. P. (2018). Corporate social responsibility excites 'exponential' positive employee engagement: The matthew effect in CSR and sustainable policy. *Corporate Social Responsibility and Environmental Management*, *25*(4), 339–354. doi:10.1002/csr.1464

Chapter 4
Social Responsibility Reporting in Higher Education Institutions:
A Systematic Literature Review

José Vale
Porto Accounting and Business School, Polytechnic of Porto, Portugal

Rui Bertuzi
https://orcid.org/0000-0002-1544-5614
Porto Accounting and Business School, Polytechnic of Porto, Portugal

Albertina Paula Monteiro
Porto Accounting and Business School, Polytechnic of Porto, Portugal

ABSTRACT

This chapter analyzes research in social responsibility (SR) reporting in higher education institutions (HEI), addressing different aspects: a longitudinal assessment, the theoretical approaches, the adopted methodologies, and its main results. A systematic literature review is undertaken. To do so, the ISI Web of Knowledge and Scopus databases were used to retrieve the articles for analysis. The articles were limited to business and management research area. Findings show that literature on SR reporting in HEIs is still in its infancy and it is very heterogeneous, with only 24 articles addressing this theme. Most articles resorted to qualitative methodologies, emphasizing the case study. Findings also show a lack of normalization regarding reporting. Stakeholders' theory and the seek for legitimacy are crucial in SR disclosing in HEIs. Several contributions emerge, namely the provision of a comprehensive review of the current state of research on SR reporting in HEIs and, consequently, a call for increasing the awareness of such organizations towards the importance of this theme.

DOI: 10.4018/978-1-7998-2128-1.ch004

INTRODUCTION

In the last few years, different entities, such as governments and organizations, or even the civil society are engaged in an intense debate focused on environmental and social problems. In fact, the United Nations agenda for the 2030 sustainable development encompasses, in its goals, the development of initiatives to address such problems. Nowadays, it is expected that organizations show transparency and act in a socially responsible fashion. Organizations are increasingly being pressured namely by external stakeholders, who seek to hold companies accountable for social problems and to highlight the financial risks that may arise for those who incur in misconduct (Porter and Kramer, 2006). In other terms, there is a pressure to engage in what is called "Corporate Social Responsibility (CSR)". CSR, as a research field, emerged in the 1950s, namely due to the publication of Howard R. Bowen's seminal book "Social Responsibilities of the Businessman" (Bowen, 1953) and, in the 1960s, this theme gained relevance in academic and practical terms. However, research on CSR related to management is relatively recent (Wang et al., 2016).

Research on CSR has been addressing different types of organizations, with different sizes (Nejati et al., 2011). However, most of this research has been focusing on private and for-profit organizations, although it is a fact that other types of organizations are, nowadays, pressured to act in a social responsible way and, accordingly, disclose their actions and initiatives: such is the case of Higher Education Institutions (HEIs) (Dahlsrud, 2008; Duff, 2016). In fact, organizations have different motivations to undertake and disclose CSR activities, namely, to gain support from stakeholders and obtain legitimacy (Frynas and Yamahaki, 2016; Branco and Rodrigues, 2008). Specifically, some companies consider that if they have good relationships with their stakeholders, such will lead to the development of intangible resources capable of generating financial benefits and competitive advantages. CSR actions can be used as an instrument of legitimacy, in order to show that companies are in line with the standards and expectations of their stakeholders about how operations should be performed (Branco and Rodrigues, 2008). Hence, this chapter focuses on SR disclosure in HEIs.

Higher Education Institutions are considered as centers of knowledge creation and diffusion and, consequently, their role in todays' society is crucial. However, the higher education sector has been under deep changes. International organizations claim that HEIs should be leading the development of solutions for a greater sustainability and that they should integrate this concept in their procedures (Rodríguez Bolívar et al., 2013). HEIs can, nowadays, be compared to big businesses which have to attend their stakeholders' needs (namely students, employees and society) in order to be sustainable (Asrar-ul-Haq et al., 2017). Their internal governance, their performance or even their accountability and transparency are issues which are now stressed by public opinion (Ntim et al., 2017; Asrar-ul-Haq et al., 2017). Thus, many top world HEIs consider SR as a serious theme, adopting different strategies and developing CSR activities, such as including CSR in their curricula or using different reports and digital platforms to disclose their practices (Nejati et al., 2011; Asrar-ul-Haq, 2017). However, although HEIs "are now integrating the concepts of social responsibility within the university educational system whilst also training professionals in educational ethics, social values and concern about the repercussion of business activity on the environment" (Rodríguez Bolívar et al., 2013, p. 552), CSR "is yet to be proven in the higher education industry" (Othman and Othman, 2014, p. 1), namely when pressures to report their actions are increasing.

The field of research in SR and its disclosure is increasing and expanding to different types of organizations. Since CSR reporting in HEIs is still in its infancy, a systematic review of the body of literature in such context proves to be relevant since, as long as the authors are aware, this is the first study addressing SR disclosure in this context, something which can, potentially, open new avenues for further research. Specifically, this literature review is focused on 4 different themes: the assessment of the literature along time; the main theories (when) used; the methodologies adopted, and the results achieved. Therefore, through the review of all the papers eligible to develop this chapter, the following research questions were proposed:

Research Question 1: how has literature on SR reporting in HEIs evolved in a longitudinal stance?
Research Question 2: what are the main theoretical approaches used in the literature on SR reporting in HEIs?
Research Question 3: what are the main methodologies adopted in studies on SR reporting in HEIs?
Research Question 4: what are the main results of studies on SR reporting in HEIs?

This study contributes to describe the diversity of understandings about SR in higher education institutions and, thereby, to make more organized the current body of literature on the aforementioned theme. Also, it contributes to develop a roadmap to guide further researches. In fact, researchers need to find new ways of addressing the theme and explore it in innovative ways.

The chapter proceeds with the conceptual background, followed by the method adopted for the systematic literature review. Then, the main results of the articles under analysis are described and discussed. Finally, in the last section, some concluding remarks and some cues for further research are offered.

Conceptual Background

Since the 1960s, CSR has been gaining the attention of both academics and practitioners (Wang et al., 2016), with most business literature on this theme being published in the last two decades (Malik, 2015). SR is a multidimensional concept, which encompasses different issues such as business ethics, environmental sustainability or corporate citizenship. Therefore, and due to its evolving nature, defining it is troublesome (Malik, 2015; Asrar-ul-Haq et al., 2017). Votaw (1972, p. 25) stressed such difficulty by claiming that "it means something, but not always the same thing to everybody. To some it conveys the idea of legal responsibility or liability; to others, it means socially responsible behavior in the ethical sense; to still others, the meaning transmitted is that of 'responsible for' in a causal mode; many simply equate it with a charitable contribution; some take it to mean socially conscious; many of those who embrace it most fervently see it as a mere synonym for legitimacy in the context of belonging or being proper or valid; a few see a sort of fiduciary duty imposing higher standards of behavior on businessmen than on citizens at large".

CSR can be broadly defined as a "concept whereby companies decide voluntarily to contribute to a better society and a cleaner environment" (European Commission, 2011, p.4), i.e. it aims to implement activities that can improve the welfare of communities, going beyond organizations' financial interests (Carroll and Shabana, 2010). This fact does not prevent CSR to be considered and used as an instrument to create organizational value, in line with most literature on accounting, finance and management (Malik, 2015).

Organizations may have different motivations to implement CSR activities, such as the possibility of obtaining potential benefits (e.g. better image), and thus competitive advantages (Branco and Rodrigues, 2006; Asrar-ul-Haq et al., 2017). Driven by these motivations, several frameworks and practices have been developed along time and several theories have been applied, namely the so-called general theories, although there is no consensus regarding the appropriate classification (Frynas and Yamahaki, 2016). Grounded in previous studies, namely the one of Mellahi et al. (2016), Frynas and Yamahaki (2016) distinguish two categories of theories: the ones aiming to explain external drivers of CSR and the others aiming to explain the internal drivers. On the one hand, stakeholder, institutional, legitimacy, as well as resource dependence theories are commonly used by organizations to explain the external drivers of CSR, namely getting the support of their stakeholders, legitimize their actions and guarantee the flow of critical resources. These theories, which focus on the relationship between organization and society, are, according to Frynas and Yamahaki (2016), the most used in CSR research, namely when combined (e.g. stakeholder theory combined with legitimacy theory). On the other hand, resource-based view and agency theory have been used from an internal perspective, focused on internal processes (Frynas and Yamahaki, 2016).

CSR reporting traditionally adopts the "external" theories. Specifically, the stakeholder theory argues that "companies have a social responsibility to consider the interests of all actors affected by their business decisions" (Donaldson and Preston, 1995, p. 85). According to Donaldson and Preston (1995, p. 68), these actors – the stakeholders – are "persons or groups with legitimate interests in procedural and/or substantive aspects of corporate activities". Freeman (1984) had already consider the disclosure of social and environmental information to help companies to better manage their relations with social and business partners. Institutional theory, according to Lincoln (1995, p. 1147) reflects "the tendency for social structures and processes to acquire meaning and stability in their own right rather than as instrumental tools for the achievement of specialized ends". This theory has become a dominant theory to study macro-organizational phenomena (Suddaby, 2010), considering that organizations respond to external pressures from their stakeholders regarding CSR practices. Such pressures can affect organizations' voluntary reporting (Tudor-Tiron and Dragu, 2014). Legitimacy theory is a variant of the institutional theory (O'Donovan, 2002). Prior studies consider that CSR is, namely, based on organizations' need to seek legitimacy (Gray et al., 1995; Duff, 2016) and increase its reputation (Carroll and Shabana, 2010). The legitimacy theory predicts that organizations continually seek to ensure that they operate within the limits and norms accepted by their community (Prasad et al., 2016). The terms legitimacy and legitimation can have different interpretations. The former can be considered a condition or status per se while the latter can be defined as the process which organizations can undertake to achieve such condition/status through specific disclosure strategies (Brown and Deegan, 1998). Based on the notion of legitimacy, Mousa and Hassan (2015), stress the importance of CSR reports for companies seeking to obtain, maintain or repair their legitimacy.

Another theory – the media agenda setting theory – and its role in CSR, can also be stressed (see Bhutta and Saeed, 2011). The media agenda setting theory emphasizes the importance of the media to disseminate several topics to the public in order to raise concern about them. Accordingly, media attention can lead to a greater community involvement (Brown and Craig, 1998). For example, this theory is broadly used in accounting research to "explain changing community expectations and the implications these changing expectations have on corporate disclosure policies" (Islam and Deegan, 2010, p. 134).

An important theme, thus, emerges: the one of SR reporting. In this chapter, CSR reporting is conceptualized as a voluntary effort that aims to produce positive effects on society and in the environment (Duff, 2016). According to Ali et al. (2017), CSR disclosure is mainly driven by the following factors: organizations' characteristics (such as dimension, activity sector, governance mechanisms or profitability), and social, economic and political factors. Nowadays, it is expected that organizations show transparency and accountability. Accordingly, they are increasingly investing on CSR practices and its reporting (Malik, 2015; Duff, 2016), knowing that their responsible behaviors and reporting are also increasingly being monitored (Nejati et al., 2011). Although a variety of instruments are, nowadays, used to report SR, most organizations still use the annual report to do so, namely with a focus on environmental issues (Duff, 2016).

According to Frynas and Yamahaki (2016), CSR has been studied at different levels of analysis, specifically micro (at the individual level), meso (at the organizational level) and macro (addressing political, economic and societal issues). Also, several types of organizations have been addressed in CSR literature, from large corporations to small companies (Nejati et al., 2011). However, most literature on SR reporting focuses on companies, something which "standardized" the use of the expression "corporate social responsibility". Furthermore, in the last few years, other types of organizations sought to report their social (and environmental) practices. Society is now more concerned with SR and, therefore, demands information not only to companies but also to other types of organizations such as HEIs (Alonso-Almeida et al, 2015).

Despite the growing interest on reporting HEIs' CSR, literature on SR regarding this context is still very scarce and even scarcer when referring to the reporting (Alonso-Almeida et al., 2015; Othman and Othman, 2014). Most literature addresses the students' perceptions of the concept, assesses the courses offered or the specific actions undertaken by HEIs (Rodríguez Bolívar et al., 2013). This is intriguing, since HEIs can, in fact, influence society through the knowledge it creates and transfers, grounded in a properly developed mission or relying on the individual initiatives of their staff. Through teaching, researching or collaboration, HEIs can help society's improvement in a sustainable fashion, by promoting social responsible policies included in their vision, mission and strategies and training graduates which will be future managers and leaders (Rodríguez Bolívar et al., 2013; Deus et al, 2016; Alonso-Almeida et al., 2015; Othman and Othman, 2014). In fact, in the context of HEIs, CSR can be defined as "the capacity of the university to disseminate and implement a body of principles and general and specific values, by means of four key processes – management, teaching, research and university extension – thus responding to the needs of the university community and of the country as a whole" (Rodríguez Bolívar et al., 2013, p. 554). Furthermore, national and international competition "forces" HEIs to use CSR as a "marketing tool", which can enhance their reputation and their ability to attract students and funds (Ntim et al., 2017; Othman and Othman, 2014).

The need to improve transparency and accountability is demanded by HEI's different stakeholders (Rodríguez Bolívar et al., 2013) and, as such, the need to report SR has increased. HEIs have different reasons to voluntary report information: to reflect their social actions, reputation, image or public goodwill, through public accountability and transparency (in line with the legitimacy theory); to reflect the benefits of reporting, by gaining support from the main stakeholders, something which is crucial to the HEI survival (see stakeholder theory) or; to access to important resources (see resource-based theory) (Ntim et al., 2017). Despite these reasons, reporting has been namely focused on financial information, which does not consider SR issues. HEIs typically use the annual report to provide information, namely of financial nature, despite stakeholders' pressures to develop sustainability and SR reports (Rodríguez Bolívar et al., 2013). In general terms, research on reporting in the Higher Education Context is still in its infancy (Mion et al., 2019) and HEIs appear to be reporting SR issues only to fulfil basic policy demands, to gain legitimacy and enhance their image (Rodríguez Bolívar et al., 2013). According to Alonso-Almeida et al. (2015, p. 152), "while hundreds of universities in more than fifty countries have signed the Declaration of the "Higher Education Sustainability Initiative for Rio 20," only a small number of universities are reporting their sustainability efforts".

METHOD

Systematic literature reviews are becoming increasingly popular in the field of business and management. Regarding CSR, there are several examples addressing different themes such as its global nature (Pisani et al., 2017) or the type of companies it addresses (Vázquez-Carrasco and López-Pérez, 2013). Systematic literature reviews allow to extract and analyze literature in a precise and reliable fashion (Mays et al., 2005; Liberati et al., 2009). A systematic literature review can be done in three steps: first by selecting the journals (or the databases) and articles, then by choosing the search keywords and, finally, by selecting the relevant articles, which are then coded and analyzed (Grant and Booth, 2009).

In this study, we followed the Preferred Reporting Items for Systematic Reviews and Meta-Analyses (PRISMA) method, which was originally applied to the healthcare sector (see Liberati et al., 2009). Its flowchart is portrayed in Figure 1 (see below). The ISI Web of Knowledge and the Scopus databases were selected to retrieve the articles to be reviewed and, in order to do so, the following keywords were combined: 'social responsib*', 'report*', 'disclos*', 'CSR', 'higher education' and 'universit*'. Although no temporal limitation was imposed, the selection encompassed articles published and available until the 15th March 2019, date in which they were retrieved. Furthermore, in this search, literature was filtered by area of research, specifically: 'management and business'; 'finance'; 'accounting'; 'economics'; 'social sciences'; 'decisions sciences'; 'education'; 'ethics'; 'environmental'. Then, 406 references from the ISI Web of Knowledge database and 396 from Scopus were identified. After removing duplicates, a total of 701 references were identified. The documents were, then, screened according to their title, keywords and, namely, abstract. During the screening stage, conference proceedings were removed (n = 185) and the remaining documents were not eligible namely because they did not fit with the mix of the search keys. Only 25 references were eligible to be included in the final sample and, since we could not have access to 1 book chapter, a total of 24 articles were selected to be analyzed in-depth.

Finally, the information needed to develop this research was gathered in an online spreadsheet (developed by all the authors). It included various items such as year, authors, title, abstract, theoretical approaches, adopted methodologies, sample or results. Then, it was coded according to different themes in line with the research questions. In order to avoid any potential bias, the following procedures were adopted: first, the articles were retrieved by one author. Then, two others extracted the information deemed relevant to develop the spreadsheet. Finally, the final sample was reviewed by all authors. It should be noted that, although CSR research and its reporting has been object of vast contributions, the same theme applied to HEIs is emerging as a new topic of discussion. In fact, the first article exploring SR reporting in HEIs dates from 2001. Furthermore, the remaining articles that constitute the final sample were published since 2011. Table 1 summarizes the articles which were subject of analysis.

Figure 1.

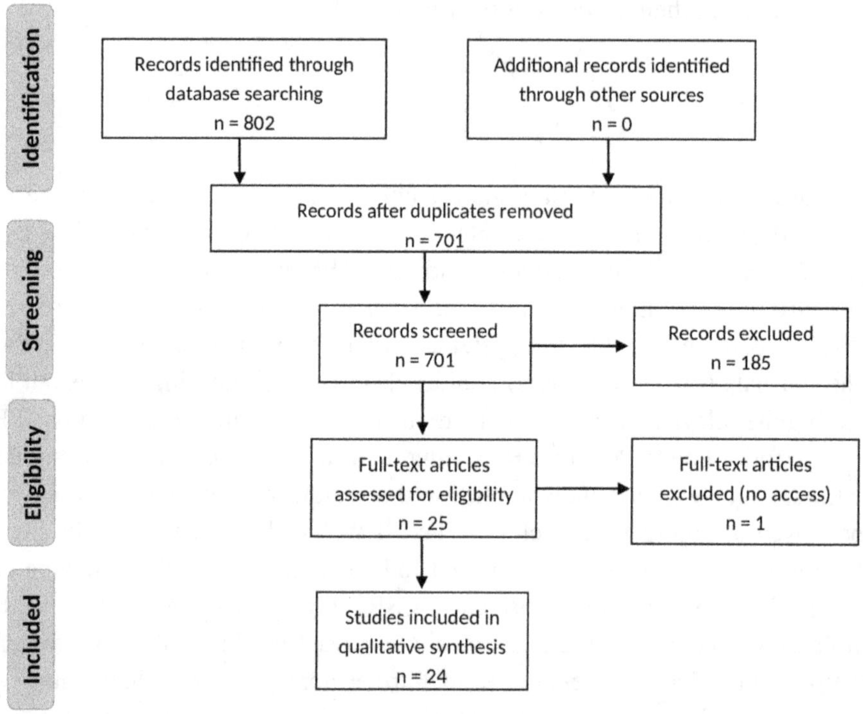

RESULTS AND DISCUSSION

The results of the systematic literature review were assessed and discussed according to four themes:

First, a longitudinal assessment of the literature was conducted to depict its evolution along time, allowing to identify the number of articles published *per* year, the number of authors participating in each article and the number of times each article was cited. Next, the theoretical approaches used in each article were described and discussed. A third theme referred to the adopted methodologies and, finally, the results of each article pertaining to the systematic literature review were described and discussed.

Longitudinal Assessment of the Literature

This section aims to describe how SR reporting literature has evolved in a longitudinal stance. As depicted in Figure 2, findings show an increase in studies in the last decade. In total, 24 articles were analyzed and, although the first article to address SR reporting in HEIs dates from 2001 (see Coy et al., 2001), research in this topic began to grow after 2011. The years 2014 and 2018 were the ones in which more articles were published, with 4 and 6 articles, respectively. Also, it should be noted that the year 2019 only encompasses articles published until 15th March 2019. As it can be noticed, there is a decade mediating the publication of Coy et al.'s (2001) article and Nejati et al.'s (2011). This does not mean that, regarding the theme of this chapter, no other article was published during this period. In fact, it should be stressed that the final sample only encompasses articles retrieved from the ISI web of knowledge and Scopus databases that meet the inclusion criteria, as mentioned in the Method section.

Table 1. Summary of the articles under analysis

Year	Authors	Journal	Title
2001	Coy, Fischer and Gordon	Critical Perspectives on Accounting	Public accountability: A new paradigm for college and university annual reports
2011	Nejati, Shafaei, Salamzadeh and Daraei	African Journal of Business Management	Corporate social responsibility and universities: A study of top 10 world universities' websites
2013	Garde Sánchez, Rodríguez Bolívar and López-Hernández	Environmental Education Research	Online disclosure of university social responsibility: a comparative study of public and private US universities
2013	Lange and Kerr	Social Responsibility Journal	Accounting and incentives for sustainability in higher education: An interdisciplinary analysis of a needed revolution
2013	Rodríguez Bolívar, Sanchez and Hernandez	Journal of Environmental Policy & Planning	Online Disclosure of Corporate Social Responsibility Information in Leading Anglo-American Universities
2014	Othman and Othman	International Journal of Business and Society	Higher education institutions and social performance: Evidence from public and private universities
2014	Wigmore-Álvarez and Ruiz-Lozano	Sage Open	The United Nations Global Compact progress reports as management control instruments for social responsibility at Spanish universities
2014	Lopatta and Jaeschke	International Journal of Education Economics and Development	Sustainability reporting at German and Austrian universities
2014	Bisogno, Citro and Tommasetti	Global Business and Economics Review	Disclosure of university websites. Evidence from Italian data
2015	Alonso-Almeida, Marimon, Casani and Rodriguez-Pomeda	Journal of Cleaner Production	Diffusion of sustainability reporting in universities: current situation and future perspectives
2016	Jiménez, Martinez and Lopez	Ciriec-espana Revista de Economia Publica Social y Cooperativa	Proposal for University Social Responsibility indicators according to GRI G4 guidelines: the case of the University of Cordoba (Spain)
2016	Deus, Battistelle and Silva	International Journal of educational Management	Sustainability insights from the mission statements of leading Brazilian Universities
2017	Ntim, Soobaroyen and Broad	Accounting Auditing & Accountability Journal	Governance structures, voluntary disclosures and public accountability: The case of UK higher education institutions
2017	Huerta-Riveros and Gaete-Feres	Revista Iberoamericana de Educacion Superior	Social accountability through the Global Reporting Initiative's sustainability reports: The experiences of a public university
2018	Ferrero-Ferrero, Fernandez-Izquierdo, Munoz-Torres and Belles-Colomer	International Journal of Sustainability in Higher Education	Stakeholder engagement in sustainability reporting in higher education: An analysis of key internal stakeholders' expectations
2018	Lopéz and Martin	Business and Society Review	University Mission Statements and Sustainability Performance
2018	Sassen and Azizi	International Journal of Sustainability in Higher Education	Assessing sustainability reports of US universities
2018	Sepasi, Rahdari and Rexhepi	Sustainable Development	Developing a sustainability reporting assessment tool for higher education institutions: The University of California
2018	Zorio-Grima, Sierra-Garcia and Garcia-Benau	International Journal of Sustainability in Higher Education	Sustainability reporting experience by universities: a causal configuration approach
2018	Alnodel, Elobaid, Elawady and Alhdaif	International Journal of Engineering Business Management	Business colleges and their community: Content analysis of websites of business colleges in the MENA region
2018	Corraza	World Review of Entrepreneurship, Management and Sustainable Development	The process of social accounting and reporting at University of Torino: Main challenges and managerial implications
2019	Mion, Broglia and Bonfanti	Sustainability	Do Codes of Ethics Reveal a University's Commitment to Sustainable Development? Evidence from Italy
2019	Miotto, López and Rodríguez	Sustainability	Gender Equality and UN Sustainable Development Goals: Priorities and Correlations in the Top Business Schools' Communication and Legitimation Strategies
2019	Sepasi, Braendle and Rahdari	Social Responsibility Journal	Comprehensive sustainability reporting in higher education institutions

For example, although Gordon et al.'s (2002) article examines the extension of disclosures by private and public universities in the USA, they do not address SR as the main topic. Therefore, this article was not included in our sample.

Figure 2.

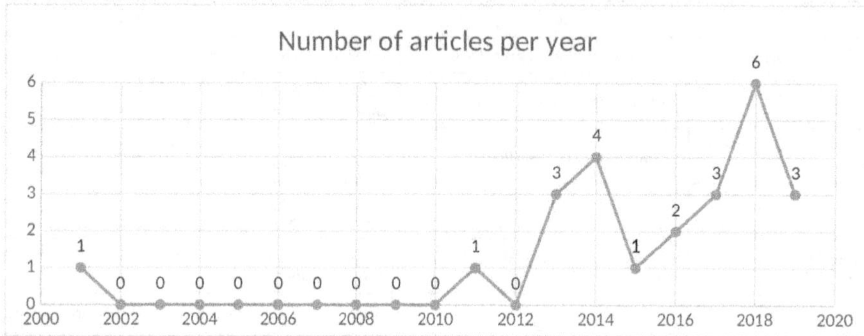

Furthermore, it was found that most of the articles (70,84%) were published by three or more authors, 20,83% were published by two authors and only 8,33% by one author (see Figure 3). More specifically, 13 articles were written by three authors, 5 articles were written by two authors and 4 articles by four authors, and finally 2 articles were written by one author. These results can suggest that collaboration between authors can be of due importance regarding research on SR disclosure in HEI. This theme can intersect different disciplines, thus needing the collaboration of authors pertaining to different areas of expertise and possessing knowledge about specific topics such as voluntary disclosure of information or SR management (see Manton and English, 2007). This fact stresses the importance of co-authoring in research not only in broader terms, but also regarding SR reporting in HEIs, something which is in line with Manton and English's (2007) study. In fact, these authors consider that more than 80% of articles published in business journals are done in co-authorship. Furthermore, according to this chapter's authors, collaboration can increase the quality of the articles in this area of research.

Finally, regarding the number of citations (retrieved in the 20th of June 2019 from google scholar) for the 24 articles under analysis, the findings suggest that the most cited articles are Coy et al. (2001), Alonso-Almeida (2015), Nejati et al. (2011) and Ntim et al. (2017). The number of citations for the 24 articles are portrayed in Table 2. Coy et al. (2001) developed a theoretical framework encompassing both older and recent ideas/notions of public responsibility and SR, thus contributing to a new paradigm regarding reporting in HEIs. Alonso-Almeida et al. (2015) analyzed the current situation as well as future

Figure 3.

perspectives about the diffusion of sustainability reporting in HEIs. Nejati et al. (2011) assessed the websites of the top 10 world universities ranked by Times Higher Education. Ntim et al. (2017) studied the extent of voluntary disclosures in HEIs' annual reports in United Kingdom (UK), also examining if internal governance structures affect reporting in periods that follows reforms or years where there is a lack of funding. Although Ntim et al.' (2017) article is a recent one, it has been already cited by several authors, something that can potentially be justified by the type of journal where the article was published – accounting – and its audience. In fact, only another article was published in an accounting-oriented journal, which was the one of Coy et al. (2001): the most cited article (see Table 1 above). Furthermore, it is also important to stress that both these articles address North American and United Kingdom HEIs (see Table 2). According to Garde Sánchez et al. (2013), the best practice of disclosure belongs to the Anglo-American universities, which usually are the most active regarding the CSR related information. Finally, although it is possible that older articles should be the most cited ones, it is the authors' opinion that several factors such as the access to the articles, their quality or contributions can affect the number of citations (see for example Wigmore-Álvarez and Ruiz-Lozano, 2014).

Theoretical Approaches

A theoretical framework can be considered as a structure based on the theoretical foundation that sustains a particular topic in a study (Mertens, 1998). This is true for SR research. In fact, several theories can be applied in this area, such as the stakeholder theory, the institutional theory, the legitimacy theory or the media agenda setting theory (Tanggamani et al., 2018; Bhutta and Saeed, 2011; Lange and Kerr, 2013). Stakeholder theory and legitimacy theory have been extensively used in research regarding social and environmental reporting (Frynas and Yamahaki, 2016) in several contexts, such as the one of HEIs.

The systematic literature review of the 24 articles shows that only 6 refer to theories that can be considered as external drivers of CSR, namely aiming to obtain legitimacy regarding the stakeholders. More specifically, only 3 theories are mentioned in these 6 articles: the institutional theory (see Mioto et al., 2019), the legitimacy theory (see Ntim et al., 2017) and the stakeholder theory (see Lopatta and Jaeschke, 2014; Ntim et al., 2017; Ferrero-Ferrero et al., 2018; Lopéz and Martin, 2018; Corraza, 2018). This means that more than 76% are not explicitly grounded in any theoretical background. The media agenda setting theory was not referred by any article, although Watson's (2011, pp.95-96) claim that "the voluntary disclosures can be explained by applying legitimacy theory and media agenda-setting theory". These findings are in line with Frynas and Yamahaki (2016), who considers that most theories used in CSR research aim to explain the external drivers of the phenomenon under analysis.

Furthermore, stakeholder theory is the most mentioned theory in the sample, with five articles explicitly mentioning it. Surprisingly, only one article mentions the legitimacy theory (see Ntim et al., 2017), which is one of the most used along with the stakeholder theory, namely when combined with each other (see Frynas and Yamahaki 2016). Theories mentioning drivers of CSR of internal nature are sparsely mentioned. On the one hand Coy et al. (2001) mention the accounting theory and agency theory as drivers of CSR of internal nature. On the other hand, Ntim et al. (2017) are the only ones to mention drivers of CSR of both external and internal nature (e.g. agency theory; resource dependence theory). Lange and Kerr (2013) briefly mention the critical social theory in an accounting and educational context.

Table 2. Number of citations per article and sample

Authors	Number of citations	Sample
Coy et al. (2001)	260	100 United States college and universities
Alonso-Almeida et al. (2015)	133	47 universities pertaining to 18 countries
Nejati et al. (2011)	109	Top 10 world universities ranked by Times Higher Education
Ntim et al. (2017)	46	164 United Kingdom HEIs
Garde Sánchez et al. (2013)	42	The first 25 universities in the webometrics ranking, pertaining to Australia, Canada, Ireland, New Zealand, United Kingdom and the United States of America
Othman and Othman (2014)	34	2 universities in Malaysia
Lopatta and Jaeschke (2014)	29	4 universities of Germany and 2 universities of Austria
Rodriguéz Bolivar et al. (2013)	21	154 United States universities (105 public and 49 private)
Lange and Kerr (2013)	9	Conceptual study
Bisogno et al. (2014)	8	55 Italian Universities
Sassen and Azizi (2018)	8	23 United States universities
Deus et al. (2016)	7	30 Brazilian universities
Huerta-Riveros et al. (2017)	5	1 Chile university
Wigmore-Álvarez and Ruiz-Lozano (2014)	3	14 Spain universities
Ferrero-Ferrero et al. (2018)	3	10 HEI's from: Australia, Brazil, Chile, USA, Spain, Philippines, Italy and Portugal.
Jiménez et al. (2016)	1	1 Spanish university
Lopez and Martin (2018)	1	347 universities from the United States of America
Sepasi et al. (2018)	1	227 HEIs' sustainability reports publish according to the university sustainability assessment framework
Alnodel et al. (2018)	1	142 business colleges from 20 countries in the MENA (Middle East and North Africa) region
Corraza (2018)	1	1 Italian university
Miotto et al. (2019)	1	50 business schools worldwide according to the "Financial Times Global MBA Ranking 2016"
Zorio-Grima et al. (2018)	0	49 public Spain universities
Mion et al. (2019)	0	64 Italian public universities
Sepasi et al. (2019)	0	1 United States university

Adopted Methodologies

The systematic literature review allowed to assess different types of methodologies which were adopted across the final sample (24 articles). Four different types of methodologies were considered for the analysis, namely: the conceptual study; the qualitative study; the quantitative study and the mixed-method study. Figure 4 depicts the adopted methodologies in terms of how frequent they were used in the final sample, encompassing the period ranging from 2001 to 2019. The year 2019 shows a trend which was not seen in previous years: the adoption of different methodologies. Specifically, two articles adopted a qualitative approach and two others adopted a mixed-method one.

Figure 4.

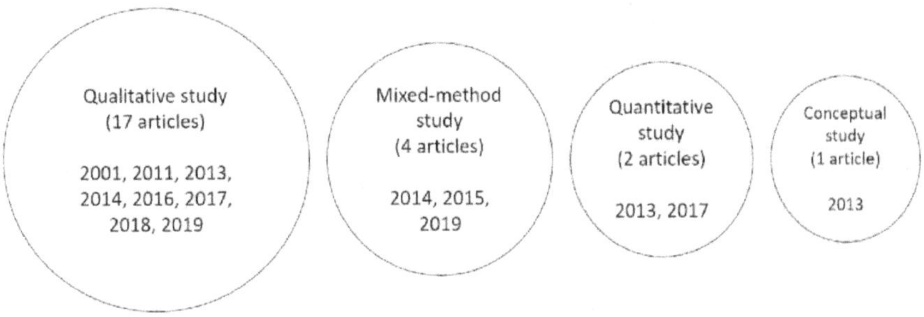

Results suggested that the most common methodology used was the qualitative one, with 17 articles using it. Also, the case study method was adopted in 8 studies (e.g. Alonso-Almeida et al., 2015; Huerta-Riveros and Gaete-Feres, 2017; Jiménez et al., 2016). The case study is a research technique that allows to study a phenomenon in a particular context and in a deep stance (Yin, 2009). The second most used methodology was the mixed method (4 articles), which possesses several advantages. Qualitative studies can be more robust when resourcing to different data sources, i.e. data triangulation, which allows the results to have a stronger validation level due to the combination of both quantitative and qualitative analysis (Jick, 1979; Modell, 2005; Suter and Data, 2011; Mason, 2002). The less used methodologies were the quantitative one and the conceptual study, being used in 2 and 1 articles, respectively.

This type of studies (voluntary reporting) usually make use of qualitative methodologies. Typically, such studies resort to content analysis, which is a very used method in social sciences research, namely related to qualitative studies (Miles & Huberman, 1994). Content analysis has been the most popular method for collecting data in order to assess the quantity and quality of CSR reporting (Nejati et al., 2011; Duff, 2016). In order to do so, it includes factors such as the form or type of quantification (e.g. monetary; non-monetary; narrative) (Duff, 2016). Content analysis can be defined as "a research method for the subjective interpretation of the content of text data through the systematic classification process of coding and identifying themes and patterns" (Shannon, 2014, p. 1278). In fact, when referring to data analysis, content analysis was the most common approach used in this study with 14 articles. Therefore, our results are in line with the literature which make use of content analysis. Hence, the presence of only 2 quantitative articles and 1 conceptual study. It is the authors' opinion that quantitative analysis could be better explored in further studies on SR reporting in HEI (e.g. using multiple linear regressions or structural equations models to assess effects between variables).

Finally, regarding data collection, the most used data sources were documents, websites and surveys (see Corraza, 2018, Ferrero-Ferrero et al., 2018 and Coy et al., 2001). Surprisingly, only 3 articles claimed that direct observation was used to collect data (e.g. Deus et al., 2016). Therefore, further research should make more use of observation of the setting or the interviews' reactions in order to allow data triangulation and, thus, to be aligned with the aforementioned mixed method (see Yin, 2009).

Main Results

This section refers to the main results suggested in the 24 articles, which is summarized in Table 3 (see below).

Table 3. Summary of results

<table>
<tr><th>Year</th><th>Author</th><th>Title</th></tr>
<tr><td>2001</td><td>Coy, Fischer and Gordon</td><td>Public accountability: A new paradigm for college and university annual reports</td></tr>
<tr><td colspan="3">Results suggest that HEI should not limit themselves to a "traditional" decision public accountability. It is crucial for them to disclose a more comprehensive information and reach a wider audience. Results also suggest that reporting in such settings (HEIs) should focus on aspects such as fairness or accessibility.</td></tr>
<tr><td>2011</td><td>Nejati, Shafaei, Salamzadeh and Daraei</td><td>Corporate social responsibility and universities: A study of top 10 world universities' websites</td></tr>
<tr><td colspan="3">The 10 analyzed HEIs are committed with SR and provide enough information on most of the CSR core areas, specifically "organizational governance", "human rights", "labor practices", "environment", "fair operating practices" and "consumer issues". All the HEIs disclosed these aspects. However, only one was deemed to engage with "community and development".</td></tr>
<tr><td>2013</td><td>Garde Sánchez, Rodríguez Bolívar and López-Hernández</td><td>Online disclosure of university social responsibility: a comparative study of public and private US universities</td></tr>
<tr><td colspan="3">Results suggest that there is not a strong commitment by public and private HEIs in USA regarding reporting through web pages.</td></tr>
<tr><td>2013</td><td>Lange and Kerr</td><td>Accounting and incentives for sustainability in higher education: An interdisciplinary analysis of a needed revolution</td></tr>
<tr><td colspan="3">Results suggest that, although seeing advantages in voluntary information disclosure, the rigidness of the conventional accounting practices is a great obstacle to such disclosure in HEIs.</td></tr>
<tr><td>2013</td><td>Rodríguez Bolívar, Sanchez and Hernandez</td><td>Online Disclosure of Corporate Social Responsibility Information in Leading Anglo-American Universities</td></tr>
<tr><td colspan="3">This study focuses on CSR disclosure through online means. Results suggest that HEIs attach little importance to such type of disclosure.</td></tr>
<tr><td>2014</td><td>Othman and Othman</td><td>Higher education institutions and social performance: Evidence from public and private universities</td></tr>
<tr><td colspan="3">Findings show that the two analyzed HEIs responded differently to CSR. While the more traditional public university focused on its internal social responsibilities (namely students and staff), the private one followed a legitimacy strategy focused on all stakeholders, thus including the outside communities.</td></tr>
<tr><td>2014</td><td>Wigmore-Álvarez and Ruiz-Lozano</td><td>The United Nations Global Compact progress reports as management control instruments for social responsibility at Spanish universities</td></tr>
<tr><td colspan="3">Results suggest that, on the one hand, the 14 analyzed HEIs disclosed information in accordance with the UN Global Compact principles. However, on the other hand, not all made the effort to specify their actions despite being educational institutions.</td></tr>
<tr><td>2014</td><td>Lopatta and Jaeschke</td><td>Sustainability reporting at German and Austrian universities</td></tr>
<tr><td colspan="3">Results show that sustainability reporting in HEIs is still in its infancy in quantity and quality terms. Furthermore, it is argued that reports focus on the environmental, economic and educational dimensions rather than on social equity.</td></tr>
<tr><td>2014</td><td>Bisogno, Citro and Tommasetti</td><td>Disclosure of university websites. Evidence from Italian data</td></tr>
<tr><td colspan="3">The study reveals that Italian HEIs achieve a satisfactory rate in disclosing information related with research and teaching activities. It also suggests that complexity and SR are the factors that mostly affect the disclosure level.</td></tr>
<tr><td>2015</td><td>Alonso-Almeida, Marimon, Casani and Rodriguez-Pomeda</td><td>Diffusion Of sustainability reporting in universities: current situation and future perspectives</td></tr>
<tr><td colspan="3">The results indicate that the diffusion of sustainability reporting is still at an early stage in HEIs, and future expectations do not seem to be positive, despite the increasing concerns. Therefore, some actions need to be taken to persuade HEIs in adopting reporting standards, such as the GRI guidelines, and to highlight the benefits and necessity of sustainability reporting.</td></tr>
<tr><td>2016</td><td>Jimenez, Martinez and Lopez</td><td>Proposal for University Social Responsibility indicators according to GRI G4 guidelines: the case of the University of Cordoba (Spain)</td></tr>
<tr><td colspan="3">The authors identified a set of performance indicators aiming to facilitate the adjustment to the GRI G4 guidelines for SR reports.</td></tr>
<tr><td>2016</td><td>Deus, Battistelle and Silva</td><td>Sustainability insights from the mission statements of leading Brazilian Universities</td></tr>
<tr><td colspan="3">This study focused on the analysis of HEIs' mission statements. Results suggested that only 10% of such statements report, in a clear fashion, sustainability aspects.</td></tr>
<tr><td>2017</td><td>Ntim, Soobaroyen and Broad</td><td>Governance structures, voluntary disclosures and public accountability. The case of UK higher education institutions</td></tr>
<tr><td colspan="3">Results suggested that there is a need for a major shift in HEIs' governance, reporting and voluntary disclosure practices, and also that governments, executives and managers play a crucial role to achieve this purpose. Hence, the authors emphasized the need to create voluntary disclosure guidelines and also to develop a regulatory framework in order to harmonize HEIs' reports.</td></tr>
<tr><td>2017</td><td>Huerta-Riveros and Gaete-Feres</td><td>Social accountability through the Global Reporting Initiative's sustainability reports: The experiences of a public university</td></tr>
<tr><td colspan="3">This research mentioned that sustainability reports made under the GRI G3 guidelines demonstrates the so-called "social footprint". The studied HEIs used these reports to include the various initiatives which were taken in order to show their commitment towards sustainability.</td></tr>
<tr><td>2018</td><td>Ferrero-Ferrero, Fernandez-Izquierdo, Munoz-Torres and Belles-Colomer</td><td>Stakeholder engagement in sustainability reporting in higher education: An analysis of key internal stakeholders' expectations</td></tr>
<tr><td colspan="3">This study improved the knowledge about stakeholders' engagement in HEIs. Results helped to identify the relevant impacts of such engagement, as well as enhancing the quality of reporting and encouraging a real dialogue with those stakeholders.</td></tr>
<tr><td>2018</td><td>Lopéz and Martin</td><td>University Mission Statements and Sustainability Performance</td></tr>
<tr><td colspan="3">This research suggested the need for a balance between the three domains of sustainability: economic, environmental and society.</td></tr>
<tr><td>2018</td><td>Sassen and Azizi</td><td>Assessing sustainability reports of US universities</td></tr>
<tr><td colspan="3">The results suggest that sustainability reports need to be improved, since information on the social dimension is still low. Furthermore, ical incentives could be used to improve the quality of reports.</td></tr>
<tr><td>2018</td><td>Sepasi, Rahdari and Rexhepi</td><td>Developing a sustainability reporting assessment tool for higher education institutions: The University of California</td></tr>
</table>

continued on following page

Table 3 continued

Year	Author	Title
Results suggest that sustainability reports are gaining strength among HEIs. In fact, the number of HEIs reporting their practices are increasing, aiming, among others, to share their social practices with their stakeholders. However, although such increase is an evidence, the number of HEIs doing such reports is still very low when compared with private organizations.		
2018	Zorio-Grima, Ana; Sierra-Garcia, Laura; Garcia-Benau, Maria A.	Sustainability reporting experience by universities: a causal configuration approach
The authors claimed that HEIs are very important organizations to promote social practices. Therefore, it is suggested that regulators become aware of the need to increase sustainability reporting, with an emphasis in the social dimension.		
2018	Alnodel, Elobaid, Elawady and Alhdaif	Business colleges and their community: Content analysis of websites of business colleges in the MENA region
The results show that HEIs use their websites to disclose information. However, the authors argue that this means of communication, although important, does not reach all stakeholders.		
2018	Corraza	The process of social accounting and reporting at University of Torino: Main challenges and managerial implications
Results suggest that stakeholders' pressures led to the development of new governance tools in HEIs and new social accounting and reports techniques, as well as the need to search for new forms of reporting, such as intellectual capital reports, campuses sustainability assessments or sustainability reports. The authors also consider that reporting aims to seek legitimacy.		
2019	Mion, Broglia and Bonfanti	Do Codes of Ethics Reveal a University's Commitment to Sustainable Development? Evidence from Italy
The authors consider that codes of ethics allow to minimize sustainable impacts and limit the commitment of HEIs to a formal level. Furthermore, they claim that the role of HEIs is complex since they have important responsibilities in promoting social, economic and environmental development.		
2019	Miotto, López and Rodríguez	Gender Equality and UN Sustainable Development Goals: Priorities and Correlations in the Top Business Schools' Communication and Legitimation Strategies
Results suggest that HEIs use sustainability reports to engage a conversation with their stakeholders and acquire legitimacy. However, although, in HEIs, social reporting and sustainable practices are considered very important and necessary, they still do not get the popularity that is wished.		
2019	Sepasi, Braendle and Rahdari	Comprehensive sustainability reporting in higher education institutions
Results suggest that increasing disclosure quality in HEIs is critical to better comprehend it and to help in better understanding future trends in sustainability reporting practices.		

Several findings can be withdrawn from the results mentioned above. It is important to stress the heterogeneity of the studies and, hence, of the results. One common finding can be highlighted: research in SR reporting in HEIs is still very scarce (Lopéz and Martin, 2018; Alonso-Almeida et al., 2015; Sassen and Azizi, 2018). Furthermore, several articles stress the importance of stakeholders in SR reporting, namely to seek legitimacy. Visibility towards stakeholders, pressures HEIs to promote such reporting and increase its quality (e.g. Sepasi et al., 2018, Miotto et al., 2019, Ferrero-Ferrero et al., 2018). However, it is also a fact that most public HEIs still use the traditional public accountability which tends to hinder voluntary reporting and a better engagement with external stakeholders (e.g. Coy et al., 2001; Lange and Kerr, 2013, Othman and Othman, 2014, Ferrero-Ferrero et al., 2018; Nejati et al., 2011). Hence, further research could seek for new ways to better interact with external stakeholders and to address the importance or SR reporting from the stakeholders' perspective, namely in order to know how they use different power dimensions to exert such pressures. Findings also stress the importance of HEIs to conduct new initiatives to promote SR reporting (e.g. Huerta-Riveros and Gaete-Feres, 2017; Zorio-Grima et al., 2018). In fact, in HEIs, knowledge is both an input and output, which makes these organizations as an important vehicle to transfer such knowledge to both internal and external stakeholders. In fact, this type of organizations can affect society in both direct and indirect ways. On the one hand, and in a direct way, knowledge about SR can be transferred to society (e.g. through collaborative engagement with external organizations). On the other hand, such knowledge can be transferred, in an indirect stance, through the graduated students which will be the future professionals in organizations. Thus, they can potentially put in action all knowledge that they have learned about CSR. Therefore, organizations may include new initiatives about this theme in their strategies and serve as benchmarks.

The lack of normalization on the CSR disclosure is an aspect which is also argued as an obstacle to organizational reporting, although the GRI guidelines have been minimizing such problem, allowing organizations to report CSR aspects in a standard fashion (Morhardt, 2010). With the change of guidelines to standards, the GRI has gained more relevance, the quality of reporting has increased and, consequently, trust on such reporting by the stakeholders (see stakeholder theory) (The portal for Sustainability Reporting, 2017). The articles' results also suggest that, on the one hand, most studies focus on North American and UK organizations. However, and on the other hand, it is important to notice that the European HEIs have been pioneers in the adoption of the GRI standards (Alonso-Almeida et al., 2015).

Finally, the articles' findings suggest that different means are used by HEIs to report SR practices (Corraza, 2018). Besides the traditional annual reports, which are the most common, nowadays online reporting is also considered as an important mean of communication, although according to Rodríguez Bolívar et al. (2013) it is not the best one to disclose CSR information. Therefore, future studies should consider alternative and effective means to report SR by HEIs.

CONCLUSION

This chapter addresses SR disclosure in a specific context: the one of HEIs. This type of organization differentiates from other types, namely because they use knowledge as both an input and an output. Therefore, is crucial that, they not only implement and develop new socially responsible practices for themselves, but also report such practices to their stakeholders. Therefore, it is the aim of this study to make a systematic review of the literature on SR disclosure in HEIs, focused on four different themes.

First, it was found that only 24 articles (indexed to the ISI web of knowledge and Scopus databases) address SR disclosure in the aforementioned context. Furthermore, these studies have a heterogeneous nature, namely regarding their goals. Research on SR reporting in HEIs is still in its infancy, even though, in the past decades, this theme has addressed other type of organizations, namely private and pro-profit ones. Also, collaboration between authors are an evidence regarding the analyzed articles. Second, although most articles do not refer any of the commonly used theories in CSR research, stakeholder theory is the more mentioned one. It is a fact that different organizations have different stakeholders and can also have different motives to report their social practices. Third, the analyzed studies used different research methodologies. However, the focus on qualitative studies is highlighted in more than two thirds of the articles analyzed. Fourth, regarding the main results of the analyzed studies, several insights can be withdrawn from this chapter. The scarcity of studies in this area and the lack of normalization on CSR disclosure was an aspect many times suggested as an obstacle to HEIs reporting. Furthermore, another important aspect regards the country of origin of the studied HEIs. Most HEIs belong to the United States and the UK. In fact, the United States are one of the countries which more value the CSR issues, since the half of the XX century (Crane et al., 2008). This aspect is in line with the nationality of some main authors in the CSR field such as Archie Carroll, who developed some notorious CSR frameworks (e.g. Pyramid of Corporate Social Responsibility), which inspired other studies.

Hence, this chapter contributes to the literature in different ways. It provides a summed-up description about how literature on SR in HEIs evolved along time, what are the main theoretical approaches adopted, the main methodologies used and the results from all the articles that encompassed the final sample, providing a comprehensive review of the current state of research in SR reporting in HEIs. Also, it is given methodological details of how a literature review on this theme should be conducted. Finally, it contributes to increase the awareness of HEIs towards the importance of this theme.

This study is not without limitations. First, only academic journal articles retrieved from the ISI Web of Knowledge and Scopus databases were included in the systematic review and belong. Second, although it is believed that the right terms have been used in the literature search, different codes may have been missed. Finally, several cues for further research have been given along the chapter in order to help to develop this theme in a still underexplored setting. However, normalization/standardization of CSR reporting in HEIs is needed and future studies should address this theme. Furthermore, besides websites, new platforms (namely of a digital nature) could be used to make such reporting. Further studies could explore this theme.

REFERENCES

Ali, W., Frynas, J. G., & Mahmood, Z. (2017). Determinants of corporate social responsibility (CSR) disclosure in developed and developing countries: A literature review. *Corporate Social Responsibility and Environmental Management*, *24*(4), 273–294. doi:10.1002/csr.1410

Alnodel, A. A., Elobaid, D. E., Elawady, S. I., & Alhdaif, S. A. (2018). Business colleges and their community: Content analysis of websites of business colleges in the MENA region. *International Journal of Engineering Business Management*, *10*, 1–10. doi:10.1177/1847979018800891

Alonso-Almeida, M., Marimon, F., Casani, F., & Rodriguez-Pomeda, J. (2015). Diffusion of sustainability reporting in universities: Current situation and future perspectives. *Journal of Cleaner Production*, *106*, 144–154. doi:10.1016/j.jclepro.2014.02.008

Asrar-ul-Haq, M., Kuchinke, K. P., & Iqbal, A. (2017). The relationship between corporate social responsibility, job satisfaction, and organizational commitment: Case of Pakistani higher education. *Journal of Cleaner Production*, *142*, 2352–2363. doi:10.1016/j.jclepro.2016.11.040

Bhutta, N. T., & Saeed, M. M. (2011). Accounting scandals in the context of corporate social reporting. *Journal of Database Marketing & Customer Strategy Management*, *18*(3), 171–184. doi:10.1057/dbm.2011.25

Bisogno, M., Citro, F., & Tommasetti, A. (2014). Disclosure of university websites. Evidence from Italian data Disclosure of university websites. *Global Business and Economics Review*, *16*(4), 452–470. doi:10.1504/GBER.2014.065365

Bowen, H. (1953). *Social Responsibilities of the Businessman*. New York: Harper.

Branco, M. C., & Rodrigues, L. L. (2006). Corporate social responsibility and resource-based perspectives. *Journal of Business Ethics*, *69*(2), 111–132. doi:10.100710551-006-9071-z

Branco, M. C., & Rodrigues, L. L. (2008). Factors influencing social responsibility disclosure by Portuguese companies. *Journal of Business Ethics*, *83*(4), 685–701. doi:10.100710551-007-9658-z

Brown, N., & Deegan, C. (1998). The public disclosure of environmental performance information-a dual test of media agenda setting theory and legitimacy theory. *Accounting and Business Research*, *29*(1), 21–41. doi:10.1080/00014788.1998.9729564

Carroll, A. B., & Shabana, K. M. (2010). The business case for corporate social responsibility: A review of concepts, research and practice. *International Journal of Management Reviews*, *12*(1), 85–105. doi:10.1111/j.1468-2370.2009.00275.x

Corazza, L. (2018). The process of social accounting and reporting at University of Torino: Main challenges and managerial implications. World Review of Entrepreneurship, Management and Sust. *Development, 14*(1/2), 171–186.

Coy, D. A. C., Ischer, M. A. R. Y. F., & Ordon, T. E. G. (2001). Public accountability: A new paradigm for college and university annual reports. *Critical Perspectives on Accounting, 12*(1), 1–31. doi:10.1006/cpac.2000.0416

Crane, A., McWilliams, A., Matten, D., Moon, J., & Siegel, D. S. (Eds.). (2008). *The Oxford handbook of corporate social responsibility*. Oxford University Press on Demand.

Dahlsrud, A. (2008). How corporate social responsibility is defined: An analysis of 37 definitions. *Corporate Social Responsibility and Environmental Management, 15*(1), 1–13. doi:10.1002/csr.132

Deus, R. M., Battistelle, R. A. G., & Silva, G. H. R. D. (2016). Sustainability insights from the mission statements of leading Brazilian Universities. *International Journal of Educational Management, 30*(3), 403–415. doi:10.1108/IJEM-05-2014-0065

Donaldson, T., & Preston, L. E. (1995). The stakeholder theory of the corporation: Concepts, evidenc. *Academy of Management.the Academy of Management Review, 20*(1), 65–91. doi:10.5465/amr.1995.9503271992

Duff, A. (2016). Corporate social responsibility reporting in professional accounting firms. *The British Accounting Review, 48*(1), 74–86. doi:10.1016/j.bar.2014.10.010

European Commission. (2011). Communication from the commission to the European Parliament, the Council, the European Economic and Social Committee and the Committee of the Regions: A renewed EU strategy 2011-14 for corporate social responsibility COM (2011) 681 final. Brussels: EC.

Ferrero-Ferrero, I., Fernández-Izquierdo, M. A., Muñoz-Torres, M. J., & Bellá-Colomer, L. (2018). Stakeholder engagement in sustainability reporting in higher education: An analysis of key internal stakeholders' expectations. *International Journal of Sustainability in Higher Education, 19*(2), 313–336. doi:10.1108/IJSHE-06-2016-0116

Freeman, R. E. (1984). *Strategic Management: A stakeholder approach*. Boston: Pitman.

Frynas, J. G., & Yamahaki, C. (2016). Corporate social responsibility: Review and roadmap of theoretical perspectives. *Business Ethics (Oxford, England), 25*(3), 258–285. doi:10.1111/beer.12115

Garde Sánchez, R., Rodriguéz Bolívar, M. P., & López-Hernández, A. M. (2013). Online disclosure of university social responsibility: A comparative study of public and private US universities. *Environmental Education Research, 19*(6), 709–746. doi:10.1080/13504622.2012.749976

Gordon, T., Fischer, M., Malone, D., & Tower, G. (2002). A comparative empirical examination of extent of disclosure by private and public colleges and universities in the United States. *Journal of Accounting and Public Policy, 21*(3), 235–275. doi:10.1016/S0278-4254(02)00051-0

Grant, M. J., & Booth, A. (2009). A typology of reviews: An analysis of 14 review types and associated methodologies. *Health Information and Libraries Journal, 26*(2), 91–108. doi:10.1111/j.1471-1842.2009.00848.x PMID:19490148

Gray, R., Kouhy, R., & Lavers, S. (1995). Corporate social and environmental reporting: A review of the literature and a longitudinal study of UK disclosure. *Accounting, Auditing & Accountability Journal, 18*(2), 47–77. doi:10.1108/09513579510146996

Huerta-Riveros, P., & Gaete-Feres, H. (2017). Responsabilidad social universitaria a través de los reportes de sostenibilidad del Global Reporting Initiative: Experiencia de una universidad pública. *Revista Iberoamericana de Educación Superior, 8*(23), 120–137. doi:10.22201/iisue.20072872e.2017.23.3014

Islam, M. A., & Deegan, C. (2010). Media pressures and corporate disclosure of social responsibility performance information: A study of two global clothing and sports retail companies. *Accounting and Business Research, 40*(2), 131–148. doi:10.1080/00014788.2010.9663388

Jick, T. D. (1979). Mixing Qualitative and Quantitative Methods: Triangulation in Action. *Administrative Science Quarterly, 24*(4), 602–611. doi:10.2307/2392366

Jiménez, C. G., Martinez, A. G., & López, M. A. (2016). Propuesta de indicadores de la Responsabilidad Social Universitaria conforme a la guía G4 del GRI: El caso de la Universidad de Córdoba. *C.I.R.I.E.C. España*, (87), 103–137.

Lange, E. A., & Kerr, S. G. (2013). Accounting and incentives for sustainability in higher education: An interdisciplinary analysis of a needed revolution. *Social Responsibility Journal, 9*(2), 210–219. doi:10.1108/SRJ-08-2011-0058

Liberati, A., Altman, D., Tetzlaff, J., Mulrow, C., Gøtzsche, P., Ioannidis, J., ... Moher, D. (2009). The PRISMA statement for reporting systematic reviews and meta-analyses of studies that evaluate health care interventions: Explanation and elaboration. *Journal of Clinical Epidemiology, 6*(7), 1–28. doi:10.1016/j.jclinepi.2009.06.006 PMID:19631507

Lincoln, J. R. (1995). Book review—Walter W. Powell & Paul DiMaggio (Eds.): The new institutionalism in organizational research. Social Forces, 73, 1147-1148.

Lopatta, K., & Jaeschke, R. (2014). Sustainability reporting at German and Austrian universities. *Int. J. Education Economics and Development, 5*(1), 66–90.

Lopéz, Y. P., & Martin, W. F. (2018). University mission statements and sustainability performance. *Business and Society Review, 132*(2), 341–368. doi:10.1111/basr.12144

Malik, M. (2015). Value-enhancing capabilities of CSR: A brief review of contemporary literature. *Journal of Business Ethics, 127*(2), 419–438. doi:10.100710551-014-2051-9

Manton, E. J., & English, D. E. (2007). The Trend Toward Multiple Authorship in Business Journals. *Journal of Education for Business, 82*(3), 164–168. doi:10.3200/JOEB.82.3.164-168

Mason, J. (2002). Qualitative Researching (2nd ed.). Sage Publications. Retrieved from http://www.uk.sagepub.com/booksProdDesc.nav?prodId=Book224801

Mays, N., Pope, C., & Popay, J. (2005). Systematically reviewing qualitative and quantitative evidence to inform management and policy-making in the health field. *Journal of Health Services Research & Policy, 10*(1), 6–20. doi:10.1258/1355819054308576 PMID:16053580

Mellahi, K., Frynas, J. G., Sun, P., & Siegel, D. (2016). A review of the nonmarket strategy literature: Towards a multi-theoretical integration. *Journal of Management*, *42*(1), 143–173. doi:10.1177/0149206315617241

Mertens, D. M. (1998). *Research methods in education and psychology: Integrating diversity with quantitative and qualitative approaches*. London: Sage.

Miles, M. B., & Huberman, A. M. (1994). *Qualitative Data Analysis*. Sage Publications.

Mion, G., Broglia, A., & Bonfanti, A. (2019). Do Codes of Ethics Reveal a University's Commitment to Sustainable Development? *Evidence from Italy. Sustainability*, *11*(4), 1134. doi:10.3390u11041134

Miotto, G., Polo, M., & Rom, J. (2019). Gender Equality and UN Sustainable Development Goals: Priorities and Correlations in the Top Business Schools' Communication and Legitimation Strategies. *Sustainability*, *11*(302), 2–18.

Modell, S. (2005). Triangulation between case study and survey methods in management accounting research: An assessment of validity implications. *Management Accounting Research*, *16*(2), 231–254. doi:10.1016/j.mar.2005.03.001

Morhardt, J. E. (2010). Corporate social responsibility and sustainability reporting on the internet. *Business Strategy and the Environment*, *19*(7), 436–452.

Mousa, G., & Hassan, N. T. (2015). Legitimacy theory and environmental practices: Short notes. *International Journal of Business and Statistical Analysis*, *2*(01), 41–53. doi:10.12785/ijbsa/020104

Nejati, M., Shafaei, A., Salamzadeh, Y., & Daraei, M. (2011). Corporate social responsibility and universities: A study of top 10 world universities' websites. *African Journal of Business Management*, *5*(2), 440–447.

Ntim, C. G., Soobaroyen, T., & Broad, M. J. (2017). Governance structures, voluntary disclosures and public accountability: The case of UK higher education institutions. *Accounting, Auditing & Accountability Journal*, *30*(1), 65–118. doi:10.1108/AAAJ-10-2014-1842

O'Donovan, G. (2002). Environmental disclosures in the annual report: Extending the applicability and predictive power of legitimacy theory. *Accounting, Auditing & Accountability Journal*, *15*(3), 344–371. doi:10.1108/09513570210435870

Othman, R., & Othman, R. (2014). Higher education institutions and social performance: Evidence from public and private universities. *International Journal of Business & Society*, *15*(1), 1–1.

Pisani, N., Kourula, A., Kolk, A., & Meijer, R. (2017). How global is international CSR research? Insights and recommendations from a systematic review. *Journal of World Business*, *52*(5), 591–614. doi:10.1016/j.jwb.2017.05.003

Porter, M. E., & Kramer, M. R. (2006). The link between competitive advantage and corporate social responsibility. *Harvard Business Review*, *84*(12), 78–92. PMID:17183795

Prasad, M., Mishra, T., & Kalro, A. D. (2017). Environmental disclosure by Indian companies: An empirical study. *Environment, Development and Sustainability*, *19*(5), 1999–2022. doi:10.100710668-016-9840-5

Rodríguez Bolívar, M. P., Garde Sánchez, R., & López Hernández, A. M. (2013). Online disclosure of corporate social responsibility information in leading Anglo-American universities. *Journal of Environmental Policy and Planning*, *15*(4), 551–575. doi:10.1080/1523908X.2013.817945

Sassen, R., & Azizi, L. (2018). Assessing sustainability reports of US universities. *International Journal of Sustainability in Higher Education*, *19*(7), 1158–1184. doi:10.1108/IJSHE-06-2016-0114

Sepasi, S., Braendle, U., & Rahdari, A. H. (2019). Comprehensive sustainability reporting in higher education institutions. *Social Responsibility*, *15*(2), 155–170. doi:10.1108/SRJ-01-2018-0009

Sepasi, S., Rahdari, A., & Rexhepi, G. (2018). Developing a sustainability reporting assessment tool for higher education institutions: The University of California. *Sustainable Development*, *26*(6), 672–682. doi:10.1002d.1736

Shannon, S. E. (2014). Three Approaches to Qualitative Content Analysis. *Qualitative Health Research*, *15*(9), 1277–1288. PMID:16204405

Suddaby, R. (2010). Challenges for institutional theory. *Journal of Management Inquiry*, *16*(1), 14–20. doi:10.1177/1056492609347564

Suter, W. N., & Data, Q. (2011). *Introduction to Educational Research: A Critical Thinking Approach*. SAGE Publications.

Tanggamani, V., Amran, A., & Ramayah, T. (2018). The Corporate Social Responsibility and Corporate Financial Performance Virtuous Loop: A Theoretical Framework. *Global Business and Management Research: An International Journal*, *10*(1), 331–344.

The portal for Sustainability Reporting (2017). *The GRI Standards: One year on*. Retrieved from https://www.sustainability-reports.com/the-gri-standards-one-year-on/

Tudor-Tiron, A., & Dragu, I. (2014). From sustainability to integrated reporting – the political perspective of institutional theory. *Studia Universitatis Babes-Bolyai*, *59*(2), 20–33.

Vázquez-Carrasco, R., & López-Pérez, M. E. (2013). Small & medium-sized enterprises and Corporate Social Responsibility: A systematic review of the literature. *Quality & Quantity*, *47*(6), 3205–3218. doi:10.100711135-012-9713-4

Votaw, D. (1972). Genius becomes rare: A comment on the doctrine of social responsibility pt. 1. *California Management Review*, *150*(2), 25–31. doi:10.2307/41164415

Wang, H., Tong, L., Takeuchi, R., & George, G. (2016). Corporate social responsibility: An overview and new research directions: Thematic issue on corporate social responsibility. *Academy of Management Journal*, *59*(2), 534–544. doi:10.5465/amj.2016.5001

Watson, S. (2011). Conflict diamonds, legitimacy and media agenda: An examination of annual report disclosures. *Meditari Accountancy Research*, *19*(1), 94–111. doi:10.1108/10222521111178655

Wigmore-Álvarez, A., & Ruiz-Lozano, M. (2014). The United Nations Global Compact Progress Reports as Management Control Instruments for Social Responsibility at Spanish Universities. *SAGE Open*, (April-June): 2–12.

Yin, R. K. (2009). *Case Study Research - Design and Methods* (4th ed.). Thousand Oaks, CA: Sage.

Zorio-Grima, A., Sierra-García, L., & Garcia-Benau, M. A. (2018). Sustainability reporting experience by universities: A causal configuration approach. *International Journal of Sustainability in Higher Education*, *19*(2), 337–352. doi:10.1108/IJSHE-07-2016-0142

KEY TERMS AND DEFINITIONS

Legitimacy Theory: a theory that advocates that organizations seek to act within the limits and norms accepted by the community;

Stakeholder Theory: a theory that argues that organizations have the responsibility of considering the interests of all affected by their activities;

Social Responsibility Reporting: the means by which organizations seek to disseminate information to its stakeholders, about their social responsibility performance and strategies;

Systematic Literature Review: a research method that allows to identify, evaluate and interpret all available evidence in the literature regarding a particular topic.

Chapter 5
Anything Goes in Cause Related Marketing?
The Case of the 'Solidarity' Traffic Radar

M. Mercedes Galan-Ladero
University of Extremadura, Spain

Clementina Galera-Casquet
https://orcid.org/0000-0001-5113-1885
University of Extremadura, Spain

ABSTRACT

Cause-related marketing (CRM) is currently considered one of the main initiatives of corporate social responsibility (CSR). CRM programs offer numerous advantages for all the parties involved: companies, non-profit organizations, and consumers. Examples of CRM programs can be found in virtually every country in the world. Although most CRM campaigns succeeded, several of them were involved in some scandals. In Spain, an example of the controversy caused by CRM campaigns resurfaced with the installation of the so-called "solidarity traffic radar." The aim of this chapter is to offer a case study about this campaign, where a private company managed this traffic radar. Half of the money that was raised in fines was given to the Town Council, which in turn decided to donate it to needy local families, that is, it was allocated to social aid. Thus, this case study discusses if anything goes in CRM, or there is sometimes a trivialization of solidarity.

INTRODUCTION

Corporate Social Responsibility (CSR), defined as "the voluntary integration, by enterprises, of social and environmental concerns in their business operations and their interaction with their stakeholders" (Commission of the European Communities, 2001, p. 7), is nowadays a key aspect for all kind of companies that integrated it into their corporate mission and organizational culture. CSR concept is an "umbrella" where different activities are included.

DOI: 10.4018/978-1-7998-2128-1.ch005

Cause-related marketing (CRM) is currently considered as one of the main initiatives of CSR (Kotler & Lee, 2005; Nelson & Vilela, 2017; Rego, 2017; Galan & Galera, 2018), with an important growth in the last years (Rego, 2017; Duarte & Silva, 2018). CRM is defined as "an agreement between a company and a non-profit organization to collaborate in a social cause and get mutual benefit. The commitment of the company focuses on contributing (financially or in kind) to the cause in terms of sales. Therefore, the donation will depend on consumer behaviour" (adapted from Santesmases, 1999, p. 1004; Kotler and Lee in Galan, 2012).

Thus, CRM is not social marketing (Santesmases, 1999), and its most relevant characteristics are (Galan & Galera, 2018): (1) there is a link between a for-profit organization (a company) and a non-profit organization (a NPO), in order to support a social cause, and obtaining a mutual benefit (Penelas et al., 2012); and (2) the donation is conditioned by sales (CRM ultimately depends on consumer behaviour if he/she buys the product linked to the CRM campaign).

The theoretical development of CRM is based on the evolution of the marketing concept toward the social perspective (social dimension of marketing), the emergence of non-business marketing, the importance of CSR, and the influence of paradigms such as marketing orientation, marketing relationships, stakeholder orientation, holistic marketing orientation, and sustainability (Galan et al., 2013). Theories such as stakeholder theory, resource-advantage theory (Hunt & Morgan, 1995; Ferrell, 2010), or legitimacy theory (Liu, 2013, p. 248) are considered fundamental for this development; and also approaches such as the instrumental dominant logic (that considers CRM as "a commercial marketing campaign, focused on influence consumers' purchase intention; that is, attracting customers' attention to generate sales" – Liu, 2013, pp. 243-244, 257) and relational dominant logic (that considers CRM as "a management strategy, focused on building relationships with the target stakeholders through the enhancement of a firm's legitimacy" - Liu, 2013, pp. 243-244, 257).

CRM emerged in the USA in the 1980s (American Express copyrighted the term "cause-related marketing" (Varadarajan and Menon, 1988, p. 58)) and it was quickly imitated by other companies. Nowadays, examples of CRM programs can be found in virtually any country in the world.

CRM campaigns have evolved along this time (Kropp et al., 1999, p. 71; Bennett et al., 2008), and many types of CRM programs can be distinguished, according to different criteria, such as the donation type (a fixed amount of money, a percentage of sales, a percentage of profits, etc.), the number of products linked to the campaign (a specific product, some products, or all the products of the company), firms or non-profit organizations involved (only one firm and one non-profit organization, or several ones), its duration (a short / long period of time, indefinitely), its geographical scope (local, regional, national, international or global campaign), the supported cause (childhood in need, research about a certain disease, fight against hunger, environment protection, education, etc.) (Galan et al., 2013).

CRM programs offer numerous advantages for all the parts implied: companies, non-profit organizations, and consumers (Galan et al., 2013):

- For companies: tax incentives, purchase motivation (new values are added to the product and offered to the consumers); increase on sales and market share; promotion of the product / brand / corporation; customer loyalty and expansion of the customer base; employee motivation, commitment, and loyalty (low turnover); improvement of organizational image, reputation, and positioning; a competitive advantage (differentiation from competitors, based on ethical and social dimensions); access to the media (better conditions or, indeed, free advertising) and visibility; attraction of good investors; improvement of relationships with stakeholders, etc.

- For non-profit organizations: diversification of funding sources; logistical support; an increase of program effectiveness; cause / mission spreading; visibility and better access to the media; enhancement of their image and participation in society; an increase on the number of partners, donors, and volunteers; learning from the company (e.g. management, professionalism, etc.); awareness about a social cause; education on values; improvement of relations with society, etc.
- For consumers: new values added to the product; ability to participate in charitable causes; knowledge about the situation of certain groups and populations from other countries; purchase awareness and satisfaction; etc.

Thus, CRM has become an important strategy for all kind of organizations from any sector.

Although most CRM campaigns had an important success, several of them were involved in some scandals. For example, in Spain, we can highlight the following cases:

- The 'For 0.7' campaign (by Fortuna), at the end of 1990s.

  This CRM campaign was developed by Fortuna, a tobacco brand that offered to collaborate to humanitarian projects in the Third World, donating the 0.7 percent of cigarettes sales.

  This program was heavily criticized by different social groups and non-profit organizations, because the product was considered unethical (tobacco seriously harms health), the campaign was focused on young people, and the Third World was the new target for tobacco companies (because of the restrictions to tobacco consumption in North America and European Union).
- The 'No child without milk' campaign (by Ram), also at the end of the 1990s.

  This first CRM campaign between Ram, a milk brand, and UNICEF was criticized for using shocking images (a malnourished and starving child).
- The 'Action Man' campaign (by Hasbro), at the beginning of the 2000s.

  In this program, a line of war toys (Action Man) was linked with a non-profit organization (Asociación España con ACNUR – Spain with UNHCR Association, in English) that precisely helps refugees and victims of armed conflicts in the world.

In other countries, there have also been controversial campaigns, such as:

- 'Buy a sex toy, save a child' campaign (in the USA, in 2009).

  An online adult toy retailer, Sinlesstouch.com, created a project to support children in Third World countries. On October 15, all profits from product sales would be donated to this program. In addition, during checkout, customers had the option to round up their purchases and donate electronic 'spare change' to this charitable cause (Olathe, 2009).

  The 'Adopt A Child Charity' Program tried to help empower children from the Third World to raise themselves from poverty. Each of the adopted children could be viewed on Sinless Touch web site (Olathe, 2009).

This charitable campaign was strongly criticized for linking sex toys and kids.

- *Or some restaurants, which fine those customers who do not eat everything they order, wasting food.* For example:

In Australia (Excelencias Gourmet, 2010).

Wafu´s owner, an Australian restaurant in Sydney, specializing in organic and free-gluten, -dairy, -sugar and -egg Japanese food, was tired of seeing the remains of food left by her customers ('vegetables and salads are not decorative, they are also part of the meal'). Therefore, she decided to change the policy of the restaurant: Customers should terminate all dishes, or pay a fine of $30 and choose another restaurant next time.

As it was explained on the web site, the commitment adopted was to serving meals that nurture and respect the body, but also prevent the expense and seriously consider environmental responsibility.

- *In Saudi Arabia* (Periodismo.com, 2011).
  An Arab restaurant in Dammam decided to charge an extra fee to those customers who did not eat everything they had ordered.
  Restaurant owners adopted this policy to "educate" their customers, because there was the custom in that city to order large amounts of food and hearty dishes at restaurants just to impress other diners and customers, and thus, increase their social prestige. The owners, tired of their customers to order food just to try and leave, made this decision to educate their customers that they should not waste food, because people are starving in other parts of the world. Therefore, the chosen cause was the fight against hunger and malnutrition in Somalia (fines applied, depending on the leftovers, would be donated to this cause).
  The idea was considered by the Saudi Arabian lawmakers to extend it to the whole country.
- *In Japan* (Planetacurioso.com, 2013)
  Hachikyo, a seafood restaurant in Sapporo, also announced that customers would fine if they did not end the food served. It was explained on the menu that the working conditions of fishermen were hard and dangerous. Therefore, to show gratitude and appreciation for the food provided, to leave food in the bowl was strictly forbidden (not even a single grain of rice!).
  The fine for failing to meet this represented a donation equivalent to $20.
- *In United Kingdom* (diariodigitaldeasturias.com, 2016).
  Chinese food restaurant Kylin, located in Ocean Road, South Shields, had as its slogan 'all you can eat.' If someone left food on the plate, he/she would be fined (£20).
- In Spain (April, 2016), the controversy resurfaced again with the installation of the called 'solidarity traffic radar', which is the case study that it will be developed in this chapter.

Thus, the aim of this chapter is to offer a case study focused on this controversial CRM campaign, where a private company managed this traffic radar. Half of the money that was raised in fines, was given to the Town Council, which in turn decided to donate it to needy local families, that is, it was allocated to social aid.

Using the analysis of secondary data (from mass media, mainly) as research method, the final purpose of this case study is to discuss and reflect about these questions: Anything goes in CRM? Is there any trivialization of solidarity?

STUDY CASE: THE "SOLIDARITY" TRAFFIC RADAR

The Town Council of a small village in Cantabria, Santa Maria de Cayon, made headlines in the media in April 2016 for having installed the first 'solidarity traffic radar' in Spain.

The reason was to publicly release that part of the revenue obtained from fines imposed with this speed detector will be targeted to the neediest families in the area, that is, for social aid.

Background

A road (CA-142), the busiest one in Cantabria, crosses this village. And it does so in the confluence between two educational facilities: a primary school and a high school, where more than 1,600 students attend (ABC, 2016).

The high speed with which cars usually circulate around that area has led, for years, numerous requests from parents and the educational community. They called for regulation of the situation and a reduction of the speed of the cars, at least when they go through the school zone. These demands were increased after an outrage suffered by a student in 2012 at the pedestrian crossing, which also had a traffic light. The School Board requested the Town Council that would increase road safety, taking steps to regulate traffic and prevent new accidents (San Miguel, 2016).

Finally, the Town Council handled these requests and decided to place a traffic radar at that point in early April 2016.

The "Solidarity" Traffic Radar

The solution to the existing problem came in the firm Vialine, a service company specialising in technology-based development of management systems for Public Administration, and whose motto was "We think about the citizen" (Vialine, 2016).

According to its corporate website, this company is dedicated to (Vialine, 2016):

- Mobility management, with systems for the surveillance, regulation and control of traffic and parking on urban roads, as well as the registration of infractions.
- The management of traffic sanctions, collaborating and providing technical assistance to the local police and facilitating the collection of fines.
- The tax management of the income and taxes of the municipal administrations, providing computer assistance and logistic support.
- Applications and mobile devices to improve services for citizens (lost property service, online incident manager, broken streetlights, broken tiles, wastepaper boxes in poor condition).

In this case, the first two services were contracted in this town (Santa Maria de Cayon).

The company, which was already working with other town councils in the area, proposed to take over management of the fine collection, yielding road safety devices to municipalities (each device was valued at about 70,000 Euros). Finally, the Town Council selected it to promote road safety in the council.

But the traffic radar placed in the area was not an ordinary one, but rather a photo-red camera. This type of device did not measure the speed of vehicles, but took advantage of the traffic lights that were put red when the speed limit is exceeded. The device connected to the traffic light and fined those drivers that left it out in red. The fine was 200 Euros and involved the removal of 4 points from the driving license.

In addition to installing a warning signal of the existence of a traffic radar, to deter drivers and avoid possible accidents, it was publicized and announced in the media and social networks, so that everyone knew the initiative.

The private company that managed and was responsible for maintaining, took half of the money raised, that is, it distributed it to 50 per cent with the Town Council, which in turn referred sanctions to the Provincial Office of the Directorate General of Traffic (DGT), where the points of the sanctioned driver were subtracted.

Therefore, it was a variable amount, where the company charges based on the proceeds. In this village, the Town Council decided that its half was intended to needy local families (180, approximately – Lopez, 2016), that is, it would be allocated to social aid.

And as the objective of the town council was not to have a tax collection effort but avoid a tragedy, the responsible ones were in charge of the traffic radar being well indicated (with a visible traffic signal warning of its existence to the drivers). They also made it known in all the media (local, regional, and national), as well as in social networks, so that the initiative was known by everyone.

RESULTS

After several months, it was known that 76 vehicles were fined in the first two days after installation (37 cars, on April 4, 2016; and 39 cars, on April 5, 2016), reaching therefore a fund of 15,200 Euros, and subtracting 304 points. However, it was expected that as time passed, these figures declined significantly, when the "word spread" of that point was controlled.

However, sabotage was detected several weeks later, at the end of April. Someone manipulated the traffic light device. Regardless of the speed which the car was circulating at, even if it was stopped, the traffic light remained red. So, since that day, the number of fines skyrocketed.

The numerous complaints of the neighbours about the traffic light (more than 20, in a single day – Lopez, 2016) led the company to carry out an inspection and detect sabotage. Due to this, the company had to cancel all the sanctions imposed from that day (April 14) and until it was repaired a few days later (April 18, at noon). In total, 139 fines (San Miguel, 2016). Since it went back to work, there were 4 fines on that same day, and 9 penalties the following day (April 19). Thereafter, no other incident was made public again, and the traffic radar continued to function normally.

The town council resolved, in the Commission of Health and Social Services, on September 20, 2017, the concession of 13,177 Euros to those families who requested Council Economic Aid from the Supply and Solidarity Radar Fund, from June 30 to September 19 (Ayuntamiento de Santa Maria de Cayon, 2017).

In January 2018, it was published that the solidarity traffic radar had collected almost 18,000 Euros (17,180 Euros, exactly (Tresgallo, 2018a)), which had been allocated to social spending, for families in need (Tresgallo, 2018b).

However, since April 2017, the solidarity traffic radar was without service (although it still had a deterrent effect), with the expiration of the first year of contract with Vialine. Although the reason pointed out was the delay (due to lack of time) in bidding for the control service and imposition of sanctions, it seems that the real reason was the doubt about the legality of this radar. Although it was authorized and the Directorate General of Traffic (DGT) homologation was not needed, and the Town Council was also who assumed the processing of sanctions and was responsible for the traffic radar (Tresgallo, 2018a), some similar equipment, from other towns, was giving rise to sentences declaring null the fines (by the strength of the test), so the town council was waiting for a "consultation to know if the prototype was legal".

But the most important aspect of this case was the generated opinions, both for (some neighbours were delighted with the action taken) and against (there were many criticisms, especially through social networks) – El Diario Montañes (2016):

- In favour: locals, in general, and neighbours and the educational community of that area, in particular, concerned about the high speed at which cars circulated and the presence of many children in this area. These citizens also applauded the joint initiative of the mayor, considering it a great idea.

In addition, some people even believed that the system was perfect: there was no cost to the Town Council, and therefore it had no impact on taxpayers (a business installed it free, which was also responsible for maintaining and managing fines). It also helped to reduce accidents in the area, to raise aware of drivers to reduce their speed in urban areas, and to ensure the pedestrian safety. In addition, part of the proceeds would be donated to charity purposes.

In short, everything depended on the drivers, whether or not they respected traffic rules.

- Against: those that indicated that a fine is a punishment, and it should not be mixed with charity. Or who criticized the company to manage to "hide" their profitable interests under the term "solidarity". Or people who directly saw hypocrisy, or even a 'charade', or even a robbery to drivers. Also those who would have preferred another solution to the problem (to build a roundabout, to use the other exits from the primary school and the high school, to develop social marketing campaigns, etc.), rather than collecting fines.

Also, those who believed that the aid to families in need should not depend on the income generated by traffic fines, but it should be independent of all this, and come from other sources more stable and permanent over time. In their opinion, this initiative did not solve the structural problems of these families in the long term.

FINAL REFLECTIONS

This case was chosen for its creative and 'solidarity' solution to the road safety problem detected in this village. It was the first time that a private company and a town council collaborated in a CRM campaign in Spain. Although it was really working only one year, many questions arouse: Would it be "copied" by other councils? Would it be a new business opportunity?

Other news has immediately jumped to the media: Town Council of L'Arboç (in Tarragona) also studied to implement the 'solidarity' radar for social assistance (CiU, a political party, proposed to allocate 25 per cent of fines to actions decided by neighbours) (Diari de Tarragona, 2016)).

A fine is a sanction, but if revenue goes to solidarity purposes, Would the drivers´ attitude towards these traffic fines change? Would they be less reluctant to pay them? Would they pay more eager? Would they be 'happier' when they paid these fines? Would the 'solidarity' fines be a new trend in Spain?

Proceeds depended neither the Town Council nor the business, it only depended on the drivers. If all drivers respected the traffic rules, then there would be no sanctions, there would be road safety for pedestrians, and the company would not obtain benefits (but also no money would be allocated to help needy families).

Therefore, the main advantages for the different parties involved can be summarized as follows:

- For pedestrians, in the area: greater safety when crossing the road, reducing the risk of being run over.
- For the Town Council: extra income, which could be allocated to help the most disadvantaged families in the town. In addition, this initiative could help to develop social responsibility in the Public Administration context.

And the dissemination of this local initiative also gave publicity to this small town, being now well-known for this initiative of solidarity.

- For the company (Vialine): it contributes to road safety with this activity, improving the quality of life of citizens.
- For drivers: greater awareness of the need of driving at a moderate speed through the urban area.
- For society, in general: the dissemination of this type of initiatives helps to become aware of the importance of compliance with traffic regulations for road safety and accident prevention.

But there are also several drawbacks for the different parts implied:

- For the business (Vialine): a negative image, if citizens considered it was a purely commercial strategy, opportunistic or even immoral (to "hide" its economic objectives under the term "solidarity").
- For the Town Council: also a negative image for the local Government, if people considered that there was a hidden tax collection character behind the word "solidarity." It could also be accused of evading its responsibility with the most disadvantaged people in the town, forcing drivers to be the ones who financed social services, when it was really the Town Council that should do it.

Basic social benefits should be financed otherwise, because if fines decreased in the long-term, then the social aid would also decrease. Thus, other ways of financing should be assured. Therefore, this system did not really solve the social problems of these families in need.

In addition, transparency should be offered: to give enough information about the destination of the funds is basic for credibility. In this way, all this would be an example of how Town Councils also assume their social responsibility.

- For drivers: to pay without losing their driving misbehaviour, or to 'clean' conscience (guilt feelings by bad driving were reduced – "it's not so bad what I've done, because at least I'm helping a good cause"). They actually paid the cost of the social actions for people in need in the village, when it was the obligation of the Town Council.
- For pedestrians: the road safety could be improved. But they could be considered as the responsible promoters of sanctions by some drivers.

The idea of a "solidarity" traffic radar had a great impact on the media and on society in general. And it was spread to other towns.

Therefore, anything goes in CSR in general, and CRM in particular? Could any cause be linked with a CRM program, just for appearance, excuse or pretext of solidarity, just because the raised money is donated to a good cause?

Non-Governmental Organizations (NGOs) have codes of conduct to regulate relations with companies. But, in situations like the one we discussed above, in which the non-profit part is a Town Council, should specific codes of conduct be also adopted?

Could the 'solidarity' traffic radar also become a social marketing tool? Could the 'solidarity' traffic radar help drivers to raise awareness about the importance of circulating at a moderate speed in town, and to change their attitude and behaviour towards greater respect for traffic rules?

We should think about this, to avoid situations that some authors, such as Ballesteros (2001), called "trivialisation of solidarity".

CONCLUSION, IMPLICATIONS, LIMITATIONS AND FURTHER RESEARCH

Conclusion

Among the main conclusions, the following ones stand out:

- CRM can be considered an initiative where the holistic marketing approach is applied: companies assume CSR and sustainability principles. CRM seeks a benefit for the company involved (higher profits, better corporate image and reputation), for the non-profit organization (new fundraising sources), for the consumers (sharing values), and for society in general (encouraging the defense of social causes and the general welfare).
- Although CRM has extended to different sectors and other types of organizations are also involved in CRM programs (public and non-profit organizations, such as Town Councils or Universities), aspects such as coherence, long-term commitment and communication, following ethical codes, are always critical to avoid any controversy in CRM campaigns.

After analyzing the "solidarity" traffic radar case, the question is if anything goes in CRM. Does the end justify the means?

Theoretical Contributions and Managerial Implications

This chapter contributes to broaden the scope of the CRM literature, studying its extension to new fields and with new types of organizations involved (town councils, in this case).

The analysis of controversial campaigns can help organizations to be conscious about the opportunities and threats that CRM can offer in "difficult" situations, e.g. where a specific social behavior is also sought, and the punishment for not to do it could be "softer" with a solidarity orientation. Thus, CRM can be complementary to social marketing campaigns.

Limitations and Further Research

This chapter is only a case study. It would be necessary to do a more complete search about other controversial CRM campaigns, to have a deeper vision of the CRM effects and consequences in this type of situations.

Therefore, it would be interesting to develop a cross-cultural study to observe and compare reactions toward several controversial campaigns in different countries; or to compare CRM programs developed by corporations versus CRM campaigns developed by public or nonprofit organizations (e.g. universities, town councils, etc.), to have a widen vision of the current CRM concept.

REFERENCES

ABC. (2016, April 6). El primer radar 'solidario' de España. *ABC Sociedad*. Retrieved from http://www.abc.es

Ayuntamiento de Santa María de Cayón. (2017). *Ordenanza Reguladora de las Ayudas Económicas Municipales de Carácter Excepcional con cargo al Fondo de Suministros y al Radar Solidario*. Retrieved from http://www.santamariadecayon.es

Bennett, R., Mousley, W., & Ali-Choudhury, R. (2008). Transfer of marketing knowledge within business – nonprofit collaborations. *Journal of Nonprofit & Public Sector Marketing*, *20*(1), 37–70. doi:10.1080/10495140802165352

Diari de Tarragona. (2016). *L'Arboç estudia implantar el 'radar solidario' para ayudas sociales*. Retrieved from http://www.diaridetarragona.com

Duarte, P., & Costa e Silva, S. (2018). The role of consumer-cause identification and attitude in the intention to purchase cause-related products. *International Marketing Review*. doi:10.1108/IMR-04-2018-0159

El Diario Cantabria. (2016). *Santa María de Cayón instala el primer radar de recaudación solidaria en España*. Retrieved from http://eldiariocantabria.es

El Diario Montañés. (2016). *Foro*. Retrieved from http://eldiariomontanes.es

Ferrell, O. C. (2010). Shelby Hunt's Resource Advantage Theory. University of New Mexico.

Galan-Ladero. M. (2012). *Variables que influyen en la actitud hacia el marketing con causa y determinantes de la satisfacción y la lealtad en la "compra solidaria"* [Doctoral Thesis]. University of Extremadura.

Galan-Ladero. M. (2013). Marketing con Causa: ¿Oportunidad o Solidaridad? In J.M. Rey-Pino & A.I. Polo-Peña (Eds.), Marketing y Sociedad: Aplicaciones Sectoriales del Marketing No Lucrativo (pp. 15-24). Granada: Servicio de Publicaciones de la Universidad de Granada.

Galan-Ladero, M. & Galera-Casquet, C. (2016). The Case of the 'Solidarity' Radar: Anything Goes in a Cause-Related Marketing? In *Proceedings of the 15th International Congress on Public and Nonprofit Marketing*. Academic Press.

Galan-Ladero, M. & Galera-Casquet, C. (2018). Corporate Social Responsibility and Digital Tools. The Cause-Related Marketing Case. In L. Carvalho & P. Isaias (Eds.), Handbook of Research on Entrepreneurship and Marketing for Global Reach in the Digital Economy (Ch. 1, pp. 1-16). Hershey, PA: IGI Global.

Galan-Ladero, M. & Galera-Casquet, C. (2019). Marketing para el cambio social. In L.M. Cerda-Suarez & M. Ramírez-Ramírez (Eds.), Fundamentos para un nuevo marketing (Ch. 11, pp. 251-284). Madrid: Sinderesis.

Galan-Ladero, M.M., Galera-Casquet, C., Valero-Amaro, V., & Barroso-Mendez, M.J. (2013). Sustainable, socially responsible business: The cause-related marketing case. A review of the conceptual framework. *Journal of Security and Sustainability Issues*, *2*(4), 35–46. doi:10.9770/jssi.2013.2.4(4)

Hunt, S. D., & Morgan, R. M. (1995). The Comparative Advantage Theory of Competition. *Journal of Marketing*, *59*(2), 1–15. doi:10.1177/002224299505900201

Kotler, P., & Lee, N. (2005). *Corporate Social Responsibility*. Wiley.

Kropp, F., Holden, S. J. S., & Lavack, A. M. (1999). Cause – related marketing and values in Australia. *International Journal of Nonprofit and Voluntary Sector Marketing*, *4*(1), 69–80. doi:10.1002/nvsm.57

La Sexta. (2016, April 6). *Instalan el primer radar de tráfico solidario de España, lo recaudado irá para familias necesitadas*. Retrieved from http://www.lasexta.com

Liu, G. (2013). Impacts of Instrumental Versus Relational Centered Logic on Cause-Related Marketing Decision Making. *Journal of Business Ethics*, *113*(2), 243–263. doi:10.100710551-012-1292-8

López, N. (2016). Sabotean el primer radar solidario de España. *AutoBild.es*. Retrieved from http://www.autobild.es/noticias/primer-radar-solidario-espana-286723

MAPFRE. (2015, December 1). Todas las infracciones con retirada de puntos. *Canal Motor*. Retrieved from http://www.motor.mapfre.es

Moral, J. (2016, April 6). *Nace el primer radar solidario: recaudará para fines sociales*. Retrieved from http://www.autopista.es

Nelson, M. R., & Vilela, A. M. (2017). Exploring the interactive effects of brand use and gender on cause-related marketing over time. *International Journal of Nonprofit and Voluntary Sector Marketing*, *22*(3), 1–13. doi:10.1002/nvsm.1580

Penelas-Leguia. A., Galera-Casquet, C., Galan-Ladero, M., & Valero-Amaro, V. (2012). Marketing Solidario. El marketing en las organizaciones no lucrativas. Madrid: Piramide.

Rego, M. (2017). The Impact of Cause-Related Marketing on Global Consumers: A Meta-Analysis [Doctoral Dissertation]. University of Connecticut (USA).

San Miguel, A. (2016, April 7). El 'radar solidario' de Cayón se estrena con 76 multas en dos días. *El Diario Montañés*. Retrieved from http://www.eldiariomontanes.es

San Miguel, A. (2016, April 20). Sabotean el 'radar solidario' de Cayón y obligan a la empresa a anular 139 multas. *El Diario Montañés*. Retrieved from http://www.eldiariomontanes.es/bahia-centropas/201604/20/sabotean-radar-solidario-cayon-20160419231211.html

Santesmases, M. (1999). *Marketing. Conceptos y Estrategias*. Madrid: Piramide.

Tresgallo, E. (2018a, February 6). El Ayuntamiento de Cayón duda de la legalidad de su radar solidario. *El Diario Montañés*. Retrieved from https://www.eldiariomontanes.es/region/valles-pasiegos/ayuntamiento-cayon-duda-20180206211807-ntvo.html

Tresgallo, E. (2018b, January 17). El radar solidario de Cayón recauda 18.000 euros que se destinan a familias necesitadas. *El Diario Montañés*. Retrieved from https://www.eldiariomontanes.es/region/valles-pasiegos/radar-solidario-cayon-20180117214925-ntvo.html

Varadarajan, P.R., & Menon, A. (1988). Cause-related marketing: A coalignment of marketing strategy and corporate philanthropy. *Journal of Marketing*, *52*(3), 58–74. doi:10.1177/002224298805200306

Vialine. (2016). *Corporate information*. Retrieved from http://www.vialine.es

Viz-Blanco. M.J. (2016, April 13). *El radar solidario*. Retrieved from http://www.elcorreogallego.es

ADDITIONAL READING

Galan - Ladero, M., Galera - Casquet, C., Valero - Amaro, V. & Barroso - Mendez, M.J. (2013). Sustainable, socially responsible business: The cause-related marketing case. A review of the conceptual framework. *Journal of Security and Sustainability Issues*, *2*, 35–46.

Galan – Ladero. M. & Galera – Casquet, C. (2018). Chapter 1: Corporate Social Responsibility and Digital Tools. The Cause-Related Marketing Case. In Carvalho, L.; Isaias, P. (edit.): Handbook of Research on Entrepreneurship and Marketing for Global Reach in the Digital Economy, pp. 1-16. USA: IGI Global.

KEY TERMS AND DEFINITIONS

Cause-Related Marketing (CRM): a CSR initiative that consists of an agreement between a company and a nonprofit organization to collaborate on a social cause, obtaining a mutual benefit. The company's commitment is focused on contributing (monetary or in kind) to the cause in terms of sales (therefore the donation will depend on consumer behavior).

Controversial campaigns: ad campaigns involved in some scandals (because of the product involved in the campaign, the images or messages included in campaign ads, the social cause chosen for the campaign, etc.).

Corporate Social Responsibility (CSR): the voluntary integration of economic, social and environmental concerns in the firm's operations, its value chain, and the interaction with its stakeholders.

For-profit Organization: an entity whose main aim is to obtain monetary profit (e.g. a company that seeks an economic purpose).

Nonprofit Organization (NPO): an entity whose main aim is not to obtain monetary profit (e.g. a Non-Governmental Organization – NGO – that seeks a social purpose).

Social Cause: an idea, opinion, attitude, value, or behavior that is socially desirable.

'Solidarity' Traffic Radar: system that uses radio waves to control traffic (e.g. speed) and records traffic violations. Offenders receive fines later. But, in this case, the traffic radar adds the term "solidarity" because part of the money raised in fines is given for social aid, for a social cause.

Town Council: local government. It can be considered a public nonprofit organization.

Chapter 6
Corporate Social Responsibility and Disclosure of Socioenvironmental Risks by Credit Unions

Rodrigo Gaspar de Almeida
https://orcid.org/0000-0002-9122-8507
Universidade Estadual de Maringá, Brazil

Marguit Neumann
https://orcid.org/0000-0003-1246-3769
Universidade Estadual de Maringá, Brazil

Simone Leticia Raimundini Sanches
https://orcid.org/0000-0002-7363-2573
Universidade Estadual de Maringá, Brazil

Valéria Gama Fully Bressan
Universidade Federal de Minas Gerais, Brazil

ABSTRACT

This study aimed to investigate which groups of stakeholders Sicredi has included in its assessment of socioenvironmental risks. To that end, the content analysis technique was applied for primary sources, interviews with Sicredi's superintendent and the supervisor of Brazil's Central Bank, and secondary sources e.g. organizational reports. Results evidenced that stakeholders—credit union members, employees, government, community and the media—were included in Sicredi's socioenvironmental risk disclosure. As theoretical contributions, this study provides discussions around corporate social responsibility and socioenvironmental risks at credit unions. The target audience of this study can be those in academia, practitioners, business managers, professionals from the financial industry, and corporate social responsibility researchers.

DOI: 10.4018/978-1-7998-2128-1.ch006

INTRODUCTION

Corporate Social Responsibility prescribes that credit unions (Financial Institutions) shall operate under the Triple Bottom Line (TBL) of Sustainable Development, which entails equitably fulfilling economic growth, environmental quality and social equality, including transparency when disclosing information to stakeholders (positive and negative impacts). It is identified by the establishment of organizational policies that seek the wellbeing of society and must comprise: preservation of environmental and cultural resources for future generations, respect for biodiversity, fight against social inequalities, and inclusion of socioenvironmental information in accounting reports (Carroll, 2015; Clarkson, 1995; Deegan, 2017; Elkington, 2012; Freeman & Evan, 1990; Gray, 2001).

Within the scope of credit unions, socioenvironmental risk is defined as the possibility that an event related to environmental or social aspects may unfavorably impact their objectives. This risk may be direct or indirect. Direct socioenvironmental risks of credit unions result from the impact caused by the use of natural resources such as water, paper and electricity to render services, as well as from employee relations. Indirect socioenvironmental risks arise from the impacts from financed projects; therefore, they are related to financial intermediation services, which are the main business of credit unions (Federação Brasileira dos Bancos, 2015; Nogueira, Conceição & Imbroisi, 2015; Sanchéz, 2011).

It should be noted that joint and several (legal) liability of credit unions has already existed with regard to socioenvironmental damages arising from the projects they finance (article 3) since the enactment of Law no. 6,938, of August 31, 1981. Furthermore, the Central Bank of Brazil (BACEN) enacted Resolution 4.327, of April 25th, 2014, making it compulsory for Financial Institutions to disclose their socioenvironmental policy, including socioenvironmental risks (BACEN, 2014; Brasil, 1981; Nogueira et al., 2015; Ribeiro & Martins, 1993).

The manifestation of socioenvironmental risks can result in financial and socioenvironmental losses for the credit union and its stakeholders. Therefore, Corporate Social Responsibility embraces the need to develop mechanisms for these financial institutions to identify and mitigate socioenvironmental risks, by seeking to provide liquidity to the credit union, promoting socioenvironmental wellbeing, and acting under the *Triple Bottom Line* (Carroll, 2015; Elkington, 2012; FEBRABAN, 2015; Nogueira et al., 2015; Sanchéz, 2011).

The process of disclosing socioenvironmental risks demands that credit unions identify who their stakeholders are and how they are affected (Clarkson, 1995; Gray, 2001). Barakat, Boaventura & Polo (2017) argue that Financial Institutions expose themselves to these risks due to their client portfolio. For this reason, the identification of stakeholders affected by the activities of credit unions and the profile of member portfolios reinforce the need to disclose socioenvironmental risks.

From this perspective, Stakeholder Theory (normative view) seeks to identify who the stakeholders are in order to help an organization disclose how it understands and treats their demands or needs. Additionally, communication that aims to serve stakeholders is a CSR practice (Freeman & Evan, 1990).

In that regard, highlight is given to the operation in Brazil by the Sicredi, which structured a plan (2016-2020) with 3 main goals: 1) relationship and cooperativism; 2) responsible solutions (socioenvironmental risk management); and 3) local development (Sustainability Report-RS, 2017). This planning contributed to the investigation on the socioenvironmental risks of credit unions, as well as stakeholder engagement and CSR.

In this context, the following research question was raised: Which groups of stakeholders has the Sicredi included in their disclosure of socioenvironmental risks? To answer the proposed question, the following general objective was set: Investigate which groups of stakeholders the Sicredi has included in their disclosure of socioenvironmental risks. Data were collected by means of interviews (with Sicredi's superintendent and the supervisor of Brazil's Central Bank) and organizational reports: 2015 Socioenvironmental Responsibility Policy, 2017 Risk Management Structure, 2017 Financial Statements, and 2017 Sustainability Report, all treated using content analysis (Bardin, 2016).

Results evidenced that the stakeholders—members, employees, government, community and the media—were included in Sicredi's socioenvironmental risk disclosure. Another result to highlight is that indirect socioenvironmental risks had a smaller proportion in the disclosure, opposing theoretical perspectives according to which indirect socioenvironmental risks have the capacity to escalate impact, considering they arise from financial intermediation services.

The importance and originality of this study are founded on the scarcity of research studies relating credit unions and socioenvironmental risks. Investigations addressing socioenvironmental risks at Financial Institutions do not target credit unions (Elshahat, Parhizgari & Hong, 2012; Guimarães, 2015; Kalapodas & Thomson, 2006; Nogueira et. al, 2015) or focus solely on financial risks (Bressan, Braga, Bressan e Resende Filho, 2011; Mahajan, 1981; Sollenberger, 2005; Wen, 2015). Moreover, Veiga (2009), Sanchéz (2011, 2017), Hessou and Lai (2017), and Weber (2017) state that the discussion around socioenvironmental risks is still incipient.

The theoretical contributions expected to be provided by this study comprise the discussion around CSR at credit unions, application of Stakeholder Theory to credit unions, and the socioenvironmental risks posed by these institutions. As for practical contributions, this study brings the application of the socioenvironmental risk theme to the context of credit unions, supports the disclosure of socioenvironmental risks by credit unions, and helps verify whether Resolution 4.327/2014 (BACEN, 2014) has already influenced credit unions' disclosure processes. Furthermore, this research is expected to contribute to society by discussing socioenvironmental risks, as their materialization may cause financial and socioenvironmental losses to members and indirectly affect other credit union stakeholders.

BACKGROUND

Corporate Social Responsibility and the Stakeholder Theory

Corporate Social Responsibility (CSR) emerged as a concept in 1953 following World War II, and is fully evolving. In the organizational context, CSR has been influenced by the advancement of civil rights, women's rights, consumer rights, environmental movements, as well as World Environment Conferences of the United Nations (UN) (Almeida, Neumann & Sanches, 2018; Carroll, 1999; Elkington, 2012).

According to Carroll (1979), Corporate Social Responsibility of business encompasses economic, ethical, legal and discretionary responsibilities at a given point in time. Thus, an organization is deemed socially responsible when it applies organizational practices in the scope of the four CSR categories (Wood, 1991).

Elkington (2012) pointed out that a socially responsible organization must concomitantly aim at economic growth, environmental quality and social equality – the Triple Bottom Line. Indicators based on the Triple Bottom Line came to be used by organizations starting in 1995 and emphasize dialogue with stakeholders and CSR (Elkington, 2012).

Table 1. Synthesis of advantages and disadvantages related to CSR

CSR as advantage to the organization	CSR as disadvantage to the organization
Staff motivation and ease of hiring and retaining employees.	CSR understood by consumers as business as usual or greenwashing.
Goodwill toward consumers and loyal clients.	Expenses with CSR practices consume the organization's financial resources that belong to partners.
Improved financial performance and competitive advantage.	
Reduces the organization's exposure to risks (operational, legal, financial, market, socioenvironmental).	Over time, and due to increased expenses with CSR, capital cost rises and the organization's value consequently drops.
Long-term organizational policies and objectives.	
Rationalization of productive processes, bringing about efficiency and cost reduction.	
Benchmarking (with the organization itself and with other entities from the same industry).	
Improvement to the organization's reputation and legitimacy.	
Show society how the organization influences and is affected (proactive attitude in meeting social demands).	
Value creation by means of synergies.	

Source: Designed from Carroll (1999), Carroll & Shabama (2010), Fatemi, Fooladi, & Tehranian (2015), Kurucz, Colbert, & Wheeler (2008), McGuire, Sundgreen, & Schneewels (1998).

Gray (2001) claimed that the sustainability reports of organizations have evolved in the sense of evidencing the needs of stakeholders and describing policies on stakeholder relationship and engagement, but they are still incipient, and areas such as Social Auditing still need to evolve. Deegan (2017) emphasized that the intention of maximizing profits may result in income inequality and hunger; thus, Accounting needs to advance by shifting its normative accountability focus (complying with legislation), in which Corporate Social Responsibility is detrimental to the organization, toward an integrative focus on accountability to stakeholders, aiming at the sustainable development of current and future generations, in such a way that Corporate Social Responsibility becomes an organizational advantage (Table 1).

In addition to its advantages, Corporate Social Responsibility involves actions that may bring future benefits to the organization and its stakeholders, such as: staff motivation, cost reduction, process rationalization, improved reputation, value creation to the cooperative organization and its members. Moreover, Corporate Social Responsibility has the potential to create mechanisms for the credit union to engage with its stakeholders (members, employees, suppliers, among others) such as transparency, cultural actions in the community, donations, etc.

Stakeholders are, from the perspective of Stakeholder Theory, any group or individual that influences and is influenced by organizations (Freeman, Harrison, Wicks, Parmar, & De Colle, 2010). Still under the perspective of groups or persons, Clarkson (1995) described stakeholders as those who have or claim rights, ownership or interests concerning past, present or future activities of an organization (such demands may be legal or moral).

Clarkson (1995) also categorized stakeholders as primary (investors, employees, consumers, suppliers, government, and society) and secondary (media). That author further argued that organizations must give their attention to primary stakeholders, but that secondary ones may bring benefits (or risks) as well and therefore must not be neglected. Barakat et. al. (2017), Porter and Kramer (2006), Gray (2001) and Elkington (2012) stated that Corporate Social Responsibility practices must be voluntarily extended by the organization to the following stakeholders: consumers, employees, suppliers, government, and local communities (primary stakeholders). Tilling (2004) classified the media as a critical stakeholder, given its power to spread information (secondary stakeholder).

Considering the theoretical dissonance as to who stakeholders are, this study took into account the groups of stakeholders mentioned by Clarkson (1995) (both primary and secondary). When it comes to how stakeholders act or are affected, Chia (2011) argued that they need to know that they have been included in organizational practices, and that such a perception may occur by means of a disclosure addressed to them. Milani Filho (2007) stated that disclosure is crucial to dialogue with stakeholders.

To BACEN (2014) and FEBRABAN (2015), credit unions must disclose socioenvironmental risks to their internal and external audiences, that is, stakeholders. To do so, it is of paramount importance that stakeholders are identified in the information disclosure process. Therefore, Stakeholder Theory comprises theoretical perspectives concerning the disclosure of information to stakeholders, risks and Corporate Social Responsibility (Clarkson, 1995; Freeman, et al., 2010), which are applicable to credit unions and to the socioenvironmental risk to which these organizations are subject.

Credit Unions and Their Exposure to Socioenvironmental Risks

Credit unions are groups of people that associate with each other (voluntarily) to save and loan money, allowing members to participate democratically in decision making (Bressan et al., 2011; Gonçalves & Braga, 2008; Organization of Brazilian Cooperatives (OCB), 2017). Also, they make access to credit easier and less onerous by reinvesting (or distributing) surplus, which positively affects members, employees, society and the local economy (Bauer, Miles, & Nishikawa, 2009; Bialoskorski Neto, Barroso, & Rezende, 2012).

The structural organization of credit unions can take place through Central Credit Unions, Credit Union Confederations, or Credit Union Banks, in order to achieve a staggered increase in their activities, not oriented towards profit but rather to values, which include meeting the needs of its members by providing services and products (Brasil, 2009; Duguid & Balkan, 2016). However, they are inserted in a competitive environment and depend on the positive results of their activities (surplus) in order to fulfill their social role. This context demands best practices in accountability to members and stakeholder engagement, encompassing the disclosure of socioenvironmental risks (International Cooperative Alliance (ICA), 2015).

It is worth stressing that credit unions are guided by the 7 Cooperative Principles, which reinforces the socioenvironmental emphasis of these Financial Institutions. The Rochdale Principles are accepted worldwide among cooperatives and were published by the International Cooperative Alliance (2015), namely: 1) voluntary and open membership, 2) democratic member control, 3) economic participation, 4) autonomy and independence, 5) education, training and information, 6) cooperation among cooperatives, and 7) concern for the community. It is important to highlight that the 5th and the 7th Rochdale principles set forth that credit unions shall disclose information to stakeholders.

Credit unions, just as other Financial Institutions, are exposed to the risks of the financial industry and to the socioenvironmental risks inherent in the relationship with members, employees, organizations located in the credit union's area of operation, and society; therefore, they must comply with BACEN resolutions (2014), which include disclosing socioenvironmental risks to stakeholders.

Socioenvironmental risk is the possibility of an event related to environmental or social aspects occurring and preventing an organization from reaching its goals. Socioenvironmental risks have a

Figure 1. Socioenvironmental risks of Financial Institutions.
Source: designed from FEBRABAN, 2015; Nogueira et al., 2015; Sanchéz, 2011.

macroeconomic or microeconomic nature, are intrinsic of any enterprise and may be manageable or not (Carroll & Sabhama, 2010). Sánchez (2011) defined socioenvironmental risks as those arising from adverse (undesired) effects on health (human life), environment and material goods.

BACEN's report (2014) reinforced the need to manage socioenvironmental risks at credit unions, whether for compliance with the law or to foster CSR practices for stakeholders by these institutions. The socioenvironmental risks of credit unions may be classified into direct and indirect, which derive from their activities, as shown in Figure 1.

Due to the nature of their economic activities, Financial Institutions do not cause significant direct socioenvironmental impacts; however, this is not the case for indirect socioenvironmental risks (resulting from financial intermediation services), which have the capacity to escalate impact and may affect all economic sectors (systemic crisis), consequently impacting the whole society. Given the existence of joint and several liability in Brazil (1981), should a credit union member cause social or environmental impacts, the credit union may incur a socioenvironmental risk. This highlights the importance of creating mechanisms to mitigate indirect socioenvironmental risks (FEBRABAN, 2015; Nogueira et. al., 2015; Sanchéz, 2011; Weber, 2017).

To identify socioenvironmental risks at Financial Institutions, including credit unions, it is necessary to compile information about client profiles (company size, number of employees, economic sector, and others), because socioenvironmental risks impact a variety of segments at different degrees. Stakeholder engagement may assist in this step (FEBRABAN, 2015; Sánchez, 2011).

At Financial Institutions, indirect socioenvironmental risk is associated with financial variables such as liquidity, default and extending credit because, by preventing such risks organizations reach their goal of maximizing capital and providing investors and society with security (Guimarães, 2015; Nogueira et al., 2015). However, at credit unions, there is still concern about maximizing the socioenvironmental value, which is one of their specificities (Fuller, 1998; Goddard, Mckillop & Wilson, 2008).

MAIN FOCUS OF THE CHAPTER

This is a descriptive and single case study (Yin, 2010), carried out at the Sicredi Credit Union System, known as Sicredi for short, headquartered in the city of Porto Alegre, in the state of Rio Grande do Sul, Brazil. Sicredi was founded in 1902 in the city of Nova Petrópolis, also in the state of Rio Grande do Sul. In 2016, it featured over 3.6 million members, 24.3 thousand employees, 117 affiliated credit unions, and more than 1,500 points of service (Sustainability Report, 2017), in 21 Brazilian states.

Given its structural organization, Sicredi operates through a Credit Union Bank, Credit Union Confederations, Central Credit Unions, and Single Credit (all of these credit unions comprise the Sicredi Credit Union System). It is noteworthy that it is Sicredi (the case under study) that devises and implements the socioenvironmental (PRSA, 2015) and socioenvironmental risk policies that are disseminated to the other levels of its credit union structure.

In addition to investigating the Sicredi case, this study also collected primary data on socioenvironmental risks from the Central Bank of Brazil (BACEN), which is an autonomous federal agency, safe keeper of Brazil's values and member of the National Financial System. Among the main attributions of the Central Bank are: keeping inflation under control, assuring a solid and efficient financial system, monitoring other banks (Bank of Banks), and issuing currency. BACEN was responsible for publishing Resolution 4327/2014, which made it compulsory for credit unions to devise a socioenvironmental responsibility policy and disclose socioenvironmental risks.

The research data were collected from primary sources (semi-structured interview with Sicredi's superintendent on March 5, 2018 and with the supervisor of the Central Bank of Brazil on April 23, 2018), as well as secondary sources (Sicredi's reports: 2015 Socioenvironmental Responsibility Policy, 2017 Risk Management Structure, 2017 Financial Statements, and 2017 Sustainability Report).

Both interviews were held via Skype®, and the interviewees gave their free and informed consent. Sicredi's interviewee works in the socioenvironmental risk field and has a degree in Economics. BACEN's supervisor holds a master's degree in Accounting from the University of São Paulo (USP) and has worked at BACEN since 2003; some of his roles include supervising and implementing BACEN (2014) at credit unions. Both interviewees proved to have knowledge on the subject under investigation, and their discourses express personal opinions based on past and current experiences and do not reflect the opinions and stances of the institutions and organizations for which they work.

The research protocol for the semi-structured interviews was validated by three masters and four PhDs from the accounting field, who attempted to identify ambiguous questions or those that did not contribute to meet the objectives. The script of the semi-structured interviews is displayed in Table 2.

The documents (secondary sources) were collected on January 15, 2018 at the Sicredi website and are public domain (Table 3):

Primary and secondary data were treated using the content analysis technique (Bardin, 2016). To define the analysis categories and units of the Content Analysis (Table 4), this study employed: TBL as proposed by Elkington (2012), the stakeholders referred to by Clarkson (1995), and the types of socioenvironmental risks of Financial Institutions addressed by Nogueira et. al (2015), Sanchéz (2011).

To support the analysis categories and units established herein, this research resorted to Archel, Fernández & Larrinaga (2008) and Mathuva, Mboya & McFie (2017), who analyzed socioenvironmental disclosure based on the TBL proposed by Elkington (2012). The groups of stakeholders referred to by Clarkson (1995) were applied to the studies conducted by Barakat et al., (2017) and Tilling (2004). The categories of socioenvironmental risks were approached by Sanchéz (2011) and Nogueira et al. (2015)

Table 2. Script for the semi-structured interview with Sicredi's superintendent and BACEN's supervisor.

Question	Content Analysis Categories	References
Script for the interview with Sicredi's superintendent		
Block I		
Identification of the respondent's profile and his work on Sicredi's socioenvironmental risks.		
Block II		
1. What do you understand by socioenvironmental risks?	Identification of Socioenvironmental Risks.	BACEN (2014), FEBRABAN (2015), Ribeiro & Martins (1993).Sanchéz (2011), Wood (1991).
2. Which groups of stakeholders does Sicredi consider to be affected by its activities?		
3. How do you identify socioenvironmental risks?		
4. How is the process of disclosing socioenvironmental risks to stakeholders?	Disclosure of Socioenvironmental Risks.	BACEN (2014); Carroll (1979, 2015). FEBRABAN (2015)
5. How does the disclosure of socioenvironmental risks relate to CSR?		
6. How was the process of drafting the Socioenvironmental Responsibility Policy?	Specificities of Credit Unions.	BACEN (2014); Decker (2004); Fuller (1998); Mahajan (1981); Rymza (2015); Simmons & Birchall (2008);
7. Which factors influence Sicredi Confederation's disclosure of socioenvironmental risks?		
Script for the interview with BACEN's supervisor		
Block I		
Identification of the respondent's profile and his work on BACEN's socioenvironmental risks.		
Block II		
1. Why was Brazil the first country to make the disclosure of socioenvironmental risks compulsory?	Disclosure of Socioenvironmental Risks	BACEN (2014); Bressan et al. (2011); Decker (2004); FEBRABAN (2015); Fuller (1998); Mahajan (1981); Rymza (2015); Simmons & Birchall (2008)
2. How does the disclosure of socioenvironmental risks relate to CSR?		
3. How can the process of disclosing socioenvironmental risks be taken as a stakeholder engagement practice?		
4. Do the specificities of credit unions (constituted by members, oriented toward satisfying members, democracy, surplus, etc.) influence the disclosure of socioenvironmental risks?	Specificities of Credit Unions	BACEN (2014); Carroll (1979, 2015)

Source: designed by the authors themselves.

Table 3. Analyzed secondary sources.

Title	Year	Nature	Description
Política de Responsabilidade Socioambiental [Socioenvironmental Responsibility Policy] (PRSA, 2015).	2015	Compulsory	Established principles and guidelines that orient best socioenvironmental practices (including socioenvironmental risk management).
Estrutura de Gerenciamento de Riscos Pilar III [Risk Management Structure Pillar III] (EGR, 2017)	2017		Meets BACEN's requirements (Circular 3.678/13). It addresses risk management and presents the main procedures on risk management.
Demonstrações Financeiras Padronizadas [Standardized Financial Statements] (DFP, 2017).	2016		Encompass compulsory statements. Emphasis was given to explanatory notes (risk disclosure).
Relatório de Sustentabilidade [Sustainability Report] (RS, 2017).	2016	Voluntary	Complied with GRI guidelines (G4), and the indicators followed 3 themes: CSR, stakeholder relationship, and socioenvironmental risks. It covers Sicredi's operations and business model (01/01/2016 to 31/12/2016).

Source: designed by the authors themselves.

Table 4. Analysis categories and units of the content analysis

Socio environmental Risks		Stakeholders					
		Member (investor) (consumer)	Employee	Supplier	Government	Community	Media
		(A)	(B)	(C)	(D)	(E)	(F)
Direct							
TBL	Environmental						
	Economic						
	Social						
Indirect							
TBL	Environmental						
	Economic						
	Social						

Source: designed from BACEN (2014), Clarkson (2015), Elkington (2012), FEBRABAN (2015)

Table 5. Operationalization of content categories and units

Categories		Operationalization Description on ATLAS.ti
Corporate Social Responsibility	Direct Socioenvironmental Risk	Excerpts from the analyzed sources were selected, specifically those containing the word 'risk' or correlated ones, such as: impact, uncertainty, lack, decrease, low, damages, harmful, affect, dangerous, bad. Additionally, they had to fit in one of the TBL categories (environmental, economic and social).
	Indirect Socioenvironmental Risk	Besides characterizing Socioenvironmental Risk, the excerpts should contain the word 'indirect' (before or after).
	Environmental	Excerpts containing descriptions about a) critical natural capital and b) renewable natural capital were highlighted. Similar terms: natural, nature, environmental, environment, critical, renewable and natural resources.
	Economic	Excerpts containing descriptions about the economic pillar (represented by profit or production factors) were highlighted. Guiding terms were: economic activities, profitability, income, money, Capital, machines, product, services, production, surplus, profits, economy, Gross Domestic Product (GDP), loans, financing, financial, cash flow.
	Social	Excerpts containing descriptions of human capital were highlighted. In addition to the term 'social', correlate ones were considered: health, skills, education, job, minorities, human rights and women's rights.
Analysis Units		**Operationalization Description**
Stakeholder Engagement	Members	The highlighted excerpts about socioenvironmental risks should also contain these terms: union members, associates, consumers, investors, owners, partner, member.
	Employees	The highlighted excerpts about socioenvironmental risks should also contain these terms: employees, collaborators, human capital.
	Suppliers	The highlighted excerpts about socioenvironmental risks should also contain the terms: suppliers, producer, carrier. It is worth underscoring that this study considered Suppliers of Materials for Credit Unions (such as paper, disposable cups, coffee, etc.). Union members' suppliers were not included (within the members' value chain).
	Government	The highlighted excerpts about socioenvironmental risks should contain these terms: government, Union, State, Municipalities, public administration, policies, legislation, regulation, Central Bank of Brazil.
	Community	The highlighted excerpts about socioenvironmental risks should contain these terms: community, society, public, people.
	Media	The highlighted excerpts about socioenvironmental risks should contain these terms: media, communication, social networks, television, radio, internet.

Source: designed from BACEN (2014), Clarkson (2015), Elkington (2012), FEBRABAN (2015).

(direct and indirect socioenvironmental risks) and match the ones described by BACEN (2014) and FEBRABAN (2015).

The operationalization of analysis categories and units had the aid of ATLAS.ti software, version 8, and encoding (codes) was guided by the following precepts (Table 5):

After encoding all excerpts from the primary and secondary sources on ATLAS.ti software, based on Table 5, triangulation was performed – that is, a confrontation between findings and theoretical perspectives, allowing the researchers to make inferences (Yin, 2010).

RESULTS AND DISCUSSION

The presentation of study results is organized into groups of stakeholders related to socioenvironmental risk, mechanisms to identify and disclose socioenvironmental risks, examples of CSR practices enabled by the identification and disclosure of socioenvironmental risks, and, finally, discussion of results.

Groups of Stakeholders Related to Socioenvironmental Risks

Socioenvironmental risks were disclosed by means of qualitative information (narratives and descriptions) or quantitative information (indicators from the Global Reporting Initiative –

GRI (version 4), risk measurements, rates, and others). The groups of stakeholders included in Sicredi's socioenvironmental risk disclosure were: members, employees, government, communities and the media. Considering the collection instrument, direct socioenvironmental risks were the most frequently mentioned, and indirect socioenvironmental risks (derived from financial intermediation services) were the least recurrent. On the other hand, the specificities of credit unions (democracy and autonomy, surplus destination, cooperative education, promotion of cooperative culture) were related to socioenvironmental risk factors.

Sicredi considers as groups of stakeholders: "its internal audience, members, institutional partners, suppliers, regulatory and supervisory agents, the government, class associations and the community" (Socioenvironmental Responsibility Policy, 2015, p. 3). Other stakeholders included in the reports were external consultants (Sustainability Report, 2017, p. 6) and universities (Sustainability Report, 2017, p. 37, 86); however, no socioenvironmental risks, which are object of this study, were listed.

The Members group of stakeholders (investors and consumers in Clarkson, [1995]) was included in the following categories: Direct Risk (social, environmental and economic) and Indirect Risk (social and economic). Although, in secondary sources, no information about the indirect socioenvironmental risk of the environmental pillar has been provided, only the Sustainability Report (2017, p. 7) states: "the environment theme is fundamental to our indirect impact".

Employees (or collaborators) comprise the second most recurrent group of stakeholders on the analyzed reports. Nevertheless, no information has been provided about indirect socioenvironmental risks, only direct ones (social and economic). The Government stakeholder was identified in economic socioenvironmental risks (direct and indirect), whereas the social and environmental pillars were not addressed.

The Communities (or society) stakeholder was related only to direct socioenvironmental risks (environmental and economic). The Media stakeholder was identified only in Direct Economic Socioenvironmental Risks.

Table 6 presents a synthesis of results found.

No environmental risks related to the Supplier group of stakeholders were disclosed. However, socioenvironmental information and engagement practices for this group were included in the analyzed reports, namely: search for improving supplier management (Sustainability Report, 2017, p. 9), priority of hiring Suppliers that are also members. In 2016, 26% of the suppliers were from cities whose populations were smaller than 200,000 inhabitants (Sustainability Report, 2017, p. 87). Such aspects were not considered as risks.

The analyzed results showed that direct socioenvironmental risks, especially social and economic ones, were the most frequently disclosed. In contrast, indirect socioenvironmental risks, for employees and suppliers, were not even mentioned. These findings contradict Stakeholder Theory, which emphasizes that socioenvironmental risks have the capacity to escalate impact because they derive from financial intermediation services (a credit union's main activity).

Identification and Disclosure of Socioenvironmental Risks

Sicredi defined socioenvironmental risk on its reports as "the possibility of institutions suffering losses resulting from socioenvironmental damages" (Socioenvironmental Responsibility Policy, 2015, p. 3) and that analyses must assess "the associate's compliance with the environmental and social legislation in force, the risks of the industry and the associate's capacity to manage them and seize opportunities" (Socioenvironmental Responsibility Policy, 2015, p. 3). In his interview, Sicredi's superintendent described socioenvironmental risk as any type of impact that Sicredi may suffer, directly or indirectly, as a result of social or environmental matters, similarly to Carroll & Shabama (2010), FEBRABAN (2015), Sánchez (2011) and Weber (2017).

About the identification of Sicredi's environmental risks, the credit union's superintendent highlighted three types of processes (Table 7):

As for Sicredi's disclosure of socioenvironmental risks, it is internal and/or external, according to the superintendent (Table 8):

Analyzing Table 8, it is possible to infer that BACEN (2014) promoted changes within Sicredi's scope and that the process of socioenvironmental disclosure needs further enhancement. It is worth pointing out that compulsory disclosure of socioenvironmental risks is a recent theme in the Brazilian scenario (from 2014), even though the country was the first to institute such a requirement (FEBRABAN, 2015). An excerpt from the interview with BACEN's supervisor illustrates this evidence:

Brazil, for this leadership [...], in environmental terms, brought this (socioenvironmental risk) as a conversation topic to the Financial Institution business. European and North American entities do not have that as a compulsory thing, the enforcement of a policy, but they are way ahead of us in the sense that this comes from the Financial Institutions themselves. It has already been identified as a risk situation, and the Institutions have already incorporated this socioenvironmental issue. And, in Brazil, what we see is that this does not happen like that, [...] despite having been required compulsorily.

The proactivity of European and North American organizations is aligned with the ethical and philanthropic responsibilities discussed by Carroll (1979), while, in Brazil, such a practice would initially fit into legal responsibility. Compliance is considered a CSR practice and stakeholder engagement. Sicredi, even though it is forced to disclose this information, may also turn this requirement into an opportunity for CSR practices, generating socioenvironmental value and mitigating socioenvironmental losses to stakeholders.

Table 6. Overall Synthesis of Results for the Content Analysis

Group of Stakeholders	Socioenvironmental Risk	Indicators	Triangulation	
			Analyzed Source	References
Members (investors) (consumers) (A)	Direct Environmental	Ecoefficient Management at Agencies Failure to comply with environmental laws Droughts Ecological disasters	Documental Analysis BACEN Interview Sicredi Interview	FEBRABAN (2015), Nogueira et al. (2015), Sanchéz (2011), PRSA (2015, p.2), Ribeiro & Martins (1993);
	Direct Economic	Credit Risk Economic loss Surplus destination Provision for liabilities and litigations Operational Risk Market Risk Liquidity Risk Legal Risk Reputation and Image Risk Risk Management Costs	Documental Analysis Sicredi Interview BACEN Interview	Bialoskorski Neto et al.(2012), Carroll (1999), Carroll & Shabana (2010), Decker (2004), DFP (2017, p. 3, 13, 30, 36, 45, 46 47, 48), EGR (2017 p. 2, 15-39), Elkington (2012), Elshahat, Hessou & Lai (2017), FEBRABAN (2015), Fatemi et. al (2015), Fuller (1998), GRI (2017), Goodard et al (2008), Kurucz et. al. (2008), Mahajan (1981), Mcguire et. al (1998), Nogueira et al. (2015), RS (2017, p. 3, 8, 9, 41. 65, 76, 77), Ribeiro & Martins (1993), Sanchéz(2011).
	Direct Social	Democracy Communication Profile diversity (NP and LP) Conflicts due to new standards (requirements) Lack of natural resources	Documental Analysis Sicredi Interview BACEN Interview	Barakat et al (2017), Chia (2011), Clarkson (1995), Deegan (2017), Elkington (2012), FEBRABAN (2015), Gray (2001), Mathuva et al. (2017), PRSA (2015, p.2), Rymsza (2015), RS (2017, p. 34), Weber (2017).
	Indirect Environmental	Failure to comply with the demarcation of permanent preservation areas (PPA) Impacts to Agribusiness Environmental bans Illegal deforestation	Documental Analysis Sicredi Interview BACEN Interview	Brasil (1981), Ribeiro & Martins (1993), Sanchéz (2011,2017).
	Indirect Economic	Indirect impact of products Economic losses with fines, sanctions Harvest losses due to fires Financial losses	Documental Analysis Sicredi Interview BACEN Interview	Decker(2004) , FEBRABAN (2015), Fuller (1998), Kurucz et al. (2008), Nogueira et. al., (2015), RS(2017, p.7), Simmons & Birchall(2008), Weber (2017)
	Indirect Social	Indirect impact of products Conflicts between associates and public/ social organs or entities	Documental Analysis Sicredi Interview BACEN Interview	Decker(2004), FEBRABAN (2015), Fuller (1998), RS(2017, p.7), Nogueira et. al., (2015), Sanchéz (2011), Simmons & Birchall(2008)
Employees (B)	Direct Environmental	Jobs lost to droughts	BACEN Interview	Bialoskorski Neto et al. (2012), ICA (2015)

continued on following page

Table 6. Continued

Group of Stakeholders	Socioenvironmental Risk	Indicators	Triangulation	
			Analyzed Source	References
Employees (B)	Direct Economic	Labor actions Use of financial resources Relationship with associates and communities	Documental Analysis Sicredi Interview BACEN Interview	Carroll (1979, 1999), Decker (2004), Elkington (2012), FEBRABAN (2015), Nogueira et. al., (2015), PRSA (2015, p. 4), Sanchéz (2011).
	Direct Social	Health Organizational climate Compensation Turnover rate Neglected education	Documental Analysis BACEN Interview	Clarkson (1995), Elkington (2012), GRI (2016), Nogueira et al. (2015), RS (2017,p. 49,50, 52, 54-57)
	Indirect Environmental	None		
	Indirect Economic	None		
	Indirect Social	None		
Suppliers (C)	Direct Environmental	None		
	Direct Economic	None		
	Direct Social	None		
	Indirect Environmental	None		
	Indirect Economic	None		
	Indirect Social	None		
Government (D)	Direct Environmental	• Discussion on the Forest Code • Biome-Preserving Entities • Agribusiness entities	Sicredi Interview	Brasil (1981), Ribeiro & Martins (1993), Sanchéz (2011, 2017)
	Direct Economic	• Economic crisis • GDP retraction • Basel indicators • Regulatory risk	Documental Analysis Sicredi Interview BACEN Interview	Carroll (1979, 1999), DFP (2017, p. 49), EGR (2017, p. 3), FEBRABAN (2015), Kalapodas & Thomson (2006), Nogueira et al. (2015), RS (2017, p. 4),
	Direct Social	• Fight against slave labor • Funding of activities concerning tobacco, alcohol and non-certified wood	Sicredi Interview	Elkington (2012), FEBRABAN (2015)
	Indirect Environmental	None		
	Indirect Economic	• Sectorial norms • Losses reducing investments in society	Documental Analysis Sicredi Interview	BACEN (2014), Bialoskorski Neto et al. (2012) FEBRABAN (2015), Nogueira et al (2015), Barakat et al. (2017), Hessou & Lai (2017), ICA(2015), RS (2017), Rymza (2015)
	Indirect Social	None		
Community (E)	Direct Environmental	• CO^2 emission • Use of paper • Energy consumption • Loss of productive capacity	Documental Analysis Sicredi Interview BACEN Interview	FEBRABAN (2015), Nogueira et al. (2015), RS (2017, p. 7), Sanchéz (2011)

continued on following page

Table 6. Continued

Group of Stakeholders	Socioenvironmental Risk	Indicators	Triangulation	
			Analyzed Source	References
Community (E)	Direct Economic	• Use of financial resources • Financial inclusion • Disregard for society's expectations • Business losses	Documental Analysis Sicredi Interview BACEN Interview	Carroll (1979, 1999), Elkington (2012), Fuller (1998), Goddard et al. (2008), Kurucz et al. (2008), ICA (2015), Nogueira et al. (2015), Ribeiro & Martins (1993), PRSA (2015, p. 2, 4), RS (2017, p. 86), Sanchéz (2011).
	Direct Social	• Conflicts between associates and natives and *quilombolas [inhabitants of rural communities populated by the descendants of runaway slaves]* • Fauna and flora losses	Sicredi Interview BACEN Interview	Carroll (1979,1999), Decker (2004), Fuller (1998), GRI (2016), Kurucz et al. (2008), Simmons & Birchall (2008)
	Indirect Environmental	• Incorrect waste disposal • Demographic impact due to production or activity (uncommon at cooperatives)	BACEN Interview	Carroll (1979,1999), Fuller (1998), Kurucz et al. (2008), Simmons & Birchall (2008).
	Indirect Economic	• Financial losses reducing investments in society	Sicredi Interview	Bialokorski Neto et. al (2012), ICA (2015)
	Indirect Social	• Interdiction of places • Impacts caused by funded activities • Conflicts caused in indigenous areas or *quilombolas*	Sicredi Interview	Bialokorski Neto et. al (2012), Carroll (1979,1999), Decker (2004), ICA (2015), Kurucz et al. (2008), Simmons & Birchall (2008)
Media (F)	Direct Environmental	None		
	Direct Economic	• Risk perception at Fitch and Moody's • Damages (loss of value) to the Sicredi brand	Documental Analysis Sicredi Interview	Freeman et. al (2010), GRI (2016), Kurucz et al (2008), RS (2017, p. 93), Tilling (2004)
	Direct Social	• It integrates Sicredi's Strategic Planning	Sicredi Interview	Kurucz et al (2008), RS (2017, p. 93), Tilling (2004)
	Indirect Environmental	None		
	Indirect Economic	• Damages (loss of value) to the Sicredi brand due to associates' actions	Sicredi Interview	Freeman et. al (2010), RS (2017, p. 93), Tilling (2004)
	Indirect Social	• Damages (credibility) to the Sicredi brand due to associates' actions	Sicredi Interview	RS (2017, p. 93), Tilling (2004)

Source: designed by the authors themselves with study data.

Table 7. Ways of disclosing socioenvironmental risks at Sicredi.

Identification	Process Description	Triangulation
1) Identification of credit union members' profiles	Questionnaire application to members (14 questions) in 21 Brazilian states, which made it possible to design the Risk Map. Members were classified according to industry of operation and the socioenvironmental characteristics of the geographical region.	Barakat et al. (2017); Carroll & Shabama, 2010; Sanchéz (2011); Sustainability Report (2017).
2) Granting credit blocked or hindered	Based on the borrower's socioenvironmental characteristics, rather than the geographical region. A checklist is applied. Block situations mentioned: being included on lists of slave-like labor, producing in banned areas, and violating environmental laws.	Sustainability Report (2017); Socioenvironmental Responsibility Policy (2015).
3) Geodesic coordinates – Georeferencing	Applied to decision making involving rural credit. It aims to prevent or limit rural funding in specific regions and biomes.	Sustainability Report (2017); Hessou & Lai (2017) and Sanchéz (2011).

Source: designed from the interview with Sicredi's superintendent.

Table 8. Ways of disclosing socioenvironmental risks at Sicredi

Disclosure	Level	Examples
External	Advanced	Sustainability Report (4 years) and biannual gadgets to the World Bank (statistical data).
Internal (from the Confederation to Central Cooperatives and Single Cooperatives)	Intermediate	Reports from the Confederation to single cooperatives, explaining how the socioenvironmental risk is affecting Sicredi, as well as risk mitigation tools. Internal crossings, such as applied questionnaires x non-applied questionnaires
Internal and External (Accounting records - FEBRABAN SARB 14)	Incipient	Accounting records on likely socioenvironmental impact. Despite existing, they are isolated cases, very irrelevant and small.

Source: designed from the interview with Sicredi's superintendent.

Examples of CSR Practices Enabled by the Identification of Socioenvironmental Risks.

In the interview with Sicredi, examples of CSR practices resulting from identification of socioenvironmental risks were provided, as shown in Table 9:

With respect to the cooperative nature and socioenvironmental risks, BACEN's supervisor argued that:

Furthermore, and this is the great benefit, so to speak, that, when you have a cooperative, comparatively to other institutions, the Cooperative System is one step ahead because it already has a social standpoint, which is way greater than that of other Financial Institutions, and this can be very positive.

By triangulating primary sources, secondary sources and theory, it was possible to infer that the specificities of the credit union influence the management of socioenvironmental risks (Duguid & Balkan, 2016, Decker, 2004; Rymza, 2015).

FEBRABAN (2015) also addressed cuts to tobacco funding as a CSR practice. Sicredi's interviewee described how the credit union has acted in these cases:

In the case of tobacco, we have 2 specific regions. They are small for the credit unions but are used for growing tobacco; one of them is in Rio Grande do Sul, and the other one, in Paraná. So, these regions have a relevant number of associates. What we did at those meetings was this: keep a policy that is gradual, that, over time, encourages those Associates to quit this activity. This takes 10, 15 years.

Table 9. Specificities of Cooperatives and CSR practices involving socioenvironmental risks

Corporate Social Responsibility Practice	Specificities of Credit Unions
Blocks against Borrowers with their names on lists of slave-like labor	Concern for Community
Banned areas (or environmental fines)	
Restrictions by international organs, which limit portfolios – e.g., for tobacco.	
Limit financing for production at an Integral Protection Conservation Unit, a national park, a biosphere reserve.	
Limit loans in Areas belonging to natives or *quilombolas*, that have demarcation of indigenous lands or have a process underway.	
Limit loans in Production conservation units (Environmental Conservation Areas) or Areas of Relevant Ecological Interest.	
Not finance production in contaminated lands and eroded regions.	
Transparency, which consists of providing proper and timely information to the relevant audience, strengthening the cooperative culture.	Education, training and information Concern for Community
Financial inclusion.	Economic participation Concern for community
Prioritization of activities with positive impact on the value chain.	
Fight against fraud and corruption.	Economic participation
Management of Agencies' Ecoefficiency.	
Meetings with members to define means for implementing the socioenvironmental policy.	Participation and Democratic Management

Source: designed by the authors themselves, with study data.

After giving examples on how socioenvironmental risks may corroborate society's environmental issues, Sicredi's superintendent identified, during the interview, an example on factors linked to the social realm:

Today we have been looking at the other side of the prism, that is, looking at this in a different way, because I would not like to have a 10-year-old child working there, or I would not like to have the river bank eroding as the riparian forest disappears, which sometimes is 2-3-5 meters, right? With a simple way, you protect and make your property more productive.

Sicredi's interviewee talked about how the credit union carries out CSR practices by means of socioenvironmental risk management:

Our role here is to spread more and more practices that we consider/judge as correct, so that this somehow permeates an environment in the everyday life of our associates. How do we do that? Sometimes we do it simply through conflict, so, if something is illegal, for us, we have little tolerance; even if the norm was released yesterday, today, or a year ago, if we say it is prohibited, for example, to grow things on the banks of river A, B or C, we cut funds. (...)

It is worth stressing that Sicredi has considered socioenvironmental disclosure as a practice of stakeholder engagement by means of its Mission and Value (Sustainability Report, 2017, p. 11), which state that the cooperative system values the relationship with members and contributes to improving the quality of life of associates and society. The need for society to recognize that Sicredi operates under such prescriptions and to have access to socioenvironmental information (Sustainability Report, 2017, p.11) corroborates with Chia (2011) and Milani Filho (2007).

A characteristic of credit unions is their orientation to maximization of value for members, who are among their stakeholders (Decker, 2004; Fuller, 1998; Goddard et. al, 2008). The reports brought evidence about stakeholder engagement, for instance: a) they were consulted as to the definition of material themes, and b) there is a channel for comments, feedback and suggestions (Sustainability Report, 2017, p. 6). Such practices are considered as stakeholder engagement (FEBRABAN, 2015; Freeman et. al, 2010).

Another evidence of stakeholder engagement was the contacts made with BACEN (supervision aspects) and with the International Finance Cooperation for the implementation of the socioenvironmental risk norm. The contact with the International Finance Corporation corroborated with indicators geared toward socioenvironmental risk assessment (Sustainability Report, 2017, p. 78). It is worth highlighting that the socioenvironmental risk norm (Socioenvironmental Risk Policy, 2015) was drafted in pilot format because the enhancement of socioenvironmental risk management involves identifying the profile of Sicredi Confederation's members (Barakat, et. al, 2017).

It is important to note that BACEN (2014) and FEBRABAN (2015) argue that stakeholder engagement is inherent of the process of identifying, mitigating, managing and disclosing socioenvironmental risks. Here is an example of socioenvironmental risk mitigation at Sicredi, promoted by stakeholder engagement (Sicredi, members, local community and government):

In Paraná itself, there is an Environmental Conservation Area (ECA) called Environmental Conservation Area of Ilhas e Várzeas do Rio Paraná, located near Ilha Grande National Park. [...] This Environmental Conservation Area has 1 million hectares. So we have 4 Sicredi cooperatives within the Environmental Conservation Area, […] About 2 months ago, we visited the Environmental Conservation Area and had an actual meeting with the local community, the city government, the Paraná Institute of Technical Assistance and Rural Extension [Instituto Paranaense de Assistência Técnica e Extensão Rural] (EMATER), the Brazilian Agricultural Research Corporation [Empresa Brasileira de Pesquisa Agropecuária] (EMBRAPA), the Chico Mendes Institute of Biodiversity Conservation [Instituto Chico Mendes de Conservação da Biodiversidade] (ICMBio), […] This is what we did: last year, we blocked funding within that area for about 2 weeks, […] then we reached out to the environmental organ, which said, 'no, it is fine, release it, but under this and this conditions' […] we reached an environmental agreement to keep production and obviously, not to impair the city's Gross Domestic Product (GDP), but also looking at specific things. […] Without this dialogue, and that is obviously what we want, we would have been given a 'no' and a 'yes', and production within the region would have come to an end, with the possibility of a series of impacts, not only to our image, but legal as well.

These results reveal that the identification and disclosure of socioenvironmental risks involved Corporate Social Responsibility practices. These practices contribute to reducing Sicredi's exposure to socioenvironmental risks and help the cooperative fulfill its social and legal roles, since the materialization of these risks may cause financial losses to members, to the National Financial System and to society.

FUTURE RESEARCH DIRECTIONS

This section was structured based on the results obtained and considering the theoretical perspectives employed. It is designed to relate implications of this study for future research.

One of the discoveries of this study was that the Suppliers stakeholder group was not linked to socioenvironmental risks at Sicredi. Nevertheless, in the literature, Suppliers, can affect or be affected by credit union activities. Porter & Kramer (2006) noted that any organization that operates in the socioenvironmental field must consider the impact of the value chain, which includes the impacts of Suppliers. In that regard, this study can corroborate to perfect Sicredi disclosures (inclusion of socioenvironmental risks indicators related to Suppliers). It should be highlighted that it was mentioned that in RS (2017) Sicredi gives priority to contracting sustainable suppliers, which may mean that Suppliers can also be sources of socioenvironmental risks.

The Sicredi superintendent stated that the practice of identifying socioenvironmental risks led to engagement with stakeholders. He mentioned meetings with members, discussions with government entities such as the International Finance Corporation, and communications geared towards Employees. Considering these evidences, this study contributed to advance Stakeholder Theory by identifying engagement practices with stakeholders among primary and secondary sources, as well as information directed to stakeholders.

Socioenvironmental risks can change according to the portfolio profile of credit union customers – members will be more or less exposed to socioenvironmental risks depending on the economic sector in which the member operates. Nevertheless, Table 4, which features a model to support content analysis, and Table 6, which compiled socioenvironmental risk indicators, can be used to analyze the disclosure of socioenvironmental risks by other credit unions and be adapted according to their reality. Moreover, it can promote debate at Sicredi contribute for future disclosures in reports.

The research aided the literature on the mechanisms to identify socioenvironmental risks by highlighting practices by Sicredi such as: use of checklists, portfolio risk map, and georeferencing. Future studies may be able to detect different or similar practices in the process of identifying socioenvironmental risks and compare them to the findings of this study.

With regard to Corporate Social Responsibility, this study contributed to the literature by demonstrating that Sicredi considered the impacts of its decisions on local communities, met the legal disclosure requirements set by BACEN concerning socioenvironmental risks, and promoted socioenvironmental education in ecological parks.

CONCLUSION

The objective of this study was to investigate which groups of stakeholders were included in the disclosure of socioenvironmental risks by the Sicredi. Results evidenced that stakeholders – members, employees, government, community and the media – were included in Sicredi's disclosure of socioenvironmental risks.

CSR and socioenvironmental risk themes have gained importance in the realm of Brazilian credit unions, particularly after the enactment of Brazilian Central Bank Resolution no. 4327/2014. The results of this study demonstrated that the disclosure of socioenvironmental risks by Sicredi can still be perfected to include other stakeholders and consequently outros types of socioenvironmental risks (direct and indirect).

The literature on socioenvironmental risk disclosure by credit unions is still emerging. Studies geared toward this field and CSR have the potential to contribute to society – by understanding how stakeholders are impacted, measures can be taken to prevent these impacts, corroborating to action on the Triple Bottom Line of Sustainable Development.

As a suggestion, future studies could track further publications by Sicredi Confederation, with the conduction of longitudinal researches. The main limitations concerned the method of data analysis (qualitative analysis), documents, and the choice of case. The qualitative analysis has limitations because only two participants were interviewed. The limitation of document analysis exists because it was a cross section and no data from other exercises (prior and subsequent) were compared. Because the case studied herein was chosen due to convenience, this study does not allow for generalization; therefore, the results refer only to Sicredi.

The originality of the research lies on it addressing credit unions and socioenvironmental risks simultaneously. The audience of this study may be the academy (scholars, professors, researchers and postgraduate students), practitioners (organizations), business managers, professionals from the financial industry, and Corporate Social Responsibility researchers.

REFERENCES

Almeida, R., Neumann, M., & Sanches, S. (2018). O que é evidenciado no Brasil sobre a Responsabilidade Social Corporativa advinda da Política Nacional de Resíduos Sólidos (PNRS) nos formulários de referência e Relatos Integrados? *Sociedade. Contabilidade e Gestão, 13*(3). doi:10.21446cg_ufrj.v13i3.13855

Archel, P., Fernadez, M., & Larrinaga, C. (2008). The organizational and operational boundaries of triple bottom line reporting: A survey. *Environmental Management, 41*(1), 106–117. doi:10.100700267-007-9029-7 PMID:17990022

Banco Central do Brasil. (2014). Resolução nº 4.327, de 25 de abril de 2014. Retrieved from http://www.bcb.gov.br/pre/normativos/res/2014/pdf/res_4327_v1_O.pdf

Barakat, S. R., Boaventura, J. M. G., & Polo, E. F. (2017). Alinhamento estratégico da responsabilidade social corporativa: Um estudo de caso no setor bancário brasileiro. *Revista Eletrônica de Administração, 86*(1), 206–233.

Bardin, L. (2016). Analise de Conteúdo. Edições 70.

Bauer, K. J., Miles, L. L., & Nishikawa, T. (2009). The effect of mergers on credit union performance. *Journal of Banking & Finance, 33*(12), 2267–2274. doi:10.1016/j.jbankfin.2009.06.004

Bialoskorski Neto, S., Barroso, M. F. G., & Rezende, A. J. (2012). Cooperative governance and management control systems: An agency costs theoretical approach. *Brazilian Business Review, 9*(2), 68–87. doi:10.15728/bbr.2012.9.2.4

Brasil. (1981). Lei nº 6.938, de 31 de agosto de 1981. Retrieved from http://www.planalto.gov.br/ccivil_03/leis/l6938.htm

Brasil. (2009). Lei Complementar nº 130, de 17 de abril de 2009. Retrieved from http://www.planalto.gov.br/ccivil_03/leis/LCP/Lcp130.htm

Brasileira dos Bancos, F. (FEBRABAN). (2015). Normativo SARB Nº 14 de 28 de agosto de 2014. Retrieved from: https://portal.febraban.org.br/pagina/3083/45/pt-br/prsa

Bressan, V. G. F., Braga, M. J., Bressan, A. A., & Resende Filho, M. A. (2011). Uma aplicação do sistema PEARLS às cooperativas de crédito brasileiras. *Revista de Administração da Universidade de São Paulo, São Paulo, 46*(3), 258–274.

Carroll, A. B. (1979). A three dimensional conceptual model of corporate social performance. *Academy of Management Review*, *16*(4), 497–505. doi:10.5465/amr.1979.4498296

Carroll, A. B. (1999). Corporate social responsibility: Evolution of a definitional construct. *Business & Society*, *38*(3), 268–295. doi:10.1177/000765039903800303

Carroll, A. B. (2015). Corporate social responsibility: The centerpiece of competing and complementary frameworks. *Organizational Dynamics*, *44*(2), 87–96. doi:10.1016/j.orgdyn.2015.02.002

Carroll, A. B., & Sabhama, K. M. (2010). The Business Case for Corporate Social Responsibility: A Review of Concepts, Research and Practice. *International Journal of Management Reviews*, *12*(1), 85–105. doi:10.1111/j.1468-2370.2009.00275.x

Chia, J. (2011). Communicating, connecting and developing social capital for sustainable organisations and their communities. *Australasian Journal of Regional Studies*, *17*(3), 330–351.

Clarkson, M. B. E. (1995). A Stakeholder Framework for Analyzing and Evaluating Corporate Social Performance. *Academy of Management Review*, *20*(1), 92–117. doi:10.5465/amr.1995.9503271994

Decker, O. S. (2004). Corporate social responsibility and structural change in financial services. *Managerial Auditing Journal*, *19*(6), 712–728. doi:10.1108/02686900410543840

Deegan, C. (2017). Twenty five years of social and environmental accounting research within critical perspectives of Accounting: Hits, misses and ways forward. *Critical Perspectives on Accounting*, *43*, 65–87. doi:10.1016/j.cpa.2016.06.005

Duguid, F. & Balkan, D. (2016). Talking the talk: canadian cooperatives and sustainability reporting. *Journal of cooperative accounting and reporting*, *4*(1), 1-34.

Elkington, J. (2012). *Sustentabilidade, canibais com garfo e faca*. São Paulo: M. Books do Brasil Editora Ltda.

Elshahat, A., Parhizgari, A., & Hong, L. (2012). The information content of the banking regulatory agencies and the depository credit intermediation institutions. *Journal of Economics and Business*, *64*(1), 90–104. doi:10.1016/j.jeconbus.2011.06.003

Fatemi, A., Fooladi, I., & Tehranian, H. (2015). Valuation effects of corporate social responsibility. *Journal of Banking & Finance*, *59*, 182–192. doi:10.1016/j.jbankfin.2015.04.028

Freeman, R. E., & Evan, W. (1990). Corporate governance: A stakeholder interpretation. *The Journal of Behavioral Economics*, *19*(4), 337–359. doi:10.1016/0090-5720(90)90022-Y

Freeman, R. E., Harrison, J., Wicks, A., Parmar, B., & De Colle, S. (2010). *Stakeholder theory the state of Art*. New York: Cambridge University Press. doi:10.1017/CBO9780511815768

Fuller, D. (1998). Credit union development: Financial inclusion and exclusion. *Geofonm*, *29*(2), 145–157.

Global Reporting Initiative (GRI). (2016). GRI: standards glossary. Retrieved from https://www.globalreporting.org/standards/media/1035/gri-standards-glossary-2016.pdf

Goddard, J., Mckillop, D., & Wilson, J. O. S. (2008). The diversification and financial performance of US credit unions. *Journal of Banking & Finance*, *32*(9), 1836–1849. doi:10.1016/j.jbankfin.2007.12.015

Gonçalves, R. M. L., & Braga, M. J. (2008). Determinantes de Risco de Liquidez em Cooperativas de Crédito: Uma Abordagem a partir do Modelo Logit Multinomial. *Revista de Administração Contemporânea*, *12*(4), 1019–1041. doi:10.1590/S1415-65552008000400007

Gray, R. (2001). Thirty years of social accounting, reporting, and auditing: What (if anything) have we learnt? *Business Ethics (Oxford, England)*, *10*(1), 9–15. doi:10.1111/1467-8608.00207

Guimarães, G. L. E. (2015). *Gerenciamento do risco socioambiental nas instituições financeiras bancárias no Brasil. Dissertação de Mestrado*. Universidade Federal de Brasília.

Hessou, H., & Lai, V. S. (2017). Basel III capital buffer requirements and credit union Prudential regulation: Canadian evidence. *Journal of Financial Stability*, *30*, 92–110. doi:10.1016/j.jfs.2017.05.002

International Cooperative Alliance (ICA). (2015). Guidance notes to the cooperative principles. Retrieved from https://ica.coop/sites/default/files/publication-files/ica-guidance-notes-en310629900.pdf

Kalapodas, E., & Thomson, M. E. (2006). Credit risk assessment: A challenge for financial institutions. *IMA Journal of Management Mathematics*, *17*(1), 25–46. doi:10.1093/imaman/dpi026

Kurucz, E. C., Colbert, B. A., & Wheeler, D. (2008). *The business case for corporate social responsibility*. Oxford: Oxford University Press.

Mahajan, Y. L. (1981). A Macro-Econometric Model of the Credit Unions. *Atlantic Economic Journal*, *9*(2), 40–48. doi:10.1007/BF02301207

Mathuva, D. M., Mboya, J. K., & McFie, J. B. (2017). Achieving legitimacy through cooperative governance and social and environmental disclosure by credit unions in a developing country. *Journal of Applied Accounting Research*, *18*(2), 162–184. doi:10.1108/JAAR-12-2014-0128

Mcguire, J. B., Sundgreen, A., & Schneewels, T. (1998). Corporate social responsibility and firm financial performance. *Academy of Management Journal*, *31*(4), 869–882.

Milani Filho, M. A. F. (2007). Responsabilidade Social e investimento social privado: Entre o discurso e a evidenciação. *Revista Contabilidade & Finanças*, *19*(47), 89–101. doi:10.1590/S1519-70772008000200008

Nogueira, J. M., Conceição, P. H. Z., & Imbroisi, D. (2015). Crédito bancário, risco ambiental e sustentabilidade empresarial: O caminho percorrido pelas instituições financeiras no Brasil. *Business and Management Review*, *4*(8), 734–744.

Organização das Cooperativas do Brasil (OCB). (2017). Site OCB, aba O que é Cooperativismo. Retrieved from http://www.somoscooperativismo.coop.br/#%2Fo-que-e-cooperativismo

Porter, M., & Kramer, M. K. (2006). Strategy and society: The link between competitive advantage and corporate social responsibility. *Harvard Business Review*, *84*(12), 78–92. PMID:17183795

SicrediReport. (2017). Retrieved from https://www.sicredi.com.br/html/conheca-o-sicredi/relatorios/

Ribeiro, M. A., & Martins, E. (1993). A informação como instrumento de contribuição da contabilidade para a compatibilização no desenvolvimento económico e a preservação do meio ambiente. Caderno de Estudos FIPECAFI, 9.

Risk Management Structure Pillar (EGR). (2017). Retrieved from https://www.sicredi.com.br/html/conheca-o-sicredi/relatorios/

Rymsza, M. (2015). The role of social enterprises in shaping social bonds. *International Journal of Social Economics*, *42*(9), 830–840. doi:10.1108/IJSE-03-2015-0059

Sanchéz, L. E. (2011). *Avaliação de impacto ambiental: conceitos e métodos*. São Paulo: Oficina de textos.

Sanchéz, L. E. (2017). Por que não avança a avaliação ambiental estratégica no Brasil? *Estudos Avançados*, *31*(89), 167–183. doi:10.15900103-40142017.31890015

Simmons, R., & Birchall, J. (2008). The role of co-operatives in poverty reduction: Network perspectives. *Journal of Socio-Economics*, *37*(6), 2131–2140. doi:10.1016/j.socec.2008.04.016

Socioenvironmental Responsibility Policy (PRSA). (2015). Retrieved from https://www.sicredi.com.br/html/conheca-o-sicredi/relatorios/

Sollenberger, H. M. (2005). Building a consensus on credit union capital adequacy: At the appropriate level, risks are covered and competitive capability is enhanced. *Bank Accounting & Finance*, *18*(5), 1–15.

Standardized Financial Statements (DFP). (2017). Retrieved from https://www.sicredi.com.br/html/conheca-o-sicredi/relatorios/

Tilling, M. V. (2004). Refinements to Legitimacy Theory in Social and Environmental Accounting.

Veiga, J. E. (2009). Indicadores socioambientais: Evolução e perspectivas. *Revista de Economia Política*, *29*(4), 421–435. doi:10.1590/S0101-31572009000400007

Weber, O. (2017). Corporate sustainability and financial performance of Chinese banks. *Sustainability. Accounting. Management and Policy Journal*, *8*(3), 358–385.

Wen, Y. (2015). Money, liquidity and welfare. *European Economic Review*, *76*, 1–24. doi:10.1016/j.euroecorev.2015.01.012

Wood, D. J. (1991). Corporate Social Performance Revisited. *Academy of Management Review*, *16*(4), 691–718. doi:10.5465/amr.1991.4279616

Yin, R. K. (2010). Estudo de caso: planejamento e métodos (4th ed.). Porto Alegre: Bookman.

KEY TERMS AND DEFINITIONS

Corporate Social Responsibility: It is about how an organization operates in the economic, environmental and social spheres with its value chain, including compliance with legal requirements on (compulsory) disclosure and voluntary disclosure to stakeholders, which involves socioenvironmental risks. Besides, it is identified by short, mid- and long-term organizational policies compatible with Sustainable Development.

Credit Unions: Financial Institutions whose objective is to provide financial services to their members and develop the community of which they are a part; to do so, they need to engage with their stakeholders by disclosing socioenvironmental risks.

Disclosure: Practice through which an organization provides its users with relevant information to guide decisions.

Stakeholders: All groups or people that affect and are influenced by the activities of organizations. Examples of stakeholders: union members, owners, investors, employees, government, society, media and suppliers.

Stakeholder Engagement: It refers to an organization's capacity to understand and meet the demands of the audience that affects and is influenced by its activities.

Socioenvironmental Risk: It refers to the possibility of an event related to environmental or social aspects occurring and preventing an organization from reaching its goals. It causes adverse (undesired) effects on health (human life), the environment and material goods, has a macroeconomic and microeconomic nature, is intrinsic of any enterprise and involves Corporate Social Responsibility practices and stakeholder engagement.

Solidary Responsibility: Sharing of legal responsibility with a third party (person or organization), concerning a certain act – for instance, debt or legal agreement. When one of the parties violates laws, both may be prosecuted.

Section 2

Applied Perspectives: The Contexts of Countries, Regions, and Cities

Chapter 7
Linking Corporate Social Responsibility Reporting With the UN Sustainable Development Goals:
Evidence From the Portuguese Stock Market

Sónia Monteiro
Research Center on Accounting and Taxation, Portugal

Verónica Ribeiro
Research Center on Accounting and Taxation, Portugal

Kátia Lemos
https://orcid.org/0000-0002-3961-5964
Research Center on Accounting and Taxation, Portugal

ABSTRACT

The approval of the 17 Sustainable Development Goals (SDG) within the 2030 United Nations Agenda represents a historic mark for sustainable development, allowing to companies to seek solutions that add value and solve the greatest global challenges, by linking organizational strategies and global priorities. Thus, listed companies will need to be able to assess their impact on the SDGs and review their strategies accordingly. Therefore, reporting can play a key role by informing the progress of listed companies in alignment with the SDGs. This article aims to analyse how Portuguese listed company reporting includes their contributions toward the SDGs. The study methodology is based on content analysis of the sustainability reports (SR) and non-financial statements (NFS) published in 2017, seeking to characterize the Portuguese listed companies that are concerned with SDG-related disclosure. The results indicate that from a sample of 46 listed companies, only 12 published SR or NFS, but 9 companies made the alignment with the UN goals.

DOI: 10.4018/978-1-7998-2128-1.ch007

INTRODUCTION

In 2015, Member States of the United Nations (UN) adopted an ambitious agenda for poverty eradication and global economic, social and environmental development until 2030, known as Agenda 2030, containing 17 Sustainable Development Goals (SDGs) and 169 targets. This agenda, adopted by almost all countries in the world, define the priorities and requires global action by governments, business, and civil society.

The SDGs provides an opportunity to create and implement solutions and technologies that address the greatest global challenges, helping to link organizational strategies and global priorities. It is therefore important at this point to assess how organizational practices can be developed in order to meet the goals. The SDGs provide an integrated framework for future-oriented Corporate Social Responsibility (CSR) engagement (Schönherr et al., 2017). CSR assumes a voluntary character of the organizations towards the impacts of their activities in society and the environment, through a transparent and ethical behavior that contributes to Sustainable Development. CSR and SDGs together have potential to develop an interconnected model for sustainable growth. CSR creates a balance between economic interests, environmental needs and social expectations by integrating the spirit of Sustainable Development into the business strategy (Behringer & Szegedi, 2016).

The way in which organizations evaluate their contributions to the SDGs is the key to informing and shaping future engagement and action. Thus, organizations will need to be able to assess their impact on the achievement of the SDGs and review their strategies and practices accordingly, wich requires to collect and report new data. In this sense, it is important to align the organizations' strategy and the corporate reporting with the SDGs, giving the stakeholders the current level of commitment to these goals.

Among the goals of Agenda 2030, the target 12.6 that encourages companies to adopt sustainable practices and to integrate sustainability information into their reporting cycle. The development of CSR/ sustainability reporting models in the last years leads companies wordwide to disseminate information related to sustainable developmemt (KPMG, 2017). However, none of the sustainability/non-financial reporting frameworks (such as those of the Global Reporting Initiative and the International Integrated Reporting Council) include specific guidance on SDGs disclosures. Thus, the linkage of SDGs into corporate reporting is still at a very embryonic stage and it is, therefore, necessary to promote their progress.

The main level of the 2030 Agenda implementation being undoubtedly national, each country has to establish how the SDGs should be implemented. Portugal embodies its strategic priorities for the implementation of the 2030 Agenda for Sustainable Development in the SDG 4, 5, 9, 10, 13, and 14. As other UN member states, Portugal has been strongly involved in the international efforts undertaken to align their respective policies and instruments to the SDGs. A first UN report produced in 2019 by independent scientists, titled "The Future is Now: Science for Sustainable Development,", assess the compliance with the SDGs adopted four years ago. The 10 most sustainable developing countries are members of the European Union: the first on the list is Denmark; Sweden, Finland, France and Austria are the following countries.

With 76.4 points out of a maximum of 100, this report ranks Portugal among the 30 most sustainable countries of the world (position 26th out of 162 countries evaluated). A concerted and effective corporate action towards Sustainable Development is, therefore, possible if Portuguese companies align their activities to incorporate the SDGs, meeting the mission defined at national level. Thus, it is important to analyze whether companies are monitoring and reporting their impacts in relation to their alignment with the SDGs.

SDGs reporting being an emerging phenomenon there are few empirical studies exploring SGDs reporting practices . To the best of the authors' knowledge this is the first paper that provides some insights into reporting's linkage with the SDGs from a Portuguese perspective. This study aims to verify if Portuguese listed companies are disclosing information about theirs practices to promote SDGs and about the impact of their activities on SDGs achievement. For this purpose, a content analysis of their sustainability reports and/or non-financial statetments will be conducted, seeking to characterize the listed companies that are concerned with SDGs-related disclosure.This study adds to the international research on SDG reporting by providing empirical data from a country, Portugal, where empirical evidence is still relatively limited.

This paper is structured as follows: after this introduction, the second section, related to the background, discusses the evolution of sustainabibility/integrated reporting frameworks, the SDGs the relation between them. The third section presents the empirical literature review. In the fourth section, the research design is presented, following by the empirical results and discussion. Finally, the main conclusions are presented.

BACKGROUND

Traditionally, the assessment and reporting of organization performance has been based on the financial accounting model. However, the growing interest in sustainability matters has led to the evolution of accountability mechanisms and new reporting models to address the non-financial information needs of stakeholders. Organizations have been disseminating information in reports of CSR/sustainability to meet the growing demand for transparency and accountability by stakeholders (KPMG, 2008).

A Sustainability report should include economic, social and environmental information about the management of the institution on its interest groups, as well as the corporate governance and management systems implemented. The guidelines/standards developed by the Global Reporting Initiative (GRI) are singled out as the world's foremost internationally recognized and globally accepted sustainability reporting framework (KPMG, 2015). Since 2000, GRI has developed a continuous improvement of the framework, updating the guidelines to version G3 and G4. In 2016, GRI launched the first global standards for sustainability reporting, based on a modular structure that can be kept up-to-date and relevant. It is basically a restructuring of the G4 into a new Standards architecture with the aim of making the content clearer and more logical, in a more flexible and easily adaptable structure over time.

The KPMG study (2015) states that GRI guidelines continue to be the most popular voluntary reporting framework worldwide but notes that GRI usage has fallen among the largest companies in the world. This decline may be related to the introduction of the GRI G4 structure, because it is considered more complex than the previous GRI structure, or because the companies have started to make integrated reports. This idea is reinforced in the KPMG study (2017), whereby some countries seem to be embracing the concept of integrated financial and "non-financial" reporting, in many cases driven by stock market regulation/guidance.

Traditionally companies have been publishing separate financial reports and sustainability reports because the strategic link between them was not recognized. In fact, the information disclosed in the sustainability reports is not always presented in a strategic context, making it difficult for the stakeholders understand how sustainability (social, economic or environmental) can affect the value creation process of an organization (Eccles & Serafeim, 2015). In this context, the concept of Integrated Report emerges as a model that values the reporting of financial and non-financial information, under duly defined parameters, interconnecting investment decisions with the strategic and operational options and the conduct of the organization.

In 2013, the International Integrated Reporting Council (IIRC) published "The International <IR> Framework", the guidelines for the elaboration of an Integrated Report, defining it as a concise capable of assessing the value creation capacity of organizations, identify strategic key points and anticipate risks and opportunities, internal or external, in business. The IR aims to increase the relevance, consistency and comparability of information, adding in the same report all the "Capitals"(Natural, financial, human, intellectual, social and manufactured-) that contribute effectively to business success and to value creation, not only in the short but also in the medium and long term. The integrated reporting enables organizations to think in an integrated way about their strategy, facilitating more informed decision making, good risk management, increasing the confidence of the various stakeholders, with the main objective of improving the performance of the organization as a whole (Guthrie et al., 2017). The IR seems to be the organizational report of the future (Rossi, 2017), complementing the sustainability reporting.

Regarding the non-financial reporting, reference should again be made to Directive 2014/95 / EU, on the disclosure of non-financial information and diversity information by certain large companies and groups. This directive requires certain companies to include in the annual management report a non-financial statement or, alternatively, to prepare a separate report containing the information required for the non-financial statement. This Directive had to be transposed into the legislation of the various EU Member States by the end of 2016, applying to large companies which are public interest entities or to large groups which, at the date of disclosure of their balance sheet (individual or consolidated, respectively) have an average of more than 500 employees. The directive suggests that companies can use national, EU or international systems to prepare this non-financial statement[1], such us the GRI Standards, and the IR framework.

Based on the disclosure requirements of the Directive, the guidelines proposed in that document make an important contribution to the SDGs of Agenda 2030. This Agenda 2030 covers all areas and sectors of any country, and it requires comparable and reliable data reflecting companies' performance concerning the SDGs agreed by the UN member States.

Relevant data on companies' contribution towards the SDGs is critical for assessing the progress of the SDGs implementation, and this have a direct impact on the accounting and reporting agenda. Target 12.6 explicitly encourages companies, especially large and transnational companies, to adopt sustainable practices and to integrate sustainability information into their reporting cycles. Indicator 12.6.1 requires data on the number of companies publishing sustainability reports. Although many companies mention the sustainable development in their annual or sustainability/integrated reports, particularly on topics related to climate change, sustainable water management or employment (PwC, 2018), organizations need a reporting approach that takes into account not only the importance of specific SDGs, but also how to measure the level of progress against them. The report needs to evolve in order to quantify, verify and effectively communicate the impact that companies have on SDGs (KPMG, 2017).

Rosati and Faria (2019a) discuss the potential role of sustainability reporting in the advancement of the SDGs. The authors define SDGs reporting as the practice of disclose publicly on how an organization addresses the SDGs. Therefore, transparent and relevant reports on SDGs are important both to provide internal feedback and to communicate to investors and regulators how companies are meeting the goals.

Integrating the SDGs into the companies reports represents, therefore, one of the biggest challenges on reporting agenda. However, the different sustainability frameworks (from the GRI, the International

Organization for Standardization, IIRC and the United Nations Global Compact-UNGGC) present different ways to approach reporting on sustainability, but none of them include specific guidance on SDGs disclosures.

To bridge this gap, and to integrate business into the sustainable development GRI, the UNGC and World Business Council for Sustainable Development (WBCSD) established an international network of professionals as well as perspectives of forward-thinking companies from around the world in 2015. The aim of it was to produce an implementation guide on impact assessment, KPI selection and goal setting, a publication that will support businesses in assessing their impacts, aligning their strategies with the SDGs and setting company goals. This innovative initiative entitled "The SDG Compass: the guide for business action on the SDGs", guides companies so they can align their strategies, measure and manage their contribution to achieving the SDGs, and put sustainability at the center of their business strategy. It also helps companies to identify the GRI standards that can be used to publicize their actions in order to reach the SDGs.

Sustainability reporting can thus be seen as an enabler of SDGs actions. Thus, in order to facilitate the integration of the SDGs in the Organizational Report, the UN Global Compact Network together with the GRI have developed two key documents ("Business Reporting on the SDGs: An Analysis of the Goals and Targets" and "A Practical Guide to Defining Priorities and Reporting")[2] that should be used together as part of the business reporting cycle. It is not intended to create a new reporting structure, but to help companies to highlight their contribution to SDGs and provide relevant information to stakeholders through qualitative and quantitative disclosures for the SDGs targets that are likely to be relevant to business, regardless of the size, sector or location of operations. Organizations can use these documents to disclose their impacts and contributions to the SDGs, for example, reporting according to GRI standards and/or the 10 principles of the UN Global Compact.

However, according to Adams (2017), SDG Compass does not help reporters in deciding how to integrate the SDGs into reports, in accordance with UNGC principles or GRI guidelines/standards. Moreover, the language used in the document is much closer to the language of integrated reporting than to the language of sustainability reporting. In this sense, the author considers that the integrated report is a promising approach for the dissemination of the contribution of organizations to the SDGs. Therefore, she states that organizations should report their contribution to SDGs targets along with the 6 "capitals" provided in the Integrated Report Framework (IIRC, 2013), as demonstrated in the figure below:

The need for a common set of performance indicators is crucial for stakeholders, to compare the contributions of companies to the achievement of SDGs. The SDG reporting frameworks already developed are still at a very embryonic stage (Amey & Whooley, 2018) and it is therefore necessary to improve their maturity.

The most recent development in this matter was promoted by the Corporate Reporting Dialogue (CRD)[3], which brings together the main international organizations and normalizers at the reporting level. In February 2019, the CRD released a position paper entitled "SDGs and the Future of Corporate Reporting" to support the development of better reporting guidelines for the SDGs. The document mentions how corporate reports can illustrate which SDGs are relevant to a company's business model, but also clarifies how companies and investors can focus on SDGs with a bigger probability of affecting their financial performance. The document also stresses the importance of promoting the integration of financial and non-financial information to demonstrate value creation for stakeholders, over the short and long-term. The authors of this document have committed themselves to working together to develop

Figure 1.
Source: Adams (2017, p. 14)

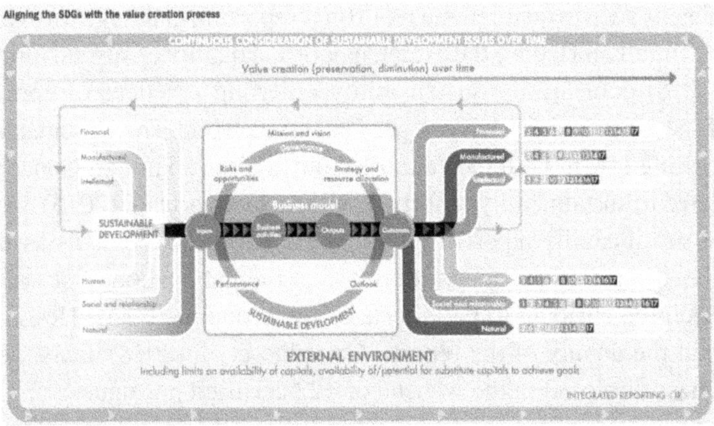

a guide and a structure that will make companies more transparent and accountable, and ensure better decision making that promotes financial stability and sustainable development.

EMPIRICAL LITERATURE REVIEW

Chersan (2017) conclude that companies which operate in Europe and in Asia are ranked on the top position as far as publication of reports in GRI database. There are several studies related to sustainability developed in the last years, using as sample listed companies. Gati and Seele (2014) conducted a content analysis on 329 CSR/sustainability reports from 50 leading European companies from Euro Stoxx 50 that were published between the beginning of online CSR/sustainability reporting in 1998 and 2010. The results indicates that the use of social and environment-related terms occurred more frequently in the past and demonstrates the establishment of sustainability in corporate non-financial reporting. Kiliç & Kuzey (2017) study the sustainability reporting practices of Turkish non-financial companies listed on Borsa Istanbul (during the years 2004 to 2015). The findings indicate that a growing number of companies publish stand-alone sustainability reports, most of them using the GRI framework. However, the percentage of companies which did not produce a separate sustainability is still relatively hight. The findings revealed that listing on the Corporate Governance Index (CGI), having a sustainability committee, the type of industry, the size of the company and profitability are significant determinants of stand-alone sustainability reporting, whereas leverage is not . The study of Wang (2017) focus on a sample of Taiwan listed companies examined the relationship between firm characteristics and sustainability reporting for. The results indicated that several corporate governance and business characteristics (including board size, the percentage of independent directors, the existence of an audit committee, export sales percentage, foreign shareholdings, firm growth, and the average age of assets) are positively related to publishing a sustainability report. In Sri Lanka, Dissnayke et al. (2019) study the key company characteristics which influence sustainability reporting by 84 listed companies from 2012 to 2015. The results indicate that size and the use of GRI guidelines are found to be the most relevant company characteristics associated with sustainability reporting. Also in Kasakistan, Orazalin & Mahmood (2019) analyzes data from publicly traded companies at the Kazakhstani Stock Exchange for the years 2013–2015, analysing the extent and determinants of sustainability performance disclosures, by using the GRI framework. The results indicate that determinants such as stand-alone reporting, reporting language, firm profitability, firm size and auditor type substantially influence the extent, nature and quality of sustainability-reporting process.

Bhatia & Tuli (2018) compare the sustainability reporting practices of companies, listed on the Stock Exchanges of the USA and the UK, as per GRI framework. The findings suggest that the level of sustainability reporting low in both the countries, but is almost similar. Concerning to our country, Portugal, studies related to sustainability reporting are few. Gomes et al. (2015) analyse the main trends in the publication of sustainability reports by Portuguese firms as well as its assurance for the period 2008-2011. The authors found evidende of a decrease of the publication of sustainability reports, during these period, which the attribute to the effects of the economic crisis. However, they found signs of a steady increase in the quality of the reports. Carvalho et al. (2018) analysise the information on sustainable development disclosed in the website of 422 certified portuguese organizations. Conclude that little information is disclosed and the larger organizations disclose more information. Portugal, the organizational factors, such as the activity sector, geographic location and media ranking (i.e., media exposure) are not relevant explanatory factors to explain the disclosure of information on SD. Gomes (2016) discusses the sustainability reporting practices in the financial sector in Portugal and Spain from 2012 to 2014, analyzing 36 sustainability reports and 78 annual reports. The study also reveals that the disclosure of CSR is different between banks of the two countries: Spanish banks disclose more indicators than the Portuguese banks, but both countries closely follow the standards of GRI.

Specificaly related to Portuguese stock market, Dias (2009) sheds light upon the quantity and quality of corporate infor- mation composed by a sample which gathers 49 companies listed on the Portuguese Official Stock Market in 2005. Evidence unfolds that only 45% of the listed companies provide reports on issues which somehow relate to its sustainability whilst hinting that the sus- tainability corporate report is not their major concern. Also Dias et al. (2016), analyse the evolution and extent of CSR reporting practices of Portuguese listed companies before the global financial crisis (2005-2008) and during crisis (2008-2011). The results found reporting decreased only slightly during the period of financial crisis. This was because companies tended to disclose more information about their community engagement obligations and corruption.

Concerning integrated reporting, globally, there is still limited research on integrated reporting. Publicly listed companies are the most commonly researched organisations. Regarding the country of research, the European Union is the most active region, followed by Australasia. South Africa is not at the IR research forefront as expected, even though it is a pioneering country of IR and the only country that currently requires publicly listed companies to issue an integrated report on an "apply or explain" basis (Roman, 2019).[4] Setia et al. (2015), examine whether the integrated reports prepared in accordance with the King III Code of corporate governance regulation are providing the information intended of an integrated report. Annual/integrated reports of the top 25 JSE listed companies for the years 2009/2010 and 2011/2012 were content-analysed for the presence of information on capitals. The results show that the introduction of IR in South Africa has resulted in an increase in the extent of disclosure of human, social and relational, natural and intellectual capital information of the listed companies. Buitendag et al. (2017) analyse the IR of the top 100 entities listed on Johannesburg Stock Exchange (JSE) for the financial peridos 2013- 2015. The results show that the type of industry the entity finds itself in, the size and profitability of the entity, as well as the composition of the members of the board, have an effect on the quality of the integrated report. Also Wang et al. (2019), using a sample of integrated reports published between 2012 and 2015 by listed companies on the JSE, find that traditional governance mechanisms such as the board and the audit committee are positively related to the reporting quality of IR. Bananuka el al. (2019) condutect an analysis of annual reports of listed firms on Uganda Securities Exchange (USE) from 2010 to 2016, in order to to establish why firms in developing countries are slow to adopt integrated reporting. Results suggest that, firms are slow to adopt integrated reporting because of the scarce and minimal resources, culture and leadership, stakeholders demand, the regulatory requirement, the effect of globalization and the mindset, lack of awareness about IR and the nature of business and size.

Lopes & Coelho (2018) provide evidence on geographic and firm-level characteristics within organizations using IR (2011 to mid-2015), based on a sample of 224 organizations across 26 countries. The results indicate that the majority of IR reporters are from South Africa, the United Kingdom, Spain and the Netherlands. However the majority of companies classified as Reference Reporters are from Europe, are larger, have a higher market value, are more profitable and less leveraged. Roman et al. (2019) analyse 30 integrated reports (extracted randomly from the IR database set up by IIRC) refered to the financial year 2017, that belong to companies from different continents, operating in different industry groups. The results show that the higher the revenues of the reporting company, the more balanced their integrated reports, while younger companies use a more optimistic tone when reporting. Additionally, entities based in countries with a stronger tendency towards transparency surprisingly provide less readable integrated reports. It was also revealed that companies operating in non-environmentally sensitive industries, as well as International Financial Reporting Standards adopters deliver foggier and thus less readable integrated reports. Bratu (2017) assess the compliance level of the integrated reports published for 2015 by 30 European companies which have adopted the IIRC Framework.The results reveal that the companies are in different stages regarding the conformity with the IIRC requirements. Moreover, some companies analyzed in this study are in the vanguard of the initiative whereas others produce "combined" rather than "integrated" reports.

In our country, studies on IR are few. Leocádio (2017) analyses five portuguese companies that published integrated reports, in order to evaluate what types of Integrated Reports are being elaborated at this stage. However, the quality of their IR was far away from the autor's expectations, since in some respects they are limited to complying with the GRI guidelines.

In the scope of SDGs reporting, empirical research in this area is still very embryonic, comparative to the empirical studies on sustainability reporting (Hahn & Kühnen, 2013; Coulmont et al., 2015; KPMG, 2017) or IR reporting (Stacchezzini et al., 2016, Bananuk et al., 2019) fields.

A PwC (2017) study refers that a third (38%) of companies a global level (sample of 470) and more than half of the 35 Portuguese companies surveyed (57%) did not mention the SDGs in their report. KPMG (2018) has developed a study to provide a base level view of SDGs reporting majority among the G250 large companies worldwide. The KPMG study concludes that 4 in 10 (40%) of the world's largest companies already reference the SDGs in their corporate reporting (specially talking about their positive impacts on the SDGs). These results suggest that business interest in the SDGs has grown quickly since their launch in 2015. However, there is not yet an established process, benchmark or standard for reporting on the SDGs. Large companies from Europe (Germany, France and the UK) are significantly more likely to report on the SDGs than companies in other countries. However the numbers are currently too low to draw meaningful regional or sector conclusions.

Bebbington and Unernam (2018) highlight some of the large companies that have readily incorporated the SDGs into their sustainability reports, for example Telecoms group, BT and Unilever. Also Schramade (2017) mentioned Novozymes, as one of the few companies that has clear impact targets derived from the SDGs . Another two leaders in SDGs integration are Safaricom and Philips. Schramade (2017) found that only a minority of companies currently mention the SDGs in their reports. He found that "40% of the Dow 30, 28% of the Eurostoxx 50, and 28% of the largest 30 companies in the Nikkei 225 mentioned the SDGs in their 2015 reporting". The author concluded that one of the key challenge in terms of SDGs and implementation is linking them with specific incentives that might influence the choice to invest in the SDGs.

Calvo Centeno et al. (2018) analyzed the degree of contribution to the SDGs of the groups listed in the IBEX 35, through the non-financial information disclosed in the consolidated non-financial report required by Spanish legislation (Decree-Law 18/2017 following 2014/95 / EU Directive[5]). A disclosure index based on the 17 SDGs of Agenda 2030 was developed to measure the degree of compliance with the SDGs. The results indicate that 6 of the 35 (17,14%) companies of the IBEX 35 do not mention any of the SDGs included in Agenda 2030 and 2 companies (Telefónica and Iberdrola) include all of the 17 SDGs. However, 50% of IBEX 35 companies incorporate less than 41.18% of the SDGs in their reports.

Concerning the determinants factors of SDGs reporting we can highlit the studies of Rosati & Faria (2019a and b). In their first study, Rosati & Faria (2019a) investigated the relationship between adoption of SDGs reporting and some internal organizational factors. Using a logit model based on data from 408 organizations worldwide, the study concluded that only 16% of the sample addressed the SDGs in the reports published in 2016. SDGs reporting is related to a larger size, a higher level of intangible assets, a higher commitment to sustainability frameworks and external assurance, a higher share of female directors, and a younger board of directors. The second study of Rosati &Faria (2019b) contributes to understand the relationship between an organization's willingness to address the SDGs in its sustainability report and some external institutional factors related to the organization's country. The authors conduct an analysis of the country-level institutional factors related to the decision to address the SDGs in sustainability reports. The research was undertaken by considering 27 institutional factors belonging to six different national institutional systems, and it relies on data from 2413 sustainability reports published by organizations located in 90 different countries. The results shows that SDGs reporting are more likely to be located in countries with higher levels of climate change vulnerability, national corporate social responsibility, company spending on tertiary education, indulgence and individualism, and lower levels of market coordination, employment protection, power distance and long-term orientation.

RESEARCH DESIGN

Based on the above empirical literature, the sample of this study includes the portuguese listed companies, that satisfy the following condition: the company published a sustainability report, an integrated report or a non-financial statement. The authors used 2017 as the reference year for the analysis (year of entry into force of the DL 89/2017, related to non-financial information), in order to identify the fastest adopters of SDGs, which were announced in 2015.

In 11th November 2018, the main Portuguese stock exchange market, Euronext Lisbon, included a total of 47 companies. None of the companies had integrated reports, one company (Vista Alegre) published separately a non-financial statement, and 11 companies published a sustainability report (one of them denominate it "Sustainability report and Non-financial statement"). It should also be noted that some companies (6) use the sustainability report to simultaneously comply with the DL 89/2017, regarding the disclosure of non financial information, and do not present this statement separately. Thus, the authors focused on those 12 reports.

In collecting data, the authors applied a content analysis approach, as it is the most commonly used technique in studies that evaluate social/environmental an sustainability information disclosure.

EMPIRICAL RESULTS AND DISCUSSION

By analyzing the content of the 12 reports, it was observed that only 3 (25%) did not make any reference to the SDGs, so they will be excluded from our detailed analysis. This represents an higher percentage, compared to the results of Calvo Centeno et al. (2018), in the spanish stock market (only 17% companies of the IBEX 35 did not mention the SDG in their 2017 corporate reporting). Thus, our study will be focus on the content analysis of 9 reports (sustainability reports and/or non-financial statetments), in order to characterize the portuguese listed companies that are concerned with SDGs-related disclosure.

In this sense, our preliminary results are in accordance to Schramade (2017), who found that only a minority of companies currently mention the SDGs in their reports. In fact, from the 47 portuguese companies listed companies, only 9 (19%) mentioned the SDGs in their 2017 reporting.

Table 1 summarizes the analysis of SDGs-related disclosure. Considering the 9 reports under analysis, only 2 (Vista Alegre and Semapa) have a briefly mention to the SDGs; but in the others cases, the reporting it is done in alignment with the SDGs.

It can be observed that all companies that use sustainability reports to refer to SDGs use the GRI Framework, and in some cases they also disclose information in accordance to the DL 89/2017. Only one company (CTT) use de GRI – G4; in most cases the sustainability reporting is based on the GRI Standards 2016. Only in 2 companies (Navigator and EDP), the selection of the indicators was made in order to adopt the most demanding option of GRI, corresponding to the highest level of comprehensiveness: in Accordance-Comprehensive; the other companies use the option "In accordance – Core". In most cases, reports had an external verification by GRI. In our opinion, collecting data is important but request verification of that data to a competent entity makes the process more credible.

The authors find that the companies are not in the same stage of SDGs reporting. In other words, although 7 companies align their reporting into SDGs, most have their mission/strategy aligned with the UN goals, however 3 of them (SONAE, Media Capital and Sporting) do not prioritized their SDGs. A PwC study (2017) concludes that 37% of companies globally (in a sample of 470 companies) selected specific SDGs as priorities in their reporting. But when compared to Portugal, they found that only 26% of the 35 companies surveyed selected specific SDGs as a priority in their financial or sustainability reporting. We share PwC's (2017) view that in companies that fail to prioritize their critical goals, this may suggest that there is no significant level of commitment to them. PwC add that it is therefore a challenge for Portuguese companies to identify which objectives are most relevant to their business and then prioritize it and define how to approach it.

Table 2 shows a detailed analysis of the 9 listed companies' reporting that demonstrates their linkage with the SDGs. The UN goals allow companies to report information about their involvement and contribution to sustainable development, using common indicators and a set of shared priorities.

Table 1. SDG in Corporate Reports: summary

	Vista Alegre	Navigator	SONAE	Semapa	Media Capital	EDP	CTT	Corticeira Amorim	Sporting
Report type	Non-financial statement	Sustainability report	Sustainability report	Sustainability report	Sustainability report	Sustainability report	Sustainability report	Sustainability report	Sustainability report
Publication date	2017	2016/17	2017	2017	2017	2017	2017	2017	106/17
Framework used	DL 89/2017	• GRI Standards 2016 • DL 89/2017	• GRI Standards 2016 • DL 89/2017	GRI Standards 2016	• GRI Standards 2016 and sectorial supplement Media G4 • DL 89/2017	• GRI Standards 2016 • DL 89/2017	• GRI -G4	• GRI Standards 2016 • DL 89/2017	GRI Standards 2016
No. of pages	20	130	105	83	97	171	80	53	105
Level of declaration (GRI)	Not applied	In accordance - Comprehensive	In accordance - Core	In accordance - Core	In accordance - Core	In accordance - Comprehensive	In accordance - Core	In accordance - Core	In accordance - Core
External verification (GRI)	Auditor declaration	yes	yes	no	no	yes	yes	yes	no
Alignment with SDGs	No (Brief mention to SDGs)	yes	sim	No (Brief mention to SDGs)	Yes	Yes	yes	Yes (mention to SDGs, without alignment)	yes
Mission/vision/ strategy	no	yes	no	no	yes	yes	yes	yes	yes
Prioritary SDGs definition	no	yes	no	no	no	yes	yes	yes	no
Reference to SDG compass	yes	no	no	no	no	no	yes	no	no

CONCLUSION

The 17 SDGs were adopted in 2015, they were designed to be universal and to be applied to all countries. The integration between sustainability initiatives and business goals is progressively happening in practice. An increasing number of organizations are aligning their corporate purpose with the execution of sustainable strategies and the SDGs (Busco, 2018). Sustainability reports can thus lend themselves very well to measuring, understanding and communicating organization SDGs efforts towards more sustainable development. At the same time, the SDGs can also play an important role in the advancement of corporate reporting.

Given that the SDGs are still relatively new, there is as yet no benchmark or framework that is widely accepted as the standard for SDG reporting. There are, however, many and various initiatives that seek to establish such frameworks. Standard or common practice will no doubt emerge over time (KPMG, 2018).

At the moment, SDG- reporting is yet in its infancy, with a minority of companies now mentioning the SDGs in their reporting. The results of our study indicate that from a sample of 46 listed companies, none published integrated reports, and only 12 published Sustainability Reports or Non Finantial Statements. But 9 of those companies refer to the SDGs in their reports. The companies adopted the GRI framework, and some use SR to acomplish to the portuguese law (nº 89/2017) related to Non-financial information.Of the 9 companies SGDs-related reporting, not all are in the same stage. On the one hand, although 7 companies report linking with the SDGs, not all are in the process of implementing their sustainability strategy in line with the SDGs. Companies that are at a more advanced stage: aligning the

Table 2. Analysis of the information disclosed on SDGs

Vista Alegre	**Non-Financial Statement 2017** In paragraph 6- Commitments to the future, it is stated: "The United Nations Sustainable Development Goals, ratified by almost all countries, including Portugal, have identified 17 priority themes aimed at ensuring sustainable development. The SDGs explicitly assume the importance of companies and economic agents in achieving their goals. Vista Alegre assumes its responsibility in this process and the commitment to society, intending to be an active part in the pursuit of these goals. Vista Alegre has the perfect notion of which goals to prioritize and where to concentrate its efforts, always keeping in mind its capabilities and the value chain of its subsidiaries. Under this commitment, based on the SDG Compass methodology and taking into account the nature of Vista Alegre's activity, the Sustainable Development Goals considered as priority will be identified. "
Navigator	**Sustainability Report 2016/17** "The Company is aligned with the United Nations Sustainable Development Goals, which are identified and associated with the broad lines of action and objectives along its value chain" (page11) Presents its sustainability road map (pages 17-18). To do this, a table shows 27 commitments made for sustainability related to 10 most relevant topics (materials), establishing the action line, goals and key performance indicators (KPI) that allow monitoring the implementation of actions. It should be noted that each of the commitments associates the corresponding SDG (s). In the scope of its mission / vision it has "taken into account the major market trends and the needs of our stakeholders and is in line with SDGs" (page 26) Under item 5: Challenges of the international agenda, a sub-item is dedicated to the 13 SDGs identified as priorities for the company. It presents a detailed analysis of each material topic in identifying the applicable SDGs, the goals to be fulfilled and what the stakeholders say.
Sonae	**Sustainability Report 2017** "The activity report shows our performance at the level of the UNGC Principles and the SDGs" (page 4). The GRI Supplement, which appears in the report, presents the indicators around a set of 5 axes, where the interconnection with the UNGC principles and the respective SDGs are made.
Semapa	**Sustainability Report 2017** "Semapa assumes the sustainable development goals defined by the United Nations in its strategy, investments and operations" (page 28). Semapa assumes its responsibility towards society in this common project, committing itself to being an active part in pursuing these goals. It is our intention to align our sustainability strategy with the SDGs, establishing goals and programs of action. "Point 4.3: Agenda 2030 states that a work program with short and medium-term actions, structured in 4 pillars and in the material topics identified, is being developed. The company undertakes to incorporating their approaches to the SDGs. Bearing in mind the resources, value chain and evaluation of the material topics, will during the next exercise identify the goals to be prioritized and where to focus their efforts.
Media Capital	**Sustainability Report 2017** "Our contribution to the United Nations' 2030 Sustainable Development Goals is to empower all our resources in raising awareness and empowering consumers to respond collectively to the major environmental and social challenges facing the future" (page 1) The assessment of the material themes for Media Capital's stakeholders was based, inter alia, on "(...) the objectives defined by the United Nations in the context of its global sustainable development initiatives - Sustainable Development Goals (SDGs) and United Nations Global Compact (UNGC) "(page 14). The GRI table, which appears at the end of the report, presents the different indicators, and is matched with both DL 89/2017 and their respective SDGs. The report concludes by referring to "Media Capital intends during 2018 to define a sustainability governance strategy and model, aligned with the Group's business strategy for the next three years. In this first exercise, an initial approach is taken to map the Contribution of the Media Capital Group to the United Nations Sustainable Development Goals. However, in 2018 the Group will develop its internal approach, as well as a base of key indicators, objectives and targets for monitoring their contributions to the implementation of the United Nations Agenda 2030 "(page 97).
EDP	**Sustainability Report 2017** The report "Includes the commitments made to goals and targets and their relationship to the United Nations' 2030 Sustainable Development Goals" (page 4). In the framework of the strategy, "these objectives also correspond to contributions to the common agenda established by the United Nations Sustainable Development Goals (SDGs), which EDP endorsed at the launch of this initiative in 2015" (page 39) "(...) EDP's commitment to 8 of the 17 Sustainable Development Goals "(page 101). It presents contributions to SDGs 7,9, 12 (on the axis of economic value creation); SDGs 5 and 8 (in the eizo: developing people); SDGs 13 and 15 (how to manage climate and environment); SDGs 11 and 17 (to strengthen confidence) (page 39) "Through its Social Investment Policy, EDP actively contributes to the United Nations Sustainable Development Goals, namely for SDG11, SDG13 and SDG15." (page 109)
CTT	**Sustainability Report 2017** In the President's message it refers "We were one of the first Portuguese and industry companies to integrate the United Nations Sustainable Development Goals (SDGs) into their business strategy." (page 5). "In the case of CTT, we mapped and prioritized the SDGs to our value chain using the SDG Compass methodology developed by the WBCSD, UN Global Compact and GRI. We have identified the SDGs targets that can contribute to promote positive impacts or minimize / avoid negative impacts and allocate them to each stage of the value chain, taking into account risks and opportunities "(...) Consultation with SDG Compass supported the identification and selection of the specific indicators and objectives of CTT "(page 20). They present targets for SDGs 3, 4, 7, 8, 13 and 16. The 3rd edition of the participatory carbon offset initiative in 2018 "confirms the alignment of CTT with UN SDGs 12 and 13, which CTT subscribes to" (page 14). Among other initiatives (conferences, trainings, workshops ..) there is also the "publication of two case studies of CTT (SDG 12-Ecoportfolio and SDG 13-Drivers' Challenge), in a document BCSD Europe on SDGs." (page 58)
Corticeira Amorim	**Sustainability Report 2017** "This circular profile of Corticeira Amorim contributes in a very relevant way to the SDG 12 ... However, from the crossing of the SDGs with the areas of operation of the organization we verified that the sustainability strategy is clearly in line with other 10 SDGs ... "(page 103). This is reinforced on page 117: "The sustainability strategy of Corticeira Amorim is particularly aligned with 11 of the SDGs". The strategic priorities .... taking into account the alignment with the United Nations SDGs "(page 117). "(...) the company has begun a detailed analysis of its practices, which is still ongoing, and therefore considers it appropriate not to proceed in this report to the concrete definition of objectives and targets for the following years "(page 117) During the year 2017 (...) it took the first step towards aligning its sustainability strategy according to the 17 SDGs, crossing them with its material areas of action"
Sporting	**Sustainability Report 2016/17** In his message, the President states that it is a strategic concern, "... to ensure that we are aligned and committed to the United Nations Sustainable Development Goals. In the GRI table, which appears at the end of the report, it presents the different indicators and is matched with the respective SDGs.

reporting with the SDGs, considering them in their strategy and prioritizing the most important goals are EDP, ED and CTT.

The contribution of this paper is to provide a first initial evidence of SGDs reporting in the Portuguese stock market context. By analyzing the SDGs reporting from portuguese listed companies, this study will help non-listed companies to benchmark their own reporting against this global leadership group. The authors expect that (listed and non-listed) Portuguese companies will increasingly report on their contributions to the goals in the next few years. For that, professional accountants have an important role to play. The International Federation of Accountants (IFAC, 2016) presents a snapshot of the accountancy profession's contribution toward the 2030 Agenda. According to IFAC (2016, p. 7) "the profession is an essential driver of strong and sustainable organizations, financial markets, and economies. As a result, it inherently has a crucial role in achieving the SDGs and meeting the targets". "The opportunities for the global profession to contribute to the SDGs involve at least eight of the SDGs: Goal 4: Quality Education; Goal 5: Gender Equality; Goal 8: Decent Work and Economic Growth; Goal 9: Industry, Innovation, Infrastructure; Goal 12: Responsible Consumption and Production;Goal 13: Climate Action; Goal 16: Peace and Justice and Strong Institutions; Goal 17: Partnerships For The Goals" (IFAC, 2016, p. 9). Also, Bebbington & Unernan (2018), recently proposed an accounting research agenda for the SDGs by emphasizing the enabling role of accounting scholars for the implementation and achievement of the SDGs. According to Bebbington & Unernan the SDGs have the potential to inform and advance research and practice on sustainability accounting and reporting. They state "Academic investigation is needed to help understand where specific SGD-related accounting initiatives lie on the continuum between pure rhetoric and meaningful action, and to inform the most effective use of the SDGs by a broad range of organizations in developing policies and practices that will contribute toward achievement of the SDGs (2018, p. 10).

Those authors also state thaht ".., it is important for accounting academics to appreciate that much of the information and underlying data that will need to be used within meaningful SDG-related accounting practice will probably come from systems that have so far been beyond the boundaries of entity-level sustainability accounting and reporting. Where such systems have been outside the purview of social and environmental accounting academics, this makes embracing interdisciplinarity even more important in a research agenda seeking to enhance the role of accounting in achievement of the SDGs (Bebbington & Unernan (2018, p. 12).

In view of the above, major challenges are placed on organizations and professionals in identifying priority SDGs for their activities and stakeholders, incorporating them into their strategy, setting goals for their success, measuring and reporting on their progress.

Integrating the SDGs evaluation into the corporate reporting implies showing their effective performance to the stakeholders, using emerging non-financial reporting models. The 2030 Agenda gives a new impetus towards aligning harmonization of sustainability reporting with the SDG monitoring framework. Whether through sustainability reports, integrated reports or new reporting structures, the authors believe that there is an urgent need to align the corporate reporting reports with the structure and scope of the SDGs. Further development of a SDG-reporting framework is a process that requires time and the possibility of refinement as knowledge and data availability improve. Therefore should be a priority research area for the future.

FUTURE RESEARCH DIRECTIONS

A limiation of the study is that it only consider listed companies, which may represent a bias, because portuguese stock market is very small . Thus, further research might focus on all GRI reporting organizations, that might be willingness to address the SDGs in their reporting. In the future the authors also aspire to shed light on the relationship that exists between SDG reporting and corporate governance attributes (like size, economic performance, board of directors, etc.), in order to understand the characteristics that are related to the decision to engage SDGs early in sustainability frameworks.

REFERENCES

Adams, C. (2017). *The Sustainable Development Goals, integrated thinking and the integrated report.* International Integrated Reporting Council and ICAS. Retrieved from www.theiirc.org

Amey, M., & Whooley, N. (2018). Corporate reporting on the SDGs: mapping a sustainable future. *PIMCO.*

Bananuka, J., Tumwebaze, Z., & Orobia, L. (2019). The adoption of integrated reporting: A developing country perspective. *Journal of Financial Reporting and Accounting, 17*(1), 2–23. doi:10.1108/JFRA-09-2017-0089

Behringer, K., & Szegedi, K. (2016). The role of CSR in achieving sustainable development – theoretical approach. *European Scientific Journal, 12*(22), 1857–7881. doi:10.19044/esj.2016.v12n22p10

Bratu, A. (2017). Empricial study regarding the integrated reporting practices in Europe. *Audit Financiar, XV, 4*(148), 613–627. doi:10.20869/AUDITF/2017/148/613

Buitendag, N., Fortuin, G. S., & De Laan, A. (2017). Firm characteristics and excellence in integrated reporting. *South African Journal of Economic and Management Sciences, 20*(1). doi:10.4102ajems.v20i1.1307

Busco, C., Granà, F., & Izzo, M. F. (2018). Make Sustainable Development Goals happen through Integrated Thinking: an introduction. In *Sustainable Development Goals and Integrated Reporting* (pp. 11–30). Routledge.

Calvo Centeno, M., Gragera Pizarro, E., Romero Ramos, E., & Ropero Moriones, E. (2018). Informaci6n no financiera divulgada por las empresas del IBEX 35: análisis de la contribuci6n a los objetivos de desarrollo sostenible de Naciones Unidas. In Proceedings of the XVIII Encuentro Internacional AECA. Academic Press.

Carvalho, F., Santos, G., & Gonçalves, J. (2018). The disclosure of information on sustainable development on the corporate website of the certified portuguese organizations. *International Journal of Qualitative Research, 12*(1), 253–276.

Chersan, I. (2017). Integrated reporting in europe – from voluntary to mandatory? Journal of Public Administration, *Finance and Law,* (3), 19-30

Coulmont, M., Loomis, S., Berthelot, S., & Gangi, F. (2015). Determinants and Impacts of Sustainability Disclosure. In *Studies in Managerial and Financial Accounting* (pp. 25-79). Academic Press.

Decreto-Lei. n.º 89/de 28 de julho - Divulgação de informações não financeiras e de informações sobre a diversidade por grandes empresas e grupos. (2017).

Dias, A. (2009). O Relato da Sustentabilidade Empresarial: Evidência empírica nas empresas cotadas em Portugal. *Portuguese Journal of Accounting & Management*, *8*(1), 111–150.

Dias, A., Rodrigues, L., & Craig, R. (2016). Global financial crisis and corporate social responsibility disclosure. *Social Responsibility Journal*, *12*(4), 654–667. doi:10.1108/SRJ-01-2016-0004

Diretiva 2014/95/UE do Parlamento Europeu e do Conselho, de 22 de outubro de 2014, que altera a Diretiva 2013/34/UE no que se refere à divulgação de informações não financeiras e de informações sobre a diversidade por parte de certas grandes empresas e grupos. (2014).

Dissanayake, D., Tilt, C., & Qian, W. (2019). Factors influencing sustainability reporting by Sri Lankan companies. *Pacific Accounting Review*, *31*(1), 84–109. doi:10.1108/PAR-10-2017-0085

Eccles, R. G., & Serafeim, G. (2015). Corporate and integrated reporting: a functional perspective. In *Mohrman, S., O'Toole, J. e Lawler, E., Corporate Stewardship: Organizing for Sustainable Effectiveness* (pp. 156–173). Sheffield, UK: Greenleaf Publishing. doi:10.9774/GLEAF.9781783532605_10

European Commission. (2011). *Corporate social responsibility: a new EU strategy for the period 2011-2014.* COM (2011) 681 final. Retrieved from http://www.europarl.europa.eu/meetdocs/2009_2014/documents/com/com_com(2011)0681_/com_com(2011)0681_pt.pdf

European Commission (COM). (2016). Communication from de Commission to the European Parliament, the Council, the European Economic and Social Committee and Committee of the Regions. Next steps for a sustainable European future. European action for sustainability.

Gatti, L., & Seele, P. (2014). Evidence for the prevalence of the sustainability concept in European corporate responsibility reporting. *Sustainability Science*, *9*(1), 89–102. doi:10.100711625-013-0233-5

Gomes, S. (2016). *Relato de Sustentabilidade – Práticas no Setor Financeiro em Portugal e Espanha.* Dissertação de Mestrado em Finanças Empresariais, Instituto Politécnico de Leiria.

Gomes, S., Eugénio, T., & Branco, M. (2015). Sustainability reporting and assurance in Portugal, Corporate Governance. *The International Journal of Business in Society*, *15*(3), 281–292.

Guthrie, J., Manes-Rossi, F., & Orelli, R. L. (2017). Integrated reporting and integrated thinking in Italian public sector organisations. *Meditari Accountancy Research*, *25*(4), 553–573. doi:10.1108/MEDAR-06-2017-0155

Hahn, R., & Kühnen, M. (2013). Determinants of sustainability reporting: A review of results, trends, theory, and opportunities in an expanding field of research. *Journal of Cleaner Production*, *59*, 5–21. doi:10.1016/j.jclepro.2013.07.005

International Federation of Accountants, IFAC. (2016). *The 2030 Agenda for Sustainable Development. A Snapshot of the Accountancy Profession's Contribution.*

International Integrated Reporting Council (IIRC). (2011). *Towards Integrated Reporting: Communicating Value in the 21stCentury*. International Integrated Reporting Council. Retrieved from http://integratedreporting.org/wp-content/uploads/2011/09/IR-Discussion-Paper-2011_spreads.pdf

International Integrated Reporting Council (IIRC). (2013). *The International <IR> Framework*. Retrieved from www.theiirc.org

Jan, B., & Unerman, J. (2018). Achieving the United Nations Sustainable Development Goals: An enabling role for accounting research. *Accounting, Auditing & Accountability Journal*, *31*(1), 2–24. doi:10.1108/AAAJ-05-2017-2929

Kiliç, M., & Kuzey, C. (2017). Factors influencing sustainability reporting: evidence from Turkey. In K. Tunca Çaliyurt & S. G. Günay (Eds.), *Recent Issues in Accounting Finance and Auditing* (pp. 139–175). Edirne: Trakya University.

KPMG. (2008). *KPMG international survey of corporate sustainability reporting 2008*.

KPMG. (2015). *KPMG survey of corporate responsibility reporting 2015*. Retrieved from https://home.kpmg/content/dam/kpmg/pdf/2015/12/KPMG-survey-of-CR-reporting-2015.pdf

KPMG. (2017). *KPMG survey of corporate responsibility reporting 2017*. Retrieved from https://assets.kpmg/content/dam/kpmg/xx/pdf/2017/10/kpmg-survey-of-corporate-responsibility-reporting-2017.pdf

KPMG (2018). How to report on the SDGs. What good looks like and why it matters. February 2018. Retrieved from kpmg.com/sdgreporting

Leocádio. (2017). *Relato Integrado em Portugal, Dissertação de Mestrado em Contabilidade e Controlo de Gestão*. Porto: FEP.

Lopes, A. I., & Coelho, A. M. (2018). Engaged in integrated reporting? Evidence across multiple organizations. *European Business Review*, *30*(4), 398–426. doi:10.1108/EBR-12-2016-0161

PricewaterhouseCoopers PWC. (2017). *Os desafios das empresas portuguesas na priorização dos ODS e no* relato não-financeiro 2017. Estará a sua empresa preparada?

PricewaterhouseCoopers PWC (2018). *SDG Reporting Challenge 2018. From promise to reality. Does business really care about the SDGs? And what needs to happen to turn words into action*. Retrieved from https://www.pwc.com/gx/en/sustainability/SDG/sdg-reporting-2018.pdf

Roman, A., Mocanu, M., & Hoinaru, R. (2019). Disclosure Style and Its Determinants in Integrated Reports. *Sustainability*, *11*(7), 1960. doi:10.3390u11071960

Rosati, F., & Faria, L. (2019a). Business contribution to the Sustainable Development Agenda: Organizational factors related to early adoption of SDG reporting. *Corporate Social Responsibility and Environmental Management*, 1–10.

Rosati, F., & Faria, L. (2019b). Addressing the SDGs in sustainability reports: The relationship with institutional factors. *Journal of Cleaner Production*, *215*, 1312–1326. doi:10.1016/j.jclepro.2018.12.107

Rossi, F. M. (2017). *From sustainability reporting to integrated reporting: the public sector experience*. University of Salerno.

Schönherr, N., Findler, F., & Martinuzzi, A. (2017). Exploring the Interface of CSR and the Sustainable Development Goals. *Transnational Coorporations*, *24*(3), 33–48. doi:10.18356/cfb5b8b6-en

Schramade, W. (2017). Investing in the UN Sustainable Development Goals: Oppor- tunities for companies and investors. *Journal of Applied Corporate Finance*, *29*(2), 87–99. doi:10.1111/jacf.12236

Setia, N., Abhayawansa, S., & Anh, H. (2015). Integrated reporting in South Africa: Some initial evidence", Sustainability Accounting. *Management and Policy Journal*, *6*(3), 397–424.

Stacchezzini, R., Mellon, G., & La, A. (2016). Sustainability management and reporting: The role of integrated reporting for communicating corporate sustainability management. *Journal of Cleaner Production*, *136*, 102–110. doi:10.1016/j.jclepro.2016.01.109

UN Global Compact Network and GRI. (2018). Business Reporting the SDGs -Analysis of the Goals and Targets. Retrieved from https://www.globalreporting.org/resourcelibrary/GRI_UNGC_Business-Reporting-on-SDGs_Analysis-of-Goals-and-Targets.pdf

UN Global Compact Network and GRI. (2018). Integrating the Sustainable Development Goals into Corporate Reporting: A Practical Guide. Retrieved from http://globalcompact.pt/images/pdf/Practical_Guide_SDG_Reporting_08_2018.pdf

Wang, M. (2017). The relationship between firm characteristics and the disclosure of sustainability reporting. *Sustainability*, *9*(4), 624. doi:10.3390u9040624

Wang, R., Zhou, S., & Wang, T. (2019). Corporate Governance, Integrated Reporting and the Use of Credibility-enhancing Mechanisms on Integrated Reports. *European Accounting Review*, 1–33. doi:10.1080/09638180.2019.1668281

KEY TERMS AND DEFINITIONS

Agenda 2030: The 2030 Agenda for Sustainable Development was approved by the United Nations General Assembly, in September 2015, and represents a new commitment to fighting poverty and promoting a truly sustainable and global development model. Endorsed by the 193 UN member countries, this Agenda includes 17 Sustainable Development Goals (SDG) and 169 measures, which must be implemented in all countries of the world.

Sustainable Development: It is a development model that enables us to meet the needs of the present without compromising the ability of future generations to meet their own needs. The concept of sustainable development seeks to harmonize the objectives of economic development, social development and environmental conservation. This concept waa internationally recognized and formalized by the United Nations in the Brundtland Report (1987).

Sustainability Report: It is one of the main ways for an organization to report on its sustainability practices. Through the report the organization disclosures social, economic and environmental indicators resulting from its activity. When prepared according to clear guidelines, such as the Global Reporting Initiative (GRI), it is an important communication and management tool.

ENDNOTES

1 Such us: the United Nations Global Compact, the Organization for Economic Co-operation and Development guidelines for multinational enterprises, the ISO 26000 Social Responsibility standard of the International Organization for Standardization, the Global Reporting Initiative (GRI) on Sustainability Reporting or other recognized international frameworks (such as the Integrated Reporting) and the methodological reporting guidelines developed by the European Commission.

2 UN Global Compact Network and GRI, "Integrating the Sustainable Development Goals into Corporate Reporting: A Practical Guide", http://globalcompact.pt/images/pdf/Practical_Guide_SDG_Reporting_08_2018.pdf e "Business Reporting the SDGs "Analysis of the Goals and Targetshttps://www.globalreporting.org/resourcelibrary/GRI_UNGC_Business-Reporting-on-SDGs_Analysis-of-Goals-and-Targets.pdf

3 CDP, Climate Disclosure Standards Board, Global Reporting Initiative (GRI), International Integrated Reporting Council (IIRC), International Organization for Standardization and the Sustainability Accounting Standards Board (IASB).

4 South Africa stands out as the pioneer country, by imposing the King III Code, to require the annual preparation and publication of the Integrated Report (or provide reasons for not doing so) to companies listed on the Johannesburg Stock Exchange (JSE) (Setia et al., 2015)

5 In Portugal, the transposition of Directive was made to the Portuguese legal system by Decree-Law no. 89/2017, of July 28. The diploma creates two non-financial reporting obligations, one related to environmental, social and labor aspects, and the other is centered on the diversity policies of members of higher corporate bodies. Specifically, Decree-Law (DL) No. 89/2017 stipulates that companies must present a non-financial statement, as a general rule included in the management report, as from 2018, with reference to the financial year 2017, but may be presented in a separate report (either as an annex to the management report or thereafter, not later than six months after the balance sheet closure date). The information requested in this non-financial statement includes a description of the business model, policies, risks, environmental and social performance, as well as measures aimed at workers, respect for human rights, gender equality and anti-corruption and bribery.

Chapter 8
Integrated Reports and Board Diversity:
An International Perspective

Ana Isabel Lopes
Business Research Unit, Instituto Universitário de Lisboa, Portugal

Maria João Braz
Instituto Universitário de Lisboa, Portugal & Caixa Geral de Depósitos, Portugal

ABSTRACT

Organizations currently must report to a broader audience, capturing the attention of several categories of stakeholders, who want to know why, where, and how companies create and add value, and how they deal with responsibility and sustainability issues, contributing to the emerging of integrated reporting (IR). IR is as an innovation in promoting a holistic and integrated vision of the business, where the Board of Directors must play an important role. This chapter covers diversity of directors seated on the board of integrated reporters, comparing two groups: those who are IR references and those that are IR regular reporters. The results show that organizations with larger boards, higher proportions of non-executive directors, and a higher proportion of women on the board have an higher probability of preparing IR reference reports, while the duality role of CEO inverts the probability, and no relationship is found with board experience.

INTRODUCTION

Corporate social responsibility and corporate sustainability are distinct concepts, but the literature exposes a growing tendency towards a more integrated approach to both topics that incorporates social, environmental and economic perspectives. This integrate approach can be potentially achieved through the preparation of the so-called "integrated report," a recent channel used by Organizations to communicate the way they create value through short, medium and long term. Organizations currently must report to a broader audience than shareholders, capturing the attention of several categories of stakehold-

DOI: 10.4018/978-1-7998-2128-1.ch008

ers, who want to know why, where and how companies create and add value, and how they deal with responsibility and sustainability issues, contributing to the emerging of integrated reporting. While it is still voluntary in almost all the world, it is indeed gradually encouraged and supported by regulators, institutional investors and organizations, as an innovative nature in promoting a holistic and integrated vision of the organization, where the Board of Directors must play an important role (defining strategies, promoting policies and implementing best practices).

The main issue addressed in this chapter is an analysis of the different characteristics of Directors seated on the Board of Organizations preparing Integrated Reports." As such, two different groups are created: the main focus, comprising all the organizations that prepared an integrated report that is considered a benchmark or that has obtained a premium; the control group, covering all the other organizations that also prepare an integrated report. The sample includes almost 380 entities all over the world identified as IR preparers, from whom people expect to be accountable for the transparency of their external communication process. Characteristics such has the role duality, the board size, the independence, the gender diversity and the experience of boards members are stressed and compared. Results show that larger Boards, with a larger proportion of non-executive directors and a higher proportion of women as directors on the board have higher likelihood of producing an integrated report that is highlighted as IR reference, while the dual role of the CEO negatively influences the recognition of leading practices of the integrated reports. This last result is not maintained if unlisted entities are removed. Due to the international context of all the entities included in the sample, institutional characteristics of the countries are also used for control issues. The findings will be of practical interest to investors (shareholders) and executives when evaluating the board composition and the perspectives of being engaged with the integrated reporting commitment.

Background

Social, environmental and economic perspectives of firms running businesses are traditionally included in the scope of corporate social responsibility and corporate sustainability concepts. Beyond their importance, there are an awareness about how to facilitate the dialogue between reporting companies, users and other relevant stakeholders. Some Organizations are engaged in promoting communication not just about the perspectives mentioned, but about value creation, assuming that this would be the next step in the evolution of corporate reporting. The most important Organization leading this process is the International Integrated Reporting Council (IIRC), a global coalition of regulators, investors, companies, standard setters, the accounting profession and even NGOs.

The role of IIRC has been increasing since its foundation in 2010. Currently, the IIRC intends to establish integrated reporting and thinking within 'mainstream business practice'. This integrate approach can be potentially achieved through the preparation of the so-called "integrated report," a recent channel used by Organizations to communicate the way they create value through short, medium and long term. Organizations currently must report to a broader audience than shareholders, capturing the attention of several categories of stakeholders, who want to know why, where and how companies create and add value, and how they deal with responsibility and sustainability issues, contributing to the emerging of Integrated Reporting. Since the Board of Directors represent the interest of the shareholders, and act in the firm's social interest, one key is to outline a value creation pattern. So, the board of directors should have an active role in the integrated thinking phase (strategic orientations) and in the drafting of integrated report (relevant financial and non-financial information on critical issues).

Characteristics of Directors seated on the Board of Organizations preparing "Integrated Reports", such has the role duality, the board size, the independence, the gender diversity and the experience of boards members, are stressed and compared. Due the international context of all the entities included in the sample, institutional characteristics of the countries where their companies are playing are also used for control issues.

literature review

Overview about Integrated Reporting

Integrated reporting (IR) is "an evolution of corporate reporting, with a focus on conciseness, strategic relevance and future orientation" (IIRC, 2019). In order to make IR easy to embrace and comparable across different companies, the international IR framework was developed. According to Professor Mervyn King, IIRC Chairman, this "Framework is a tool for the better articulation of strategy, and to engage investors on a long-term journey to attract investment that will be crucial to achieving sustained, and sustainable, prosperity."

Companies are requiring an evolution in the reporting system, facilitating the communication to stakeholders without the complexity of current reporting requirements. According to IIRC, integrated reporting has been created to enhance accountability, stewardship and trust, and harness the information flow and transparency of business that technology has brought to the modern world. Integrated reporting is an emerging international corporate reporting initiative to address limitations to existing corporate reporting approaches (Zhou, Simnett, & Green, 2017), with a focus on conciseness, strategic relevance and future orientation. Integrated reporting requires an integrated thinking within the organization, enabling a better understanding of the organization's ability to create value over time. Integrated thinking is defined by IIRC as "the active consideration by an organization of the relationships between its various operating and functional units and the capitals that the organization uses or affects" (IIRC, 2013, p. 2). Integrated thinking implies a change of thinking within the company, shifting its focus to aligning profit maximization with environmental and social issues (Adams, 2015), leading to better integrated decision-making and actions in view to the creation of value over the short, medium and long term.

The traditional financial report alone is no longer enough to meet the needs of all stakeholders, neither to provide a full picture of the company (Roxana-Ioana & Petru, 2017). Integrated reporting aims to add to the current financial reporting model additional information about a company's strategy, governance and performance. In order to provide a full picture of the company, integrated reporting has been progressively adopted by companies, since the concern with environmental, social and governance (ESG) issues has been gaining importance.

The concern with ESG issues was first introduced by sustainability reporting, being in the origins of integrated reporting. According to Global Reporting Initiative (GRI), a sustainability report is a report published by a company or organization about the economic, environmental and social impacts caused by its everyday activities. A sustainability report also presents the organization's values and governance model and demonstrates the link between its strategy and its commitment to a sustainable global economy. Companies have started formal reporting of their sustainability-related activities through the sustainability report, which is a stand-alone report that intends to supplement the financial information of annual reports. However, this separation of disclosure has led to some criticism, because seems that the non-financial information is not considered with the same priority and relevance as financial information (Pavlopoulos, Magnis, & Iatridis, 2017). Eccles and Serafeim (2014) showed some concerns related to sustainability reports and defended that this stand-alone report tends to be published with a lag of several months compared to financial reports, and the information is rarely presented in the context of the business model and the strategy of an organization. This makes it difficult for investors to understand how ESG performance related to financial performance and how sustainability issues affect the value creation process in an organization. Integrated reporting aims to enhance corporate reporting by emphasizing interconnections between different types of information currently reported in stand-alone reports (Zhou et al., 2017).

To prepare a report with these characteristics, there is an international IR framework, which is a voluntary principles-based document, establishing a set of guiding principles and content elements that guide the overall content of an integrated report and explain the fundamental concepts that underpin them (IIRC, 2013). By producing this framework, IIRC does not intend to prescribe a structure that companies should follow strictly, but rather to suggest a set of elements and principles that guide companies to produce their integrated reports (Roxana-Ioana & Petru, 2017).

To better understand the process of value creation, IIRC defines some fundamental concepts, such as the capitals that a company uses and affects, the value creation for the organization and for others and the company's business model. According to IIRC, the capitals contribute to the success for all organizations, and the six capitals are: financial (the source of funds), manufactured (the manufactured physical objects), intellectual (the organizational intangibles), human (the people's competencies and experience), social and relationship (relationships between stakeholders), and natural (the environmental resources). The process of value creation is dependent on an organization's business model, which is the system that transform inputs into outputs and outcomes through the business activities of the organization (IIRC, 2013).

South Africa was the first country to require the mandatory regime for integrated reporting, in March 2010, to all listed companies on the Johannesburg Stock Exchange (JSE), on an "apply or explain" approach (Slack & Tsalavoutas, 2018). Integrated reporting is also part of the listing demands in Brazil (PwC, 2015; Robertson, 2015), country where companies need to explain why they did not prepare an integrated report. Countries strongly supporting the practice of integrated reporting include United Kingdom, Netherlands, Australia, Spain, Singapore, Japan and United States of America (Robertson, 2015).

The works of de Villiers, Venter, and Hsiao (2017) and of Cheng et al. (2014) discuss the background to this new tool of communication, and why it is an area of interest for accounting profession, investors, regulators, among others, providing an overview of the literature on the origins of integrated reporting.

Earlier Research about Integrated Reporting

Research about integrated reporting has been emerging, namely, about motivations and benefits. Internal benefits (better resource allocation decisions, greater engagement with shareholders and other stakeholders and lower reputational risk), external market benefits (sustainability indices, report accurate non-financial information), and managing regulatory risk (responding to requests from stock exchanges) are examples of benefits (Eccles & Saltzman, 2011), although external market benefits are harder to measure because few companies have been practicing integrated reporting at the time (Eccles & Armbrester, 2011). Also, Krzus (2011) and Morros (2016) present theoretical benefits of integrated reporting, most of them contributing to the development of a culture of collaboration, getting senior executives sited on the Board engaged with reported issues. Some recent papers (e.g., Velte and Stawinoga, 2017; Vitolla, Raimo, &

Rubino, 2019) present systematics literature reviews that are helpful to understand the state of the art on integrated reporting, using a wider perspective than the topic explored in this chapter.

A strand of research has produced empirical studies investigating the impact that integrated reporting may have on the reporting practices. Stacchezzini, Melloni, and Lai (2016) obtained unenthusiastic evidences about the ability of this type of report to integrate corporate sustainability management and did not see the integrated report as the most appropriate accounting mechanism for the creation of ethically correct corporate cultures, arguing that in some companies the use of integrated reports is a way to opportunistically manage public impressions on corporate behavior. Maniora (2017) examined the impact of integrated reporting on the integration of ESG issues into the business model and the related economic and ESG performance changes and concluded that companies do not benefit in terms of economic and sustainability performance by switching from stand-alone ESG reporting to integrated reports.

The influence of corporate governance on corporate disclosure arises from the role of the Board of directors in deciding what should be disclosed in annual reports, managing the disclosure of a wide range of information that will have an impact on capital providers (Fasan & Mio, 2016; Hurghis, 2017) and overseeing the creation and execution of management's plans to balance the interests of multiple stakeholders, acting as representatives of shareholders (Harjoto, Laksmana, & Lee, 2015). From the agency theory perspective, company disclosure is one of the main tools used to harmonize the interests of managers and shareholders. From a stakeholder theory perspective, the board is responsible for balancing the interests of all stakeholders and safeguarding their interests.

The relationship between corporate governance and board diversity is a relatively new topic (Bing & Amran, 2017). According to Prado-Lorenzo & Garcia-Sanchez (2010), diversity is a characteristic that refers to the board of directors of an organization, characterized by the existence of differences on its members' traits. Therefore, diversity in boards of directors contributes to a greater variety of backgrounds and knowledges, implying different points of view that lead to better strategic decision making (Pechersky, 2016). Rao and Tilt (2016) stated that the diversity of board members provides broad and heterogeneous perspectives to the decision-making process, which is crucial for voluntary and more complex decisions. In this line, some researchers looked to the relationship between board characteristics and the production of integrated reporting. Frías-Aceituno, Rodríguez-Ariza, and García-Sánchez (2013) examined the influence of some board of directors' characteristics in the degree of information integration and they found that board size and gender diversity are the most influential factors in the decision to disclosure integrated information. Hurghis (2017) investigated whether the production of an integrated report might be influenced by the characteristics of the company's board of directors and he found that only the size of the board have an influence on the extent to which the issued integrated report is in accordance with the international IR framework, arguing that one possible reason for these results is because the IR framework is not mandatory for all the companies. Pavlopoulos et al. (2017) investigated the relationship between integrated reporting disclosure quality and corporate governance mechanisms, found that some characteristics are likely to increase the quality of accounting information, namely, the higher the percentage of independent directors on boards. So far, the best it is known, no study has examined how the diversity characteristics of boards can influence the best practices of integrated reporting. This study intends to fill this gap, investigating whether some characteristics of diversity contribute to a report presenting a higher recognition.

Board's Diversity Evidence

Objective and Sample

The main objective of this chapter is to describe the effect of different characteristics of diversity of Board of directors - board size, board independence, gender diversity, role duality and board experience - on the probability of the integrated reports became recognized by leading practices of the organizations where those boards belong to, distinguishing between IR reference reports (the higher quality ones) and IR regular reports. The IR reference reports are those reports that are highlighted in the IIRC examples database and considered as "best practices" by the IIRC or by a reputable award process or through benchmarking. The IR regular reports are all the other integrated reports that are available in the IIRC examples database as examples of companies engaged with the IR process. To perform this chapter, the integrated reports were hand-collected from the IIRC Examples Database, and all the data about the characteristics of boards of directors was hand-collected directly from those integrated reports. The sample comprises a total of 377 integrated reports, equivalent to 377 integrated reporters, since only the most recent integrated report for each company were collected.

Geographic Dispersion

Figure 1 shows the geographical dispersion of the sample. Africa is the most representative region (34%) followed by Europe (31%), both representing more than half of the total sample (65%). The geographical analysis is in line with the literature review. The African continent should be where there is a greater predominance of integrated reports, since as from March 2010 all companies listed on the JSE were required to adopt the Integrated Reporting (Hoffman, 2012). Looking within each region, the number of IR reference reporters is equal or exceeds the number of IR regulars reporters only in Europe, Australasia, and Americas.

Mapping the Board Diversity

This section highlights the characteristics used in prior research related with the potential influence of board diversity in the likelihood of providing voluntary disclosures related with CSR or sustainability reporting. These variables are used but now applied to the context of disclosures related with reporters engaged with the IR process. So, firstly the characteristics are explained, and then they are mapped into two groups or organization as follows: i) for each characteristic, the descriptive measure is presented comparing the group of IR reference reporters with the group of IR regular reporters; ii) the results are then decomposed into a map to show diversity along geographic dispersion.

Board Size

The Board Size represents the size of the board of directors and is measured by the number of board members (Frías-Aceituno et al., 2013; Prado-Lorenzo & Garcia-Sanchez, 2010). Larger boards contribute with different backgrounds that provide broader perspectives in controlling area (Pechersky, 2016). Some prior researches suggest a positive association between the size of the board and voluntary disclosure (e.g. Akbas, 2016; Akhtaruddin et al., 2009; Allegrini & Greco, 2013; Handajani, Subroto, Sutrisno,

Figure 1. Geographic dispersion

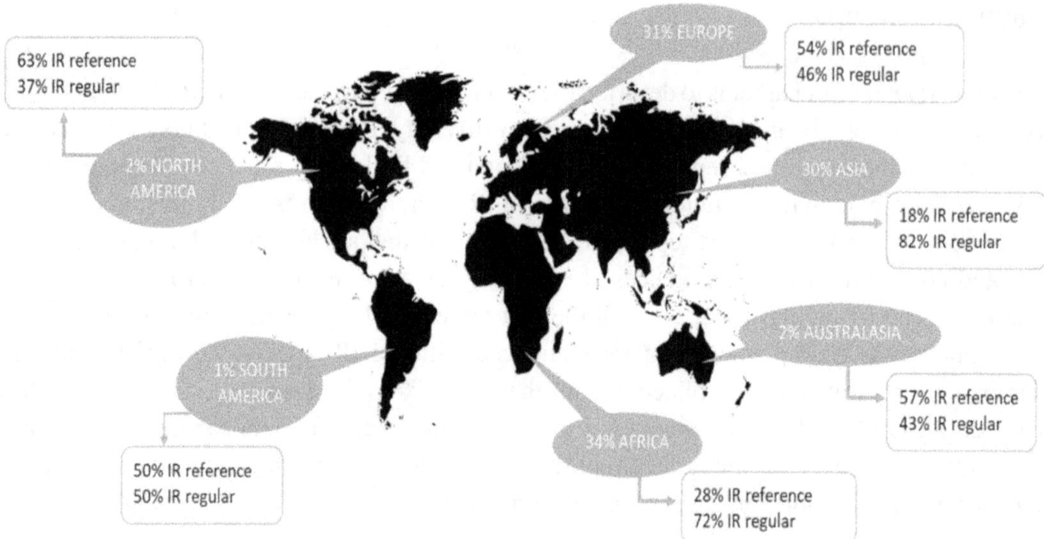

& Saraswati, 2014; Jizi, Salama, Dixon, & Stratling, 2014; Samaha, Khlif, & Hussainey, 2015), while others found no association between both variables (e.g. Cheng & Courtenay, 2006), but Janggu, Darus, Zain, and Sawani (2014) found that board size is the strongest determinant of sustainability disclosures.

Board independence

Some previous studies suggest a positive association between the proportion of independent directors on the board and the probability of publish or level of voluntary disclosures (e.g. Akhataruddin et al., 2009; Cheng & Courtenay, 2006; Donnelly & Mulcahy, 2008; Lim, Matolcsy & Chow, 2007; Samaha et al., 2015). Furthermore, Herda, Taylor, and Winterbotham (2012) found that companies with more independent directors are more likely to publish stand-alone sustainability reports and even to publish higher quality sustainability reports, in line with Jizi et al. (2014) for on the quality of CSR disclosure and Fuente, García-Sánchez, and Lozano (2017) on the CSR information disclosed according to the GRI. However, other studies did not find any association between the independence of board members and the level or quality of voluntary disclosures (including CSR disclosures) (e.g., Allegrini & Greco, 2013; Haniffa & Cooke, 2005; Janggu et al., 2014; Mahmood, Kouser, Ali, Ahmad, & Salman, 2018; Michelon & Parbonetti, 2012).

Gender Diversity

Gender diversity became a widely recognized characteristic of board diversity (Mahmood et al., 2018), and one of the most important factors in the integrated dissemination of information (Frías-Aceituno et al., 2013). One of the issues the earlier literature has explored widely is whether the presence of women on the board of directors has an impact on board performance and on voluntary disclosures. Prior findings suggest better level of CSR reporting (Dienes & Velte, 2016; Fernandez-Feijoo, Romero, & Ruiz-

Blanco, 2014), and higher quality sustainability reports (Al-Shaer & Zaman, 2016). On the other hand, Handajani et al. (2014), found that the increasing number of women on board of directors does not have a positive impact on corporate social disclosure.

Role Duality

Duality exists when the same person occupies cumulatively the positions of CEO and chairman (Prado-Lorenzo & Garcia-Sanchez, 2010). Empirical studies on the relationship between CEO duality and the level of disclosure are mixed. Cheng and Courtenay (2006) and Michelon & Parbonetti (2012) demonstrated that CEO duality is not associated with voluntary disclosure. On the other hand, while Allegrini & Greco (2013) and Samaha et al. (2015) obtained evidences of a negative impact of CEO duality on voluntary disclosures, Jizi et al. (2014) found that CEO duality have a positive impact on the CSR disclosure.

Board Experience

Age diversity can be seen as a mean of gaining new insights for boards of directors, bringing together younger and older groups, in order to promote the wider level of knowledge of the group as a whole (Hagendorff & Keasey, 2012; Kang, Cheng, & Gray, 2007). Age is a feature that reflects directors' business experience, evidencing their maturity in directing the business (Hafsi & Turgut, 2013). Hafsi and Turgut (2013) suggest that age diversity has a significant negative effect on corporate social performance, while Kang et al. (2007) found a preference for directors in the older age, and Post, Rahman, and Rubow (2011) found that boards whose directors average closer to 56 years in age tend to report more environmental corporate social responsibility information. The age of directors of the boards is used as a proxy variable for the board's experience.

Map

The results for the board diversity characteristics are summarized in Table 1. On average, the Board of IR reporters has more directors than the Board of IR Regular reporters. Concerning independence, IR reference reporters have higher (lower) percentages of non-executive (executive) directors, from which the percentage of independent non-executive are also higher, compared with IR regular reporters. The percentage of cases with women seated on the Board is also higher in IR reference reporters, where the percentage of reporters for which the CEO is not the same person as the chairman is lower, and the Boards are slightly younger.

The pattern across the geographic regions is presented in Figure 2. The prior conclusions are not equal in every region. The average number of seats in the board of directors in IR reporters is lower in Asia and Australasia, but the percentage of non-executive directors is in line with the prior evidence. Also, South America is the only region where the average percentage of non-executive directors is lower in the group of IR reference reporters than IR regular reporters, and this lower percentage is extensible to independent non-executive directors not only in South America but also in North America and Australasia. The percentage of women seated on the board of directors in Australasian and South America is lower in the <IR> Reference reporters' group. Differences also exist in duality: there is no such role in Africa and Australasia.

Table 1. Summary of board diversity characteristics between groups

	Board size	Board Independence (%)			Gender diversity (%)	Role Duality (%)	Board experience
	Average number of directors	*Executive directors*	*Non-executive directors*	*Independent non-executive directors*	*Woman on board*	*CEO duality*	*Average age of board directors*
IR reference reporters	11,89	28	72	58	22	8	57,6
IR regular reporters	10,58	35	65	52	16	13	58,5
Full sample	11,03	33	67	54	18	11	58,2

Figure 2. Summary of board diversity characteristics between geographic regions

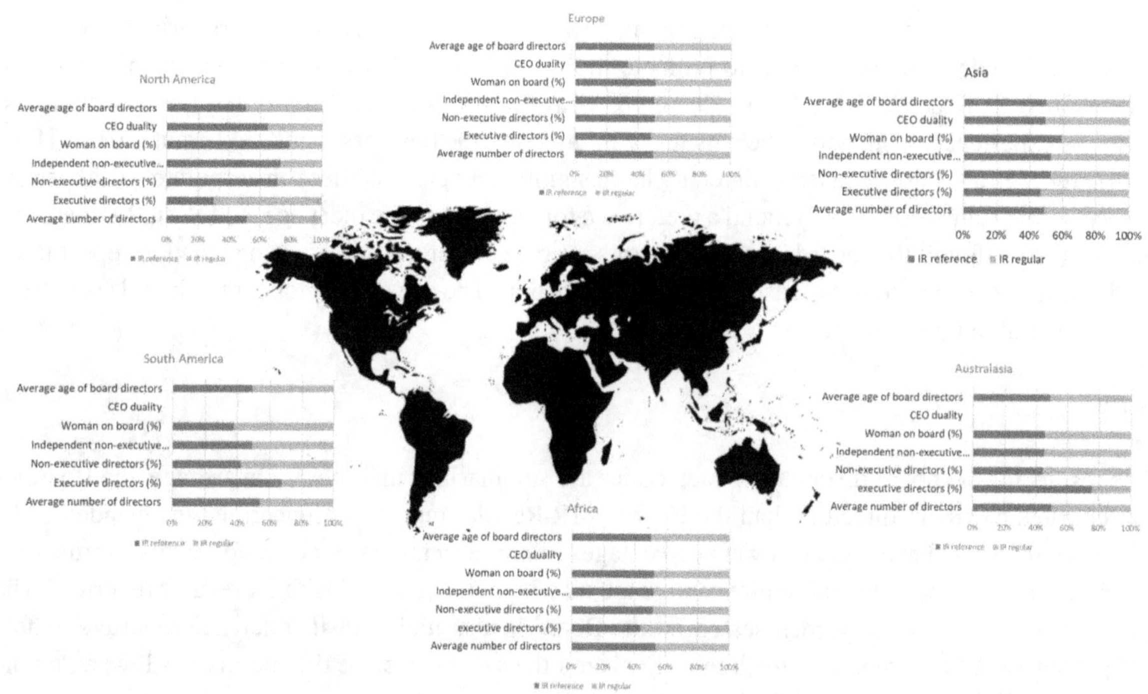

Testing the Hypothesis

Prior research used diversity to explore its relationship with voluntary CSR disclosures, sustainability practices, and similar issues. The relationship with integrated reporting is very scarce. This study explores this issue, considering the range of organizations preparing <IR>, and considering that board diversity potential has an impact on the probability of the <IR> Report is considered of better quality. So, the unique hypothesis is the following:

Hypothesis: There is an association between board diversity and the higher recognition of leading practices of the integrated reports.

In order to test the Hypothesis, each characteristic is included as an independent variable. The following logistic regression model (1) is estimated:

$$RECOGN = \alpha_0 + \alpha_1 BSIZE + \alpha_2 BINDEP + \alpha_3 GENDER + \alpha_4 DUALITY + \alpha_5 BEXPER + \alpha_6 STATUSLIST + \alpha_7 COUNTRY + \varepsilon \quad (1)$$

where:

RECOGN is the dependent variable that represents the recognition of leading practices of the integrated reports and is a dummy variable that equals 1 if the entity is considered a <IR> reference reporter and 0 if the entity is considered a IR regular reporter.

BSIZE represents the size of the board of directors and is measured by the number of board members (Frías-Aceituno et al., 2013; Prado-Lorenzo & Garcia-Sanchez, 2010).

BINDEP represents the independence of the board of directors and is measured by the percentage of non-executive directors (Frías-Aceituno et al., 2013; Haniffa & Cooke, 2005).

GENDER represents the gender diversity of the board of directors and is measured by the percentage of women directors (Al-Shaer & Zaman, 2016; Nadeem, Zaman & Saleem, 2017; Setó-Pamies, 2015).

DUALITY represents the role duality of the CEO and is a dummy variable that assumes 1 if the entity's CEO is also the chairman of the board of directors and 0 otherwise (Nadeem et al., 2017; Prado-Lorenzo & Garcia-Sanchez, 2010).

BEXPER represents the board experience and is measured by the average age of board members (Post et al., 2011).

In addition, the status listing and the country institutional variables are included as control variables, as follows:

STATUSLIST is a dummy variable that assumes 1 if the entity is listed on a stock exchange and 0 otherwise. This variable is used to control the differences between listed and unlisted entities.

COUNTRY represents the country institutional variables. The proxy for the institutional variables with the impact on the recognition of the integrated reports follows the same methodology as in De Villiers & Marques (2016) and Cahan et al. (2016), which considered the impact of some nation-level characteristics in CSR disclosures (not tabulated).

Table 2 reports the descriptive statistics of the variables used in the empirical analysis of Equation (1), for the entire sample and for the two subgroups of reporters analyzed: IR Reference reporters and IR regular reporters. On average, 37% of the IR reporters are IR reference reporters. This table details more deeply the numbers plugged in Table 1, adding typical statistic descriptive measures. Analyzing the entire sample, on average, boards are composed of about 11 directors, with the smallest board only with 2 members, and the largest with 31 members. It is notable a high percentage of independence of the board (67%) on the selected entities but there is a weak presence of women as directors (18%). The proportion of entities in which the CEO is also the chairman of the board is not high (11%). This reveals that the dual role is not a very common practice in the entities of this study, which is mainly due to the agency theory that defends the separation of both functions (Shrivastav & Kaise, 2016). The boards of directors in the sample have an average age of 58 years, with the youngest board having an average age

Table 2. Descriptive statistics

Variable	Mean	Std. Dev.	Median	Min	Max
<IR> Reporters (n=377)					
Main variables:					
RECOGN	0.37	0.48	-	-	-
BSIZE	11.03	3.92	11.00	2.00	31.00
BINDEP	0.67	0.21	0.71	0.00	1.00
GENDER	0.18	0.13	0.18	0.00	0.81
DUALITY[a]	0.11	0.31	-	-	-
BEXPER	58.2	4.27	57.79	41.88	72.67
IR Reference Reporters (n=140)					
Main variables:					
BSIZE	11.89	4.02	11.00	3.00	26.00
BINDEP	0.82	0.19	0.78	0.00	1.00
GENDER	0.22	0.14	0.23	0.00	0.81
DUALITY[a]	0.08	0.26	-	-	-
BEXPER	57.6	3.79	57.68	44.45	66.80
IR Regular Reporters (n=237)					
Main variables:					
BSIZE	10.58	3.83	10.00	2.00	31.00
BINDEP	0.65	0.22	0.67	0.00	1.00
GENDER	0.16	0.12	0.16	0.00	0.56
DUALITY[a]	0.12	0.33	-	-	-
BEXPER	58.5	4.49	57.92	41.88	72.67

RECOGN is the recognition of the integrated reports; BSIZE is the number of board members; BINDEP is the proportion of non-executive directors; GENDER is the proportion of women directors; DUALITY assumes 1 if the CEO is also the chairman of the board and 0 otherwise; BEXPER is the medium age of board members; [a]These variables, because they are binary, present minimum and maximum values of 0 and 1, respectively.

of 42 years, and the oldest being approximately 73 years. According to Kang et al. (2007), most of the boards are mature and middle-aged. Correlation (not tabulated) between the main independent variables are low, which indicates that multicollinearity problems are minimal.

Table 3 presents the regression results of Equation (1) after removing outliers by eliminating the observations whose standardized residuals were superior to 2 in absolute value. The coefficient of the variable BSIZE is statistically significant at a significance level of 10% (coefficient = 0.061; p-value = 0.053), suggesting that larger boards contributes positively to the higher recognition of leading practices of the integrated reports. In earlier literature, larger boards are generally positively associated with voluntary disclosures (Akhtaruddin, Hossain & Yao, 2009; Allegrini & Greco, 2013; Samaha et al., 2015), sustainability disclosures (Janggu et al., 2014) and CSR disclosures (Jizi et al., 2014). This result confirms that this positive association also occurs in the relationship between larger boards and the production of integrated reports, leading them to be considered as reference reports. This result is consistent with Frías-Aceituno et al. (2013), who argued that larger boards contribute to better integrating corporate information into integrated reports, being one of the most important factors in integrated information dissemination, and with Hurghis (2017), who argued that board size have an influence on issuing an integrated report according to the IR framework.

The variable BINDEP is statistically significant at a significance level of 1% (coefficient = 2.121; p-value = 0.002) suggesting that a higher proportion of non-executive directors on the board positively contributes to the higher recognition of leading practices of the integrated reports. This result is in line with most of the literature review, which suggested that a higher level of independence of the board of directors contributes positively to better disclosure of non-financial information (Lim et al., 2007). This finding supports the study of Pavlopoulos et al. (2017) that defended that a higher proportion of independent directors on board leads to a greater alignment of the integrated reports with the IR framework. However, this conclusion does not support the findings obtained by Frías-Aceituno et al. (2013), who argued that greater independence of the board does not contribute to the integration of corporate information. The results are similar if this variable is substituted by the average number of independent non-executive directors (and if both are included, one is dropped).

The variable GENDER is statistically significant at a significance level of 1% (coefficient = 3.995; p-value = 0.000) indicating that a higher proportion of women directors on the board have a positive influence of the higher recognition of leading practices of the integrated reports. This conclusion supports the study of Frías-Aceituno et al. (2013), who defended that gender diversity is one of the most important factors in the integrated dissemination of information. This conclusion is in agreement with different studies that supported the conclusion that a higher proportion of women on board of directors has a positive influence on the disclosure strategy by companies, in terms of sustainability and corporate social responsibility (Al-Shaer & Zaman, 2016; Dienes & Velte, 2016; Fernandez-Feijoo et al., 2014; Nadeem et al., 2017; Setó-Pamies, 2015).

The variable DUALITY is statistically significant at a significance level of 5% (coefficient = -1.227; p-value = 0.027), suggestive of an association between the CEO's duality and the recognition of leading practices of integrated reports. The coefficient of this variable is negative, so it is concluded that entities that have a CEO who is also the chairman of the board of directors tend to produce integrated reports that are not benchmarked. This conclusion seems to show that the concentration of power on only one person compromises the effectiveness of the board (Haniffa & Cooke, 2002), which is reflected in the result of its integrated reports.

The variable BEXPER is not statistically significant (coefficient = -0.046; p-value = 0.175), so, it is not possible to conclude on the cause-effect relationship (positive or negative), with the dependent variable.

FUTURE RESEARCH DIRECTIONS

The following step to open an avenue to future research is to extent the hypotheses to include a new approach concerning the importance of <IR> to the capital markets. Taking into consideration the existence of some characteristics related to board diversity on the probability of producing a report that is considered as of high quality and supported in best leading practices, the impact of the disclosure of these practices on the market value of organizations is a question for future research.

Table 3. Regression results

Variables	Coefficient	p-value
Constant	-0.960	0.643
Main variables:		
BSIZE	0.061	0.053
BINDEP	2.121	0.002
GENDER	3.995	0.000
DUALITY	-1.227	0.027
BEXPER	-0.046	0.175
Control variables:		
STATUSLIST	Included	Included
COUNTRY	Included	Included
LR Statistic	410.102	
Nagelkerke R^2	0.229	
BSIZE is the number of board members; BINDEP is the proportion of non-executive directors; GENDER is the proportion of women directors; DUALITY assumes 1 if the CEO is also the chairman of the board and 0 otherwise; BEXPER is the medium age of board members; STATUSLIST assumes 1 if the entity is listed on a stock exchange and 0 otherwise; COUNTRY represents the country institutional variables.		

CONCLUSION

This study examines the influence of some boards' diversity characteristics – board size, board independence, gender diversity, role duality and board experience - on the recognition of leading practices of the integrated reports, distinguishing between IR Reference reports (those of higher quality) and IR Regular reports (all the others), based on a sample of IR Reporters extracted from the IIRC Examples Database. Considered as a whole, the full sample reveals that the average number of directors on the Board is around 11 people, and 18% of the sample have women on that Board. The average age is 58 years. The non-executive directors represent about 67% of the total seats, from which around more than half (54%) are independent. These percentages however are not exactly similar between IR Reference reporters and IR Regular reporters, and some diversity across different geographic regions also exist.

The results of a logit regression show that larger Boards, with a larger proportion of non-executive directors and a higher proportion of women on the board have higher likelihood of producing an Integrated report that is highlighted as IR Reference, thus, of higher quality. This means that the composition of the Board has potential to contribute to the engagement and commitment with the integrated reporting and integrating thinking processes, leading to a better communication between the Boards and all the other stakeholders. However, the results also show that the duality role of the CEO/Chairman negatively influences the recognition of leading practices of the integrated reports, which means that the entities in which the CEO and the chairman of the board are the same person tend to produce integrated reports that are not awarded or considered leading (IR regular reporter). On the contrary, when the CEO and the chairman of the board are different, the probability of producing an integrated report of higher recognition (IR reference reporter) is greater. However, this relationship changes if unlisted entities are removed, mislaying its significance for the model (results not tabulated). This result suggests that in listed companies, the dual role of the CEO has no influence on the quality of the IR. Finally, the results do not find a relationship between the board experience and the likelihood of producing a IR report considered as reference.

This study contributes to the literature on the integrated reporting, a new concept that has been growing over the years, requesting new studies to add to the existing literature. It adds to the debate about the relationship between the board's characteristics and the recognition of leading practices of the integrated reports, analyzing if these certain characteristics on the company's board have an influence to produce integrated reports in a way that they are classified a IR reference reports. However, suffers from some limitations. First, the IIRC Examples Database only includes the companies that voluntarily send their integrated reports to the database. Second, the choice of the board's diversity characteristics for the study was also limited by the availability of information, having been chosen the variables that allowed to get the maximum of information possible.

ACKNOWLEDGMENT

This research was supported by the *Fundação para a Ciência e a Tecnologia* [grant number UID/GES/00315/2013 and UID/GES/00315/2019].

REFERENCES

Adams, C. A. (2015). The international integrated reporting council: A call to action. *Critical Perspectives on Accounting*, *27*, 23–28. doi:10.1016/j.cpa.2014.07.001

Akbas, H. E. (2016). The relationship between board characteristics and environmental disclosure: Evidence from Turkish listed companies. *South East European Journal of Economics and Business*, *11*(2), 7–19. doi:10.1515/jeb-2016-0007

Akhtaruddin, M., Hossain, M., & Yao, L. (2009). Corporate governance and voluntary disclosure in corporate annual reports of Malaysian listed firms. *Journal of Applied Management Accounting Research*, *7*(1), 1–19.

Al-Shaer, H., & Zaman, M. (2016). Board gender diversity and sustainability reporting quality. *Journal of Contemporary Accounting and Economics*, *12*(3), 210–222. doi:10.1016/j.jcae.2016.09.001

Allegrini, M., & Greco, G. (2013). Corporate boards, audit committees and voluntary disclosure: Evidence from Italian listed companies. *The Journal of Management and Governance*, *17*(1), 187–216. doi:10.100710997-011-9168-3

Bing, N. S., & Amran, A. (2017). The role of board diversity on materiality disclosure in sustainability reporting. *Global Business & Management Research*, *9*(4), 96–109.

Cahan, S. F., De Villiers, C., Jeter, D. C., Naiker, V., & Van Staden, C. J. (2016). Are CSR disclosures value relevant? Cross-country evidence. *European Accounting Review*, *25*(3), 579–611. doi:10.1080/09638180.2015.1064009

Cheng, E. C. M., & Courtenay, S. M. (2006). Board composition, regulatory regime and voluntary disclosure. *The International Journal of Accounting*, *41*(3), 262–289. doi:10.1016/j.intacc.2006.07.001

Cheng, M., Green, W., Conradie, P., Konishi, N., & Romi, A. (2014). The International Integrated Reporting Framework: Key Issues and Future Research Opportunities. *Journal of International Financial Management & Accounting*, *25*(1), 90–119. doi:10.1111/jifm.12015

De Villiers, C., & Marques, A. (2016). Corporate social responsibility, country-level predispositions, and the consequences of choosing a level of disclosure. *Accounting and Business Research*, *46*(2), 167–195. doi:10.1080/00014788.2015.1039476

De Villiers, C., Venter, E. R., & Hsiao, P.-C. (2017). Integrated reporting, measurement issues, approaches and an agenda for future research. *Accounting and Finance*, *57*(4), 937–959. doi:10.1111/acfi.12246

Dienes, D., & Velte, P. (2016). The impact of supervisory board composition on CSR reporting. Evidence from the German two-tier system. *Sustainability*, *8*(1), 1–20. doi:10.3390u8010063

Donnelly, R., & Mulcahy, M. (2008). Board structure, ownership, and voluntary disclosure in Ireland. *Corporate Governance*, *16*(5), 416–429. doi:10.1111/j.1467-8683.2008.00692.x

Eccles, R. G., & Armbrester, K. (2011). Integrated reporting in the cloud. *IESE Insight*, (8), 13–20.

Eccles, R. G., & Saltzman, D. (2011). Achieving sustainability through integrated reporting. *Stanford Social Innovation Review*, *9*(3), 56–61.

Eccles, R. G., & Serafeim, G. (2015). Corporate and integrated reporting: A functional perspective. In *Corporate Stewardship*. Sheffield, UK: Greenleaf Publishing.

Fasan, M., & Mio, C. (2016). Fostering stakeholder engagement: The role of materiality disclosure in integrated reporting. *Business Strategy and the Environment*, *26*(3), 288–305. doi:10.1002/bse.1917

Fernandez-Feijoo, B., Romero, S., & Ruiz-Blanco, S. (2014). Women on boards: Do they affect sustainability reporting? *Corporate Social Responsibility and Environmental Management*, *21*(6), 351–364. doi:10.1002/csr.1329

Frías-Aceituno, J. V., Rodríguez-Ariza, L., & García-Sánchez, I. M. (2013). The role of the board in the dissemination of integrated corporate social reporting. *Corporate Social Responsibility and Environmental Management*, *20*(4), 219–233. doi:10.1002/csr.1294

Fuente, J. A., García-Sánchez, I. M., & Lozano, M. B. (2017). The role of the board of directors in the adoption of GRI guidelines for the disclosure of CSR information. *Journal of Cleaner Production*, *141*, 737–750. doi:10.1016/j.jclepro.2016.09.155

Hafsi, T., & Turgut, G. (2013). Boardroom diversity and its effect on social performance: Conceptualization and empirical evidence. *Journal of Business Ethics*, *112*(3), 463–479. doi:10.100710551-012-1272-z

Hagendorff, J., & Keasey, K. (2012). The value of board diversity in banking: Evidence from the market for corporate control. *European Journal of Finance*, *18*(1), 41–58. doi:10.1080/1351847X.2010.481471

Handajani, L., Subroto, B., Sutrisno, T., & Saraswati, E. (2014). Does board diversity matter on corporate social disclosure? An Indonesian evidence. *Journal of Economics and Sustainable Development, 5*(9), 8–17.

Haniffa, R., & Cooke, T. (2002). Culture, corporate governance and disclosure in Malaysia corporations. *Abacus, 38*(3), 317–349. doi:10.1111/1467-6281.00112

Haniffa, R., & Cooke, T. (2005). The impact of culture and governance on corporate social reporting. *Journal of Accounting and Public Policy, 24*(5), 391–430. doi:10.1016/j.jaccpubpol.2005.06.001

Harjoto, M., Laksmana, I., & Lee, R. (2015). Board diversity and corporate social responsibility. *Journal of Business Ethics, 132*(4), 641–660. doi:10.100710551-014-2343-0

Herda, D. N., Taylor, M. E., & Winterbotham, G. (2012). The effect of board independence on the sustainability reporting practices of large U.S. firms. *Issues in Social & Environmental Accounting, 6*(3/4), 25–44.

Hoffman, B. M. (2012). *Integrated Reporting in practice: The South African story*. Retrieved from https://home.kpmg.com/content/dam/kpmg/pdf/2013/04/the-south-african-story.pdf

Hurghis, R. (2017). Integrated reporting and board features. *Audit Financiar, 15*(145), 83–92. doi:10.20869/AUDITF/2017/145/83

International Integrated Reporting Council (IIRC). (2013). *The international integrated reporting framework*. London: IIRC.

International Integrated Reporting Council (IIRC). (2019). *What? The tool for better reporting*. Retrieved from https://integratedreporting.org/what-the-tool-for-better-reporting/

Janggu, T., Darus, F., Zain, M. M., & Sawani, Y. (2014). Does good corporate governance lead to better sustainability reporting? An analysis using structural equation modeling. *Procedia: Social and Behavioral Sciences, 145*, 138–145. doi:10.1016/j.sbspro.2014.06.020

Jizi, M. I., Salama, A., Dixon, R., & Stratling, R. (2014). Corporate governance and corporate social responsibility disclosure: Evidence from the US banking sector. *Journal of Business Ethics, 125*(4), 601–615. doi:10.100710551-013-1929-2

Kang, H., Cheng, M., & Gray, S. J. (2007). Corporate governance and board composition: Diversity and independence of Australian boards. *Corporate Governance, 15*(2), 194–207. doi:10.1111/j.1467-8683.2007.00554.x

Krzus, M. P. (2011). Integrated reporting: If not now, when? *IRZ, 6*(6), 271–276.

Lim, S., Matolcsy, Z., & Chow, D. (2007). The association between board composition and different types of voluntary disclosure. *European Accounting Review, 16*(3), 555–583. doi:10.1080/09638180701507155

Mahmood, Z., Kouser, R., Ali, W., Ahmad, Z., & Salman, T. (2018). Does corporate governance affect sustainability disclosure? A mixed methods study. *Sustainability, 10*(1), 1–20. doi:10.3390u10010207 PMID:30607262

Maniora, J. (2017). Is integrated reporting really the superior mechanism for the integration of ethics into the core business model? An empirical analysis. *Journal of Business Ethics*, *140*(4), 755–786. doi:10.100710551-015-2874-z

Michelon, G., & Parbonetti, A. (2012). The effect of corporate governance on sustainability disclosure. *The Journal of Management and Governance*, *16*(3), 477–509. doi:10.100710997-010-9160-3

Morros, J. (2016). The integrated reporting: A presentation of the current state of art and aspects of integrated reporting that need further development. *Intangible Capital*, *12*(1), 336–356. doi:10.3926/ic.700

Nadeem, M., Zaman, R., & Saleem, I. (2017). Boardroom gender diversity and corporate sustainability practices: Evidence from Australian securities exchange listed firms. *Journal of Cleaner Production*, *149*, 874–885. doi:10.1016/j.jclepro.2017.02.141

Pavlopoulos, A., Magnis, C., & Iatridis, G. E. (2017). Integrated reporting: Is it the last piece of the accounting disclosure puzzle? *Journal of Multinational Financial Management*, *41*, 23–46. doi:10.1016/j.mulfin.2017.05.001

Pechersky, A. (2016). Diversity in board of directors: Review of diversity as a factor to enhance board performance. *Studia Commercialia Bratislavensia*, *9*(33), 88–101. doi:10.1515tcb-2016-0009

Post, C., Rahman, N., & Rubow, E. (2011). Green governance: Boards of directors' composition and environmental corporate social responsibility. *Business & Society*, *50*(1), 189–223. doi:10.1177/0007650310394642

Prado-Lorenzo, J. M., & García-Sánchez, I. M. (2010). The role of the board of directors in disseminating relevant information on greenhouse gases. *Journal of Business Ethics*, *97*(3), 391–424. doi:10.100710551-010-0515-0

PwC. (2015). *Implementing integrated reporting*. Retrieved from https://www.pwc.com/gx/en/audit-services/publications/assets/pwc-ir-practical-guide.pdf

Rao, K., & Tilt, C. (2016). Board composition and corporate social responsibility: The role of diversity, gender, strategy and decision making. *Journal of Business Ethics*, *138*(2), 327–347. doi:10.100710551-015-2613-5

Robertson. (2015). *What is Integrated Reporting and why does it matter?* ICAS. Retrieved from https://www.icas.com/ca-today-news/what-is-integrated-reporting-why-it-matters

Roxana-Ioana, B., & Petru, S. (2017). Integrated reporting for a good corporate governance. *Ovidius University Annals Series Economic Sciences*, *17*(1), 424–428.

Samaha, K., Khlif, H., & Hussainey, K. (2015). The impact of board and audit committee characteristics on voluntary disclosure: A meta-analysis. *Journal of International Accounting, Auditing & Taxation*, *24*, 13–28. doi:10.1016/j.intaccaudtax.2014.11.001

Setó-Pamies, D. (2013). The relationship between women directors and corporate social responsibility. *Corporate Social Responsibility and Environmental Management*, *22*(6), 334–345. doi:10.1002/csr.1349

Shrivastav, S. M., & Kalsie, A. (2016). The relationship between CEO duality and firm performance: An analysis using panel data approach. *IUP Journal of Corporate Governance*, *15*(2), 37–58.

Slack, R., & Tsalavoutas, I. (2018). Integrated reporting decision usefulness: Mainstream equity market views. *Accounting Forum*, *42*(2), 184–198. doi:10.1016/j.accfor.2018.01.005

Stacchezzini, R., Melloni, G., & Lai, A. (2016). Sustainability management and reporting: the role of integrated reporting for communicating corporate sustainability management. *Journal of Cleaner Production*, *136*(Part A), 102–110.

Velte, P., & Stawinoga, M. (2017). Integrated reporting: The current state of empirical research, limitations and future research implications. *Journal of Management Control*, *28*(3), 275–320. doi:10.100700187-016-0235-4

Vitola, F., Raimo, N., & Rubino, M. (2017). Appreciations, criticisms, determinants, and effects of integrated reporting: A systematic literature review. *Corporate Social Responsibility and Environmental Management*, *26*(2), 518–528. doi:10.1002/csr.1734

Zhou, S., Simnett, R., & Green, W. (2017). Does integrated reporting matter to the capital market? *Abacus*, *53*(1), 94–132. doi:10.1111/abac.12104

ADDITIONAL READING

Adams, C. A., Potter, B., Singh, P. J., & York, J. (2016). Exploring the implications of integrated reporting for social investment (disclosures). *The British Accounting Review*, *48*(3), 283–296. doi:10.1016/j.bar.2016.05.002

Baboukardos, D., & Rimmel, G. (2016). Value relevance of accounting information under an integrated reporting approach: A research note. *Journal of Accounting and Public Policy*, *35*(4), 437–452. doi:10.1016/j.jaccpubpol.2016.04.004

Bernardi, C., & Stark, A. W. (2018). Environmental, social and governance disclosure, integrated reporting, and the accuracy of analyst forecasts. *The British Accounting Review*, *50*(1), 16–31. doi:10.1016/j.bar.2016.10.001

Brown, J., & Dillard, J. (2014). Integrated reporting: On the need for broadening out and opening up. *Accounting, Auditing & Accountability Journal*, *27*(7), 1120–1156. doi:10.1108/AAAJ-04-2013-1313

Chaidali, P., & Jones, M. J. (2017). It's a matter of trust: Exploring the perceptions of Integrated Reporting preparers. *Critical Perspectives on Accounting*, *48*, 1–20. doi:10.1016/j.cpa.2017.08.001

Rinaldi, L., Unerman, J., & de Villiers, C. (2018). Evaluating the integrated reporting journey: Insights, gaps and agendas for future research. *Accounting, Auditing & Accountability Journal*, *31*(5), 1294–1318. doi:10.1108/AAAJ-04-2018-3446

Rowbottom, N., & Locke, J. (2016). The emergence of <IR>. *Accounting and Business Research*, *46*(1), 83–115. doi:10.1080/00014788.2015.1029867

Stubbs, W., & Higgins, C. (2014). Integrated Reporting and internal mechanisms of change. *Accounting, Auditing & Accountability Journal*, *27*(7), 1068–1089. doi:10.1108/AAAJ-03-2013-1279

Tweedie, D., & Martinov-Bennie, N. (2015). Entitlements and time: Integrated reporting's double-edged agenda. *Social and Environmental Accountability Journal*, *35*(1), 49–61. doi:10.1080/0969160X.2015.1007466

KEY TERMS AND DEFINITIONS

Board of Directors: A group of people with powers, duties, and responsibilities to decide and supervise the activities (strategic and operational) of an organization.

Corporate Reporting: There is no unique definition, but includes the communication helping an organization to demonstrate to shareholders and potential investors its capabilities, opportunities, as well as the management's ability to deal with changes in the business environment.

IIRC: The International Integrated Reporting Council (IIRC) is a global coalition of regulators, investors, companies, standard setters, the accounting profession and NGOs, promoting communication about value creation as the next step in the evolution of corporate reporting.

Integrated Report: A summarizing communication about how an organization's strategy, governance, performance and forecasts, lead to the creation of value in the short, medium and long term.

Integrated Reporting: A process founded in integrated thinking resulting in a periodic integrated report published by an organization about the value creation over time and other related concerns.

Integrated Reporter: An organization that prepares and publish integrated reports.

Integrated Thinking: Is the active attention by an organization of the relationships between its various operating and functional units and the capitals that the organization uses or affects and leads to integrated decision-making and actions that consider the creation of value over the short, medium and long term.

IR Reference Report: It is an integrated report considered by IIRC as being prepared under best practices or awarded by an external indepe006Edent organization, as included in the IIRC Examples Database.

IR Reference Report: It is an integrated report included in the IIRC Examples Database but not considered as IR Reference Report.

Chapter 9
Corporate Social Responsibility Reporting and Climate Change:
Carbon Emissions Disclosures by Portuguese Companies

Ana Florindo
Research Center on Accounting and Taxation, Portugal

Kátia Lemos
https://orcid.org/0000-0002-3961-5964
Research Center on Accounting and Taxation, Portugal

Sónia Monteiro
Research Center on Accounting and Taxation, Portugal

Verónica Ribeiro
Research Center on Accounting and Taxation, Portugal

ABSTRACT

This article aims to investigate the extent of carbon emissions disclosures in Portuguese companies operating in environmentally sensitive industries, from 2008 to 2012. Additionally, the chapter aims to explore the factors that explain the extent of such disclosures. The research sample is based upon Portuguese companies that had been continuously integrating in the PNALE I and II, over the twelve-year period. A content analysis of their annual/sustainability reports was conducted to explore the carbon emissions-related disclosures. The study also uses a disclosure index to investigate the extent of disclosure and a panel data regression model was performed to determine the factors that influence carbon emissions reporting. The results show a relatively high level of disclosure and the influence of size, activity sector, concentration of capital and economic period on the level of disclosure presented.

DOI: 10.4018/978-1-7998-2128-1.ch009

INTRODUCTION

Global climate change has become the epicentre of the concerns of global governments as they pose a threat to humanity. These changes can have natural and/or anthropogenic causes to which technological innovation, subject to constant change, has contributed, which obliges companies to join in order to face the competition that takes place in an increasingly globalized market.

In the sense of mitigating the environmental impacts caused by the emission of gaseous pollutants, the Kyoto Protocol of 1997 implied the commitment of several countries to reduce atmospheric emissions. Within the European Union (EU), Member States have committed to reduce their emissions by 8% over the period 2008-2010 compared to 1990 levels. In this context, Directive 2003/87/ EC, of 13 October, established a European Greenhouse Gas Emissions Trading Scheme (EU ETS).

This market allows entities that exceed established targets to buy contamination rights from entities that have achieved reductions above fixed limits. In this way, the emissions market starts to stimulate the economy, with more than one million licenses (about 23 million euros) being traded in 2006 (year after its entry into service). In the second period, the quantity of allowances allocated decreases and the price of the ton of carbon has increased. The price of licenses is very variable, being influenced by political, economic, climate, among others (Santos, 2013). With the evolution of the EU ETS for the third period (2013-2020) the allowances are no longer allocated free of charge (as they were in the first two phases: 2005-2007 and 2008-2012) and are now auctioned.

With regard to the accounting of CO_2 emission allowances, there is no accounting regulation in this area at both European and international level[1]. The absence of a specific accounting standard, set by the International Accounting Standards Board (IASB), which regulates the accounting treatment of allowances has led to the adoption of different accounting treatments by the contracting entities. In this sense, some Member States (such as Portugal, Spain, Belgium, France and the United Kingdom) felt the need to develop specific regulations applicable in these countries for the accounting treatment of such licenses.

In Portugal, following the approval of the Accounting Standardization System (Sistema de Normalização Contabilística, SNC), Decree Law (DL) No. 158/2009, of 13 July, amended by DL 98/2105, published Accounting and Financial Reporting Standard (Norma Contabilística e de Relato Financeiro, NCRF) No. 26 - Environmental Matters, with has an appendix dedicated to the accounting of CO_2 emission allowances.

In view of the above, this topic has been catching the interest of researchers who are looking to see if companies disclose information about GHG emissions and the impact of certain company characteristics on the disclosure level presented (Giorgios & Dimitrios, 2009); Prado Lorenzo et al., 2009; Luo et al., 2012; Luo et al., 2013; González-González & Zamora Ramírez, 2016; Kalu et al., 2016; Liesen et al., 2015; Hermawan et al., 2018; Faisal et al., 2018; Akbas & Canikli, 2018; Hapsoro & Ambarwati, 2018; Borhei et al., 2018; Hasih et al., 2019; Kiliç & Kuzey, 2019).

In this sense, this paper pretends to contribute to the greenhouse gas (GHG) disclosure literature by analysing the level of disclosure about Emission Allowances (EA) in Portuguese companies that have been covered by National Plan for the Allocation of Emission Licenses (Plano Nacional de Atribuição de Licenças de Emissão, PNALE) and to identify the determinants of disclosure level.

This research provides empirical evidence on the determinants of GHG emission licenses disclosure, which could be useful for organizations and regulatory bodies, especially in Portugal's commitment to reduce emission of GHG. These findings may be useful in the definition of policies that seek to minimize greenhouse gas emissions.

After this introduction, the structure of this work is organized in three points. In the first point, an approach is taken with regard to the functioning of the carbon market and the accounting framework for CO_2 emission allowances. The second point is dedicated to the literature review and the development of research hypothesis. Following is the research design, namely the presentation of the selected sample and the research methodology developed. Finally, the results are analyzed and discussed, and the solutions and recommendations, the clues for future research and the conclusion are presented.

THE CARBON MARKET AND THE ACCOUNTING FRAMEWORK FOR CO_2 EMISSION LICENSES

The European Carbon Market

The EU ETS, created by Directive 2003/87/EC, is a revolutionary application with an unparalleled dimension with regard to environmental policy instruments, mainly for global pollutants such as CO_2 (carbon dioxide).

In order to comply with the Kyoto Protocol, to reduce its CO_2 emissions by 8% compared to 1990, the EU sought to define a set of measures and policies with the aim of minimizing the costs to be borne by Member States. The creation of a market for the transaction of CO_2 emissions was one of the most important measures.

After a number of discussions on the subject, the EU ETS was legally established in 2003, with Directive 2003/87/EC of the European Parliament and of the Council of 13 October 2003. This market came into force in 2005, with the initial Directive being amended by Directive 2004/101/EC and later by Directive 2009/29/EC, which regulated the post-2012 period by introducing more greenhouse gases (GHGs) and more sectors (Santos, 2013).

It is possible to distinguish three important stages in the implementation of this market (Monast et al., 2009):

- Phase I, which ran from 2005 to 2008, which corresponded to a pilot phase pre-Kyoto Protocol and is considered as the learning phase, with free allocation of EA.
- Phase II, which took place between 2008 and 2012, and corresponds to the period of validity of the Kyoto Protocol. During this phase the free allocation have been reduced in 10%.
- Phase III, between 2013 and 2020, which represents a unilateral EU commitment to reduce greenhouse gas emissions and was negotiated under the Kyoto Protocol. The commitment for this phase is to reduce emissions in 20% in 2020, compared to 2005.

The Directive defines the concept of Emission Allowance as the right to emit a tonne of carbon dioxide (CO_2) or any other greenhouse gas having an equivalent effect for a given period.

The possession of a license issued for that purpose by the competent authorities has been required to greenhouse gas installations, which operate one of the activities listed in Annex I to the Directive and which form part of a national allocation plan, since the beginning of 2005. As regards the emission allowance limits to be allocated to each sector and the method of allocation, the Directive states that both will be established by each Member State and should be based on objective and clear criteria.

In the EU Carbon Market, the cap-and-trade system is applied, with a limited number of licenses being granted to the entities for a given period, which may sell the surplus allowances or acquire them if they are not sufficient (Fernandes et al., 2009).

According to KPMG UK (2008), cap-and-trade establishes a maximum value for total pollutant emissions in a given period, which is translated into allowances distributed across facilities. It is then determined that the respective pollutant company must hold the emission allowances corresponding to the polluting emissions carried out. If there is an excess of licenses, that is to say, it holds more licenses than the emissions that it plans to carry out, it can sell them in the market, as it can buy if there is a deficit of licenses.

On the other hand, with regard to the form of allocation of licenses, the directive establishes, in addition to the cap-and-trade system in the EU, the free distribution - grandfathering - as a rule to be followed. In other words, each Member State allocates free-of-charge CO_2 allowances (initial allocation), with an auction of 5% of the CO_2 emission allowances in the first phase (2005-2008) and 10% in the second phase (2008-2012).

The Directive, which led to the creation of the EU ETS, also imposed on Member States the responsibility to ensure the free movement of allowances within the European Community, and also made it obligatory for plant operators to deliver the allowances corresponding to their total emissions in the course of the previous year, for later annulment, until 30 April of each year. It is therefore essential that at the end of each year, facility operators inform the responsible authorities about their actual emission levels.

Directive 2003/87/EC, of October 13th is currently transposed into the Portuguese legal system through DL no. 233/2004, of December 14th (with the amendments introduced by DL no. 24-A/2004, of December 31st and DL no. 230/2005, of December 29th) and applies from 1st January of 2005 to a number of installations in the industrial and electro producing sectors.

Following this legislation, in 2005, through the Resolution of the Council of Ministers no. 53/2005 of March 3rd, the first National Plan for the Allocation of Emission Licenses (PNALE) for the period 2005-2007 was approved, and for a later period, from 2008 to 2012, PNALE II was approved, through the Resolution of the Council of Ministers no. 1/2008, of January 4th. These plans define the methodology and criteria for the free allocation of allowances to plants in Portuguese territory. The companies covered by the PNALE are granted a quantity of licenses, which represent the "cap" that each can emit of CO_2, being able to acquire licenses in the EU ETS if they surpass this "cap", or to sell licenses if they do not reach the total quantities attributed. Portugal under the Kyoto Protocol has set a target of not exceeding its emissions by 27% in the period 2008-2012, compared to the reference year 1990. To this end, it has drawn up the National Climate Change Plan (PNAC), approved in 2004 and reformulated in 2006 (Santos, 2013).

With the publication of the new Directive 2009/29/EC, included in the Energy Climate Package, the rules change considerably, starting on January 1st, 2013, to a new period of application of the EU ETS regime: 2013-2020 period.

This period is governed by new rules, in particular as regards the monitoring and reporting of greenhouse gas emissions from all activities listed in Annex I to Directive 2009/29/EC of April 23rd. These rules for the monitoring and reporting of emissions are set out in Commission Regulation (EU) No 601/2012 of June 21st.

In general, there is an extension of the scope with the introduction of new gases and new sectors, the total quantity of allowances determined at Community level and the allocation of allowances by means of an auction, remaining marginally free allocation, based on benchmarks defined at Community level.

Accounting Standard for CO_2 Emission Allowances

At an international level, the IASB has published several International Accounting Standards that determine accounting principles and provisions applicable to the treatment of environmental matters[2]. However, they are not sufficient to respond to the specific treatment of emission allowances, and an international regulatory vacuum of the IASB remains with regard to the specific treatment of these matters. In 2004, the IFRIC 3 "Emission Rights" was issued by the IASB, which dealt with the issue of GHG emission allowances.

However, the European Financial Reporting Advisory Group (EFRAG) was reluctant to apply it in the European Union, exposing its disagreement as to the reliability of the financial information that IFRIC 3 intended to implement and it was repealed by the IASB in June 2005.

Within the EU, entities with securities admitted to trading on a regulated market are obliged to adopt regulations issued by the IASB, which is accepted by the EU, pursuant to Regulation No. 1606/2002 of the European Parliament and of the Council, of July 19th. Therefore, listed companies also lack specific accounting regulations to deal with EA.

Reference should, however, be made to the European Commission Recommendation of May 30th, 2001, providing an accounting standard-setting framework for the recognition, measurement and dissemination of environmental matters, with some countries having accepted the recommendation in their national legislation.

In Portugal, the Accounting Directive (Diretriz Contabilística, DC) 29 - Environmental Matters, approved in 2002, accepted that recommendation, thus imposing an accounting framework designed for environmental matters. In addition, Technical Interpretation (TI) No. 4 - Emission rights of greenhouse gases: accounting for emission allowances was issued. Subsequently, the Accounting Standardization System was approved by DL no. 158/2009, of July 13rd, repealing this guideline. The SNC is composed of 28 accounting and financial reporting standards, adapted from IAS / IFRS and accepted in the EU, which includes NCRF 26 - Environmental Matters, which is an almost complete transcription of DC 29, the appendix of which is identical to Technical Interpretation (TI) no.4.

Table 1 summarizes the main aspects provided in the national accounting standard for CO_2 emission allowances.

LITERATURE REVIEW AND HYPOTHESIS DEVELOPMENT

Recently, several studies have been developed with the intent to identify the determinants of GHG emission disclosure in certain countries, like China (Li et al., 2018; Zhou et al., 2018), Turkey (Akbas & Canikli, 2018; Kiliç & Kuzey, 2019), Malaysia (Kalu et al., 2016), Indonesia (Hermawan et al., 2018, Nasih et al. 2019) and Australia (Borghei, et al., 2018), or in more than one country (Prado-Lorenzo et al., 2009; Luo et al., 2012; Luo et al., 2013; Liesen et al., 2015; Hapsoro & Ambarwati, 2018).

Some of these studies indicate a great tendency for choosing samples composed by listed companies (Prado-Lorenzo & García-Sanchez, 2010; Kalu et al., 2016; Broadstock et al., 2018; Faisal et al., 2018; Borghei et al., 2018; Nasih et al., 2019; Kiliç & Kuzey, 2019) or by companies that have participated in CDP (Prado-Lorenzo & García-Sanchez, 2010; Luo et al., 2012; Li et al., 2018; Akbas & Canikli, 2018), also considering companies belonging to certain sectors of activity (Kalu et al., 2016; Zhou et al., 2018; Hermawan et al., 2018; Nasih et al., 2019) or considered more polluting (Hapsoro & Ambarwati, 2018).

Table 1. Accounting treatment of GHG emission allowances (NCRF 26 and its appendix)

Recognition	GHG Emission Allowances	Recognition of an intangible asset.
	Licenses acquired free of charge	Recognition of a subsidy evidenced in equity. The allowance will be charged to income on the basis of the depreciation recorded (NCFF 22).
Measurement	Initial measurement of licenses acquired free of charge	Measurement at Fair Value.
	Initial measurement of licenses acquired for a fee	Measurement at fair value, which is assumed to coincide with the acquisition cost.
Subsequent Measurement	Subsequent Measurement	Period expense (amortization of intangible assets) measured by the cost of the licenses, on a FIFO basis.
	Subsequent Measurement	Recognition of a provision and an expense for the best estimate of expenditure (NCRF 21)
	Cost Model vs. Revaluation Model	Missing (however, these models are set out in IFRS 6 - Intangible assets)
Derecognition	Delivery of licenses	Derecognition of the carrying amount of the IIA (accumulated amortization and intangible assets).
	Alienation of Licenses	Derecognition of Intangible assets, and recognition of other income and gains / expenses and losses, and recognition of net financial debt. Derecognizing the allowance against a revenue and earnings account (if it is a free allocation)
	Cancellation of unused licenses (purchased free of charge)	Derecognition of the subsidy and the intangible asset.
	Cancellation of unused licenses (purchased for a fee)	Recognition of the expense or loss and derecognition of the intangible asset.
	Cancellation of licenses that you do not have	Recognition of new licenses acquired, the provision, as well as the IA, are derecognized for the licenses issued (not available at the date of issue)
Disclosure	Disclosure	- Emissions of greenhouse gases in tonnes of carbon dioxide equivalent; - EA sold in the year in tonnes of carbon dioxide and their price; - EA acquired in the year in tonnes of carbon dioxide and their price; - Fines, and ancillary sanctions related to the emission of greenhouse gases; - Fair value of the licenses held.

Source: Adapted from Boas and Monteiro (2012)

The influence of some firm characteristics in GHG emission disclosure has been proved by several authors that have identified some determinants of disclosure, such as the size of the company (Liu & Anbumozhi, 2009; Giorgios & Dimitrios, 2009; Prado Lorenzo et al., 2009; Luo et al, 2012; Luo et al, 2013; González-González & Zamora Ramíorez, 2016; Kalu et al., 2016; Liesen et al., 2015; Hermawan et al., 2018; Faisal et al., 2018; Akbas & Canikli, 2018; Nasih et al., 2019; Kiliç & Kuzey, 2019), the activity sector (Giorgios & Dimitrios, 2009; Liesen et al., 2015; Faisal et al., 2018; Kiliç & Kuzey, 2019), profitability (Luo et al., 2013; Liesen et al., 2015; González-González & Zamora Ramírez, 2016; Kalu et al., 2016; Hermawan et al., 2018; Hapsoro & Ambarwati, 2018; Faisal et al., 2018; Borghei et al., 2018; Akbas & Canikli, 2018) and leverage (Kalu et al., 2016; Hapsoro & Ambarwati, 2018; Faisal et al., 2018).

This paper aims to investigate the extent of carbon emissions disclosure in Portuguese companies operating in environmentally sensitive industries, from 2008 to 2012, and to identify its determinant factors.

Based on a joint and complementary perspective of Institutional (isomorphism coercive) and Legitimacy theories, the paper aims to explore the factors that explain the extent of such disclosures.

The NCRF 26 is the standard that regulates environmental matters accounting, and thus it is intended to analyze the degree of disclosure in relation to CO_2 emission licenses, based on the items outlined in the appendix of the NCRF 26.

Thus, it starts with the general hypothesis that associates the disclosure on emission allowances to certain organizational characteristics, developing a model that considers a quantitative variable that measures the degree of disclosure [which is referred to as the Carbon Emissions Disclosure Index (CEDI)] as the dependent variable. This model considers as independent variables, the variables associated with different factors, such as: social pressure factor, shareholders' pressure factor, market pressure factor and institutional pressure factor.

Following we present the research hypotheses defined to measure the impact of these factors on the degree of disclosure on CO_2 emission licenses, based on the following variables:

- Social pressure factor: size, sector and environmental certification
- Shareholders' pressure factor: capital concentration
- Market pressure factor: profitability, leverage and Carbon Disclosure Project
- Institutional pressure factor: economic period

Social Pressure Factor

External social pressure, especially of society in general, is more felt in larger companies and / or in those that carry out more polluting activities. These companies, on the one hand, are more subject to regulations by governments and, on the other hand, are under more observation from the stakeholders. Being more exposed, they tend to be more controlled by society in terms of the information they disclose abroad and also through the media. Thus, there tends to be a positive relation between the size of the company and the disclosure of information, in this case, environmental (Prado Lorenzo et al., 2009). Similarly, there is empirical evidence of an association between the disclosure of GHG emissions and the activity sector (Giorgios & Dimitrios, 2009; Liesen et al., 2015; Faisal et al., 2018; Kiliç & Kuzey, 2019).

Particularly in more polluting companies, the issue of environmental certification comes up with some importance, insofar as international studies argue that companies with environmental management committees or environmental control and management systems make these companies more environmentally aware, making not only a greater attempt to improve environmental aspects but also in their dissemination (Rankin et al., 2011). Authors such as Monteiro (2006) and Del Brio et al. (2001) conclude that companies with an environmental certificate tend to give greater importance to the environmental issue and, therefore, tend to do more about this.

Size

The size of the company is the variable most frequently considered in studies related to environmental disclosure in general (Brammer & Pavelin, 2008; Stanny & Ely, 2008; Liu & Anbumozhi, 2009), and on GHG emission in particular (Liu & Anbumozhi, 2009; Giorgios & Dimitrios, 2009; Prado Lorenzo et al., 2009; Luo et al, 2012; Luo et al, 2013; González-González & Zamora Ramíorez, 2016; Kalu et al., 2016; Liesen et al., 2015; Hermawan et al., 2018; Faisal et al., 2018; Akbas & Canikli, 2018; Nasih et al., 2019; Kiliç & Kuzey, 2019).

From the point of view of Hackston and Milne (1996), in the theory of legitimacy there are indications about the existence of an influence of size in environmental disclosure. In fact, large companies, because of an organizational structure and audit and auditing processes, are more inclined to better inform of their environmental performance in their annual accounts. Thus, predicting a positive relationship between the size of the company and the disclosure of CO_2 EA, it is expected to prove the following hypothesis:

H1.1.: Larger companies have a greater degree of disclosure on CO_2 EA.

Activity Sector

The sector where the activity of a company is inserted can be a determining factor in the disclosure of environmental information, and there is empirical evidence of a significant association between the disclosure of GHG and the activity sector (Giorgios & Dimitrios, 2009; Liesen et al., 2015; Faisal et al., 2018; Kiliç & Kuzey, 2019). In the concrete case of the potentially most polluting sectors, these tend to be forced to publish more environmental information, since they are exposed to a growing environmental normative (Wilmshurst & Frost, 2000; Archel & Lizarraga, 2001; Campbell, 2003).

As far as this study is concerned, all the sectors included in the sample, because they belong to the PNALE II list, are considered to be potentially polluting, making it difficult to distinguish those which will have a more significant environmental impact and which can therefore be reflected in a greater degree of disclosure. Thus, it is formulated the following hypothesis, without predicting the association sign:

H1.2.: The level of disclosure on CO_2 EA is related to the sector of activity in which the company operates.

Environmental Certification

Monteiro (2006) and Del Brio et al. (2001) argue that companies that have environmental certification are more likely to give the environment greater prominence, both at the accounting level and at the organizational level. Archel and Lizarraga (2001) also indicate that an entity that has certification of standards such as ISO 14001 or EMAS has substantial additions to the level of environmental disclosure, since the standards themselves impose requirements at that level. In this way, it can be assumed that the same will happen regarding the release of CO_2 EA.

Although the variable "Environmental Certification" has not been the subject of any empirical study that seeks to determine if it is a determinant factor of the degree of EA in concrete, there are already some empirical studies that designate the certification as an explanatory factor of the disclosure on environmental in general (Archel & Lizarraga, 2001; Mitchell & Hill, 2009; Serrat & Aliberch, 2010; Monteiro & Guzmán, 2010a); Barros & Monteiro, 2012). Thus, and based on these studies, we believe that the possession of environmental certification may also influence the disclosure of CO_2 emission licenses.

In view of the above, we decided to include this variable in our study, formulating the following hypothesis:

H1.3.: Companies with environmental certification have a higher level of disclosure on CO_2 EA.

Shareholders Pressure Factor

Shareholders play an important role in promoting and lobbying for the disclosure on environmental matters by companies (Lee et al., 2015). This type of information can be useful for attracting investors, which can, in turn, guarantee the profitability of shareholders, as well as value their investments (Lee et al., 2015).

Gonzalez-Gonzalez & Zamora Ramirez (2016) conducted a study where they analyzed the environmental disclosure, analyzing on the one hand the significance of the companies listed on the stock exchange and, on the other hand, the significance of the concentration of capital. They concluded that there is a positive relationship between stock market quotation and environmental disclosure, and in terms of concentration of capital, there was a negative correlation, that is, the more the concentration of capital in shareholders, the less environmental disclosure. Taking into account that the sample used in this study is mainly composed of listed companies, only the impact of capital concentration on the level of disclosure on CO_2 emission licenses will be analysed.

Concentration of Capital

Some studies claim that a smaller group of shareholders leads to greater disclosure of voluntary information (Baek et al., 2009; Borghei & Leung, 2013). On the other hand, other studies affirm that a greater number of shareholders will lead to greater pressure for the transparency of the company, namely at the level of disclosure (Prencipe, 2004; Cormier et al., 2005) This is further supported by Reverte (2009) who argues that, in the case of a large number of shareholders, a higher level of disclosure leads to a reduction of agency risks between managers and shareholders. The study by Brammer and Pavelin (2008) associated this variable with the disclosure of specifically environmental information and González-González & Zamora Ramírez (2016) obtained empirical evidence of a negative association between GHG disclosure and ownership concentration. Thus, we tried to test the following hypothesis of investigation:

H2.1. Companies with the lowest concentration of capital have a higher degree of disclosure on CO_2 EA.

Market Pressure Factor

This factor is reflected in the pressure that investors and creditors exert on companies' managers (Lee et al., 2015). Given the importance of current climate change, the disclosure of information becomes a point that may be favourable to companies in their quest for foreign investment. This disclosure may also be significantly correlated, positively or negatively, with its profit, financial risk, among other economic-financial ratios (Luo et al., 2012)

Analyzing the financial performance is interesting, since, according to some studies, companies with greater profit are better positioned to face the costs related to CO2 emissions and indirectly with disclosure (Bewley & Li, 2000; Cormier et al., 2004). Theories such as legitimacy give strength to the interest of companies to disclose environmental matters in order to have the approval of third parties, and the companies with the best financial position are the ones that most disclose their business and financial information. (Magness, 2006; Stanny & Ely, 2008). Ismail and Chandler (2005) have found evidence that there is a positive relationship between disclosure and profit.

Profitability

The influence of profitability on environmental disclosure has been the subject of many studies, although they are not conclusive on the positive profitability relation - environmental disclosure (Gray et al. 1995a; Moneva & Llena, 1996; Hackston & Milne, 1996; Archel & Lizarraga, 2001). Giorgios e Dimitrios (2009) report in their study that there is a positive association between the release of CO_2 EA and profitability. Furthermore, the studies carried out by Luo et al. (2013), Liesen et al. (2015), González-González & Zamora Ramírez (2016), Kalu et al. (2016), Hermawan et al. (2018), Hapsoro & Ambarwati (2018), Faisal et al. (2018), Borghei et al. (2018), and Akbas & Canikli (2018) have proven a positive association between profitability and GHG disclosure. Thus, following this study, we formulate the following hypothesis:

H3.1: The most profitable companies have a greater degree of disclosure on CO_2 EA.

Carbon Disclosure Project

Climate change is a social concern today, and stakeholders have different expectations in this regard, exerting pressure on organizations for these to disclose relevant information (Prado Lorenzo et al., 2009; Luo et al., 2013). Disclosure of environmental information for stakeholders, and the disclosure of information through CDP, is strategic for organizations. Carbon disclosure can be used by the organizations' managers to show their compliance to social expectations in regard to climate change and thus achieve legitimacy (Luo et al., 2012).

Thus, following this study, we formulate the following hypothesis:

H3.2.: Companies responding to the CDP survey present a greater degree of disclosure on CO2 EA.

Leverage

In heavily leveraged companies there is greater pressure from creditors to provide more detailed information about their activity, since disclosure reduces the existing asymmetries between companies and their potential creditors, thereby reducing financing costs (Sengupta, 1998). According to stakeholder theory, the greater the leverage of the company, the greater the pressure from the creditor to the company (Prasetya &Yulianto, 2018).

Gonzalez-Gonzalez e Zamora Ramírez (2016) argue that more leveraged companies are subject to more scrutiny by their investors and creditors and therefore tend to disclose more information on GHG emissions to meet the requirements of these stakeholders. Furthermore, Kalu et al. (2016), Hapsoro and Ambarwati (2018), and Faisal et al. (2018) found empirical evidence of a positive relation between GHG disclosure and leverage. In this way, the following hypothesis is formulated:

H3.3.: Companies with higher levels of leverage present a greater degree of disclosure on $_{CO2}$ EA.

Institutional Pressure Factor

Many of the procedures and policies adopted by organizations result from pressures exerted by public opinion, by the entities with which they have commercial relations, by social prestige and by existing laws and standards. Through the design of a formal structure that adheres to the myths prescribed by the institutional environment, the organization demonstrates that it acts correctly and adequately (Carpenter & Feroz, 2001).

One of the basic concepts of Institutional Theory is that of isomorphism, which consists of the process by which a unit of a given population is forced to resemble other units facing the same environmental conditions. One of the basic propositions of this theory is that isomorphism is a form of legitimation (DiMaggio & Powell, 1983; Meyer & Rowan, 1977) and that organizations that deviate from institutionalized prescriptions face considerable costs of legitimacy (Meyer & Rowan, 1977).

Institutional Theory has been used on several empirical studies on accounting and environmental management (Delmas & Toffel, 2004; Ribeiro, 2007; Barros & Monteiro, 2012), with the objective of identifying and studying the institutional pressures that can explain the behavior of organizations with a view to legitimization, as well as the environmental accounting practices adopted in the process of organizational change.

Some authors (Delmas & Toffel, 2004; Marshall et al., 2005) believe that institutional and normative pressures may be, even indirectly, the main reason for the implementation of environmental management practices by organizations. Thus, by analogy, we consider that both the very specificities of an organization and the legislative pressures (coercive isomorphism) can trigger the adoption of accounting practices and dissemination of environmental information, more specifically, the dissemination of information on CO_2 emission licenses. On the other hand, Petty and Cuganesan (2005) argue that the reporting of information by the best companies encourages other companies to reproduce their benchmarking in order to be among the best market practices (mimetic isomorphism).

Economic Period

Taking into account the possible increase in the contracting of CO_2 emission allowances, as a result of the change in the way they are attributed and the possible increase of the experience acquired by the companies in their negotiation, it is expected that the levels of disclosure on these licenses increase over the period 2008 to 2017, with a special focus on the period from 2013 to 2017.

On the other hand, taking into account the basic concepts of Institutional Theory, it is expected that the non-disclosing companies feel pressured to follow the example of the disclosing companies and that there is a gradual increase in isomorphism with regard to the disclosure of information on emission allowances, with an increase in the number of disclosing companies during the period under study.

In view of the above, the following hypothesis of investigation is formulated:

H4.1.: The level of disclosure on CO_2 EA will be higher in the period 2013 to 2017 compared to the period 2008 to 2012.

Table 2, sums up the defined hypothesis and the predicted sign to the association of each firm characteristic with disclosure level on EA.

RESEARCH DESIGN

Sample

Most of the studies on compulsory environmental disclosure are about entities of the industrial activity sectors, since the sector of activity where the company is inserted positively influences the environmental disclosure (Archel & Lizarraga, 2001; Campbell, 2003; Cho & Patten, 2007; Brammer & Pavelin, 2008; Zeng et al., 2010) or GHG disclosures (Hapsoro & Ambarwati, 2018).

Luo et al. (2012) study shows that firms operating with an emission trading scheme are more likely to disclose carbon-related information. It is presumed, therefore, that Portuguese companies that are

Table 2. Hypothesis summary

Factor	Hypothesis	Firm characteristic	Predicted sign	References
Social Pressure	H1.1	Size	+	Giorgios & Dimitrios (2009); Prado Lorenzo et al. (2009); Luo et al. (2012); Luo et al. (2013); González-González & Zamora Ramírez (2016); Kalu et al. (2016); Liesen et al. (2015); Hermawan et al. (2018); Faisal et al. (2018); Akbas & Canikli (2018); Hasih et al. (2019); Kiliç & Kuzey (2019)
	H1.2	Activity sector	?	Giorgios & Dimitrios (2009); Liesen et al. (2015); Faisal et al. (2018); Kiliç & Kuzey (2019)
	H1.3	Environment certification	+	Archel & Lizarraga (2001); Mitchell & Hill (2009); Serrat & Aliberch (2010); Monteiro & Guzmán (2010a)
Shareholders pressure	H2.1	Concentration of capital	-	González-González & Zamora Ramírez (2016)
Market pressure	H3.1	Profitability	+	Luo et al. (2013); Liesen et al. (2015); González-González & Zamora Ramírez (2016); Kalu et al. (2016); Hermawan et al. (2018); Hapsoro & Ambarwati (2018); Faisal et al. (2018); Borhei et al. (2018); Akbas & Canikli (2018)
	H3.2	Carbon Disclosure Project	+	Prado Lorenzo et al. (2009); Luo et al. (2012); Luo et al. (2013)
	H3.4	Leverage	+	Kalu et al. (2016); Hapsoro & Ambarwati (2018); Faisal et al. (2018)
Institutional Pressure	H4.1	Economic period	+	

included in PNALE, belong to potentially polluting sectors[3], and are therefore subject to greater pressure from stakeholders to improve their environmental performance.

There are also studies where the criterion, in the choice of the sample, covers not only the sector of activity but also the size (Freitas et al., 2007; Beck et al., 2010; Monteiro & Guzmán, 2010b; Barros & Monteiro, 2012) or stock quote (Frost, 2007). Some studies analysed indicate the great tendency for the choice of samples composed by listed companies (Djama & Martinez, 2007; Freitas et al., 2007; Frost, 2007; PWC & IETA, 2007; Lovell et al., 2010; Zeng et al.,2010; Gonçalves & Góis, 2011; Reis & Lopes, 2011; Prado-Lorenzo & García-Sanchez, 2010; Kalu et al., 2016; Broadstock et al., 2018; Faisal et al., 2018; Borghei et al., 2018; Nasih et al., 2019; Kiliç & Kuzey, 2019) or by companies that have participated in CDP (Prado-Lorenzo & García-Sanchez, 2010; Luo et al., 2012; Li et al., 2018; Akbas & Canikli, 2018).

In view of the above, it is assumed that companies quoted and / or included in PNALE, are more likely to provide information related to the environment (Campbell, 2003; Cho & Patten, 2007; Zeng et. al., 2010), in this case in particular, on the CO_2 emission allowances.

Our study focuses on the companies included in the PNALE I and II lists. As mentioned previously, environmental policies regarding emission allowances have gone through several phases of EU ETS, with different specificities, and the post-2012 period may bring differences in the behavior of companies in their reporting practices, in view of the new rules of implementation of the EU ETS scheme. It is therefore important to examine whether there are significant differences in the form / type of environmental information disclosed between the EU ETS periods (2008-2012 and 2013-2020).

In order to carry out this study, it was sought to obtain, in the respective sites, the reports and accounts for the years 2008 to 2017 of the companies that, continuously, were part of PNALE I and II, during that period. Our sample is made up of 5 companies: Cimpor, Secil, EDP, Navigator, Galp.

Methodology

As mentioned above, the disclosure of emission allowances made in 5 companies during the period 2008-2017 will be the object of study, making a total of 48 observations, to be treated as panel data.

In order to assess the type and degree of disclosure of CO_2 EA, we have used the content analysis of the information disclosed in the reports and accounts for the periods 2008 to 2017, in particular in the Management Report and in the notes to the financial statements.

The report and accounts, as an analysis tool, have been pointed out in the literature (Wilmshurst & Frost, 2000; Deegan et al., 2002; Holland & Foo, 2003) as the best source to be used in this type of empirical studies, which deal with environmental disclosure, not only by the obligation of its elaboration and presentation but also because it is information that is easily accessible by researchers. The notes to financial statements will therefore be the source of our study, and from the point of view of several authors (Llena et al., 2007; Serrat & Aliberch, 2010) it is mainly in this document that information on environmental matters in general and on specific licenses is reported.

Content analysis is undoubtedly the most commonly used methodology in Corporate Social Reporting (Gray et al., 1995b), allowing an adequate description of the type of environmental disclosure carried out by companies (Mathews, 1997), and in emission allowances. This method consists of analyzing the content of documents by encoding environmental information into predefined attributes or categories (which may, for example, be consistent with the categories of information required by accounting regulations).

This methodology has been used by several studies about GHG disclosures, such as Prado-Lorenzo et al. (2009), Luo et al (2013), Liesen et al. (2015), Kalu et al. (2016), Hapsoro and Ambarwati (2018), Hermawan et al. (2018), Faisal et al. (2018), and Kiliç & Kuzey (2019).

Generally, this type of analysis is used to prove the practices of environmental disclosure from a quantitative perspective (for example, it allows to quantify the level of disclosure in terms of words, phrases and / or pages), facilitating the statistical treatment of data.

Our research focuses on the information released taking into account clearly defined and codified information categories based on NCRF 26, giving a clear emphasis to the content of the appendix of this standard, designed exclusively for EA.

In our study, we chose to adopt a methodology that gives relevance to the breadth of environmental information disclosed, but not to the extent of it, by using a disclosure index for carbon emission licenses. This methodology has been used previously by several authors such as Prado-Lorenzo et al. (2009), Kalu et al. (2016), Hermawan et al. (2018), Faisal et al. (2018), Borghei et al. (2018), Nasih et al. (2019), and Kiliç & Kuzey (2019).

Thus, to measure the degree of disclosure of EA, a non-weighted index, Carbon Emissions Disclosure Index (CEDI) was created. This index was based on the analysis of the information on emission allowances required in NCRF 26, which were grouped into 5 information items, as described in Table 3.

For the construction of the index a score was assigned according to the following criteria: 1 if the company discloses information about the item in question and 0 if it does not. The total CEDI value is therefore the result of the division of the total score obtained by each company by the maximum number of assigned points (5), as described below in Table 4:

Table 3. Information items on greenhouse gas emission allowances

Licenses allocated (in each PNALE)
EA alienation disclosure
EA acquisition disclosure
Fines related to EA
Fair value of EA

Table 4. Disclosure index determination formula

$CEDIj = \sum_{n=1}^{i} in / i$	CEDI j	Carbon Emissions Disclosure Index - Company Total j
	i_n	Item i under analysis. Dichotomous dummy variable with value 1 if the company discloses information about the element and value 0 if the company does not disclose information about the element
	i	Maximum number of items (5)

Model and Variables

In order to analyze the factors that influence the degree of disclosure on CO_2 EA of the companies that make up the study sample, a model was developed in which CEDI was considered as a dependent variable. On the other hand, the following variables were considered as independent variables (possible explanatory factors) (Table 5), which were the basis of the previously formulated research hypotheses. In order to identify the factors that, according to the hypotheses formulated, determine the degree of disclosure of the CO_2 EA, a multivariate analysis was carried out using STATA software, to verify if the independent variables together explain the level of emission allowances disclosure. Thus, similar to studies on environmental disclosure in general (Liu & Anbumozhi, 2009; Monteiro & Guzmán, 2010a; Barros & Monteiro 2012), the following multiple linear regression model was developed (see Table 5)

ANALYSIS AND DISCUSSION OF RESULTS

At this point we will proceed to the analysis and discussion of the results obtained in our study. We begin with a global analysis of the degree of disclosure on CO_2 emission licenses, made by companies in the period under review, measured through CEDI.

Descriptive Analysis

Regarding the quantitative variables, as can be seen in Table 6, the average value of the asset logarithm stands at 18.23, the average value of the capital concentration is 69,91%, the average level of ROA is 2,40% and of leverage is 197,61%.

Concerning the dichotomous variables, as shown by the analysis presented in Table 7, with regard to Environmental certification, it is verified that, of the 48 companies in the sample, 34 have this certification. However, only 15 of the companies studied answered the Carbon Disclosure Project survey. As

Table 5. Multiple linear regression model

$CEDI = \alpha_0 + \beta_1 SIZE + \beta_2 AS + \beta_3 EC + \beta_4 COC + \beta 5 ROA + \beta 6 CDP + \beta 7 LEV + \beta 8 PERIOD + \varepsilon_i$	
$CEDI_{Total}$	Total Disclosure Index - 2008-2017 period.
SIZE	Size, measured by the logarithm of total assets.
AS	Activity sector.
EC	Environmental Certification - dummy variable, which assumes the value 1, if the company holds an environmental certification, and 0, otherwise.
COC	Concentration of capital - measured by the % of capital held by the 3 largest shareholders.
ROA	Variable calculated according to the formula of the ratio of the Return of the assets.
CDP	Dummy variable, which assumes the value 1, if the company responded to the CDP survey, and 0, otherwise.
LEV	Variable calculated according to the debt ratio formula.
PERIOD	Dummy variable, which assumes the value 1, if the observation refers to the period 2013-2017, and 0, if the observation refers to the period 2008-2012.
α_0	Constant.
α_i	Residual random variable.

regards the period, 23 observations relate to the period 2008 to 2012 and the remaining 25 observations relate to the period from 2013 to 2017.

Concerning the disclosure of information on carbon emissions, all of the 48 companies disclosed any type of information. CEDI has an average value of 0,5958333 (table 8), with a maximum value of 1, which indicates that Portuguese companies are concerned about compliance with the disclosure requirements contained in the applicable standards, yet do not disclose all the information required.

Regarding the comparison of our results, related to the disclosure on GHG, with that obtained by Borghei et al. (2018), Hagih et al. (2019) and Kiliç e Kuzey (2019) it is higher, since these authors had concluded by lower levels of disclosure. On the other hand, this result is close to the study of Faisal et al. (2018), who have concluded that the mean disclosure is relatively high.

Multivariate Analysis

Based on the previously delineated linear regression model, panel data treatment was used, and the results were estimated taking into account the random effects model and the fixed effects model.

Table 6. Descriptive statistics: quantitative variables

	SIZE	COC	ROA	LEV
N	48	47	48	48
Average	18,22646	69,91%	2,40%	197,61%
Standard deviation	2,478762	21,25%	4,66%	335,74%
Minimum	15,29668	31,61%	-15,79%	-1317,05%
Maximum	21,76045	97,10%	9,00%	1712,62%

Table 7. Descriptive statistics: dichotomous variables

		N	%
EC	Yes	34	70,83
	No	14	29,17
	Total	**48**	**100.0**
CDP	Yes	15	31,25
	No	33	68,75
	Total	**48**	**100.0**
PERIOD	2008-2012	23	47,92
	2013-2017	25	52,08
	Total	**48**	**100.0**

The random effects model considers the individual effects as resulting from a series of random and unobservable factors (Marques, 2000) and, therefore, does not consider the existence of an unobservable individual effect for all periods (Martins, 2006). This model is based on two assumptions: the unobserved individual effects are random, and the explanatory variables are strictly exogenous. This means that the error terms are not correlated with the past, present and future values of the regressors (Hsiao, 2003).

The fixed effects model considers that the coefficients can vary from individual to individual or in time, although they remain fixed, therefore, non-random constants (Marques, 2000). In this model, "it is assumed that errors ... are explained by two unobservable components: (...) an individual effect that is constant over time and (...) a noise variable for each individual i and period t." (Martins, 2006).

It should be noted that the AS variable was taken from the fixed effects model because it is a business characteristic that remains fixed throughout all the considered periods, being automatically eliminated by the statistical software in the estimation of the model. In addition, the model considers only 47 observations because it was not possible to obtain the information on the capital concentration for one of the companies analyzed.

As can be seen in Table 9, in the random effects model, for a significance level of 5%, SIZE, AS, COC and PERIOD present a significant association with CEDI. In the fixed effects model, only the PERIOD has a significant association with the dependent variable. The fact that SIZE, AS and COC variables are no longer significant in this model can be explained by the fact that they are business characteristics that did not suffer significant variations over the period.

Thus, as expected, the level of disclosure presented is greater in larger companies, in companies with lower capital concentration and is related to the sector of activity to which the company belongs, and, therefore, it is possible to validate H1.1, H2.1 and H1.2. However, contrary to our expectations,

Table 8. License Disclosure Index (CEDI)

N	Average	Minimum	Maximum	Standard deviation
48	0,5958333	0	1	0,1956531

Table 9. Results of the Multiple Regression Model

	Random effects		Fixed effects	
CEDI	**Coeff.**	**Sig.**	**Coeff.**	**Sig.**
SIZE	0,0528664	0,000	0,0007939	0,995
AS	-0,780472	0,000		
EC	-0,0553884	0,259	-0,0540658	0,318
COC	-0,0032719	0,034	0,0008116	0,698
ROA	-0,0080313	0,172	-0,0102674	0,066
CDP	0,1075563	0,090	0,1312049	0,060
LEV	0,0000694	0,237	0,0000589	0,302
PERIOD	-0,1461293	0,000	-0,150228	0,000
Cons	0,1377754	0,426	0,7408153	0,767
Number of observations		47	47	
Number of groups		5	5	
R-Sq	**within**	0,3166	0,3796	
	between	0,8368	0,0142	
	overall	0,6299	0,0421	
	Wald chi2	64,68	**F (7,35)**	3,06
	Prob>chi2	0,000	**Prob>F**	0,0128

the level of disclosure is higher during the period from 2008 to 2012 and it is not possible to validate hypothesis H4.1.

For a level of significance of 10%, the fact that the company has responded to the survey of the Carbon Disclosure Project is also an explanatory factor for the level of disclosure, in the two estimated models, validating H3.2.

The table below (Table 10) summarizes the results obtained from the multivariate analysis.

The level of significance of the Wald Chi2 and F tests (shown in Table 9) allows us to validate the models in global terms and to conclude that the estimated models are adequate to describe the relationship between the explanatory variables and the dependent variable.

The R^2 values allow us to conclude that the random effects model explains, overall, 62.99% of the CEDI value, 83.68% of the differences between companies and 31.66% of the variations between time periods for the same company, and that the fixed-effects model accounts for 4.21% of the CEDI value, 1.42% of the differences between firms and 37.96% of the variances between periods of time for the same company.

After analyzing the results, we can conclude that:

- Size is an explanatory factor for the level of disclosure about emission allowances. This result was also confirmed by Prado Lorenzo et al. (2009), Luo et al. (2012), Luo et al. (2013), González-González & Zamora Ramírez (2016), Kalu et al. (2016), Liesen et al. (2015), Hermawan et al. (2018), Faisal et al. (2018), Akbas and Canikli (2018), Nasih et al. (2019) and Kiliç and Kuzey (2019);

Table 10. Determining factors for the degree of disclosure on CO_2 EA

Independent variables	Hypothesis	Multivariate analysis	Hypothesis validation
Size	H1.1	Significant *	Yes
Activity sector	H1.2	Significant *	Yes
Environmental certification	H1.3	Not significant	No
Concentration of capital	H2.1	Significant *	Yes
ROA	H3.1	Not significant	No
Carbon Disclosure Project	H3.2	Significant **	Yes
Leverage	H3.3	Not significant	No
Period	H4.1	Significant	No

* only in the random effects model.
** for a significance level of 10%.

- The Activity Sector was also evidenced as an explanatory factor of Total CEDI, thus validating Hypothesis 1.2. This result is in line with the results obtained by Giorgios & Dimitrios (2009), Liesen et al. (2015), Faisal et al. (2018) and Kiliç and Kuzey (2019);
- The concentration of capital negatively influences the level of disclosure presented, and it is possible to validate H2.1. This result is in line with the results obtained by González-González and Zamora Ramirez (2016);
- The period is evidenced as a determinant factor of CEDI, but, contrary to our expectations, has a negative association with the disclosure index, and it is not possible to validate H4.1. In this way, it can be concluded that the fact that the EU ETS has developed into a third period, with different allocation rules, has negatively influenced the level of disclosure;
- The fact that the company responded to the Carbon Disclosure Project survey is also an explanatory factor for CEDI, but for a level of significance of 10%, revealing that these companies are concerned about disclosing to stakeholders their role in the carbon market, to increase or maintain its legitimacy (Luo et al., 2012);
- Our results are not consistent with the results obtained by other authors, who have concluded by a significant positive association of GHG disclosures with profitability (Luo et al., 2013; Liesen et al., 2015; González-González & Zamora Ramírez, 2016; Kalu et al., 2016; Hermawan et al., 2018; Hapsoro & Ambarwati, 2018; Faisal et al., 2018; and Akbas & Canikli, 2018, Boghei et al., 2018), and leverage (Kalu et al., 2016; Hapsoro & Ambarwati, 2018; Faisal et al., 2018).

After this comparative analysis of our results, we try to interpret them based on some of the most important theories. Considering that our study is focused on companies with high public visibility, that is companies belonging to contaminating sectors that are part of PNALE I and II, it was expected, according to the Theory of Legitimacy, that this type of companies, and in particular the certified ones, would be more likely to disclose information that reflects their environmental responsibility in order to improve their image. In fact, in the case of companies with greater exposure and public pressure, the greater the need to legitimize themselves before the different stakeholders, and therefore, the disclosure is one way of demonstrating an environmentally responsible performance. Thus, the use of annual accounts as a vehicle for the disclosure on CO_2 EA and the predominantly narrative and positive character of the disclosed aspects as a way of improving the company's image and reputation are supported by the Theory of Legitimacy.

SOLUTIONS AND RECOMMENDATIONS

In Portugal, NCRF 26 (and its appendix) harmonized the accounting treatment and disclosure of data related to CO_2 emission trading by Portuguese companies' subject to the SNC. However, there is still a lack of accounting standards for companies that apply the IASB standards and which hold CO_2 emission licenses.

In that sense, it was important for the IASB to express its views on this issue and to develop an international standard defining the criteria for recognition, measurement and disclosure on environmental matters and in particular on emission allowances.

FUTURE RESEARCH DIRECTIONS

We are aware that the study carried out has some limitations, so the results should be analyzed and interpreted with some care. We are sure that data from only 5 companies may not be sufficient to reach decisive conclusions on the extent of CO_2 emission allowances in the annual accounts. In addition, there may be other variables not considered in this study, which may better explain the disclosure on this topic. However, this study has the advantage that, like other studies (Larrinaga et al., 2002; Frost, 2007; Llena et al., 2007), has taken into account the evolution of disclosure on CO_2 EA.

In this sense, it is suggested, for future research, the analysis of disclosure by a broader set of companies, including companies from other countries, allowing an analysis at international level, including other factors that also characterize the country of origin of the companies under study.

On the other hand, we suggest the extension of the period beyond 2017, in order to verify whether the levels of disclosure presented remain stable over the period after 2013, or if there is any significant evolution in the disclosure during the third period of the EU ETS.

CONCLUSION

Using the content analysis technique of the information disclosed in the reports and accounts, we have developed an index of information on CO_2 EA (CEDI), composed of 5 items, in accordance with NCRF 26. Based on this index, considered as the dependent variable, a linear regression model was developed with the objective of identifying potential determinants of the degree of disclosure on CO_2 EA.

Our sample included a total of 5 Portuguese companies that are included in the list of PNALE I and II, during the period 2008-2017, making a total of 48 observations.

The descriptive statistics reveal that all companies make some kind of disclosure about CO_2 EA.

Overall, the disclosure index has relatively high average values, with CEDI Total being 0.5958, that is, the sample companies make disclosures about more than half of the information items that make up the index.

In this way, we can affirm that the results of our study reveal some influence of the normative accounting in the practices of disclosure on emission allowances, following the existent empirical evidence in the matter of obligatory environmental report (Holland & Foo, 2003; Cowan & Gadenne, 2005; Yeoh, 2005; Freitas et al., 2007; Frost, 2007; Llena, 2007; Criado-Jiménez et al., 2008; Jorgensen & Soderstrom, 2008; Damak-Ayadi, 2010; Monteiro & Guzmán, 2010b; Serrat & Aliberch 2010).

Regarding the determinants of disclosure level, we have concluded that size, activity sector, capital concentration and the period of analysis are shown as determining factors of CEDI, at a significance level of 5%. The fact that the company participated in the Carbon Disclosure Project also proved to be a determining factor, at a significance level of 10%.

Thus, as predicted, it was possible to prove that larger firms tend to disclose more information about GHG emission seeking to legitimize themselves (validating hypothesis H1.1). The sector of activity also proved to be an explanatory factor for the disclosure level, as well as the lower degree of capital concentration, being possible to validate the hypotheses H1.2 and H2.1.

Although it was not possible to validate hypothesis H4.1, since the association obtained for the variable period was contrary to the expected one, since Portuguese companies have lower disclosure levels in the period 2013-2017.

Our results are consistent to the results obtained by Giorgios and Dimitrios (2009), Prado Lorenzo et al. (2009), Luo et al. (2012), Luo et al. (2013), González-González and Zamora Ramírez (2016), Kalu et al. (2016), Liesen et al. (2015), Hermawan et al. (2018), Faisal et al. (2018), Akbas & Canikli (2018), Nasih et al. (2019) and Kiliç & Kuzey (2019).

However, they are not consistent with the results obtained by other authors, who have concluded for the influence of profitability (Luo et al., 2013; Liesen et al., 2015; González-González & Zamora Ramírez, 2016; Kalu et al., 2016; Hermawan et al., 2018; Hapsoro & Ambarwati, 2018; Faisal et al., 2018; and Akbas & Canikli, 2018, Boghei et al., 2018) or leverage (Kalu et al., 2016; Hapsoro & Ambarwati, 2018; Faisal et al., 2018) in GHG emission disclosure.

In this sense, it can be concluded that social pressure (size and sector of activity), pressure from shareholders (concentration of capital) and market pressure (Carbon Disclosure Project) influence the disclosure of CO_2 emission licenses in Portuguese companies. However, contrary to expectations, the institutional pressure factor seems to have no influence on this type of disclosure.

REFERENCES

Accounting Standardization Committee. (2002). Accounting Directive No. 29 - Environmental Matters, June 5, CD-ROM of the Order of Official Accountants.

Akbas, H., & Canikli, S. (2018). Determinants of voluntary greenhouse gas emission disclosure: An empirical investigation in Turkish firms. *Sustainability*, *11*(1), 107. doi:10.3390u11010107

Archel, P., & Lizarraga, D. (2001). Algunos determinantes de la información medioambiental divulgada por las empresas españolas cotizadas. *Revista de Contabilidad*, *4*(7), 139–153.

Baek, H., Johnson, D. R., & Kim, J. (2009). Managerial ownership, corporate governance, and voluntary disclosure. *Journal of Business & Economic Studies*, *15*(2), 44–61.

Barros, C., & Monteiro, S. (2012). Determinant factors of mandatory environmental reporting: the case of Portuguese primary metal and steel industry. In A.M. Gil-Lafuente, J. Gil-Lafuente, & J.M. Merigó-Lindahl (Eds.), Soft Computing in Management and Business Economics (pp. 123-147). Springer Berlin Heidelberg.

Beck, A., Campbell, D., & Shrives, P. (2010). Content analysis in environmental reporting research: Enrichment and rehearsal of the method in a British-German context. *The British Accounting Review*, *42*(3), 207–222. doi:10.1016/j.bar.2010.05.002

Bewley, K. & Li, Y. (2000). Disclosure of environmental information by Canadian manufacturing companies: a voluntary disclosure perspective. *Advances in Environmental Accounting & Management*, *1*(1), 201-226.

Boas, S.; Monteiro, S. (2012). O relato sobre licenças de emissão de CO2: o caso das empresas portuguesas do PNALE II. In *XV Encontro AECA - Novos caminhos para a Europa: O papel das empresas e dos governos*. Academic Press.

Borghei, Z., & Leung, P. (2013). An empirical analysis of the determinants of greenhouse gas voluntary disclosure in Australia. *Accounting and Finance Research*, *2*(1), 110.

Borghei, Z., Leung, P., & Guthrie, J. (2018). Voluntary greenhouse gas emission disclosure impacts on accounting-based performance: Australian evidence. *Australasian Journal of Environmental Management*, *25*(3), 321–338. doi:10.1080/14486563.2018.1466204

Brammer, S., & Pavelin, S. (2008). Factors influencing the quality of corporate environmental disclosure. *Business Strategy and the Environment*, *17*(2), 120–136. doi:10.1002/bse.506

Campbell, D. (2003). Intra- and intersectoral effects in environmental disclosures: Evidence for legitimacy theory*? Business Strategy and the Environment*, *12*(6), 357–371. doi:10.1002/bse.375

Carpenter, V. L., & Feroz, E. H. (2001). Institutional theory and accounting rule choice: An analysis of four US state governments' decisions to adopt generally accepted accounting principles. *Accounting, Organizations and Society*, *26*(7-8), 565–596. doi:10.1016/S0361-3682(00)00038-6Cho, C., & Patten, D. (2007). The role environmental disclosures as tools of legitimacy: A research note. *Accounting, Organizations and Society*, *32*(7-8), 639–647. doi:10.1016/j.aos.2006.09.009

Commission of the European Communities. (2001). Commission Recommendation of 30 May 2001 on the recognition, valuation and reporting of environmental matters in the annual accounts and the annual report on the management of companies,, L 156, 13.06.01.

Committee on Accounting Standardization. (2006). Technical Interpretation No. 4 - Greenhouse gas emission allowances: accounting for emission allowances, Published in Diário da República II Series, May 25, 2006 -Despacho n.º 11 384/2006 (2nd series).

Committee on Accounting Standardization. (2009). Accounting and Financial Reporting Standard 26 - Environmental Matters, CD of the Order of Chartered Accountants.

Cormier, D., Gordon, I. M., & Magnan, M. (2004). Corporate environmental disclosure: Contrasting management's perceptions with reality. *Journal of Business Ethics*, *49*(2), 143–165. doi:10.1023/B:BUSI.0000015844.86206.b9

Cormier, D., Magnan, M., & Van Velthoven, B. (2005). Environmental disclosure quality in large German companies: Economic incentives, public pressures or institutional conditions? *European Accounting Review*, *14*(1), 3–39. doi:10.1080/0963818042000339617

Cowan, S., & Gadenne, D. (2005). Australian corporate environmental reporting: A comparative analysis of disclosure practices across voluntary and mandatory disclosure systems. *Journal of Accuonting & Organizational Change*, *1*(2), 165–179. doi:10.1108/18325910510635344

Criado-Jiménez, I., Fernández-Chulián, M., Husillos-Carqués, F., & Larrinaga-González, C. (2008). Compliance with mandatory environmental reporting in financial statements: The case of Spain (2001–2003). *Journal of Business Ethics*, *79*(3), 245–262. doi:10.100710551-007-9375-7

Damak-Ayadi, S. (2010). Social and environmental reporting in the annual reports of large companies in France. *Accounting and Management Information Systems*, *9*(1), 22–44.

Decree-Law no. 158/2009, of July 13, Diário da República, 1st series, no. 133. (2009).

Decree-Law no. 230/2005 of 29 December, Diário da República, 1st series, no. 249. (2005).

Decree-Law no. 233/2004 of December 14, Diário da República, 1st series, no. 291. (2004).

Decree-Law no. 24/2004, of January 23, Diário da República, 1st Series - A, no. 19. (2004).

Decree-Law no. 35/2005, of 17 of February, Diário da República, 1st series, nº 133. (2005).

Decree-Law no. 98/2015, of June 2, Diário da República, 1st series, no. 106. (2015).

Deegan, C., Rankin, M., & Tobin, J. (2002). An examination of the corporate social and environmental disclosures of BHP from 1983-1997: A test of legitimacy theory. *Accounting, Auditing & Accountability Journal*, *15*(3), 312–343. doi:10.1108/09513570210435861

Del Brio, J. A., Fernández, E., Junquera, B., & Vázquez, C. J. (2001). Environmental managers and departments as driving forces of TQEM in Spanish industrial companies. *International Journal of Quality & Reliability Management*, *18*(5), 495–511. doi:10.1108/02656710110392638

Delmas, M., & Toffel, M. W. (2004). Stakeholders and environmental management practices: An institutional framework. *Business Strategy and the Environment*, *13*(4), 209–222. doi:10.1002/bse.409

Dimaggio, P., & Powell, W. W. (1983). The iron cage revisited: Institutional isomorphism and collective rationality in organizational fields. *American Sociological Review*, *48*(2), 147–160. doi:10.2307/2095101

Djama, C., & Martinez, I. (2007). *La comptabilisation des quotas d'émission de gaz à effet de serre: véritable incitation de lutte contre le réchauffement climatique?* Universités Toulouse et Poitiers.

Directive 2003/87/EC of the European Parliament and of the Council of 13 October. (2003).

Directive 2009/29/EC of the European Parliament and of the Council of 23 April. (2009).

Faisal, F., Andiningtyas, E., Achmad, T., Haryanto, H., & Meiranto, W. (2017). The content and determinants of greenhouse gas emission disclosure: Evidence from Indonesian companies. *Corporate Social Responsibility and Environmental Management*, *25*(6), 1397–1406. doi:10.1002/csr.1660

Fernandes, M. T., Veloso, A. B., & Pinto, L. C. (2009). *O mercado de direitos de emissão de CO2: um estudo experimental* [PhD Thesis]. Universidade do Minho.

Fernando, A.; Albuquerque, F.; Almeida, M.; Delgado, S. (2010). Tratamento contabilístico das licenças de emissão de gases com efeito de estufa: o caso português. In *XIV Encuentro AECA*. Academic Press.

Freitas, A. (2007). *Análise das divulgações ambientais nos relatórios anuais das maiores empresas Portuguesas* [Master Dissertation]. Instituto Superior de Ciências do Trabalho e da Empresa.

Frost, G. R. (2007). The introduction of mandatory environmental reporting guidelines: Australian evidence. *Abacus*, *43*(2), 190–216. doi:10.1111/j.1467-6281.2007.00225.x

Georgios, X., & Dimitrios, X. (2009). *Accounting treatment of emission credits*. International Hellenic University.

Gonçalves, A. G., & Góis, C. G. (2011). *Licenças de emissão de CO2: o caso português perspetiva legal e contabilística*. Instituto Superior De Contabilidade E Administração De Coimbra.

Gonzalez-Gonzalez, J., & Zamora Ramírez, C. (2016). Voluntary carbon disclosure by Spanish companies: An empirical analysis. *International Journal of Climate Change Strategies and Management*, *8*(1), 57–79. doi:10.1108/IJCCSM-09-2014-0114

Gray, R., Kouhy, R., & Lavers, S. (1995a). Corporate social and environmental reporting. A review of the literature and a longitudinal study of UK disclosure. *Accounting, Auditing & Accountability Journal*, *8*(2), 47–77. doi:10.1108/09513579510146996

Gray, R., Kouhy, R., & Lavers, S. (1995b). Methodological themes. Constructing a research database of social and environmental by UK companies. *Accounting, Auditing & Accountability Journal*, *8*(2), 78–101. doi:10.1108/09513579510086812

Hackston, D., & Milne, M. (1996). Some determinants of social and environmental disclosures in New Zealand companies. *Accounting, Auditing & Accountability Journal*, *9*(1), 77–108. doi:10.1108/09513579610109987

Hapsoro, D., & Ambarwati, A. (2018). Antecedents and consequences of carbon emissions' disclosure: Case study of oil, gas and coal companies in non-annex 1 member countries. *Journal of Indonesian Economy and Business*, *33*(2), 99–111. doi:10.22146/jieb.28756

Hermawan, A., Aisyah, I., Gunardi, A., & Putri, W. (2018). Going green: Determinants of carbon emission disclosure in manufacturing companies in Indonesia. *International Journal of Energy Economics and Policy*, *8*(1), 55–61.

Holland, L., & Foo, Y. B. (2003). Differences in environmental reporting practices in the UK and the US: The legal and regulatory context. *The British Accounting Review*, *35*(1), 1–18. doi:10.1016/S0890-8389(02)00127-0

Hsiao, C. (2003). *Analysis of panel data (2ª ed.)*. University of Southern California, Cambridge University Press. doi:10.1017/CBO9780511754203

Ismail, K., & Chandler, R. (2005). Disclosure in the quarterly reports of Malaysian companies, *Financial Reporting. Regulation & Governance*, *4*(1), 1–26.

Jorgensen, B., & Soderstrom, N. (2008). *Environmental disclosure within legal and accounting contexts: an international perspective.* University of Colorado at Boulder.

Kalu, J., Buang, A., & Aliagha, G. (2016). Determinants of voluntary carbon disclosure in the corporate real estate sector of Malaysia. *Journal of Environmental Management*, *182*, 519–525. doi:10.1016/j.jenvman.2016.08.011 PMID:27529312

Kiliç, M., & Kuzey, C. (2019). The effect of corporate governance on carbon emission disclosures: Evidence from Turkey. *International Journal of Climate Change Strategies and Management*, *11*(1), 35–53. doi:10.1108/IJCCSM-07-2017-0144

KMPG UK. (2008). *Accounting for carbon – The impact of carbon trading on financial statements.*

Larrinaga, C., Carrasco, F., Correa, C., Llena, F., & Moneva, J. (2002). Accountability and accounting regulation: The case of Spanish environmental disclosure standard. *European Accounting Review*, *11*(4), 723–740. doi:10.1080/0963818022000001000

Lee, S., Park, Y., & Klassen, R. (2015). Market responses to firms' voluntary climate change information disclosure and carbon communication. *Corporate Social Responsibility and Environmental Management*, *22*(1), 1–12. doi:10.1002/csr.1321

Li, D., Huang, M., Ren, S., Chen, X., & Ning, L. (2018). Environmental legitimacy, green innovation, and corporate carbon disclosure: Evidence from CDP China 100. *Journal of Business Ethics*, *150*(4), 1089–1104. doi:10.100710551-016-3187-6

Liesen, A., Hoepner, A., Patten, D., & Figge, F. (2015). Does stakeholder pressure influence corporate GHG emissions reporting? Empirical evidence from Europe. *Accounting, Auditing & Accountability Journal*, *28*(7), 1047–1074. doi:10.1108/AAAJ-12-2013-1547

Liu, X. & Anbumozhi, V. (2009). Determinant factors of corporate environmental information disclosure: an empirical study of Chinese listed company. *Journal of Cleaner Production*, 593-600/8.

Llena, F., Moneva, J. M., & Hernandez, B. (2007). Environmental disclosures and compulsory accounting standards: The case of Spanish annual reports. *Business Strategy and the Environment*, *16*(1), 50–63. doi:10.1002/bse.466

Lovell, H., Aguiar, T. S., Bebbington, J., Larrinaga-Gonzalez, C. (2010). Accounting for carbon. *Certified Accountants Educational Trust for the Association of Chartered Certified Accountants.*

Luo, L., Lan, Y., & Tang, Q. (2012). Corporate incentives to disclose carbon information: Evidence from the CDP Global 500 report. *Journal of International Financial Management & Accounting*, *23*(2), 93–120. doi:10.1111/j.1467-646X.2012.01055.x

Luo, L., Tang, Q., & Lan, Y. (2013). Comparison of propensity for carbon disclosure between developing and developed countries: A resource constraint perspective. *Accounting Research Journal*, *26*(1), 6–34. doi:10.1108/ARJ-04-2012-0024

Magness, V. (2006). Strategic posture, Financial performance and environmental disclosure: An empirical test of legitimacy theory. *Accounting, Auditing & Accountability Journal*, *19*(4), 540–563. doi:10.1108/09513570610679128

Marques, L. D. (2000). *Modelos dinâmicos com dados em painel: revisão de literatura*. Centro de Estudos Macroeconómicos e Previsão, Faculdade de Economia do Porto. Retrieved fro http://www.fep.up.pt/investigacao/workingpapers/wp100.pdf

Marshall, S. R., Cordano, M., & Silverman, M. (2005). Exploring individual and institutional drivers of proactive environmentalism in the US wine industry. *Business Strategy and the Environment*, *14*(2), 92–109. doi:10.1002/bse.433

Martín, J.A.J., Martín, Z., Maria, P., & Léon, C. (2007). *Tratamiento contable de los derechos de emisión: la aplicación de la resolución de 8 de febrero de 2006 del ICAC en el sector eléctrico español*. Universidad de Huelva.

Martins, L. F. (2006). *Modelos com dados em painel*. Instituto Superior de Ciências do Trabalho e da Empresa.

Mathews, M. R. (1997). Twenty-five years of social and environmental accounting research: Is there a silver jubilee to celebrate? *Accounting, Auditing & Accountability Journal*, *10*(4), 481–531. doi:10.1108/EUM0000000004417

Meyer, J. W., & Rowan, B. (1977). Institutionalized organizations: Formal structure as myth and ceremony. *American Journal of Sociology*, *83*(2), 340–363. doi:10.1086/226550

Mitchell, C. G., & Hill, T. (2009). Corporate social and environmental reporting and the impact of internal environmental policy in South Africa. *Corporate Social Responsibility and Environmental Management*, *16*(1), 48–60. doi:10.1002/csr.179

Monast, J., Anda, J., & Profeta, T. (2009). U.S. Carbon Market Design: regulating emission allowances as financial instruments. Nicholas Institute for Environmental Policy Solutions, Duke University.

Moneva, J. M., & Llena, F. M. (1996). Análisis de la información sobre responsabilidad social en las empresas industriales que cotizan en Bolsa. *Revista Española de Financiación y Contabilidad*, *XXV*(87), 361–401.

Monteiro, S. (2006). *El Medio Ambiente como factor clave en la definición de las estratégias empresariales y sus implicaciones en la gestión y el sistema de información contable. Una perspectiva del caso Portugués* [Tesis Doctoral]. Universidad de Santiago de Compostela.

Monteiro, S., & Guzman, B. (2010a). The influence of the Portuguese environmental accounting standard on the environmental disclosures in the annual reports of large companies operating in Portugal: A first view. *Management of Environmental Quality*, *21*(4), 414–435. doi:10.1108/14777831011049070

Monteiro, S., & Guzman, B. (2010b). Determinants of environmental disclosure in the annual reports of large companies operating in Portugal. *Corporate Social Responsibility and Environmental Management, 17*(4), 185–204. doi:10.1002/csr.197

Nasih, M., Harymawan, I., Paramitasari, Y., & Handayani, A. (2019). Carbon emissions, firm size, and corporate governance structure: Evidence from the mining and agricultural industries in Indonesia. *Sustainability*, 11.

Pestana, M., & Gageiro, J. (2008). *Análise de dados para Ciências Sociais – A complementaridade do SPSS* (5th ed.). Lisboa: Edições Sílabo.

Petty, R., & Cuganesan, S. (2005). Voluntary disclosure of intellectual capital by Hong Kong companies: Examining size, industry and growth effects over time. *Australian Accounting Review, 15*(2), 40–50. doi:10.1111/j.1835-2561.2005.tb00291.x

Prado Lorenzo, J., Rodríguez-Domínguez, L., Gallego-Álvarez, M., & García Sánchez, I. (2009). Factors influencing the disclosure of greenhouse gas emissions in companies world-wide. *Management Decision, 47*(7), 1133–1157. doi:10.1108/00251740910978340

Prasetya, R. A., & Yulianto, A. (2018). Analysis of the factors affecting the disclosure of corporate carbon emission in Indonesia. *Journal Dinamika Akuntansi, 10*(1), 71–81. doi:10.15294/jda.v10i1.12653

Prencipe, A. (2004). Proprietary costs and determinants of voluntary segment disclosure: Evidence from Italian listed companies. *European Accounting Review, 13*(2), 319–340. doi:10.1080/0963818042000204742

Pricewaterhousecoopers, & International Emissions Trading Association (PWC & IETA). (2007). *Trouble-Entry Accounting – Revisited - Uncertainty in accounting for the EU Emissions Trading Scheme and Certified Emission Reductions.*

Rankin, M., Windsor, C., & Wahyuni, D. (2011). An investigation of voluntary corporate greenhouse gas emissions reporting in a market governance system. *Accounting, Auditing & Accountability Journal, 24*(8), 1037–1070. doi:10.1108/09513571111184751

Regulation (EC) 1606/2002 of the European Parliament and of the Council of 19. (2002).

Regulation (EU) 601/2012 of the European Parliament and of the Council of 21. (2012).

Reis, C., Lopes, A. (2011). Fatores económicos e contabilísticos que influenciam a qualidade da informação ambiental: um estudo com empresas Admitidas à cotação na Euronext Lisbon que tenham títulos de Emissão de gases com efeito de estufa. In *XVI Encuentro AECA*. Academic Press.

Resolution of the Council of Ministers no. 1/2008, of January 4, Diário da República, 1st series. (2008).

Resolution of the Council of Ministers no. 53/2005, of March 3, Diário da República, 1st series. (2005).

Reverte, C. (2009). Determinants of corporate social responsibility disclosure ratings by Spanish listed rms. *Journal of Business Ethics, 88*(2), 351–366. doi:10.100710551-008-9968-9

Ribeiro, V. (2007). *La gestión medioambiental en las entidades públicas locales portuguesas. Una perspectiva contable* [Tesis Doctoral]. Universidad de Santiago de Compostela.

Santos, A. (2013). O comércio de licenças de emissão em Portugal. *International Business and Economics Review:Revista Internacional de Gestão e Comunicação*, *4*, 62–77.

Sengupta, P. (1998). Corporate Disclosure Quality and the Cost of Debt. *The Accounting Review*, *73*(4), 459–474.

Serrat, N., & Aliberch, A. (2010). Análisis de la responsabilidad social corporativa, en su aspecto medioambiental, en empresas del mercado continuo Español. In XIV Encuentro AECA, Informaci6n Financiera de Calidad: Señalando el Camino de la Recuperaci6n. Academic Press.

Stanny, E., & Ely, K. (2008). *Corporate Environmental disclousures about the effects of climate change*. Rohnert Park, CA: Sonoma State University.

Steenkamp, N., Rahman, A., & Kashyap, V. (2010). *Recognition, measurement and disclosure of carbon emission allowances under the eu ets – an exploratory study*. School of Commerce and Law – CQUniversity.

Teoh, H. Y., Pin, F. W., Joo, T. T., & Ling, Y. Y. (1998). Environmental disclosures-financial performance link: further evidence from industrialising economy perspective. In *Proceedings of the Second Asian Pacific Interdisciplinary Research in Accounting Conference* (APIRA). Academic Press.

Wilmshurst, T. D., & Frost, G. R. (2000). Corporate environmental reporting. a test of Legitimacy Theory. *Accounting, Auditing & Accountability Journal*, *13*(1), 10–26. doi:10.1108/09513570010316126

Yeoh, J. (2005). Compliance with mandatory disclosure requirements by New Zealand listed companies. *Advances in International Accounting*, *18*, 245–262. doi:10.1016/S0897-3660(05)18012-X

Zeng, S., Xu, X., Dong, Z., & Tamb, V. (2010). Towards corporate environmental disclosure: An empirical study in China. *Journal of Cleaner Production*, *18*(12), 1142–1148. doi:10.1016/j.jclepro.2010.04.005

Zhou, Z., Zhou, H., Peng, D., Chen, X., & Li, S. (2018). Carbon disclosure, financial transparency, and agency cost: Evidence form Chinese manufacturing listed companies. *Emerging Markets Finance & Trade*, *54*(12), 2669–2686. doi:10.1080/1540496X.2018.1428796

ADDITIONAL READING

Ahmed, K., & Courtis, J. K. (1999). Associations between corporate characteristics and disclosure levels in annual reports: A meta-analysis. *The British Accounting Review*, *31*(1), 35–61. doi:10.1006/bare.1998.0082

Chavent, M., Ding, Y., Fu, L., Stolowy, H., & Wang, H. (2005). *Disclosure and determinants studies: an extension using the divisive clustering method (DIV)*. France: University of Bordeaux.

Marston, C., & Shrives, P. (1991). The use of disclosure indices in accounting research: A review article. *The British Accounting Review*, *23*(3), 195–210. doi:10.1016/0890-8389(91)90080-L

KEY TERMS AND DEFINITIONS

Cap-and-trade system: a system whereby a limited number of allowances are granted to entities for a given period, and those entities may sell surplus licenses or acquire other licenses if they are not sufficient.

Disclosure Index: Indicator of the extent of the disclosure presented by a certain company, relative to certain information, measured by the sum of the items disclosed on the total items considered.

Emission allowance: the right to emit one tonne of carbon dioxide (CO_2) or any other greenhouse gas (GHG) having an equivalent effect for a given period.

EU Emission Trading Scheme: Market established by Directive 2003/87 / EC of 13 October, which allows entities that exceed established targets to purchase pollution rights from entities that have achieved reductions above the limits set.

ENDNOTES

1 In December 2004, the International Financial Reporting Interpretations Committee (IFRIC) of the International Accounting Standard Board (IASB) issued the only interpretative standard specifically dedicated to environmental issues, designated as IFRIC No. 3 - Emission Rights, referring to accounting for emission rights. However, this interpretation was withdrawn in July 2005, in the face of the negative opinion of the European Financial Reporting Advisory Group (EFRAG), and no other standard or interpretation has yet been issued on this subject.

2 IAS 20, entitled "Accounting for Government Grants and Disclosure of Government Assistance" of the IASB, is understood as a response to accounting for CO_2 emission allowances. This standard suggests that C02 emission allowances should not be, when assigned free of charge, at the time of receipt, generating any asset. IAS 20 also indicates that the subsidies received must be recognized at their nominal value. In this sense, since the licenses are allocated free of charge by the states, their nominal value will be zero, that is, there will be no recognition of the subsidy. Whereas, as long as the company has licenses equivalent to its emissions, no liability will be recognized. When you do not have sufficient license, you should recognize a provision for the market value of the required licenses.

3 The sectors of activity are classified in the PNALE as follows: (1) Paper and Folder; (2) Cements and lime; (3) Energy and Combustion; (4) Energy / Thermal Power Plants; (5) Energy / Cogeneration; (6) Ceramics and (7) Ferrous Metals. In our study, we consider companies belonging to the sectors of paper and folder, of cements and lime and of energy.

Chapter 10
Which Local Governments Provide Suitable Promotion of Entrepreneurship?

Mª Teresa Nevado Gil
Universidad de Extremadura, Spain

María Pache Durán
https://orcid.org/0000-0002-6670-5818
Universidad de Extremadura, Spain

Inna Sousa Paiva
https://orcid.org/0000-0002-9980-7503
Instituto Universitário de Lisboa, Portugal

Luisa Cagica Carvalho
https://orcid.org/0000-0002-9804-7813
Institute Polytechnic of Setubal, Portugal

ABSTRACT

The main objective of this final degree project is to analyze the information that the city councils of the 50 capitals of Spanish provinces offer to entrepreneurs through their institutional pages, using the content analysis technique. The results obtained corroborate the existence of an implication, although still modest, of the municipalities of the Spanish provincial capitals in relation to the promotion of entrepreneurship and business ecosystems. These results should help the municipalities to reflect on the important work they perform, and in the future these studies will serve to reflect the deficiencies observed in order to improve the information offered.

DOI: 10.4018/978-1-7998-2128-1.ch010

INTRODUCTION

Every day, hour, minute and second that passes, present-day society increases in competitiveness, causing greater complexity of the labour market and consequently preventing the young population from finding employment. It is clear that self-employment or, in other words, the development of an entrepreneurial activity, can become an important tool to combat this series of problems. This undertaking is not an easy task and so requires a foothold. Local governments thus contribute to this work, since the development of entrepreneurial activity will cause a significant improvement in their locality. Traditionally, entrepreneurship has been related to the capacity that different individuals have in order to take advantage of certain business situations, gaining profitability in their development (Dimova and Pela, 2018). This identification of business opportunities usually causes entrepreneurship to be commonly associated with the face of business creation (Domenichelli, 2012), considered by some authors as the most appropriate method to analyse it (Gartner, 1990).

Undertaking this is a complicated task that requires the gathering of different knowledge by the entrepreneur, such as the operation of the sector where you want to invest, the knowledge of the financial system that surrounds you, or the possibility of obtaining financing, among others. In this case, the lack of information is one of the problems of development of their company which face entrepreneurs in a region (Carvalho, Pérez, and Pache, 2019). Therefore, the support that entrepreneurs receive during all the stages of their adventure will be decisive and must be provided by local governments in the first place "since they play an important role of support and promotion in the creation of companies" (Nevado, Gallardo and Carvalho, 2019, p. 98). On the other hand, these authors affirm that a very useful ally for the transmission of information is new technologies, especially the internet. In view of the above, and considering local governments as a fundamental support factor for entrepreneurial work, the objective of this study is to analyse the information they provide to entrepreneurs in their institutional web portals.

As regards the sample, the local governments of the Spanish provincial capitals were chosen of which, as established in article 141 of the Spanish Constitution, there are 50. To carry out our study we will use the content analysis technique, used in previous research (Moneva and Martín, 2012; Nevado, Gallardo and Sánchez, 2013; Beuren and Angonese, 2015; García-Sánchez, Frías-Aceituno and Rodríguez-Domínguez, 2013; among others). Data collection was carried out through access via search engine of the home page of each local entity between the months of January and April 2015, collecting information related to entrepreneurship. To provide this information, the indicators proposed by Carvalho, Gallardo and Nevado (2018) were used, comprising a total of 49 indicators grouped into 5 dimensions. With the information collected, information disclosure indices are prepared in order to obtain the degree and type of information they disclose. The results show that the local governments of the capitals of Spanish provinces offer information to entrepreneurs through their websites; however, the degree of information they disclose is low. Attending to the results of this study we are able to conclude that information disclosure is related to the communication with entrepreneurs and are scarce the information provided about resources and active entrepreneurship. This chapter is divided in introduction, literatura review about entrepreneurship, methodology, results, final remarks and new avenues for future research.

Figure 1. Evolution of companies growth in Spain by year
Source: INE, 2017.

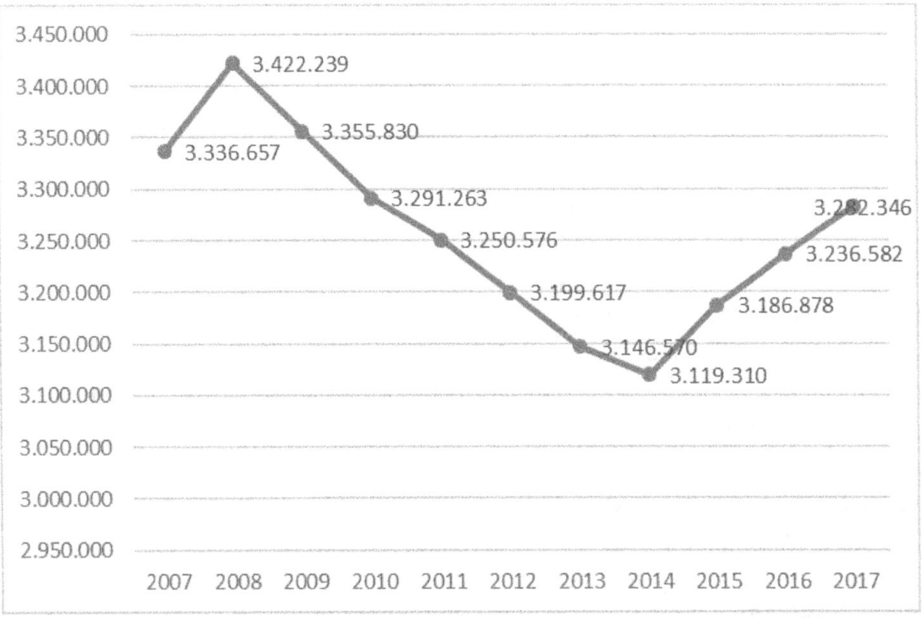

LITERATURE REVIEW

Nowadays competitive society, it is undoubtedly true that the person with entrepreneurial skills has a position of special relevance (Lazear, 2005), and self-employment can be constituted by an important source of job creation in different areas. In addition, literature highlighted a growth in the approaches regarding entrepreneurship and their contribute to the economies (Sullivan and Meek, 2012). The Royal Spanish Language Academy defines entrepreneurship as the act of undertaking and commencing a work, a business, a job, especially if it is difficult to do[1].

Usually entrepreneurship had been related to the capability of some individuals benefit with entrepreneurial situations and obtain reantability with this development (Dimova and Pela, 2018). This identification of business opportunities can lead to the fact that entrepreneurship is commonly associated with the business creation facet (Palos-Sánchez, Baena-Luna and Casablanca Peña, 2019), considered by some of the authors as the most appropriate method for analyze entrepreneurship (Gartner, 1990). In particular, three key elements can be highlighted in the process of creating a new business (Timmons, 2003): a) the niche market, identified as the latent business opportunity, b) the entrepreneurial character and the group that accompanies it and c) a fundamental element, the resources available for the pursuit of the entrepreneurial idea.

The Spanish National Institute of Statistics (INE) has found that as of 2014, six consecutive years of reduction in the number of companies in Spain have been achieved, reaching more than the last decade, in particular, as it stands. in 3,119,310. In the last three years available, I can see a trend in relation to the number of companies created, in the last available date corresponding to the year 2017, where there are 3,282,346 companies, however less than the data. existing in 2009 (See Figure 1).

Becomes an entrepreneur implies a hard work and the acess to a set of resources. Thus, the lack of information can be considered as one of the problems facing entrepreneurs and access to information about the rules, conditions, and opportunities available in a region for the development of their business (Carvalho, Pérez and Pache, 2019). Therefore, it will be crucial to support entrepreneurs during all the stages of their adventure which, at a first moment, could be provided by public administrations "... who play an important role in supporting and fostering business creation, and new technologies –especially the internet– enable the transmission of information, thereby converting it into an ally of great utility to boost entrepreneurship "(Nevado, Gallardo and Carvalho, 2019, p. 98). In this context, is fundamental support entrepreneurship in a regional context and public administration could be important and disclosure relevant information to the entrepreneurs using web institutional portals.

Entrepreneurial activity depends on a set of elements, such as financial aspects, risk management, risk of failure, etc. (Block, Sandner and Spiegel, 2015).

In order to be able to define entrepreneurial process it is necessary to start from the idea of entrepreneurial activity, it could be defined as "the entrepreneurial initiative there is that creativity and innovation are introduced in existing markets, which change them, and including that creen new markets. Thus, fostering entrepreneurship is considered a key element for economic and social development (Alemany, Álvarez, Planellas and Urbano, 2011). Shane and Venkataraman (2000) considered that the entrepreneurial initiative includes the study of opportunities, the processes of discovery, the evaluation and exploitation of opportunities, and the people who discover, evalue and exploit them. Entrepreneurial initiative does not require, but may include, the creation of new organizations.

The entrepreneurial iniative it is also named as entrepreneurial spirit, defined as a strong motivation to create new companies, innovate and identify new oportunities (Stam, Suddie, Hessels, and Van Stel, 2006). Literature also highlights a positive correlation between economic growth and entrepreneurial spirit with a positive impact in development of new markets (Minniti, 2012).

It is also necessary to make a brief mention of the fundamental characteristics of the entrepreneur. These entrepreneurial characteristics or competencies can be defined as those that seek the autonomy of the person and are oriented towards the self-realization of the subject, as a way to carry out a vital project focused on the production of goods and services that meet the needs of the community (Martínez and Carmona, 2009). Some authors divide entrepreneurs in two large groups: those related to the domain of business skills and basic economic concepts and those related to the ability to create companies (Fernández and Fernández, 2010), standing out, in addition, by the academy that, although competencies can be different types, must be acquired in a balanced situation (Balmaceda, 2018). Concerning competences some authors identified at least five elements: a person's own knowledge; a know-how, consisting in the application of the person's own knowledge to the resolution of problems; a know-how, where it should behave based on the procedures established in each organization; a want to know, where you should want to apply the activities developed optimally by the competition and, a power to do, where the entrepreneur must have the means at his disposal to develop the competition (Pereda and Berrocal, 2001).

Regardless, the potential competencies of the entrepreneur, it is also important to highlight his possible motivations to undertake (Marulanda, Montoya and Vélez, 2019). Thus, personal motivations can be found, such as the needs of achievement and wealth, the desire to reach new challenges or the desire to overcome (Varela and Bedoya, 2006), although the need for the entrepreneur of obtain an independence (Manolova, Brush and Edelman, 2008); motivations related to knowledge, normally acquired by the entrepreneur thanks to his work experience (Shepherd, 2005), although as will be discussed later, more academic training in this regard would be appropriate, especially in the university field; motivations related to the perception of an opportunity that could provide profitability (Shane and Venkataraman, 2000), motivations related to the availability of resources, both financial, technical or related to obtaining a positive network of relationships (Farmer, Yao and Kung-Mcintyre, 2011) and, the differentiation between two types of motivations carried out by the Global Entrepreneurship Monitor (GEM) should also be highlighted, since they distinguish between entrepreneurship by necessity, since it must survive, or entrepreneurship by opportunity. Concerning the values and skills of an entrepreneur, and the GEM report of the year 2014 referring to Spain referred, first, to the state of alertness to the new opportunities in which an entrepreneur must be found by definition, "state of alert conditioned by a series of individual characteristics (knowledge, skills, fear of failure, reference models, etc.) and contextual (standards of life, the image of the entrepreneur in society, etc.). In this way, both elements are combined over time to become a series of values, perceptions and skills that a population has linked to the entrepreneurial activity in their environment[2].

METHODOLOGY

The objective of this study is to analyze the information that the capitals of Spanish provinces provide to entrepreneurs in their institutional web portals. The following research questions are proposed to be resolved: Do the municipalities selected through their institutional portal provide information related to entrepreneurship? What is the degree of said information disclosed? What is its nature?

In relation to the sample, the local governments of the Spanish provincial capitals have been chosen which, as established in article 141 of the Spanish Constitution, are 50. As described above, the web pages of the selected municipalities will be analyzed, looking for information related to entrepreneurship, using the content analysis technique (Moneva and Martín, 2012). The data was collected during the months of February to May 2015, assigning to each indicator a dichotomous scale, that is, the value 1 if the item is in the analyzed institutional portal and, giving the value 0 in the case that was not present (Frías-Aceituno, Conceição-Marques, and Rodríguez-Ariza, 2013).

In relation to the indicators proposed in this study, it has been based on those prepared by Carvalho, Gallardo, and Nevado (2018), thus obtaining five different analysis axes that have a total of 49 indicators. In this way, the axis of analysis 1 has 10 indicators, where the general information described in the web pages is measured; analysis axis 2, meanwhile, measures the resources and support to the entrepreneur and has a total of 12 indicators; axis 3, related to active entrepreneurship, is made up of 10 indicators; the axis of analysis 4, with 6 indicators related to digital entrepreneurship and, finally, axis 5, related to the dissemination and communication to the entrepreneur, which has a total of 11 indicators. This information can be summarized in Table 1.

Once the institutional web portals of the different selected municipalities have been analyzed, a series of dissemination indices (Nevado, Gallardo and Sánchez, 2016) are prepared, in order to obtain the type and degree of information on entrepreneurship that they provide, and That your support work is essential for the entrepreneur. Thus, a measurement of the dissemination of information will be carried out at two levels (Pache and Nevado, 2019) measuring, on the one hand, the disclosure by city council in each of the dimensions from a starting index (IDGE) and, subsequently, calculating a new index in order to obtain the information of each City Council selected in the present study (IDG). On the other hand, we will proceed to calculate the disclosure obtained by each indicator (IDI), subsequently building

Table 1. Study analysis axis

Axis of analysis	Number of indicators	Index weight	Weighing
1) General information	10	20,42%	20%
2) Resources and support to the entrepreneur	12	24.46%	20%
3) Active entrepreneurship	10	20,42%	20%
4) Digital entrepreneurship	6	12,24%	20%
5) Disclosure and communication with the entrepreneur	11	22,46%	20%
Total	49	100%	100%

Source: Adapted from Carvalho et al., 2018.

from this, another indicator for each of the dimensions set forth above (IDE), completing the task by measuring the total disclosure of the sample (IDT). The indices can be observed as follows in Table 2.

Where, M = number of items that make up each axis of analysis; E = number of analysis axes; Aij = takes the value of 1 if the characteristic that defines the indicator (i) is present in the local government (j), and 0 in the opposite case; N = number of local governments; Having no empirical evidence on the importance of the different partial indices that make up the total index, the same specific weight has been assigned for each of the dimensions (p = 20%).

Table 2. Disclosure indexes

Indexes	Concept	Expression
Disclosure index by local government and analysis axis (IDGE)	Measure the percentage of total disclosure of each local government in each of the analysis axes	$IDGE_j = \left(\frac{\sum_{i=1}^{M}(Aij)}{M} * p \right) * 100$
Disclosure index by local government (IDG)	Measure the total disclosure of each local government	$IDG_j = \sum_{i=1}^{E}(IDGE_j)$
Disclosure index by item (IDI)	Measure the percentage of local governments that report each item	$IDI_i = \frac{\sum_{i=1}^{N}(Aij)}{N} * 100$
Disclosure index by analysis axis (IDE)	Measure the total disclosure of each axis of analysis	$IDE_i = \left(\frac{\sum_{i=1}^{M}(IDI_i)}{M} * p \right) * 100$
Total disclosure index (IDT)	Measure the total disclosure of the sample	$IDT = \sum_{i=1}^{E}(IDE_i)$

Source: Adapted from Carvalho, Gallardo y Nevado (2018)

Figure 2. Analysis axis 1 indexes (See Annex I)
Source: Own elaboration

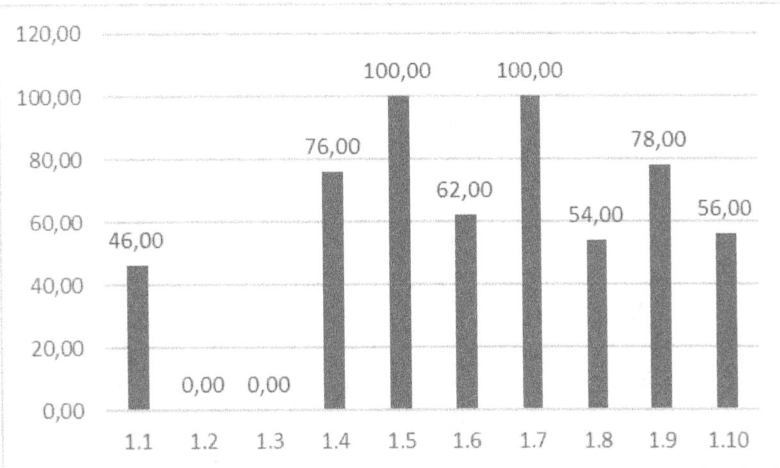

RESULTS

Annex 1 shows the results obtained in the different indexes of information disclosure by items (IDI). However, it is convenient to make a graphic breakdown of the information on entrepreneurship that the municipalities of Spain describe in each dimension. Thus, in the first of them, Figure 2, where the general information existing on their web pages has been measured, it should be noted that 76% of them have both a map, and with their own search engine on their pages, a fact that facilitates enormously the search for information related to entrepreneurship. In all municipalities there is an internal search engine that

Figure 3. Analysis axis 2 indexes (See Annex I)
Source: Own elaboration

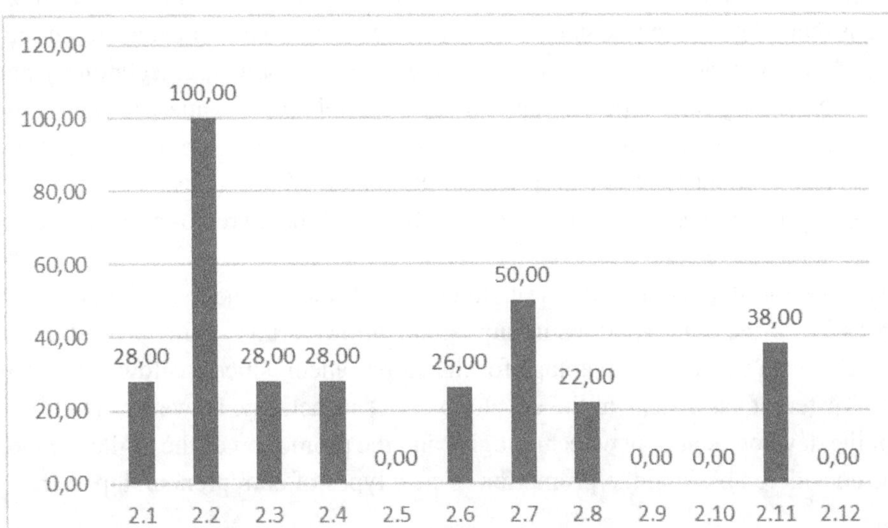

Figure 4. Analysis axis 3 indexes (See Annex I)
Source: Own elaboration

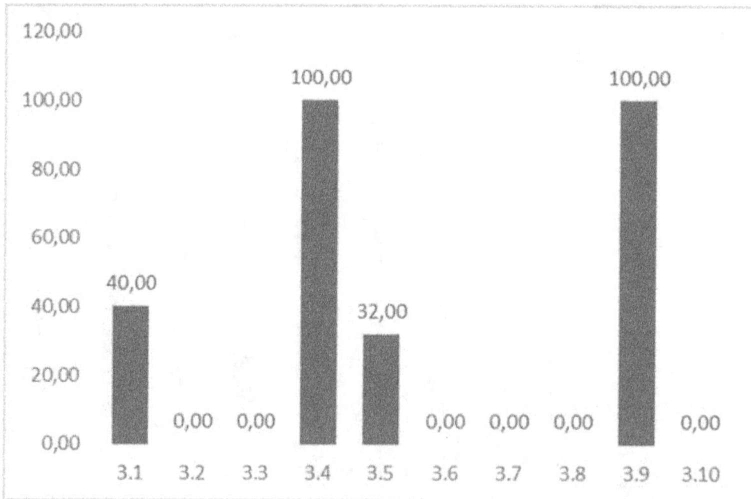

facilitates the search for information and links for social networks. From a more negative point of view, it should be noted that, only 46% of the municipalities have a statement from the head of the same, on the importance of promoting entrepreneurship and economic development.

In relation to the second axis of analysis related to resources and support to the entrepreneur (Figure 3), the results show that the regulations regarding the creation of companies are available on all the websites of the municipalities. Half of the municipalities report on the contacts of interest and the rest of the information regarding this block is quite deficient, only 28% of the proposed indicators are disclosed. There are few municipalities in which there is an entrepreneur support cabinet, and in which reference is made to the existence of a space available for the beginning of the activity.

The analysis of the third axis related to active entrepreneurship (Figure 4), it should be noted that the results obtained continue along the same lines as those previously analyzed, since there is very little information regarding the items under study. Thus, it can be mentioned that the aspect most covered by the town halls, is that related to the existence of contests, awards or similar events to publicly recognize businessmen and the existence of an incubator, business nest or municipal technology park. It should be noted negatively, among other aspects, that none of the municipalities analyzed has on their websites tutorials related to the creation of companies, courses available to develop the skills of entrepreneurs, clarity about priorities and the type of entrepreneurship that the Municipality wants to encourage, there are no days of exchange of experiences and good practices and there are no initiatives to encourage the sustainable behavior of companies.

In relation to the fourth axis of analysis related to digital entrepreneurship (Figure 5), it should be mentioned that 40% of the municipalities in our sample allow certain online procedures to be carried out, which can cause an enormous advantage for the entrepreneur, since it allows him save time in the performance of different basic steps in the development of its activity. However, no city councils have campaigns for the development of new technologies and the promotion of the digital economy, an issue that should be considered basic in the promotion of new types of entrepreneurship in the 21st century.

Figure 5. Analysis axis 4 indexes (See Annex I)
Source: Own elaboration

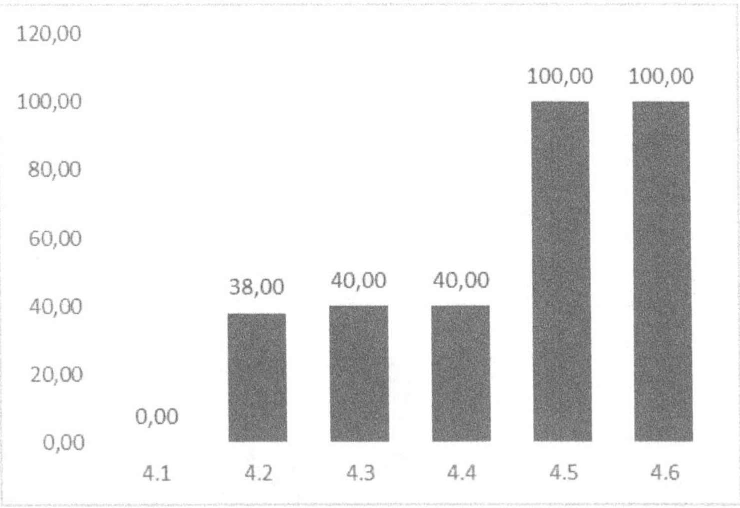

On the other hand, in all municipal websites there is a citizen mailbox or a section for complaints, suggestions and a platform for business exchange, business portals, fairs, associations and business clubs.

The last indicator is the one related to the dissemination and communication with the entrepreneur, where the results are also quite high, since the entrepreneur needs important support for the promotion and development of his activity. In this regard, it should be noted that all municipalities have an insti-

Figure 6. Analysis axis 5 indexes (See Annex I)
Source: Own elaboration

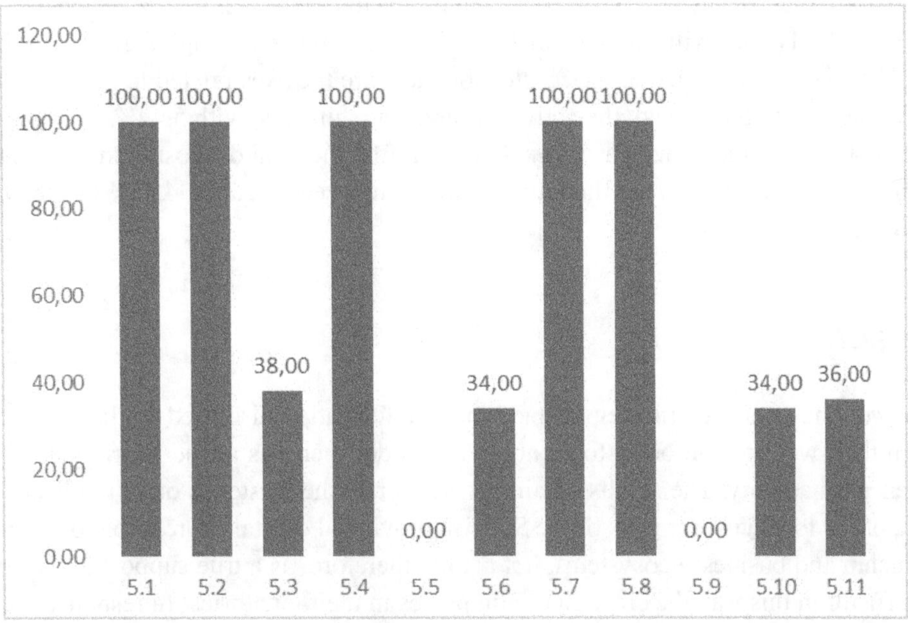

Figure 7. Disclosure index by analysis axis
Source: Own elaboration

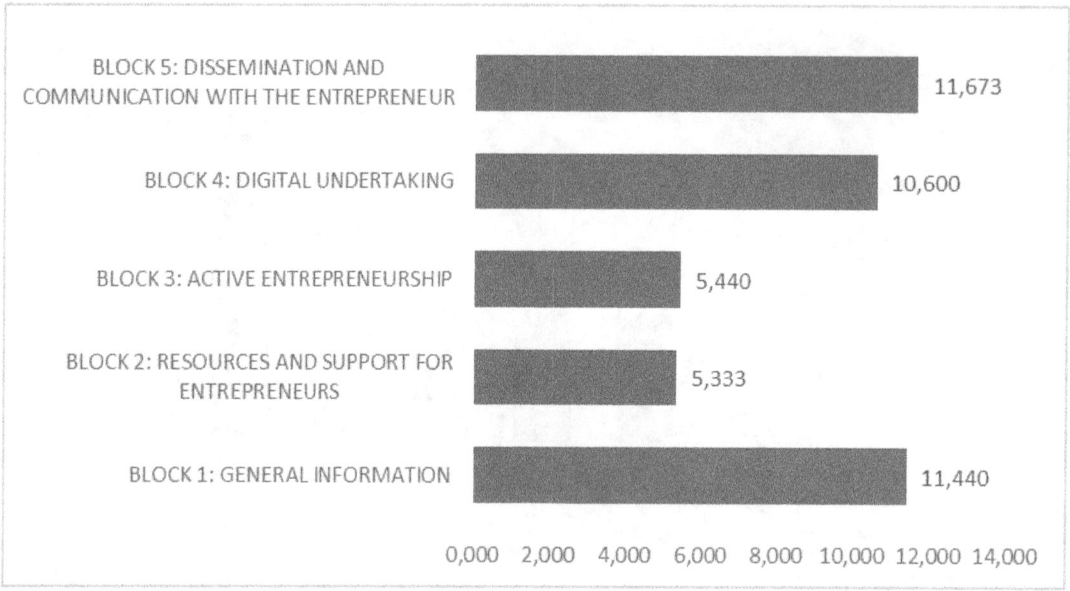

tutional section in their institutional portal and are accessible on the web and easy to locate. All report on the news such as new approved projects, outstanding news, publish a Municipal Bulletin with news related to the business activity and inform about what is necessary to start an activity. On the other hand, none of the councils disseminate or publicize the newly created companies (Figure 6).

Also, the disclosure rates for each axis of analysis can be found in Annex 1, which include the contribution of each axis to the total disclosure index. Thus, in Figure 7 shown below, it can be seen that the axis related to disclosure and communication with the entrepreneur is the most widely disclosed by the municipalities, specifically with 11.67%, secondly, it is found the axis related to general information, with 11.44%. In third place, with an index of 10.60%, the axis related to digital entrepreneurship and in fourth and fifth place, almost tied in the results obtained, are the axes related to resources and support to the entrepreneur with 5.33% and, the active entrepreneurship axis, with 5.44%.

In addition, based on the above, in Annex 2 you can find the total disclosure index (RTD), where it has been obtained, which on average the municipalities analyzed disclose 44.48% of the total information on entrepreneurship.

CONCLUSION

The present work has analyzed the degree and type of information disclosed by the Spanish city councils, through their websites, in order to be able to consider them, as a true instrument of support for the entrepreneurial activity. The results obtained corroborate the existence of an implication, although still modest, of the local governments of the Spanish provincial capitals in relation to the promotion of entrepreneurship and business ecosystems, not acting, therefore, as a true support to the entrepreneur, making it difficult in this way the creation of companies in their territories. In response to the research questions raised, it should first be noted that the municipalities of the Spanish provincial capitals provide little information regarding entrepreneurship, thus obtaining a degree of disclosure of 44.48%, as evidenced by the ITD Regarding the nature of the information disclosed, it has been obtained that the most detailed is the one related to the dissemination and communication with the entrepreneur, while in the last place there may be the one related to resources and support for the entrepreneur and active entrepreneurship. These results should serve so that the selected municipalities reflect on the important work they perform and, in the future, these studies serve to reflect the deficiencies observed in order to improve the information disclosed. The main limitation of this study is its purely descriptive nature, since it uses cross-sectional data that does not allow inferences. It is proposed, therefore, an interesting line of work focused on the analysis of the explanatory factors of the development of these dissemination practices, considering their evolution over time and evidencing their contribution to economic development and job creation in the territory under study through entrepreneurship. Finally, the work provides a new reference to the literature on entrepreneurship, deepening the core of entrepreneurship support that local corporations represent.

REFERENCES

Alemany, L., Álvarez, C., Planellas, M., & Urbano, D. (2011). *Libro Blanco de la iniciativa emprendedora en España*. Barcelona: editado por la Fundación Príncipe de Girona.

Balmaceda, F. (2018). Entrepreneurship: Skills and financing. *Small Business Economics, 50*(4), 871–886. doi:10.100711187-017-9915-1

Beuren, I.M. & Angonese, R. (2015). Instruments for determining the disclosure index of accounting information. *Revista Eletrônica de Estratégia e Negócios, 8*(1), 120-144.

Block, J., Sandner, P., & Spiegel, F. (2015). How do risk attitudes differ within the group of entrepreneurs? The role of motivation and procedural utility. *Journal of Small Business Management, 53*(1), 183–206. doi:10.1111/jsbm.12060

Carvalho, L., Gallardo, V. D., & Nevado, G. M. T. (2018). Local municipalities' involvement in promoting entrepreneurship: An analysis of web page orientation to the entrepreneurs in Portuguese municipalities. In L. Carvalho (Ed.), Handbook of Research on Entrepreneurial Ecosystems and Social Dynamics in a Globalized World. Hershey PA: IGI Global.

Carvalho, L., Pérez, E., & Pache, M. (2019). Implicación de los gobiernos locales en la promoción del emprendimiento: Evidencia para España. *Revista Espanola la de Documentacion Cientifica, 42*(1), 1–16.

Dimova, R., & Pela, K. (2018). Entrepreneurship: Structural transformation, skills and constraints. *Small Business Economics, 51*(1), 203–220. doi:10.100711187-017-9916-0

Domenichelli, R.N. (2012). Factores condicionantes de la actividad emprendedora. *Revista de treball, economia i societat*, (64), 1-16.

Farmer, S. M., Yao, X., & Kung-Mcintyre, K. (2011). The behaioral impact of entrepreneur Identy aspiration and prior entrepreneurial Experience. *Entrepreneurship Theory and Practice, 35*(2), 245–273. doi:10.1111/j.1540-6520.2009.00358.x

Fernández, L. S., & Fernández, E. F. (2010). Competencias emprendedoras y desarrollo del espíritu empresariales en los centros educativos. *Educación XX1. Revista da Faculdade de Educação*, *13*(1), 15–38.

Frías-Aceituno. J., Conceicao Marques, M., & Rodríguez-Ariza, L. (2013). Divulgación de información sostenible: ¿Se adapta a las expectativas de la sociedad? Spanish Accounting Review, 16(2), 147-158.

García-Sánchez, I.-M., Frías-Aceituno, J.-V., & Rodríguez-Domínguez, L. (2013). Determinants of Corporate Social Disclosure in Spanish Local Governments. *Journal of Cleaner Production*, *39*, 60–72. doi:10.1016/j.jclepro.2012.08.037

Gartner, W. B. (1990). What are we talking about when we talk about emtrepreneurship? *Journal of Business Venturing*, *5*(1), 15–28. doi:10.1016/0883-9026(90)90023-M

Gil, N. (2019). Emprendimiento en la administración local: Un estudio empírico de la información contenida en los portales electrónicos de los municipios del Alentejo, región de Portugal. *Revista Innovar*, *29*(71), 97–112. doi:10.15446/innovar.v29n71.76398

Instituto Nacional de Estadística (2017). Estadísticas PYME. Evolución e indicadores.

Lazear, E. P. (2005). Entrepreneurship. *Journal of Labor Economics*, *23*(4), 282–305. doi:10.1086/491605

Manolova, T., Brush, C., & Edelman, L. (2008). What do women entrepreneurs want? *Strategic Change*, *17*(3), 69–82. doi:10.1002/jsc.817

Martínez, M., & Carmona, G. (2009). Aproximación al concepto de competencias emprendedoras: Valor social e implicaciones educativas. *Revista Electrónica Iberoamericana sobre Calidad, Eficacia y Cambio en Educación*, *7*(3), 82–98.

Marulanda, F. A., Montoya, I. A., & Vélez, J. M. (2019). El individuo y sus motivaciones en el proceso emprendedor. *Revista Universidad y Empresa*, *21*(36), 10–24.

Minniti, M. (2012). El emprendimiento y el crecimiento económico de las naciones. *Revue d'Economie Industrielle*, *383*, 23–32.

Moneva, J., & Martín, E. (2012). Universidad y Desarrollo sostenible: Análisis de la rendición de cuentas de las universidades públicas desde un enfoque de responsabilidad social. *Revista Iberoamericana de Contabilidad de Gestión*, *10*(19), 1–18.

Nevado-Gil, M. T., Gallardo Dolores, L., & Isabel Sánchez, M. (2013). La administración local y su implicación en la creación de una cultura socialmente responsable. *Revista Prisma Social Revista de Ciencias Sociales*, *10*, 64–118.

Nevado-Gil, M.T., Gallardo Dolores, L., y Isabel Sánchez, M. (2016). Análisis del grado de divulgación de información sobre responsabilidad social en las webs de los principales municipios extremeños. *Auditoría pública*, (67), 77-92.

Pache-Durán, M., & Nevado-Gil, M. T. (2019). Divulgación de información responsable por los gobiernos locales españoles. *Revista Bibliotecológica*, *33*(81), 111–134.

Palos- Sánchez, P.R., Baena-Luna, P., & Casablanca Peña, A. (2019). *Factores determinantes para la mejora de la capacidad emprendedora a partir de las competencias*. Cáceres: editada por Extremadura Avante Servicios Avanzados.

Pereda, S. & Berrocal, F. (2001). *Gestión de Recursos Humanos por Competencias*. Madrid: editado por el Centro de Estudios Ramón Areces.

Shane, S., & Venkataraman, S. (2000). The promise of Entrepreneurship as a Field of Research. *Academy of Management Review*, *25*(1), 217–226.

Shepherd, D., & DeTienne, D. R. (2005). Prior Knowlegde, Potential Financial Reward, and Opportunity Identification. *Entrepreneurship Theory and Practice*, *29*(1), 91–112. doi:10.1111/j.1540-6520.2005.00071.x

Stam, E., Suddie, K., Hessels, S. J., & Van Stel, A. (2006). Los emprendedores con potencial de crecimiento y el desarrollo económico: Políticas públicas de apoyo a los emprendedores. *Ekonomiaz: Revista Vasca de Economía*, *62*, 124–149.

Sullivan, D. M., & Meek, W. R. (2012). Gender and entrepreneurship: A review and process model. *Journal of Managerial Psychology*, *27*(5), 429–452. doi:10.1108/02683941211235373

Timmons, J. (2003). *Entrepreneurial thinking: can entrepreneurship be taught*? Coleman Chicago: Coleman Foundation.

Varela, R., & Bedoya, O. (2006). Modelo conceptual de desarrollo empresarial basado en competencias. *Revista Estudios Generales*, *22*(100), 21–47.

KEY TERMS AND DEFINITIONS

Disclosure of information: reveal of information

Entrepreneurship: the activity of setting up a business or businesses, taking on financial risks in the hope of profit.

Local Public administration: is the implementation of government policy in a local level

WebPage: is a document commonly written in HTML (Hypertext Markup Language) that is accessible through the Internet or other networks using an Internet browser.

ENDNOTES

1. Diccionario de la Real Academia Española de la Lengua, available on: http://lema.rae.es/drae/srv/search?id=F77BO4xYqDXX2BpwCGRr, (20/09/2019).
2. GEM Report for Spain 2014, page 37, available: http://www.gem-spain.com/wp-content/uploads/2015/04/GEM_es_2014.pdf, (10/09/2019).

APPENDIX

Disclosure Rates by Items and by Analysis Axis

Total Disclosure Index

IDT = 11,44 + 5,33 + 5,44 + 10,60+ 11,67 = 44,48

Table 3. Analysis axis 1: General information about the municipal corporation

		IDI
1.1	There is a statement from the head of responsibility for the importance of entrepreneurship and economic development	46,00
1.2	Priorities and strategies to be achieved are included in this statement.	0,00
1.3	Events, achievements and failures recorded by the entity are included	0,00
1.4	There is a map of the website itself	76,00
1.5	There is an internal search engine to facilitate your navigation	100,00
1.6	There is the possibility of listening to the page	62,00
1.7	There are links for social networks	100,00
1.8	There is a list of companies in the territory	54,00
1.9	Key economic information such as GDP or unemployment rate is published	78,00
1.10	It informs about the strategic aspects or reasons to invest in that municipality	56,00
Disclosure index of analysis axis 1 (IDE)		**11,44**

Table 4. Analysis axis 2: Information on resources and support for entrepreneurs

		IDI
2.1	Is there any cabinet or organ supporting the entrepreneur	28,00
2.2	The regulations for the creation of a company are available	100,00
2.3	Reference is made to the availability of some physical space for the beginning of the activity	28,00
2.4	There are specific objectives on the procedures to follow for the creation of a business	28,00
2.5	There are specific objectives and measurable objectives to increase business activity, including social entrepreneurship and its impact on the economy	0,00
2.6	Information on entrepreneurship is disseminated, including social entrepreneurship and its impact on the economy	26,00
2.7	The contacts of interest are informed	50,00
2.8	Specific needs of young people, women and other target groups are recognized	22,00
2.9	The tax incentives of the investment (risk capital financing solutions) are reported	0,00
2.10	There is information on knowledge protection, brand etc.	0,00
2.11	Formalities for business creation are reported	38,00
2.12	Reference is made to the time and cost of starting a business	0,00
Disclosure index of analysis axis 2 (IDE)		**5,33**

Table 5. Analysis axis 3: Information on active entrepreneurship

		IDI
3.1	There are mechanisms, such as multi-stakeholder forums to promote dialogue about entrepreneurship	40,00
3.2	Help tutorials are available for starting a business	0,00
3.3	There are courses available to develop the skills of entrepreneurs	0,00
3.4	There are contests, awards or similar events to publicly recognize entrepreneurs	100,00
3.5	The municipality offers services to help the creation of companies in compliance with regulatory requirements	32,00
3.6	There is clarity about the priorities and the type of entrepreneurship that the municipality wants to encourage	0,00
3.7	Days of exchange of experiences and good practices are held	0,00
3.8	There are education programs for entrepreneurship in younger schools	0,00
3.9	There is an incubator, business nest or municipal technology park	100,00
3.10	There are initiatives to encourage corporate SR	0,00
Disclosure index of analysis axis 3 (IDE)		**5,44**

Table 6. Analysis axis 4: Information on digital entrepreneurship

		IDI
4.1	There are awareness raising and capacity development campaigns in the use of ICT and digital economy	0,00
4.2	The municipality facilitates support for the improvement of technology in small businesses	38,00
4.3	Possibility of administrative procedures, permits, licenses online	40,00
4.4	Online monitoring of the processing status and incidents of the proposed procedure	40,00
4.5	There is a citizen mailbox or section for complaints, suggestions	100,00
4.6	There is a platform for business exchange, business portals, fairs, associations and business clubs	100,00
Disclosure index of the analysis axis 4 (IDE)		**10,60**

Table 7. Analysis axis 5: Information on dissemination and communication with the entrepreneur

		IDI
5.1	There is a specific area for the entrepreneur	100,00
5.2	It is accessible on the web and is easy to identify	100,00
5.3	Investment opportunities are disclosed	38,00
5.4	News is reported as new approved projects, outstanding news ...	100,00
5.5	There is a space for user satisfaction for the improvement of GAE	0,00
5.6	There is a space to express user opinions	34,00
5.7	A municipal newsletter about business activity news is published	100,00
5.8	You are informed about what is necessary to start an activity	100,00
5.9	Newly created new businesses are disseminated or publicized	0,00
5.10	There is a link to the university or the institute of higher education	34,00
5.11	Campaigns are carried out to promote entrepreneurship	36,00
Disclosure index of the analysis axis 5 (IDE)		**11,67**

Chapter 11
An Exploratory Study About Corporate Governance and Integrated Reporting in the Mozambican Context:
What Mozambique Has Done in Corporate Governance

Angélica Violeta Chiau
University of Minho, Portugal

Graça Azevedo
Higher Institute of Accounting and Administration, University of Aveiro, Portugal

ABSTRACT

This article gives an overview of corporate governance in Mozambique. The mandatory disclosure of sustainability information leads to an increase in the social responsibility of managers. In this sense, the measure can possibly improve the ethical behaviour of the companies, while at the same time allowing for the reduction of the levels of corruption. The reputation in the business world creates a good image and can be transmitted in a reduction of risks to shareholders, and attraction of investments. This work contributes to the literature, and a greater understanding of sustainability in developing countries, particularly in Mozambique.

INTRODUCTION

This article intends to give an overview of corporate governance in Mozambique. Despite the good examples of the adoption of the integrated reporting, as noted in South Africa and in Brazil, in Mozambique these reports are not yet mandatory. The mandatory disclosure of sustainability information leads

DOI: 10.4018/978-1-7998-2128-1.ch011

to an increase in the social responsibility of managers. In this sense, the measure can possibly improve the ethical behaviour of the companies, while at the same time allowing the reduction of the levels of corruption. There is evidence of the relationship between, the adoption of the integrated reporting and the reputation of the companies in the capital markets. The reputation in the business world creates a good image and can be transmitted in a reduction of risks to shareholders, and attraction of investments.

In addition to the reasons previously presented, the study is relevant, because Mozambique, is facing a phase of great economic, political and social changes. It is in this context of changes, that the pressure on the part of society in general is evident, in order for the country to adopt measures to improve the performance of enterprises, with a significant impact on the competitiveness of country through higher reliable. Mozambique, in the last two decades, has been attracting foreign investment. Thus, it becomes important to adopt the corporate governance code, in that the good management practices recommended in the code can enhance economic growth. However, the relationship between transparency and attraction of new investments should be taken into consideration. This occurs as a general rule, investors are looking for markets that are considered transparent and/or secure.

It should be noted that we seek previous studies that address this subject, focusing on Mozambique. However, we find studies such as those of Esperança (2011) that address the topic with a focus on Lusophony space, examines the extent to which publicly listed companies across Sub-Saharan African countries have adopted "good corporate governance" practices; Munisi and Randøy, (2013) examines the extent to which publicly listed companies across Sub-Saharan African countries have adopted "good corporate governance" practices. Dues to the lack/ absence of studies focused in Mozambique, we started this exploratory study in order to launch the debate and to contribute to the continuous improvement of corporate governance and the integrated reporting in Mozambique. We conclude that, despite the progress observed in the sense, encourage the Mozambican companies to adopt the corporate governance code, still persists at low adherence to code in reference. In addition, in the context of Mozambique, the reports disclosed by most of these companies demonstrate the low or non-existent concern with social and environmental issues. In some cases, irrelevant information, is disclosed in order to try to legitimize your behaviour, by means of reports depicting a socially responsible image, regardless of actual behaviour.

The study is structured in six parts. We began by doing the contextualization of the debate around the topic, showing some ideas and reflections on the adoption of the corporate governance code, and the importance of the elaboration and dissemination of the integrated reporting; secondly, we address the financial aspects and the impact of the dissemination of the integrated reporting. The example of South Africa is then presented as one of the countries with the best adoption of the integrated reporting. This is justified according to the corporate governance code in Mozambique, being partly inspired by the South African. After that, the process of adoption of the integrated reporting in the country is explored, and some examples of dissemination are presented by the largest companies in the country. Finally, the limitations of the study, recommendations, clues to future works and some final considerations are presented.

LITERATURE REVIEW

The revision of the literature aims to make a survey and its synthesis of the scientific production of the thematic area. Thus, the mechanisms of corporate governance and the integrated reporting that contribute to the sustainability of companies will be described. We begin by discussing the importance of corporate governance and the integrated reporting.

The Importance of Corporate Governance and the Integrated Reporting

The corporate governance theme (CG) and sustainability is vast and raises discussions between scholars and entities linked to economic forums. In terms of the concept of corporate governance, the Organization for Economic Cooperation and Development (OECD) presents what appears to be the most widely accepted by the nations. The OECD (2004) states that corporate governance involves a set of relationships between the management of a company, the board of Directors, shareholders and other constituents, providing a structure through which the company's objectives are Established and the means of reaching them are determined.

A key aspect of the governance process inside organizations and markets is the measurement and disclosure of important metrics and information (Ioannou and Serafeim, 2017). The discussion on corporate governance covers mainly the trade-offs between the benefits provided by the best corporate governance practices and the tangible and intangible costs for disclosure of information and the establishment of corporate governance system (Idowu and Adedoyin, 2015).

Regarding the integrated reporting (IR) Adams and Simnett (2011) consider that it is a new reporting paradigm that is holistic, strategic, responsive, material and relevant across multiple time frames. The IR provides a basis to address the range of issues and opportunities affecting long-term business value by re-focussing reporting around an organization's business model and operational priorities (Hoffman, 2012). Is an expression of the "integrated thinking," a reflexion of the management's capacity to monitor, manage and disclose the entire complexity of the value creation process and how it contributes to success in time (Dumitru et al., 2013).

According to International Integrated Reporting Council (IIRC, 2013) the aim of IR is to communicate the full range of factors that affect an organization's ability to create value over time. With this in mind, the organization should understand how it defines and creates value before it can meaningfully define reporting content. Eccles and Armbrester (2011) corroborate the previous by advocating that the integrated reporting is the best way for a company to create value for shareholders in the long term.

Integrated reporting companies are different from traditional sustainability reporting (TSR) companies with regard to several country-level determinants. In particular, investor and employment protection laws, the intensity of market coordination and ownership concentration, the level of economic, environmental and social development, the degree of national corporate responsibility and the value system of the country of origin proved to be relevant (Jensen and Berg, 2012). Aside from creating profit, sustainable company leaders capture other qualitative, non-financial criterion as references for their performance, such as quality of management, corporate governance structures, reputation, human capital management, stakeholder relations, environmental protection and corporate social responsibility (Lo and Sheu, 2007).

More than adopting the integrated reporting is the success or impact that this instrument should have in the business. The key to successful IR implementation is the ability of the business to achieve integrated thinking and integrated management in the organization. From the practical perspective, implementing IR could be complex, but what it can do for business entities those are notable (Hoque, 2017). The Association of Chartered Certified Accountants (ACCA, 2017) lists the benefits of adopting IR: More integrated thinking and management; Greater clarity on business issues and performance; Improved corporate reputation and stakeholder relationships; More efficient reporting for both users and preparers of reports; etc.

This requires getting the different disciplines within the business to work together and break down the silos that are evident in many organizations (Hoffman, 2012). Therefore, and on the basis of the statements of the authors mentioned above, it can be concluded that the communication of the performance of enterprises in the economic, social and environmental fields is a process that implies a series of challenges. However, it cannot be disposed of, therefore, it allows greater visibility of the company and probably greater competitiveness.

Financial Aspects: What Really Impacts the Dissemination of the Integrated Reporting

Integrated reporting combines financial and non-financial information with a forward-looking perspective that's designed to help readers understand all the components of business value – and how they may be affected by future opportunities and exposures (KPMG, 2012). It should be noted that the percentage of companies to publish their reports relating to their non-financial performance varies depending on the country. According to Eccles and Saltzman (2011) European countries, Australia, Brazil, and Japan has being more active than China, India, and the United States. These authors also add that the European Commission is considering making the disclosure compulsory. Currently, Australia and Brazil have the largest number of companies to publish non-financial performance reports.

Still in the context of disclosure of financial reports and transparency Rossouw, Watt and Malan (2002) they consider it advisable that the managers responsible for disseminating the information in the IR to all stakeholders, such as shareholders, employees, potential investors, etc. According to Kaplan and Norton (1992) this measure is justified, to the extent that the disclosures of companies do not represent the reality of these, that is, companies tell incomplete stories about their performance and future prospects. Similar opinion is expressed by Krzus (2011) to the extent that, it considers that transparency in communication is an important vehicle for the reconstruction of public trust. Transparency also means that the firm discloses its activities as they occur, thus allowing stakeholders to create a stock of positive moral capital before bad acts occur (Godfrey, 2005). In this sense, Rossouw, Watt and Malan (2002) indicate that as companies are encouraged to constantly fight for transparency, this objective is likely to be achieved by the dissemination of relevant accounts.

Still in the context of disclosure Guerreiro (2012) point the downside of the reports. This author considers that the adoption of sustainability reports for reasons of image improvement and the firm's reputation increase, with its consequent exploitation as a marketing tool, distorts the concept of sustainability and its incorporation in the business strategies, not producing results in the long run. In this sense, it can be concluded that the adoption of the integrated reporting cannot be interpreted by the companies as a politically correct measure, but rather as an obligation to society.

Integrated Reporting and Sustainability: Relevance and Contribution to the Continuity of Business

When we deal with the integrated reporting and sustainability, we are essentially dealing with complementary issues. Good corporate governance requires an acknowledgement that an organisation doesn't operate in a vacuum, but is an integral part of society and therefore has accountability towards current and future stakeholders (PwC, 2016). In fact, the principal motivation of the bodies that founded the IRC (the GRI and A4S) was to improve the reporting of sustainability (Flower, 2015). Nowadays the literature is very developed in this aspect of sustainability as demonstrated by (Fifka, 2013) there are large number of empirical studies exist today.

In this sense, the communication of the operations and results of the companies is fundamental in the business world. Disclosure of sustainability information is increasingly the basis of good business conduct. Financial reporting alone is insufficient as a measure of value. It needs to be complemented with sustainability information – on economic, social and environmental performance (KPMG, 2011). The crucial point is the meaning given to the word 'value'; possible alternative interpretations are 'value to society' (which is consistent with social and environmental accounting), 'value to stakeholders' (which is consistent with the stakeholder theory of the firm), and 'value to present and future generations' - which is consistent with sustainability – (Flower, 2015).

This is positive and shows the concern in improving the performance of companies. The evidence shows that the past 30 years have seen substantial progress made by companies in complementing financial reporting with a broader range of non-financial information (Setia et al., 2015; Albertini, 2014). In fact, at the heart of the IR conceptual framework is the notion that companies should expand their reporting to include all of the resources they use as inputs to their business activities (Cheng et al., 2014).

Krzus (2011) affirms that the concept underlying the term "integrated reporting" is in the fact that it integrates fully financial and non-financial information (including environmental, social and intangible governance). A communication intended mainly for investors in which top management provides its views on how sustainability issues and initiatives are expected to contribute to the long-term growth strategy of the business (Churet, and Eccles, 2014). According to Tinker and Gary (2003) sustainability – in the sense of a system of deep-rooted social justice and a fair and responsible allocation and use of ecological resources – requires a political philosophy adequate to its unique task in effecting change. Despite attempts to provide answers to social issues, the improvement of the concept to include the use of environmental and social resources is hampered by the limitations or difficulties of measuring environmental damage, for instance. The lack of systematic disclosure of corporate value creation processes and intangible drivers of value, such as intellectual capital, is another limitation that has been highlighted (Setia *et al*, 2015). So, some solutions are discussed. Ioannou and Serafeim (2014) states that the obligation of the integrated reporting can promote socially responsible management practices and can improve the perception of social responsibility by stakeholders. In this context, the question is the following:

"To what extent are socially responsible management practices contributing to the sustainability of businesses?"

The available literature shows the various attempts to give an answer to this question. According to (Krzus, 2011) the IR allows to better understand the cause and effect, for example, of the relations between the financial performance and the sustainability of the companies. Furthermore, IR should explain the story of reaching the organisation's vision, underpinned by its values, enacted by management, monitored by governance, and using facets of resources relating to financial capital, intellectual capital, social capital, and environmental capital (Abeysekera, 2013).

As far as sustainability is concerned, Guerreiro (2012) indicates that the dissemination of financial and non-financial information involves not only a source of reduction of operational and financial costs, but also responds to a wider range of stakeholders who find in financial information and non-financial, especially in the latter, increasingly important factors of decision-making at the most diverse levels, which affect the lives of companies. In this sense, Adams and McNicholas (2007) argue that the report can be a catalyst for change in the sense of performance and improvement of sustainability. Jensen and

Berg (2012) argue that the extent of ownership concentration in a company influences the form of sustainability reporting.

Within this panorama, it can be concluded that the disclosure of the company's account has consequences. Therefore, in the process of elaborating and disseminating the company's account, it is essential to understand and take into account the expectations of investors and stakeholders. Thus, all stakeholders should be aware that the company, although it has to generate profit, has on the other hand social obligations, which can allow the continuity of this.

METHODOLOGY

In order to investigate whether good management practices are in any way related to the integrated reporting and the sustainability of the business, qualitative research, of an interpretative nature, was adopted and based on the analysis of bibliographic material. Fundamentally, the data were analysed using qualitative content analysis of the corporate sustainability reports and the corporate governance codes of Mozambique and South Africa. For the support of the work, we rescue ourselves from the following theories: Theory of legitimacy, theory of stakeholders and institutional theory. The theory of legitimacy allowed to explain the practices of disclosure of corporate reports. Agrawal and Hockerts (2013) consider that practitioners can use legitimacy to reflect on the social network, stakeholders, and sources of funding. The institutional theory is useful, in the light of, in this particular work, to explain the social performance, that is, to focus on the sustainability of the Mozambican companies. The application of institutional theory has proven to be especially helpful to entrepreneurial research (Bruton, Ahlstrom and Li, 2010). And also, it proposes that the relationship between the sustainability determinants and the level of sustainability initiatives is mediated by coercive, mimetic and normative isomorphic pressures (Horak, Arya and Ismail, 2018). Other authors use the institutional theory with the same approach (Brammer, Jackson, and Matten, 2012; Campbell, 2007). Thus, we analyse the reports of some companies considered the ten largest in the country according to KPMG, namely: Aluminium Foundry Company (MOZAL), the electricity of Mozambique (EDM), the mining company VALE, the oil firm (SASOL), the Cahora Bassa Hydroelectric Power Plant, Mota-Engil construction, Mozambique Beers (CDM), Mozambique Ports and Railways (CFM), Millennium BIM Bank and Grindrod Terminals. VALE's sustainability report is one of the most comprehensive, as the content of the report covers the guidelines and commitments related to the United Nations Global Compact, the International Mining and Metals Council (ICMM), the Sustainable Development Goals (ODS). In addition, it considers the Agenda 2030, a document of the United Nations (UN) that presents concrete measures to promote sustainable development and achieve a more viable world for all, taking the year 2030 as a horizon. Another example of better reports is that of Grindrod. The group sustainability review provides a balanced and reasonable representation of Grindrod's ESG policies, practices and performance, and covers the group company activities around the world, including impacts on communities and the environment. This is important to the extent that in the last few years, Grindrod has moved towards a more holistic, integrated and stakeholder-driven approach to managing the ESG and sustainability aspects of its business, in the firm belief that these are inextricably linked to long-term shareholder value. The examples previously presented were fundamental to the extent that among the largest companies operating in Mozambique few are clear with regard to their sustainability reports. The most curious is that these companies although they are operating in Mozambican territory are not of national origin, overcoming those that are entirely national in the issues of sustainability.

South Africa: The Practical Example of Adopting the Integrated Reporting

Despite its geographical location, South Africa, with regard to the adoption of the IR has been the pioneer. Therefore, it can be stated that South Africa is the example of a fairly progressive regulation with regard to the adoption of the integrated reporting. IR published compulsorily in South Africa (although not yet following the Framework) provide a more holistic way of thinking about the business, than an array of unconnected reports (Adams, 2015).

KPMG (2004) indicates that in some areas of corporate citizenship, South Africa is considered to be a global leader. In this sense, it can serve as an example to the countries of the African continent that seek greater visibility in the world markets. South Africa is an emerging market economy, with the 10th largest stock market in the world, the richest and most economically developed country on the African continent (Dawkins e Ngunjiri, 2008). Due to the country's visibility, Hoffman (2012) indicates that the companies listed on the Johannesburg Stock Exchange (JSE) are required to adopt the integrated reporting since 1st March 2010. The catalyst for this measure was the Code of Governance principles for South Africa, released in 2009, called (King III). However, South Africa has evolved greatly in the issues related to the integrated report, and is currently in the fourth version in order to accompany international modifications. In this context, from the day 1st April 2017 is the effective date of King IV. The Report highlights the importance of integrated thinking, integrated reporting and value creation and uses the definitions contained in the International <IR> Framework (Atkins and Maroun, 2015).

According to Ioannou and Serafeim (2015) The South African regulators in the code highlight the importance of the need for a fundamental change in the way the Managers act. In this sense the PricewaterhouseCoopers (PwC,2013; PwC,2014) similarly, surveys of integrated reporting trends by leading South African companies have revealed a number of shortcomings in disclosure trends and have identified opportunities for better integration of key performance measures.

The experience of the South companies with regard to the adoption of the integrated reporting was positive. Dawkins and Ngunjiri (2008) corroborate stating that the South African experience shows the favourable impact of government and institutional regulation on the issue of reports. Nevertheless, the overall impact of the South African approach cannot be determined in the short term in its economy. On the other hand, Herbst (2005) draws attention to the disadvantage of the adoption of the reports. According to this author, the information requirements are too costly. The costs inherent in the reports in question may in other countries be of justification for the non-adoption of the practice.

According to Hoffman (2012), the implementation of integrated reporting indicates positive experience for companies that have established a clear business approach. In this manner, most of the companies in question have a clear perception of the areas that need improvement. Following the South African example, many companies worldwide began to adopt the integrated reporting thinking about decision-making (Ridehalgh, 2011). In this sense, managers are provided with information that allows them to safely take strategic decisions on the direction of companies. In order to demonstrate the differences between the two countries follows table 1 which presents the fundamental principles for good corporate governance.

The table above compares the adoption of the Corporate governance code between South Africa and Mozambique. As can be seen the code of South Africa seeing being updated frequently, having been the

Table 1. Comparison between the fundamental principles of the South African and Mozambican code

Some principles toward of good corporate governance in South Africa (KING IV)	Explanation	Some principles toward of good corporate governance in Mozambique	Explanation
The Board should lead ethically and effectively;	The Board leads by example and has adopted a code of ethics and conduct so as to commit the business practices which the company will follow to writing as well as the standards of behaviour required by others within the company. Agility, integrity, trust, simplicity and accountability are all relevant words and concepts within the company.	The Principle of transparency	Refers to the rules and regulations governing decisions taken and their supervision, taking into account that the information (credible) should be made available to all persons and entities affected by decision-making and their supervision.
The Board should govern the ethics of the organisation in a way that supports the establishment of an ethical culture	The Board assumes responsibility for the governance of ethics. The Board has adopted a code of ethics which clearly sets out the business practices which the company will follow as well as the standards of behaviour for all persons within the company. The Board ensures that the code of ethics is well communicated and understood.	The Principle of participation	Refers to equal participation that men and women should exercise in governance activities, contemplating direct or indirect participation, through legitimate institutions or representatives, in a framework of freedom of expression and association in Organised civil societies.
The Board should govern compliance with applicable laws and adopted, non-binding rules, codes and standards in a way that supports the organisation's being ethical and a good corporate citizen.	The company has a dedicated legal resource that monitors compliance and remains appraised of any new legislation, non-binding rules and codes which may be of application to the company. Pre-emptive action is taken where possible so as to be prepared in advance of the implementation date of new legislation, regulation or codes.	The principle of responsibility	Refers to the design of governance structures in the sense that all persons affected by business decisions should be treated in a situation of equality and non-discrimination.
The Board should ensure that assurance services and functions enable an effective control environment, and that these support the integrity of information for internal decision making and of the organisation's external reports.	ERES, the company's outsourced property manager, have an internal audit department which provides assurance on the internal controls of ERES.	The principle of effectiveness	Refers to the production of results that conform to the best possible use of the resources mobilised and the needs of the beneficiaries of undertakings, including environmental protection and the use of USAD resources them in a sustainable way
In the execution of its governance role and responsibilities, the Board should adopt a stakeholder inclusive approach that balances the needs, interests and expectations of material stakeholders in the best interests of the organisation over time.	The Chair of the Board attends all shareholder meetings. The executive directors have an open-door policy and regularly engage with tenants and meet monthly with the property managers	The principle of coherence	Refers to the question of the search for consensus in social relations so that the different interests in question are mediated, in a framework of agreement and coherence with regard to the best options to be taken and taking into account the long-term aim of sustainable human development.

last updated held in 2016. A latest version called King IV includes in its entirety seventeen principles. The constant update of the South Africa Codex has thus allowed to accompany the changes that occur in the country and in some way better meet the expectations of international investors. However, Mozambique has not updated its principles for more than ten years in the sense of accompanying the economic changes that have occurred in the country. In this sense, it would be essential to revise the codex by demonstrating in this way the preoccupation that the country has to ensure good governance and thereby attract more and better international investors. We believe that Mozambique has much to learn from the South African experience, and the geographic proximity and commercial interests can reinforce this cooperation in the sense of best grandad in the code of corporate governance in Mozambique.

THE INTEGRATED REPORTING IN MOZAMBIQUE: WHAT ADVANTAGES FOR THE COUNTRY

The adoption of the integrated reporting reflects the reality of the companies operating in a multidimensional world, that is, in a global economy, in which the business is based on value creation. According to Adams (2015) implementing integrated reporting requires the development of new accountings and management processes. Therefore, the Global Reporting Initiative (GRI) is the institution that creates the guidelines and indicators for the elaboration of sustainability reports. It should be noted that, effectively, on its foundation, the IRC's principal objective was the promotion of sustainability accounting (Flower, 2015). In the Mozambican context, the corporate governance code recommends all companies to adopt the reporting. According to the Institute of Directors of Mozambique (IODmz, 2011) it is recommended the annual disclosure of the report, communicating in a transparent way to its stakeholders the level of performance or development of the society according to its goals of sustainability, ss well as their practices, policies and projects. Furthermore, the report must point to positive contributions to the environment and society, as well as the dimensions that require improvement. Unfortunately, the recommendations of IODmz (2011) do not seem enough to stop the lack of transparency and the ethical problems noted in Mozambican companies.

Compared to South Africa, Mozambique does not place the disclosure of reports as mandatory for companies operating in its territory. This happens in the light of the Corporate governance code in Mozambique, following the principle of self-regulation, which empowers the voluntary adherence and adoption of corporate governance. In this sense, and taking into account the experience of the partner countries in the development of the corporate governance code in Mozambique, namely South Africa, Brazil and Portugal, Mozambican regulators should consider the incorporation of changes in the sense that Mozambican companies should be obliged to publish the IR. Another important issue for Mozambique is related to ethics and transparency, which are fundamental to the security or confidence of international investors. Socially responsible management practices reinforce the competitiveness of a country. More importantly, the finding of Ioannou and Serafeim (2015) that the mandatory disclosure of the integrated reporting takes:

- Increase in the social responsibility of business managers
- Prioritization of sustainable development
- Prioritization of employee training
- More efficient supervision of managers by the boards of directors
- Increase in the implementation of ethical practices by companies
- Reduction of corruption
- Improvement of management and credibility within the society

Doane (2002) advocates the compulsory disclosure of the reports, and furthermore, consider that mandatory reporting will allow the market to operate more effectively – by making sure that relevant and transparent information is provided to all. However, cultural factors should be considered fundamentals in the reporting. According to Yusoff, Othman, and Yatim (2014), there is significant influence of culture in the practices of disseminating information. These authors also added that an examination of culture and its impact on corporate environmental reporting practices (ENRPs) could add knowledge about the potential success of environmental accounting and reporting systems as a whole. In this sense,

Adams and McNicholas (2007) indicate that an integrated reporting team includes individuals from different roles within the company. This practice is advantageous because its perspectives are different and often challenged. In this sense, the choice of members of the teams responsible for generating the reports implies increased care on the part of the top management. Therefore, it can be concluded that the best management practices have the potential to lead businesses to success. It should be noted that companies should recognize that the integrated reporting is a way of achieving the best performance. So, all the actors involved should conduct the process of adopting and implementing the reporting, bearing in mind that this is not a mere matter of normative compliance.

CONCLUSION

Corporate governance, as a set of laws that regulate corporate management, allows business sustainability. It was based on this premise of accounting, which we seek to establish and achieve the objective of this work. Thus, the main objective was to explore social issues, specifically the relationship between corporate governance and sustainability in the Mozambican context. For this, a revision of the literature was made in the field of accounting regulation, within which the theme falls. Despite the progress made to encourage Mozambican companies to adopt the corporate governance code, the low adherence to the code in reference still persists. In Mozambique, governance is particularly important, as the country, considered one of the world's poorest, is in need of attracting foreign investment. In this context, it is essential, that the Mozambican regulators, consider the change in the application of the code in question, that is, it should move from the principle of self to the compulsory regime, as in South Africa.

In the context of the companies, the obligation can probably translate into "greater control" of the actions of the managers and consequent accountability of them for the illicit acts, if they are detected, that is, when the Managers Act for the purpose of to harm shareholders or other interested parties. As far as the integrated reporting is concerned, we seek to understand, to what extent the dissemination of sustainability information has significant consequences on managerial practices. Therefore, throughout the work, the perception was that, in the Mozambican context, the reports disclosed by most of these companies highlight the little or non-existent concern with social and environmental issues. In some cases, irrelevant information is disseminated in order to try to legitimize its behaviour through the reports depicting a socially responsible image regardless of actual behaviour. The dissemination of the reports is part of the commitment that companies have to society.

Thus, it is important that managers have the perception of the relationship between the adoption of the integrated reporting and the reputation of the companies in the capital markets. The IR can be used as a tool for the construction of communication channels, between the company and its stakeholders, making the company more transparent. Thus, it can be said that transparency will allow greater credibility and confidence in the market, contributing to the attraction of investments. At sustainability level, it will promote economic development, with medium-and long-term benefits for all stakeholders. In this sense, we can conclude that adopting the principles of governance and the integrated reporting, produces at an enterprise level a competitive advantage, and at a country level, increase of reputation in the markets, and can be translated into greater attraction of investments. Transparency is fundamental and goes far beyond the simple publication of information that promotes a good image of the company. This information should translate the real image of the company, whether the financial situation is good or not. Despite the topic under discussion to be present and worthy of further developments it is considered that the work serves as a starting point for a further study. It is expected as a contribution to literature, a greater understanding of sustainability in developing countries, specifically in Mozambique.

REFERENCES

Abeysekera, I. (2013). A template for integrated reporting. *Journal of Intellectual Capital, 14*(2), 227–245. doi:10.1108/14691931311323869

Adams, C. A. (2015). The international integrated reporting council: A call to action. *Critical Perspectives on Accounting, 27*, 23–28. doi:10.1016/j.cpa.2014.07.001

Adams, C. A., & McNicholas, P. (2007). Making a difference: Sustainability reporting, accountability and organisational change. *Accounting, Auditing & Accountability Journal, 20*(3), 382–402. doi:10.1108/09513570710748553

Adams, S., & Simnett, R. (2011). Integrated Reporting: An Opportunity for Australia's Not-for-Profit Sector. *Australian Accounting Review, 21*(3), 292–301. doi:10.1111/j.1835-2561.2011.00143.x

Agrawal, A., & Hockerts, K. (2013). Institutional theory as a framework for practitioners of social entrepreneurship. In *Social Innovation* (pp. 119–129). Springer. doi:10.1007/978-3-642-36540-9_11

Albertini, E. (2014). A descriptive analysis of environmental disclosure: A longitudinal study of French companies. *Journal of Business Ethics, 121*(2), 233–254. doi:10.100710551-013-1698-y

Atkins, J., & Maroun, W. (2015). Integrated reporting in South Africa in 2012: Perspectives from South African institutional investors. *Meditari Accountancy Research, 23*(2), 197–221. doi:10.1108/MEDAR-07-2014-0047

Brammer, S., Jackson, G., & Matten, D. (2012). Corporate social responsibility and institutional theory: New perspectives on private governance. *Socio-economic Review, 10*(1), 3–28. doi:10.1093er/mwr030

Bruton, G. D., Ahlstrom, D., & Li, H. L. (2010). Institutional theory and entrepreneurship: Where are we now and where do we need to move in the future? *Entrepreneurship Theory and Practice, 34*(3), 421–440. doi:10.1111/j.1540-6520.2010.00390.x

Campbell, J. L. (2007). Why would corporations behave in socially responsible ways? An institutional theory of corporate social responsibility. *Academy of Management Review, 32*(3), 946–967. doi:10.5465/amr.2007.25275684

Churet, C., & Eccles, R. G. (2014). Integrated reporting, quality of management and financial performance. *Journal of Applied Corporate Finance, 26*(1), 56–64.

Dawkins, C., & Ngunjiri, F. W. (2008). Corporate Social Responsibility Reporting in South Africa a Descriptive and Comparative Analysis. *Journal of Business Communication, 45*(3), 286–307. doi:10.1177/0021943608317111

Doane, D. (2002). Market failure: The case for mandatory social and environmental reporting. *Presentation at Institute for Public Policy Research seminar*. Academic Press.

Dumitru, M., Glavan, M. E., Gorgan, C., & Dumitru, V. F. (2013). International integrated reporting framework: A case study in the software industry. *Annales Universitatis Apulensis Series Oeconomica*, *15*(1), 24.

Eccles, R. G., & Armbrester, K. (2011). Integrated Reporting in the Cloud: Two disruptive ideas combined. *IESE insight*, *8*.

Eccles, R. G., & Saltzman, D. (2011). Achieving sustainability through integrated reporting. *Stanford Social Innovation Review*, (Summer), 56–61.

Fifka, M. S. (2013). Corporate responsibility reporting and its determinants in comparative perspective–a review of the empirical literature and a meta-analysis. *Business Strategy and the Environment*, *22*(1), 1–35. doi:10.1002/bse.729

Flower, J. (2015). The international integrated reporting council: A story of failure. *Critical Perspectives on Accounting*, *27*, 1–17. doi:10.1016/j.cpa.2014.07.002

Godfrey, P. C. (2005). The relationship between corporate philanthropy and shareholder wealth: A risk management perspective. *Academy of Management Review*, *30*(4), 777–798. doi:10.5465/amr.2005.18378878

Guerreiro, A. (2012). O Relato de Sustentabilidade, o Técnico Oficial de Contas e a OTOC. IV *Congresso dos TOC.*

Herbst, J. (2005). Mbeki's South Africa. *Foreign Affairs*, *84*(6), 93–105. doi:10.2307/20031779

Hoffman, M. (2012). Integrated Reporting in practice: The South African story. *KPMG: Integrated Reporting: Performance insight through Better Business Reporting*, (2), 1-42.

Hoque, M. E. (2017). Why Company Should Adopt Integrated Reporting? International. *Journal of Economics and Financial Issues*, *7*(1).

Horak, S., Arya, B., & Ismail, K. M. (2018). Organizational Sustainability Determinants in Different Cultural Settings: A Conceptual Framework. *Business Strategy and the Environment*, *27*(4), 528–546. doi:10.1002/bse.2018

Idowu, S. O., & Adedoyin, O. (2015). *Key Initiatives in Corporate Social Responsibility*. Springer.

International Integrated Reporting Council (2013). The international IR- Framework.

Ioannou, I., & Serafeim, G. (2015). The impact of corporate social responsibility on investment recommendations: Analysts' perceptions and shifting institutional logics. *Strategic Management Journal*, *36*(7), 1053–1081. doi:10.1002mj.2268

Ioannou, I., & Serafeim, G. (2017). The Consequences of Mandatory Corporate Sustainability Reporting. *Harvard Business School Research*. Retrieved from https://papers.ssrn.com/

IODmz. (2007). Corporate Governance Como Instrumento Chave: Plano Estratégico e de Negócios do IoDmz. Retrieved from http://iodmz.com

Jensen, J. C., & Berg, N. (2012). Determinants of traditional sustainability reporting versus integrated reporting. An institutionalist approach. *Business Strategy and the Environment*, *21*(5), 299–316. doi:10.1002/bse.740

Kaplan, R. S., & Norton, D. P. (1992). The balanced scorecard - Measures that drive performance. *Harvard Business Review*, *70*, 71–79. PMID:10119714

KPMG. (2011). *International Survey of Corporate Responsibility Reporting 201*. KMPG International.

KPMG. (2012). Integrated Reporting: Performance Insight Through Better Business Reporting (Issue 2).

Krzus, M. P. (2011). Integrated reporting: If not now, when? *Zeitschrift fuer Internationale Rechnungslegung*, *6*, 271–276.

Lo, S. F., & Sheu, H. J. (2007). Is Corporate Sustainability a Value-Increasing Strategy for Business? *Corporate Governance*, *15*(2), 345–358. doi:10.1111/j.1467-8683.2007.00565.x

Munisi, G., & Randøy, T. (2013). Corporate governance and company performance across Sub-Saharan African countries. *Journal of Economics and Business*, *70*, 92–110. doi:10.1016/j.jeconbus.2013.08.003

Organisation for Economic Co-operation and Development. (2004). The OECD Principles of Corporate Governance.

PwC. (2013). The value creation journey: a survey of JSE Top-40 companies integrated reports. Retrieved from www.pwc.co.za/en_ZA/za/assets/pdf/integrated-reporting-august-2013

PwC. (2014). Value creation: the journey continues: A survey of JSE Top-40 companies' integrated reports. Retrieved from www.pwc.co.za/en_ZA/za/assets/pdf/integrated-reporting-survey-2014

PwC. (2016). King IV - Steering point: A summary of the King IV Report on Corporate Governance for South Africa. Retrieved from https://www.pwc.co.za/en/publications/king4.html

Ridehalgh, N. (2011). Active Governance: the core of Better Business Reporting. KPMG.

Rossouw, G. J., van der Watt, A., & Malan, D. P. (2002). Corporate Governance in South Africa. *Journal of Business Ethics*, *37*(3), 289–302. doi:10.1023/A:1015205511601

Setia, N., Abhayawansa, S., Joshi, M., & Huynh, A. V. (2015). Integrated reporting in South Africa: Some initial evidence. Sustainability Accounting. *Management and Policy Journal*, *6*(3), 397–424.

Tinker, T., & Gray, R. (2003). Beyond a critique of pure reason: From policy to politics to praxis in environmental and social research. *Accounting, Auditing & Accountability Journal*, *16*(5), 727–761. doi:10.1108/09513570310505952

Yusoff, H., Othman, R., & Yatim, N. (2014). Culture and accountants' perceptions of environmental reporting practice. *Business Strategy and the Environment*, *23*(7), 433–446. doi:10.1002/bse.1793

Chapter 12
CEO Duality and Firm Performance:
Portuguese Evidence

Sandra Alves
University of Aveiro, Portugal

ABSTRACT

Two divergent theories emerge from the literature on CEO duality. The agency theory advocates that a dual CEO negatively affects corporate performance, because it compromises the monitoring and control of the CEO, whilst the stewardship theory suggests the contrary effect due to the unity of command it presents. For a sample of 26 non-financial listed Portuguese firms from 2002 to 2016, this study draws on agency and stewardship theories to evaluate the relationship between CEO duality and firm performance, proxied by Tobin's Q. Using ordinary least square (OLS) and two stage least squares (2SLS) techniques to control potential problems simultaneity between CEO duality and firm performance, the author finds a negative relationship between CEO duality and Tobin's Q. This suggests that investors perceive no value in having a concentration of power with a dual leadership structure. Therefore, this study recommends that the positions of chairman and CEO should be separated for listed Portuguese firms.

INTRODUCTION

Whether dual leadership structure is better for corporations is one of the most controversial topics in corporate governance literature. The board leadership structure, as it relates to whether the chief executive officer (CEO) and chairman position is combined or held by separate individuals, is an important and visible instrument of CEO power over the board. The effectiveness of the board fulfilling its monitoring and disciplining functions depends on CEO power relative to the board (Finkelstein, Hambrick, & Cannella, 2009). Therefore, the decision to adopt CEO duality or non-duality is a vital internal governance decision regarding the power structure of the firm and determines the ability of the board to fulfill its monitoring role (He, 2008).

DOI: 10.4018/978-1-7998-2128-1.ch012

Regulators and governance activists are pressuring firms to abolish CEO duality. Although CEO duality is considered an impediment to good corporate governance, it remains common practice in Portugal. In fact, CEO duality is observed in the majority (56,6%) of Portuguese listed companies in analysis. Consequently, CEO duality continues to exist and an examination of the consequences is relevant and valuable. In addition, the code of corporate governance for listed firms in Portugal is silent on whether the CEO should (or should not) be appointed as the board chair. It is therefore important for Portuguese firms to be aware of the likely performance outcomes from adopting the dual leadership structure.

Drawing on agency and stewardship theories, this study aims to evaluate the impact of CEO duality on firm performance for a sample of listed Portuguese firms from 2002 to 2016. Additionally, it is also examined whether firms that changed their leadership structure from duality to non-duality have differences in firm performance. Agency theory suggests that combining the two positions would constrain board independence and weaken board control, implying a negative effect on firm performance. Duality roles allow CEOs to dominate the board of directors, and they provide them with an opportunity to satisfy their own individual objectives in lieu of the best interests of its shareholders (Abels & Martelli, 2013). This also suggests that, firms that switch to a non-dual leadership structure should experience an improvement in performance following the leadership structure change. In contrast, stewardship theory argues that duality promotes strong, unambiguous leadership which facilitates organizational effectiveness in a potentially dynamic business environment (Finkelstein & D'Aveni, 1994). In addition, CEO duality leads to a considerable firm-specific knowledge and experience retained by the CEO. The cost of transferring this knowledge to a separate chairman of the board is high (Brickley, Coles, & Jarrell, 1997). Therefore, combining the two roles avoids these costs and should therefore improve corporate performance. Consequently, according stewardship theory, firms that switch to a non-dual leadership structure should experience no improvement in performance following the leadership structure change.

The choice of Portugal as research context is motivated by a number of reasons. The majority of literature on CEO duality and firm performance to date has been conducted in the Anglo-American context, characterized by dispersed ownership. Thus, board leadership issues seem to be particularly relevant in the Portuguese corporate environment, characterized by concentrated ownership. In addition, Portugal is a unique setting because corporate governance recommendations are not mandatory. Moreover, the code of corporate governance for listed firms in Portugal is silent on whether the CEO should (or should not) be appointed as the board chair. This lack of recommendation means that leadership structure practices may be more variable than in regulatory environments recommending specific leadership structure. Therefore, findings based on Portuguese data help build a more expansive international understanding of the effect of CEO duality on firm performance.

The study makes some contributions to the existing literature. First, this study draws on agency and stewardship theories to evaluate the relationship between CEO duality and firm performance and whether firms that changed their leadership structure from duality to non-duality have differences in firm performance. Second, the majority of literature on CEO duality and firm performance to date has been conducted in the Anglo-American context. This environment is characterized by dispersed ownership. Hence, this study provides the opportunity to examine an environment where listed firms typically have large shareholders (concentrated ownership). Third, the Portuguese institutional setting provides an interesting framework for the study of duality, as companies can freely choose to unify or split CEO and Chairman positions within a unitary board (as in the US model) or a two-tier board (as in the German model). Four, this study is a valuable addition to recent cross-national governance research, which contributes to the limited Portuguese corporate governance literature by examining the impact of

CEO duality on firm performance. Findings based on Portuguese data also help build a more expansive international understanding of the effect of CEO duality on firm performance. Fifth, the literature lacks clear evidence on the impact of CEO duality on firm performance due to endogeneity issues (Adams, Hermalin, & Weisbach, 2010; Hermalin & Weisbach, 2003). Hence, this paper also addresses the potential simultaneity problem between CEO duality and firm performance, using two stage least squares (2SLS) techniques. Finally, the findings of this study can provide useful information for auditors, regulators, standard setters and shareholders, mainly whether the CEO duality enhance or reduce firm performance, especially in firms with highly concentrated equity ownership.

LITERATURE REVIEW AND TESTABLE HYPOTHESES

CEO Duality and Firm Performance

The impact of CEO duality on firm performance has been controversial from an academic perspective. Mainly, there are two competing views about CEO duality based on the perception of whether a firm is best served by monitoring effectively (agency theory), or by strong leadership (stewardship theory).

Agency theorists suggest that managers may act in their own interests and pursue private benefits that depart from shareholder interests (Fama & Jensen, 1983; Jensen & Meckling, 1976). Jensen (1993) argues that the board of directors is an efficient counter-weight to any decisions that may harm shareholders' value. The board of directors is the apex of the decision control system of modern corporations, which mitigates agency problems due to the separation of ownership and control (Fama & Jensen, 1983). Hence, the role of the board is to monitor management to ensure a lack of deviation from shareholders' interests. The effectiveness of the board fulfilling its monitoring and disciplining functions depends on CEO power relative to the board (Finkelstein et al., 2009). The chairman of the board is responsible for running the board and monitoring and evaluating managerial activities, while the CEO is responsible for executing the company's policies and running the company. The position of board chairman wields power, influence and responsibility (Lechem, 2002). Therefore, combining the functions of decision and control reduces the board's ability to effectively monitor the decisions and actions of the CEO, thus giving the latter more latitude to satisfy his own interests rather than those of shareholders (Fama & Jensen, 1983; Jensen, 1993). In fact, CEO duality represents a conflict of interest in which a CEO who is responsible for the overall strategic management of a firm is also in a position to evaluate the effectiveness of that strategy (Bliss, 2011; Yasser, Mamun, & Suriya, 2014). CEO duality increases CEO power/control over the board (Giannarakis, 2014). In such a situation, the board can no longer efficiently monitor and control decisions if the CEO has significant influence. That is, CEOs can reduce the oversight power of the board, allowing pursuit of personal interests at the expense of shareholders. Really, CEO power enhances managerial ability to extract personal benefits at the expense of shareholders and is negatively associated with firm value (Jensen & Meckling, 1976). In this sense, prior research shown that CEO duality is associated with higher levels of CEO performance payments (Broye, François, & Moulin, 2017; Lee, 2009) and lower earnings quality (Alzoubi, 2016; Anderson, Gillan, & Deli, 2003; Cornett, Marcus, & Tehranian, 2008; Klein, 2002; Sarkar, Sarkar, & Sen, 2008). In addition, CEO duality can increase the potential for entrenchment, reducing board monitoring effectiveness. Outside directors are largely dependent on the CEO for information. Hence, CEO duality allows the CEO to effectively control information available to other board members, and thus may obstructs effective monitoring (Eisenhardt,

1989; Kim, Al-Shammari, Kim, & Lee, 2009). Accordingly, agency theorists emphasize the necessity for separation between roles of CEO and board chair (Mallette & Fowler, 1992). These arguments suggest a negative relationship between CEO duality and firm performance. Consistent with this, several studies find that CEO duality affect negatively the firm performance in the US (Desai, Kroll, & Wright, 2003; Rechner & Dalton, 1991; Rutledge, Karim, & Lu, 2016), in China (Bai, Liu, Lu, Song, & Zhang, 2004; Lew, Yu, & Park, 2018; Shao, 2019), in Pakistan (Singh, Tabassum, Darwish, & Batsakis, 2018), in Taiwan (Hsu, Lin, Chen, & Huanh, 2019) and in Bangladesh (Rashid, 2010).

Unlike agency theory, stewardship theory assumes that managers are stewards and are not motivated by individual goals; rather their behaviors are aligned with organizations' principals (Davis, Schoorman, & Donaldson, 1997; Zahra, Hayton, Neubaum, Dibrell, & Craig, 2008). Stewardship theory argues that duality promotes unity of leadership, facilitating organizational effectiveness (Donaldson & Davis, 1991). The unity of command helps establish clear lines of authority and responsibility within the firm and thus has substantive and symbolic values (Pfeffer, 1981). It enhances the power of the CEO, which can create value by making speedy decision and responding quickly to changes in market conditions (Boyd, 1995; Finkelstein & D'Aveni, 1994). That is, combining the roles of CEO and board chair may result in fast paced implementation of strategic decisions (Daily & Dalton, 1997; Desai et al., 2003; Donaldson & Davis, 1991). Duality helps to create an enabling and empowering structure which encourages the CEO to act pro-organizationally as a steward (Davis et al., 1997; Donaldson & Davis, 1991). In addition, CEO duality can create an image of firm stability, install confidence in the firm's management, and promote better communication with the board (Bhagat & Black, 2001; Brickley et al., 1997; Stoeberl & Sherony, 1985). CEOs and directors are also interested to protect their reputation as expert decision makers (Daily, Dalton, & Canella, 2003). Thus, a reputable CEO is less likely to engage in value-diminishing or self-serving behavior. As a result, CEOs operate the firm in a manner that maximizes financial performance, including shareholder returns, as firm performance directly impacts perception about CEOs' individual performance. Hence, arguments based on the stewardship theory suggest a positive association between CEO duality and firm performance. Several studies find that CEO duality affect positively the firm performance in the US (Boyd, 1995; Brickley et al., 1997; Donaldson & Davis,1991; Faleye, 2007), in China (Peng, Zhang, & Li, 2007; Tian, & Lau, 2001), in Malaysia (Chang, 2015) and in Australia (Nguyen, Rahman, & Zhao, 2018).

Summing up, the agency theory perspective suggests that CEO duality increases the potential for self-serving behavior by the CEO at the expense of shareholders and therefore, it can negatively impact firm performance. In contrast, stewardship theory suggests that duality promotes unity of leadership, facilitating organizational effectiveness. Duality encourages CEO to serve their firms more vigorously. This can be associated with greater firm performance. Consequently, there are presented the following competing alternative hypotheses regarding the effect of CEO duality on firm performance:

Hypothesis 1a **(Agency theory):** The relationship between CEO duality and firm performance is negative.
Hypothesis 1b **(Stewardship theory):** The relationship between CEO duality and firm performance is positive.

Leadership Structure Change and Firm Performance

Firms may change their board leadership structures for several reasons. Changes in the business environment of firms, such as changes in the information environment or changes in the bargaining power of the CEO, may alter the cost benefit tradeoff of their existing leadership structure.

Agency theory suggests that a non-dual leadership structure will be more efficiently to control the agency problems associated with the separation of ownership and control. Therefore, under agency theory it is expected that firms that switch to a non-dual leadership structure should experience an improvement in performance following the leadership structure change. Fosberg and Nelson (1999) find that firms that switch to a non-dual leadership structure show an improvement in performance after the leadership structure change. Palmon and Wald (2002) find that a change from a dual to non-dual leadership structure induces positive abnormal returns for large firms.

On the other hand, stewardship theory suggests that a dual role of the CEO may enhance a firm's financial performance since the CEO has a thorough knowledge of the strategies and the operations of the firm. Consequently, according stewardship theory, firms that switch to a no-dual leadership structure should experience no improvement in performance following the leadership structure change. In this sense, Chen, Lin and Yi (2008) find no improvement in firm performance after change in leadership structure. Dey, Engel and Liu (2011) find that firms splitting the titles have worse post-announcement performance.

Consequently, there are presented the following competing alternative hypotheses regarding the effect of leadership structure change on firm performance:

***Hypothesis 2a* (Agency theory):** A change from a dual to non-dual leadership will improve firm performance.

***Hypothesis 2b* (Stewardship theory):** A change from a dual to non-dual leadership will not improve firm performance.

Endogeneity Relative to Leadership Structure and Firm Performance

An analysis of the impact of CEO duality on firm performance may face the endogeneity challenge. Previous literature has addressed the influence of CEO duality on firm performance, whereas only a few studies have investigated whether reciprocal relationships exist between firm performance and CEO duality (Chen et al., 2008; Drakos & Bekiris, 2010). More specifically, board leadership structure is most likely endogenous. For instance, firm performance may be both a result of CEO duality and, itself, a driver that influences a firm's decision to adopt CEO duality (Hermalin & Weisbach, 2003). This endogeneity creates estimation problems when the decision of board leadership structure is made on the basis of latent factors that correlate with the error term in the regression (Adams et al., 2010). To address the potential endogeneity problem, the author estimates a simultaneous equation system of CEO duality and performance using the 2SLS method.

Table 1. Sample selection criteria during the years 2002-2016

Sample selection	Number of firm years
Firms listed on the Euronext Lisbon	749
(-) Financial companies	(69)
(-) Foreign companies	(49)
(-) Football club companies	(11)
(-) Firms not having shares listed in the previous year and firms whose shares were delisted in the following year	(220)
(-) Firms with missing data	(10)
Number of firm-year observations in the final sample	390

SAMPLE AND RESEARCH DESIGN

Sample Selection

Table 1 details how the selection criteria resulted in a final sample of 390 firm-year observations to test hypothesis 1. Information on managerial ownership, CEO duality, non-executive directors, total assets, common equity, liabilities, operating income and board size are collected from the Annual Report and Corporate Governance Report. Both Annual Report and Corporate Governance Report are available online at www.cmvm.pt. Stock price data are obtained from the Euronext Lisbon, which allows measuring the market value of common equity.

To test hypothesis 2, there are considered only firms that changed their leadership structure, during the sample period. It was identified 12 firms that changed their leadership structure (from dual to non-dual or vice versa). 10 firms switch from a dual to a non-dual leadership structure over the sample period, while 2 firms switch from a non-dual to a dual leadership structure. Therefore, the number of firm-year observations that switch from a dual to a non-dual leadership structure during the sample period (16 years) is 160 in total.

Research Design

Measuring CEO Duality

CEO duality (*Duality*) is measured as an indicator variable taking the value of 1 when the CEO and the chairman of the board is the same person and 0 otherwise.

Measuring Leadership Structure Change

Change_to_Non-Dual (*Change_to_Non-Dual*) is measured as an indicator variable taking the value of 1 when firms switch from a dual to non-dual leadership structure and 0 otherwise.

Measuring Firm Performance

Following previous studies (e.g. Faleye, 2007; Guillet, Seo, Kucukusta, & Lee, 2013; Iyengar & Zampelli, 2009; Mura, 2007; Yang & Zhao, 2014), firm performance is measured by Tobin's Q, calculated as the market value of common equity minus book value of common equity plus book value of total assets, over book value of total assets. Tobin's Q is used as measure of firm performance because it is the conventional proxy for firm performance in accounting and corporate finance literature, including studies on the impact of the board of directors on firm performance (e.g., Faleye, 2007; Iyengar & Zampelli, 2009; Yang & Zhao, 2014; Yermack, 1996).

Control Variables

Given that the *CEO duality* is not the only factor affecting firm performance, several control variables are introduced to isolate other factors that may influence the firm performance. Previous research suggests that managerial ownership, non-executive directors, board size, leverage and firm size are associated with firm performance (Adams & Ferreira, 2009; Detthamrong, Chancharat, & Vithessonthi, 2017; Eisenberg, Sundgren, & Wells, 1998; Ibhagui & Olokoyo, 2018; Kalsie & Shrivastav, 2016; Lam & Lee, 2008; Li, Moshirian, Nguyen, & Tan, 2007; Mura, 2007; Muravyev, Talavera, & Weir, 2016; Rashid, 2010; Wahba, 2014; Yermack, 1996).

Managerial ownership (Managerial). Jensen and Meckling (1976) point out that managers deviate from shareholder wealth-maximization by consuming perquisites when they do not have an ownership stake in the firm. Consequently, more managerial ownership aligns managerial interests with shareholder interests. This suggest that, more managerial ownership results in higher firm performance. Cole and Mehran (1998), Li et al. (2007), and Wahba (2014) find that managerial ownership has a positive effect on firm performance.

Non-executive directors (Non-Executive). Boards dominated by non-executive directors are arguably in a better position to monitor and control managers. Therefore, the proportion of non-executive directors on a board should be positively related to firm performance. In this regard, for example, Lee and Lee (2009), Mura (2007), and Muravyev et al. (2016) find that the proportion of non-executives on the board is significantly and positively related to firm performance. However, boards dominated by non-executive directors may result in oppressive strategic actions, excessive monitoring, lack of business knowledge and real independence (Haniffa & Cooke, 2002). Adams and Ferreira (2009), and Agrawal and Knoeber (1996) find a negative relationship between non-executive directors and firm performance.

Board Size (BSize). Board size can affect boards' functions and potentially firm performance (Jensen, 1993). A larger board would introduce problems of communication and coordination, as well as of decision-making (Eisenberg et al., 1998; Forbes & Milliken, 1999; Jensen, 1993). This suggests that smaller boards can be more effective than larger boards. In this vein, for example, Eisenberg et al. (1998), Lee and Lee (2009), Rashid (2010), and Yermack (1996) provide evidence that firm performance is negatively related to board size.

Leverage. Leverage can have a negative or positive influence on firm performance. Agency theory suggests that the use of debt financing can improve performance by inducing better monitoring by creditors (Agrawal & Knoeber, 1996; Jensen & Meckling, 1976). In this sense, Detthamrong et al. (2017), Ibhagui and Olokoyo (2018), and Margaritis and Psillaki (2010) find that higher leverage is positively associated with firm performance. However, agency costs can also exist from conflicts between debt and equity investors. These conflicts arise when there is a risk of default. The risk of default may aggravate the underinvestment problem (Jensen, 1986; Myers, 1977). In this case, debt may have a negative effect on firm performance. Bhatt and Bhattacharya (2017), Evgeny (2015), and Zeitun and Tian (2007) find that leverage has a negative effect on firm performance.

Firm Size (Size). Large firms are likely to have more resources and market opportunities. Larger firms may also benefit from the economies of scale. This suggests that larger firms perform better. Chen et al. (2008), Drakos and Bekiris (2010), Kalsie and Shrivastav (2016), Lan and Zhang (2013), Lee (2009), and Zeitun and Tian (2007) find that firm size is positively associated with firm performance.

Regression Models

To test hypothesis 1, which examines the relationship between CEO duality and firm performance, it is first run an ordinary least squares (OLS) regression (equation 1). Additionally, to address the potential endogeneity problem, it is estimated a simultaneous equation system of CEO duality and performance using the 2SLS method. 2SLS method is used as an alternative estimation method when there is a potential simultaneity problem between firm performance and CEO duality. If firm performance and CEO duality is simultaneously determined, then the OLS estimated coefficients on *Duality* in equation (1) will be biased and inconsistent.

Variables influencing the dual/non-dual decision were chosen in accordance with the antecedents to duality literature. Thus, following the previous literature, apart from the firm performance variable, some control variables are also included: ownership concentration (*Concentration*), board size (*BSize*), managerial ownership (*Managerial*) and firm size (*Size*) (Chen et al., 2008; Drakos & Bekiris, 2010; Iyengar & Zampelli, 2009; Monem, 2013).

Therefore, the simultaneous equation system can be expressed as follows:

$$Firm\ Performance_{it} = \beta_0 + \beta_1(Duality_{it}) + \beta_2(Managerial_{it}) + \beta_3(Non\_Executive_{it}) + \beta_4(BSize_{it}) + \beta_5(Leverage_{it}) + \beta_6(Size_{it}) + \varepsilon_{it} \quad (1)$$

$$Duality_{it} = \lambda_0 + \lambda_1\ (Firm\ Performance_{it}) + \lambda_2\ (Concentration_{it}) + \lambda_3\ (BSize_{it}) + \lambda_4\ (Managerial_{it}) + \lambda_5\ (Size_{it}) + \gamma_{it} \quad (2)$$

To test hypothesis 2, which examines whether firms that changed their leadership structure have differences in performance, it is estimated the following OLS regression:

$$Firm\ Performance_{it} = \beta_0 + \beta_1(Change\_to\_Non\text{-}Dual_{it}) + \beta_2(Managerial_{it}) + \beta_3\ (Non\_Executive_{it}) + \beta_4\ (BSize_{it}) + \beta_{0=5}\ (Leverage_{it}) + \beta_6\ (Size_{it}) + \varepsilon_{it} \quad (3)$$

where:

Firm Performance$_{it}$ = is the Tobin's Q for firm *i* for period *t*;

Duality$_{it}$ = value of 1 when the CEO and the chairman of the board is the same person and 0 otherwise;

Change_to_Non-Dual$_{it}$ = value of 1 when firms switch from a dual to non-dual leadership structure and 0 otherwise;

Table 2. Summary of Descriptive Statistics

	Mean	Median	Min.	Max.
Duality	0.566	1.000	0.000	1.000
Managerial	0.050	0.001	0.000	0.641
Non-Executive	0.414	0.461	0.000	0.888
BSize	8.250	8.000	3.000	23.000
Leverage	0.775	0.729	0.062	4.148
Size	19.910	18.743	12.429	23.517

Duality dummy variable which takes a value 1 when the CEO and the chairman of the board is the same person and 0 otherwise; *Managerial* represents the equity held by executive managers; *Non-executive* represents the ratio between the number of non-executive directors and the total number of board members; *BSize* is the number of members of the board; *Leverage* represents the ratio between the book value of all liabilities and the total assets; *Size* represents the firm's size.

$Managerial_{it}$ = proportion of the company's shares owned by the executive managers of firm *i* for period *t*;

$Non\text{-}Executive_{it}$ = ratio between the number of non-executive directors and the total number of board members of firm *i* for period *t*;

$Concentration_{it}$ = proportion of stocks owned by shareholders who own at least 2% of the common stock of firm *i* for period *t*;

$BSize_{it}$ = number of members on the board of firm *i* for period *t*;

$Leverage_{it}$ = ratio between the book value of all liabilities and the total assets of firm *i* for period *t*;

$Size_{it}$ = logarithm of market value of equity of firm *i* for period *t*.

RESULTS AND DISCUSSION

Descriptive Statistics and Correlations

Table 2 presents the sample descriptive statistics for the variables used in this research. Spearman correlations between the explanatory variables are documented in Table 3.

Table 2 shows that the CEO is also the chairman of the board in 56.6% of the sample. The mean (median) managerial ownership (*Managerial*) is 5.0% (0.1%), with a minimum of 0.0% and a maximum of 64.1%. The difference between the mean and the median reveals a considerable skewed nature, suggesting the existence of large percentages of shares held by managers in some companies (as can be confirmed by the maximum of the variable). About 41.4% (with a median of 46.1%) of the members of the board are non-executive directors (*Non-Executive*), with a minimum of 0.0% and a maximum of 88.8%, suggesting that there is a large difference across different firms for this variable. Board size (*BSize*) is comprised of approximately 8 members (with a median of 8 members). Because the minimum number of members on the board is 3 but the maximum number of members is 23, there exist large differences across different firms for this variable, too. *Leverage* variable represents on average 0.775 of the total assets of the company (with a median of 0.729). The mean of firm size (*Size*) is about EUR 980 million with a minimum of EUR 250 thousand and a maximum of EUR 16.345 million.

Table 3. Pearson Correlation Coefficients Matrix

	Managerial	Non-Executive	BSize	Leverage	Size
Managerial	1				
Non-Executive	-0.168**	1			
BSize	-0.211***	0.478**	1		
Leverage	-0.046	-0.060	-0.129*	1	
Size	-0.303**	0.324**	0.142**	-0.155**	1

Managerial represents the equity held by executive managers; *Non-executive* represents the ratio between the number of non-executive directors and the total number of board members; *BSize* is the number of members of the board; *Leverage* represents the ratio between the book value of all liabilities and the total assets; *Size* represents the firm's size.

*** Correlation is significant at the 0.01 level (2-tailed); ** Correlation is significant at the 0.05 level (2-tailed).

The analysis of Table 3 shows that there are some significant correlations between the variables. The binary variable *Duality* is not included in the Table 3, given that the Pearson correlation coefficient is not computed to nominal variables.

Managerial is negatively correlated with *Non-Executive*, *BSize* and *Size*, suggesting that managers' equity interest in the firm is declining as number of non-executive directors on the board, board size and firm size increases. *Non-Executive* is positively associated with board size (*BSize*), suggesting that larger boards have more non-executive directors. *Size* is positively correlated with both *BSize* and *Non-Executive*, suggesting that large firms have greater board size and higher number of non-executive directors on the board.

A negative correlation between *Leverage* and *BSize* indicates that firms with high leverage tend to have smaller boards. *Size* is negatively associated with *Leverage*, suggesting that larger firms have lower leverage constraint levels. Correlation coefficients are, in general, low (below the 0.9 threshold) (Tabachnick & Fidell, 2001), suggesting the absence of serious statistical problems related with multicollinearity.

Regression Results

Table 4 presents both OLS and 2SLS regressions estimate for equation 1. Table 5 reports the multiple regression of equation (3) results of the sample firms that changed their leadership structure (from a dual to a non-dual).

The results in Table 4 show that CEO duality is negatively related to Tobin's Q. The Hypothesis 1*a* predicts a negative relationship between CEO duality and firm performance. The findings support this hypothesis, which suggests that CEO duality diminishes the monitoring role of the board of directors over the executive manager. Therefore, this provides support for those opposing duality and is consistent with agency theory. This result is in line with recent findings of studies conducted in the Chinese context (e.g. Lew et al., 2018; Shao, 2019), in the Taiwan context (e.g. Hsu et al., 2019), in the Pakistani context (Singh et al., 2018) and in the Jordanian context (e.g. Qadorah & Fadzil, 2018), characterized also by concentrated ownership.

The results no support for stewardship theory (Hypothesis 1*b*), that investors perceive value in having a concentration of power with an individual who possesses superior knowledge and is motivated to maximize profits.

Table 4. Regression Results: Dependent variable Tobin's Q (Number of observations: 390, Period: 2002-2016)

	OLS estimates		2SLS estimates	
Dependent variable	**Tobin's Q**		**Tobin's Q**	
Independent variables	**Coefficient**	**t-values**	**Coefficient**	**t-values**
Constant	0.648	6.245***	0.715	2.204**
Duality	-0.089	-2.161**	-0.156	-3.861**
Managerial	0.185	1.579	0.193	1.673*
Non-Executive	-0.069	-0.890	-0.068	-0.899
BSize	-0.038	-6,126***	-0.041	-6.811***
Leverage	-0.005	-2.211**	-0.005	-2.470**
Size	0.062	5.337***	0.058	5.114***
R-squared	0.154		0.148	
Adjusted R-squared	0.141		0.135	
F-statistic	11.651***			

Tobin's Q represents the firm's performance; *Duality* dummy variable which takes a value 1 when the CEO and the chairman of the board is the same person and 0 otherwise; *Managerial* represents the equity held by executive managers; *Non-executive* represents the ratio between the number of non-executive directors and the total number of board members; *BSize* is the number of members of the board; *Leverage* represents the ratio between the book value of all liabilities and the total assets; *Size* represents the firm's size.

*** Significant at the 1-percent level; ** Significant at the 5-percent level; * Significant at the 10-percent level.

Table 5. Regression Results: Dependent variable Tobin's Q (Number of observations: 160, Period: 2002-2016)

Dependent variable	**Tobin's Q**	
Independent variables	**Coefficient**	**t-values**
Constant	-0.207	-0.518
Change_to_Non-Dual	0.169	2.403**
Managerial	1.226	3.434***
Non-Executive	0.020	1.047
BSize	-0.044	-6.167***
Leverage	-0.002	-0.351
Size	0.069	3.110***
R-squared	0.119	
Adjusted R-squared	0.094	
F-statistic	8.892***	

Tobin's Q represents the firm's performance; *Change_to_Non-Dual* dummy variable which takes a value 1 when the firm switches from a dual to no-dual and 0 otherwise; *Managerial* represents the equity held by executive managers; *Non-executive* represents the ratio between the number of non-executive directors and the total number of board members; *BSize* is the number of members of the board; *Leverage* represents the ratio between the book value of all liabilities and the total assets; *Size* represents the firm's size.

*** Significant at the 1-percent level; ** Significant at the 5-percent level; * Significant at the 10-percent level.

Table 5 shows that switches from a dual to a non-dual leadership are positively associated with performance. This result supports the Hypothesis 2*a* which suggests that firms that switches to a non-dual leadership structure should experience an improvement in performance following the leadership structure change. This finding is also consistent with agency theory, suggesting that the market places higher valuations on companies that change to a non-dual leadership structure.

The control variables, board size, is negatively and significantly associated with Tobin's Q consistent with other studies (e.g. Eisenberg et al., 1998; Rashid, 2010; Yermack, 1996). As in other studies (e.g. Bhatt and Bhattacharya, 2017; Evgeny, 2015), leverage has a negative and significant effect on Tobin's Q for the equation (1), suggesting that the market places a lower value on firms with high leverage. In line with the findings of previous studies (e.g. Chang, 2015; Mura, 2007), firm size is positively related to firm performance indicating that larger firms are more profitable.

DISCUSSION

This study examines the relationship between CEO duality and firm performance as well as whether firms that changed their leadership structure have differences in firm performance using agency and stewardship theoretical frameworks. These theories differ significantly in their assessment of the effectiveness of CEO duality in performing their duties. Agency theory provides a framework that posits that managers act in their own interests and suggests a negative role for CEO duality. On the other hand, stewardship theory provides a framework that presumes that managers maximize their utility to achieve organizational rather than self-serving objectives and suggests a positive role for CEO duality. In line with the competing theoretical research dedicated to CEO duality, the empirical literature provides no consensus on the effects of these on firm performance.

The findings of this research show evidence that support the notion that CEO duality intensifies the agency problem. In line with agency theory perspective on CEO duality, duality is negatively related to firm performance. This suggests that the market places a lower value on companies with CEO duality, and offer support for those opposing CEO duality. Duality may constrain board independence, thereby reducing the effectiveness of the oversight and governance mechanisms, and this in turn may have a negative effect on firm performance. Therefore, the existence of a dominant personality where the CEO is also the chairman of the board may bring negative outcomes.

In line with agency theory perspective, the results of this study also suggest that firms that switch to a non-dual leadership structure experience an improvement in performance following the leadership structure change. Therefore, this finding is consistent with the notion that a non-dual leadership structure is associated with better performance. Based on the research findings, it is suggested that companies should give greater consideration to choose leadership structure. This study recommends that the positions of chairman and CEO should be separated for listed Portuguese firms.

Overall, this study suggests that non-dual leadership structure seems to be more beneficial than dual leadership structure. However, despite the alleged superiority of the non-dual leadership structure, the majority of Portuguese listed companies in analysis maintain a dual leadership structure. Possible explanations for the persistence of the CEO duality structure may be: (1) dual leadership structure reflects the traditional influence of firm management in board composition; (2) the board may be indifferent to the dual structure issue if it is convinced that the CEO has the capacity to engage both positions effectively; (3) dual leadership structure avoids (a) the agency cost of monitoring the behaviour of the non-CEO chairman, (b) the information cost of transferring critical information between the CEO and the chairman; (4) the lack of independent leadership in a firm with a dual structure may reduce monitoring by the board and makes it difficult for the board to change the leadership structure; and (5) though a non-dual structure may be superior to a dual structure, firms may have other control mechanisms in place to reduce managerial opportunism that may arise from a dual structure. However, this other control mechanisms may not be effective in the presence of CEO duality.

SENSITIVITY ANALYSES

To ensure the robustness of results, the author performs several sensitivity checks. The first sensitivity analysis tests the impact of using alternative definition for the firm performance and firm size variable on regression results. Return on equity is used as the measure of firm performance in place of Tobin's Q. The central findings of this study are similar with the initial ones. The results are also robust to using either the value of assets or reported sales as alternative proxies of firm size.

The second sensitivity analysis examines the effect of influential observations on results. Where outliers are found (namely in the variables *BSize and Leverage*), a winserization method is used to test the robustness of the results. Extreme values (defined as values that are more than three standard deviations away from the mean) are replaced by values that are exactly three standard deviations away from the mean. The results (not reported here) do not differ from results presented previously. Thus, the influential observations do not seem affect the results.

The next sensitivity analysis examines the effects of sales growth on firm performance. Bhatt and Bhattacharya (2017), and Yang and Zhao (2014) suggest that sales growth is likely to affect firm performance. The effect of sales growth on firm performance will be positive, because higher sales growth likely increases firm value. The *Sales Growth* variable is the annual percentage change in sales. All coefficient and average coefficient estimates retain their sign and significance levels. As in Bhatt and Bhattacharya (2017), and Yang and Zhao (2014), the *Sales Growth* is significantly positively related to firm performance, which suggests that high sales growth leading to increases in firm performance. Thus, all conclusions remain even after controlling for sales growth.

Overall, the several sensitivity analyses conducted largely corroborate the results presented previously.

CONCLUSION

This research draws on agency and stewardship theories to examine: (1) the relationship between CEO duality and firm performance, and (2) whether firms that changed their leadership structure have differences in firm performance. Agency theory provides a framework that posits that managers act in their own interests and suggests a negative role for CEO duality. On the other hand, stewardship theory provides a framework that presumes that managers maximize their utility to achieve organizational rather than self-serving objectives and suggests a positive role for CEO duality.

The paper aims to contribute to the literature investigating the impact of duality choice on firm performance and whether leadership structure change have impact on performance, with a focus on the specific Portuguese context. Portuguese listed firms are characterized by large shareholders. This presents a unique setting for studying the impact of CEO duality and leadership structure change on firm performance. Understanding the influence of CEO duality on the financial performance of the firm and the impact of leadership structure change on firm performance have important implications for top managers, shareholders, corporate boards and policy makers.

Using ordinary least square (OLS) and two stage least squares (2SLS) techniques to control potential simultaneity problems between CEO duality and firm performance, the author finds a negative relationship between CEO duality and Tobin's Q. This suggests that the market places a lower value on companies with dual leadership structure. Hence, the findings of this study offer support for those opposing duality and is consistent with agency theory, which suggests that duality may constrain board independence and vigilance, leading to more agency problems and, ultimately, poor firm performance. Consistent with agency theory, this study also finds that firms that switch to a non-dual leadership structure experience an improvement in performance following the leadership structure change. Consequently, this study recommends that the positions of chairman and CEO should be separated for listed Portuguese firms.

The results of this study make the following contributions. First, this study contributes to the growing literature on leadership structure by providing a multi-year analysis on the influence of CEO duality on firm performance in the Portuguese context. Second, in contrast with the most previous studies, this study uses OLS and 2SLS techniques to control potential simultaneity problems between CEO duality and firm performance. Third, the results show lower firm performance for dual than for non-dual CEO. Fourth, the findings suggest that firms that switch to a non-dual leadership structure experience an improvement in performance. Fifth, this paper has also implications for cross-national governance research. The results of this study show that leadership structure significantly impacts firm performance in Portugal. Sixth, the findings are relevant for countries with an institutional environment similar to that of Portugal. Seventh, the findings have practical implications for regulators and practitioners who publicly debate the benefits and costs of duality, and commonly advocate the separation of titles as the best practice to ensure "good" corporate governance. Finally, it may also help regulators in the European Union to identify the strengths and weaknesses of alternative models given the recent movement toward greater freedom of choice about board structure among member states (Belot, Ginglinger, Slovin, & Sushka, 2014). Specifically, the findings of this study can be of use to practitioners seeking a better understanding of the interdependences between CEO duality and firm performance.

REFERENCES

Abels, P. B., & Martelli, J. T. (2013). CEO duality: How many hats are too many? *Corporate Governance: The International Journal of Business in Society*, *13*(2), 135–147. doi:10.1108/14720701311316625

Adams, R., & Ferreira, D. (2009). Women in the boardroom and their impact on governance and performance. *Journal of Financial Economics*, *94*(2), 291–309. doi:10.1016/j.jfineco.2008.10.007

Adams, R., Hermalin, B., & Weisbach, M. (2010). The role of boards of directors in corporate governance: A conceptual framework and survey. *Journal of Economic Literature*, *48*(1), 58–107. doi:10.1257/jel.48.1.58

Agrawal, A., & Knoeber, C. R. (1996). Firm performance and mechanisms to control agency problems between managers and shareholders. *Journal of Financial and Quantitative Analysis*, *31*(3), 377–397. doi:10.2307/2331397

Alzoubi, E. S. S. (2016). Audit quality and earnings management: Evidence from Jordan. *Journal of Applied Accounting Research, 17*(2), 170–189. doi:10.1108/JAAR-09-2014-0089

Anderson, K. L., Gillan, S. L., & Deli, D. (2003). Boards of Directors, Audit Committees, and the Information Content of Earnings. Weinberg Center for Corporate Governance. Retrieved from https://ssrn.com/abstract=444241

Bai, C. E. B., Liu, Q., Lu, J., Song, F. M., & Zhang, J. (2004). Corporate governance and market valuation in China. *Journal of Comparative Economics, 32*(4), 599–616. doi:10.1016/j.jce.2004.07.002

Belot, F., Ginglinger, E., Slovin, M., & Sushka, M. (2014). Freedom of choice between unitary and two-tier boards: An empirical analysis. *Journal of Financial Economics, 112*(3), 364–385. doi:10.1016/j.jfineco.2014.02.011

Bhagat, S., & Black, B. (2001). The non-correlation between board independence and long-term firm performance. *The Journal of Corporation Law, 27*(2), 231–273.

Bhatt, R. R., & Bhattacharya, S. (2017). Family firms, board structure and firm performance: Evidence from top Indian firms. *International Journal of Law and Management, 59*(5), 699–717. doi:10.1108/IJLMA-02-2016-0013

Bliss, M. A. (2011). Does CEO duality constrain board independence? Some evidence from audit pricing. *Accounting and Finance, 51*(2), 361–380. doi:10.1111/j.1467-629X.2010.00360.x

Boyd, B. K. (1995). CEO duality and firm performance: A contingency model. *Strategic Management Journal, 16*(4), 301–312. doi:10.1002mj.4250160404

Brickley, J. A., Coles, J. L., & Jarrell, G. (1997). Leadership structure: Separating the CEO and chairman of the board. *Journal of Corporate Finance, 3*(3), 189–220. doi:10.1016/S0929-1199(96)00013-2

Broye, G., François, A., & Moulin, Y. (2017). The cost of CEO duality: Evidence from French leadership compensation. *European Management Journal, 35*(3), 336–350. doi:10.1016/j.emj.2017.01.007

Chang, A. (2015). The Role of Internal and External Corporate Governance Mechanisms on Firm's Financial Performance in Malaysia. *Asian Journal of Accounting and Governance, 6*, 55–65. doi:10.17576/AJAG-2015-6-06

Chen, C. W., Lin, J. B., & Yi, B. (2008). CEO duality and firm performance - An endogenous issue. *Corporate Ownership & Control, 6*(1), 58–65. doi:10.22495/cocv6i1p6

Cole, R. A., & Mehran, H. (1998). The effect of changes in ownership structure on performance: Evidence from the thrift industry. *Journal of Financial Economics, 50*(3), 291–317. doi:10.1016/S0304-405X(98)00039-7

Cornett, M. M., Marcus, J. A., & Tehranian, H. (2008). Corporate governance and pay-for-performance: The impact of earnings management. *Journal of Financial Economics, 87*(2), 357–373. doi:10.1016/j.jfineco.2007.03.003

Daily, C. M., & Dalton, D. R. (1997). Separate, But Not Independent: Board leadership structure in large corporations. *Corporate Governance, 5*(3), 126–136. doi:10.1111/1467-8683.00053

Daily, C. M., Dalton, D. R., & Canella, A. A. (2003). Corporate Governance: Decades of Dialogue and Data. *Academy of Management Review*, *28*(3), 371–382. doi:10.5465/amr.2003.10196703

Davis, J. H., Schoorman, F. D., & Donaldson, L. (1997). Toward a stewardship theory of management. *Academy of Management Review*, *22*(1), 20–47. doi:10.5465/amr.1997.9707180258

Desai, A., Kroll, M., & Wright, P. (2003). CEO duality, board monitoring, and acquisition performance: A test of competing theories. *The Journal of Business Strategy*, *20*(2), 137–156.

Detthamrong, U., Chancharat, N., & Vithessonthi, C. (2017). Corporate governance, capital structure and firm performance: Evidence from Thailand. *Research in International Business and Finance*, *42*, 689–709. doi:10.1016/j.ribaf.2017.07.011

Dey, A., Engel, E., & Liu, X. (2011). CEO and board chair roles: To split or not to split? *Journal of Corporate Finance*, *17*(5), 1595–1618. doi:10.1016/j.jcorpfin.2011.09.001

Donaldson, L., & Davis, J. H. (1991). Stewardship theory or agency theory: Corporate governance and shareholder returns. *Australian Journal of Management*, *16*(1), 49–64. doi:10.1177/031289629101600103

Drakos, A. A., & Bekoris, F. V. (2010). Endogeneity and the Relationship Between Board Structure and Firm Performance: A Simultaneous Equation Analysis for the Athens Stock Exchange. *Managerial and Decision Economics*, *31*(6), 387–401. doi:10.1002/mde.1492

Eisenberg, T., Sundgren, S., & Wells, M. T. (1998). Larger Board Size and Decreasing Firm Value in Small Firms. *Journal of Financial Economics*, *48*(1), 35–54. doi:10.1016/S0304-405X(98)00003-8

Eisenhardt, K. M. (1989). Agency Theory: An Assessment and Review. *Academy of Management Review*, *14*(1), 57–74. doi:10.5465/amr.1989.4279003

Evgeny, I. (2015). The impact of financial leverage on firm performance: Evidence from Russia. *Journal of Corporate Finance Research*, *34*(2), 24–36.

Faleye, O. (2007). Does one hat fit all? The case of corporate leadership structure. *The Journal of Management and Governance*, *11*(3), 239–259. doi:10.100710997-007-9028-3

Fama, E. F., & Jensen, M. C. (1983). Separation of ownership and control. *The Journal of Law & Economics*, *26*(2), 301–325. doi:10.1086/467037

Finkelstein, S., & D'Aveni, R. A. (1994). CEO duality as a double-edged sword: How boards of directors balance entrenchment avoidance and unity of command. *Academy of Management Journal*, *37*(5), 1079–1108. doi:10.5465/256667

Finkelstein, S., Hambrick, D. C., & Cannella, A. A. (2009). *Strategic leadership: Theory and research on executives, top management teams and boards*. New York, NY: Oxford University Press.

Forbes, D. P., & Milliken, F. J. (1999). Cognition and Corporate Governance: Understanding Boards of Directors as Strategic Decision-Making Groups. *Academy of Management Review*, *24*(3), 489–505. doi:10.5465/amr.1999.2202133

Fosberg, R. H., & Nelson, M. R. (1999). Leadership structure and firm performance. *International Review of Financial Analysis*, *8*(1), 83–96. doi:10.1016/S1057-5219(99)00007-1

Giannarakis, G. (2014). Corporate governance and financial characteristic effects on the extent of corporate social responsibility disclosure. *Social Responsibility Journal*, *10*(4), 569–590. doi:10.1108/SRJ-02-2013-0008

Guillet, B. D., Seo, K., Kucukusta, D., & Lee, S. (2013). CEO duality and firm performance in the U.S. restaurant industry: Moderating role of restaurant type. *International Journal of Hospitality Management*, *33*, 339–346. doi:10.1016/j.ijhm.2012.10.004

Haniffa, R. M., & Cooke, T. E. (2002). Culture, corporate governance and disclosure in Malaysian corporations. *Abacus*, *38*(3), 317–349. doi:10.1111/1467-6281.00112

He, L. (2008). Do founders matter? A study of executive compensation, governance structure and firm performance. *Journal of Business Venturing*, *23*(3), 257–279. doi:10.1016/j.jbusvent.2007.02.001

Hermalin, B., & Weisbach, M. (2003). Boards of directors as an endogenously determined institution: A survey of the economic literature. *Federal Reserve Bank of New York Economic Policy Review*, *9*, 7–26.

Hsu, S., Lin, S. W., Chen, W. P., & Huanh, J. W. (in press). CEO Duality, Information Costs, and Firm Performance. *The North American Journal of Economics and Finance*. doi:10.1016/j.najef.2019.101011

Ibhagui, O. W., & Olokoyo, F. O. (2018). Leverage and firm performance: New evidence on the role of firm size. *The North American Journal of Economics and Finance*, *45*, 57–82. doi:10.1016/j.najef.2018.02.002

Iyengar, R. J., & Zampelli, E. M. (2009). Self-selection, endogeneity, and the relationship between CEO duality and firm performance. *Strategic Management Journal*, *30*(10), 1092–1112. doi:10.1002mj.776

Jensen, M. C. (1986). Agency costs of free cash flow, corporate finance, and takeovers. *The American Economic Review*, *76*(2), 323–329.

Jensen, M. C. (1993). The Modern Industrial Revolution, Exit, and the Failure of Internal Control Systems. *The Journal of Finance*, *3*(48), 831–880. doi:10.1111/j.1540-6261.1993.tb04022.x

Jensen, M. C., & Meckling, W. H. (1976). Theory of the Firm: Managerial Behavior, Agency and Ownership Structure. *Journal of Financial Economics*, *3*(4), 305–360. doi:10.1016/0304-405X(76)90026-X

Kalsie, A., & Shrivastav, S. M. (2016). Board size and firm performance: Evidence from NSE companies using panel data approach. *Indian Journal of Corporate Governance*, *9*(2), 148–172. doi:10.1177/0974686216666456

Kim, K. H., Al-Shammari, H. A., Kim, B., & Lee, S. H. (2009). CEO duality leadership and corporate diversification behaviour. *Journal of Business Research*, *62*(11), 1173–1180. doi:10.1016/j.jbusres.2008.10.017

Klein, A. (2002). Audit committee, board of director characteristics, and earnings management. *Journal of Accounting and Economics*, *33*(3), 375–400. doi:10.1016/S0165-4101(02)00059-9

Lam, T. Y., & Lee, S. K. (2008). CEO duality and firm performance: Evidence from Hong Kong. *Corporate Governance: The International Journal of Effective Board Performance*, *8*(3), 299–316. doi:10.1108/14720700810879187

Lan, X., & Zhang, T. (2013). An Empirical Study on the Endogeneity of Corporate Governance Mechanisms and Firm Performance. In *Proceedings of the 19th International Conference on Industrial Engineering and Engineering Management* (pp. 485-495). Academic Press.

Lechem, B. (2002). *Chairman of the Board: A Practical Guide*. New Jersey, NJ: John Wiley & Sons, Inc.

Lee, J. (2009). Executive performance-based remuneration, performance change and board structures. *The International Journal of Accounting*, *44*(2), 138–162. doi:10.1016/j.intacc.2009.03.002

Lee, K. W., & Lee, C. F. (2009). Cash holdings, corporate governance structure and firm valuation. *Review of Pacific Basin Financial Markets and Policies*, *12*(3), 475–508. doi:10.1142/S021909150900171X

Lew, Y. K., Yu, J., & Park, J. Y. (2018). The impacts of independent director and CEO duality on performance in the Chinese post-institutional-transition era. *Canadian Journal of Administrative Sciences*, *35*(4), 620–643. doi:10.1002/cjas.1468

Li, D., Moshirian, F., Nguyen, P., & Tan, L. W. (2007). Managerial ownership and firm performance: Evidence from China's privatizations. *Research in International Business and Finance*, *21*(3), 296–413. doi:10.1016/j.ribaf.2007.02.001

Mallette, P., & Fowler, K. L. (1992). Effects of board composition and stock ownership on the adoption of poison pills. *Academy of Management Journal*, *35*(5), 1010–1035. doi:10.5465/256538

Margaritis, D., & Psillaki, M. (2010). Capital structure, equity ownership and firm performance. *Journal of Banking & Finance*, *43*(3), 621–632. doi:10.1016/j.jbankfin.2009.08.023

Monem, R. M. (2013). Determinants of board structure: Evidence from Australia. *Journal of Contemporary Accounting & Economics*, *9*(1), 33–49. doi:10.1016/j.jcae.2013.01.001

Mura, R. (2007). Firm Performance: Do Non-Executive Directors Have Minds of their Own? Evidence from UK Panel Data. *Financial Management*, *36*(5), 81–112. doi:10.1111/j.1755-053X.2007.tb00082.x

Muravyev, A., Talavera, O., & Weir, C. (2016). Performance effects of appointing other firms' executive directors to corporate boards: An analysis of UK firms. *Review of Quantitative Finance and Accounting*, *46*(1), 25–45. doi:10.100711156-014-0460-6

Myers, S. (1977). Determinants of corporate borrowing. *Journal of Financial Economics*, *5*(2), 147–175. doi:10.1016/0304-405X(77)90015-0

Nguyen, P., Rahman, N., & Zhao, R. (2018). CEO characteristics and firm valuation: A quantile regression analysis. *The Journal of Management and Governance*, *22*(1), 133–151. doi:10.100710997-017-9383-7

Palmon, O., & Wald, J. K. (2002). Are two heads better than one? The impact of change in management structure on performance by firm size. *Journal of Corporate Finance*, *8*(3), 213–226. doi:10.1016/S0929-1199(01)00042-6

Peng, M. W., Zhang, S., & Li, X. (2007). CEO Duality and Firm Performance during China's Institutional Transitions. *Management and Organization Review*, *3*(2), 205–225. doi:10.1111/j.1740-8784.2007.00069.x

Pfeffer, J. (1981). *Power in organizations*. Boston: Pitman.

Qadorah, A. A. M., & Fadzil, F. H. (2018). The Relationship Between Board Size and CEO Duality and Firm Performance: Evidence from Jordan. *International Journal of Accounting. Finance and Risk Management*, *3*(3), 16–20. doi:10.11648/j.ijafrm.20180303.11

Rashid, A. (2010). CEO duality and firm performance: Evidence from a developing country. *Corporate Ownership and Control*, *8*(1), 163–175. doi:10.22495/cocv8i1c1p1

Rechner, P. L., & Dalton, D. R. (1991). CEO duality and organizational performance: A longitudinal analysis. *Strategic Management Journal*, *12*(2), 155–160. doi:10.1002mj.4250120206

Rutledge, R. W., Karim, K. E., & Lu, S. (2016). The Effects of Board Independence and CEO Duality on Firm Performance: Evidence from the NASDAQ-100 Index with Controls for Endogeneity. *Journal of Applied Business and Economics*, *18*(2), 49–71. doi:10.33423/jabe.v18i2.838

Sarkar, J., Sarkar, S., & Sen, K. (2008). Board of Directors and Opportunistic Earnings Management: Evidence from India. *Journal of Accounting, Auditing & Finance*, *23*(4), 517–551. doi:10.1177/0148558X0802300405

Shao, L. (2019). Dynamic study of corporate governance structure and firm performance in China. *Chinese Management Studies*, *13*(2), 299–317. doi:10.1108/CMS-08-2017-0217

Singh, S., Tabassum, N., Darwish, T. K., & Batsakis, G. (2018). Corporate Governance and Tobin's Q as a Measure of Organizational Performance. *British Journal of Management*, *28*(1), 171–190. doi:10.1111/1467-8551.12237

Stoeberl, P. A., & Sherony, B. C. (1985). Board efficiency and effectiveness. In E. Mattar & M. Ball (Eds.), Handbook for Corporate Directors. New York: McGraw-Hill.

Tabachnick, B. G., & Fidell, L. S. (2001). *Using Multivariate Statistics*. New York, NY: Allyn and Bacon.

Tian, J. J., & Lau, C. M. (2001). Board Composition, Leadership Structure and Performance in Chinese Shareholding Companies. *Asia Pacific Journal of Management*, *18*(2), 245–263. doi:10.1023/A:1010628209918

Wahba, H. (2014). Capital structure, managerial ownership and firm performance: Evidence from Egypt. *The Journal of Management and Governance*, *18*(4), 1041–1061. doi:10.100710997-013-9271-8

Yang, T., & Zhao, S. (2014). CEO duality and Firm performance: Evidence from an exogenous shock to the competitive environment. *Journal of Banking & Finance*, *49*, 534–552. doi:10.1016/j.jbankfin.2014.04.008

Yasser, Q. R., Mamun, A. A., & Suriya, A. R. (2014). CEO duality structure and firm performance in Pakistan. *Asian Journal of Accounting and Governance*, *5*(1), 57–68. doi:10.17576/AJAG-2014-5-05

Yermack, D. (1996). Higher market valuation of companies with a small board of directors. *Journal of Financial Economics*, *40*(2), 185–211. doi:10.1016/0304-405X(95)00844-5

Zahra, S. A., Hayton, J. C., Neubaum, D. O., Dibrell, C., & Craig, J. (2008). Culture of family commitment and strategic flexibility: The moderating effect of stewardship. *Entrepreneurship Theory and Practice*, *32*(6), 1035–1054. doi:10.1111/j.1540-6520.2008.00271.x

Zeitun, R., & Tian, G. G. (2007). Capital structure and corporate performance: Evidence from Jordan. *Australasian Accounting*. *Business and Finance Journal*, *1*(4), 41–61.

ADDITIONAL READING

Abdullah, S. A. (2004). Board Composition, CEO Duality and Performance among Malaysian Listed Companies. *Corporate Governance*, *4*(4), 47–61. doi:10.1108/14720700410558871

Dahya, J., & Travlos, N. G. (2000). Does the one man show pay? Theory and evidence on the dual CEO revisited. *European Financial Management*, *6*(1), 85–88. doi:10.1111/1468-036X.00113

Daily, C. M., & Johnson, J. L. (1997). Sources of CEO power and firm financial performance: A longitudinal assessment. *Journal of Management*, *23*(2), 97–117. doi:10.1177/014920639702300201

Muth, M., & Donaldson, L. (2008). Stewardship Theory and Board Structure: A contingency approach. *Corporate Governance*, *6*(1), 5–28. doi:10.1111/1467-8683.00076

Pucheta-Martínez, M. C., & Gallego-Álvarez, I. (2019). Do board characteristics drive firm performance? An international perspective. *Review of Managerial Science*, *13*(47), 1–47. doi:10.100711846-019-00330-x

Vandewaerde, M., Voordeckers, W., Lambrechts, F., & Bammens, Y. (2011). Board Team Leadership Revisited: A Conceptual Model of Shared Leadership in the Boardroom. *Journal of Business Ethics*, *104*(3), 403–420. doi:10.100710551-011-0918-6

Wang, G., DeGhett, K., Ellen, B. P., & Lamont, B. T. (2018). Board Antecedents of CEO Duality and the Moderating Role of Country-level Managerial Discretion: A Meta-analytic Investigation. *Journal of Management Studies*, *56*(1), 172–202. doi:10.1111/joms.12408

Yu, M., & Ashton, J. K. (2015). Board leadership structure for Chinese public listed companies. *China Economic Review*, *34*, 236–248. doi:10.1016/j.chieco.2015.01.010

KEY TERMS AND DEFINITIONS

CEO Duality: When the CEO and the chairman of the board is the same person.

Dual Leadership Structure: In a dual leadership structure, the roles of chief executive officer and chairman are held simultaneously by the same person.

Manager: An individual who exercises executive managerial functions.

Non-dual Leadership Structure: In a non-dual leadership structure, the leadership role is split into two positions held by different individuals.

Chapter 13
Best Practices to Become a Sustainable Smart City:
The Case of Singapore

Jannis Elm
South Westphalia University of Applied Sciences, Germany

Luísa Cagica Carvalho
https://orcid.org/0000-0002-9804-7813
Instituto Politécnico de Setúbal, Portugal & CEFAGE – Universidade de Évora, Portugal

ABSTRACT

The world´s population is growing, day by day, and the latest trends in pertinent magazines show people preferring cities more and more than the countryside. This brings us to take a closer look on the effects brought with this urban sprawl. Cities grow in a dimension; city planners have to excogitate more and more innovative city concepts and solutions in order to cope with this increase of population and with maintain the cities infrastructure and systems. This has led to the term, Smart City, which was coined to reflect or at least promote innovative and smart solutions not only for today but for coming generations. This chapter reflects on a case study of an Asian city that developed a plan to become a smart city. This research focused essentially on the sustainable perspective of a smart city and present some results and best practices that could be implemented by other cities that aim to become smart.

INTRODUCTION

Nowadays, the population in the cities worldwide is growing more and more. Percentage of the population in the city increases more than in the countryside. There are mega metropolises around the world which cause many problems. ONU (2012) forecast a population growth from 7 to 9 billion in 2040, especially in developed countries. Nevertheless, cities are regional spaces to suitable to promote innovation, knowledge and creativity and the biggest cities in the world manage 60% of worlds GDP in 2025 (McKinsey, 2011).

DOI: 10.4018/978-1-7998-2128-1.ch013

The Mega-cities are facing problems such as poverty, poor infra-structure which has often impact on the economy and thus the prosperity of the city. Furthermore, the sustainable development of the city plays an increasingly important role nowadays.

This case study was prepared to share best practices to become to a city become sustainable and environmental smart and to present these implemented ideas and governance practices to other cities that's wants to become a smart city. Singapore could be considered as a role model and an example of how to manage population growth and cope with the challenges related with such fields like infrastructure, mobility, pollution and energy, with a view to sustainability.

In order to show a clear path with good results, data from the government, international and private organizations were evaluated and shown, using the smart solutions, Singapore has found for this with an example and future models. The models and solutions which are presented are not directly transferable to other cities, as they may have differences in culture, geography and economic aspects, but these possible future paths can show how the large population growth can be mastered sustainably. The case study deals with the topic's mobility, pollution, energy, infrastructure and space problems. These were selected because they are the biggest and most common problems worldwide. The question "Is Singapore a smart city and still sustainable" was addressed in each of the points. The investigations began with the problem identification and then the way in which the individual problems were solved with which methods and how they affected the population of Singapore.

Background

Smart City Definition and General Problems

What is a smart city? The term "smart city" is not clearly definable, but the characteristics and generally concepts of smart cities try to face mostly the same problems and there is no universally accepted definition and some authors have registered a "lack of definitorial precision" (Hollands, 2008). Cities use this discrepancy and try to self-define themselves as smart cities (Hollands, 2008; Caragliu et al., 2011; Tranos and Gertner, 2012).

According to Carvalho (2017), a smart city is a smart regional ecosystem that includes several interconnected stakeholders that develop collaborative networks (firms, citizens, public organizations, cultural, economic and social infrastructures) to create an open and creative environment which is useful for improving the population's quality of life and for developing smart and innovative businesses and social projects. These regions present high standards respecting some indicators associated with innovation, creativity, environment, quality of life, entrepreneurial activities and support facilities.

In the context of Urbanization almost all cities around the world get a fast-growing higher population. This phenomenon has to be managed and bring a lot of challenges with it. For instance, modernizing cities and making them more livable with the help of the possibilities offered by new technological developments, information and communication technologies with regard to ecology, social coexistence, political participation. This includes, for example, the more sustainable use of resources by coordinating traffic flows through intelligent systems or using lighting only when it is needed, as well as the digitalization of administration so that services, for which a personal consultation was previously necessary, can in future be carried out online.

One of the most important points of metropoles nowadays is not only infrastructure problems and lack of habitats, but also it covers almost every aspect of society, security, energy and resource management.

Table 1. Smart cities dimensions

Dimension	Authors
ICT (use and availability)	Bakici et al., 2013; Caragliu et al., 2011; Hollands, 2008; Komninos, 2002; Thite, 2011; Tranos and Gertner, 2012.
Entrepreneurial ecosystems (entrepreneurial activities and business creation)	Carvalho, 2016; Gottdiener, 2001; Klein, 2000; Monbiot, 2000; Hollands, 2008; Lombardi et al., 2012; Thite, 2011.
E-government and resident inclusion	Bakici et al., 2013; Caragliu et al., 2011; Hollands, 2008; Schaffers et al., 2011.
Creative industries and high tech	Hollands, 2008; Florida, 2002; Winters, 2011
Human capital and community	Bolisani and Scarso, 2000; Kourtit et al., 2012.
Social capital and relationships	Coe et al., 2001; Kourtit et al., 2012.
Social and environmental sustainability	Caragliu et al., 2011; Nathan, 2013; Sen et al., 2012; Shafiullah et al., 2013; Sivaram et al., 2013.; Strielkowski, 2017

Source: Carvalho, 2017, adapted

Singapore is known as one of the smartest cities in the world and for many countries it is a role model. It is an indisputable leader when it comes to smart mobility, safety, and the long-term planned infrastructure. Singapore boasts the most capable and intelligent mobility system that is marveled around the world.

In concert with its prepared solution how to make prices for the house more affordable for people and commitment to become suitable location for smart urban technologies to be explored, Singapore has deserved rank of one of the smartest, most sustainable and safest cities - equally with cities like Paris and San Francisco.

Today's view of Singapore can't be clearer: during the last few decades, the city absolutely proved itself to be at the helm among others, with the best living conditions and competitiveness. This case study shows how has handled the rapid population growth, how government has solved the problems step by step and can be a kind of user manual for other cities.

Figure 1. Smart city Singapore at night view showing all its glance and beauty

The long-term planning is described and the problems it has brought with it in the areas of infrastructure, living conditions, mobility, pollution and energy supply. The main focus is on these issues, as Singapore has mastered them in a critical view of environmental friendliness and the well-being and standard of living of the population.

How and Why Did Singapore Become a Smart City? Sharing Best Practices

At the beginning of the 19th century, after the Dutch and Portuguese, the British began to expand their Commonwealth to Southeast Asia. When Sir Thomas Stamfort Raffle's in 1819 took possession of Singapore and acquired the right from the British government, to establish a trading base there, there were already about 100 small houses and huts at the Singapore-River. Singapore was an important trade route for China, India, Europe and British Colonial from the beginning of the history.

Already in the year 1822 there were the first urban development plan for Singapore: the government functions were located in the shore zone, the business districts to the south of the Singapore River and the residential districts to the north, which were strictly separated according to ethnic groups. The individual functional areas were also separated from each other by public green areas. The strict segregation of residential areas was intended to create social tensions between population groups (Chinese, Europeans, Malay, Indians, Arabs). In the process, a ghetto formation was also purchased.

Since the ethnic separation also brought with it a spatial concentration of identical building forms, it is still possible today to differ between the individual quarters: the Europeans lived in large detached houses, while the Chinese and Indians lived in "shophouses".

In 1823, the area of Singapore comprised just 1.28 km^2 along the rest of the island belonged to the Malaysian rulers. One hundred years later the area already covers between 72 and 96 km^2. By 1950, the area had increased by more than 60-fold compared with 1819 (Westerholt, 1995, p. 307). Since 1923, Singapore was connected by a dam to the Malaysian mainland, which was very important for the development of the city. Today this dam is used not only for railway and car traffic but also for electricity and drinking water supply and sewage disposal.

The population increased even more rapidly in the course of time, mainly as a result of immigrants from the southern Chinese provinces. In the 19th century it came to overpopulation in particular of the Chinese quarter and to the formation of at the edge of cities and even slums in the inner-city areas. It was not until the beginning of the 20th century that the promotion of private and public housing began to be introduced in order to remedy this situation, after a nationwide survey had shown that there were overcrowded dwellings, too little free green space, too little light, air and inadequate sanitary facilities (Westerholt, 1995, p. 308) in the town.

The successes were very limited until the outbreak of the Second World War and the Japanese occupation 1942 but with housing for only 6000 people rather modest. The air raids by the Japanese destroyed large parts of Singapore, especially production facilities and the railway network. The economy lay on the ground until the surrender. In 1945 unemployment, inflation and the black market prevailed.

After the capitulation of the Japanese in 1945, Singapore received the status of a crown colony. At the same time, the British had to do an enormous amount of reconstruction work, as the bombardments by the Allies had destroyed the port and infrastructure. The continuing immigration intensified a further increase in the housing problem in the city, which was currently being rebuilt. At that time there lived about a third of the population (approx. 300,000 p.e.) "living on 4 km^2 in the city centre with a

Figure 2. Private and public housing joined together

medium-sized population density of 75,000 P.E./km^2 in rows of houses without spaces at the back and with extreme densities up to 250,000 EW/km^2."

In 1955, the first development plan, the so-called "master plan", was presented, which was valid for 20 years and got reviewed every 5 years to face the over density and the resulting problems out of that. Open spaces for satellite cities had been created. At the same time, the population density in of the inner city through resettlement measures and at the same time to create a green belt for the inner-city boundary.

This decentralization measures have been implemented until today in Singapore, in the first years there were, however, substantial problems with the implementation of the master plan, which was only ratified in 1958.

This meant an area redevelopment in the inner-city areas, which did not take into consideration the historical buildings, but without an overall concept for Singapore, the old town was replaced it with new high-rise housing estates, hotels and office buildings.

In 1971 the Master Plan was replaced by the Concept Plan. For the first time, this plan included wide Urban planning areas, such as the development of high-performance traffic concepts, the expansion of the New Towns into urban sub-centres and thus the provision of affordable housing, as well as the designation of open spaces for local recreation and drinking water production to make Singapore smarter.

The Concept Plan was based on a continuous expansion of the urban area a limitation was no longer foreseen. In addition, the residential densities were to be further increased in order to deal economically with the limited space available and to provide a targeted transport and supply infrastructure.

Figure 3. A typical old town view nowadays in Singapore

IS SINGAPORE AS A SMART CITY STILL SUSTAINABLE?

Infrastructure and Space Problems

One of the biggest problems that Singapore's government wanted to solve with the master plan was the lack of apartments. From the very beginning, Singapore has been committed to providing housing for all people, especially for the lower income citizens. At the beginning of the large housing program the main objective was to build as many standardized, cost-minimized apartments as possible in order to eliminate the slums in the city center.

Today, Singapore is one of the greenest cities in the world. Parks are built on skyscrapers to protect native animal species and another function of the green roof terraces and the parks between the residential complexes is on the one hand, a recreation area and it cools the city, as well as the buildings. This reduces the need for air conditioning and emissions.

In 2030, Singapore will be much greener than today when 80% of its buildings is certified green - that is, energy and water efficient, with a high quality and healthy indoor environment, integrated with green spaces and constructed from eco-friendly materials.

Since 2008, a law has stipulated that every new building must be planted, for example on the roof, as a vertical garden or overgrown walls. This means that up to a third of emissions, 40% of global energy and resources and 25% of water consumption can be reduced.

The number of Green Mark certified buildings in Singapore has increased exponentially over the years. As of 1 September 2013, about eight and a half years after the introduction of the certification

Figure 4. Infrastructure view in the evening

program, Singapore has more than 1,650 Green Mark certified building projects totaling some 49 million square meters and accounting for 21 percent of total existing building floor space.

But not only the housing living conditions were improved, nowadays developments have been extended to the whole country instead of concentrating exclusively on the central area. Western Singapore has been designed as an industrial area and north-western Singapore as a recreational area to preserve nature and create a pleasant quiet retreat. This results in a very high quality of life and a good “work - life balance”.

All these different areas are connected with the Mass Rapid Transit metro system, and its one of the fastest, most efficient and cleanest in the world. This results in a very high quality of life and good “work -life balance”

Singapore is almost impossible to grow in terms of land area, although land is being built up diligently. That’s why Singapore is growing upwards. But this leads to an increasing density of living space and traffic. Intelligent infrastructure in urban areas will have a positive impact on our lives in the future. Singapore has a strong motivation to control the immense traffic flows from people and vehicles with digitally optimized traffic management, sensor data and data analysis makes it possible. As early as 2014, the administration officially launched the ‘Smart Nation’ initiative. Smart City is Singapore’s state doctrine and the only way out is if the city doesn’t want to collapse on its own attraction.

A Smart City does not only consist of digital traffic concepts, even if the traffic regulation in Singapore is particularly in the foreground. Singapore is a pioneer in autonomous driving of public transport. It is also the safest city in the world, both in terms of cyber security and infrastructure security (fire protection, power grid, water supply, etc.) as well as crime prevention. This is only possible through a high degree of networking and intelligent analysis of security-relevant devices (smart meters, fire detectors, security cameras).

Singapore’s Smart Nation Initiative benefits from the fact that it can draw on an excellent, state-of-the-art digital infrastructure that is hardly possible in any other city. For example, was one of the first

Figure 5: The fast trains in Singapore are most innovative

cities to offer comprehensive free WLAN access. The broadband network is one of the first and best developed in the world. Since the beginning of its Tiger State development, Singapore has placed the highest national priority on creating optimal conditions for a seamless digital business environment. The digital infrastructure not only attracted companies but is now also paying off in the conversion to Smart City.

Mobility

Over the past few decades, Singapore's land transport has evolved from traffic-clogged roads and unreliable bus services to one which has a world-known reputation for mobility and efficiency. This transformation was not achieved accidentally, but through foresight, reasonable planning, infrastructure developments and the sustained implementation of policies. To ensure sustainable mobility of Singapore, they are demanding complex and unpopular decisions.

Development of Singapore's transport policies is a consequence of the country's economic development. It's progress can be seen as a simple cultivation of transport infrastructure – from trams, buses to trains. From this perspective, the main policy challenges are planning and integration. Transport also designed to meet individual needs, social aspiration and population's needs in mass transport in combination with negative external factors such as congestion and environmental pollution. These needs often conflict each other, and integration on this level means that meeting competing needs in land roads in Singapore have to compete with habitation and industry. In this case there are presented dynamic, processes and institutional framework which helped to solve these issues.

The linear development presents a historical and chronological map of transport policy changes in Singapore. In this case traces this development, highlighting policy dilemmas between public and private transport, as well as between roads and other uses of land have led to policy problems and innovations over the years. Singapore's transport policies have two main elements. First, they provide a world class public transport system to cater for mass movement. Singapore's first challenge was in terms of land and funding constraints for increasing capacities to meet a growing economy and population. Transportation policy and infrastructure also impacted economic and social development.

Second, there is also the policy challenge of managing demands for cars, including the choice and structure of public and private transport. As such, regulatory and economic institutions were put in place to achieve public goals of mobility, equity and development. Transport policy came through those two broad phases, due to changing needs, as well as interests and principles. Though changes in the earlier years were seen to be reaction to market demand, the later years were more complicated. Public transport is a large-scale network industry, that better operates as a natural monopoly.

Singapore's transport system, however, did not start from this foundation, but developed in the direction of series of experiments, adaption and sometimes mistakes. In the mid of 20th century people have been depending on public transport, which was unfortunately had poor service. They complained a lot about unsustainable bus schedule that was because of drivers who were going on strike to demand a higher pay and improvement working conditions. It was a result of having transport planning out of priority list.

In the year 1963 was the end of a 144-year period on British rule in Singapore. This independence gave the Singaporean Government an impetus for a considerable urban renewal program. Public housing was built to get rid of slums and road developments were implemented to improve availability.

Taxi

Taxi industry in the 1950s was free and easy to regulate. Because of high unemployment, large number of people wanted to become a taxi driver and private cars also were transporting passengers. The main question was rapid growth of "pirate taxis."

There were private cars working as taxi with no license. Pirate taxi drivers were employed by gangster owners, who had up to 100 those cars. Although they had poor service standards, posed safe road movement and irregular fare structure, they met public needs, because public transport service in those times was inadequate.

Traffic Management

To help keep Singapore's roads free from traffics, besides regulating vehicle growth and encouraging to use public transport, Electronic Road Pricing (ERP) is also an important tool. It is based on a pay-as-you-use principle, motorists are charged when they use priced roads during peak hours.

Purpose of ERP

ERP system ensure targeted solution for congestion prices. It allows to understand where the most overloaded places are and change prices depending on this. Therefore, costs would increase or decrease, depending on traffic jam level on the road.

Now Singapore's Government is thinking about more effective and responsive solution to manage congestion. It has to be less expensive to build and maintain, and more space efficient. The next-generation ERP system (ERP2) due to advanced technology will provide more flexibility in managing traffic congestion. This will more equitable that the current system.

Figure 6: One private taxi rolling by

Parking System

The LTA (Land Transport Authority) of Singapore launched the Parking Guidance System (PGS) in 2008 in response to rising congestion in the city-state. At various car parks across Singapore, the PGS collects information on available parking spaces. It helps driver do find the parking place even being on the way.

In addition to the PGS, the Government of Singapore has taken other parking measures aimed at reducing vehicle use. It has reduced the number of parking spaces required for new developments, so that if all of Singapore's buildings fell under new development restrictions, the City is evaluated to have only 29,000 parking spaces instead of the 49,000 currently supplied. Nevertheless, Singapore still has a large number of parking spaces, and parking prices are low in comparison to other global cities. For example, season parking in Singapore's Central Business District (CBD) is an average of S$160-200 per month, compared to S$720-850 in Hong Kong, and there are 165 parking spaces per 1,000 jobs in the CBD versus 85 in London. In the future, the Government of Singapore plans to gradually draw down the parking supply in the CBD.

Zero cars Growth in Singapore

On 23 the October 2017 Singapore declared its decision to suspend increase in the number of private cars and motorcycles on the roads. The news has shocked global media, while Singaporeans reacted to this calmly. The reason is that governance during last years has undertaken efficient work to prepare citizens for this unavoidable policy decision.

The Land Transport Authority (LTA) extradites permissions, known as Certificates of Entitlement, that give vehicle owners the right to have their vehicle for ten years. The highest price that people paid in auction for having just benefits of being able to have a car was $41,617. The reason, according to the governance's opinion, is that there is not enough land area. The LTA stated: "In view of land constraints and competing needs, there is limited scope for further expansion of the road network." Nowadays the roads occupy twelve percent of a city's total land area. There are more than 600,000 private and rental cars on this limited road space. Limitation on new cars will make it more difficult to own a car in Singapore, which is still one of the most expensive places to own a vehicle. According to Reuters, mid-range vehicles can cost four times more that the same vehicle in the US. Though, this change will have some positive effects, at least with regard to environment. Less cars on the Singapore's road mean less pollution.

Pollution

In today´s world, big cities become more and more places with over billions of people. These people consume tons of goods and -this is the logical consequence- produce a massive amount of waste. It is one of our biggest tasks to shrink this amount as well as to create a feeling of sustainability and awareness to have a brighter future and cleaner world. Singapore is one of those examples strengthening those authors, who say that it is possible to create a city wherein at least most of the people care of the environment. This means in first stage to care about rubbish. So then how can rubbish and cleanliness be linked together?

Cleanliness in Singapore has a lot to do with education. In the early years of the school system, pupils are taught to care about their waste and as their belongings. One of the most important sentences in Singapore is the following: "We good people must not allow the evil and ugly people to make our city dirty." Because of this education, people learn to not throw their rubbish into the nature but to put it in bins and baskets. And when you look at the numbers and fact sheets, the viewer recognize that the streets and the benches really seem licked.

But of course, education is not all the business. Those who don´t think well of Singaporeans, who pollute their environment by simply dropping waste, have to pay up to 2,000 Singapore dollars the first time. This is about 1300 Euro. The second and the third time the punishment will increase up to $ 10,000, so 6500 in Euro. Such high punishments pay off and keep people from throwing away their rubbish and waste in the nature and on the streets.

Another really innovative idea which was established a few decades ago is to let the cleaning be done by volunteers and convicts together. The polluters can also be condemned to clean parks for twelve hours. Preferably directly in their neighborhood, so that they are publicly exposed. The "public shaming" was the motivation behind the introduction of this punishment.

Punishment lurks on very many places: smoking in the wrong place, spitting on the floor or even in illegal paintings. Two Germans, who graffiti-decorated a subway in Singapore more than three years ago, were sentenced to three sticks and nine months imprisonment. Singapore should be a clean city. One must ensure that Singapore stays beautiful, says one of the voluntary city cleaners.

Figure 7. This garden is located right in the centre of Singapore

In addition to these punishment treatments, a whole movement has been formed: "Keep Singapore Clean Movement", it is called. On weekends, entire school classes go to the "food courts", large gatherings of food stalls, sing a song or write a poem to appeal to the eaters to clean up their rubbish. Keeping Singapore clean also improves the quality of life, residents see it. It is the pride of their thriving city that motivates many Singaporeans. "The Garden City" is her name as well, the city as a garden where everyone can enjoy themselves, which leads to great prosperity. Because the city cannot rely on volunteers alone, a huge army of cheap labor sweeps, cleans, cleans and cleans every sidewalk and every park path. In view of such measures, it is not surprising that Singapore is not only the probably cleanest city in the world, but also considered to be very safe.

When we compare the So2-emissions of Singapore with other countries in the world, we can see that the town meets the objectives: Within the last ten years it was possible to decrease the SO2-intensity from 192 in 2000 to 52 in the year 2010. This is immense, if you compare this achievement with Uruguay for

Figure 8. The centre garden from Singapore by night8

example, which had to face a tremendous increase of almost 70 over this time. The exact trends can be seen in the graphic below.

Looking at the main emissions produced in Singapore there are four main categories to focus on. The main and most important is characterized by the industry. It is important to state that power generation is one main aspects of the industry. Because of its high importance, the topic of "power generation" will be discussed at a later point deeper. The industry causes over 60 percent of all emissions in Singapore, followed by the building producing nearly 14 percent. The third party is represented by transports such as cars or busses or trains. Another producer of emissions is the household that causes nearly eight percent.

One last category named "others" includes waste, water and other electricity use.

Whereas most countries in the world like the US, China and Korea use coal to generate their energy and satisfy their energy needs, Singapore declines coal. This is not only innovative as burning coal is a dirty way to produce electricity. Moreover, it proves Singapore to be a city that cares about environmental topics and issues.

Energy

Energy can simply be defined as "ability to do a work". Therefore, to provide a good functioning, every country needs to produce energy by using some sources. These sources can be divided into two different categories which are renewable and non-renewable energy. Solar energy, wind energy, hydropower, geothermal energy and biomass are considered as main sources of renewable energy. On the other hand, the examples of the main sources of non-renewable energy can be given as nuclear energy, coal, natural gas etc. We can state that not all these energy sources are good for the environment, so not for the sustainability too. To ensure a better future, the best way usually is to choose the renewable energy sources. Since one of the aims of the smart cities is resource optimization, using the renewable energy sources is the most common and favorite one in the smart cities.

Figure 9. The energy system is connected as wide as the traffic system

In Singapore, which is the chosen smart city, to provide a livable future, the most preferred and suitable renewable energy source is the solar energy. The government focuses on the improvement of the existed solar energy system.

To do that, the government invests a lot of money on this issue. For example, under the Innovation and Enterprise 375 million dollars have been invested for key research, development and deployment initiatives in the energy space, focusing on areas such as solar, energy storage, smart grids, and green buildings. Due to lack of enough area in the city and the high cost of producing electricity from solar energy, the progress of this issue is very important for the government in order to continue being sustainable. For example, one solution of lack of sufficient area is that installing solar panels on rooftops.

Recognizes to all these investments, the government states that the current solar deployment, which is 47 MWp, will increase to 350 MWp by 2020. Moreover, it is also stated that, probably by 2030, these systems will be able to contribute up to 8% of Singapore's peak electricity demand.

Singapore is a role-model country in the field of renewable energy. In the figure below, you can see its emission comparison between other countries. Since in Singapore, renewable energy is preferable energy type, emission amount is really low. Moreover, Singapore also tries to use biofuel resource which is another renewable energy source. They try to improve in this area to and they are already in top 16 countries in global. Furthermore, Singapore continues to be a role-model for other countries with its laws and regulations in energy field. For example, in 2017, the Singapore Government announced plans to implement a carbon tax to these facilities which emit 25,000 tons or more of carbon dioxide from 2019. Also, the other example is, in 2014, the Economic Development Board of Singapore (EDB) announced the Renewable Energy Integration Demonstrator – Singapore (REIDS) which is a platform for researchers and industry to develop, test and demonstrate the integration of renewable energy sources. However, the main problem is that solar energy is not enough for the city, and since they cannot use any other renewable sources, they need other energy sources which are not renewable energy sources. In 2018, the most common non-renewable energy sources were natural gas, petroleum products and coal in Singapore. The natural gas is imported from all of from other countries like Austria and US, and a part of the petroleum products and coal are imported, too. From the figure above, one can see the percentages of the sources which are used in generation of electricity. As it can be seen, natural gas has the highest percentage and the all of the energy sources are non-renewable. Therefore, we can say that, this situation is an obstacle for being a totally sustainable city. However, Singapore is able to produce electricity with the amount of it needs. So, it is able to provide itself with self-produced energy.

To conclude, Singapore uses both renewable and non-renewable energy sources, and the government always tries to improve the usage of the renewable energy source, which is the solar energy. For now, solar energy cannot satisfy the demand, so non-renewable energy sources are used because of this reason. Due to this situation, Singapore is not totally sustainable in the field of energy. However, every year it gets better with new technology and implementations. In the future, being totally sustainable is not a dream for Singapore city. Present your perspective on the issues, controversies, problems, etc., as they relate to theme and arguments supporting your position. Compare and contrast with what has been or is currently being done as it relates to the chapter's specific topic and the main theme of the book.

SOLUTIONS AND RECOMMENDATIONS

Taking into account the main characteristics shown in the study above, the importance of being innovative and future-orientated becomes very clear. Central elements like the energy or the mobility sector are characterized to be smart. That means that Singapore in this matter goes new ways and tries to solve its problems as efficient as possible. This is the first step.

Caring about what is not going well. Then, in the second step, it is about solving the problem as best as possible. So did Singapore. They not only created a "green"-environmental focused behavior with their citizens but developed new ways to relieve infrastructure and solve space problems. This great afford can be used to with other cities want to become a smart city too. It is not only about the facts, not only about measuring the status quo, but about the real motivation and group identity of inhabitants of the city.

Of course, at first you have to come up with needed information and meetups where represents talk about the idea and the change these methods and new ways will cause. But if you are able to persuade the citizens about a new idea for their town, everything becomes possible. This is a process and you have to start it in the early days of a human´s life, which is in school. If you are able to create a feeling for sustainability and attention, everything becomes possible. Being taught these values, the rising generation will never drop waste on the streets again and will keep the town safe and clean.

Additionally, it is really important to think about green energy. Solar panels can be placed for example easily on the top roofs of the buildings. This will prevent your town from coping with dust and high CO2-emissions. Electric cars will improve the air condition as well as it keeps the air clean because fossils burned are not more needed. As Singapore is a town with many electric stations, you have to think about the infrastructure as well. It is mandatory to become a smart city to have spots where people can charge their electric cars. On top of that -and this is something really important- you have to participate the people in such innovative projects. Being part of it, you have a high motivation and you put a big effort of energy in it. So, keeping this in mind, your town will improve and improve and one day will become a smart city too.

FUTURE RESEARCH DIRECTIONS

Nowadays, every city faces a big problem, which is fast-growing population. That is the most important reason for increasing number of smart cities. Because, every city tries to be sustainable to win this challenge and being a smart city is the best way of doing it. To understand the concept of smart cities better, we can give some examples. For instance, The UK Department for Business, Innovation and Skills (BIS) considers smart cities a process rather than a static outcome, in which increased citizen engagement, hard infrastructure, social capital and digital technologies make cities more livable, resilient and better able to respond to challenges. Moreover, it is also defined as "a smart city is a place where traditional networks and services are made more efficient with the use of digital and telecommunication technologies for the benefit of its inhabitants and business" according to European Commission.

CONCLUSION

In our case, firstly we explained how Singapore became a smart city. There were two plans to become a smart city which are Master Plan and Concept Plan. Then, we tried to learn whether Singapore is sustainable as being a smart city or not. We searched this subject by dividing it into four subtopics. These were infrastructure and space problems, mobility, pollution and energy. In every subtopic, we gave some examples for other countries from Singapore case to be a role model to them.

We can sum up these subtopics and problems. Firstly, in Singapore, for infrastructure the government is trying to provide houses for everyone and also, they have green rooftops to be green city. They have digitally optimized traffic management to face the traffic problem with growing population. Secondly for mobility, the government has two main policies. The first one is providing a very good public transport system to cater for mass movement and the second one is managing demands for cars, including the choice and structure of public and private transport. Thirdly, for pollution they start teaching about this subject in the school. Moreover, the government applies some penalties for the citizens who cause pollution. Lastly, for energy the country really favors renewable energy to be sustainable and there are many regulations and laws to increase the usage of renewable energy. In conclusion, Singapore is a smart city which is trying hard to be totally sustainable. With this progress, it seems it will happen in very soon future.

REFERENCES

Asheim, B. T., & Isaksen, A. (1997). Location, agglomeration and innovation: Towards regional innovation systems in Norway? *European Planning Studies*, *5*(3), 299–330. doi:10.1080/09654319708720402

Bakici, T., Almirall, E., & Wareham, J. (2013). A Smart City initiative: The case of Barcelona. *Journal of the Knowledge Economy*, *4*(2), 135–148. doi:10.100713132-012-0084-9

Batty, M., Axhausen, K. W., Giannotti, F., Pozdnoukhov, A., Bazzani, A., Wachowicz, M., ... Portugali, Y. (2012). Smart Cities of the Future. *The European Physical Journal. Special Topics*, *214*(1), 481–518. doi:10.1140/epjst/e2012-01703-3

Bernardez, M. (2009). *The power of entrepreneurial ecosystems: Extracting booms from busts*. Expert 2 business. Retrieved from www.expert2business.com/itson/Articles/Ecosystems.pdf

Bolisani, E., & Scarso, E. (2000). Electronic communication and knowledge transfer. *International Journal of Technology Management*, *20*(1–2), 116–133. doi:10.1504/IJTM.2000.002855

Caragliu, A., Del Bo, C., & Nijkamp, P. (2011). Smart Cities in Europe. *Journal of Urban Technology*, *18*(2), 65–82. doi:10.1080/10630732.2011.601117

Caragliu, A., Del Bo, C., & Nijkamp, P. (2011). Smart Cities in Europe. *Journal of Urban Technology*, *18*(2), 65–82. doi:10.1080/10630732.2011.601117

Carvalho, L. (2017). Entrepreneurial Ecosystems. Lisbon as a Smart Start-up City. In L. Carvalho (Ed.), *Handbook of Research On Entrepreneurial Development and Innovation within Smart Cities* (pp. 1–24). Hershey, PA: IGI Global. doi:10.4018/978-1-5225-1978-2.ch001

Caughill, P. (2017). Singapore will stop adding new cars to its roads in 2018. Retrieved from https://futurism.com/singapore-will-stop-adding-new-cars-to-its-roads-in-2018

Centre for Cities. (2014). Smart cities definitions. Retrieved from https://www.centreforcities.org/reader/smart-cities/what-is-a-smart-city/1-smart-cities-definitions/

Consultants Private Limited. (2014). World Cities Summit. Retrieved from http://www.scp.com/page.aspx?s=en&cid=19&id=450

European Commission. (2018). Smart cities. Retrieved from https://ec.europa.eu/info/eu-regional-and-urban-development/topics/cities-and-urban-development/city-initiatives/smart-cities_en

Hollands, R. G. (2008). Will the real Smart City please stand up? City: Analysis of Urban Trends, Culture, Theory. *Policy and Action*, *13*(3), 303–320.

Ivan. (1970). Flashback: Wildlife news in 1960s Singapore. Retrieved from http://lazy-lizard-tales.blogspot.com/2013/06/flashback-wildlife-news-in-1960s.html

McKinsey Global Institute. (2011). *Urban World: Mapping the Economic Power of Cities*. MGI.

Nino. (2016). Singapore - the first smart nation in the world. Tanaza. Retrieved from https://www.tanaza.com/blog/singapore-the-first-smart-nation-in-the-world/

ONU. (2012). Resilient People, Resilient Planet: A Future Worth Choosing, Relatório do Painel de alto Nível sobre Sustentabilidade Global do Secretário-geral das Nações Unidas.

Petronzio, M., & Petronzio, M. (2014). 54% of the World's Population Now Lives in Cities [CHART]. Retrieved from https://mashable.com/2014/07/18/urbanization-city-growth/?europe=true#nvfGudR5lGqz

Sennhauser, P. (2018). EINE EINFÜHRUNG. Suisse Digital. Retrieved from https://www.suissedigital.ch/fileadmin/user_upload/suissedigital/public/de/Smart_City-DE-1_04-20181204.pdf

Singfat, C. (2017). Zero car growth: Only in Singapore? Policy Forum. Retrieved from https://www.policyforum.net/zero-car-growth-only-in-singapore/

The Economist Newspaper. (2017): The Safe Cities Index 2017. Retrieved from http://safecities.economist.com/safe-cities-index-2017

Tranos, E., & Gertner, D. (2012). Smart networked cities? *Innovation (Abingdon)*, *25*(2), 175–190. doi:10.1080/13511610.2012.660327

Wong, K., Meng, T. W., Kiat, Y. B. A., & Gledhill, L.L.P. (2018). *Practical Law*. Thomson Reuters. Retrieved from https://uk.practicallaw.thomsonreuters.com/7-637-5107?transitionType=Default&contextData=(sc.Default)&firstPage=true&comp=pluk&bhcp=1#co_anchor_a734811

ADDITIONAL READING

Aguilera, G., Galán, J.L., Campos, J.C., & Rodríguez, P. (2013). An Accelerated-Time Simulation for Traffic Flow in a Smart City. FEMTEC, 26.

Ahvenniemi, H., Huovila, A., Pinto-Seppä, I., & Airaksinen, M. (2017). What are the differences between sustainable and smart cities? *Cities*, *60*, 234-245.

Al Nuaimi, E., Al Neyadi, H., Mohamed, N., & Al-Jarrodi, J. (2015). Applications of big data to smart cities. *Journal of Internet Services and Applications*, 6–25.

Bakıcı, T., Almirall, E., & Wareham, J. (2013). A smart city initiative: The case of Barcelona. *Journal of the Knowledge Economy*, *4*(2), 135–148. doi:10.100713132-012-0084-9

Brkljačić, T., Majetić, F., & Tarabić, B. (2017). Smart Environment: Cyber Parks (Connecting Nature and Technology). In L. Carvalho (Ed.), *Handbook of Research On Entrepreneurial Development and Innovation within Smart Cities* (pp. 160–183). Hershey, PA: IGI Global. doi:10.4018/978-1-5225-1978-2.ch008

European Parliament. (2014). *Mapping Smart Cities in the EU*. Directorate General For Internal Policies. Policy Department. Retrieved from http://www.europarl.europa.eu/RegData/etudes/etudes/join/2014/507480/IPOL-ITRE_ET(2014)507480_EN.pdf

Lazaroiu, G., & Roscia, M. (2012). Definition methodology for the smart cities model. *Energy*, *47*(1), 326–332. doi:10.1016/j.energy.2012.09.028

Pawlikowska-Piechotka. (2017). *A Smart City Initiative: Urban Greens and Evaluation Method of the Sport and Recreation Potentials (SEM)*. In L. Carvalho (Ed.), *Handbook of Research On Entrepreneurial Development and Innovation within Smart Cities* (pp. 580–602). Hershey, PA: IGI Global.

Prado-Lorenzo, J., García-Sanchez, I., & Cuadrado-Ballesteros, B. (2011). Sustainable cities: Do political factors determine the quality of life? *Journal of Cleaner Production*, *21*(1), 34–44. doi:10.1016/j.jclepro.2011.08.021

Winters, J. V. (2011). Why are smart cities growing? Who moves and who stays. *Journal of Regional Science*, *51*(2), 253–270. doi:10.1111/j.1467-9787.2010.00693.x

KEY TERMS AND DEFINITIONS

Best practice: commercial or professional procedures that are accepted or prescribed as being correct or most effective.

Smart City: It's a smart regional ecosystem that includes several partners and stakeholders interconnected. They develop collaborative networks (firms, citizens, public organizations, cultural, economic and social infrastructure) to create an open and creative environment useful to live and to develop smart and innovative businesses and social projects. These regions present high standards attending to some indicators associated with innovation, creativity, environment, life quality, entrepreneurial activities and support infrastructures.

Sustainable development: Development that meets the needs of the present human beings, without compromising future generations to meet their own needs.

Urban Plannning: is a technical and political process concerned with the development and design of land use and the built environment, including air, water, and the infrastructure passing into and out of urban areas, such as transportation, communications, and distribution networks.

Chapter 14
The Impact of Firm Performance and Corporate Governance on Corporate Social Responsibility:
Evidence From France

Souhaila Kammoun
IHEC, CODECI, University of Sfax, Tunisia

Sahar Loukil
University of Sfax, Tunisia

Youssra Loukil
University of Sfax, Tunisia

ABSTRACT

Based on the behavioral aspect of the governance theory, this chapter explores the effect of the firm performance and corporate governance (CG) on corporate social responsibility (CSR) engagement by investigating their causal effects. Using annual reports of a large and extensive sample of French firms for the year 2014-2016, we find that firm performance significantly improves that firm's social responsibility, but it has a significant and negative impact when we consider corporate government as a contingency factor. The results show that the existence of institutional administrator is in favor of CSR while it is the inverse effect when we consider the other independent administrators. However, we fail to find any significant impact of administrator's expertise. Our results suggest that pressures exerted by outsiders and corporate governance mechanisms influence CSR practices. Overall, our study implies that corporate governance attributes play a vital role in ensuring organizational legitimacy through CSR. The study findings should be of interest to regulators and policy makers.

DOI: 10.4018/978-1-7998-2128-1.ch014

INTRODUCTION

With the increasing social awareness, firms and academics have increasingly been required to attach importance to more understand social problems. In an attempt to go more socially responsible, firms make active efforts to involve social concern into their corporate landscapes and strategic decision-making processes. As results, firms become to involve social and responsible actions through the implementation of corporate social responsibility (CSR).

The theoretical foundations based on the nature and direction causality of the relationship between CSR and firm performance have been the subject of a large number of empirical validations (Allouche and Larouche, 2005). Some researchers were interested in studying the association between CSR and performance such as operational performance and environmental, marketing and financial performance (Iwata and Okada, 2011; Johns and Khojastehpour, 2014; Amores-Salvadó et al., 2014; Rashid et al., 2015, Martínez Conesa et al., 2016; Wei et al., 2017; Chuang and Huang, 2018 and Wu et al., 2018). Other researchers have focused on relationship between corporate governance and CSR.

The underlying aim of this chapter is twofold. First, we investigate CSR reporting information of private French firms with a view to observe the levels and varieties of CSR information. Second, we examine the variability of CSR reporting information for CG elements considering the nature of corporate governance mechanisms and the moderating effect of performance. Thus, our study might be inclined to construct few inferences for firm's strategies in order to promote CSR performance.

This chapter is expected to contribute to the literature on the relationship between social performance and financial performance in the following ways. This study's analysis of administrator type and CSR performance extends the largely literature to the French context. Our study also contributes to the ongoing discussion about causality direction between CSR and firm performance. We assess whether firm performance impacts greater influence on social ratings. Results suggest that while firms' performance has a positive impact on CSR commitments, it has got a negative impact when we consider governance mechanisms. To be more precise, contrary to the upward effect of institutional administrators, the presence of independent administrators significantly decreases CSR ratings. We thus extend the literature on the type of governance mechanisms to a new domain. This contribution is important given the literature's emphasize on the role of CG in CSR performance. Finally, our empirical analysis is expected to provide implications to policy makers, managers, and academicians in the French context.

The chapter is set out as follows. The next section documents a short review of the association between CSR reporting, CG and firm performance. Next, the details of the research method used in the study are discussed. In the final section, it reviews the finding of the study together with the implications, limitations and the further scope of study.

BACKGROUND

In this overview, we provide a brief summary of the background literature relevant to our study in order to distinguish some determinants of social performance such as corporate governance and firm performance. We begin by first setting out the evolution of CSR in Europe and France. We then present the conflicting studies of the CSR-firm performance link, despite the fact, that many empirical researches have been conducted on this topic. Herein, we outline the main findings from empirical studies related to the relationship between CSR and firm performance. Afterwards, we proceed to review empirical studies on the relationship between CSR and corporate governance.

The Evolution of CSR in Europe and France

Corporate Social Responsibility (CSR) has generated great interest for many practitioners and researchers. Despite a wide variation in definitions of CSR, a clear universal definition of what CSR exactly is still lacking (Dahlsrud, 2008; van Marrewijk, 2013; Kooskora et al., 2019). In his study, Dahlsrud (2008) identified 37 different definitions of CSR from 27 studies. The concept of CSR was first introduced in the European Union (EU) through the July 2001 Green Paper. CSR is defined as the voluntary integration by companies of social and environmental concerns into their business activities and their relations with their stakeholders and as "the responsibility of enterprises for their impacts on society" (European Commission, 2011). Following some researches on CSR, we consider that engagement in CSR depends on a combination of external pressures and factors internal to the firm (Aguilera et al., 2007; Brown et al., 2010 and Graafland & Noorderheaven, 2019). In Europe, there are already regulations concerning the disclosure of CSR in countries such as Sweden, Norway, Finland, Denmark, Germany, France, the United Kingdom, Switzerland and France. As noted by Dardour et al. (2018) and Noronha et al. (2013), governments play important role relevant standards regarding CSR disclosure requirements.

The Global Compact, launched by the United Nations Secretary-General in 2000, encourages businesses to "adopt, support and implement a set of core values within their sphere of influence in the areas of human rights, labor standards and the environment and the fight against corruption". According to the Organisation for Economic Co-operation and Development (OECD) Guidelines for Multinational Enterprises, revised in 2011, "To ensure that the activities of these enterprises are in harmony with government policies, strengthen the basis of mutual trust between enterprises and companies in which they operate, contribute to improving the climate of foreign investment and enhance the contribution of multinational enterprises to sustainable development."

This policy was aimed at strengthening sustainable development in projects, assessing their impacts, reducing negative impacts and integrating international standards into AFD's[1] activities. It also aimed at improving dialogue with stakeholders, better managing controversies and increasing the transparency of the agency, subject to its legal and banking framework. In addition, the AFD Group has begun to include CSR criteria in its calls for tenders. From the beginning, the French CSR policy, launched in the early 2000s, aimed to establish a legal framework governing the social and environmental transparency of companies.

France adopted a national action plan for the implementation of the Guiding Principles on Business and Human Rights on April 26, 2017 and participates in a working group to develop a binding treaty on human rights and business in the United Nations. It adopted the directive requiring certain large companies and certain groups to disclose non-financial information on July 21, 2017. The government is committed to becoming a country at the 2013 G8 summit. It has even actively promoted CSR adoption in the definition of the Sustainable Development Goals (SDGs), and in particular the target 12.6 of the SDGs. Finally, France has been invited to become a member of the government's advisory group, which aims to facilitate government discussions on actions to promote corporate transparency in the social and environmental fields.

In this chapter, we are interested in exploring the nature and the course of association shared between the CSR, corporate governance and financial performance by French companies.

The Link Between CSR and Financial Performance

The relationship between financial performance and CSR has given rise to a considerable academic literature and the findings and areas studied vary as evidenced by the many literature reviews devoted to this topic for several decades (Orlitzky et al., 2003, Preston and O'Bannon, 1997; Portney, 2008; Margolis et al. 2009; Galant and Cadez, 2017: Maqbool and Zameer, 2017; Kooskora, M., Juottonen, M., & Cundiff, 2019; Akben-Selcuk, 2019; Cho, Chung and Young, 2019). The question to raise however is as to which effect prevails. A literature revue will enable us to shed light on the direction of causality between CSR and firm performance. In this context, there are several core bodies of literature which are relevant. The underlying aim of this chapter is to explore the nature and the course of association shared between the CSR and firm performance since empirical studies on the relationship between corporate social responsibility (CSR) and corporate financial performance are still inconclusive regarding the causality and different dimensions of CSR (Galant & Cadez, 2017; Broadstock et al., 2019).

A first review of existing research findings on the impact of firm performance on CSR reveals that a high level of financial performance implies greater commitment to socially responsible actions (Allouche and Larouche, 2005). From the point of view of to the theory of "Slack organization", a profusion of financial resources encourages the company to invest more in social issues. McGuire et al, (1988) also argued that financial performance, through the profitability criterion, can optimize the level of social performance. From this point of view, financial performance becomes a prerequisite for the implementation of socially responsible actions (McGuire et al., 1988). According to Waddock and Grave (1997), when a company's financial performance improves, slack resources will be available to enable the company to conduct corporate social performance such as society and community relation, employee relation, and environment performance (Fauzi & Idris, 2009).

Other evaluated empirical studies suggest both a potentially negative or positive relationship between CSR and financial performance, while other studies have found no significant relationship. The first documented research found that CSR has a positive impact on financial performance in a view that CSR enhances financial performance of the firm (Freeman, 1984; Shen and Chang, 2009; Gillan, Hartzell, Koch, and Starks, 2010; Ameer and Othman, 2012; Rodriguez-Fernandez, 2016; Akben-Selcuk, 2019.). According to this line of thinking, if companies do not engage in CSR, they can compromise their brand image and reputation, a fact that would deteriorate their profitability in the short and long term. The second set of studies has found that CSR and financial performance are negatively connected since social action involves costs. In fact, Costs incurred in different CSR activities (charity, ecofriendly equipment, better working conditions, pollution control) will squeeze the profitability and deteriorate firm performance (Maqbool and Zameer, 2018). The third set of studies argues that there is no significant association between CSR and financial performance (FP) (Soloman and Hansen 1985; Nelling and Webb, 2009; Soana, 2011). Makni et al. (2009) found no significant positive relationship and even identify in some cases a strong negative impact of the environmental dimension on financial performance. The combination of these different questions about the causal relationship between CSR and financial performance is summarised in Table 1.

As illustrated in the table above, empirical studies on the link between CSR and FP presented divergent results. The intense debate over whether there is a real link between CSR and FP is still generating debate among researchers (Lu et al., 2013; Broadstock et al., 2019). It is at this point useful to bring attention to concerns of methodology, assessments of FP, and measurements of CSR. To understand how firms

Table 1. Main findings of the empirical literature review on the CSR- FP link

Nature of the CSR-FP link	Empirical studies
Positive	Belkaoui, 1976; McGuire et al. 1988; Johnson and Greening, 1999; Preston and O'Bannon, 1997; Waddock and Graves, 1997; Simpson and Kohers 2002; Margolis et al., 2009; Karagiorgos 2010; Rodgers et al., 2013; Rodriguez-Fernandez, 2016; Akben-Selcuk, 2019.
Negative	Vance, 1975; Kedia and Kuntz, 1981; Shane and Spicer, 1983; Lopez et al. 2007; Makni et al. 2009; Baird, Geylani, & Roberts, 2012; Peng & Yang, 2013; Moore, 2019.
No significant link	Alexander & Buchholz, 1978; Aupperle et al., 1985; McWilliams & Siegel, 2000; Nelling and Webb, 2009; Soana, 2011; Kooskora et al., 2019.

Source: Authors' development based on empirical findings

can succeed in both financial and extra-financial terms it is necessary to circumvent many difficulties highlighted by the previous researches.

According to Karyawati et al. (2018), inconsistent results are due to the complexity of relationship between the two variables and this complexity stems from the nature of CSR, which is unseparable from its environment. Furthermore, it is noteworthy that the performance and CSR are both multidimensional and there is a wide variety of ways to measure the relationship between CSR and FP (Kooskora et al., 2019). For instance, empirical researches have proposed different CSR measurements such as Fortune reputation ratings (Preston and O'Bannon (1997), Business Ethics magazine ratings (Murphy and Verschoor, 1998) or the Kinder, Lyndenburg and Domini (KLD) index (used by Waddock and Graves, 1997).

Similarly, measurements of FP include both accounting and shareholder wealth factors. As performance measure, we can cite return on assets (ROA) and return on equity (ROE) (Banker, Chang, and Majumdar, 1996) and shareholder wealth factors (Hillman and Keim, 2001). Moreover, some studies have become seriously criticized for combining positive and negative dimensions of CSR. In fact, while positive CSR involves proactive stakeholder relationship management, negative CSR involves reactive compliance with minimum standards, and hence these should not be combined. Bénabou and Tirole (2010) argue that firms can be proactive on some dimensions and set back on others. Previous research (e.g., Waddock and Graves, 1997) suggests that well performed firms are more likely to invest in CSR. In a global way, Artiach et al. (2010) postulate that financial performance can be correlated with CSR performance[2]. According to Rhou et al. (2016) stakeholders' CSR awareness can gain more benefits from a firm's CSR initiatives, thereby improving firm performance.

The Link Between CSR Strategy, Corporate Governance and Firm Performance

A key question in the literature is to identify why companies have an interest in engaging CSR strategies. According to Wang (2017), CSR is a growth strategy for companies as for their business grows. Thus, large companies are called upon to adopt a CSR strategy while ensuring that it has a positive impact on their financial performance. Henceforth, CSR is seen as a real strategic necessity (Falkenberg and Brunsael, 2011). Nowadays, the development of sustainable finance is a crucial issue for the promotion of responsible social criteria, but also in terms of governance in companies and markets. It reflects the continued efforts of investors, legislators, businesses and all stakeholders in corporate social responsibility (CSR) over the last two decades (Abad et al., 2017; Bonnet et al., 2017 and Cavaco et al., 2017).

Corporate Governance and CSR Performance

According to Bonn and Fisher (2005), corporate governance is fundamental when establishing the corporate and strategic focus of CSR and business ethics. Herein, the board of directors is responsible for the implementation of the CSR strategy (Elkington, 2006; Zubeltzu-Jaka, 2018).

Admittedly, the relationship between CSR and CG and especially the question of the real impact of managers on the company's CSR strategy were widely discussed in the literature. On this topic, two opposing points of view stand out: the strategic current (Andrews, 1971) postulates a strong impact whereas the neo-institutional and ecological theories (Hannan and Freeman, 1977; Dimaggio and Powell, 1983) postulate the absence of a real influence. Hambrick and Finkelstein (1987) propose to reconcile the two approaches and explain that the influence of the leaders is strong when their managerial discretion is great (strong latitude of action), and weak when this discretion is weak. In this vein, the study of Harjoto and Jo (2011) is one of the few studies to have jointly studied a governance mechanism (the change of leader) and CSR performance in the context of an advanced economy[3].

Moreover, pressures have increased in recent years to increase the number of independent directors on boards of the largest companies. Even for Barnea and Rubin (2010) who were interested in the boards of directors structure and the shareholder / manager relationship and noted that the internal directors would be interested in investing in CSR to build a good reputation citizens, potentially to the detriment of the shareholders, while reinforcing the overconfidence of the managers. On the contrary, independent directors, playing an effective monitoring role, would limit investment in CSR. A significantly different argument can also be used to find this relationship between internal and independent directors and CSR: internal directors, whose main function is to provide company-specific information to outside directors, are likely to adopt a more cautious strategy, minimizing the risk of accidents and lawsuits, and therefore investing more in CSR (Krüger, 2010, Ansari et al., 2013).

Following the studies of Jo and Harjoto (2011) and Gomes and Novaes (2001), major shareholders and majority block-holders, because of their stronger incentives to do so and their more effective means of control, are likely to have interests that are quite distant from the minority shareholders and will have a stronger influence on the strategic decisions of the company than small and diversified shareholders. Based on a sample of American companies over the period (1993-2004), Jo and Harjoto (2012) show that CSR choices are positively correlated with institutional ownership. Studying a sample of 118 Korean firms in 2005, Oh et al. (2011) show a positive relationship between CSR and institutional or foreign shareholding and a negative relationship between CSR and managerial shareholding. Using a sample of 691 European companies in 2005, Dam and Scholtens (2013) show that the concentration of capital is associated with lower CSR performance. Crifo et al. (2015) similarly show, on a sample of 898 companies worldwide, over the period 2004-2012, that a higher shareholding concentration has a negative impact on CSR performance. Crifo et al. (2015) similarly show that Environment, Social and Governance (ESG) factors asymmetrically impact the value of unlisted companies, with firms having relatively more to lose from ESG mismanagement than to gain from good management.

On this particular issue, there is a wide variety of empirical studies (Jo and Harjoto, 2011; Khan et al., 2013; Giannarakis, 2014, Jizi et al., 2014; Lau and Lu, 2014; Rees and Rodionova, 2014; Jain and Jamali, 2016; Liao et al., 2016; Liu and Zhang, 2017; Shahab et al., 2018; Alotaibi et al., 2019). In this vein, what we are concerned with is the nature of board members as institutional and independent members. Nevertheless, empirical results concerning the effect of institutional administrator are paradoxical. Johnson and Greening (1999) argue that some categories of institutional administrators are more concerned with a firm's social performance because it may impact financial performance over time. While some research found that institutional owners reduce CSR expenditures, given the long-term horizons and uncertain outcomes, others argue that institutional administrator undertake more CSR in order to mitigate the risk of adverse regulatory action, higher compliance costs, consumer retaliation because they cannot exit easily the firm. For instance, Guinness et al. (2016) support that qualified foreign institutional administrator deploys social engagement in non-SOEs to build competitive advantage and that gender diversity on boards promotes Chinese firms' social performance. Based on a social rating from Rankings (RKS) for a sample of 2412 Chinese firms during 2009-2013, they found that CSR performance exhibits positive (negative) relation with a listed entity's size and age (leverage and lagged return-on-equity) but virtually no connection with independent board representation.

In summary, as further encapsulated in the research of Arora and Dharwadkar (2011), the relationship between various governance mechanisms and CSR is still far from clear. Moreover, as outlined by Zubeltzu-Jaka (2018), the direction of causality between CG and CSR has not been adequately approached. In fact, some researchers have tried to put light on CG's causal relation with the CSR (Jo and Harjoto, 2012) without analyzing the causal relation from the opposite side (Jo and Harjoto, 2012). Other researchers such as Rees & Rodionova (2014) have tried to approach the study of causality but they were unable to demonstrate the direction of causality.

Association Between CG, FP and CSR

As mentioned previously, the relationship between the CG and the CSR and, similarly, between the CSR performance and the FP was investigated worldwide. However, each relationship has been universally studied in different ways and with different methods. Thus, despite ample empirical enquiry into the nature and the causality direction of each relationship, the empirical studies fail to provide conclusive results (Galant, & Cadez, 2017; Zubeltzu-Jaka et al., 2018) and no common ground has been obtained.

Due to the mixed findings of empirical studies on relation among CSR, corporate governance and firm performance, some researchers have tried to explain why companies integrate CSR activities and how CSR relates to corporate governance, financial performance, and stakeholders (Harjoto and Jo, 2011). Admittedly, as a topic of debate, the link between corporate governance mechanisms, firm performance and CSR investigated in some studies, but lacks insights from an empirical perspective on the effect of firm performance and corporate governance on CSR. In this regard, Kooskora et al. (2019) underline that a vital issue in corporate governance is the influence that CSR has on financial performance. In a similar way, Rodriguez-Fernandez (2016) notes that social policies increment financial resources, and vice versa, that increased financial performances lead to greater social benefits which will encourage all board members to weigh investing financial resources in developing social policies. In the same line of thinking, Zubeltzu-Jaka et al. (2018) conclude that a promotion of governance recommendations has positive effects on firms' CSR activities and firms which integrate CSR practices will improve their corporate performance.

Employing a sample of large American and European companies, Sahut et al., (2018) study the link between governance, corporate social responsibility (CSR) and financial performance. The findings indicate that governance and some financial variables are prerequisites for CSR. Corporate governance is a determining factor of CSR. Furthermore, Sahut et al. (2018) underline that CSR practices have an impact on financial performance, but there is a dual impact, direct and indirect, of governance on financial performance. In a nutshell, the more a company has strong governance practices, the more the company apply CSR practices, the more the company gains in performance.

In this chapter, we address this question with the idea that not only corporate governance mechanisms are not a bloc and their potential effects are different, but we also consider the moderating effect of governance index on the firm performance effect. We globally extend the literature results by putting in evidence that CG mechanisms and firm performance are key determinants of CSR performance depending on their different types and interactions between them and that the links between governance and CSR are crucial for sustainable development.

DATA AND METHODOLOGY

The data for the study consists of a firm level panel data set of 99 companies listed in the stock exchanges of France. The observations were collected from annual reports of a large and extensive sample of French firms. We also used the Data Stream database for accounting and financial information. Missing reports are downloaded from company websites. In addition, for the collection of social data, we referred to special reports: sustainable development, environmental and social responsibility reports. The operationalization of CSR refers to the international standard ISO 26000, "Corporate Social Responsibility Guidelines". This standard identifies seven central issues: governance, human rights, labor relations and conditions, the environment, fair practices, consumer issues, societal engagement.

The analysis grid used includes the different items and sub-items as determined by the standard, to understand the concept of CSR. Each item corresponds to one aspect of CSR and each sub-item represents a societal action defined by ISO 26000. If the company has published in its sustainable development report, information describing that it has carried out this action, we will give it the value of "1". If no, it is given the value "0". Thus, the CSR score corresponds to the sum of the alternative responses of the social action divided by the number of sub-items (for more details see Appendix 1). On the other hand, the governance variable is expressed by an index, called "Corporate Governance Score" and provided by the Thomson Reuters-ASSET 4 database. This index brings together a number of governance mechanisms:

- The characteristics (composition / structure) of the board of directors
- The ownership structure
- Stakeholder relations and rights
- Financial transparency and disclosure of information

The governance index gives each company a score for each of the criteria of the index that the company meets reported to the total number of criteria.

Several motivations are behind our action research. First, corporate social responsibility emerges as an important issue revealing from the objectives of durable development. In this sense, several researchers argue that financial performance and corporate governance could determine the firm's aptitude to respect the seven CSR principal questions according to the ISO 26000 as mentioned below:

- Governance of the organization (including compliance, transparency, accountability and stakeholder engagement),
- Human rights

Table 2. Variables, indications and measurements

Variable	Indication	Measurement
Corporate Social Responsibility	CSR	The CSR score corresponds to the sum of the alternative responses of the social action divided by the number of sub-items.
Return on Equity	ROE	Return on equity (ROE) is a measure of financial performance calculated by dividing net income by shareholders' equity.
Governance Scope	GOV	Governance score provided by the Thomson Reuters-ASSET 4 database.
Administrator Expertise	EXPERT	A dummy variable indicating if the administrator is an expert in board management.
Independence of	INDEP. *Administrator*	Percentage of independent administrators on the board of directors
	INST. *Administrator*	Percentage of institutional administrators on the board of directors.
	SIZE	Natural logarithm of total assets.
Mandate	MANDATE	A dummy variable indicating if the administrator has got a mandate in the board of directors the last year.

Source: Authors' development

- Working conditions and relationships
- The environment
- Good business practices (including the fight against corruption)
- Consumer issues
- Societal commitment

Moreover, corporate governance mechanisms have the potential to carry out structural changes, modify some aspects of the firm social commitment strategy. At last and not at least, the relationship between firm performance, corporate governance mechanisms and social responsibility is not a clearly understood notion by both academia and the media. Despite the well documented amount of research, only a small number of academic researchers have investigated this relationship and preciously in France. This chapter is supposed to shed more light on this topic in France and evaluate determinants of the ISO 26000 implementation. The table below presents variables used in our regression.

THE STUDY FINDINGS

In this study, the relationship between corporate governance, firm performance and corporate social responsibility is viewed and analyzed from the equilibrium model approach (e.g. Albuquerque et al., 2018). The main purpose of this study is to examine the impact of firm performance and certain internal corporate governance mechanisms on corporate social responsibility rating according to the ISO 26000. We approximate firm performance (FP) through the return on equity ratio (ROE) while we approximate corporate governance mechanisms through a set of variables that measure the governance scope, the existence of independent or institutional administrators, their expertise and if they got a previous mandate. Finally, we introduce the measure of the firm size as a control variable.

Table 3. Summary statistics for all variables

Variable	Obs.	Mean	Std. Dev.	Min	Max
CSR	99	0.932966	0.0529901	0.6590909	1
INDEP. *Administrator*	99	0.5199747	0.1485251	0.125	0.8
INST. *Administrator*	99	0.3417603	0.1784113	0	0.86
SIZE	99	9.937837	1.064239	7.720462	12.27759
ROE	99	0.1624175	0.5103706	-0.2515883	5.126214
GOV	99	69.82515	18.17594	26.76	97.26
EXPERT	Proportion	Std. Err.	[95% Conf. Interval]	EXPERT	Proportion
0	0.4444444	0.0501949	0.3448343	0	0.4444444
1	0.5555556	0.0501949	0.4559454	1	0.5555556

Source: Authors' calculations

The relationship between CG, FP and CSR in this study is viewed and analyzed from the equilibrium model approach (Fika, 2013; Taoukif, 2015; Frimousse and Peretti, 2015, Noronha 2013; Wang, 2017, bouaziz and Jarboui, 2019). The main purpose of this chapter is to examine the impact of firm performance and certain internal CG mechanisms on CSR rating. In order to assess this relationship, the following model can be written as:

$$CSR = f\ (FP, CGV, CV) \tag{1}$$

where corporate social responsibility (CSR) is a function of firm performance (FP), corporate governance variables (CGV) and other control variables (CV) supposed to be related to CSR.

For a panel regression model, Model (1) can be written as:

$$CSR\ it = \alpha_0 + \beta\ i\ FP\ it + \lambda\ i\ CGV\ it + \varepsilon\ it \tag{2}$$

where i is the cross-section dimension (i =1,...n), t is time dimension (1,...8), y is the dependent variable (CSR) for firm i and period t, FP is a the firm performance, CGV it correspond to the mechanisms of governance, β and λ are coefficients to be estimated and ε it is the error term. The parameters of the empirical model are estimated using Ordinary Least Squares (OLS) regression (also employed by Lee and Cho, 2016; Elkelish and Hassan, 2015; Al, Pesqueux, 2018; Tahri and El Khamlichi, 2019 and Jarboui and Bouaziz, 2019).

Our analysis of data begins with descriptive statistics of all the dependent and independent variables employed in the study in order to judge the spread and trend of the data employed. The table 3 below presents statistics and proportions for all variables. To be more precise, the table reports the number of observations, mean, standard deviation, minimum and maximum values for continuous variables and proportions for binary ones.

An overview of the table 3 clearly depicts a significant social responsibility of French firms with a mean value of 0.93. Thus, it varies from minimum value of 0.65 to a maximum value of 1. This observation reflects the high social commitment of those firms. Concerning the index of governance, we notice that on average 69.82 varying from 26.76 to 97.26. These values reflect the wide range distribution of firm's index and consequently the diversity of our sample. We also can easily observe the significant presence of institutional administrator (34.17%) and independent administrators (51.99%) in the structure of the board of directors. On the other hand, the firm performance measured by ROE is on average low (16.24%) with a high standard deviation reflecting that the values are spread out over a wider range of values. This suggest that firms are differently distributed in terms of performance varying from a negative ROE (-0.25) to a positive one (5.12). This diversity allows us to analyze the association between firm performance and its social commitment.

Before an OLS regression, some diagnostic tests such as test for multicollinearity and autocorrelation are initially performed (see Tables 4 and 5). The correlation coefficient measures the strength and direction of a linear relationship between two variables. All coefficients are under 0.5 suggesting a moderate downhill (positive or negative) relationship between couple of variables. On the other hand, we run the collinearity test implying that two variables are near perfect linear combinations of one another. In fact, when more than two variables are correlated it is often called multicollinearity, although the two terms are often substitutable. In our empirical research, we use the STATA command VIF after the regression to check for multicollinearity. VIF stands for variance inflation factor. As a rule of thumb, when VIF values of variable are greater than 10, further investigation merit to be applied. Tolerance, defined as 1/VIF, is also used by to check on the colinearity degree. Tolerance values are superior than 0.1 and VIF are lower to 10 suggesting that variables can' be considered as a linear combination of other independent variables.

Under those results for both tests (see tables 4 and 5) we apply the OLS regression. Table 6 reports the OLS estimation results of the general models developed for each CSR firm based on firm performance (FP), corporate governance mechanisms (CG) and interaction between both factors.

From the regression outputs it may be concluded that the model explain 21, 69% of the CRS variation through the variation of some CG mechanisms, financial performance measure and control variables. The Wald Test Statistics reveal a Chi-square ($\chi2$) distribution significant beyond 1% level rejecting the null hypothesis that all the exogenous variables are equal to zero. Moreover, this result indicates that the explanatory power of FP firm performance in combination with CG mechanisms and control variables are significant in terms of elucidating the variation in CSR. Table 6 reveals that of the 6 variables tested, four variables emerge statistically different from zero (ROE, GOV*ROE, INDEP. Administrator, INST. Administrator, MANDATE).

We globally prove that the development of sustainable finance is a crucial issue for the promotion of responsible social criteria and that institutional board member would be interested in CSR investing to build a good reputation, potentially to the detriment of independent ones, while reinforcing the overconfidence of the citizens. It seems that the implementation of the CSR concept is of great importance for institutional administrators to the extent that this task was included as an independent function known as Corporate Social Responsibility Administrator.

The results show that the FP variable ROE has positive and significant relationship with CSR (0.405247 at 1%) endorsing that performing firms are interested in respecting their social commitments, consistent with the findings by (Sabbaghi and Xu, 2013; Dewi et al., 2014 and Resmi, 2018). This result is very important since it has implications for decision makers on a strategic plan. Thus, to enhance social welfare, governments are supposed to promulgate investment incentives improving firm's performance. While when, we consider the governance index as a contingency factor, GOV*ROE exhibits negative and statistically significant relationship at 1% (0.0054363). We conclude that as whole corporate governance

Table 4. Correlation matrix of Pearson

	CSR	ROE	GOV	EXPERT	INDEP. *Administrator*	INST. *Administrator*	SIZE	MANDATE
CSR	1							
ROE	-0.0863	1						
	0.3959							
GOV	-0.3096*	0.0243	1					
	0.0018	0.811						
EXPERT	0.037	-0.1	0.024	1				
	0.7162	0.3247	0.8135					
INDEP. *Administrator*	-0.2937*	-0.0655	0.2151*	-0.1014	1			
	0.0032	0.5195	0.0325	0.3178				
INST. *Administrator*	-0.0167	-0.1892	0.2971*	-0.0296	0.4790*	1		
	0.8699	0.0607	0.0028	0.7709	0			
SIZE	-0.0228	-0.0158	0.1557	-0.0002	0.2957*	0.1242	1	
	0.8231	0.8764	0.1237	0.9984	0.003	0.2207		
MANDATE	-0.2192*	0.0795	0.0887	0.0137	0.2518*	0.2488*	0.0409	1
	0.0293	0.434	0.3826	0.8929	0.0119	0.013	0.6875	

***, **, * denotes statistical significance at the 1%, 5% and 10% levels, respectively

Source: Authors' calculations

mechanisms reduce the improving effect of firm performance on CSR. This result is in line with other CG related studies by Barnea and Rubin (2010), Chang and Martynov (2011), Harjoto and Jo (2011) and Muttakin and Siddiqui (2013).

In order to be more precise, we choose to analyze the separate effect of different corporate governance mechanisms and we find that board size, duality of function for administrators, managerial propriety, quality of external audit and institutional have no impact on firm's CSR. In fact, we do find significant impact only for MANDATE, INDEP. Administrator and INST. Administrator. On the literature level, our finding is in line with the strategic current (Andrews, 1971) who postulates a strong impact of managers on CSR whereas the neo-institutional and ecological theories (Hannan and Freeman, 1977, DiMaggio

Table 5. Variance inflation factors and tolerance

Variable	VIF	1/VIF
INDEP. *Administrator*	1.45	0.68751
INST. *Administrator*	1.38	0.723163
MANDATE	1.12	0.89616
SIZE	1.1	0.910111
ROE	1.07	0.935269
EXPERT	1.03	0.974485
Mean VIF	1.19	

Source: Authors' calculations

Table 6. Regression results with firm CSR for French firms

	Coef.	Std. Err.	Statistic value	P-value	[95% Conf. Interval]
ROE	0.405247***	0.1419257	2.86	0.005	0.1233702 0.6871237
GOV*ROE	-0.0054363***	0.0018593	-2.92	0.004	-0.0091289 -0.0017437
EXPERT	0.0021098	0.0100994	0.21	0.835	-0.0179484 0.0221681
INDEP. *Administrator*	-0.1451604***	0.0398197	-3.65	0.000	-0.2242457 -0.0660751
INST. *Administrator*	0.070945**	0.0335913	2.11	0.037	0.0042298 0.1376601
SIZE	0.0062816	0.0049672	1.26	0.209	-0.0035836 0.0161468
MANDATE	.0174833*	.0104567	1.67	0.098	.0382541 .0032876
cons.	0.9176495***	0.0491413	18.67	0.000	0.8200506 1.015248
R-squared	0.2169				
Test of the nullity of the parameters	3.60*** (0.001)				

***, **, * denotes statistical significance at the 1%, 5% and 10% levels, respectively
Source: Authors' calculations

and Powell, 1983) postulate the absence of a real influence. MANDATE and INST. Administrator have respectively emerged a positive and statistically significant coefficient (0.070945 and .0174833) at 1% and 5% level with CSR while INDEP. Administrator coefficient is significantly negative (-0.1451604) at 1% level. This explains the source of the negative impact of GOV index.

But, with respect to INDEP. admin, the coefficient is consistently negative and significant (-0.1451604) at 1% level. This presumes that in contrary to institutional administrator independent administrator's mentality is not one that supports the crucial role of firms in social development.

Table 6 further shows that the firm's size does not have a significant impact on firm's CSR. This result is supported by Saidi and Elabbadi, (2016), France stratégie (2018) and Pesqueux, (2018).

Finally, the relationship between CSR and CG mechanisms is found to be inconclusive globally unless we reason in terms of each mechanism. Our empirical results suggest that the firm performance and institutional administrators unlike independent administrators exhibit better CSR performance due to their awareness of the importance of social function of firms in developing society.

Our findings allow us to conclude that institutional administrators are more motivated to improve social responsibility of firms. A literature review of previous studies shows that there are several reasons for these motivations like the willingness of reducing the managerial latitude of managers and improving the reputation of financial institutions through the firm's social commitments. Further investigation on this issue should be applied in order to point out the reasons behind the real motivations of institutional to promote corporate social responsibility. The chapter concludes with the findings, practical implications and some directions for future research.

CONCLUSION AND PRACTICAL IMPLICATIONS

The prime motive of the chapter is to examine the main determinants of CSR among CG mechanisms and firm performance. We try to demystify the arena of social engagement and the widespread presence of CSR reforms. The study uses firm level panel data set of 99 companies listed in the stock exchanges of France for the period 2014-2016. Results estimated by OLS regression reveal that the firm performance emerged as a vital determinant of CSR. Our principal contribution is to investigate on the moderating effect of CG mechanisms such as institutional administrators and mandate. We highlight significant results. We consider that these facts would help academics to arrive at some important conclusions. Empirical results show find that the more the firm is performing the more there is socially committed. But, this potential impact is not absolute. In fact when we consider CG index the effect become negative on CSR suggesting the reducing effect, as a hole, of governance. But we were more precise by distinguishing between the effects of each mechanism. We prove that institutional administrators have a supporting mentality to social welfare through firm's social commitments and are more interested in improving their reputation among citizens. On the other hand, this issue is not a priority for independent administrators.

Our results are interesting since they support the positive relation from firm performance to CSR and expand our understanding of the potential determinants of CSR through the moderating effect of corporate governance mechanisms. Doing so, this chapter aims to provide academics, policymakers and practitioners with a valuable discussion on the determinants of CSR and so the social welfare. These implications are structured around three main axes.

First, in line with several previous researches, we find that performing firms are more interested in CSR. It seems that social engagement is profitable. French companies create economic value by creating social value. The more efficient is the economic fabric, the more likely it is to achieve goals in terms of human development, the well-being of the local population and the protection of nature. According to these findings, a special attention is needed to channel remittance investment towards social investments.

Second, it would be important to sensitize independent administrators about the social commitment of the firm either through an internal strategy (reputation among citizens; financial leverage effect of CSR; etc.) of motivation or governmental one through rules and financial incentives.

Last but not least, on the basis of this chapter's findings, we can validate the significant effect of close relationship with administrators through the number of mandates. We can postulate that the more the directors have links with the company and the more the feeling of belonging to the firm is developed the more there are a tendency to improve its societal reputation.

Further investigations should be applied to generalize our results and there are several ways in which this study might be extended. We propose that future researchers explore other corporate governance mechanisms on CSR and shed more lights on the moderating effect of social and political factors of the country since the literature covering this subject is quite limited at the moment.

REFERENCES

Abad, D., Lucas-Pérez, M. E., Minguez-Vera, A., & Yagüe, J. (2017). Does Gender Diversity on Corporate Boards Reduce Information Asymmetry in Equity Markets? *Business Research Quarterly*, *20*(3), 192–205. doi:10.1016/j.brq.2017.04.001

Aguilera, R., Rupp, D., Williams, C., & Ganapathi, J. (2007). Putting the S back in corporate social responsibility: A multilevel theory of social change in organizations. *Academy of Management Review, 32*(3), 836–863. doi:10.5465/amr.2007.25275678

Akben-Selcuk, E. (2019). Corporate Social Responsibility and Financial Performance: The Moderating Role of Ownership Concentration in Turkey. *Sustainability, 11*(13), 1–10. doi:10.3390u11133643

Albuquerque, R., Koskinen, Y., & Zhang, C. (2018). Corporate Social Responsibility and Firm Risk: Theory and Empirical Evidence. *Management Science, 65*(10), 4451–4949. doi:10.1287/mnsc.2018.3043

Alexander, G. J., & Buchholtz, R. A. (1978). Corporate Social Responsibility and Stock Market Performance. *Academy of Management Journal, 21*(3), 479–486.

Allouche, J., & Laroche, P. (2005). A meta-analytical investigation of the relationship between corporate social and financial performance. *Revue de Gestion des Ressources Humaines, 57*, 18–41.

Alotaibi, A., Edum-Fotwe, F., & Price, A. D. F. (2019). Critical Barriers to Social Responsibility Implementation within Mega-Construction Projects: The Case of the Kingdom of Saudi Arabia. *Sustainability, 11*(6), 1755. doi:10.3390u11061755

Ameer, R., & Othman, R. (2012). Sustainability practices and corporate financial performance: A study based on the top global corporations. *Journal of Business Ethics, 108*(1), 61–79. doi:10.100710551-011-1063-y

Amores-Salvadó, J., Martín-de Castro, G., & Navas-López, J. E. (2014). Green corporate image: Moderating the connection between environmental product innovation and firm performance. *Journal of Cleaner Production, 83*(15), 356–365. doi:10.1016/j.jclepro.2014.07.059

Andrews, K. R. (1971). *The concept of corporate strategy*. Homewood, IL: Irwin.

Ansari, S., Wijen, F., & Gray, B. (2013). Constructing a climate change logic: An institutional perspective on the Tragedy of the commons. *Organization Science, 24*(4), 1014–1040. doi:10.1287/orsc.1120.0799

Arora, P., & Dharwadkar, R. (2011). Corporate governance and corporate social responsibility (CSR): The moderating roles of attainment discrepancy and organization slack. *Corporate Governance, 19*(2), 136–152. doi:10.1111/j.1467-8683.2010.00843.x

Artiach, T., Lee, D., Nelson, D., & Walker, J. (2010). The determinants of corporate sustainability performance. *Accounting and Finance, 50*(1), 31–51. doi:10.1111/j.1467-629X.2009.00315.x

Aupperle, K. E., Caroll, A. B., & Hatfield, J. D. (1985). An Empirical Examination of The Relationship Between Corporate Social Responsibility and Profitability. *Academy of Management Journal, 28*(2), 446–463.

Baird, Ph., Geylani, P., & Roberts, J. (2012). Corporate Social and Financial Performance Re-Examined: Industry Effects in a Linear Mixed Model Analysis. *Journal of Business Ethics, 109*(3), 367–388. doi:10.100710551-011-1135-z

Banker, R. D., Chang, H., & Majumdar, S. K. (1996). A Framework for Analyzing Changes in Strategic Performance. *Strategic Management Journal, 17*(9), 693–712. doi:10.1002/(SICI)1097-0266(199611)17:9<693::AID-SMJ847>3.0.CO;2-W

Barnea, A., & Rubin, A. (2010). Corporate Social Responsibility as a Conflict Between Shareholders. *Journal of Business Ethics, 97*(1), 71–86. doi:10.100710551-010-0496-z

Belkaoui, A. (1976). The Impact of the disclosure of the environmental effects of oragnizational behavior on the market. *Financial Management, 5*(Winter), 26–30. doi:10.2307/3665454

Bénabou, R., & Tirole, J. (2010). Individual and corporate social responsibility. *Economica, 77*(305), 1–19. doi:10.1111/j.1468-0335.2009.00843.x

Bonnet, C., Seville, M & Wirtz, P. (2017). Genèse et fonctionnement du conseil d'administration d'une firme entrepreneuriale: le rôle des identifications sociales des administrateurs. *Finance Contrôle Stratégie, 20*(3).

Broadstock, D. C., Matousek, R., Meyer, M., & Tzeremes, N. G. (2019). Does corporate social responsibility impact firms' innovation capacity? The indirect link between environmental & social governance implementation and innovation performance. *Journal of Business Research.* doi:10.1016/j.jbusres.2019.07.014

Brown, D. L., Vetterlein, A., & Roemer-Mahler, A. (2010). Theorizing transnational corporations as social actors: An analysis of corporate motivations. *Business and Politics, 12*(1), 1–37. doi:10.2202/1469-3569.1302

Cavaco, S., Crifo, P., Reberioux, R. & Roudaut, G. (2014). Independent directors: less informed, but better selected? New evidence from a two-way director-firm fixed effect model. *Cahier, 29.*

Cho, S. J., Chung, C. Y., & Young, J. (2019). Study on the relationship between CSR and financial performance. *Sustainability, 11*(2), 343. doi:10.3390u11020343

Chuang, S. P., & Huang, S. J. (2018). The Effect of Environmental Corporate Social Responsibility on Environmental Performance and Business Competitiveness: The Mediation of Green Information Technology Capital. *Journal of Business Ethics, 150*(4), 991–1009. doi:10.100710551-016-3167-x

Crifo, P. & Rebérioux, A. (2015). Gouvernance et responsabilité sociétale des entreprises: nouvelle frontière de la finance durable ? *Revue d'économie financière*, (117), 205-223.

Dahlsrud, A. (2008). How Corporate Social Responsibility Is Defined: An Analysis of 37 Definitions. *Corporate Social Responsibility and Environmental Management, 15*(1), 1–13. doi:10.1002/csr.132

Dardour, A. & Husser, J. (2016). Does It Pay to Disclose CSR Information? Evidence from French Companies. *Management international, 20*, 94-108.

Dewi, D.M., & Sudarma, M., Djumahir, & Ganis, E. (2014). CSR Effect on Market and Financial Performance. *International Journal of Business and Management Invention, 3*(1), 56–66.

Dimaggio, P. J., & Powell, W. W. (1983). The Iron Cage Revisited: Institutional Isomorphism and Collective Rationality in Organizational Fields. *American Sociological Review, 48*(2), 147–160. doi:10.2307/2095101

ElKelish, W. W., & Hassan, K. M. (2015). Corporate governance disclosure and share price accuracy: Empirical evidence from the United Arab Emirates. *Journal of Applied Accounting Research, 16*(2), 265–286. doi:10.1108/JAAR-02-2013-0015

EU. (2001). Promoting a European framework for corporate social responsibility. *Commission of the European Communities.*

European Commission. (2011). Communication from the Commission to the European Parliament, the Council, the European Economic and Social Committee and the Committee of the Regions.

Fauzi, H., & Idris, K. (2009). The Relationship of CSR and Financial Performance: New Evidence from Indonesian Companies (October 18, 2010). *Issues in Social and Environmental Accounting*, *3*(1). Retrieved from https://ssrn.com/abstract=1694284

Galant, A., & Cadez, S. (2017). Corporate social responsibility and financial performance relationship: A review of measurement approaches. *Economic Research-Ekonomska Istraživanja, 30*(1), 676–693. doi:10.1080/1331677X.2017.1313122

Giannarakis, G. (2014). Corporate governance and financial characteristic effects on the extent of corporate social responsibility disclosure. *Social Responsibility Journal, 10*(4), 569–590. doi:10.1108/SRJ-02-2013-0008

Gillan, S., Hartzell, J. C., Koch, A., & Starks, L. T. (2010). Firms' environmental, social and governance (ESG) choices, performance and managerial motivation. Retrieved from http://www.business.pitt.edu/faculty/papers/koch 3. pdf

Gomes, A., & Novaes, W. (2001). Sharing of Control as a Corporate Governance Mechanism. *PIER*, *29*(1), 01-12.

Graafland, J., & Noorderheaven, N. (2019). Technological Competition, Innovation Motive and Corporate Social Responsibility: Evidence from Top Managers of European SMEs. *De Economist*, 1–22. doi:10.100710645-019-09351-z

Guinness, M., & Hogan, T. (2014). Bank credit and trade credit: Evidence from SMEs over the financial crisis. *International Small Business Journal, 34*(4).

Hambrick, D. C., & Finkelstein, S. (1987). Managerial discretion: A bridge between polar views of organizational outcomes. *Research in Organizational Behavior*, *9*, 369–406.

Hannan, M., & Freeman, J. (1977). The Population Ecology of Public Organizations. *American Journal of Sociology*, *82*(5), 929–964. doi:10.1086/226424

Harjoto, M. A., & Jo, H. (2011). Corporate governance and CSR nexus. *Journal of Business Ethics*, *100*(1), 45–67. doi:10.100710551-011-0772-6

Hillman, A., & Kleim, G. (2001). Shareholder stakeholder value management and social issues what's the bottom line. *Strategic Management Journal*, *22*(2), 125–139. doi:10.1002/1097-0266(200101)22:2<125::AID-SMJ150>3.0.CO;2-H

Iwata, H. & Okada, K. (2010). How does environmental performance affect financial performance? Evidence from Japanese manufacturing firms. *MPRA*.

Jain, T. & Jamali, D. (2016). Looking Inside the Black Box: The effect of Corporate Governance on Corporate Social Responsibility. *Review of corporate governance*, *24*(3), 253–273

Jarboui, A. & Bouaziz, S. (2019). The moderating effect of audit quality on the relation between shareholder activism and earnings management: Evidence from France. *Contemporary economics*, *13*(1), 63-78.

Jizi, M., Salama, A., Dixon, A., & Stratling, R. (2014). Corporate governance and corporate social responsibility disclosure: Evidence from the US banking sector. *Journal of Business Ethics*, *125*(4), 601–615. doi:10.100710551-013-1929-2

Jo, H., & Harjoto, M. A. (2011). Corporate Governance and Firm Value: The Impact of Corporate Social Responsibility. *Journal of Business Ethics*, *103*(3), 351–383. doi:10.100710551-011-0869-y

Jo, H., & Harjoto, M. A. (2012). The causal effect of corporate governance on corporate social responsibility. *Journal of Business Ethics*, *106*(1), 53–72. doi:10.100710551-011-1052-1

Johns, R., & Khojastehpour, M. (2014). CSR Reasons, Practices and Impact to Corporate Reputation. *Social and Behavioral Sciences*, *213*, 503–508.

Johnson, R. A., & Greening, W. D. (1999). The Effect of Corporate Governance and Institutional Ownership Types on Corporate Social Performance. *Academy of Management Journal*, *42*(5), 564–576.

Karagiorgos, Th. (2010). Corporate Social Responsibility and Financial Performance: An Empirical Analysis on Greek Companies. *European Research Studies Journal*, *04*(4), 85–108. doi:10.35808/ersj/301

Karyawati, P. G., Subroto, B., Sutrisno, T., & Saraswati, E. (2018). The Complexity of Relationship between Corporate Social Responsibility (CSR) and Financial Performance. *Emerging Markets Journal*, *8*(2), 2018. doi:10.5195/emaj.2018.155

Kedia, B. L., & Kuntz, E. C. (1981). The context of social performance: an empirical study of Texas Banks. In P. Lee (Ed.), Research in Corporate Social Performance and Policy (Vol. 3, pp. 133-154). Greenwich, CT: JAI Press.

Khan, A., Muttakin, M. B., & Siddiqui, J. (2013). Corporate Governance and Corporate Social Responsibility Disclosures: Evidence from an Emerging Economy. *Journal of Business Ethics*, *114*(2), 207–223. doi:10.100710551-012-1336-0

Kooskora, M., Juottonen, M., & Cundiff, K. (2019). The Relationship Between Corporate Social Responsibility and Financial Performance (A Case Study from Finland). *Social Responsibility and Sustainability*, 471–491. doi:10.1007/978-3-030-03562-4_25

Krüger, C. (2010). Corporate social responsibility and the board of directors.

Lau, C. H., & Lu, Y. (2014). Corporate Social Responsibility in China: A Corporate Governance Approach. *Journal of Business Ethics*, *125*(4), 207–221.

Liao, L., Lin, T. P., & Zhang, Y. (2016). Corporate board and corporate social responsibility assurance: Evidence from China. *Journal of Business Ethics*, *150*(1), 211–225. doi:10.100710551-016-3176-9

Lopez, M. V., Garcia, A., & Rodriguez, L. (2007). Sustainable development and corporate performance: A study based on the Dow Jones sustainability index. *Journal of Business Ethics*, *75*(3), 285–300. doi:10.100710551-006-9253-8

Lu, W. M., Wang, W. K., & Lee, H. L. (2013). The relationship between corporate social responsibility and corporate performance: Evidence from the US semiconductor industry. *International Journal of Production Research*, *51*(19), 5683–5695. doi:10.1080/00207543.2013.776186

Makni, R., Francoeur, C., & Bellavance, F. (2009). Causality between corporate social performance and financial performance: Evidence from Canadian firms. *Journal of Business Ethics*, *89*(3), 409–422. doi:10.100710551-008-0007-7

Maqbool, S., & Zameer, M. N. (2017). An Empirical Examination of the Relationship between Corporate Social Responsibility and Profitability: Evidence from Indian Commercial Banks. *Pacific Business Review International*, *9*(12), 39–47.

Maqbool, S., & Zameer, M. N. (2018). Corporate social responsibility and financial performance: An empirical analysis of Indian banks. *Future Business Journal*, *4*(1), 84–93. doi:10.1016/j.fbj.2017.12.002

Margolis, J. D., Elfenbein, H. A., & Walsh, J. P. (2009). Does It Pay to Be Good and Does It Matter? A Meta-Analysis of the Relationship between Corporate Social and Financial Performance.

McGuire, J. B., Sundgren, A., & Schneeweis, T. (1988). Corporate social responsibility and firm financial performance. *Academy of Management Journal*, *31*(4), 854–872.

McWilliams, A., & Siegel, D. (2000). Corporate social responsibility and financial performance: Correlation or misspecification? *Strategic Management Journal*, *21*(5), 603–609. doi:10.1002/(SICI)1097-0266(200005)21:5<603::AID-SMJ101>3.0.CO;2-3

Moore, M. (2019). CSR & Company Financial Performance (April 25, 2019). Retrieved from https://ssrn.com/abstract=3377842

Muttakin, M. B., Khan, A., & Azim, M. I. (2015). Corporate social responsibility disclosures and earnings quality. Are they a reflection of managers' opportunistic behavior. *Managerial Auditing Journal*, *30*(3), 277–298. doi:10.1108/MAJ-02-2014-0997

Nelling, E., & Webb, E. (2009). Corporate social responsibility and financial performance: The "virtuous circle" revisited. *Review of Quantitative Finance and Accounting*, *32*(2), 197–209. doi:10.100711156-008-0090-y

Noronha, C., Tou, S., Cynthia, M. I., & Guan, J. (2013). Corporate Social Responsibility Reporting in China: An Overview and Comparison with Major Trends. *Corporate Social Responsibility and Environmental Management*, *1*(1), 29–42. doi:10.1002/csr.1276

Oh, W. Y., Chang, Y. K., & Martynov, A. (2011). The effect of ownership structure on corporate social responsibility: Empirical evidence from Korea. *Journal of Business Ethics*, *104*(2), 283–297. doi:10.100710551-011-0912-z

Orlitzky, M., Frank, L., Schmidt, F. L., Sara, L., & Rynes, S. L. (2003). Corporate social and financial performance: A meta-analysis. *Organization Studies*, *24*(3), 403–441. doi:10.1177/0170840603024003910

Peng, C.-W., & Yang, M.-L. (2013). The Effect of Corporate Social Performance on Financial Performance: The Moderating Effect of Ownership Concentration. *Journal of Business Ethics*, *123*(1), 171–182. doi:10.100710551-013-1809-9

Portney, P. R. (2008). The (Not So) New Corporate Social Responsibility: An Empirical Perspective. *Review of Environmental Economics and Policy*, *2*(2), 261–275. doi:10.1093/reep/ren003

Rashid, A., & Rehman, Z. (2015). Analyzing Performance of Banks in Pakistan: Conventional versus Islamic Banks. *Journal of Islamic Business and Management*, *5*(2), 17–42. doi:10.12816/0026416

Rees, W., & Rodionova, T. (2014). The influence of family ownership on corporate social responsibility: An international analysis of publicly listed companies. *Corporate Governance*, *23*(3), 184–202. doi:10.1111/corg.12086

Resmi, S. I., Begum, N. N., & Hassan, M. M. (2018). Impact of CSR on Firm's Financial Performance: A Study on Some Selected Agribusiness Industries of Bangladesh. *American Journal of Economics. Financial Management*, *4*(3), 74–85.

Rhou, Y., Singal, M., & Koh, Y. (2016). CSR and Financial Performance: The Role of CSR Awareness in the Restaurant Industry. *International Journal of Hospitality Management*, *57*(1), 30–39. doi:10.1016/j.ijhm.2016.05.007

Rodgers, W., Choy, H. L., & Guiral, A. (2013). Do Investors Value a Firm's Commitment to Social Activities? *Journal of Business Ethics, 114*(4), 607-623. 10.100710551-013-1707-1

Rodriguez-Fernandez, M. (2016). Social responsibility and financial performance: The role of good corporate governance. *BRQ Business Research Quarterly*, *19*(2), 137–151. doi:10.1016/j.brq.2015.08.001

Sabbaghi, O., & Xu, M. (2013). ROE and Corporate Social Responsibility: Is There a Return On Ethics? *Journal of Accounting and Finance*, *13*(4), 82–95.

Sahut, J. M., Mili, M., & Teulon, F. (2018). Gouvernance, RSE et performance financière: Vers une compréhension globale de leurs relations? *Management & Avenir*, *101*(3), 39. doi:10.3917/mav.101.0039

Saidi, C., & Elabbadi, B. (2016). CSR as a dimension of perceived quality: A model of societal determinants of perceived quality to predict customer satisfaction in the context of commercial and industrial utilities. *International Journal of Innovation and Applied Studies*, *17*(3), 838–851.

Scholtens, B., & Kang, F. C. (2013). Corporate Social Responsibility and Earnings Management: Evidence from Asian Economies. *Corporate Social Responsibility and Environmental Management*, *20*(2), 95–112. doi:10.1002/csr.1286

Shahab, Y., & Ye, C. (2018). Corporate social responsibility disclosure and corporate governance: Empirical insights on neo-institutional framework from China. *International Journal of Disclosure and Governance*, 1–17.

Shen, C. H., & Chang, Y. (2009). Ambition versus conscience, does corporate social responsibility pay off? The application of matching methods. *Journal of Business Ethics*, *88*(S1), 133–153. doi:10.100710551-008-9826-9

Simpson, W. G., & Kohers, T. (2002). The link between corporate social and financial performance: Evidence from the banking industry. *Journal of Business Ethics*, *35*(2), 97–109. doi:10.1023/A:1013082525900

Soana, M.-G. (2011). The Relationship Between Corporate Social Performance and Corporate Financial Performance in the Banking Sector. *Journal of Business Ethics*, *104*(1), 133–148. doi:10.100710551-011-0894-x

Tahri, W. & El khamlichi, A. (2019). Disclosure and Communication of the Corporate Social Responsibility (CSR) in Morocco: The Case of a Bank. In *ICT for a Better Life and a Better World* (pp. 247-261). Springer Nature.

Van Marrewijk, M. (2013). Concepts and definitions of CSR and corporate sustainability: between agency and communion. *Journal of Business Ethics*, 641–655.

Vance, S. C. (1975). Are socially responsible corporations good investment risks? *Management Review*, *64*, 18–24.

Waddock, S. A., & Graves, B. (1997). The corporate social performance-financial performance link'. *Strategic Management Journal*, *18*(4), 303–319. doi:10.1002/(SICI)1097-0266(199704)18:4<303::AID-SMJ869>3.0.CO;2-G

Wei, Z., Shen, Zhou, H. & Li, J.J. (2017). How does environmental corporate social responsibility matter in a dysfunctional institutional environment? Evidence from China. *Journal of Business Ethics*, *140*(2), 209-223.

Wu, W., Liu, Y., Chin, T., & Zhu, W. (2018). Will Green CSR Enhance Innovation? A Perspective of Public Visibility and Firm Transparency. *International Journal of Environmental Research and Public Health*, *15*(2), 268. doi:10.3390/ijerph15020268 PMID:29401714

Zubeltzu-Jaka, E., Andicoechea-Arondo, L., & Alvarez Etxeberria, I. (2018). Corporate social responsibility and corporate governance and corporate financial performance: Bridging concepts for a more ethical business model. *Business Strategy & Development*, *1*(3), 214–222. doi:10.1002/bsd2.29

KEY TERMS AND DEFINITIONS

Corporate Governance (CG): The organization of the control and management of the company. Corporate governance is one of the essential means of reducing agency costs resulting from the relationship between shareholders and managers.

Corporate Social Responsibility (CSR): CSR encompasses all the practices put in place by a firm in order to uphold the principles of sustainable development which implies that the firm needs to be economically viable, have a positive impact on society, and preserve the environment.

Correlation coefficient: A statistical measure that calculates the strength of the relationship between two variables.

Financial Performance (FP): A measure of a firm's profitability position at any given period. FP can be measured through various financial indicators. The most commonly used metrics are ROA (Retun on Assets) and ROE (Return on Equity).

Multi-colinearity: The existence of a perfect linear relationship between two or more explanatory variables of the model. It usually occurs when there is little variation in the variables within the sample.

ENDNOTES

1 AFD is The French Development Agency (in French, Agence Française de Développement).

2 This link can be explained in several ways; the financial benefits from investing in CSR outweigh the costs (McGuire et al., 1988), investing in CSR can generate positive financial benefits from better stakeholder management or firms that invest in CSR have more resources (Waddock and Graves, 1997).

3 Not in an emerging economy like Khan et al. (2013) or Meng Substitutability et al. (2013).

APPENDIX 1

ISO (the International Organization for Standardization) is a worldwide federation of national standards bodies (ISO member bodies). The work of preparing International Standards is normally carried out through ISO technical committees. Each member body interested in a subject for which a technical committee has been established has the right to be represented on that committee. International organizations, governmental and non-governmental, in liaison with ISO, also take part in the work. ISO collaborates closely with the International Electro-technical Commission (IEC) on all matters of electro-technical standardization.

Table 7. ISO 26000 outline

Clause title	Clause number	Description of clause contents
Scope	Clause 1	Defines the scope of this International Standard and identifies certain limitations and exclusions.
Terms and definitions	Clause 2	Identifies and provides the definition of key terms that are of fundamental importance for understanding social responsibility and for using this International Standard.
Understanding social responsibility	Clause 3	Describes the important factors and conditions that have influenced the development of social responsibility and that continue to affect its nature and practice. It also describes the concept of social responsibility itself - what it means and how it applies to organizations. The clause includes guidance for small and medium-sized organizations on the use of this International Standard.
Principles of social responsibility	Clause 4	Introduces and explains the principles of social responsibility.
Recognizing social responsibility and engaging stakeholders	Clause 5	Addresses two practices of social responsibility: an organization's recognition of its social responsibility, and its identification of and engagement with its stakeholders. It provides guidance on the relationship between an organization, its stakeholders and society, on recognizing the core subjects and issues of social responsibility and on an organization's sphere of influence.
Guidance on social responsibility core subjects	Clause 6	Explains the core subjects and associated issues relating to social responsibility. For each core subject, information has been provided on its scope, its relationship to social responsibility, related principles and considerations, and related actions and expectations.
Guidance on integrating social responsibility throughout an organization	Clause 7	Provides guidance on putting social responsibility into practice in an organization. This includes guidance related to: understanding the social responsibility of an organization, integrating social responsibility throughout an organization, communication related to social responsibility, improving the credibility of an organization regarding social responsibility, reviewing progress and improving performance and evaluating voluntary initiatives for social responsibility.

Figure 1. Schematic overview of the steps to take by an organization in an ISO 26000 approach
Source: www.iso.org

Chapter 15
The Relationship Between CSR, Corporate Governance, and Firm Performance:
Evidence From Moroccan Listed Firms

Souhaila Kammoun
IHEC, CODECI, University of Sfax, Tunisia

Sahar Loukil
University of Sfax, Tunisia

Youssra Ben Romdhane
University of Sfax, Tunisia

Abdelmajid Ibenrissoul
ENCG, University Hassen II, Casablanca, Morocco

ABSTRACT

Research has been conducted to extend our understanding of CSR by revealing CG mechanism antecedent effects on firm social engagements. In spite of this, few studies aimed to understand the impact of the performance of those mechanisms on CSR. To our knowledge, our study is the first to measure CG performance and its role in the expansion of CSR in an emerging country. We also analyze some component of firm performance that could potentially affect a firm's social commitment. Using a data survey questionnaire consisting of 37 items assessing CSR engagement measured by a self- constructed index and firm level data of 76 listed Moroccan firms, empirical results underline the impact of corporate governance performance and firm's performance on CSR. These results suggest that governance mechanism performance and firm performance are principal drivers of CSR particularly for big business. Debts have shown a reducing effect. Thus, our study of CSR commitment index allows for a clearer and more robust assessment of CG on Moroccan firm CSR activities.

DOI: 10.4018/978-1-7998-2128-1.ch015

INTRODUCTION

Corporate Social Responsibility (CSR) has generated great interest for many practitioners and researchers in the last two or three decades and has become a widespread movement in both developed and developing countries. Undoubtedly, there is a large body of theoretical and empirical research on the topic, especially now that the term of CSR has expanded to entail social, environmental and economic interests at both macro and micro levels (Rok, 2019).

From a theoretical standpoint, we have witnessed a growing interest in this area and various definitions for CSR have been proposed. Some sociologists speak of an elastic concept and thus by nature is easy to transpose in different intellectual, social or institutional contexts and therefore easy to disseminate in all developed countries. The OECD sees that CSR can mean different things to different groups, sectors and stakeholders and is always evolving. In this context, the study of Dahlsrud (2008) identified 37 definitions from 27 authors. According to the author, 'confusion is not so much about how CSR is defined, as about how CSR is socially constructed in a specific context'. If, there is no clear consensus on a universal definition of CSR, it should be noted that all definitions relate to how business takes into account the economic, social and environmental dimensions in the way it acts up, maximising the economic benefits and minimising the downsides. For our framework, we focus on definitions of CSR that included more description of the nature of the practice. In this line of thinking, Carroll (1979) placed CSR within a framework of corporate social performance; including four types of CSR: economic, legal, ethical and discretionary. Similarly, Drucker (1984) defined CSR as a way of tackling social problem(s) to realise positive 'economic benefit(s)' and wealth'. In 2002, the European Commission defines CSR as 'the voluntary integration by companies of social and environmental concerns into their business activities and their relations with their stakeholders'. Additionally, Jamali and Mirshak (2007) characterised CSR as a set of management practices that extend beyond the normal legal, ethical, commercial and public demands. They outlined that a firm can create economic growth and therefore should have moral duty to undertake practices which may increase both opportunity and economic growth in a fair and sustainable way. In a similar vein, Frimousse and Peretti (2017) recognised that CSR can create value by taking into account the broader conception of performance, the development of partnership between companies.

From an empirical standpoint, the notion of CSR expresses an awareness of the negative impacts that the activities of industrial companies can have on human communities and the environment (Ibenrissoul and Alami, 2016). Nowadays, a growing number of firms acknowledge the relevance of implementing CSR practices and many firms have re-branded their fundamental values to integrate social responsibility. Furthermore, several companies dedicate a part of their websites to communicate the CSR commitment (Coupland, 2005). Within the Moroccan context, listed firms started considering the social responsibility aspect in their annual reports till the end of 2006 (Tahri and El Khamlichi, 2019). Compared to unlisted firms, it is important to notice the greater interest to CSR of listed firms.

In this chapter, neither do we review the full repertoire of research on CSR literature. Rather, building on the previous theoretical and empirical underpinnings of the corporate social responsibility (CSR), we intend to discuss how governance mechanisms performance and firm's performance are principal drivers of CSR particularly for big business.

In this light, the underlying aim of this chapter is to explore key CSR practices implemented by 74 Moroccan listed firms and analyze CSR potential determinants in order to extend empirical literature on CSR levers. Therefore, the main contribution of this chapter is to advance in the knowledge about the implementation of CSR practices in Morocco examining whether governance mechanisms and firm performance underlie the CSR performance measured by a self- constructed index. In Section 2, we provide an overview of the empirical literature on CSR, governance and performance of Moroccan firms to provide the theoretical basis for the study. In Section 3, we present the data sources and some summary statistics of the variables used in our empirical work, and discuss the data and methodology issues in Section 4. Finally, we highlight the empirical results, state the main conclusions of the research, and provide some policy implications.

BACKGROUND

The Relationship Between CSR, Corporate Governance and Firm Performance

Corporate governance, firm performance and corporate social responsibility have been of great interest to researchers (Judge, Gaur, and Muller-Kahle, 2010; Sahut and Gharbi, 2011; Gantchev, Gredil and Jotikasthira, 2015; Prevost, Wongchoti and Marshall, 2016). In fact, Waddock and Graves, (1997) confirmed that the effectiveness of governance can ensure trust for resource providers and therefore the financial performance of companies. Krafft et al. (2010) noted that good governance results from the practices of control of managers by the stakeholders which impacts firm performance.

Nevertheless, if several researchers have studied the relationship between corporate governance and results management (González and García-Meca, 2014; Lin, Liu and Noronha 2016) and showed that specific governance mechanisms are associated with profit management behaviour (Bouaziz and Jarboui, 2019; Hadani, Goranova and Khan, 2011; Toumi, 2017), other researches have confirmed the hypothesis that CSR can add value to businesses in several areas such as management, marketing and property. In this context, several studies have confirmed the existence of other practices such as results management (Khanchel and Seboui, 2009) and Corporate Social Responsibility (Fika, 2013) and have found that both practices can avoid a situation of poor performance. Choi et al. (2013) emphasized that failing business management is the result of the personal goals of opportunistic managers through excessive investment in corporate social responsibility.

The inclusion of CSR in the company's objectives has become the new element for examining the performance of a modern enterprise, but the debate on CSR is still going on recently. Wang (2017) highlights the positive relationship between company performance and CSR and underlines that CSR needs to be integrated with business operations and also has a growth factor for companies as their business grows. Therefore, companies should assume more responsibility for the economic and societal environment through improving business growth, Carroll (1979). Examining the relationship between CSR and corporate governance mechanisms condition in a broad cross-section of listed companies, Rashid et al. (2017) have confirmed that CSR activities can play the role of the right marketing program to improve sales revenue and the reputation of the company. Jo and Harjoto (2011) find that after controlling for various characteristics of the firm, several governance mechanisms have a direct positive effect on CSR.

Several authors have analyzed the relationship between governance and corporate social responsibility. Rashid et al. (2017) chose the Pakistan context and found that governance in listed companies has a positive effect on CSR and has a vital role in social engagement choices. In addition, he said that better-governed companies have greater disclosure of CSR compared to smaller companies that control insider ownership. According to Wang (2006), social responsibility can increase the portfolios of listed companies. As a result, CSR is becoming a growth strategy for businesses as companies grow. Mallin and Michelon (2011) and Giannarakis (2014) confirmed that the board's commitment to CSR, corporate size and profitability has a positive effect on the extent of disclosure of corporate social responsibility but the financial leverage and disclosure of CSR are inversely related.

According to Ullman (1985), the relationship between financial performance and CSR can be based on the sector in which the firm operates (turnover) and size. From Branco and Rodrigues' point of view (2008), the size of the firm is a determining factor for both types of disclosure. He found that the financial leverage has a negative impact on the extent of the information provided on the websites and also, he asserted that the factor of exposure to the media is an important feature for the annual reports. Reverte (2009) finds that the type of sector, the size of the firm and the media coverage are the most important determinants of the extent of disclosure of CSR information. Mallin and Michelon (2011) examine whether the reputation of the board of directors (board diversity, leadership, composition, skill and structure) affects the social performance of companies. The results suggest that for firm size, most of the key concepts and tools related to CSR were developed by and in the context of large firms (OPME, 2002). Sahut et al. (2016) confirmed that size of the firm is a better determinant of CSR practices. They found that research and development costs and also operating income may indicate that CSR expenditures can be considered as intangible investments. Pae and Choi, (2011) noted that responsible governance is a very important determinant for CSR, even if this result is inconsistent with other published results according to which certain elements of governance have no effect on financial performance.

The Evolution of CSR in the Moroccan Context

Moroccan firms are also aware that CSR can add value to the country's economy by developing its attractiveness and strengthening its competitiveness, Tlemçani (2009). This socially responsible movement is mainly linked to the massive integration of large companies to the Moroccan economic fabric (Ben Abdallah and Makati, 2018). Indeed, large firms have developed several initiatives on the human, social and cultural levels and environmental policies are designed to address CSR issues and challenges (Ibenrissoul and Alami, 2016) and today, CSR has become a very important and unavoidable theme that generate interest among both companies and their stakeholders (Benraiss-Noailles and Bentaleb, 2014; Cherkaoui, 2014).

Based on this premise, it is but fitting to understand how CSR is being developed and acted upon in Morocco. Since 2006, General Confederation of Moroccan Companies (CGEM) has adopted a charter of social responsibility. This charter refers to the ISO 26000 standard defining the guidelines of social responsibility of organizations. The charter of CGEM Label for CSR is structured in 9 pillars or overarching objectives of commitment: promoting Human Rights, improving labour conditions, protecting the environment, support ethical business conduct and preventing corruption, respecting the rules of healthy competition, reinforcing the transparency of corporate governance, respecting the interests of customers and consumers, promoting corporate responsibility of suppliers and subcontractors and developing societal commitment (Tahri and El Khamlichi, 2019). According to the CGEM, the attribution of the label requires the adoption of an ethical and transparent conduct which: i) participates in sustainable development; ii) considers the expectations of all stakeholders; iii) respects the laws in force in line with the international standards of Conduct; and iv) is included throughout the firm and implemented in its relationships (AFNOR, 2006). Through this charter, CGEM aims to promote the factors of attractiveness of productive investment and long-term growth (Ben Abdallah and Makati, 2018). Henceforth, Moroccan firms are expected to innovate not only in terms of their core business operations but also in terms of their corporate social responsibility activities by putting in place different initiatives (economic, environmental, and social responsibility).

Conscious of the advantages of CSR, Moroccan listed firms have implemented a communication policy focused on CSR practices (Binkkour and Messaoudi, 2013) and nowadays more than 70 companies have awarded the CSR label (Tahri and El Khamlichi, 2019). To be more precise, the CGEM awarded its CSR Label to companies that acknowledge that they observe, defend and promote the universal principles of social responsibility in their economic activities, their social relationships and, more generally, in their contribution to value creation (Ben Aicha, 2017).

Previous empirical literature on Moroccan firms has focused the analyses about CSR initiatives, according to their size or their financial performance or profit purpose. In this regard, Taoukif (2015) confirmed that the company's social behavior depends on its differentiated profitability and that the impact of CSR on the company's turnover is reflected in sales growth and also in margin growth. Additionally, Taoukif (2015) found that the economic results of companies depend on promoting CSR. In a similar vein, Mouatassim-Lahmini and Ibenrissoul (2016) confirmed that CSR has a positive and significant impact on financial performance (on economic profitability) but it has no effect on stock market performance. Studying CSR practices of Casablanca's SMEs, Cherkaoui (2016) found that the degree of knowledge of CSR depends closely on the company size. In his study, turnover is expressed by firm size (number of employees). The larger the size of the company, the more CSR is steeped in the company. Nevertheless, Cherkaoui, (2016) concluded that CSR practices in Moroccan companies are limited to the legal minimum, taking into account the expectations of employees (i.e. the social dimension), but ignoring those of other stakeholders and the community (i.e. social and environmental dimensions).

In the same context, Yassin and Ibenrissoul (2018) studied the perception of executives on the social responsibility of the listed companies in which they work. They used a survey of 74 Moroccan executives who carried 37 items presented in the form of a Likert scale based on Carroll's (1991) theoretical model of social responsibility. Empirical results show that Moroccan executives working in listed companies do not have the same perception on CSR and companies that operate in the industrial sector are less observant about the respect of the laws and ethical values than the companies that operate in the service sector.

In an attempt to shed more light on CSR practices in Morocco, this chapter approaches the idea of analyzing the performance of management systems and its role in the development of CSR in Moroccan listed firms. The main contribution of this chapter is to measure Corporate Governance (CG) performance and test its role in the expansion of CSR in an emerging country. Taking into account the key CSR dimensions used by 74 Moroccan listed firms; this research intends to examine the impact of the performance of the corporate governance, turnover and the firm performance on the development of a social commitment. Finally, we explore the implications for the evolution of CSR in Morocco and note emergent pressures in developing a culture tuned to CSR and sustainability initiatives within both listed and non-listed firms in response to a spectrum of stakeholder interests.

DATA DESCRIPTION AND STUDY METHODOLOGY

Sample Selection and Variables

In recent years, worldwide social issues have brought an increasing challenge for firms to engage in social commitments. Following previous researches, we intend to analyze CSR potential determinants in order to extend empirical literature on CSR levers. Our procedure is quiet unique since this study is based on the results of a data survey. The sample is composed from 74 Moroccan listed firms to whom was addressed a questionnaire. It consists essentially of 37 items presented in the form of a five-point response scale assessing CG performance and CSR engagement. We also collected firm level data from annual reports downloaded from Morocco stock exchange website. We examine whether governance mechanisms and firm performance underlie the CSR performance measured by a self- constructed index.

To score the variable CSR, the method of additional rankings assuming that the items have the same weight was adopted. The score consists of 5 sub-indexes that are measured through several items. Below, we present the dimensions used in our study:

- Dimension 1: societal commitment: Community and local development
- Dimension 2: consumer issues
- Dimension 3: loyalty of practices
- Dimension 4: environment
- Dimension 5: human rights
- Dimension 5: Governance

In order to study the potential effect of corporate governance performance on CSR engagement, considered as our principal contribution, we approximate the corporate governance performance through the following three items noted on the Likert scale from 1 to 5:

- Commitment to producing products respecting environmental standards.
- Commitment to create jobs.
- Commitment to create value for shareholders.

Finally, we measure the impact of firm performance on CSR commitment. Unlike previous studies that consider a different proxy for firm performance each time, we base our study on several regressions where we introduce one firm performance proxy in every regression model. This proceeding will allow us to determine which measure has the most explaining power. The following table presents all variables included in our 5 models.

Regression Model

The main purpose of this chapter is to examine the impact of firm performance and certain internal CG mechanisms on CSR rating. To recap, we will test the impact of the performance of the corporate governance and the firm performance on the development of a social commitment. This brings us to test the two following guiding hypotheses:

H_1: The performance of corporate governance mechanisms contribute to the improvement of social commitment.

H_2: The firm performance is a key determinant of its involvement in social development (Gantchev, Gredil and Jotikasthira, 2015).

Table 1. Variable definitions and measures

Variable	Indication	Measurement
Corporate social responsibility	CSR	An index constructed from 5 sub-indexes each one consists of several items.
Governance performance	GOV1	A note according to the scale of Likert from 1 to 5 to the Item "My company is committed to producing eco-products, i.e. goods or services that respect quality standards, safety and the environment."
	GOV2	A note according to the scale of Likert from 1 to 5 to the Item "My company helps create job opportunities"
	GOV3	A note according to the scale of Likert from 1 to 5 to the Item "My company creates value for its shareholders."
Firm Performance	EQUITY	Firm's own funds
	TURNOVER	Total sales
	OP. PROFIT	Operational profit
	LIAB	Total liabilities

Source: Authors' development

Based on a multiple regression to estimate, our study uses a generalized least square regression (GLS). The multiple regression models for estimating the main effects of CG mechanisms and performance on CSR have the following form:

$$CSR = f\,(FP, CGV, CV) \qquad (1)$$

where corporate social responsibility (CSR) is a function of firm performance (FP), corporate governance variables (CGV) and other control variables (CV) supposed to be related to CSR. For a regression model, Model (1) can be written as:

$$CSR_{it} = \alpha_0 + \beta FP_i + \lambda_i CGV_i + \sigma_i CV_i + \varepsilon_i \qquad (2)$$

where:

α_0 – intercept or constant amount
β_i – coefficients of the firm performance variables
λ_i – coefficients of the corporate governance variables
σ_i – coefficients of control variables
ε– error term
i – cross-section dimension (i =1,...N)

The parameters of the empirical model are estimated using panel GLS regression. In this purpose, some diagnostic tests such as test for autocorrelation and multicollinearity are initially performed. Table 2 shows the correlation between the independent variables. The three governance items are significantly correlated at 10% level. This is expected since all items refer to the assessment of the performance of corporate governance mechanisms through the ethic production and job and stakeholders value creation.

Table 2. Tolerance Value and Variance Inflation Factor

Variables	MODEL 1		MODEL 2		MODEL 3		MODEL 4		MODEL 5	
	VIF	1/VIF	VIF	1/VIF	VIF	1/VIF	VIF	1/VIF	VIF	1/VIF
GOV1	2.14	0.4676	2.14	0.4676	2.14	0.4676	2.14	0.4676	2.14	0.4676
GOV2	1.79	0.5571	1.79	0.5571	1.79	0.5571	1.79	0.5571	1.79	0.5571
GOV3	1.76	0.5669	1.76	0.5669	1.76	0.5669	1.76	0.5669	1.76	0.5669
LIAB	1.01	0.9898								
TURNOVER			1.06	0.9419						
OP. PROFIT					1.05	0.94806				
NET PROFIT							1.05	0.9519		
EQUITY									1.01	0.9898
MEAN VIF	1.67		1.70		1.69		1.69		1.70	

Source: Authors' development

Generally, the pairwise correlation coefficients are low. A high correlation is considered when the correlation coefficient exceeds 0.80 according to Kennedy (2003). A low correlation coefficient indicates the absence of multicollinearity problem in the analysis. We further performed the variance inflation factor analysis to justify that there is no multicollinearity. We then carry out the Variance Inflation Factor (VIF) analysis as recommended by Gujarati (2003) to test for multicollinearity. Unless the VIF is above 10 and the tolerance value is below 0.10, there is a multicollinearity problem among variables. However, the values of VIF are all below 10 and the tolerance values are above 0.10.

Results and Discussion

First, we begin our discussion with the interpretation of descriptive variables. Our sample includes data for 74 Moroccan listed firms from a questionnaire survey and firm's annual reports. Sample firms are from a broad variety of industries. Table 2 presents the descriptive statistics for the key variables including the minimum value, the maximum value, the mean value (the average of the data values of each variable) and the standard deviation (indicate the variation or dispersion of the data values of each variable) of the testing variables in our model. We notice that respectively on average the total equity, turnover, operational profit, net profit and total liabilities are about 4178, 4015, 1437, 922 and 3347 million Moroccan dinars.

The governance performance and CSR self- constructed scores range from one to 5 as defined in the questionnaire. The maximum CG scores in our sample are 4.461681 on "Commitment to producing products respecting environmental standards" with a standard deviation of 0.089261 and 4.290269 on "Commitment to create jobs" with a standard deviation of 0.1049616 and 4.453213 on "Commitment to create value for shareholders" with a standard deviation of 0.0850121. This reflects the high corporate governance performance as assessed by responders. Our sample also presents a mean CSR index of 0.8359588 with a standard deviation of 0.0117688. This indicate that CSR is low (even less than 1) since the evaluation varies from 1 to 5 according to the Likert scale. Even the low value of the standard deviation confirms our remark. We conclude that in Morocco CSR is still in his first steps. This high-

Table 3. Descriptive Statistics

	Mean	Std. Err.	[95% Conf. Interval]	
EQUITY	4178 MD	1.13E+09	1.92E+09	6.43E+09
TURNOVER	4015 MD	9.99E+08	2.02E+09	6.01E+09
OP. PROFIT	1437 MD	4.30E+08	5.79E+08	2.30E+09
NET PROFIT	922 MD	2.81E+08	3.61E+08	1.48E+09
LIAB	3347 MD	9.31E+08	1.49E+09	5.20E+09
GOV1	4.283784	0.089261	4.105887	4.461681
GOV2	4.081081	0.1049616	3.871893	4.290269
GOV3	4.283784	0.0850121	4.114355	4.453213
CSR	0.8359588	0.0117688	0.8125037	0.8594139

Source: Authors' development

lights the contribution of our study that extends empirical literature and consequently has implications for decision makers.

Second, we present regression results of the five models. Table 4 shows that for surveyed firms the results of the effect of firms' characteristics as measured by equity, turnover, operational profit, net profit and liabilities and corporate governance mechanisms (CG) on firm's social commitment (CSR). The explanatory power (R-squared) of the five regressions is quite high (0.64) which indicates that the explanatory variables included in our models explain more than 64% of the variation of the CSR in Morocco.

As presented in the table above, we find that in all regressions the first and the third items measuring corporate governance performance have significant and positive impact on CSR commitment. Results thus offer strong support for hypothesis H_1. Particularly, the more the firm's governance mechanisms orientate managers to adopt respecting environmental production strategies the more CSR is developed. Moreover, as a measure of corporate governance mechanisms performance, the commitment to create value for shareholders, that is when governance mechanisms improve profitability for own funds providers, has a positive and significant impact on CSR development. Consequently, contrary to the findings of Barnea and Rubin (2010), the firms become more socially engaged and try building a good reputation citizen not on the detriment of the shareholders. Our results supporting the positive impact of corporate governance are in line with the previous findings of (Johnson and Greening, 1999; Artiach and al. 2010; Aguinis and Glavas, 2012; Khan and al., 2013; El Mehdi, 2015 and Iness and Rabii, 2015).

Next, we test the effect of several firm level financial measures on CSR. The majority of previous studies employed one or two proxies. In order to extend empirical literature, we include five different measures. The results show that all proxies have significant impact on CSR. But interestingly the total liability has negative impact at 1% level. So, external funds so significantly downward CSR engagements. This result is consistent with that finding of Mouatassim-Lahmini and Ibenrissoul (2016) who also find a negative impact of liabilities on firm economic and exchange performance and ROE. On the other hand, they empirically find that firm financial and economic performance effect positively CSR. Thus, our study findings are in harmony with empirical literature and then we can conclude that the liabilities affect negatively CSR in Moroccan listed firms.

On the other hand, we find that the turnover, the net profit, the operational profit and the equity have respectively positive and significant impact at 5% level. All in all estimated coefficients for models 2,

Table 4. CSR rating and its association with firm performance and corporate governance performance

Independent Variables	Model 1		Model 2		Model 3		Model 4		Model 5	
	Coefficient	Significance level	Coefficient	Significance level	Coefficient	Significance level	Coefficient	Significance level	Coefficient	Significance level
GOV1	0.0810179***	0	0.0818776***	0	0.0815384***	0	0.0815424***	0	0.0795912***	0
GOV2	0.0036695	0.719	0.0012367	0.908	0.0003755	0.972	0.0004132	0.969	0.0024062	0.822
GOV3	0.0283136**	0.027	0.0266424**	0.05	0.0273534**	0.042	0.0276606**	0.04	0.026336**	0.054
LIAB	-2.96E-12***	0.001								
TURNOVER			1.82E- 12**	0.039						
OP. *PROFIT*					4.59E-12**	0.024				
NET. *PROFIT*							6.85E-12**	0.028		
EQUITY									1.62E-12**	0.041
. cons	0.3625496***	0.000	0.3587121***	0.000	0.3613561***	0.000	0.3656094***	0	0.3656094***	0.000
F(P-value)	36.41*** (0.000)		31.99*** (0.000)		32.16*** (0.000)		31.99***(0.000)		31.52*** (0.000)	
R-squared	0.6785		0.6497		0.6509		0.6497		0.6463	

*, **, and ***, denote significantly different from zero at the 0.01, 0.05 and 0.10 level, respectively
Source: Authors' development

3, 4 and 5 are all significantly positive and consequently offer strong support for the second hypothesis. This robustness check allows us to conclude about the positive impact of firm performance on CSR. Our results are consistent with previous empirical findings of (Njaya, 2014; Frimousse & Peretti, 2015 and Ghali, 2015).

Several previous researches were aiming to test the effect of CSR on firm performance. Indeed, Mouatassim-Lahmini and Ibenrissoul (2016) underline that the impact of the CSR depends from the firm performance measure. In their study, they highlight the significant effect of CSR on financial and economic performance but when considering ROE and stock performance, CSR have no significant impact.

Our main contribution to empirical literature is to test the impact of firm performance on CSR in the Moroccan context. The study findings support the positive relation from firm performance to CSR and expand our understanding of the potential determinants of CSR. Within the scope of this chapter, we hope that the findings of this research will provide academics, policymakers and practitioners with a valuable discussion on how to promote CSR through sustainable policies and decisions. More particularly in Moroccan context, it's important to know that the more the firm is performing the more the social engagement is developed the more we get to social peace. Consequently, policy makers are invited to promulgate rules and reforms assuring an appropriate environment for firm's expansions to realize social expansion. Moroccan listed or not listed companies are called on to adopt a CSR strategy or a sustainable development strategy. In this respect, Crifo and Forget (2015) argue that entrepreneurs are having more to lose from unsustainable practices than to gain from sustainable ones. In fact, for environmental and social issues, unsustainable policies decrease firm valuation by respectively 11%, 10% and 15% and sustainable policies only increase firm valuation by 5%. In this approach, sustainability is considered as a defensive strategy to protect firm value and equity access. According to Rok (2019), 'strategic CSR' is the type of CSR most firms are using in practice because it can deliver more business opportunities enabling them to build competitive advantages through social progress, redesigning products and productivity in the value chain. To some extent, the implementation of responsible and sustainable strategy can contribute to the competitiveness of SMEs and thus the development of regional economies.

CONCLUSION AND FUTURE RESEARCH DIRECTIONS

Several research studies have examined business performance and governance mechanisms and their effects on corporate social responsibility (CSR), but their results vary widely. This may stem from flawed analyses by regressing firm performance on corporate social performance, and/or perhaps from several inadequately controlled variables. Call for further investigations on these dynamic interrelations have been put on notice to provide further explanations of previous mixed findings. Our study responds to the calls for investigation by studying the effect of the performance of CG mechanisms and several aspects of firm performance.

Morocco recent promotion of Corporate Social Responsibility (CSR) has coincided with a marked stratospheric growth of the country during last twenty years. Using the data of a survey questionnaire consisting essentially of 37 items presented in the form of a five-point response scale assessing CSR engagement and firm level data of 74 listed firms, we examine whether governance and firm performance underlies the CSR performance measured by a self- constructed index.

Since, previous studies did not recognize different sources of firm performance; we apply several multiple regressions using a standard methodology devised by Aiken and West (1991). The other principal contribution is to consider corporate governance mechanisms performance and not only corporate governance proxies. Based on specific data from a questionnaire designed to Moroccan firms, our results underline two major facts. First, we find that governance mechanisms performance is a principal driver of CSR. To our knowledge, we are the first to assess this impact while previous researches consider only technical aspects of corporate governance. Second, we find strong evidence for the upward effect of own funds and own cash flow and downward effect of external funds. Thus, our study of CSR commitment index allows for a clearer and more robust assessment of CG on Moroccan firms' CSR activities. Based on these results, theoretical contributions and practical implications are outlined. Our study of the relationship between CSR, CG and firm performance, contributes to an improved understanding of the factors driving CSR. It also provides theoretical and practical guidelines to researchers and decisions makers to help them determine their necessary strategies to meet social commitment and improve social welfare.

For the sake of parsimony, we focus only on the effect on Morocco, but to generalize, it may be more useful to study the empirical determinants of CSR for a more representative sample of Moroccan firms, such as listed firms, non-listed firms and so forth. Therefore, further study is warranted to introduce socioeconomic indicators to get more robust and conclusive findings. It would also be interesting to study the other causality effect from CSR to firm performance and thus test if CSR is profitable for different stakeholders.

REFERENCES

AFNOR. (2006). Développement durable et responsabilité sociétale. SD 21000 appliqué aux collectivités territoriales. Guide pour la prise en compte des enjeux de développement durable dans la stratégie et le management des collectivités territoriales.

Andrew, P. K., Udomsak, W., & Ben, R. (2016). Does institutional shareholder activism stimulate corporate information flow? *Journal of Banking & Finance*, *70*(C), 105–117.

Bampoky, B. (2015). Enjeux et perspectives du pilotage de la RSE pour les entreprises d'une économie en développement. *Revue Congolaise de Gestion*, *20*(1), 94–129. doi:10.3917/rcg.020.0094

Ben Abdallah, A., & Makati, S. (2018). *Socially Responsible Humain Resource Management application in the Moroccan context. Actes du colloque international de recherché en économie et gestion 17* (Vol. II, pp. 419–436). Editions Universitaires Européennes.

Ben Aicha, O. (2017). La diffusion de la RSE dans les entreprises au Maroc: Facteurs déterminants, rôles et interactions des acteurs [Thèse de doctorat en Sciences de Gestion]. ISCAE.

Benraiss-Noailles, L., & Bentaleb, C. (2014). Etat des lieux de la RSE au Maroc. In *Ressources Humaines et Responsabilités sociétales*. Academic Press.

Binkkour, A., & Messaoudi, M. (2013). *La communication de la RSE: entre conviction et contraintes - Cas de la PME marocaine. Communication de la responsabilité sociale des organisations: le défi de la crédibilité*. Université Laval.

Branco, M. C., & Rodrigues, L. L. (2008). Factors influencing social responsibility disclosure by Portuguese companies. *Journal of Business Ethics*, *83*(4), 685–701. doi:10.1007/s10551-007-9658-z

Carrol, B. (1997). A Three-Dimensional Conceptual Model of Social Performance. *Academy of Management Review*. doi:10.2307/257850

Carroll, A. B. (1979). A three-dimensional conceptual model of corporate performance. *Academy of Management Review*, *4*(4), 497–505. doi:10.5465/amr.1979.4498296

Cherkaoui, A. (2016). Pratiques RSE des pme au Maroc: une analyse perceptuelle auprès des dirigeants casablancais. Question(s) de management, 3(14), 13-26. doi:10.3917/qdm.163.0013

Choi, B. B., Lee, D., & Park, Y. (2013). Corporate Social Responsibility, Corporate Governance and Earnings Quality: Evidence from Korea. *Corporate Governance*, *21*(5), 447–467. doi:10.1111/corg.12033

Choi, H., & Pae, J. (2011). Business Ethics and Financial Reporting Quality: Evidence from Korea. *Journal of Business Ethics*, *103*(3), 403–427. doi:10.1007/s10551-011-0871-4

Coupland, C. (2005). Corporate social responsibility as argument on the web. *Journal of Business Ethics*, *62*(4), 355–366. doi:10.1007/s10551-005-1953-y

Crifo, P., & Forget, V. (2019). The Economics of Corporate Social Responsibility: A firm-level perspective survey. *Journal of Economic Surveys*, *29*(1), 112–130. doi:10.1111/joes.12055

Dahlsrud, A. (2008). How Corporate Social Responsibility Is Defined: An Analysis of 37 Definitions. *Corporate Social Responsibility and Environmental Management*, *15*(1), 1–13. doi:10.1002/csr.132

Drucker, P. (1984). The new meaning of corporate social responsibility. *California Management Review*, *26*(2), 53–63. doi:10.2307/41165066

Esty, D., & Winston, A. (2009). *Green to Gold: How Smart Companies Use Environmental Strategy to Innovate, Create Value, and Build Competitive Advantage*. John Wiley & Sons.

European Commission. (2002). *Corporate Social Responsibility: A business contribution to sustainable, development*. Office for Official Publications of the European Communities.

Fifka, M. S. (2013). Corporate responsibility reporting and its determinants in comparative perspective – a review of the empirical literature and a meta-analysis. *Business Strategy and the Environment, 22*(1), 1–35. doi:10.1002/bse.729

Frimmouse, S., & Peretti, J. (2015). Regards croisés sur engagement RSE. Question(s) de management, 1(9), 65-89.

Gantchev, N., Gredil, O., & Jotikasthira, C. (2015). *Governance under the gun: Spillover effects of hedge fund activism*. European Corporate Governance Institute; doi:10.2139srn.2356544

Giannarakis, G. (2014). Corporate governance and financial characteristic effects on the extent of corporate social responsibility disclosure. Social Responsibility Journal, 10(4), 569–590. doi:10.1108/SRJ-02-2013-0008

Hadani, M., Goranova, M., & Khan, R. (2011). Institutional investors, shareholder activism, and earnings management. *Journal of Business Research, 64*(12), 1352–1360. doi:10.1016/j.jbusres.2010.12.004

Ibenrissoul, A., & Alami, F. Z. (2016). *L'évaluation économique des projets inscrits dans une perspective RSE. In 18e université de printemps de l'audit social, Audit social et mutation(s) des organisations*. Academic Press.

Jamali, D., & Mirshak, R. (2007). Corporate social responsibility (CSR): Theory and practice in a developing country context. *Journal of Business Ethics, 72*(3), 243–262. doi:10.1007/s10551-006-9168-4

Jarboui, A., and Bouaziz, S., (2019). The moderating effect of audit quality on the relation between shareholder activism and earnings management: Evidence from France. doi:10.5709/ce.1897-9254.299

Jo, H., & Harjoto, A.-M. (2011). Corporate Governance and Firm Value: The Impact of Corporate Social Responsibility. *Journal of Business Ethics, 103*(3), 351–383. doi:10.1007/s10551-011-0869-y

Judge, W. Q., Gaur, A., & Muller-Kahle, M. I. (2010). Antecedents of shareholder activism in target firms: Evidence from a multi-country study. *Corporate Governance, 18*(4), 258–273. doi:10.1111/j.1467-8683.2010.00797.x

Khanchel, I., and Seboui, S., (2009). Opportunisme dans les transferts internes et gestion de l'impression des partenaires. Gestion 2000, 26(4).

Krafft, J., Qu, Y., & Ravix, J. (2011). Gouvernance d'entreprise et performances sectorielles: une réévaluation de la fiabilité des scores et des mesures de bonne gouvernance. Retrieved from https://hal.archives-ouvertes.fr/hal-00493371

Lin, Z., Liu, M., & Noronha, C. (2016). The impact of corporate governance on informative earnings management in the Chinese market. *Abacus, 52*(3), 568–609. doi:10.1111/abac.12084

Mallin, C. A., & Michelon, G. (2016). Board Reputation Attributes and Corporate Social Performance: An Empirical Investigation of the US Best Corporate Citizens. *Accounting and Business Research*, *41*(2), 119–144. doi:10.1080/00014788.2011.550740

McWilliams, A., & Siegel, D. (2001). Corporate Social Responsibility: A Theory of the Firm Perspective. *Academy of Management Review*, *26*(1), 117–127. doi:10.5465/amr.2001.4011987

Mouatassim Lahmini, H., & Ibenrissoul, A. (2016). Y a-t-il un impact de la RSE sur la performance financière de l'entreprise: Etude empirique sur les sociétés marocaines cotées à la bourse de Casablanca. Retrieved from https://hal.archives-ouvertes.fr/hal-01351951

Murphy, K. J. (1985). Corporate Performance and Managerial Remuneration: An Empirical Analysis. *Journal of Accounting and Economics*, *7*(1-3), 11–42. doi:10.1016/0165-4101(85)90026-6

Nissim, D., & Penman, S. H. (2003). Financial Statement Analysis of Leverage and How It Informs About Profitability and Price-to-Book Ratios. *Review of Accounting Studies*, *8*(4), 531–560. doi:10.1023/A:1027324317663

Rashid, A., Khaleequzzaman, M., & Jabeen, S. (2015). Analyzing Performance of Banks in Pakistan: Conventional versus Islamic Banks. *Journal of Islamic Business and Management*, *5*(2), 17–42. doi:10.12816/0026416

Reverte, C. (2009). Determinants of corporate social responsibility disclosure ratings by Spanish listed firms. *Journal of Business Ethics*, *88*(2), 351–366. doi:10.1007/s10551-008-9968-9

Rok, B. (2019). Transition from Corporate Responsibility to sustainable strategic management. In CSR, Sustainability. Ethics and Governance. Springer Nature Switzerland. doi:10.1007/978-3-030-00440-8_1

Sáenz González, J., & García-Meca, E. (2014). Does Corporate Governance Influence Earnings Management in Latin American Markets? *Journal of Business Ethics, Springer*, *121*(3), 419–440. doi:10.1007/s10551-013-1700-8

Sahut, J., Mili, M., Ben Tekaya, S., & Teulon, F. (2016). Financial Impacts and antecedents of CSR: A PLS Path Modelling Approach. *Economic Bulletin*, *36*(2), 736–751.

Sahut, J. M., and Gharbi, H. O. (2011). Influence of French and foreign institutional shareholders on the financial performance of firms. La revue des Sciences de Gestion, (5), 51-62.

Surroca, J., Tribo, J. A., & Waddock, S. (2010). Corporate Responsibility and Financial Performance: The Role of Intangible Resources. *Strategic Management Journal*, *31*(5), 463–490. doi:10.1002/smj.820

Tahri, W., & El Khamlichi, A. (2019). Disclosure and Communication of the Corporate Social Responsibility (CSR) in Morocco: The Case of a Bank. In Y. Baghdadi & A. Harfouche (Eds.), ICT for a Better Life and a Better World: The Impact of Information and Communication Technologies on Organizations and Society (pp. 247-261). Springer International Publishing.

Taoukif, F. E. Z. (2015). Analyse perceptuelle des déterminants de l'engagement sociétal des entreprises marocaines labellisées RSE: de la performance au développement durable - cas du maroc. Retrieved from https://tel.archives-ouvertes.fr/tel-01198977

Tlemçani, A. (2009). Prise de conscience progressive des pouvoirs publics et des entreprises en matière de responsabilité sociale même si la confusion entre responsabilité sociale et responsabilité légale reste de mise. Retrieved from http://www.iteco.be/Responsabilitesociale-des-entreprises

Toumi, S. (2017). L'impact des mécanismes de gouvernance dans la gestion des risques bancaires et la performance des banques: Cas de la France, l'Allemagne et le Japon. Retrieved from https://tel.archives-ouvertes.fr/tel-01483783

Turnbull, S. (2015). Defining and Achieving Good Governance. Retrieved from http://ssrn.com/abstract=2571724

Ullmann, A. (1985). Data in search for a theory: A critical examination of the relationship among Social Performance, Social Disclosure and economic performance. *Academy of Management Review*, *10*, 540–577.

Waddock, S., & Graves, S. (1997). The corporate social performance-financial performance link. *Strategic Management Journal*, *18*(4), 303–319. doi:10.1002/(SICI)1097-0266(199704)18:4<303::AID-SMJ869>3.0.CO;2-G

Wang, Y., (2017). Taking Corporate Social Responsibility as Growth Strategy. doi:10.5772/intechopen.6902800

Yassine, A., & Ibenrissoul, A. (2018). Pratiques de la Responsabilité Sociale dans les entreprises marocaines cotées: analyse du modèle quadridimensionnel de Carroll (1991) et application au cas marocain. Retrieved from https://hal.archives-ouvertes.fr/hal-01728603v2

ADDITIONAL READING

Akben-Selcuk, E. (2019). Corporate Social Responsibility and Financial Performance: The Moderating Role of Ownership Concentration in Turkey. Sustainability, 11(13), 3643. doi:10.3390/su11133643 doi:10.3390u11133643

Al-Shuaibi, K. M. (2016). A structural equation model of CSR and performance: Mediation by innovation and productivity. Journal of Management and Sustainability, 6(2), 139. doi:10.5539/jms.v6n2p139 doi:10.5539/jms.v6n2p139

Cho, S. J., Chung, C. Y., & Young, J. (2019). Study on the relationship between CSR and financial performance. Sustainability, 11(2), 343. doi:10.3390/su11020343 doi:10.3390u11020343

Harjoto, M. A., & Jo, H. (2011). Corporate governance and CSR nexus. Journal of Business Ethics, 100(1), 45–67. doi:10.1007/s10551-011-0772-6 doi:10.100710551-011-0772-6

Hull, C. E., & Rothenberg, S. (2008). Firm performance: The interactions of corporate social performance with innovation and industry differentiation. Strategic Management Journal, 29(7), 781–789. doi:10.1002/smj.675 doi:10.1002mj.675

Husted, B. W., & Allen, D. B. (2009). Strategic corporate social responsibility and value creation. Management International Review, 49(6), 781–799. doi:10.1007/s11575-009-0016-5 doi:10.100711575-009-0016-5

Kaufmann, M., & Olaru, M. (2012). The impact of corporate social responsibility on business performance–can it be measured, and if so, how. Paper presented at the Berlin International Economics Congress. Academic Press.

López-Pérez, M., Melero, I., & Javier Sesé, F. (2017). Does specific CSR training for managers impact shareholder value? Implications for education in sustainable development. Corporate Social Responsibility and Environmental Management, 24(5), 435–448. doi:10.1002/csr.1418 doi:10.1002/csr.1418

Peng, C. W., & Yang, M. L. (2014). The effect of corporate social performance on financial performance: The moderating effect of ownership concentration. Journal of Business Ethics, 123(1), 171–182. doi:10.1007/s10551-013-1809-9 doi:10.100710551-013-1809-9

Rodriguez-Fernandez, M. (2016). Social responsibility and financial performance: The role of good corporate governance. BRQ Business Research Quarterly, 19(2), 137–151. doi:10.1016/j.brq.2015.08.001 doi:10.1016/j.brq.2015.08.001

KEY TERMS AND DEFINITIONS

Correlation coefficient: A coefficient used to measure the strength of the connection or the relationship between two variables.

Corporate governance: It refers to the way a corporation is governed. More precisely, it is the system of rules, practices, and processes by which companies are directed, managed and controlled.

Corporate social responsibility: To be socially responsible, a firm has to operate in ways that uphold the principles of sustainable development. Corporate social responsibility can take many forms depending on the firm and industry. It's a broad concept that encompasses all the practices put in place by a firm in order to be economically viable, to enhance society and preserve the environment.

Firm performance: A measure of a firm efficiency considered though several financial aggregates reflecting the firm's financing structure like total equity and total liabilities and the firm's operating cycle like firm's turnover and operational profit.

GLS Regression: Generalized least squares regression allows the OLS approach to be generalized to give the maximum likelihood estimate β when the noise is of unequal variance (heteroscedasticity).

Moroccan listed firms: Moroccan companies whose shares can be traded on a The Casablanca Stock Exchange (CSE, Morocco).

Multicollinearity: A state of very high inter-correlations or inter-associations among the independent variables. It is therefore a type of disturbance in the data, and if present in the data the statistical inferences made about the data may not be reliable.

Compilation of References

Abad, D., Lucas-Pérez, M. E., Minguez-Vera, A., & Yagüe, J. (2017). Does Gender Diversity on Corporate Boards Reduce Information Asymmetry in Equity Markets? *Business Research Quarterly*, *20*(3), 192–205. doi:10.1016/j.brq.2017.04.001

ABC. (2016, April 6). El primer radar 'solidario' de España. *ABC Sociedad*. Retrieved from http://www.abc.es

Abdelmotaleb, M., Metwally, A.B., E.M., & Saha, S. K. (2018). Exploring the impact of being perceived as a socially responsible organization on employee creativity. *Management Decision*, *56*(11), 2325–2340. doi:10.1108/MD-06-2017-0552

Abels, P. B., & Martelli, J. T. (2013). CEO duality: How many hats are too many? *Corporate Governance: The International Journal of Business in Society*, *13*(2), 135–147. doi:10.1108/14720701311316625

Abeysekera, I. (2013). A template for integrated reporting. *Journal of Intellectual Capital*, *14*(2), 227–245. doi:10.1108/14691931311323869

Accounting Standardization Committee. (2002). Accounting Directive No. 29 - Environmental Matters, June 5, CD-ROM of the Order of Official Accountants.

Adams, C. (2017). *The Sustainable Development Goals, integrated thinking and the integrated report*. International Integrated Reporting Council and ICAS. Retrieved from www.theiirc.org

Adams, C. A. (2015). The international integrated reporting council: A call to action. *Critical Perspectives on Accounting*, *27*, 23–28. doi:10.1016/j.cpa.2014.07.001

Adams, C. A., & McNicholas, P. (2007). Making a difference: Sustainability reporting, accountability and organisational change. *Accounting, Auditing & Accountability Journal*, *20*(3), 382–402. doi:10.1108/09513570710748553

Adams, R., & Ferreira, D. (2009). Women in the boardroom and their impact on governance and performance. *Journal of Financial Economics*, *94*(2), 291–309. doi:10.1016/j.jfineco.2008.10.007

Adams, R., Hermalin, B., & Weisbach, M. (2010). The role of boards of directors in corporate governance: A conceptual framework and survey. *Journal of Economic Literature*, *48*(1), 58–107. doi:10.1257/jel.48.1.58

Adams, R., Jeanrenaud, S., Bessant, J., Denyer, D., & Overy, P. (2016). Sustainability-oriented innovation: A systematic review. *International Journal of Management Reviews*, *18*(2), 180–205. doi:10.1111/ijmr.12068

Adams, S., & Simnett, R. (2011). Integrated Reporting: An Opportunity for Australia's Not-for-Profit Sector. *Australian Accounting Review*, *21*(3), 292–301. doi:10.1111/j.1835-2561.2011.00143.x

Adler, N. J. (1991). *International Dimensions of Organizational Behavior*. Boston: PWS-Kent.

AFNOR. (2006). Développement durable et responsabilité sociétale. SD 21000 appliqué aux collectivités territoriales. Guide pour la prise en compte des enjeux de développement durable dans la stratégie et le management des collectivités territoriales.

Agrawal, A., & Hockerts, K. (2013). Institutional theory as a framework for practitioners of social entrepreneurship. In *Social Innovation* (pp. 119–129). Springer. doi:10.1007/978-3-642-36540-9_11

Agrawal, A., & Knoeber, C. R. (1996). Firm performance and mechanisms to control agency problems between managers and shareholders. *Journal of Financial and Quantitative Analysis*, *31*(3), 377–397. doi:10.2307/2331397

Aguilera, R. V., Rupp, D. E., Williams, C. A., & Ganapathi, J. (2007). Putting the S back in corporate social responsibility: A multilevel theory of social change in organizations. *Academy of Management Review*, *32*(3), 836–863. doi:10.5465/amr.2007.25275678

Ahi, P., & Searcy, C. (2013). A comparative literature analysis of definitions for green and sustainable supply chain management. *Journal of Cleaner Production*, *52*, 329–341. doi:10.1016/j.jclepro.2013.02.018

Akbas, H. E. (2016). The relationship between board characteristics and environmental disclosure: Evidence from Turkish listed companies. *South East European Journal of Economics and Business*, *11*(2), 7–19. doi:10.1515/jeb-2016-0007

Akbas, H., & Canikli, S. (2018). Determinants of voluntary greenhouse gas emission disclosure: An empirical investigation in Turkish firms. *Sustainability*, *11*(1), 107. doi:10.3390u11010107

Akben-Selcuk, E. (2019). Corporate Social Responsibility and Financial Performance: The Moderating Role of Ownership Concentration in Turkey. *Sustainability*, *11*(13), 1–10. doi:10.3390u11133643

Akhtaruddin, M., Hossain, M., & Yao, L. (2009). Corporate governance and voluntary disclosure in corporate annual reports of Malaysian listed firms. *Journal of Applied Management Accounting Research*, *7*(1), 1–19.

Akin, A., & Yilmaz, İ. (2016). Drivers of Corporate Social Responsibility Disclosures: Evidence from Turkish Banking Sector. *Procedia Economics and Finance*, *38*, 2–7.

Albertini, E. (2014). A descriptive analysis of environmental disclosure: A longitudinal study of French companies. *Journal of Business Ethics*, *121*(2), 233–254. doi:10.100710551-013-1698-y

Albuquerque, J. L. (2009). *Gestão ambiental e responsabilidade social: conceitos, ferramentas e aplicações*. São Paulo: Atlas.

Albuquerque, R., Koskinen, Y., & Zhang, C. (2018). Corporate Social Responsibility and Firm Risk: Theory and Empirical Evidence. *Management Science*, *65*(10), 4451–4949. doi:10.1287/mnsc.2018.3043

Alemany, L., Álvarez, C., Planellas, M., & Urbano, D. (2011). *Libro Blanco de la iniciativa emprendedora en España*. Barcelona: editado por la Fundación Príncipe de Girona.

Alexander, G. J., & Buchholtz, R. A. (1978). Corporate Social Responsibility and Stock Market Performance. *Academy of Management Journal*, *21*(3), 479–486.

Aligleri, L. M., Aligleri, L. A., & Câmara, M. R. G. (2002). Responsabilidade Social na Cadeia Logística: uma Visão Integrada para o Incremento da Competitividade. In Proceedings of the II Encontro de Estudos Organizacionais, Recife. Academic Press.

Ali, W., Frynas, J. G., & Mahmood, Z. (2017). Determinants of corporate social responsibility (CSR) disclosure in developed and developing countries: A literature review. *Corporate Social Responsibility and Environmental Management*, *24*(4), 273–294. doi:10.1002/csr.1410

Allegrini, M., & Greco, G. (2013). Corporate boards, audit committees and voluntary disclosure: Evidence from Italian listed companies. *The Journal of Management and Governance*, *17*(1), 187–216. doi:10.100710997-011-9168-3

Allen, N. J., & Meyer, J. P. (1996). Affective, continuance, and normative commitment to the organization: An examination of construct validity. *Journal of Vocational Behavior*, *49*(3), 252–276. doi:10.1006/jvbe.1996.0043 PMID:8980084

Allouche, J., & Laroche, P. (2005). A meta-analytical investigation of the relationship between corporate social and financial performance. *Revue de Gestion des Ressources Humaines*, *57*, 18–41.

Almeida, F., & Sobral, F. (2007). Influência dos valores culturais na Responsabilidade Social das Empresas. *Revista Portuguesa e Brasileira de Gestão*, *6*(3), 52–61.

Almeida, R., Neumann, M., & Sanches, S. (2018). O que é evidenciado no Brasil sobre a Responsabilidade Social Corporativa advinda da Política Nacional de Resíduos Sólidos (PNRS) nos formulários de referência e Relatos Integrados? *Sociedade. Contabilidade e Gestão*, *13*(3). doi:10.21446cg_ufrj.v13i3.13855

Alniacik, U., Alniacik, E., & Genc, N. (2011). How corporate social responsibility information influences stakeholders' intentions. *Corporate Social Responsibility and Environmental Management*, *18*(4), 234–245. doi:10.1002/csr.245

Alnodel, A. A., Elobaid, D. E., Elawady, S. I., & Alhdaif, S. A. (2018). Business colleges and their community: Content analysis of websites of business colleges in the MENA region. *International Journal of Engineering Business Management*, *10*, 1–10. doi:10.1177/1847979018800891

Alonso-Almeida, M., Marimon, F., Casani, F., & Rodriguez-Pomeda, J. (2015). Diffusion of sustainability reporting in universities: Current situation and future perspectives. *Journal of Cleaner Production*, *106*, 144–154. doi:10.1016/j.jclepro.2014.02.008

Alotaibi, A., Edum-Fotwe, F., & Price, A. D. F. (2019). Critical Barriers to Social Responsibility Implementation within Mega-Construction Projects: The Case of the Kingdom of Saudi Arabia. *Sustainability*, *11*(6), 1755. doi:10.3390u11061755

Al-Shaer, H., & Zaman, M. (2016). Board gender diversity and sustainability reporting quality. *Journal of Contemporary Accounting and Economics*, *12*(3), 210–222. doi:10.1016/j.jcae.2016.09.001

Alzoubi, E. S. S. (2016). Audit quality and earnings management: Evidence from Jordan. *Journal of Applied Accounting Research*, *17*(2), 170–189. doi:10.1108/JAAR-09-2014-0089

Ameer, R., & Othman, R. (2012). Sustainability practices and corporate financial performance: A study based on the top global corporations. *Journal of Business Ethics*, *108*(1), 61–79. doi:10.100710551-011-1063-y

Amey, M., & Whooley, N. (2018). Corporate reporting on the SDGs: mapping a sustainable future. *PIMCO*.

Amores-Salvadó, J., Martín-de Castro, G., & Navas-López, J. E. (2014). Green corporate image: Moderating the connection between environmental product innovation and firm performance. *Journal of Cleaner Production*, *83*(15), 356–365. doi:10.1016/j.jclepro.2014.07.059

Anderson, K. L., Gillan, S. L., & Deli, D. (2003). Boards of Directors, Audit Committees, and the Information Content of Earnings. Weinberg Center for Corporate Governance. Retrieved from https://ssrn.com/abstract=444241

Andrew, P. K., Udomsak, W., & Ben, R. (2016). Does institutional shareholder activism stimulate corporate information flow? *Journal of Banking & Finance*, *70*(C), 105–117.

Andrews, K. R. (1971). *The concept of corporate strategy*. Homewood, IL: Irwin.

Ansari, S., Wijen, F., & Gray, B. (2013). Constructing a climate change logic: An institutional perspective on the Tragedy of the commons. *Organization Science*, *24*(4), 1014–1040. doi:10.1287/orsc.1120.0799

Antolín, M., & Gago, R. (2004). Responsabilidad Social Corporativa: La última innovación en management. *Universia Business Review*, *1*, 28–39.

Archel, P., Fernadez, M., & Larrinaga, C. (2008). The organizational and operational boundaries of triple bottom line reporting: A survey. *Environmental Management*, *41*(1), 106–117. doi:10.100700267-007-9029-7 PMID:17990022

Archel, P., & Lizarraga, D. (2001). Algunos determinantes de la información medioambiental divulgada por las empresas españolas cotizadas. *Revista de Contabilidad*, *4*(7), 139–153.

Argenti, P. (2014). *A comunicação empresarial: a construção da identidade, imagem e reputação*. São Paulo: Campus.

Arora, P., & Dharwadkar, R. (2011). Corporate governance and corporate social responsibility (CSR): The moderating roles of attainment discrepancy and organization slack. *Corporate Governance*, *19*(2), 136–152. doi:10.1111/j.1467-8683.2010.00843.x

Arthaud-Day, M. L. (2005). Transnational corporate social responsibility: A tri-dimensional approach to international CSR research. *Business Ethics Quarterly*, *15*(1), 1–22. doi:10.5840/beq20051515

Artiach, T., Lee, D., Nelson, D., & Walker, J. (2010). The determinants of corporate sustainability performance. *Accounting and Finance*, *50*(1), 31–51. doi:10.1111/j.1467-629X.2009.00315.x

Asgary, N., & Li, G. (2016). Corporate social responsibility: Its economic impact and link to the bullwhip effect. *Journal of Business Ethics*, *135*(4), 665–681. doi:10.100710551-014-2492-1

Asheim, B. T., & Isaksen, A. (1997). Location, agglomeration and innovation: Towards regional innovation systems in Norway? *European Planning Studies*, *5*(3), 299–330. doi:10.1080/09654319708720402

Ashley, P. A., Coutinho, R. B. G., & Tomei, P. A. (2000). Responsabilidade social corporativa e cidadania empresarial: uma análise conceitual comparativa. In Proceedings of the *XXIV Encontro da ANPAD, Florianópolis, 2000*. Florianópolis: Anais.

Asrar-ul-Haq, M., Kuchinke, K. P., & Iqbal, A. (2017). The relationship between corporate social responsibility, job satisfaction, and organizational commitment: Case of Pakistani higher education. *Journal of Cleaner Production*, *142*, 2352–2363. doi:10.1016/j.jclepro.2016.11.040

Atkins, J., & Maroun, W. (2015). Integrated reporting in South Africa in 2012: Perspectives from South African institutional investors. *Meditari Accountancy Research*, *23*(2), 197–221. doi:10.1108/MEDAR-07-2014-0047

Attig, N., Boubakri, N., El Ghoul, S., & Guedhami, O. (2016). Firm internationalization and corporate social responsibility. *Journal of Business Ethics*, *134*(2), 171–197. doi:10.100710551-014-2410-6

Aupperle, K. E., Caroll, A. B., & Hatfield, J. D. (1985). An Empirical Examination of The Relationship Between Corporate Social Responsibility and Profitability. *Academy of Management Journal*, *28*(2), 446–463.

Auranen, O., & Nieminen, M. (2010). University research funding and publication performance-An international comparison. *Research Policy*, *39*(6), 822–834. doi:10.1016/j.respol.2010.03.003

Avey, J. B., Luthans, F., & Youssef, C. M. (2010). The Additive Value of Positive Psychological Capital in Predicting Work Attitudes and Behaviors. *Journal of Management*, *36*(2), 430–452. doi:10.1177/0149206308329961

Avolio, B. J., & Gardner, W. L. (2005). Authentic leadership development: Getting to the root of positive forms of leadership. *The Leadership Quarterly*, *16*(3), 315–338. doi:10.1016/j.leaqua.2005.03.001

Ayuntamiento de Santa María de Cayón. (2017). *Ordenanza Reguladora de las Ayudas Económicas Municipales de Carácter Excepcional con cargo al Fondo de Suministros y al Radar Solidario*. Retrieved from http://www.santamariadecayon.es

Aznar-Sánchez, J. A., Velasco-Muñoz, J. F., Belmonte-Ureña, L. J., & Manzano-Agugliaro, F. (2019). Innovation and technology for sustainable mining activity: A worldwide research assessment. *Journal of Cleaner Production*, *221*, 38–54. doi:10.1016/j.jclepro.2019.02.243

Backhaus, K., Stone, B., & Heiner, K. (2002). Exploring the relationship between corporate social performance and employer attractiveness. *Business & Society*, *41*(3), 292–318. doi:10.1177/0007650302041003003

Baek, H., Johnson, D. R., & Kim, J. (2009). Managerial ownership, corporate governance, and voluntary disclosure. *Journal of Business & Economic Studies*, *15*(2), 44–61.

Bai, C. E. B., Liu, Q., Lu, J., Song, F. M., & Zhang, J. (2004). Corporate governance and market valuation in China. *Journal of Comparative Economics*, *32*(4), 599–616. doi:10.1016/j.jce.2004.07.002

Baird, Ph., Geylani, P., & Roberts, J. (2012). Corporate Social and Financial Performance Re-Examined: Industry Effects in a Linear Mixed Model Analysis. *Journal of Business Ethics*, *109*(3), 367–388. doi:10.100710551-011-1135-z

Bakici, T., Almirall, E., & Wareham, J. (2013). A Smart City initiative: The case of Barcelona. *Journal of the Knowledge Economy*, *4*(2), 135–148. doi:10.100713132-012-0084-9

Baldarelli, M. G., & Gigli, S. (2014). Exploring the drivers of corporate reputation integrated with a corporate responsibility perspective: Some reflections in theory and in praxis. *The Journal of Management and Governance*, *18*(2), 589–613. doi:10.100710997-011-9192-3

Balmaceda, F. (2018). Entrepreneurship: Skills and financing. *Small Business Economics*, *50*(4), 871–886. doi:10.100711187-017-9915-1

Bals, L., & Tate, W. (2017). Transparency. In *Implementing Triple Bottom Line Sustainability into Global Supply Chains* (pp. 90–155). Routledge. doi:10.4324/9781351285124

Bampoky, B. (2015). Enjeux et perspectives du pilotage de la RSE pour les entreprises d'une économie en développement. *Revue Congolaise de Gestion*, *20*(1), 94–129. doi:10.3917/rcg.020.0094

Bananuka, J., Tumwebaze, Z., & Orobia, L. (2019). The adoption of integrated reporting: A developing country perspective. *Journal of Financial Reporting and Accounting*, *17*(1), 2–23. doi:10.1108/JFRA-09-2017-0089

Banco Central do Brasil. (2014). Resolução nº 4.327, de 25 de abril de 2014. Retrieved from http://www.bcb.gov.br/pre/normativos/res/2014/pdf/res_4327_v1_O.pdf

Banker, R. D., Chang, H., & Majumdar, S. K. (1996). A Framework for Analyzing Changes in Strategic Performance. *Strategic Management Journal*, *17*(9), 693–712. doi:10.1002/(SICI)1097-0266(199611)17:9<693::AID-SMJ847>3.0.CO;2-W

Barakat, S. R., Boaventura, J. M. G., & Polo, E. F. (2017). Alinhamento estratégico da responsabilidade social corporativa: Um estudo de caso no setor bancário brasileiro. *Revista Eletrônica de Administração*, *86*(1), 206–233.

Barba-Sánchez, V., & Atienza-Sahuquillo, C. (2010). Integration of the environment in managerial strategy: Application of the resource-based theory of competitive advantage, dynamic capabilities and corporate social responsibilities. *African Journal of Business Management*, *4*(6), 1155.

Bardin, L. (2016). Analise de Conteúdo. Edições 70.

Barnea, A., & Rubin, A. (2010). Corporate Social Responsibility as a Conflict Between Shareholders. *Journal of Business Ethics*, *97*(1), 71–86. doi:10.100710551-010-0496-z

Barney, J. B., Ketchen, D. J. Jr, Wright, M., McWilliams, A., & Siegel, D. S. (2011). Creating and capturing value: Strategic corporate social responsibility, resource-based theory, and sustainable competitive advantage. *Journal of Management*, *37*(5), 1480–1495. doi:10.1177/0149206310385696

Bar-On, R. (1997). *The Emotional Quotient Inventory (EQ-i): a test of emotional intelligence*. Toronto: Multi-Health Systems.

Bar-On, R. (2000). Emotional and social intelligence: insights from the emotional quotient inventory. In R. Bar-On & J. D. A. Parker (Eds.), *Handbook of emotional intelligence* (pp. 363–388). San Francisco, CA: Jossey-Bass.

Barros, C., & Monteiro, S. (2012). Determinant factors of mandatory environmental reporting: the case of Portuguese primary metal and steel industry. In A.M. Gil-Lafuente, J. Gil-Lafuente, & J.M. Merigó-Lindahl (Eds.), Soft Computing in Management and Business Economics (pp. 123-147). Springer Berlin Heidelberg.

Batty, M., Axhausen, K. W., Giannotti, F., Pozdnoukhov, A., Bazzani, A., Wachowicz, M., ... Portugali, Y. (2012). Smart Cities of the Future. *The European Physical Journal. Special Topics*, *214*(1), 481–518. doi:10.1140/epjst/e2012-01703-3

Bauer, K. J., Miles, L. L., & Nishikawa, T. (2009). The effect of mergers on credit union performance. *Journal of Banking & Finance*, *33*(12), 2267–2274. doi:10.1016/j.jbankfin.2009.06.004

Baumann-Pauly, D., Wickert, C., Spence, L. J., & Scherer, A. G. (2013). Organizing Corporate Social Responsibility in Small and Large Firms: Size Matters. *Journal of Business Ethics*, *115*(4), 693–705. doi:10.100710551-013-1827-7

Bear, S., Rahman, N., & Post, C. (2010). The Impact of Board Diversity and Gender Composition on Corporate Social Responsibility and Firm Reputation. *Journal of Business Ethics*, *97*(2), 207–221. doi:10.100710551-010-0505-2

Beck, A., Campbell, D., & Shrives, P. (2010). Content analysis in environmental reporting research: Enrichment and rehearsal of the method in a British-German context. *The British Accounting Review*, *42*(3), 207–222. doi:10.1016/j.bar.2010.05.002

Behrend, T., Baker, B., & Thompson, L. (2009). Effects of pro-environmental recruiting messages: The role of organizational reputation. *Journal of Business and Psychology*, *24*(3), 341–350. doi:10.100710869-009-9112-6

Behringer, K., & Szegedi, K. (2016). The role of CSR in achieving sustainable development – theoretical approach. *European Scientific Journal*, *12*(22), 1857–7881. doi:10.19044/esj.2016.v12n22p10

Belkaoui, A. (1976). The Impact of the disclosure of the environmental effects of oragnizational behavior on the market. *Financial Management*, *5*(Winter), 26–30. doi:10.2307/3665454

Belkaoui, A., & Karpik, P. (1989). Determinants of Corporate Social Decision to Disclose Social Information. *Accounting, Auditing & Accountability Journal*, *2*(1), 09513578910132240. doi:10.1108/09513578910132240

Belot, F., Ginglinger, E., Slovin, M., & Sushka, M. (2014). Freedom of choice between unitary and two-tier boards: An empirical analysis. *Journal of Financial Economics*, *112*(3), 364–385. doi:10.1016/j.jfineco.2014.02.011

Ben Abdallah, A., & Makati, S. (2018). *Socially Responsible Humain Resource Management application in the Moroccan context. Actes du colloque international de recherché en économie et gestion 17* (Vol. II, pp. 419–436). Editions Universitaires Européennes.

Ben Aicha, O. (2017). La diffusion de la RSE dans les entreprises au Maroc: Facteurs déterminants, rôles et interactions des acteurs [Thèse de doctorat en Sciences de Gestion]. ISCAE.

Bénabou, R., & Tirole, J. (2010). Individual and corporate social responsibility. *Economica*, *77*(305), 1–19. doi:10.1111/j.1468-0335.2009.00843.x

Bennet, M., Burrit, R., & Schaltegger, S. (2006). Sustainability Accounting and Reporting. Eco-Efficient. In *Industry and Science*. Springer.

Bennett, R., Mousley, W., & Ali-Choudhury, R. (2008). Transfer of marketing knowledge within business – nonprofit collaborations. *Journal of Nonprofit & Public Sector Marketing*, *20*(1), 37–70. doi:10.1080/10495140802165352

Benraiss-Noailles, L., & Bentaleb, C. (2014). Etat des lieux de la RSE au Maroc. In *Ressources Humaines et Responsabilités sociétales*. Academic Press.

Bernardez, M. (2009). *The power of entrepreneurial ecosystems: Extracting booms from busts*. Expert 2 business. Retrieved from www.expert2business.com/itson/Articles/Ecosystems.pdf

Berthelot, S., & Robert, A. M. (2011). Climate change disclosures: An examination of Canadian oil and gas firms. *Issues in Social and Environmental Accounting*, *5*(1/2), 106–123. doi:10.22164/isea.v5i2.61

Bertoncello, S. L. T., & Chang JR, J. (2007). A importância da responsabilidade social corporativa como fator de diferenciação. *FACOM–Revista da Faculdade de comunicação da FAAP*, *17*, 70-76.

Beske, P., Land, A., & Seuring, S. (2014). Sustainable supply chain management practices and dynamic capabilities in the food industry: A critical analysis of the literature. *International Journal of Production Economics*, *152*, 131–143. doi:10.1016/j.ijpe.2013.12.026

Beuren, I.M. & Angonese, R. (2015). Instruments for determining the disclosure index of accounting information. *Revista Eletrônica de Estratégia e Negócios*, *8*(1), 120-144.

Bewley, K. & Li, Y. (2000). Disclosure of environmental information by Canadian manufacturing companies: a voluntary disclosure perspective. *Advances in Environmental Accounting & Management, 1*(1), 201-226.

Bhagat, S., & Black, B. (2001). The non-correlation between board independence and long-term firm performance. *The Journal of Corporation Law*, *27*(2), 231–273.

Bhattacharya, C. B., & Sen, S. (2004). Doing better at doing good: When. why, and how consumers respond to corporate social initiatives. *California Management Review*, *47*(1), 9–24. doi:10.2307/41166284

Bhatt, R. R., & Bhattacharya, S. (2017). Family firms, board structure and firm performance: Evidence from top Indian firms. *International Journal of Law and Management*, *59*(5), 699–717. doi:10.1108/IJLMA-02-2016-0013

Bhutta, N. T., & Saeed, M. M. (2011). Accounting scandals in the context of corporate social reporting. *Journal of Database Marketing & Customer Strategy Management*, *18*(3), 171–184. doi:10.1057/dbm.2011.25

Bialoskorski Neto, S., Barroso, M. F. G., & Rezende, A. J. (2012). Cooperative governance and management control systems: An agency costs theoretical approach. *Brazilian Business Review*, *9*(2), 68–87. doi:10.15728/bbr.2012.9.2.4

Bidwell, M. (2011). Paying more to get less: The effects of external hiring versus internal mobility. *Administrative Science Quarterly*, *56*(3), 369–407. doi:10.1177/0001839211433562

Bing, N. S., & Amran, A. (2017). The role of board diversity on materiality disclosure in sustainability reporting. *Global Business & Management Research*, *9*(4), 96–109.

Binkkour, A., & Messaoudi, M. (2013). *La communication de la RSE: entre conviction et contraintes - Cas de la PME marocaine. Communication de la responsabilité sociale des organisations: le défi de la crédibilité*. Université Laval.

Bisogno, M., Citro, F., & Tommasetti, A. (2014). Disclosure of university websites. Evidence from Italian data Disclosure of university websites. *Global Business and Economics Review*, *16*(4), 452–470. doi:10.1504/GBER.2014.065365

Bliss, M. A. (2011). Does CEO duality constrain board independence? Some evidence from audit pricing. *Accounting and Finance*, *51*(2), 361–380. doi:10.1111/j.1467-629X.2010.00360.x

Block, J., Sandner, P., & Spiegel, F. (2015). How do risk attitudes differ within the group of entrepreneurs? The role of motivation and procedural utility. *Journal of Small Business Management*, *53*(1), 183–206. doi:10.1111/jsbm.12060

Boas, S.; Monteiro, S. (2012). O relato sobre licenças de emissão de CO2: o caso das empresas portuguesas do PNALE II. In *XV Encontro AECA - Novos caminhos para a Europa: O papel das empresas e dos governos*. Academic Press.

Boccia, F., & Sarnacchiaro, P. (2018). The Impact of Corporate Social Responsibility on Consumer Preference: A Structural Equation Analysis. *Corporate Social Responsibility and Environmental Management*, *25*(2), 151–163. doi:10.1002/csr.1446

Boddy, C. (2011). *Corporate psychopaths* (1st ed.). Basingstoke: Palgrave Macmillan. Retrieved from http://www.loc.gov/catdir/enhancements/fy1114/2011003111-d.html

Boiral, O., Heras-Saizarbitoria, I., & Testa, F. (2017). SA8000 as CSR-Washing? The Role of Stakeholder Pressures. *Corporate Social Responsibility and Environmental Management*, *24*(1), 57–70. doi:10.1002/csr.1391

Bolanle, A. B. (2012). Corporate Social Responsibility and Profitability of Nigeria Banks. A Causal Relationship. *Research Journal of Finance and Accounting*, *3*(1), 6–18.

Bolisani, E., & Scarso, E. (2000). Electronic communication and knowledge transfer. *International Journal of Technology Management*, *20*(1–2), 116–133. doi:10.1504/IJTM.2000.002855

Bolton, L. E., & Mattila, A. S. (2015). How does corporate social responsibility affect consumer response to service failure in buyer-seller relationships? *Journal of Retailing*, *91*(1), 140–153. doi:10.1016/j.jretai.2014.10.001

Bonnet, C., Seville, M & Wirtz, P. (2017). Genèse et fonctionnement du conseil d'administration d'une firme entrepreneuriale: le rôle des identifications sociales des administrateurs. *Finance Contrôle Stratégie*, *20*(3).

Borger, F. G. (2001). *Responsabilidade Social: efeitos da atuação social na dinâmica empresarial* [Tese de Doutoramento]. Universidade de São Paulo, Faculdade de Economia e Administração.

Borghei, Z., & Leung, P. (2013). An empirical analysis of the determinants of greenhouse gas voluntary disclosure in Australia. *Accounting and Finance Research*, *2*(1), 110.

Borghei, Z., Leung, P., & Guthrie, J. (2016). The Nature Of Voluntary Greenhouse Gas Disclosure - An Explanation Of The Changing Rationale: Australian Evidence. *Meditari Accountability in Research*, *24*(1), 111–133.

Borghei, Z., Leung, P., & Guthrie, J. (2018). Voluntary greenhouse gas emission disclosure impacts on accounting-based performance: Australian evidence. *Australasian Journal of Environmental Management*, *25*(3), 321–338. doi:10.1080/14486563.2018.1466204

Boston College Center & EY. (2013). Value of Sustainability Reporting. Retrieved from http://www.ey.com/Publication/vwLUAssets/EY__Value_of_sustainability_reporting/$FILE/EY-Value-of-Sustainability-Reporting.pdf

Boulouta, I., & Pitelis, C. N. (2014). Who needs CSR? The impact of corporate social responsibility on national competitiveness. *Journal of Business Ethics*, *119*(3), 349–364. doi:10.100710551-013-1633-2

Bowen, H. (1953). *Social Responsibilities of the Businessman*. New York: Harper.

Bowen, H. R. (1957). *Responsabilidades sociais do homem de negócios*. Rio de Janeiro: Civilização Brasileira.

Boyack, K. W., van Eck, N. J., Colavizza, G., & Waltman, L. (2018). Characterizing in-text citations in scientific articles: A large-scale analysis. *Journal of Informetrics*, *12*(1), 59–73. doi:10.1016/j.joi.2017.11.005

Boyd, B. K. (1995). CEO duality and firm performance: A contingency model. *Strategic Management Journal, 16*(4), 301–312. doi:10.1002mj.4250160404

Brammer, S., He, H., & Mellahi, K. (2015). Corporate social responsibility, employee organizational identification, and creative effort: The moderating impact of corporate ability. *Group & Organization Management, 40*(3), 323–352. doi:10.1177/1059601114562246

Brammer, S., Jackson, G., & Matten, D. (2012). Corporate social responsibility and institutional theory: New perspectives on private governance. *Socio-economic Review, 10*(1), 3–28. doi:10.1093er/mwr030

Brammer, S., & Millington, A. (2005). Corporate reputation and philanthropy: An empirical analysis. *Journal of Business Ethics, 61*(1), 29–44. doi:10.100710551-005-7443-4

Brammer, S., & Millington, A. (2006). Firm size, organizational visibility and corporate philanthropy: An empirical analysis. *Business Ethics a European Review, 15*(1), 6–18. doi:10.1111/j.1467-8608.2006.00424.x

Brammer, S., Millington, A., & Rayton, B. (2007). The contribution of corporate social responsibility to organization commitment. *International Journal of Human Resource Management, 18*(10), 1701–1719. doi:10.1080/09585190701570866

Brammer, S., & Pavelin, S. (2008). Factors influencing the quality of corporate environmental disclosure. *Business Strategy and the Environment, 17*(2), 120–136. doi:10.1002/bse.506

Branco, M. C., & Rodrigues, L. L. (2006). Corporate social responsibility and resource-based perspectives. *Journal of Business Ethics, 69*(2), 111–132. doi:10.100710551-006-9071-z

Branco, M. C., & Rodrigues, L. L. (2008). Factors influencing social responsibility disclosure by Portuguese companies. *Journal of Business Ethics, 83*(4), 685–701. doi:10.100710551-007-9658-z

Brasil. (1981). Lei nº 6.938, de 31 de agosto de 1981. Retrieved from http://www.planalto.gov.br/ccivil_03/leis/l6938.htm

Brasil. (2009). Lei Complementar nº 130, de 17 de abril de 2009. Retrieved from http://www.planalto.gov.br/ccivil_03/leis/LCP/Lcp130.htm

Brasileira dos Bancos, F. (FEBRABAN). (2015). Normativo SARB Nº 14 de 28 de agosto de 2014. Retrieved from: https://portal.febraban.org.br/pagina/3083/45/pt-br/prsa

Bratu, A. (2017). Empricial study regarding the integrated reporting practices in Europe. *Audit Financiar, XV, 4*(148), 613–627. doi:10.20869/AUDITF/2017/148/613

Breitbarth, T., Walzel, S., Anagnostopoulos, C., & Van Eekeren, F. (2015). Corporate social responsibility and governance in sport: "Oh, the things you can find, if you don't stay behind! *Corporate Governance (Bingley), 15*(2), 254–273. doi:10.1108/CG-02-2015-0025

Bressan, V. G. F., Braga, M. J., Bressan, A. A., & Resende Filho, M. A. (2011). Uma aplicação do sistema PEARLS às cooperativas de crédito brasileiras. *Revista de Administração da Universidade de São Paulo, São Paulo, 46*(3), 258–274.

Brickley, J. A., Coles, J. L., & Jarrell, G. (1997). Leadership structure: Separating the CEO and chairman of the board. *Journal of Corporate Finance, 3*(3), 189–220. doi:10.1016/S0929-1199(96)00013-2

Broadstock, D. C., Matousek, R., Meyer, M., & Tzeremes, N. G. (2019). Does corporate social responsibility impact firms' innovation capacity? The indirect link between environmental & social governance implementation and innovation performance. *Journal of Business Research*. doi:10.1016/j.jbusres.2019.07.014

Brown, D. L., Vetterlein, A., & Roemer-Mahler, A. (2010). Theorizing transnational corporations as social actors: An analysis of corporate motivations. *Business and Politics, 12*(1), 1–37. doi:10.2202/1469-3569.1302

Browne, D., O'Regan, B., & Moles, R. (2012). Comparison of energy flow accounting, energy flow metabolism ratio analysis and ecological footprinting as tools for measuring urban sustainability: A case-study of an Irish city–region. *Ecological Economics, 83*, 97–107. doi:10.1016/j.ecolecon.2012.08.006

Brown, N., & Deegan, C. (1998). The public disclosure of environmental performance information-a dual test of media agenda setting theory and legitimacy theory. *Accounting and Business Research, 29*(1), 21–41. doi:10.1080/00014788.1998.9729564

Broye, G., François, A., & Moulin, Y. (2017). The cost of CEO duality: Evidence from French leadership compensation. *European Management Journal, 35*(3), 336–350. doi:10.1016/j.emj.2017.01.007

Bruch, H., & Walter, F. (2005). The keys to rethinking corporate philanthropy. *MIT Sloan Management Review, 47*, 48–56.

Brunsael, P. (2009). Corporate Social Responsibility as Competitive Advantage and Strategic Necessity [Dissertação]. University of Agder.

Bruton, G. D., Ahlstrom, D., & Li, H. L. (2010). Institutional theory and entrepreneurship: Where are we now and where do we need to move in the future? *Entrepreneurship Theory and Practice, 34*(3), 421–440. doi:10.1111/j.1540-6520.2010.00390.x

Brzeszczynski, J., & McIntosh, G. (2014). Performance of portfolios composed of British SRI stocks. *Journal of Business Ethics, 120*(3), 335–362. doi:10.100710551-012-1541-x

Buitendag, N., Fortuin, G. S., & De Laan, A. (2017). Firm characteristics and excellence in integrated reporting. *South African Journal of Economic and Management Sciences, 20*(1). doi:10.4102ajems.v20i1.1307

Burbano, V. C., Mamer, J., & Snyder, J. (2018). Pro bono as a human capital learning and screening mechanism: Evidence from law firms. *Strategic Management Journal, 39*(11), 2899–2920. doi:10.1002mj.2947

Busco, C., Granà, F., & Izzo, M. F. (2018). Make Sustainable Development Goals happen through Integrated Thinking: an introduction. In *Sustainable Development Goals and Integrated Reporting* (pp. 11–30). Routledge.

Café, L., & Bräscher, M. (2008). *Organização da informação e bibliometria. In Encontros Bibli: Revista Eletrônica de Biblioteconomia e Ciência da Informação* (pp. 54–75). Especial.

Cahan, S. F., De Villiers, C., Jeter, D. C., Naiker, V., & Van Staden, C. J. (2016). Are CSR disclosures value relevant? Cross-country evidence. *European Accounting Review, 25*(3), 579–611. doi:10.1080/09638180.2015.1064009

Caligiuri, P., Mencin, A., & Jiang, K. (2013). Win–win–win: The influence of company-sponsored volunteerism programs on employees, NGOs, and business units. *Personnel Psychology, 66*(4), 825–860. doi:10.1111/peps.12019

Calvo Centeno, M., Gragera Pizarro, E., Romero Ramos, E., & Ropero Moriones, E. (2018). Información no financiera divulgada por las empresas del IBEX 35: análisis de la contribución a los objetivos de desarrollo sostenible de Naciones Unidas. In Proceedings of the XVIII Encuentro Internacional AECA. Academic Press.

Campbell, B. A., Coff, R., & Kryscynski, D. (2012). Rethinking sustained competitive advantage from human capital. *Academy of Management Review, 37*(3), 376–395. doi:10.5465/amr.2010.0276

Campbell, D. (2003). Intra- and intersectoral effects in environmental disclosures: Evidence for legitimacy theory*? Business Strategy and the Environment, 12*(6), 357–371. doi:10.1002/bse.375

Campbell, J. L. (2007). Why would corporations behave in socially responsible ways? An institutional theory of corporate social responsibility. *Academy of Management Review, 32*(3), 946–967. doi:10.5465/amr.2007.25275684

Caragliu, A., Del Bo, C., & Nijkamp, P. (2011). Smart Cities in Europe. *Journal of Urban Technology, 18*(2), 65–82. doi:10.1080/10630732.2011.601117

Carpenter, V. L., & Feroz, E. H. (2001). Institutional theory and accounting rule choice: An analysis of four US state governments' decisions to adopt generally accepted accounting principles. *Accounting, Organizations and Society, 26*(7-8), 565–596. doi:10.1016/S0361-3682(00)00038-6Cho, C., & Patten, D. (2007). The role environmental disclosures as tools of legitimacy: A research note. *Accounting, Organizations and Society, 32*(7-8), 639–647. doi:10.1016/j.aos.2006.09.009

Carrol, B. (1997). A Three-Dimensional Conceptual Model of Social Performance. *Academy of Management Review*. doi:10.2307/257850

Carroll, A. B. (1979). A three-dimensional conceptual model of corporate performance. *Academy of Management Review, 4*(4), 497–505. doi:10.5465/amr.1979.4498296

Carroll, A. B. (1991). The pyramid of corporate social responsibility: Toward the moral management of organizational stakeholders. *Business Horizons, 34*(4), 39–48. doi:10.1016/0007-6813(91)90005-G

Carroll, A. B. (1999). Corporate social responsibility: Evolution of a definitional construct. *Business & Society, 38*(3), 268–295. doi:10.1177/000765039903800303

Carroll, A. B. (2008). A History of Corporate Social Responsibility: Concepts and Practices. In A. Crane, A. McWilliams, D. Matten, J. Moon, & D. Siegel (Eds.), *The Oxford Handbook of Corporate Social Responsibility* (pp. 19–46). Oxford: Oxford University Press.

Carroll, A. B. (2015). Corporate social responsibility: The centerpiece of competing and complementary frameworks. *Organizational Dynamics, 44*(2), 87–96. doi:10.1016/j.orgdyn.2015.02.002

Carroll, A. B., & Shabana, K. M. (2010). The business case for corporate social responsibility: A review of concepts, research and practice. *International Journal of Management Reviews, 12*(1), 85–105. doi:10.1111/j.1468-2370.2009.00275.x

Carvalho, L., Gallardo, V. D., & Nevado, G. M. T. (2018). Local municipalities' involvement in promoting entrepreneurship: An analysis of web page orientation to the entrepreneurs in Portuguese municipalities. In L. Carvalho (Ed.), Handbook of Research on Entrepreneurial Ecosystems and Social Dynamics in a Globalized World. Hershey PA: IGI Global.

Carvalho, F., Santos, G., & Gonçalves, J. (2018). The disclosure of information on sustainable development on the corporate website of the certified portuguese organizations. *International Journal of Qualitative Research, 12*(1), 253–276.

Carvalho, L. (2017). Entrepreneurial Ecosystems. Lisbon as a Smart Start-up City. In L. Carvalho (Ed.), *Handbook of Research On Entrepreneurial Development and Innovation within Smart Cities* (pp. 1–24). Hershey, PA: IGI Global. doi:10.4018/978-1-5225-1978-2.ch001

Carvalho, L., Pérez, E., & Pache, M. (2019). Implicación de los gobiernos locales en la promoción del emprendimiento: Evidencia para España. *Revista Espanola la de Documentacion Cientifica, 42*(1), 1–16.

Castilla-Polo, F., & Ruiz-Rodríguez, M. C. (2017). Usefulness of the Information on Intangible Assets Derived From Corporate Social Responsibility. *Paper presented at the European Conference on Intellectual Capital*. Academic Press.

Caughill, P. (2017). Singapore will stop adding new cars to its roads in 2018. Retrieved from https://futurism.com/singapore-will-stop-adding-new-cars-to-its-roads-in-2018

Cavaco, S., Crifo, P., Reberioux, R. & Roudaut, G. (2014). Independent directors: less informed, but better selected? New evidence from a two-way director-firm fixed effect model. *Cahier, 29*.

Cegarra-Navarro, J. G., Reverte, C., Gómez-Melero, E., & Wensley, A. K. P. (2016). Linking social and economic responsibilities with financial performance: The role of innovation. *European Management Journal*, *34*(5), 530–539. doi:10.1016/j.emj.2016.02.006

Centre for Cities. (2014). Smart cities definitions. Retrieved from https://www.centreforcities.org/reader/smart-cities/what-is-a-smart-city/1-smart-cities-definitions/

Chang, A. (2015). The Role of Internal and External Corporate Governance Mechanisms on Firm's Financial Performance in Malaysia. *Asian Journal of Accounting and Governance*, *6*, 55–65. doi:10.17576/AJAG-2015-6-06

Chen, C. W., Lin, J. B., & Yi, B. (2008). CEO duality and firm performance - An endogenous issue. *Corporate Ownership & Control*, *6*(1), 58–65. doi:10.22495/cocv6i1p6

Cheng, E. C. M., & Courtenay, S. M. (2006). Board composition, regulatory regime and voluntary disclosure. *The International Journal of Accounting*, *41*(3), 262–289. doi:10.1016/j.intacc.2006.07.001

Cheng, M., Green, W., Conradie, P., Konishi, N., & Romi, A. (2014). The International Integrated Reporting Framework: Key Issues and Future Research Opportunities. *Journal of International Financial Management & Accounting*, *25*(1), 90–119. doi:10.1111/jifm.12015

Chen, J. C., Patten, D. M., & Roberts, R. (2008). Corporate charitable contributions: A corporate social performance or legitimacy strategy? *Journal of Business Ethics*, *82*, 131–144. doi:10.100710551-007-9567-1

Cherkaoui, A. (2016). Pratiques RSE des pme au Maroc: une analyse perceptuelle auprès des dirigeants casablancais. Question(s) de management, 3(14), 13-26. doi:10.3917/qdm.163.0013

Chersan, I. (2017). Integrated reporting in europe – from voluntary to mandatory? Journal of Public Administration, *Finance and Law,* (3), 19-30

Chia, J. (2011). Communicating, connecting and developing social capital for sustainable organisations and their communities. *Australasian Journal of Regional Studies*, *17*(3), 330–351.

Choi, B. B., Lee, D., & Park, Y. (2013). Corporate Social Responsibility, Corporate Governance and Earnings Quality: Evidence from Korea. *Corporate Governance*, *21*(5), 447–467. doi:10.1111/corg.12033

Choi, F. D. S. (1973). Financial disclosure and entry to the European capital market. *Journal of Accounting Research*, *11*(2), 159–175. doi:10.2307/2490187

Choi, H., & Pae, J. (2011). Business Ethics and Financial Reporting Quality: Evidence from Korea. *Journal of Business Ethics*, *103*(3), 403–427. doi:10.1007/s10551-011-0871-4

Choi, S., & Ng, A. (2011). Environmental and economic dimensions of sustainability and Price effects on consumer responses. *Journal of Business Ethics*, *104*(2), 269–282. doi:10.100710551-011-0908-8

Cho, S. J., Chung, C. Y., & Young, J. (2019). Study on the relationship between CSR and financial performance. *Sustainability*, *11*(2), 343. doi:10.3390u11020343

Chuang, S. P., & Huang, S. J. (2018). The Effect of Environmental Corporate Social Responsibility on Environmental Performance and Business Competitiveness: The Mediation of Green Information Technology Capital. *Journal of Business Ethics*, *150*(4), 991–1009. doi:10.100710551-016-3167-x

Churet, C., & Eccles, R. G. (2014). Integrated reporting, quality of management and financial performance. *Journal of Applied Corporate Finance*, *26*(1), 56–64.

Clarkson, M. B. E. (1995). A Stakeholder Framework for Analyzing and Evaluating Corporate Social Performance. *Academy of Management Review*, *20*(1), 92–117. doi:10.5465/amr.1995.9503271994

Clarkson, P. M., Li, Y., Richardson, G. D., & Vasvari, F. P. (2008). Revisiting the relation between environmental performance and environmental disclosure: An empirical analysis. *Accounting, Organizations and Society*, *33*(4), 303–327. doi:10.1016/j.aos.2007.05.003

Colbert, B. A., & Kurucz, E. (2007). Three conceptions of Triple Bottom Line Business Sustainability and the Role for HRM. *HR. Human Resource Planning*, *30*(1), 21–29.

Cole, R. A., & Mehran, H. (1998). The effect of changes in ownership structure on performance: Evidence from the thrift industry. *Journal of Financial Economics*, *50*(3), 291–317. doi:10.1016/S0304-405X(98)00039-7

Collett, P., & Hrasky, S. (•••). Voluntary Disclosure of Corporate Governance Practices by Listed Australian Companies. *Corporate Governance*, *13*(2), 188–196.

Comisión de las Comunidades Europeas. (2001). *Libro Verde. Fomentar un Marco Europeo para la Responsabilidad Social de las Empresas.*

Comisión de las Comunidades Europeas. (2011). *Comunicación de la comisión al Parlamento Europeo, al consejo, al comité económico y social europeo y al comité de las regiones. Estrategia renovada de la UE para 2011-2014 sobre la responsabilidad social de las empresas.* Comisión Europea, Bruselas.

Comissão Das Comunidades Europeias. (2001). Livro Verde: Promover um quadro europeu para a responsabilidade social das empresas.

Commission of the European Communities. (2001). Commission Recommendation of 30 May 2001 on the recognition, valuation and reporting of environmental matters in the annual accounts and the annual report on the management of companies,, L 156, 13.06.01.

Commission of the European Communities. (2001). Green Paper. Promoting a European Framework for Corporate Social Responsibility. Retrieved from http://eur-lex.europa.eu

Commission of the European Communities. (2008). Communication from the commission to the council, the European parliament, the European economic and social committee, and the committee of the regions: A mid-term assessment of implementing the EC biodiversity action plan. *Journal of International Wildlife Law and Policy*, *12*(3), 216–228. doi:10.1080/13880290903199425

Commission of the European Communities. (2011). *A renewed EU strategy 2011-14 for corporate social responsibility.* Brussels: European Commission.

Committee on Accounting Standardization. (2006). Technical Interpretation No. 4 - Greenhouse gas emission allowances: accounting for emission allowances, Published in Diário da República II Series, May 25, 2006 -Despacho n.º 11 384/2006 (2nd series).

Committee on Accounting Standardization. (2009). Accounting and Financial Reporting Standard 26 - Environmental Matters, CD of the Order of Chartered Accountants.

Connely, B., Hoskisson, R., & Certo, S. (2010). Ownership as a Form of Corporate Governance. *Journal of Management Studies*, *47*(8), 1561–1589. doi:10.1111/j.1467-6486.2010.00929.x

Consultants Private Limited. (2014). World Cities Summit. Retrieved from http://www.scp.com/page.aspx?s=en&cid=19&id=450

Cooke, T. E. (1989). Disclosure in the corporate annual reports of Swedish companies. *Accounting and Business Research*, *19*(74), 113–124. doi:10.1080/00014788.1989.9728841

Corazza, L. (2018). The process of social accounting and reporting at University of Torino: Main challenges and managerial implications. World Review of Entrepreneurship, Management and Sust. *Development*, *14*(1/2), 171–186.

Corlett, J. (1988). Schefflerian ethics and corporate social-responsibility. *Journal of Business Ethics*, *7*(8), 631–638. doi:10.1007/BF00382797

Cormier, D., Gordon, I. M., & Magnan, M. (2004). Corporate environmental disclosure: Contrasting management's perceptions with reality. *Journal of Business Ethics*, *49*(2), 143–165. doi:10.1023/B:BUSI.0000015844.86206.b9

Cormier, D., Magnan, M., & Van Velthoven, B. (2005). Environmental disclosure quality in large German companies: Economic incentives, public pressures or institutional conditions? *European Accounting Review*, *14*(1), 3–39. doi:10.1080/0963818042000339617

Cornett, M. M., Marcus, J. A., & Tehranian, H. (2008). Corporate governance and pay-for-performance: The impact of earnings management. *Journal of Financial Economics*, *87*(2), 357–373. doi:10.1016/j.jfineco.2007.03.003

Coulmont, M., Loomis, S., Berthelot, S., & Gangi, F. (2015). Determinants and Impacts of Sustainability Disclosure. In *Studies in Managerial and Financial Accounting* (pp. 25-79). Academic Press.

Coupland, C. (2005). Corporate social responsibility as argument on the web. *Journal of Business Ethics*, *62*(4), 355–366. doi:10.1007/s10551-005-1953-y

Cowan, S., & Gadenne, D. (2005). Australian corporate environmental reporting: A comparative analysis of disclosure practices across voluntary and mandatory disclosure systems. *Journal of Accuonting & Organizational Change*, *1*(2), 165–179. doi:10.1108/18325910510635344

Coy, D. A. C., Ischer, M. A. R. Y. F., & Ordon, T. E. G. (2001). Public accountability: A new paradigm for college and university annual reports. *Critical Perspectives on Accounting*, *12*(1), 1–31. doi:10.1006/cpac.2000.0416

Crane, A., McWilliams, A., Matten, D., Moon, J., & Siegel, D. S. (Eds.). (2008). *The Oxford handbook of corporate social responsibility*. Oxford University Press on Demand.

Criado-Jiménez, I., Fernández-Chulián, M., Husillos-Carqués, F., & Larrinaga-González, C. (2008). Compliance with mandatory environmental reporting in financial statements: The case of Spain (2001–2003). *Journal of Business Ethics*, *79*(3), 245–262. doi:10.100710551-007-9375-7

Crifo, P. & Rebérioux, A. (2015). Gouvernance et responsabilité sociétale des entreprises: nouvelle frontière de la finance durable ? *Revue d'économie financière*, (117), 205-223.

Crifo, P., & Forget, V. (2019). The Economics of Corporate Social Responsibility: A firm-level perspective survey. *Journal of Economic Surveys*, *29*(1), 112–130. doi:10.1111/joes.12055

Cropanzano, R., Byrne, Z. S., Bobocel, D. R., & Rupp, D. E. (2001). Moral virtues, fairness heuristics, social entities, and other denizens of organizational justice. *Journal of Vocational Behavior*, *58*(2), 164–209. doi:10.1006/jvbe.2001.1791

Custodio, A. L. M., & Moya, R. (2013). *Indicadores Ethos de Responsabilidade Social Empresarial*. São Paulo: Instituto Ethos.

Daddi, T., Magistrelli, M., Frey, M., & Iraldo, F. (2011). Do environmental management systems improve environmental performance? Empirical evidence from Italian companies. *Environment, Development and Sustainability*, *13*(5), 845–862. doi:10.100710668-011-9294-8

Dahlsrud, A. (2008). How corporate social responsibility is defined: an analysis of 37 definitions. *Corporate Social Responsibility and Environmental Management, 15*, 1-13. doi:10.1002/csr/132

Dahlsrud, A. (2008). How corporate social responsibility is defined: An analysis of 37 definitions. *Corporate Social Responsibility and Environmental Management, 15*(1), 1–13. doi:10.1002/csr.132

Dahlsrud, A. (2008). How Corporate Social Responsibility Is Defined: An Analysis of 37 Definitions. *Corporate Social Responsibility and Environmental Management, 15*(1), 1–13. doi:10.1002/csr.132

Daily, C. M., & Dalton, D. R. (1997). Separate, But Not Independent: Board leadership structure in large corporations. *Corporate Governance, 5*(3), 126–136. doi:10.1111/1467-8683.00053

Daily, C. M., Dalton, D. R., & Canella, A. A. (2003). Corporate Governance: Decades of Dialogue and Data. *Academy of Management Review, 28*(3), 371–382. doi:10.5465/amr.2003.10196703

Damak-Ayadi, S. (2010). Social and environmental reporting in the annual reports of large companies in France. *Accounting and Management Information Systems, 9*(1), 22–44.

Dan Basuki, I. (2016). Carbon Emission Disclosure: Studi Pada Perusahaan Manufaktur Indonesia. *Jurnal Akuntansi dan Keuangan, 18*(2), 92-104. doi:10.9744/jak.18.2.92-104

Dardour, A. & Husser, J. (2016). Does It Pay to Disclose CSR Information? Evidence from French Companies. *Management international, 20*, 94-108.

Davis, J. H., Schoorman, F. D., & Donaldson, L. (1997). Toward a stewardship theory of management. *Academy of Management Review, 22*(1), 20–47. doi:10.5465/amr.1997.9707180258

Davis, K. (1973). The case for and against business assumption of social responsibilities. *Academy of Management Journal, 16*(2), 312–323.

Dawkins, C., & Ngunjiri, F. W. (2008). Corporate Social Responsibility Reporting in South Africa a Descriptive and Comparative Analysis. *Journal of Business Communication, 45*(3), 286–307. doi:10.1177/0021943608317111

Dawkins, J. (2005). Corporate responsibility: The communication challenge. *Journal of Communication Management, 9*(2), 108–119. doi:10.1108/13632540510621362

De Beer, P., & Friend, F. (2006). Environmental accounting. A management tool for enhancing corporate environmental and economic performance. *Ecological Economics, 58*(3), 548–560. doi:10.1016/j.ecolecon.2005.07.026

De Miguel, M. L. (2011). *La Responsabilidad Social Empresarial en la pequeña y mediana empresa: Guía de buenas prácticas. Proyecto Impulsa-RSE Pyme financiado por el Ministerio de Industria Turismo y Comercio.*

De Villiers, C., & Marques, A. (2016). Corporate social responsibility, country-level predispositions, and the consequences of choosing a level of disclosure. *Accounting and Business Research, 46*(2), 167–195. doi:10.1080/00014788.2015.1039476

De Villiers, C., Venter, E. R., & Hsiao, P.-C. (2017). Integrated reporting, measurement issues, approaches and an agenda for future research. *Accounting and Finance, 57*(4), 937–959. doi:10.1111/acfi.12246

Decker, O. S. (2004). Corporate social responsibility and structural change in financial services. *Managerial Auditing Journal, 19*(6), 712–728. doi:10.1108/02686900410543840

Decree-Law no. 158/2009, of July 13, Diário da República, 1st series, no. 133. (2009).

Decree-Law no. 230/2005 of 29 December, Diário da República, 1st series, no. 249. (2005).

Decree-Law no. 233/2004 of December 14, Diário da República, 1st series, no. 291. (2004).

Decree-Law no. 24/2004, of January 23, Diário da República, 1st Series - A, no. 19. (2004).

Decree-Law no. 35/2005, of 17 of February, Diário da República, 1st series, nº 133. (2005).

Decree-Law no. 98/2015, of June 2, Diário da República, 1st series, no. 106. (2015).

Decreto-Lei. n.º 89/de 28 de julho - Divulgação de informações não financeiras e de informações sobre a diversidade por grandes empresas e grupos. (2017).

Deegan, C. (2002). The Legitimising Effect of Social and Environmental Disclosures – A Theoretical Foundation. *Accounting, Auditing & Accountability Journal, 15*(3), 282–311. doi:10.1108/09513570210435852

Deegan, C. (2003). *Environmental management accounting: An introduction and case studies for Australia (EMAP)*. Sydney: Institute of Chartered Accountants in Australia.

Deegan, C. (2017). Twenty five years of social and environmental accounting research within critical perspectives of Accounting: Hits, misses and ways forward. *Critical Perspectives on Accounting, 43*, 65–87. doi:10.1016/j.cpa.2016.06.005

Deegan, C., Rankin, M., & Tobin, J. (2002). An examination of the corporate social and environmental disclosures of BHP from 1983-1997: A test of legitimacy theory. *Accounting, Auditing & Accountability Journal, 15*(3), 312–343. doi:10.1108/09513570210435861

Del Brio, J. A., Fernández, E., Junquera, B., & Vázquez, C. J. (2001). Environmental managers and departments as driving forces of TQEM in Spanish industrial companies. *International Journal of Quality & Reliability Management, 18*(5), 495–511. doi:10.1108/02656710110392638

Delmas, M., & Toffel, M. W. (2004). Stakeholders and environmental management practices: An institutional framework. *Business Strategy and the Environment, 13*(4), 209–222. doi:10.1002/bse.409

Desai, A., Kroll, M., & Wright, P. (2003). CEO duality, board monitoring, and acquisition performance: A test of competing theories. *The Journal of Business Strategy, 20*(2), 137–156.

Detomasi, D. A. (2008). The Political Roots of Corporate Social Responsibility. *Journal of Business Ethics, 82*(4), 807–819. doi:10.100710551-007-9594-y

Detthamrong, U., Chancharat, N., & Vithessonthi, C. (2017). Corporate governance, capital structure and firm performance: Evidence from Thailand. *Research in International Business and Finance, 42*, 689–709. doi:10.1016/j.ribaf.2017.07.011

Deus, R. M., Battistelle, R. A. G., & Silva, G. H. R. D. (2016). Sustainability insights from the mission statements of leading Brazilian Universities. *International Journal of Educational Management, 30*(3), 403–415. doi:10.1108/IJEM-05-2014-0065

Dewi, D.M., & Sudarma, M., Djumahir, & Ganis, E. (2014). CSR Effect on Market and Financial Performance. *International Journal of Business and Management Invention, 3*(1), 56–66.

Dey, A., Engel, E., & Liu, X. (2011). CEO and board chair roles: To split or not to split? *Journal of Corporate Finance, 17*(5), 1595–1618. doi:10.1016/j.jcorpfin.2011.09.001

Di Benedetto, C. A. (2017). Corporate social responsibility as an emerging business model in fashion marketing. *Journal of Global Fashion Marketing, 8*(4), 251–265. doi:10.1080/20932685.2017.1329023

Di Bitetti, M. S., & Ferreras, J. A. (2017). Publish (in English) or perish: The effect on citation rate of using languages other than English in scientific publications. *Ambio, 46*(1), 121–127. doi:10.100713280-016-0820-7 PMID:27686730

Diari de Tarragona. (2016). *L'Arboç estudia implantar el 'radar solidario' para ayudas sociales*. Retrieved from http://www.diaridetarragona.com

Dias, A. (2009). O Relato da Sustentabilidade Empresarial: práticas em Portugal [Dissertação]. Universidade Aberta, Lisboa.

Dias, A. (2009). O Relato da Sustentabilidade Empresarial: Evidência empírica nas empresas cotadas em Portugal. *Portuguese Journal of Accounting & Management*, *8*(1), 111–150.

Dias, A., Rodrigues, L., & Craig, R. (2016). Global financial crisis and corporate social responsibility disclosure. *Social Responsibility Journal*, *12*(4), 654–667. doi:10.1108/SRJ-01-2016-0004

Dienes, D., & Velte, P. (2016). The impact of supervisory board composition on CSR reporting. Evidence from the German two-tier system. *Sustainability*, *8*(1), 1–20. doi:10.3390u8010063

Dimaggio, P., & Powell, W. W. (1983). The iron cage revisited: Institutional isomorphism and collective rationality in organizational fields. *American Sociological Review*, *48*(2), 147–160. doi:10.2307/2095101

Dimova, R., & Pela, K. (2018). Entrepreneurship: Structural transformation, skills and constraints. *Small Business Economics*, *51*(1), 203–220. doi:10.100711187-017-9916-0

Directive 2003/87/EC of the European Parliament and of the Council of 13 October. (2003).

Directive 2009/29/EC of the European Parliament and of the Council of 23 April. (2009).

Diretiva 2014/95/UE do Parlamento Europeu e do Conselho, de 22 de outubro de 2014, que altera a Diretiva 2013/34/UE no que se refere à divulgação de informações não financeiras e de informações sobre a diversidade por parte de certas grandes empresas e grupos. (2014).

Dissanayake, D., Tilt, C., & Qian, W. (2019). Factors influencing sustainability reporting by Sri Lankan companies. *Pacific Accounting Review*, *31*(1), 84–109. doi:10.1108/PAR-10-2017-0085

Djama, C., & Martinez, I. (2007). *La comptabilisation des quotas d'émission de gaz à effet de serre: véritable incitation de lutte contre le réchauffement climatique?* Universités Toulouse et Poitiers.

Doane, D. (2002). Market failure: The case for mandatory social and environmental reporting. *Presentation at Institute for Public Policy Research seminar*. Academic Press.

Domenichelli, R.N. (2012). Factores condicionantes de la actividad emprendedora. *Revista de treball, economia i societat*, (64), 1-16.

Donaldson, L., & Davis, J. H. (1991). Stewardship theory or agency theory: Corporate governance and shareholder returns. *Australian Journal of Management*, *16*(1), 49–64. doi:10.1177/031289629101600103

Donaldson, T., & Preston, L. E. (1995). The stakeholder theory of the corporation: Concepts, evidenc. *Academy of Management.the Academy of Management Review*, *20*(1), 65–91. doi:10.5465/amr.1995.9503271992

Donnelly, R., & Mulcahy, M. (2008). Board structure, ownership, and voluntary disclosure in Ireland. *Corporate Governance*, *16*(5), 416–429. doi:10.1111/j.1467-8683.2008.00692.x

Dowling, J., & Pfeffer, J. (1975). Organizational Legitimacy: Social Values and Organizational Behavior. *Pacific Sociological Review*, *18*(1), 122–136. doi:10.2307/1388226

Drakos, A. A., & Bekoris, F. V. (2010). Endogeneity and the Relationship Between Board Structure and Firm Performance: A Simultaneous Equation Analysis for the Athens Stock Exchange. *Managerial and Decision Economics*, *31*(6), 387–401. doi:10.1002/mde.1492

Drucker, P. (1986). Management: Tasks, Responsibilities, Practices (Truman Tal ed.). Academic Press.

Drucker, P. (1984). The New Meaning of Corporate Social Responsibility. *California Management Review*, *26*(2), 53–63. doi:10.2307/41165066

Drucker, P. (1984). The new meaning of corporate social responsibility. *California Management Review*, *26*(2), 53–63. doi:10.2307/41165066

Duarte, A. P., Gomes, D. R., & Neves, J. G. (2014). Finding the jigsaw piece for our jigsaw puzzle with corporate social responsibility. *Management Research: The journal of the iberoamerican Academy of Management Journal*, *12*(3), 240–258.

Duarte, P., & Costa e Silva, S. (2018). The role of consumer-cause identification and attitude in the intention to purchase cause-related products. *International Marketing Review*. doi:10.1108/IMR-04-2018-0159

Dubey, R., Gunasekaran, A., Papadopoulos, T., Childe, S. J., Shibin, K. T., & Wamba, S. F. (2017). Sustainable supply chain management: Framework and further research directions. *Journal of Cleaner Production*, *142*, 1119–1130. doi:10.1016/j.jclepro.2016.03.117

Duff, A. (2016). Corporate social responsibility reporting in professional accounting firms. *The British Accounting Review*, *48*(1), 74–86. doi:10.1016/j.bar.2014.10.010

Duguid, F. & Balkan, D. (2016). Talking the talk: canadian cooperatives and sustainability reporting. *Journal of cooperative accounting and reporting*, *4*(1), 1-34.

Dumitru, M., Glavan, M. E., Gorgan, C., & Dumitru, V. F. (2013). International integrated reporting framework: A case study in the software industry. *Annales Universitatis Apulensis Series Oeconomica*, *15*(1), 24.

Eccles, R. G., & Armbrester, K. (2011). Integrated reporting in the cloud. *IESE Insight*, (8), 13–20.

Eccles, R. G., & Armbrester, K. (2011). Integrated Reporting in the Cloud: Two disruptive ideas combined. *IESE insight*, *8*.

Eccles, R. G., & Serafeim, G. (2015). Corporate and integrated reporting: A functional perspective. In *Corporate Stewardship*. Sheffield, UK: Greenleaf Publishing.

Eccles, R. G., & Saltzman, D. (2011). Achieving sustainability through integrated reporting. *Stanford Social Innovation Review*, *9*(3), 56–61.

Eccles, R. G., & Serafeim, G. (2015). Corporate and integrated reporting: a functional perspective. In *Mohrman, S., O'Toole, J. e Lawler, E., Corporate Stewardship: Organizing for Sustainable Effectiveness* (pp. 156–173). Sheffield, UK: Greenleaf Publishing. doi:10.9774/GLEAF.9781783532605_10

Eisenberg, T., Sundgren, S., & Wells, M. T. (1998). Larger Board Size and Decreasing Firm Value in Small Firms. *Journal of Financial Economics*, *48*(1), 35–54. doi:10.1016/S0304-405X(98)00003-8

Eisenhardt, K. M. (1989). Agency Theory: An Assessment and Review. *Academy of Management Review*, *14*(1), 57–74. doi:10.5465/amr.1989.4279003

El Akremi, A., Gond, J. P., Swaen, V., De Roeck, K., & Igalens, J. (2018). How Do Employees Perceive Corporate Responsibility? Development and Validation of a Multidimensional Corporate Stakeholder Responsibility Scale. *Journal of Management*, *44*(2), 619–657. doi:10.1177/0149206315569311

El Diario Cantabria. (2016). *Santa María de Cayón instala el primer radar de recaudación solidaria en España*. Retrieved from http://eldiariocantabria.es

El Diario Montañés. (2016). *Foro*. Retrieved from http://eldiariomontanes.es

El Ghoul, S., Guedhami, O., Kwok, C. Y., & Mishra, D. (2011). Does corporate social responsibility affect the cost of capital? *Journal of Banking & Finance*, *35*(9), 2388–2406. doi:10.1016/j.jbankfin.2011.02.007

ElKelish, W. W., & Hassan, K. M. (2015). Corporate governance disclosure and share price accuracy: Empirical evidence from the United Arab Emirates. *Journal of Applied Accounting Research*, *16*(2), 265–286. doi:10.1108/JAAR-02-2013-0015

Elkington, J. (1994). Towards the Sustainable Corporation: Win-Win-Win Business Strategies for Sustainable Development. *California Management Review*, *36*(2), 90–100. doi:10.2307/41165746

Elkington, J. (2000). Cannibals with forks: The triple bottom line of 21st century business. *Journal of Business Ethics*, *23*(2), 229–231. doi:10.1023/A:1006129603978

Elkington, J. (2012). *Sustentabilidade, canibais com garfo e faca*. São Paulo: M. Books do Brasil Editora Ltda.

Elshahat, A., Parhizgari, A., & Hong, L. (2012). The information content of the banking regulatory agencies and the depository credit intermediation institutions. *Journal of Economics and Business*, *64*(1), 90–104. doi:10.1016/j.jeconbus.2011.06.003

Epstein, M. J. (2008). *Making sustainability work: Best practices in managing and measuring corporate, social, environmental, and economic impacts*. San Francisco, CA: Berret-Koehler Publishers, Inc.

Erhemjamts, O., Li, Q., & Venkateswaran, A. (2013). Corporate social responsibility and its impact on firms' investment policy, organizational structure, and performance. *Journal of Business Ethics*, *118*(2), 395–412. doi:10.100710551-012-1594-x

Escribano Francés, G. (2012). Desarrollo energético sostenible y energías renovables. *Cuadernos Económicos de ICE*, *864*, 73–83.

Esty, D., & Winston, A. (2009). *Green to Gold: How Smart Companies Use Environmental Strategy to Innovate, Create Value, and Build Competitive Advantage*. John Wiley & Sons.

EU. (2001). Promoting a European framework for corporate social responsibility. *Commission of the European Communities*.

European Commission (COM). (2016). Communication from de Commission to the European Parliament, the Council, the European Economic and Social Committee and Committee of the Regions. Next steps for a sustainable European future. European action for sustainability.

European Commission. (2002). *Corporate Social Responsibility: A business contribution to sustainable, development*. Office for Official Publications of the European Communities.

European Commission. (2011). Communication from the Commission to the European Parliament, the Council, the European Economic and Social Committee and the Committee of the Regions.

European Commission. (2011). Communication from the commission to the European Parliament, the Council, the European Economic and Social Committee and the Committee of the Regions: A renewed EU strategy 2011-14 for corporate social responsibility COM (2011) 681 final. Brussels: EC.

European Commission. (2011). *Corporate social responsibility: a new EU strategy for the period 2011-2014*. COM (2011) 681 final. Retrieved from http://www.europarl.europa.eu/meetdocs/2009_2014/documents/com/com_com(2011)0681_/com_com(2011)0681_pt.pdf

European Commission. (2018). Smart cities. Retrieved from https://ec.europa.eu/info/eu-regional-and-urban-development/topics/cities-and-urban-development/city-initiatives/smart-cities_en

Evgeny, I. (2015). The impact of financial leverage on firm performance: Evidence from Russia. *Journal of Corporate Finance Research*, *34*(2), 24–36.

Faisal, F., Andiningtyas, E., Achmad, T., Haryanto, H., & Meiranto, W. (2017). The content and determinants of greenhouse gas emission disclosure: Evidence from Indonesian companies. *Corporate Social Responsibility and Environmental Management*, *25*(6), 1397–1406. doi:10.1002/csr.1660

Faleye, O. (2007). Does one hat fit all? The case of corporate leadership structure. *The Journal of Management and Governance*, *11*(3), 239–259. doi:10.100710997-007-9028-3

Fama, E., & Jensen, M. (1983). Separation of ownership and control. *The Journal of Law & Economics*, *26*(2), 301–325. doi:10.1086/467037

Farcane, N., & Bureana, E. (2015). History of Corporate Social Responsibility Concept. *Annales Universitatis Apulensis Series Oeconomica*, *2*(17), 31–48.

Farley, J., & Voinov, A. (2016). Economics, socio-ecological resilience and ecosystem services. *Journal of Environmental Management*, *183*, 389–398. doi:10.1016/j.jenvman.2016.07.065 PMID:27480914

Farmer, S. M., Yao, X., & Kung-Mcintyre, K. (2011). The behaioral impact of entrepreneur Identy aspiration and prior entrepreneurial Experience. *Entrepreneurship Theory and Practice*, *35*(2), 245–273. doi:10.1111/j.1540-6520.2009.00358.x

Farooq, O., Rupp, D. E., & Farooq, M. (2017). The multiple pathways through which internal and external corporate social responsibility influence organizational identification and multifoci outcomes: The moderating role of cultural and social orientations. *Academy of Management Journal*, *60*(3), 954–985. doi:10.5465/amj.2014.0849

Fasan, M., & Mio, C. (2016). Fostering stakeholder engagement: The role of materiality disclosure in integrated reporting. *Business Strategy and the Environment*, *26*(3), 288–305. doi:10.1002/bse.1917

Fatemi, A., Fooladi, I., & Tehranian, H. (2015). Valuation effects of corporate social responsibility. *Journal of Banking & Finance*, *59*, 182–192. doi:10.1016/j.jbankfin.2015.04.028

Fauzi, H., & Idris, K. (2009). The Relationship of CSR and Financial Performance: New Evidence from Indonesian Companies (October 18, 2010). *Issues in Social and Environmental Accounting*, *3*(1). Retrieved from https://ssrn.com/abstract=1694284

Feitosa, M. J. S., Souza, N. M. O., Santos, R. S., & Firmo, L. A. (2014). Estágio de desenvolvimento da responsabilidade social empresarial no setor bancário: Um estudo em uma agência do Banco do Brasil. *Revista Metropolitana de Sustentabilidade*, *4*(3), 15.

Feng, Y., Zhu, Q., & Lai, K. H. (2017). Corporate social responsibility for supply chain management: A literature review and bibliometric analysis. *Journal of Cleaner Production*, *158*, 296–307. doi:10.1016/j.jclepro.2017.05.018

Fernandes, M. T., Veloso, A. B., & Pinto, L. C. (2009). *O mercado de direitos de emissão de CO2: um estudo experimental* [PhD Thesis]. Universidade do Minho.

Fernandez-Feijoo, B., Romero, S., & Ruiz-Blanco, S. (2014). Women on boards: Do they affect sustainability reporting? *Corporate Social Responsibility and Environmental Management*, *21*(6), 351–364. doi:10.1002/csr.1329

Fernández, L. S., & Fernández, E. F. (2010). Competencias emprendedoras y desarrollo del espíritu empresariales en los centros educativos. *Educación XX1. Revista da Faculdade de Educação*, *13*(1), 15–38.

Fernández-Pinto, I., López-Pérez, B., & Márquez, M. (2008). Empatía: Medidas, teorías y aplicaciones en revisión. *Anales de Psicología, 24*, 284–298.

Fernando, A.; Albuquerque, F.; Almeida, M.; Delgado, S. (2010). Tratamento contabilístico das licenças de emissão de gases com efeito de estufa: o caso português. In *XIV Encuentro AECA*. Academic Press.

Ferrell, O. C. (2010). Shelby Hunt's Resource Advantage Theory. University of New Mexico.

Ferrero-Ferrero, I., Fernández-Izquierdo, M. A., Muñoz-Torres, M. J., & Bellá-Colomer, L. (2018). Stakeholder engagement in sustainability reporting in higher education: An analysis of key internal stakeholders' expectations. *International Journal of Sustainability in Higher Education, 19*(2), 313–336. doi:10.1108/IJSHE-06-2016-0116

Fifka, M. S. (2013). Corporate responsibility reporting and its determinants in comparative perspective – a review of the empirical literature and a meta-analysis. *Business Strategy and the Environment, 22*(1), 1–35. doi:10.1002/bse.729

Fifka, M. S. (2013). Corporate responsibility reporting and its determinants in comparative perspective–a review of the empirical literature and a meta-analysis. *Business Strategy and the Environment, 22*(1), 1–35. doi:10.1002/bse.729

Finkelstein, S., & D'Aveni, R. A. (1994). CEO duality as a double-edged sword: How boards of directors balance entrenchment avoidance and unity of command. *Academy of Management Journal, 37*(5), 1079–1108. doi:10.5465/256667

Finkelstein, S., Hambrick, D. C., & Cannella, A. A. (2009). *Strategic leadership: Theory and research on executives, top management teams and boards*. New York, NY: Oxford University Press.

Fischer, R. M., & Mendonça, L. R. (2002). Terceiro Setor: Inventário da Produção Brasileira. In *ISTR – Fifth International Conference: Transforming Civil Society, Citizenship And Governance: The Third Sector in an Era of Global (Dis) Order*. Academic Press.

Flammer, C., & Luo, J. (2017). Corporate social responsibility as an employee governance tool: Evidence from a quasi-experiment. *Strategic Management Journal, 38*(1), 163–183. doi:10.1002mj.2492

Flower, J. (2015). The international integrated reporting council: A story of failure. *Critical Perspectives on Accounting, 27*, 1–17. doi:10.1016/j.cpa.2014.07.002

Fombrun, C., & Shanley, M. (1990). What's in a name? Reputation building and corporate strategy. *Academy of Management Journal, 33*(2), 233–258.

Fombrun, Ch. J., & Van Riel, C. B. M. (2004). *Fame & fortune: How successful companies build winning reputations*. FT Press.

Forbes, D. P., & Milliken, F. J. (1999). Cognition and Corporate Governance: Understanding Boards of Directors as Strategic Decision-Making Groups. *Academy of Management Review, 24*(3), 489–505. doi:10.5465/amr.1999.2202133

Fosberg, R. H., & Nelson, M. R. (1999). Leadership structure and firm performance. *International Review of Financial Analysis, 8*(1), 83–96. doi:10.1016/S1057-5219(99)00007-1

Freeman, R. (1984). *Strategic management: A stakeholder approach*. Cambridge University Press.

Freeman, R. E. (1984). *Strategic Management: A Stakeholder Approach*. Boston: Pitman Publishing.

Freeman, R. E. (1984). *Strategic Management: A stakeholder approach*. Boston: Pitman.

Freeman, R. E., & Evan, W. (1990). Corporate governance: A stakeholder interpretation. *The Journal of Behavioral Economics, 19*(4), 337–359. doi:10.1016/0090-5720(90)90022-Y

Freeman, R. E., Harrison, J. S., & Wicks, A. C. (2007). *Managing for stakeholders: survival, reputation and success.* Yale University Press.

Freeman, R. E., Harrison, J., Wicks, A., Parmar, B., & De Colle, S. (2010). *Stakeholder theory the state of Art.* New York: Cambridge University Press. doi:10.1017/CBO9780511815768

Freeman, R. E., Wicks, A. C., & Parmar, B. (2004). Stakeholder theory and "the corporate objective revisited". *Organization Science, 15*(3), 364–369. doi:10.1287/orsc.1040.0066

Freitas, A. (2007). *Análise das divulgações ambientais nos relatórios anuais das maiores empresas Portuguesas* [Master Dissertation]. Instituto Superior de Ciências do Trabalho e da Empresa.

Frías-Aceituno. J., Conceicao Marques, M., & Rodríguez-Ariza, L. (2013). Divulgación de información sostenible: ¿Se adapta a las expectativas de la sociedad? Spanish Accounting Review, 16(2), 147-158.

Frias-Aceituno, J. V., Rodriguez-Ariza, L., & Garcia-Sanchez, I. M. (2013). The role of the board in the dissemination of integrated corporate social reporting. *Corporate Social Responsibility and Environmental Management, 20*(4), 219–233. doi:10.1002/csr.1294

Friedman, M. (1962). *Capitalismo e liberdade*. São Paulo: Nova Cultura.

Frimmouse, S., & Peretti, J. (2015). Regards croisés sur engagement RSE. Question(s) de management, 1(9), 65-89.

Frooman, J. (1999). Stakeholder Influence Strategies. *Academy of Management Review, 24*(2), 191–205. doi:10.5465/amr.1999.1893928

Frost, G. R. (2007). The introduction of mandatory environmental reporting guidelines: Australian evidence. *Abacus, 43*(2), 190–216. doi:10.1111/j.1467-6281.2007.00225.x

Frynas, J. G., & Stephens, S. (2015). Political Corporate Social Responsibility: Reviewing Theories and Setting New Agendas. *International Journal of Management Reviews, 17*(4), 483–509. doi:10.1111/ijmr.12049

Frynas, J. G., & Yamahaki, C. (2016). Corporate social responsibility: Review and roadmap of theoretical perspectives. *Business Ethics (Oxford, England), 25*(3), 258–285. doi:10.1111/beer.12115

Fuente, J. A., García-Sánchez, I. M., & Lozano, M. B. (2017). The role of the board of directors in the adoption of GRI guidelines for the disclosure of CSR information. *Journal of Cleaner Production, 141*, 737–750. doi:10.1016/j.jclepro.2016.09.155

Fuller, D. (1998). Credit union development: Financial inclusion and exclusion. *Geofonm, 29*(2), 145–157.

Galan-Ladero, M. & Galera-Casquet, C. (2016). The Case of the 'Solidarity' Radar: Anything Goes in a Cause-Related Marketing? In *Proceedings of the 15th International Congress on Public and Nonprofit Marketing*. Academic Press.

Galan-Ladero, M. & Galera-Casquet, C. (2018). Corporate Social Responsibility and Digital Tools. The Cause-Related Marketing Case. In L. Carvalho & P. Isaias (Eds.), Handbook of Research on Entrepreneurship and Marketing for Global Reach in the Digital Economy (Ch. 1, pp. 1-16). Hershey, PA: IGI Global.

Galan-Ladero, M. & Galera-Casquet, C. (2019). Marketing para el cambio social. In L.M. Cerda-Suarez & M. Ramírez-Ramírez (Eds.), Fundamentos para un nuevo marketing (Ch. 11, pp. 251-284). Madrid: Sinderesis.

Galan-Ladero. M. (2012). *Variables que influyen en la actitud hacia el marketing con causa y determinantes de la satisfacción y la lealtad en la "compra solidaria"* [Doctoral Thesis]. University of Extremadura.

Galan-Ladero. M. (2013). Marketing con Causa: ¿Oportunidad o Solidaridad? In J.M. Rey-Pino & A.I. Polo-Peña (Eds.), Marketing y Sociedad: Aplicaciones Sectoriales del Marketing No Lucrativo (pp. 15-24). Granada: Servicio de Publicaciones de la Universidad de Granada.

Galan-Ladero, M.M., Galera-Casquet, C., Valero-Amaro, V., & Barroso-Mendez, M.J. (2013). Sustainable, socially responsible business: The cause-related marketing case. A review of the conceptual framework. *Journal of Security and Sustainability Issues*, *2*(4), 35–46. doi:10.9770/jssi.2013.2.4(4)

Galant, A., & Cadez, S. (2017). Corporate social responsibility and financial performance relationship: A review of measurement approaches. *Economic Research-Ekonomska Istraživanja*, *30*(1), 676–693. doi:10.1080/1331677X.2017.1313122

Gallardo-Vázquez, D., & Sánchez-Hernández, M.I. (2013). Análisis de la incidencia de la responsabilidad social empresarial en el éxito competitivo de las microempresas y el papel de la innovación. *Universia Business Review, 38*, 14-31.

Gallardo-Vázquez, D., & Sánchez-Hernandez, M. I. (2014). Measuring Corporate Social Responsibility for competitive success at a regional level. *Journal of Cleaner Production*, *72*, 14–22. doi:10.1016/j.jclepro.2014.02.051

Gallardo-Vázquez, D., Sánchez-Hernández, M. I., & Corchuelo-Martínez-Azúa, M. B. (2013). Validación de un instrumento de medida para la relación entre la orientación a la responsabilidad social corporativa y otras variables estratégicas de la empresa. *Revista de Contabilidad*, *16*(1), 11–23. doi:10.1016/S1138-4891(13)70002-5

Gantchev, N., Gredil, O., & Jotikasthira, C. (2015). *Governance under the gun: Spillover effects of hedge fund activism*. European Corporate Governance Institute; doi:10.2139srn.2356544

García-Sánchez, I. M., Hussain, N., Martínez-Ferrero, J., & Ruiz-Barbadillo, E. (2019). Impact of disclosure and assurance quality of corporate sustainability reports on access to finance. *Corporate Social Responsibility and Environmental Management*, *26*(4), 832–848. doi:10.1002/csr.1724

García-Sánchez, I.-M., Frías-Aceituno, J.-V., & Rodríguez-Domínguez, L. (2013). Determinants of Corporate Social Disclosure in Spanish Local Governments. *Journal of Cleaner Production*, *39*, 60–72. doi:10.1016/j.jclepro.2012.08.037

Garde Sánchez, R., Rodriguéz Bolívar, M. P., & López-Hernández, A. M. (2013). Online disclosure of university social responsibility: A comparative study of public and private US universities. *Environmental Education Research*, *19*(6), 709–746. doi:10.1080/13504622.2012.749976

Garousi, V. (2015). A bibliometric analysis of the Turkish software engineering research community. *Scientometrics*, *105*(1), 23–49. doi:10.100711192-015-1663-x

Garriga, E., & Melé, D. (2004). Corporate Social Responsibility Theories: Mapping the Territory Social Responsibility Corporate Theories. *Journal of Business Ethics*, *53*(1/2), 51–71. doi:10.1023/B:BUSI.0000039399.90587.34

Gartner, W. B. (1990). What are we talking about when we talk about emtrepreneurship? *Journal of Business Venturing*, *5*(1), 15–28. doi:10.1016/0883-9026(90)90023-M

Gatti, L., & Seele, P. (2014). Evidence for the prevalence of the sustainability concept in European corporate responsibility reporting. *Sustainability Science*, *9*(1), 89–102. doi:10.100711625-013-0233-5

Georgios, X., & Dimitrios, X. (2009). *Accounting treatment of emission credits*. International Hellenic University.

Gharleghi, B., Jahanshahi, A. A., & Nawaser, K. (2018). The outcomes of Corporate Social Responsibility to employees: Empirical evidence from a developing country. *Sustainability*, *10*(3), 698. doi:10.3390u10030698

Giannarakis, G. (2014). Corporate governance and financial characteristic effects on the extent of corporate social responsibility disclosure. *Social Responsibility Journal*, *10*(4), 569–590. doi:10.1108/SRJ-02-2013-0008

Gietzman, M., & Irelan, J. (2005). Cost of Capital, Strategic Disclosures and Accounting Choice. *Journal of Business Finance & Accounting*, *32*(3-4), 599–634. doi:10.1111/j.0306-686X.2005.00606.x

Gillan, S., Hartzell, J. C., Koch, A., & Starks, L. T. (2010). Firms' environmental, social and governance (ESG) choices, performance and managerial motivation. Retrieved from http://www.business.pitt.edu/faculty/papers/koch 3. pdf

Gil, N. (2019). Emprendimiento en la administración local: Un estudio empírico de la información contenida en los portales electrónicos de los municipios del Alentejo, región de Portugal. *Revista Innovar*, *29*(71), 97–112. doi:10.15446/innovar.v29n71.76398

Global Reporting Index – GRI. (2006). Diretrizes para o Relatório de Sustentabilidade. Retrieved from http://www.ipai.pt/

Global Reporting Index – GRI. (2019). GRI's History. Retrieved from https://www.globalreporting.org/information

Global Reporting Initiative (GRI). (2016). GRI: standards glossary. Retrieved from https://www.globalreporting.org/standards/media/1035/gri-standards-glossary-2016.pdf

Global Reporting Initiative. (2012). Relatórios de sustentabilidade da GRI: quanto vale essa jornada?

Goddard, J., Mckillop, D., & Wilson, J. O. S. (2008). The diversification and financial performance of US credit unions. *Journal of Banking & Finance*, *32*(9), 1836–1849. doi:10.1016/j.jbankfin.2007.12.015

Godfrey, P. C. (2005). The relationship between corporate philanthropy and shareholder wealth: A risk management perspective. *Academy of Management Review*, *30*(4), 777–798. doi:10.5465/amr.2005.18378878

Gomes, A., & Novaes, W. (2001). Sharing of Control as a Corporate Governance Mechanism. *PIER*, *29*(1), 01-12.

Gomes, S. (2016). *Relato de Sustentabilidade – Práticas no Setor Financeiro em Portugal e Espanha*. Dissertação de Mestrado em Finanças Empresariais, Instituto Politécnico de Leiria.

Gomes, S., Eugénio, T., & Branco, M. (2015). Sustainability reporting and assurance in Portugal, Corporate Governance. *The International Journal of Business in Society*, *15*(3), 281–292.

Gonçalves, A. G., & Góis, C. G. (2011). *Licenças de emissão de CO2: o caso português perspetiva legal e contabilística*. Instituto Superior De Contabilidade E Administração De Coimbra.

Gonçalves, R. M. L., & Braga, M. J. (2008). Determinantes de Risco de Liquidez em Cooperativas de Crédito: Uma Abordagem a partir do Modelo Logit Multinomial. *Revista de Administração Contemporânea*, *12*(4), 1019–1041. doi:10.1590/S1415-65552008000400007

Gond, J. P., Akremi, A. E., Swaen, V., & Babu, N. (2017). The psychological microfoundations of corporate social responsibility: A person-centric systematic review. *Journal of Organizational Behavior*, *38*(2), 225–246. doi:10.1002/job.2170

Gond, J. P., Igalens, J., Swaen, V., & El Akremi, A. (2011). The Human Resources Contribution to Responsible Leadership: An Exploration of the CSR–HR Interface. In N. M. Pless & T. Maak (Eds.), *Responsible Leadership*. Dordrecht: Springer. doi:10.1007/978-94-007-3995-6_10

Gonzalez-Gonzalez, J., & Zamora Ramírez, C. (2016). Voluntary carbon disclosure by Spanish companies: An empirical analysis. *International Journal of Climate Change Strategies and Management*, *8*(1), 57–79. doi:10.1108/IJCCSM-09-2014-0114

González-Ramos, M. I., Manzanares-Donate, M. J., & Gómez-Guadamillas, F. (2014). Propuesta de una escala para la medición de la responsabilidad social corporativa. *Pecvnia*, *18*(18), 1–18. doi:10.18002/pec.v0i18.1641

Gordon, T., Fischer, M., Malone, D., & Tower, G. (2002). A comparative empirical examination of extent of disclosure by private and public colleges and universities in the United States. *Journal of Accounting and Public Policy*, *21*(3), 235–275. doi:10.1016/S0278-4254(02)00051-0

Graafland, J., & Noorderheaven, N. (2019). Technological Competition, Innovation Motive and Corporate Social Responsibility: Evidence from Top Managers of European SMEs. *De Economist*, 1–22. doi:10.100710645-019-09351-z

Grant, M. J., & Booth, A. (2009). A typology of reviews: An analysis of 14 review types and associated methodologies. *Health Information and Libraries Journal*, *26*(2), 91–108. doi:10.1111/j.1471-1842.2009.00848.x PMID:19490148

Graves, L. M., & Sarkis, J. (2012). Fostering employee proenvironmental behavior: the role of leadership and motivation. In D. R. Gallagher (Ed.), *Environmental Leadership: a Reference Handbook* (pp. 161–171). Thousand Oaks, CA: Sage. doi:10.4135/9781452218601.n18

Graves, L. M., Sarkis, J., & Zhu, Q. (2013). How transformational leadership and employee motivation combine to predict employee proenvironmental behaviors in China. *Journal of Environmental Psychology*, *35*, 81–91. doi:10.1016/j.jenvp.2013.05.002

Gray, R. (2001). Thirty years of social accounting, reporting, and auditing: What (if anything) have we learnt? *Business Ethics (Oxford, England)*, *10*(1), 9–15. doi:10.1111/1467-8608.00207

Gray, R., Kouhy, R., & Lavers, S. (1995). Corporate social and environmental reporting: A review of the literature and a longitudinal study of UK disclosure. *Accounting, Auditing & Accountability Journal*, *18*(2), 47–77. doi:10.1108/09513579510146996

Gray, R., Kouhy, R., & Lavers, S. (1995b). Methodological themes. Constructing a research database of social and environmental by UK companies. *Accounting, Auditing & Accountability Journal*, *8*(2), 78–101. doi:10.1108/09513579510086812

Greening, D. W., & Turban, D. B. (2000). Corporate social performance as a competitive advantage in attracting a quality workforce. *Business & Society*, *39*(3), 254–280. doi:10.1177/000765030003900302

Guerreiro, A. (2012). O Relato de Sustentabilidade, o Técnico Oficial de Contas e a OTOC. IV *Congresso dos TOC.*

Guillet, B. D., Seo, K., Kucukusta, D., & Lee, S. (2013). CEO duality and firm performance in the U.S. restaurant industry: Moderating role of restaurant type. *International Journal of Hospitality Management*, *33*, 339–346. doi:10.1016/j.ijhm.2012.10.004

Guimarães, G. L. E. (2015). *Gerenciamento do risco socioambiental nas instituições financeiras bancárias no Brasil. Dissertação de Mestrado*. Universidade Federal de Brasília.

Guinness, M., & Hogan, T. (2014). Bank credit and trade credit: Evidence from SMEs over the financial crisis. *International Small Business Journal*, *34*(4).

Guthrie, J., Cuganesan, S., & Ward, L. (2008). Disclosure Media for Social and Environmental Matters within the Australian Food and Beverage Industry. *Social and Environmental Accountability Journal*, *28*(1), 33–44. doi:10.1080/0969160X.2008.9651789

Guthrie, J., Manes-Rossi, F., & Orelli, R. L. (2017). Integrated reporting and integrated thinking in Italian public sector organisations. *Meditari Accountancy Research*, *25*(4), 553–573. doi:10.1108/MEDAR-06-2017-0155

Hackman, J. R., & Oldham, R. G. (1976). Motivation through the design of work: Test of a theory. *Organizational Behavior and Human Performance*, *16*(2), 250–279. doi:10.1016/0030-5073(76)90016-7

Hackston, D., & Milne, M. (1996). Some determinants of social and environmental disclosures in New Zealand companies. *Accounting, Auditing & Accountability Journal*, *9*(1), 77–108. doi:10.1108/09513579610109987

Hadani, M., Goranova, M., & Khan, R. (2011). Institutional investors, shareholder activism, and earnings management. *Journal of Business Research*, *64*(12), 1352–1360. doi:10.1016/j.jbusres.2010.12.004

Hafsi, T., & Turgut, G. (2013). Boardroom diversity and its effect on social performance: Conceptualization and empirical evidence. *Journal of Business Ethics*, *112*(3), 463–479. doi:10.100710551-012-1272-z

Hagendorff, J., & Keasey, K. (2012). The value of board diversity in banking: Evidence from the market for corporate control. *European Journal of Finance*, *18*(1), 41–58. doi:10.1080/1351847X.2010.481471

Hahn, R., & Kühnen, M. (2013). Determinants of sustainability reporting: A review of results, trends, theory, and opportunities in an expanding field of research. *Journal of Cleaner Production*, *59*, 5–21. doi:10.1016/j.jclepro.2013.07.005

Haigh, M. M., & Brubaker, P. (2010). Examining how image restoration strategy impacts perceptions of corporate social responsibility, organization-public relationships, and source credibility. *Corporate Communications*, *15*(4), 453–468. doi:10.1108/13563281011085538

Hambrick, D. C., & Finkelstein, S. (1987). Managerial discretion: A bridge between polar views of organizational outcomes. *Research in Organizational Behavior*, *9*, 369–406.

Hameed, I., Riaz, Z., Arain, G. A., & Farooq, O. (2016). How do internal and external CSR affect employees' organizational identification? A perspective from the group engagement model. *Frontiers in Psychology*, *7*, 1–13. doi:10.3389/fpsyg.2016.00788 PMID:27303345

Handajani, L., Subroto, B., Sutrisno, T., & Saraswati, E. (2014). Does board diversity matter on corporate social disclosure? An Indonesian evidence. *Journal of Economics and Sustainable Development*, *5*(9), 8–17.

Han, H., Yu, J., & Kim, W. (2019). Environmental corporate social responsibility and the strategy to boost the airline's image and customer loyalty intentions. *Journal of Travel & Tourism Marketing*, *36*(3), 371–383. doi:10.1080/10548408.2018.1557580

Haniffa, R., & Cooke, T. (2002). Culture, corporate governance and disclosure in Malaysia corporations. *Abacus*, *38*(3), 317–349. doi:10.1111/1467-6281.00112

Haniffa, R., & Cooke, T. (2005). The impact of culture and governance on corporate social reporting. *Journal of Accounting and Public Policy*, *24*(5), 391–430. doi:10.1016/j.jaccpubpol.2005.06.001

Hannan, M., & Freeman, J. (1977). The Population Ecology of Public Organizations. *American Journal of Sociology*, *82*(5), 929–964. doi:10.1086/226424

Hansen, S., Dunford, B., Boss, A., Boss, R., & Angermeier, I. (2011). Corporate Social Responsibility and the Benefits of Employee Trust: A Cross-Disciplinary Perspective. *Journal of Business Ethics*, *102*(1), 29–45. doi:10.100710551-011-0903-0

Hao, Y., Farooq, Q., & Zhang, Y. (2018). Unattended social wants and corporate social responsibility of leading firms: Relationship of intrinsic motivation of volunteering in proposed welfare programs and employee attributes. *Corporate Social Responsibility and Environmental Management*, *25*(6), 1029–1038. doi:10.1002/csr.1681

Hapsoro, D., & Ambarwati, A. (2018). Antecedents and consequences of carbon emissions' disclosure: Case study of oil, gas and coal companies in non-annex 1 member countries. *Journal of Indonesian Economy and Business*, *33*(2), 99–111. doi:10.22146/jieb.28756

Harjoto, M. A., & Jo, H. (2011). Corporate governance and CSR nexus. *Journal of Business Ethics*, *100*(1), 45–67. doi:10.100710551-011-0772-6

Harjoto, M., Laksmana, I., & Lee, R. (2015). Board Diversity and Corporate Social Responsibility. *Journal of Business Ethics*, *132*(4), 641–660. doi:10.100710551-014-2343-0

Harrison, J. S., Bosse, D. A., & Phillips, R. A. (2010). Managing for stakeholders, stakeholder utility functions, and competitive advantage. *Strategic Management Journal*, *31*(1), 58–74. doi:10.1002mj.801

Harrison, J. S., Freeman, R. E., & Abreu, M. (2015). Stakeholder theory as an ethical approach to effective management: Applying the theory to multiple contexts. *Revista Brasileira de Gestão de Negócios*, *17*(55), 858–869. doi:10.7819/rbgn.v17i55.2647

Healy, P. M. (1985). The effect of bonus schemes on accounting decisions. *Journal of Accounting and Economics*, *7*(1-3), 85–107. doi:10.1016/0165-4101(85)90029-1

Healy, P. M., & Palepu, K. G. (2001). Information Asymmetry, Corporate Disclosure, and the Capital Markets: A Review of the Empirical Disclosure Literature. *Journal of Accounting and Economics*, *31*(1-3), 405–440. doi:10.1016/S0165-4101(01)00018-0

He, L. (2008). Do founders matter? A study of executive compensation, governance structure and firm performance. *Journal of Business Venturing*, *23*(3), 257–279. doi:10.1016/j.jbusvent.2007.02.001

Henri, J.-F., & Journeault, M. (2010). Eco-control: The influence of management control systems on environmental and economic performance. *Accounting, Organizations and Society*, *35*(1), 63–80. doi:10.1016/j.aos.2009.02.001

Herbst, J. (2005). Mbeki's South Africa. *Foreign Affairs*, *84*(6), 93–105. doi:10.2307/20031779

Herda, D. N., Taylor, M. E., & Winterbotham, G. (2012). The effect of board independence on the sustainability reporting practices of large U.S. firms. *Issues in Social & Environmental Accounting*, *6*(3/4), 25–44.

Hermalin, B., & Weisbach, M. (2003). Boards of directors as an endogenously determined institution: A survey of the economic literature. *Federal Reserve Bank of New York Economic Policy Review*, *9*, 7–26.

Hermawan, A., Aisyah, I., Gunardi, A., & Putri, W. (2018). Going green: Determinants of carbon emission disclosure in manufacturing companies in Indonesia. *International Journal of Energy Economics and Policy*, *8*(1), 55–61.

Herrera, J., Larrán, M., Martínez, I., & Martínez-Martínez, D. (2016). Relationship between corporate social responsibility and competitive performance in Spanish SMEs: Empirical evidence from a stakeholders' perspective. *Business Research Quarterly*, *19*(1), 55–72. doi:10.1016/j.brq.2015.06.002

Hessou, H., & Lai, V. S. (2017). Basel III capital buffer requirements and credit union Prudential regulation: Canadian evidence. *Journal of Financial Stability*, *30*, 92–110. doi:10.1016/j.jfs.2017.05.002

Hetze, K., & Winistörfer, H. (2016). CSR communication on corporate websites compared across continents. *International Journal of Bank Marketing*, *34*(4), 501–528. doi:10.1108/IJBM-02-2015-0022

Hildebrand, D., Demotta, Y., Sen, S., & Valenzuela, A. (2017). Consumer responses to corporate social responsibility (CSR) contribution type. *The Journal of Consumer Research*, *44*(4), 738–758. doi:10.1093/jcr/ucx063

Hillman, A., & Kleim, G. (2001). Shareholder stakeholder value management and social issues what's the bottom line. *Strategic Management Journal*, *22*(2), 125–139. doi:10.1002/1097-0266(200101)22:2<125::AID-SMJ150>3.0.CO;2-H

Hoffman, B. M. (2012). *Integrated Reporting in practice: The South African story*. Retrieved from https://home.kpmg.com/content/dam/kpmg/pdf/2013/04/the-south-african-story.pdf

Hoffman, M. (2012). Integrated Reporting in practice: The South African story. *KPMG: Integrated Reporting: Performance insight through Better Business Reporting*, (2), 1-42.

Høgevold, M., Svensson, N., Wagner, G., Petzer, B. J., Klopper, D., Carlos Sosa Varela, H. B., ... Ferro, C. (2014). Sustainable business models: Corporate reasons, economic effects, social boundaries, environmental actions and organizational challenges in sustainable business practices. *Baltic Journal of Management*, *9*(3), 357–380. doi:10.1108/BJM-09-2013-0147

Holland, L., & Foo, Y. B. (2003). Differences in environmental reporting practices in the UK and the US: The legal and regulatory context. *The British Accounting Review*, *35*(1), 1–18. doi:10.1016/S0890-8389(02)00127-0

Hollands, R. G. (2008). Will the real Smart City please stand up? City: Analysis of Urban Trends, Culture, Theory. *Policy and Action*, *13*(3), 303–320.

Hopkins, M. (2003). The Planetary Bargain: Corporate Responsibility Matters (1st ed.). Academic Press. Doi:10.4324/9781849773201

Hoque, M. E. (2017). Why Company Should Adopt Integrated Reporting? International. *Journal of Economics and Financial Issues*, *7*(1).

Horak, S., Arya, B., & Ismail, K. M. (2018). Organizational Sustainability Determinants in Different Cultural Settings: A Conceptual Framework. *Business Strategy and the Environment*, *27*(4), 528–546. doi:10.1002/bse.2018

Hsiao, C. (2003). *Analysis of panel data (2ª ed.)*. University of Southern California, Cambridge University Press. doi:10.1017/CBO9780511754203

Hsu, S., Lin, S. W., Chen, W. P., & Huanh, J. W. (in press). CEO Duality, Information Costs, and Firm Performance. *The North American Journal of Economics and Finance*. doi:10.1016/j.najef.2019.101011

Huerta-Riveros, P., & Gaete-Feres, H. (2017). Responsabilidad social universitaria a través de los reportes de sostenibilidad del Global Reporting Initiative: Experiencia de una universidad pública. *Revista Iberoamericana de Educación Superior*, *8*(23), 120–137. doi:10.22201/iisue.20072872e.2017.23.3014

Hunt, S. D., & Morgan, R. M. (1995). The Comparative Advantage Theory of Competition. *Journal of Marketing*, *59*(2), 1–15. doi:10.1177/002224299505900201

Hurghis, R. (2017). Integrated reporting and board features. *Audit Financiar*, *15*(145), 83–92. doi:10.20869/AUDITF/2017/145/83

Hur, W. M., Kim, H., & Woo, J. (2014). How CSR leads to corporate brand equity: Mediating mechanisms of corporate brand credibility and reputation. *Journal of Business Ethics*, *125*(1), 1–12. doi:10.100710551-013-1910-0

Hur, W. M., Moon, T. W., & Ko, S. H. (2018). How employees' perceptions of CSR increase employee creativity: Mediating mechanisms of compassion at work and intrinsic motivation. *Journal of Business Ethics*, *153*(3), 629–644. doi:10.100710551-016-3321-5

Husted, B. W., & Allen, D. B. (2009). Strategic Corporate Social Responsibility and Value Creation. *Management International Review*, *49*(6), 781–799. doi:10.100711575-009-0016-5

Ibenrissoul, A., & Alami, F. Z. (2016). *L'évaluation économique des projets inscrits dans une perspective RSE. In 18e université de printemps de l'audit social, Audit social et mutation(s) des organisations*. Academic Press.

Ibhagui, O. W., & Olokoyo, F. O. (2018). Leverage and firm performance: New evidence on the role of firm size. *The North American Journal of Economics and Finance*, *45*, 57–82. doi:10.1016/j.najef.2018.02.002

Idowu, S. O., & Adedoyin, O. (2015). *Key Initiatives in Corporate Social Responsibility*. Springer.

Inoue, Y., & Lee, S. (2011). Effects of different dimensions of corporate social responsibility on corporate financial performance in tourism-related industries. *Tourism Management, 32*(4), 790–804. doi:10.1016/j.tourman.2010.06.019

Instituto Ethos. (2013). Responsabilidade social empresarial e sustentabilidade para a gestão empresarial. Fernanda Gabriela Borger. Retrieved from http://www3.ethos.org.br/cedoc/responsabilidade-social-empresarial-e-sustentabilidade-para-a-gestao-empresarial/#.WP0fjf9v9cv

Instituto Nacional de Estadística (2017). Estadísticas PYME. Evolución e indicadores.

International Cooperative Alliance (ICA). (2015). Guidance notes to the cooperative principles. Retrieved from https://ica.coop/sites/default/files/publication-files/ica-guidance-notes-en310629900.pdf

International Federation of Accountants, IFAC. (2016). *The 2030 Agenda for Sustainable Development. A Snapshot of the Accountancy Profession's Contribution.*

International Integrated Reporting Council (2013). The international IR- Framework.

International Integrated Reporting Council (IIRC). (2011). *Towards Integrated Reporting: Communicating Value in the 21stCentury*. International Integrated Reporting Council. Retrieved from http://integratedreporting.org/wp-content/uploads/2011/09/IR-Discussion-Paper-2011_spreads.pdf

International Integrated Reporting Council (IIRC). (2013). *The International <IR> Framework*. Retrieved from www.theiirc.org

International Integrated Reporting Council (IIRC). (2013). *The international integrated reporting framework*. London: IIRC.

International Integrated Reporting Council (IIRC). (2019). *What? The tool for better reporting*. Retrieved from https://integratedreporting.org/what-the-tool-for-better-reporting/

International Organization for Standardization – ISO. (2019). Guidance on Social Responsibility. Retrieved from https://www.iso.org/standard/42546.html

International Organization for Standardization. (2010). ISO 26000: Social Responsibility. Retrieved from: https://www.iso.org/iso-26000-social-responsibility.html

Ioannou, I., & Serafeim, G. (2017). The Consequences of Mandatory Corporate Sustainability Reporting. *Harvard Business School Research*. Retrieved from https://papers.ssrn.com/

Ioannou, I., & Serafeim, G. (2014). The impact of corporate social responsibility on investment recommendations: Analysts' perceptions and shifting institutional logics. *Strategic Management Journal, 36*(7), 1053–1081. doi:10.1002mj.2268

IODmz. (2007). Corporate Governance Como Instrumento Chave: Plano Estratégico e de Negócios do IoDmz. Retrieved from http://iodmz.com

Irigaray, H. A. R., Vergara, S. C., & Araújo, R. G. (2017). Responsabilidade Social Corporativa: O que revelam os Relatórios Sociais das Empresas. *Organizações & Sociedade, 24*(80), 73–80. doi:10.1590/1984-9230804

Islam, M. A., & Deegan, C. (2010). Media pressures and corporate disclosure of social responsibility performance information: A study of two global clothing and sports retail companies. *Accounting and Business Research, 40*(2), 131–148. doi:10.1080/00014788.2010.9663388

Ismail, K., & Chandler, R. (2005). Disclosure in the quarterly reports of Malaysian companies, *Financial Reporting. Regulation & Governance, 4*(1), 1–26.

Ivan. (1970). Flashback: Wildlife news in 1960s Singapore. Retrieved from http://lazy-lizard-tales.blogspot.com/2013/06/flashback-wildlife-news-in-1960s.html

Iwata, H. & Okada, K. (2010). How does environmental performance affect financial performance? Evidence from Japanese manufacturing firms. *MPRA*.

Iyengar, R. J., & Zampelli, E. M. (2009). Self-selection, endogeneity, and the relationship between CEO duality and firm performance. *Strategic Management Journal*, *30*(10), 1092–1112. doi:10.1002mj.776

Jabbour, C. K. C., & de Sousa Jabbour, A. B. L. (2016). Green human resource management and green supply chain management: Linking two emerging agendas. *Journal of Cleaner Production*, *112*, 1824–1833. doi:10.1016/j.jclepro.2015.01.052

Jain, T. & Jamali, D. (2016). Looking Inside the Black Box: The effect of Corporate Governance on Corporate Social Responsibility. *Review of corporate governance*, *24*(3), 253–273

Jain, T., & Jamali, D. (2016). Looking Inside the Black Box: The Effect of Corporate Governance on Corporate Social Responsibility. *Corporate Governance*, *24*(3), 253–273. doi:10.1111/corg.12154

Jamali, D. (2008). A stakeholder approach to corporate social responsibility: A fresh perspective into theory and practice. *Journal of Business Ethics*, *82*(1), 213–231. doi:10.100710551-007-9572-4

Jamali, D., & Mirshak, R. (2007). Corporate Social Responsibility (CSR): Theory and practice in a developing country context. *Journal of Business Ethics*, *72*(3), 243–262. doi:10.100710551-006-9168-4

Jamali, D., & Mirshak, R. (2007). Corporate social responsibility (CSR): Theory and practice in a developing country context. *Journal of Business Ethics*, *72*(3), 243–262. doi:10.1007/s10551-006-9168-4

Jamali, D., Safieddine, A. M., & Rabbath, M. (2008). Corporate governance and corporate social responsibility synergies and interrelationships. *Corporate Governance*, *16*(5), 443–459. doi:10.1111/j.1467-8683.2008.00702.x

Jan, B., & Unerman, J. (2018). Achieving the United Nations Sustainable Development Goals: An enabling role for accounting research. *Accounting, Auditing & Accountability Journal*, *31*(1), 2–24. doi:10.1108/AAAJ-05-2017-2929

Janggu, T., Darus, F., Zain, M. M., & Sawani, Y. (2014). Does good corporate governance lead to better sustainability reporting? An analysis using structural equation modeling. *Procedia: Social and Behavioral Sciences*, *145*, 138–145. doi:10.1016/j.sbspro.2014.06.020

Jarboui, A. & Bouaziz, S. (2019). The moderating effect of audit quality on the relation between shareholder activism and earnings management: Evidence from France. *Contemporary economics*, *13*(1), 63-78.

Jarboui, A., and Bouaziz, S., (2019). The moderating effect of audit quality on the relation between shareholder activism and earnings management: Evidence from France. doi:10.5709/ce.1897-9254.299

Jensen, J. C., & Berg, N. (2012). Determinants of traditional sustainability reporting versus integrated reporting. An institutionalist approach. *Business Strategy and the Environment*, *21*(5), 299–316. doi:10.1002/bse.740

Jensen, M. C. (1986). Agency costs of free cash flow, corporate finance, and takeovers. *The American Economic Review*, *76*(2), 323–329.

Jensen, M. C. (1993). The Modern Industrial Revolution, Exit, and the Failure of Internal Control Systems. *The Journal of Finance*, *3*(48), 831–880. doi:10.1111/j.1540-6261.1993.tb04022.x

Jensen, M., & Meckling, W. (1976). Theory of firm: Managerial behaviour, agency costs and ownership structure. *Journal of Financial Economics*, *3*(4), 305–360. doi:10.1016/0304-405X(76)90026-X

Jick, T. D. (1979). Mixing Qualitative and Quantitative Methods: Triangulation in Action. *Administrative Science Quarterly, 24*(4), 602–611. doi:10.2307/2392366

Jiménez, C. G., Martinez, A. G., & López, M. A. (2016). Propuesta de indicadores de la Responsabilidad Social Universitaria conforme a la guía G4 del GRI: El caso de la Universidad de Córdoba. *C.I.R.I.E.C. España*, (87), 103–137.

Jizi, M. I., Salama, A., Dixon, R., & Stratling, R. (2014). Corporate governance and corporate social responsibility disclosure: Evidence from the US banking sector. *Journal of Business Ethics, 125*(4), 601–615. doi:10.100710551-013-1929-2

Jo, H., & Harjoto, M. A. (2011). Corporate Governance and Firm Value: The Impact of Corporate Social Responsibility. *Journal of Business Ethics, 103*(3), 351–383. doi:10.100710551-011-0869-y

Jo, H., & Harjoto, M. A. (2012). The causal effect of corporate governance on corporate social responsibility. *Journal of Business Ethics, 106*(1), 53–72. doi:10.100710551-011-1052-1

Jo, H., Kim, H., & Park, K. (2015). Corporate environmental responsibility and firm performance in the financial services sector. *Journal of Business Ethics, 131*(2), 257–284. doi:10.100710551-014-2276-7

John, A., Qadeer, F., Shahzadi, G., & Jia, F. (2019). Getting paid to be good: How and when employees respond to corporate social responsibility? *Journal of Cleaner Production, 215*, 784–795. doi:10.1016/j.jclepro.2019.01.074

Johnson, R. A., & Greening, W. D. (1999). The Effect of Corporate Governance and Institutional Ownership Types on Corporate Social Performance. *Academy of Management Journal, 42*(5), 564–576.

Johns, R., & Khojastehpour, M. (2014). CSR Reasons, Practices and Impact to Corporate Reputation. *Social and Behavioral Sciences, 213*, 503–508.

Jones, D. A. (2010). Does serving the community also serve the company? Using organizational identification and social exchange theories to understand employee responses to a volunteerism programme. *Journal of Occupational and Organizational Psychology, 83*(4), 857–878. doi:10.1348/096317909X477495

Jones, D. A., Willness, C. R., & Madey, S. (2014). Why are job seekers attracted by corporate social performance? Experimental and filed tests of three signal-based mechanisms. *Academy of Management Journal, 57*(2), 383–404. doi:10.5465/amj.2011.0848

Jorgensen, B., & Soderstrom, N. (2008). *Environmental disclosure within legal and accounting contexts: an international perspective.* University of Colorado at Boulder.

Judge, W. Q., Gaur, A., & Muller-Kahle, M. I. (2010). Antecedents of shareholder activism in target firms: Evidence from a multi-country study. *Corporate Governance, 18*(4), 258–273. doi:10.1111/j.1467-8683.2010.00797.x

Kagan, J. (2018). Asymmetric information. Investopedia. Markets & Economy. Investopedia. Retrieved from https://www.investopedia.com/terms/a/asymmetricinformation.asp

Kalapodas, E., & Thomson, M. E. (2006). Credit risk assessment: A challenge for financial institutions. *IMA Journal of Management Mathematics, 17*(1), 25–46. doi:10.1093/imaman/dpi026

Kalsie, A., & Shrivastav, S. M. (2016). Board size and firm performance: Evidence from NSE companies using panel data approach. *Indian Journal of Corporate Governance, 9*(2), 148–172. doi:10.1177/0974686216666456

Kalu, J., Buang, A., & Aliagha, G. (2016). Determinants of voluntary carbon disclosure in the corporate real estate sector of Malaysia. *Journal of Environmental Management, 182*, 519–525. doi:10.1016/j.jenvman.2016.08.011 PMID:27529312

Kang, C., Germann, F., & Grewal, R. (2016). Washing Away Your Sins? Corporate Social Responsibility, Corporate Social Irresponsibility, and Firm Performance. *Journal of Marketing, 80*(2), 59–79. doi:10.1509/jm.15.0324

Kang, H., Cheng, M., & Gray, S. J. (2007). Corporate governance and board composition: Diversity and independence of Australian boards. *Corporate Governance*, *15*(2), 194–207. doi:10.1111/j.1467-8683.2007.00554.x

Kaplan, R. S., & Norton, D. P. (1992). The balanced scorecard - Measures that drive performance. *Harvard Business Review*, *70*, 71–79. PMID:10119714

Karagiorgos, Th. (2010). Corporate Social Responsibility and Financial Performance: An Empirical Analysis on Greek Companies. *European Research Studies Journal*, *04*(4), 85–108. doi:10.35808/ersj/301

Karyawati, P. G., Subroto, B., Sutrisno, T., & Saraswati, E. (2018). The Complexity of Relationship between Corporate Social Responsibility (CSR) and Financial Performance. *Emerging Markets Journal*, *8*(2), 2018. doi:10.5195/emaj.2018.155

Katsoulakos, P., Koutsodimou, M., Matraga, A., & Williams, L. (2004). A historic perspective of the CSR movement. CSRQuest Sustainability Framework. Retrieved from www.csrquest.net/uploadfiles/1D.pdf

Kechiche, A., & Soparnot, R. (2012). CSR within SMEs: Literature review. *International Business Research*, *5*(7), 97. doi:10.5539/ibr.v5n7p97

Kedia, B. L., & Kuntz, E. C. (1981). The context of social performance: an empirical study of Texas Banks. In P. Lee (Ed.), Research in Corporate Social Performance and Policy (Vol. 3, pp. 133-154). Greenwich, CT: JAI Press.

Keinert, C. (2008). *Corporate Social Responsibility as an International Strategy*. Leipzig, Germany: Physica-Verlag A Springer Company.

Khan, A., Muttakin, M. B., & Siddiqui, J. (2013). Corporate Governance and Corporate Social Responsibility Disclosures: Evidence from an Emerging Economy. *Journal of Business Ethics*, *114*(2), 207–223. doi:10.100710551-012-1336-0

Khanchel, I., and Seboui, S., (2009). Opportunisme dans les transferts internes et gestion de l'impression des partenaires. Gestion 2000, 26(4).

Kiliç, M., & Kuzey, C. (2017). Factors influencing sustainability reporting: evidence from Turkey. In K. Tunca Çaliyurt & S. G. Günay (Eds.), *Recent Issues in Accounting Finance and Auditing* (pp. 139–175). Edirne: Trakya University.

Kiliç, M., & Kuzey, C. (2019). The effect of corporate governance on carbon emission disclosures: Evidence from Turkey. *International Journal of Climate Change Strategies and Management*, *11*(1), 35–53. doi:10.1108/IJCCSM-07-2017-0144

Kim, A., Kim, Y., Han, K., Jackson, S. E., & Ployhart, R. E. (2017). Multilevel influences on voluntary workplace green behavior: Individual differences, leader behavior, and coworker advocacy. *Journal of Management*, *43*(5), 1335–1358. doi:10.1177/0149206314547386

Kim, K. H., Al-Shammari, H. A., Kim, B., & Lee, S. H. (2009). CEO duality leadership and corporate diversification behaviour. *Journal of Business Research*, *62*(11), 1173–1180. doi:10.1016/j.jbusres.2008.10.017

Kim, Y., Li, H., & Li, S. (2014). Corporate social responsibility and stock price crash risk. *Journal of Banking & Finance*, *43*, 1–13. doi:10.1016/j.jbankfin.2014.02.013

Kim, Y., Park, M., & Wier, B. (2012). Is earnings quality associated with corporate social responsibility? *The Accounting Review*, *87*(3), 761–796. doi:10.2308/accr-10209

Klein, A. (2002). Audit committee, board of director characteristics, and earnings management. *Journal of Accounting and Economics*, *33*(3), 375–400. doi:10.1016/S0165-4101(02)00059-9

KMPG UK. (2008). *Accounting for carbon – The impact of carbon trading on financial statements.*

Koestner, R., & Losier, G. F. (2002). Distinguishing three ways of being internally motivated: a closer look at introjection, identification, and intrinsic motivation. In E. L. Deci & R. M. Ryan (Eds.), *Handbook of Self-determination Research* (pp. 101–122). Rochester, NY: University of Rochester.

Kooskora, M., Juottonen, M., & Cundiff, K. (2019). The Relationship Between Corporate Social Responsibility and Financial Performance (A Case Study from Finland). *Social Responsibility and Sustainability*, 471–491. doi:10.1007/978-3-030-03562-4_25

Kotler, P., & Lee, N. (2005). *Corporate Social Responsibility*. Wiley.

KPMG (2018). How to report on the SDGs. What good looks like and why it matters. February 2018. Retrieved from kpmg.com/sdgreporting

KPMG. (2008). *KPMG international survey of corporate sustainability reporting 2008*.

KPMG. (2011). *International Survey of Corporate Responsibility Reporting 201*. KMPG International.

KPMG. (2012). Integrated Reporting: Performance Insight Through Better Business Reporting (Issue 2).

KPMG. (2015). *KPMG survey of corporate responsibility reporting 2015*. Retrieved from https://home.kpmg/content/dam/kpmg/pdf/2015/12/KPMG-survey-of-CR-reporting-2015.pdf

KPMG. (2017). *KPMG survey of corporate responsibility reporting 2017*. Retrieved from https://assets.kpmg/content/dam/kpmg/xx/pdf/2017/10/kpmg-survey-of-corporate-responsibility-reporting-2017.pdf

Krafft, J., Qu, Y., & Ravix, J. (2011). Gouvernance d'entreprise et performances sectorielles: une réévaluation de la fiabilité des scores et des mesures de bonne gouvernance. Retrieved from https://hal.archives-ouvertes.fr/hal-00493371

Kramer, M. R., & Porter, M. E. (2006). Estrategia y sociedad: El vínculo entre ventaja competitiva y responsabilidad social corporativa. *Harvard Business Review*, *84*(12), 42–56.

Kreitlon, M. P. (2004). A ética nas relações entre empresas e sociedade: fundamentos teóricos da responsabilidade social empresarial. In Proceedings of the XXVIII Encontro Anual da Anpad, Curitiba, 2004. Academic Press.

Kropp, F., Holden, S. J. S., & Lavack, A. M. (1999). Cause – related marketing and values in Australia. *International Journal of Nonprofit and Voluntary Sector Marketing*, *4*(1), 69–80. doi:10.1002/nvsm.57

Krüger, C. (2010). Corporate social responsibility and the board of directors.

Krzus, M. P. (2011). Integrated reporting: If not now, when? *IRZ*, *6*(6), 271–276.

Krzus, M. P. (2011). Integrated reporting: If not now, when? *Zeitschrift fuer Internationale Rechnungslegung*, *6*, 271–276.

Kurucz, E. C., Colbert, B. A., & Wheeler, D. (2008). *The business case for corporate social responsibility*. Oxford: Oxford University Press.

La Sexta. (2016, April 6). *Instalan el primer radar de tráfico solidario de España, lo recaudado irá para familias necesitadas*. Retrieved from http://www.lasexta.com

Lai, C. S., Chiu, C. J., Yang, C. F., & Pai, D. C. (2010). The effects of Corporate Social Responsibility on Brand performance: The mediating effect of industrial Brand equity and corporate reputation. *Journal of Business Ethics*, *95*(3), 457–469. doi:10.100710551-010-0433-1

Lam, T. Y., & Lee, S. K. (2008). CEO duality and firm performance: Evidence from Hong Kong. *Corporate Governance: The International Journal of Effective Board Performance*, *8*(3), 299–316. doi:10.1108/14720700810879187

Lan, X., & Zhang, T. (2013). An Empirical Study on the Endogeneity of Corporate Governance Mechanisms and Firm Performance. In *Proceedings of the 19th International Conference on Industrial Engineering and Engineering Management* (pp. 485-495). Academic Press.

Landrum, N. E., & Ohsowski, B. (2018). Identifying Worldviews on Corporate Sustainability: A Content Analysis of Corporate Sustainability Reports. *Business Strategy and the Environment*, *27*(1), 128–151. doi:10.1002/bse.1989

Lange, E. A., & Kerr, S. G. (2013). Accounting and incentives for sustainability in higher education: An interdisciplinary analysis of a needed revolution. *Social Responsibility Journal*, *9*(2), 210–219. doi:10.1108/SRJ-08-2011-0058

Lantos, G. (2001). The boundaries of strategic corporate social responsibility. *Journal of Consumer Marketing*, *18*(7), 595–632. doi:10.1108/07363760110410281

Larrinaga, C., Carrasco, F., Correa, C., Llena, F., & Moneva, J. (2002). Accountability and accounting regulation: The case of Spanish environmental disclosure standard. *European Accounting Review*, *11*(4), 723–740. doi:10.1080/0963818022000001000

Lau, C. H., & Lu, Y. (2014). Corporate Social Responsibility in China: A Corporate Governance Approach. *Journal of Business Ethics*, *125*(4), 207–221.

Lazear, E. P. (2005). Entrepreneurship. *Journal of Labor Economics*, *23*(4), 282–305. doi:10.1086/491605

Leandro, A., & Rebelo, T. (2011). A responsabilidade social das empresas: Incursão ao conceito e suas relações com a cultura organizacional. *Revista Exedra*, 11-40.

Lechem, B. (2002). *Chairman of the Board: A Practical Guide*. New Jersey, NJ: John Wiley & Sons, Inc.

Lee, J. (2009). Executive performance-based remuneration, performance change and board structures. *The International Journal of Accounting*, *44*(2), 138–162. doi:10.1016/j.intacc.2009.03.002

Lee, K. W., & Lee, C. F. (2009). Cash holdings, corporate governance structure and firm valuation. *Review of Pacific Basin Financial Markets and Policies*, *12*(3), 475–508. doi:10.1142/S021909150900171X

Lee, M. D. P. (2008). A review of the theories of corporate social responsibility: Its evolutionary path and the road ahead. *International Journal of Management Reviews*, *10*(1), 53–73. doi:10.1111/j.1468-2370.2007.00226.x

Lee, S., Park, Y., & Klassen, R. (2015). Market responses to firms' voluntary climate change information disclosure and carbon communication. *Corporate Social Responsibility and Environmental Management*, *22*(1), 1–12. doi:10.1002/csr.1321

Leocádio. (2017). *Relato Integrado em Portugal, Dissertação de Mestrado em Contabilidade e Controlo de Gestão*. Porto: FEP.

Lew, Y. K., Yu, J., & Park, J. Y. (2018). The impacts of independent director and CEO duality on performance in the Chinese post-institutional-transition era. *Canadian Journal of Administrative Sciences*, *35*(4), 620–643. doi:10.1002/cjas.1468

Liao, L., Lin, T. P., & Zhang, Y. (2016). Corporate board and corporate social responsibility assurance: Evidence from China. *Journal of Business Ethics*, *150*(1), 211–225. doi:10.100710551-016-3176-9

Liberati, A., Altman, D., Tetzlaff, J., Mulrow, C., Gøtzsche, P., Ioannidis, J., ... Moher, D. (2009). The PRISMA statement for reporting systematic reviews and meta-analyses of studies that evaluate health care interventions: Explanation and elaboration. *Journal of Clinical Epidemiology*, *6*(7), 1–28. doi:10.1016/j.jclinepi.2009.06.006 PMID:19631507

Lichtenstein, D. R., Drumwright, M., & Braig, B. M. (2004). The effect of corporate social responsibility on customer donations to corporate-supported nonprofits. *Journal of Marketing*, *68*(4), 16–32. doi:10.1509/jmkg.68.4.16.42726

Li, D., Huang, M., Ren, S., Chen, X., & Ning, L. (2018). Environmental legitimacy, green innovation, and corporate carbon disclosure: Evidence from CDP China 100. *Journal of Business Ethics*, *150*(4), 1089–1104. doi:10.100710551-016-3187-6

Li, D., Moshirian, F., Nguyen, P., & Tan, L. W. (2007). Managerial ownership and firm performance: Evidence from China's privatizations. *Research in International Business and Finance*, *21*(3), 296–413. doi:10.1016/j.ribaf.2007.02.001

Li, D., Xin, L., Chen, X., & Ren, S. (2017). Corporate social responsibility, media attention and firm value: Empirical research on Chinese manufacturing firms. *Quality & Quantity*, *51*(4), 1563–1577. doi:10.100711135-016-0352-z

Liesen, A., Hoepner, A., Patten, D., & Figge, F. (2015). Does stakeholder pressure influence corporate GHG emissions reporting? Empirical evidence from Europe. *Accounting, Auditing & Accountability Journal*, *28*(7), 1047–1074. doi:10.1108/AAAJ-12-2013-1547

Lim, S., Matolcsy, Z., & Chow, D. (2007). The association between board composition and different types of voluntary disclosure. *European Accounting Review*, *16*(3), 555–583. doi:10.1080/09638180701507155

Lincoln, J. R. (1995). Book review—Walter W. Powell & Paul DiMaggio (Eds.): The new institutionalism in organizational research. Social Forces, 73, 1147-1148.

Lins, K. V., Servaes, H., & Tamayo, A. (2017). Social Capital, Trust, and Firm Performance: The Value of Corporate Social Responsibility during the Financial Crisis. *The Journal of Finance*, *72*(4), 1785–1824. doi:10.1111/jofi.12505

Lin, Z., Liu, M., & Noronha, C. (2016). The impact of corporate governance on informative earnings management in the Chinese market. *Abacus*, *52*(3), 568–609. doi:10.1111/abac.12084

Liu, X. & Anbumozhi, V. (2009). Determinant factors of corporate environmental information disclosure: an empirical study of Chinese listed company. *Journal of Cleaner Production*, 593-600/8.

Liu, Y. S., Zhou, X., Yang, J. H., & Hoepner, A. G. F. (2016). Corporate Carbon Emission and Financial Performance: Does Carbon Disclosure Mediate the Relationship in the UK?

Liu, G. (2013). Impacts of Instrumental Versus Relational Centered Logic on Cause-Related Marketing Decision Making. *Journal of Business Ethics*, *113*(2), 243–263. doi:10.100710551-012-1292-8

Liu, M. T., Wong, I. A., Rongwei, C., & Tseng, T. H. (2014). Do perceived CSR initiatives enhance customer preference and loyalty in casinos? *International Journal of Contemporary Hospitality Management*, *26*(7), 1024–1045. doi:10.1108/IJCHM-05-2013-0222

Li, Y., Liu, B., & Huan, T. C. (2019). Renewal or not? Consumer response to a renewed corporate social responsibility strategy: Evidence from the coffee shop industry. *Tourism Management*, *72*, 170–179. doi:10.1016/j.tourman.2018.10.031

Llena, F., Moneva, J. M., & Hernandez, B. (2007). Environmental disclosures and compulsory accounting standards: The case of Spanish annual reports. *Business Strategy and the Environment*, *16*(1), 50–63. doi:10.1002/bse.466

Locke, E. A., & Latham, G. P. (1990). *A theory of goal setting and task performance*. Englewood Cliffs, NJ: Prentice Hall.

Lopatta, K., & Jaeschke, R. (2014). Sustainability reporting at German and Austrian universities. *Int. J. Education Economics and Development*, *5*(1), 66–90.

Lopes, A. I., & Coelho, A. M. (2018). Engaged in integrated reporting? Evidence across multiple organizations. *European Business Review*, *30*(4), 398–426. doi:10.1108/EBR-12-2016-0161

López, N. (2016). Sabotean el primer radar solidario de España. *AutoBild.es*. Retrieved from http://www.autobild.es/noticias/primer-radar-solidario-espana-286723

Lopez, M. V., Garcia, A., & Rodriguez, L. (2007). Sustainable development and corporate performance: A study based on the Dow Jones sustainability index. *Journal of Business Ethics*, *75*(3), 285–300. doi:10.100710551-006-9253-8

Lopéz, Y. P., & Martin, W. F. (2018). University mission statements and sustainability performance. *Business and Society Review*, *132*(2), 341–368. doi:10.1111/basr.12144

Lo, S. F., & Sheu, H. J. (2007). Is Corporate Sustainability a Value-Increasing Strategy for Business? *Corporate Governance*, *15*(2), 345–358. doi:10.1111/j.1467-8683.2007.00565.x

Lovell, H., Aguiar, T. S., Bebbington, J., Larrinaga-Gonzalez, C. (2010). Accounting for carbon. *Certified Accountants Educational Trust for the Association of Chartered Certified Accountants.*

Low, M. P., Ong, S. F., & Tan, P. M. (2017). Positioning ethics and social responsibility as a strategic tool in employees' affective commitment. Evidence from Malaysian small medium-sized enterprises (SMEs). *Annals in Social Responsibility*, *3*(1), 2–22. doi:10.1108/ASR-12-2016-0013

Luo, L., Lan, Y., & Tang, Q. (2012). Corporate incentives to disclose carbon information: Evidence from the CDP Global 500 report. *Journal of International Financial Management & Accounting*, *23*(2), 93–120. doi:10.1111/j.1467-646X.2012.01055.x

Luo, L., Tang, Q., & Lan, Y. (2013). Comparison of propensity for carbon disclosure between developing and developed countries: A resource constraint perspective. *Accounting Research Journal*, *26*(1), 6–34. doi:10.1108/ARJ-04-2012-0024

Luo, X., & Bhattacharya, C. (2006). Corporate Social Responsibility, Customer Satisfaction, and Market Value. *Journal of Marketing*, *70*(4), 1–18. doi:10.1509/jmkg.70.4.001

Luthans, F., & Youssef, C. M. (2004). Human, social and now positive psychological capital management: Investing in people for competitive advantage. *Organizational Dynamics*, *33*(2), 143–160. doi:10.1016/j.orgdyn.2004.01.003

Lu, W. M., Wang, W. K., & Lee, H. L. (2013). The relationship between corporate social responsibility and corporate performance: Evidence from the US semiconductor industry. *International Journal of Production Research*, *51*(19), 5683–5695. doi:10.1080/00207543.2013.776186

MacGregor, S. P., & Fontrodona, J. (2008). *Exploring the fit between CSR and Innovation.* Working Paper. IESE Business School University of Navarra.

Machado, M. R., Machado, M. A. V., & Santos, A. (2010). A relação entre setor econômico e investimentos sociais e ambientais. *Contabilidade, Gestão E Governança*, *13*(3), 102–115.

Madrakhimova, F. S. (2013). Evolution of the concept and definition of corporate social responsibility. In *Proceedings of the Global Conference on Business & Finance Proceedings* (pp. 113-118). Academic Press.

Magness, V. (2006). Strategic posture, Financial performance and environmental disclosure: An empirical test of legitimacy theory. *Accounting, Auditing & Accountability Journal*, *19*(4), 540–563. doi:10.1108/09513570610679128

Mahajan, Y. L. (1981). A Macro-Econometric Model of the Credit Unions. *Atlantic Economic Journal*, *9*(2), 40–48. doi:10.1007/BF02301207

Mahbuba, S., & Farzana, N. (2013). Corporate Social Responsibility and Profitability: A Case Study on Dutch Bangla Bank Ltd. *International Journal of Business and Social Research*, *3*(4), 139–145.

Mahmood, Z., Kouser, R., Ali, W., Ahmad, Z., & Salman, T. (2018). Does corporate governance affect sustainability disclosure? A mixed methods study. *Sustainability*, *10*(1), 1–20. doi:10.3390u10010207 PMID:30607262

Makni, R., Francoeur, C., & Bellavance, F. (2009). Causality between corporate social performance and financial performance: Evidence from Canadian firms. *Journal of Business Ethics*, *89*(3), 409–422. doi:10.100710551-008-0007-7

Maldonado-Guzmán, G., Pinzón-Castro, S. Y., & Leana Morales, C. (2017). Corporate Social Responsibility and Firm Reputation in Mexican Small Business. *Advances in Management and Applied Economics*, *7*(5), 29.

Malik, M. (2015). Value-enhancing capabilities of CSR: A brief review of contemporary literature. *Journal of Business Ethics*, *127*(2), 419–438. doi:10.100710551-014-2051-9

Mallette, P., & Fowler, K. L. (1992). Effects of board composition and stock ownership on the adoption of poison pills. *Academy of Management Journal*, *35*(5), 1010–1035. doi:10.5465/256538

Mallin, C. A., & Michelon, G. (2016). Board Reputation Attributes and Corporate Social Performance: An Empirical Investigation of the US Best Corporate Citizens. *Accounting and Business Research*, *41*(2), 119–144. doi:10.1080/00014788.2011.550740

Maniora, J. (2017). Is integrated reporting really the superior mechanism for the integration of ethics into the core business model? An empirical analysis. *Journal of Business Ethics*, *140*(4), 755–786. doi:10.100710551-015-2874-z

Manolova, T., Brush, C., & Edelman, L. (2008). What do women entrepreneurs want? *Strategic Change*, *17*(3), 69–82. doi:10.1002/jsc.817

Manton, E. J., & English, D. E. (2007). The Trend Toward Multiple Authorship in Business Journals. *Journal of Education for Business*, *82*(3), 164–168. doi:10.3200/JOEB.82.3.164-168

MAPFRE. (2015, December 1). Todas las infracciones con retirada de puntos. *Canal Motor*. Retrieved from http://www.motor.mapfre.es

Maqbool, S., & Zameer, M. N. (2017). An Empirical Examination of the Relationship between Corporate Social Responsibility and Profitability: Evidence from Indian Commercial Banks. *Pacific Business Review International*, *9*(12), 39–47.

Maqbool, S., & Zameer, M. N. (2018). Corporate social responsibility and financial performance: An empirical analysis of Indian banks. *Future Business Journal*, *4*(1), 84–93. doi:10.1016/j.fbj.2017.12.002

Margaritis, D., & Psillaki, M. (2010). Capital structure, equity ownership and firm performance. *Journal of Banking & Finance*, *43*(3), 621–632. doi:10.1016/j.jbankfin.2009.08.023

Margolis, J. D., Elfenbein, H. A., & Walsh, J. P. (2009). Does It Pay to Be Good and Does It Matter? A Meta-Analysis of the Relationship between Corporate Social and Financial Performance.

Mark-Herbert, C., & Von Schantz, C. (2007). *Communicating corporate social responsibility–brand management*. EJBO-Electronic Journal of Business Ethics and Organization Studies.

Marques, L. D. (2000). *Modelos dinâmicos com dados em painel: revisão de literatura*. Centro de Estudos Macroeconómicos e Previsão, Faculdade de Economia do Porto. Retrieved fro http://www.fep.up.pt/investigacao/workingpapers/wp100.pdf

Marshall, S. R., Cordano, M., & Silverman, M. (2005). Exploring individual and institutional drivers of proactive environmentalism in the US wine industry. *Business Strategy and the Environment*, *14*(2), 92–109. doi:10.1002/bse.433

Martín, J.A.J., Martín, Z., Maria, P., & Léon, C. (2007). *Tratamiento contable de los derechos de emisión: la aplicación de la resolución de 8 de febrero de 2006 del ICAC en el sector eléctrico español*. Universidad de Huelva.

Martinez-Conesa, I., Soto-Acosta, P., & Palacios-Manzano, M. (2017). Corporate social responsibility and its effect on innovation and firm performance: An empirical research in SMEs. *Journal of Cleaner Production*, *142*, 2374–2383. doi:10.1016/j.jclepro.2016.11.038

Martínez, M., & Carmona, G. (2009). Aproximación al concepto de competencias emprendedoras: Valor social e implicaciones educativas. *Revista Electrónica Iberoamericana sobre Calidad, Eficacia y Cambio en Educación*, *7*(3), 82–98.

Martínez, P., Pérez, A., & Rodríguez del Bosque, I. (2014). CSR influence on hotel brand image and loyalty. *Academia (Caracas)*, *27*(2), 267–283. doi:10.1108/ARLA-12-2013-0190

Martínez, P., & Rodríguez del Bosque, I. (2013). CSR and customer loyalty: The roles of trust, customer identification with the Company and satisfaction. *International Journal of Hospitality Management*, *35*, 89–99. doi:10.1016/j.ijhm.2013.05.009

Martins, L. F. (2006). *Modelos com dados em painel*. Instituto Superior de Ciências do Trabalho e da Empresa.

Marulanda, F. A., Montoya, I. A., & Vélez, J. M. (2019). El individuo y sus motivaciones en el proceso emprendedor. *Revista Universidad y Empresa*, *21*(36), 10–24.

Mason, J. (2002). Qualitative Researching (2nd ed.). Sage Publications. Retrieved from http://www.uk.sagepub.com/booksProdDesc.nav?prodId=Book224801

Mason, C., & Simmons, J. (2011). Forward looking or looking unaffordable? Utilising academic perspectives on corporate social responsibility to assess the factors influencing its adoption by business. *Business Ethics (Oxford, England)*, *20*(2), 159–176. doi:10.1111/j.1467-8608.2011.01614.x

Mathews, M. R. (1997). Twenty-five years of social and environmental accounting research: Is there a silver jubilee to celebrate? *Accounting, Auditing & Accountability Journal*, *10*(4), 481–531. doi:10.1108/EUM0000000004417

Mathuva, D. M., Mboya, J. K., & McFie, J. B. (2017). Achieving legitimacy through cooperative governance and social and environmental disclosure by credit unions in a developing country. *Journal of Applied Accounting Research*, *18*(2), 162–184. doi:10.1108/JAAR-12-2014-0128

Mays, N., Pope, C., & Popay, J. (2005). Systematically reviewing qualitative and quantitative evidence to inform management and policy-making in the health field. *Journal of Health Services Research & Policy*, *10*(1), 6–20. doi:10.1258/1355819054308576 PMID:16053580

Mcguire, J. B., Sundgreen, A., & Schneewels, T. (1998). Corporate social responsibility and firm financial performance. *Academy of Management Journal*, *31*(4), 869–882.

McKinsey Global Institute. (2011). *Urban World: Mapping the Economic Power of Cities*. MGI.

McWilliams, A. (2015). Corporate social responsibility. In Wiley Encyclopedia of Management. Wiley.

McWilliams, A., & Siegel, D. (2000). Corporate social responsibility and financial performance: Correlation or misspecification? *Strategic Management Journal*, *21*(5), 603–609. doi:10.1002/(SICI)1097-0266(200005)21:5<603::AID-SMJ101>3.0.CO;2-3

McWilliams, A., & Siegel, D. (2001). Corporate social responsibility: A theory of the firm perspective. *Academy of Management Review*, *26*(1), 117–127. doi:10.5465/amr.2001.4011987

McWilliams, A., & Siegel, D. (2001). Corporate Social Responsibility: A Theory of the Firm Perspective. *Academy of Management Review*, *26*(1), 117–127. doi:10.5465/amr.2001.4011987

McWilliams, A., Siegel, D. S., & Wright, P. M. (2006). Corporate social responsibility: Strategic implications. *Journal of Management Studies*, *43*(1), 1–18. doi:10.1111/j.1467-6486.2006.00580.x

Mellahi, K., Frynas, J. G., Sun, P., & Siegel, D. (2016). A review of the nonmarket strategy literature: Towards a multi-theoretical integration. *Journal of Management*, *42*(1), 143–173. doi:10.1177/0149206315617241

Melo Neto, F. P., & Fróes, E. S. C. (2001). Gestão da responsabilidade social corporativa: o caso brasileiro – da filantropia tradicional à filantropia de alto rendimento e ao empreendedorismo social. Rio de Janeiro: Qualitymark Ed.

Merco. (2014). Merco responsabilidad y gobierno corporativo. Retrieved from http://www.merco.info/br/ranking-merco-responsabilidad-gobierno-corporativo

Merminod, N., & Paché, G. (2011). Supply management and corporate social responsibility: The challenge of global chain traceability. *Journal on Chain and Network Science*, *11*(3), 213–222. doi:10.3920/JCNS2011.x201

Mertens, D. M. (1998). *Research methods in education and psychology: Integrating diversity with quantitative and qualitative approaches*. London: Sage.

Meyer, J. P., & Allen, N. J. (1991). A three-component conceptualization of organizational commitment. *Human Resource Management Review*, *1*(1), 61–89. doi:10.1016/1053-4822(91)90011-Z

Meyer, J. P., Becker, T. E., & Vandenberghe, C. (2004). Employee commitment and motivation: A conceptual analysis and integrative model. *The Journal of Applied Psychology*, *89*(6), 991–1007. doi:10.1037/0021-9010.89.6.991 PMID:15584837

Meyer, J. W., & Rowan, B. (1977). Institutionalized organizations: Formal structure as myth and ceremony. *American Journal of Sociology*, *83*(2), 340–363. doi:10.1086/226550

Michelon, G., & Parbonetti, A. (2012). The effect of corporate governance on sustainability disclosure. *The Journal of Management and Governance*, *16*(3), 477–509. doi:10.100710997-010-9160-3

Milani Filho, M. A. F. (2007). Responsabilidade Social e investimento social privado: Entre o discurso e a evidenciação. *Revista Contabilidade & Finanças*, *19*(47), 89–101. doi:10.1590/S1519-70772008000200008

Miles, M. B., & Huberman, A. M. (1994). *Qualitative Data Analysis*. Sage Publications.

Milne, M., Tregidga, H., & Walton, S. (2009). Words not actions! The ideological role of sustainable development reporting. *Accounting, Auditing & Accountability Journal*, *22*(8), 1211–1257. doi:10.1108/09513570910999292

Minniti, M. (2012). El emprendimiento y el crecimiento económico de las naciones. *Revue d'Economie Industrielle*, *383*, 23–32.

Mion, G., Broglia, A., & Bonfanti, A. (2019). Do Codes of Ethics Reveal a University's Commitment to Sustainable Development? *Evidence from Italy. Sustainability*, *11*(4), 1134. doi:10.3390u11041134

Miotto, G., Polo, M., & Rom, J. (2019). Gender Equality and UN Sustainable Development Goals: Priorities and Correlations in the Top Business Schools' Communication and Legitimation Strategies. *Sustainability*, *11*(302), 2–18.

Mitchell, C. G., & Hill, T. (2009). Corporate social and environmental reporting and the impact of internal environmental policy in South Africa. *Corporate Social Responsibility and Environmental Management*, *16*(1), 48–60. doi:10.1002/csr.179

Mitchell, R., Agle, B., & Wood, J. (1997). Toward a Theory of Stakeholders Identification and Salience: Defining the Principle of Who and What Really Counts. *Academy of Management Review*, *22*(4), 853–886. doi:10.5465/amr.1997.9711022105

Modell, S. (2005). Triangulation between case study and survey methods in management accounting research: An assessment of validity implications. *Management Accounting Research*, *16*(2), 231–254. doi:10.1016/j.mar.2005.03.001

Monast, J., Anda, J., & Profeta, T. (2009). U.S. Carbon Market Design: regulating emission allowances as financial instruments. Nicholas Institute for Environmental Policy Solutions, Duke University.

Monem, R. M. (2013). Determinants of board structure: Evidence from Australia. *Journal of Contemporary Accounting & Economics*, *9*(1), 33–49. doi:10.1016/j.jcae.2013.01.001

Moneva, J. M., & Llena, F. M. (1996). Análisis de la información sobre responsabilidad social en las empresas industriales que cotizan en Bolsa. *Revista Española de Financiación y Contabilidad, XXV*(87), 361–401.

Moneva, J., & Martín, E. (2012). Universidad y Desarrollo sostenible: Análisis de la rendición de cuentas de las universidades públicas desde un enfoque de responsabilidad social. *Revista Iberoamericana de Contabilidad de Gestión, 10*(19), 1–18.

Monteiro, S. (2006). *El Medio Ambiente como factor clave en la definición de las estratégias empresariales y sus implicaciones en la gestión y el sistema de información contable. Una perspectiva del caso Portugués* [Tesis Doctoral]. Universidad de Santiago de Compostela.

Monteiro, S., & Guzman, B. (2010a). The influence of the Portuguese environmental accounting standard on the environmental disclosures in the annual reports of large companies operating in Portugal: A first view. *Management of Environmental Quality, 21*(4), 414–435. doi:10.1108/14777831011049070

Monteiro, S., & Guzman, B. (2010b). Determinants of environmental disclosure in the annual reports of large companies operating in Portugal. *Corporate Social Responsibility and Environmental Management, 17*(4), 185–204. doi:10.1002/csr.197

Moore, M. (2019). CSR & Company Financial Performance (April 25, 2019). Retrieved from https://ssrn.com/abstract=3377842

Moral, J. (2016, April 6). *Nace el primer radar solidario: recaudará para fines sociales.* Retrieved from http://www.autopista.es

Morata, F., Vilà, B., & Suárez, C. (2010). *La responsabilidad social de la empresa a debate. Lecciones de la crisis.* Barcelona: IUEE.

Morhardt, J. E. (2010). Corporate social responsibility and sustainability reporting on the internet. *Business Strategy and the Environment, 19*(7), 436–452.

Morros, J. (2016). The integrated reporting: A presentation of the current state of art and aspects of integrated reporting that need further development. *Intangible Capital, 12*(1), 336–356. doi:10.3926/ic.700

Morsing, M., & Schultz, M. (2006). Corporate social responsibility communication: Stakeholder information, response and involvement strategies. *Business Ethics (Oxford, England), 15*(4), 323–338. doi:10.1111/j.1467-8608.2006.00460.x

Moser, D. V., & Martin, P. R. (2012, May). A Broader Perspective on Corporate Social Responsibility Research in Accounting. *The Accounting Review, 87*(3), 797–806. doi:10.2308/accr-10257

Mouatassim Lahmini, H., & Ibenrissoul, A. (2016). Y a-t-il un impact de la RSE sur la performance financière de l'entreprise: Etude empirique sur les sociétés marocaines cotées à la bourse de Casablanca. Retrieved from https://hal.archives-ouvertes.fr/hal-01351951

Mousa, G., & Hassan, N. T. (2015). Legitimacy theory and environmental practices: Short notes. *International Journal of Business and Statistical Analysis, 2*(01), 41–53. doi:10.12785/ijbsa/020104

Munisi, G., & Randøy, T. (2013). Corporate governance and company performance across Sub-Saharan African countries. *Journal of Economics and Business, 70*, 92–110. doi:10.1016/j.jeconbus.2013.08.003

Mura, R. (2007). Firm Performance: Do Non-Executive Directors Have Minds of their Own? Evidence from UK Panel Data. *Financial Management, 36*(5), 81–112. doi:10.1111/j.1755-053X.2007.tb00082.x

Muravyev, A., Talavera, O., & Weir, C. (2016). Performance effects of appointing other firms' executive directors to corporate boards: An analysis of UK firms. *Review of Quantitative Finance and Accounting*, *46*(1), 25–45. doi:10.100711156-014-0460-6

Murphy, K. J. (1985). Corporate Performance and Managerial Remuneration: An Empirical Analysis. *Journal of Accounting and Economics*, *7*(1-3), 11–42. doi:10.1016/0165-4101(85)90026-6

Murray, S. (2007). Bottom-line benefits special award corporate responsibility: Ethical concerns are a growing factor in staff motivation. *Financial Times*, 11.

Muttakin, M. B., Khan, A., & Azim, M. I. (2015). Corporate social responsibility disclosures and earnings quality. Are they a reflection of managers' opportunistic behavior. *Managerial Auditing Journal*, *30*(3), 277–298. doi:10.1108/MAJ-02-2014-0997

Myers, S. (1977). Determinants of corporate borrowing. *Journal of Financial Economics*, *5*(2), 147–175. doi:10.1016/0304-405X(77)90015-0

Myring, M., & Shortride, R. (2010). Corporate Governance and the Quality Of Financial Disclosures. Journal of Business Ethics. *International Business & Economics Research Journal.*, *9*(6), 103–110. doi:10.19030/iber.v9i6.589

Nadeem, M., Zaman, R., & Saleem, I. (2017). Boardroom gender diversity and corporate sustainability practices: Evidence from Australian securities exchange listed firms. *Journal of Cleaner Production*, *149*, 874–885. doi:10.1016/j.jclepro.2017.02.141

Nasih, M., Harymawan, I., Paramitasari, Y., & Handayani, A. (2019). Carbon emissions, firm size, and corporate governance structure: Evidence from the mining and agricultural industries in Indonesia. *Sustainability*, 11.

Needleman, S. E. (2008). The latest office perk: Getting paid to volunteer — more companies subsidize donations of time and talent; bait for millennial generation. *The Wall Street Journal Online.* Retrieved from http://online.wsj.com/article/SB120940853880850351.html

Nejati, M., Shafaei, A., Salamzadeh, Y., & Daraei, M. (2011). Corporate social responsibility and universities: A study of top 10 world universities' websites. *African Journal of Business Management*, *5*(2), 440–447.

Nelling, E., & Webb, E. (2009). Corporate social responsibility and financial performance: The "virtuous circle" revisited. *Review of Quantitative Finance and Accounting*, *32*(2), 197–209. doi:10.100711156-008-0090-y

Nelson, M. R., & Vilela, A. M. (2017). Exploring the interactive effects of brand use and gender on cause-related marketing over time. *International Journal of Nonprofit and Voluntary Sector Marketing*, *22*(3), 1–13. doi:10.1002/nvsm.1580

Nevado-Gil, M.T., Gallardo Dolores, L., y Isabel Sánchez, M. (2016). Análisis del grado de divulgación de información sobre responsabilidad social en las webs de los principales municipios extremeños. *Auditoría pública*, (67), 77-92.

Nevado-Gil, M. T., Gallardo Dolores, L., & Isabel Sánchez, M. (2013). La administración local y su implicación en la creación de una cultura socialmente responsable. *Revista Prisma Social Revista de Ciencias Sociales*, *10*, 64–118.

Nguyen, P., Rahman, N., & Zhao, R. (2018). CEO characteristics and firm valuation: A quantile regression analysis. *The Journal of Management and Governance*, *22*(1), 133–151. doi:10.100710997-017-9383-7

Nino. (2016). Singapore - the first smart nation in the world. Tanaza. Retrieved from https://www.tanaza.com/blog/singapore-the-first-smart-nation-in-the-world/

Nishitani, K., Kaneko, S., Fujii, H., & Komatsu, S. (2012). Are firms' voluntary environmental management activities beneficial for the environment and business? An empirical study focusing on Japanese manufacturing firms. *Journal of Environmental Management*, *105*, 121–130. doi:10.1016/j.jenvman.2012.03.054 PMID:22542980

Nissim, D., & Penman, S. H. (2003). Financial Statement Analysis of Leverage and How It Informs About Profitability and Price-to-Book Ratios. *Review of Accounting Studies*, *8*(4), 531–560. doi:10.1023/A:1027324317663

Nodari, P. C., Calgaro, C., & Síveres, L. (2017). *Ética, direitos humanos e meio ambiente: reflexões e pistas para uma educação cidadã responsável e pacífica*. EDUCS – Editora da Universidade de Caxias do Sul.

Nogueira, J. M., Conceição, P. H. Z., & Imbroisi, D. (2015). Crédito bancário, risco ambiental e sustentabilidade empresarial: O caminho percorrido pelas instituições financeiras no Brasil. *Business and Management Review*, *4*(8), 734–744.

Noronha, C., Tou, S., Cynthia, M. I., & Guan, J. (2013). Corporate Social Responsibility Reporting in China: An Overview and Comparison with Major Trends. *Corporate Social Responsibility and Environmental Management*, *1*(1), 29–42. doi:10.1002/csr.1276

Ntim, C. G., Soobaroyen, T., & Broad, M. J. (2017). Governance structures, voluntary disclosures and public accountability: The case of UK higher education institutions. *Accounting, Auditing & Accountability Journal*, *30*(1), 65–118. doi:10.1108/AAAJ-10-2014-1842

O'Donovan, G. (2002). Environmental disclosures in the annual report: Extending the applicability and predictive power of legitimacy theory. *Accounting, Auditing & Accountability Journal*, *15*(3), 344–371. doi:10.1108/09513570210435870

O'Reilly, C. A., & Chatman, J. (1986). Organizational commitment and psychological attachment: The effects of compliance, identification, and internalization on prosocial behaviour. *The Journal of Applied Psychology*, *71*(3), 492–499. doi:10.1037/0021-9010.71.3.492

Oh, W. Y., Chang, Y. K., & Martynov, A. (2011). The effect of ownership structure on corporate social responsibility: Empirical evidence from Korea. *Journal of Business Ethics*, *104*(2), 283–297. doi:10.100710551-011-0912-z

ONU. (2012). Resilient People, Resilient Planet: A Future Worth Choosing, Relatório do Painel de alto Nível sobre Sustentabilidade Global do Secretário-geral das Nações Unidas.

Organisation for Economic Co-operation and Development. (2004). The OECD Principles of Corporate Governance.

Organização das Cooperativas do Brasil (OCB). (2017). Site OCB, aba O que é Cooperativismo. Retrieved from http://www.somoscooperativismo.coop.br/#%2Fo-que-e-cooperativismo

Orlitzky, M., Frank, L., Schmidt, F. L., Sara, L., & Rynes, S. L. (2003). Corporate social and financial performance: A meta-analysis. *Organization Studies*, *24*(3), 403–441. doi:10.1177/0170840603024003910

Othman, R., & Othman, R. (2014). Higher education institutions and social performance: Evidence from public and private universities. *International Journal of Business & Society*, *15*(1), 1–1.

Pache-Durán, M., & Nevado-Gil, M. T. (2019). Divulgación de información responsable por los gobiernos locales españoles. *Revista Bibliotecológica*, *33*(81), 111–134.

Padgett, R., & Galán, J. (2010). The effect of R&D Intensity on Corporate Social Responsibility. *Journal of Business Ethics*, *93*(3), 407–418. doi:10.100710551-009-0230-x

Palmon, O., & Wald, J. K. (2002). Are two heads better than one? The impact of change in management structure on performance by firm size. *Journal of Corporate Finance*, *8*(3), 213–226. doi:10.1016/S0929-1199(01)00042-6

Palos- Sánchez, P.R., Baena-Luna, P., & Casablanca Peña, A. (2019). *Factores determinantes para la mejora de la capacidad emprendedora a partir de las competencias*. Cáceres: editada por Extremadura Avante Servicios Avanzados.

Pavlopoulos, A., Magnis, C., & Iatridis, G. E. (2017). Integrated reporting: Is it the last piece of the accounting disclosure puzzle? *Journal of Multinational Financial Management, 41*, 23–46. doi:10.1016/j.mulfin.2017.05.001

Pechersky, A. (2016). Diversity in board of directors: Review of diversity as a factor to enhance board performance. *Studia Commercialia Bratislavensia, 9*(33), 88–101. doi:10.1515tcb-2016-0009

Pelletier, L. G., & Aitken, N. M. (2014). Encouraging environmental actions in employees and in the working environment: a self-determination theory perspective. In E. M. Gagn (Ed.), *The Oxford Handbook of Work Engagement, Motivation, and Self-determination Theory* (pp. 314–334). Oxford: Oxford University Press.

Penelas-Leguia. A., Galera-Casquet, C., Galan-Ladero, M., & Valero-Amaro, V. (2012). Marketing Solidario. El marketing en las organizaciones no lucrativas. Madrid: Piramide.

Peng, C.-W., & Yang, M.-L. (2013). The Effect of Corporate Social Performance on Financial Performance: The Moderating Effect of Ownership Concentration. *Journal of Business Ethics, 123*(1), 171–182. doi:10.100710551-013-1809-9

Peng, M. W., Zhang, S., & Li, X. (2007). CEO Duality and Firm Performance during China's Institutional Transitions. *Management and Organization Review, 3*(2), 205–225. doi:10.1111/j.1740-8784.2007.00069.x

Pereda, S. & Berrocal, F. (2001). *Gestión de Recursos Humanos por Competencias*. Madrid: editado por el Centro de Estudios Ramón Areces.

Pereira, T. H. M., & Gonçalves, C. A. (2019). Responsabilidade social corporativa: práticas e percepções. *Revista observatorio de la economía latinoamericana*, (Enero), 01-07.

Pérez, A., & Del Bosque, I. R. (2015). How customers construct corporate social responsibility images: Testing the moderating role of demographic characteristics. *BRQ Business Research Quarterly, 18*(2), 127–141. doi:10.1016/j.brq.2014.04.003

Pérez-Ruíz, A., & Rodríguez del Bosque, I. (2012). La imagen de la Responsabilidad Social Corporativa en un contexto de crisis económica: El caso del sector financiero en España. *Universia Business Review, 33*, 14-29.

Perrini, F., & Russo, A. (2010). Investigating Stakeholder Theory and Social Capital: CSR in Large Firms and SMEs. *Journal of Business Ethics, 91*, 201–221. doi:10.100710551-009-0079-z

Pestana, M., & Gageiro, J. (2008). *Análise de dados para Ciências Sociais – A complementaridade do SPSS* (5th ed.). Lisboa: Edições Sílabo.

Petronzio, M., & Petronzio, M. (2014). 54% of the World's Population Now Lives in Cities [CHART]. Retrieved from https://mashable.com/2014/07/18/urbanization-city-growth/?europe=true#nvfGudR5lGqz

Petty, R., & Cuganesan, S. (2005). Voluntary disclosure of intellectual capital by Hong Kong companies: Examining size, industry and growth effects over time. *Australian Accounting Review, 15*(2), 40–50. doi:10.1111/j.1835-2561.2005.tb00291.x

Pfeffer, J. (1981). *Power in organizations*. Boston: Pitman.

Pfeffer, J., & Salancik, G. (1978). The External Control Of Organizations: A Resource Dependency Perspective. *Economic Journal (London), 23*, 2. doi:10.2307/2231527

Pimenta, A. A., Portela, A. R. M. R., Oliveira, C. B., & Ribeiro, R. M. (2017). A bibliometria nas pesquisas acadêmicas, SCIENTIA: Revista de Ensino. *Pesquisa e Extensão, 4*(7), 1–13.

Pisani, N., Kourula, A., Kolk, A., & Meijer, R. (2017). How global is international CSR research? Insights and recommendations from a systematic review. *Journal of World Business*, *52*(5), 591–614. doi:10.1016/j.jwb.2017.05.003

Pivato, S., Misani, N., & Tencati, A. (2008). The impact of corporate social responsibility on consumer trust: The case of organic food. *Business Ethics (Oxford, England)*, *17*(1), 3–12. doi:10.1111/j.1467-8608.2008.00515.x

Platonova, E., Asutay, M., Dixon, R., & Mohammad, S. (2018). The impact of Corporate Social Responsibility Disclosure on Financial Performance: Evidence from the GCC Islamic Banking Sector. *Journal of Business Ethics*, *151*(2), 451–471. doi:10.100710551-016-3229-0

Porter, M. E., & Kramer, M. R. (2006). The link between competitive advantage and corporate social responsibility. *Harvard Business Review*, *84*(12), 78–92. PMID:17183795

Porter, M., & Kramer, M. K. (2006). Strategy and society: The link between competitive advantage and corporate social responsibility. *Harvard Business Review*, *84*(12), 78–92. PMID:17183795

Portney, P. R. (2008). The (Not So) New Corporate Social Responsibility: An Empirical Perspective. *Review of Environmental Economics and Policy*, *2*(2), 261–275. doi:10.1093/reep/ren003

Post, C., Rahman, N., & Rubow, E. (2011). Green governance: Boards of directors' composition and environmental corporate social responsibility. *Business & Society*, *50*(1), 189–223. doi:10.1177/0007650310394642

Prado Lorenzo, J., Rodríguez-Domínguez, L., Gallego-Álvarez, M., & García Sánchez, I. (2009). Factors influencing the disclosure of greenhouse gas emissions in companies world-wide. *Management Decision*, *47*(7), 1133–1157. doi:10.1108/00251740910978340

Prado-Lorenzo, J. M., Gallego-Alvarez, I., & Garcia-Sanchez, I. M. (2009). Stakeholder engagement and corporate social responsibility reporting: The ownership structure effect. *Corporate Social Responsibility and Environmental Management*, *16*(2), 94–107. doi:10.1002/csr.189

Prado-Lorenzo, J. M., & García-Sánchez, I. M. (2010). The role of the board of directors in disseminating relevant information on greenhouse gases. *Journal of Business Ethics*, *97*(3), 391–424. doi:10.100710551-010-0515-0

Prasad, M., Mishra, T., & Kalro, A. D. (2017). Environmental disclosure by Indian companies: An empirical study. *Environment, Development and Sustainability*, *19*(5), 1999–2022. doi:10.100710668-016-9840-5

Prasetya, R. A., & Yulianto, A. (2018). Analysis of the factors affecting the disclosure of corporate carbon emission in Indonesia. *Journal Dinamika Akuntansi*, *10*(1), 71–81. doi:10.15294/jda.v10i1.12653

Prencipe, A. (2004). Proprietary costs and determinants of voluntary segment disclosure: Evidence from Italian listed companies. *European Accounting Review*, *13*(2), 319–340. doi:10.1080/0963818042000204742

PricewaterhouseCoopers PWC (2018). *SDG Reporting Challenge 2018. From promise to reality. Does business really care about the SDGs? And what needs to happen to turn words into action.* Retrieved from https://www.pwc.com/gx/en/sustainability/SDG/sdg-reporting-2018.pdf

PricewaterhouseCoopers PWC. (2017). *Os desafios das empresas portuguesas na priorização dos ODS e no* relato não-financeiro 2017. Estará a sua empresa preparada?

Pricewaterhousecoopers, & International Emissions Trading Association (PWC & IETA). (2007). *Trouble-Entry Accounting – Revisited - Uncertainty in accounting for the EU Emissions Trading Scheme and Certified Emission Reductions.*

PwC. (2013). The value creation journey: a survey of JSE Top-40 companies integrated reports. Retrieved from www.pwc.co.za/en_ZA/za/assets/pdf/integrated-reporting-august-2013

PwC. (2014). Value creation: the journey continues: A survey of JSE Top-40 companies' integrated reports. Retrieved from www.pwc.co.za/en_ZA/za/assets/pdf/integrated-reporting-survey-2014

PwC. (2015). *Implementing integrated reporting*. Retrieved from https://www.pwc.com/gx/en/audit-services/publications/assets/pwc-ir-practical-guide.pdf

PwC. (2016). King IV - Steering point: A summary of the King IV Report on Corporate Governance for South Africa. Retrieved from https://www.pwc.co.za/en/publications/king4.html

Qadorah, A. A. M., & Fadzil, F. H. (2018). The Relationship Between Board Size and CEO Duality and Firm Performance: Evidence from Jordan. *International Journal of Accounting. Finance and Risk Management*, *3*(3), 16–20. doi:10.11648/j.ijafrm.20180303.11

Rahman, S. (2011). Evaluation of Definitions: Ten Dimensions of Corporate Social Responsibility. *World Review of Business Research*, *1*(1), 166-176.

Ramdhony, D. (2018). The Implications of Mandatory Corporate Social Responsibility—A Literature Review Perspective. *Theoretical Economics Letters*, *8*(3), 432–447. doi:10.4236/tel.2018.83031

Rankin, M., Windsor, C., & Wahyuni, D. (2011). An investigation of voluntary corporate greenhouse gas emissions reporting in a market governance system. *Accounting, Auditing & Accountability Journal*, *24*(8), 1037–1070. doi:10.1108/09513571111184751

Rao, K., & Tilt, C. (2016). Board Composition and Corporate Social Responsibility: The Role of Diversity, Gender, Strategy and Decision Making. *Journal of Business Ethics*, *138*(2), 327–347. doi:10.100710551-015-2613-5

Rashid, A. (2010). CEO duality and firm performance: Evidence from a developing country. *Corporate Ownership and Control*, *8*(1), 163–175. doi:10.22495/cocv8i1c1p1

Rashid, A., & Rehman, Z. (2015). Analyzing Performance of Banks in Pakistan: Conventional versus Islamic Banks. *Journal of Islamic Business and Management*, *5*(2), 17–42. doi:10.12816/0026416

Rechner, P. L., & Dalton, D. R. (1991). CEO duality and organizational performance: A longitudinal analysis. *Strategic Management Journal*, *12*(2), 155–160. doi:10.1002mj.4250120206

Rees, W., & Rodionova, T. (2014). The influence of family ownership on corporate social responsibility: An international analysis of publicly listed companies. *Corporate Governance*, *23*(3), 184–202. doi:10.1111/corg.12086

Rego, M. (2017). The Impact of Cause-Related Marketing on Global Consumers: A Meta-Analysis [Doctoral Dissertation]. University of Connecticut (USA).

Regulation (EC) 1606/2002 of the European Parliament and of the Council of 19. (2002).

Regulation (EU) 601/2012 of the European Parliament and of the Council of 21. (2012).

Reis, C., Lopes, A. (2011). Fatores económicos e contabilísticos que influenciam a qualidade da informação ambiental: um estudo com empresas Admitidas à cotação na Euronext Lisbon que tenham títulos de Emissão de gases com efeito de estufa. In *XVI Encuentro AECA*. Academic Press.

Resmi, S. I., Begum, N. N., & Hassan, M. M. (2018). Impact of CSR on Firm's Financial Performance: A Study on Some Selected Agribusiness Industries of Bangladesh. *American Journal of Economics. Financial Management*, *4*(3), 74–85.

Resolution of the Council of Ministers no. 1/2008, of January 4, Diário da República, 1st series. (2008).

Resolution of the Council of Ministers no. 53/2005, of March 3, Diário da República, 1st series. (2005).

Reverte, C. (2009). Determinants of Corporate Social Responsibility Disclosure Ratings by Spanish Listed Firms. *Journal of Business Ethics*, *88*(2), 351–366. doi:10.100710551-008-9968-9

Reverte, C. (2009). Determinants of corporate social responsibility disclosure ratings by Spanish listed firms. *Journal of Business Ethics*, *88*(2), 351–366. doi:10.1007/s10551-008-9968-9

Reverte, C. (2012). The Impact of Better Corporate Social Responsibility Disclosure on the Cost of Equity Capital. *Corporate Social Responsibility and Environmental Management*, *19*(5), 253–272. doi:10.1002/csr.273

Reverte, C., Gómez, E., & Cegarra, J. (2016). The influence of corporate social responsibility practices on organizational performance: Evidence from Eco-Responsible Spanish firms. *Journal of Cleaner Production*, *112*, 2870–2884. doi:10.1016/j.jclepro.2015.09.128

Rhou, Y., Singal, M., & Koh, Y. (2016). CSR and Financial Performance: The Role of CSR Awareness in the Restaurant Industry. *International Journal of Hospitality Management*, *57*(1), 30–39. doi:10.1016/j.ijhm.2016.05.007

Ribeiro, M. A., & Martins, E. (1993). A informação como instrumento de contribuição da contabilidade para a compatibilização no desenvolvimento económico e a preservação do meio ambiente. Caderno de Estudos FIPECAFI, 9.

Ribeiro, C. T. L. (2001). *Responsabilidade social empresarial. Apoio às comunidades carentes. 2001*. Salvador: Universidade Federal da Bahia.

Ribeiro, V. (2007). *La gestión medioambiental en las entidades públicas locales portuguesas. Una perspectiva contable* [Tesis Doctoral]. Universidad de Santiago de Compostela.

Ridehalgh, N. (2011). Active Governance: the core of Better Business Reporting. KPMG.

Risk Management Structure Pillar (EGR). (2017). Retrieved from https://www.sicredi.com.br/html/conheca-o-sicredi/relatorios/

Rivera, J. J., Bigne, E., & Curras-Perez, R. (2016). Effects of Corporate Social Responsibility perception on consumer satisfaction with the brand. *Spanish Journal of Marketing*, *20*(2), 104-114.

Robertson. (2015). *What is Integrated Reporting and why does it matter?* ICAS. Retrieved from https://www.icas.com/ca-today-news/what-is-integrated-reporting-why-it-matters

Roberts, P. W., & Dowling, G. R. (2002). Corporate reputation and sustained superior financial performance. *Strategic Management Journal*, *23*(12), 1077–1093. doi:10.1002mj.274

Rodgers, W., Choy, H. L., & Guiral, A. (2013). Do Investors Value a Firm's Commitment to Social Activities? *Journal of Business Ethics, 114*(4), 607-623. 10.100710551-013-1707-1

Rodrigo, P., Durán, I. J., & Arenas, D. (2016). Does it really pay to be good, everywhere? A first step to understand the corporate social and financial performance link in Latin American controversial industries. *Business Ethics (Oxford, England)*, *25*(3), 286–309. doi:10.1111/beer.12119

Rodríguez Bolívar, M. P., Garde Sánchez, R., & López Hernández, A. M. (2013). Online disclosure of corporate social responsibility information in leading Anglo-American universities. *Journal of Environmental Policy and Planning*, *15*(4), 551–575. doi:10.1080/1523908X.2013.817945

Rodriguez-Fernandez, M. (2016). Social responsibility and financial performance: The role of good corporate governance. *BRQ Business Research Quarterly*, *19*(2), 137–151. doi:10.1016/j.brq.2015.08.001

Rok, B. (2019). Transition from Corporate Responsibility to sustainable strategic management. In CSR, Sustainability. Ethics and Governance. Springer Nature Switzerland. doi:10.1007/978-3-030-00440-8_1

Roman, A., Mocanu, M., & Hoinaru, R. (2019). Disclosure Style and Its Determinants in Integrated Reports. *Sustainability, 11*(7), 1960. doi:10.3390u11071960

Rosati, F., & Faria, L. (2019a). Business contribution to the Sustainable Development Agenda: Organizational factors related to early adoption of SDG reporting. *Corporate Social Responsibility and Environmental Management*, 1–10.

Rosati, F., & Faria, L. (2019b). Addressing the SDGs in sustainability reports: The relationship with institutional factors. *Journal of Cleaner Production, 215*, 1312–1326. doi:10.1016/j.jclepro.2018.12.107

Rossi, F. M. (2017). *From sustainability reporting to integrated reporting: the public sector experience*. University of Salerno.

Rossouw, G. J., van der Watt, A., & Malan, D. P. (2002). Corporate Governance in South Africa. *Journal of Business Ethics, 37*(3), 289–302. doi:10.1023/A:1015205511601

Roxana-Ioana, B., & Petru, S. (2017). Integrated reporting for a good corporate governance. *Ovidius University Annals Series Economic Sciences, 17*(1), 424–428.

Rupp, D. E., Ganapathi, J., Aguilera, R. V., & Williams, C. A. (2006). Employee reactions to corporate social responsibility: An organizational justice framework. *Journal of Organizational Behavior, 27*(4), 537–543. doi:10.1002/job.380

Rupp, D. E., & Mallory, D. B. (2015). Corporate Social Responsibility: Psychological, Person-Centric, and Progressing. *Annual Review of Organizational Psychology and Organizational Behavior, 2*(2), 11–36.

Rupp, D. E., Shao, R., Thornton, M. A., & Skarlicki, D. P. (2013). Applicants' and employees' reactions to corporate social responsibility: The moderating effects of first-party justice perceptions and moral identity. *Personnel Psychology, 66*(4), 895–933. doi:10.1111/peps.12030

Rutledge, R. W., Karim, K. E., & Lu, S. (2016). The Effects of Board Independence and CEO Duality on Firm Performance: Evidence from the NASDAQ-100 Index with Controls for Endogeneity. *Journal of Applied Business and Economics, 18*(2), 49–71. doi:10.33423/jabe.v18i2.838

Rymsza, M. (2015). The role of social enterprises in shaping social bonds. *International Journal of Social Economics, 42*(9), 830–840. doi:10.1108/IJSE-03-2015-0059

Sabbaghi, O., & Xu, M. (2013). ROE and Corporate Social Responsibility: Is There a Return On Ethics? *Journal of Accounting and Finance, 13*(4), 82–95.

Sáenz González, J., & García-Meca, E. (2014). Does Corporate Governance Influence Earnings Management in Latin American Markets? *Journal of Business Ethics, Springer, 121*(3), 419–440. doi:10.1007/s10551-013-1700-8

Sahut, J. M., and Gharbi, H. O. (2011). Influence of French and foreign institutional shareholders on the financial performance of firms. La revue des Sciences de Gestion, (5), 51-62.

Sahut, J. M., Mili, M., & Teulon, F. (2018). Gouvernance, RSE et performance financière: Vers une compréhension globale de leurs relations? *Management & Avenir, 101*(3), 39. doi:10.3917/mav.101.0039

Sahut, J., Mili, M., Ben Tekaya, S., & Teulon, F. (2016). Financial Impacts and antecedents of CSR: A PLS Path Modelling Approach. *Economic Bulletin, 36*(2), 736–751.

Saidi, C., & Elabbadi, B. (2016). CSR as a dimension of perceived quality: A model of societal determinants of perceived quality to predict customer satisfaction in the context of commercial and industrial utilities. *International Journal of Innovation and Applied Studies, 17*(3), 838–851.

Salanova, M., & Schaufeli, W. B. (2004). El engagement de los empleados: Un reto emergente para la dirección de los recursos humanos. *Estudios Financieros, 261*, 109–138.

Samaha, K., Khlif, H., & Hussainey, K. (2015). The impact of board and audit committee characteristics on voluntary disclosure: A meta-analysis. *Journal of International Accounting, Auditing & Taxation, 24*, 13–28. doi:10.1016/j.intaccaudtax.2014.11.001

San Miguel, A. (2016, April 20). Sabotean el 'radar solidario' de Cayón y obligan a la empresa a anular 139 multas. *El Diario Montañés*. Retrieved from http://www.eldiariomontanes.es/bahia-centro-pas/201604/20/sabotean-radar-solidario-cayon-20160419231211.html

San Miguel, A. (2016, April 7). El 'radar solidario' de Cayón se estrena con 76 multas en dos días. *El Diario Montañés*. Retrieved from http://www.eldiariomontanes.es

Sanchéz, L. E. (2011). *Avaliação de impacto ambiental: conceitos e métodos*. São Paulo: Oficina de textos.

Sanchéz, L. E. (2017). Por que não avança a avaliação ambiental estratégica no Brasil? *Estudos Avançados, 31*(89), 167–183. doi:10.15900103-40142017.31890015

Santesmases, M. (1999). *Marketing. Conceptos y Estrategias*. Madrid: Piramide.

Santos, A. (2013). O comércio de licenças de emissão em Portugal. *International Business and Economics Review:Revista Internacional de Gestão e Comunicação, 4*, 62–77.

Sarkar, J., Sarkar, S., & Sen, K. (2008). Board of Directors and Opportunistic Earnings Management: Evidence from India. *Journal of Accounting, Auditing & Finance, 23*(4), 517–551. doi:10.1177/0148558X0802300405

Sassen, R., & Azizi, L. (2018). Assessing sustainability reports of US universities. *International Journal of Sustainability in Higher Education, 19*(7), 1158–1184. doi:10.1108/IJSHE-06-2016-0114

Schaltegger, S., & Wagner, M. (2006). Integrative Management of Sustainability Performance, Measurement and Reporting. International Journal of Accounting. *Auditing and Performance Evaluation, 3*(1), 1–19. doi:10.1504/IJAAPE.2006.010098

Scherer, A. G., Rasche, A., Palazzo, G., & Spicer, A. (2016). Managing for Political Corporate Social Responsibility: New Challenges and Directions for PCSR 2.0. *Journal of Management Studies, 53*(3), 273–298. doi:10.1111/joms.12203

Scholtens, B., & Kang, F. C. (2013). Corporate Social Responsibility and Earnings Management: Evidence from Asian Economies. *Corporate Social Responsibility and Environmental Management, 20*(2), 95–112. doi:10.1002/csr.1286

Schönherr, N., Findler, F., & Martinuzzi, A. (2017). Exploring the Interface of CSR and the Sustainable Development Goals. *Transnational Coorporations, 24*(3), 33–48. doi:10.18356/cfb5b8b6-en

Schramade, W. (2017). Investing in the UN Sustainable Development Goals: Oppor- tunities for companies and investors. *Journal of Applied Corporate Finance, 29*(2), 87–99. doi:10.1111/jacf.12236

Sengupta, P. (1998). Corporate Disclosure Quality and the Cost of Debt. *The Accounting Review, 73*(4), 459–474.

Sennhauser, P. (2018). EINE EINFÜHRUNG. Suisse Digital. Retrieved from https://www.suissedigital.ch/fileadmin/user_upload/suissedigital/public/de/Smart_City-DE-1_04-20181204.pdf

Sepasi, S., Braendle, U., & Rahdari, A. H. (2019). Comprehensive sustainability reporting in higher education institutions. *Social Responsibility, 15*(2), 155–170. doi:10.1108/SRJ-01-2018-0009

Sepasi, S., Rahdari, A., & Rexhepi, G. (2018). Developing a sustainability reporting assessment tool for higher education institutions: The University of California. *Sustainable Development, 26*(6), 672–682. doi:10.1002d.1736

Serrat, N., & Aliberch, A. (2010). Análisis de la responsabilidad social corporativa, en su aspecto medioambiental, en empresas del mercado continuo Español. In XIV Encuentro AECA, Información Financiera de Calidad: Señalando el Camino de la Recuperación. Academic Press.

Server Izquierdo, R. J., & Capó i Vicedo, J. (2011). The interrelationship between the demands of Corporate Social Responsibility and co-operative principles and values. *CIRIEC-España. C.I.R.I.E.C. España*, *73*, 213–232.

Setia, N., Abhayawansa, S., & Anh, H. (2015). Integrated reporting in South Africa: Some initial evidence", Sustainability Accounting. *Management and Policy Journal*, *6*(3), 397–424.

Setia, N., Abhayawansa, S., Joshi, M., & Huynh, A. V. (2015). Integrated reporting in South Africa: Some initial evidence. Sustainability Accounting. *Management and Policy Journal*, *6*(3), 397–424.

Setó-Pamies, D. (2013). The relationship between women directors and corporate social responsibility. *Corporate Social Responsibility and Environmental Management*, *22*(6), 334–345. doi:10.1002/csr.1349

Shahab, Y., & Ye, C. (2018). Corporate social responsibility disclosure and corporate governance: Empirical insights on neo-institutional framework from China. *International Journal of Disclosure and Governance*, 1–17.

Shane, S., & Venkataraman, S. (2000). The promise of Entrepreneurship as a Field of Research. *Academy of Management Review*, *25*(1), 217–226.

Shannon, S. E. (2014). Three Approaches to Qualitative Content Analysis. *Qualitative Health Research*, *15*(9), 1277–1288. PMID:16204405

Shao, L. (2019). Dynamic study of corporate governance structure and firm performance in China. *Chinese Management Studies*, *13*(2), 299–317. doi:10.1108/CMS-08-2017-0217

Shehata, N. (2014). Theories and Determinants of Voluntary Disclosure. *Accounting and Finance Research.*, *3*(1), 18–26. doi:10.5430/afr.v3n1p18

Shen, C. H., & Chang, Y. (2009). Ambition versus conscience, does corporate social responsibility pay off? The application of matching methods. *Journal of Business Ethics*, *88*(S1), 133–153. doi:10.100710551-008-9826-9

Shepherd, D., & DeTienne, D. R. (2005). Prior Knowlegde, Potential Financial Reward, and Opportunity Identification. *Entrepreneurship Theory and Practice*, *29*(1), 91–112. doi:10.1111/j.1540-6520.2005.00071.x

Sheth, J. N., Sethia, N. K., & Srinivas, S. (2011). Mindful consumption: A customer-centric approach to sustainability. *Journal of the Academy of Marketing Science*, *39*(1), 21–39. doi:10.100711747-010-0216-3

Shrivastav, S. M., & Kalsie, A. (2016). The relationship between CEO duality and firm performance: An analysis using panel data approach. *IUP Journal of Corporate Governance*, *15*(2), 37–58.

SicrediReport. (2017). Retrieved from https://www.sicredi.com.br/html/conheca-o-sicredi/relatorios/

Silinske, J., Marquetto, M. F., Grohmann, M. Z., Battistella, L. F., & Madruga, L. R. da R. G. (2014). Bibliometric study about sustainability in the field of entrepreneurial economy. *Organizations and Sustainability*, *3*(2), 101–120.

Silva, E. C., Azevedo, A. S., Barros, M., & Reis, N. D. (2018). Responsabilidade social corporativa na produção de cacau: Análise das ações da indústria de chocolate. *Novo Hamburgo*, *15*(1), 183–204.

Silva, R. R., & Santos, M. J. N. (2011). A importância da responsabilidade social corporativa para a potenciação do capital social em pequenas e médias empresas. *Revista de Ciências da Administração*, *12*(27), 190–207.

Silva, V., & Lopes, W. G. (2019). Environmental accounting: Analysis of the participation in the business sustainability index (ise) and the profitability of the companies listed in in Brazil. *Revista Gestao & Tecnologia [Journal of Management and Technology], 19*(2), 109–125. doi:10.20397/2177-6652/2019.v19i2.1563

Simmons, R., & Birchall, J. (2008). The role of co-operatives in poverty reduction: Network perspectives. *Journal of Socio-Economics, 37*(6), 2131–2140. doi:10.1016/j.socec.2008.04.016

Simpson, W. G., & Kohers, T. (2002). The link between corporate social and financial performance: Evidence from the banking industry. *Journal of Business Ethics, 35*(2), 97–109. doi:10.1023/A:1013082525900

Singfat, C. (2017). Zero car growth: Only in Singapore? Policy Forum. Retrieved from https://www.policyforum.net/zero-car-growth-only-in-singapore/

Singh, S., Tabassum, N., Darwish, T. K., & Batsakis, G. (2018). Corporate Governance and Tobin's Q as a Measure of Organizational Performance. *British Journal of Management, 28*(1), 171–190. doi:10.1111/1467-8551.12237

Slack, R., & Tsalavoutas, I. (2018). Integrated reporting decision usefulness: Mainstream equity market views. *Accounting Forum, 42*(2), 184–198. doi:10.1016/j.accfor.2018.01.005

Smith, N. C., & Williams, E. (2011). Responsible consumers and stakeholder marketing: Building a virtuous circle of social responsibility. *Universia Business Review, 30*, 68–79.

Soana, M.-G. (2011). The Relationship Between Corporate Social Performance and Corporate Financial Performance in the Banking Sector. *Journal of Business Ethics, 104*(1), 133–148. doi:10.100710551-011-0894-x

Soares, G. M. P. (2004). Responsabilidade social corporativa: Por uma boa causa!? *RAE Eletrônica, 3*(2), 1–15. doi:10.1590/S1676-56482004000200007

Socioenvironmental Responsibility Policy (PRSA). (2015). Retrieved from https://www.sicredi.com.br/html/conheca-o-sicredi/relatorios/

Sollenberger, H. M. (2005). Building a consensus on credit union capital adequacy: At the appropriate level, risks are covered and competitive capability is enhanced. *Bank Accounting & Finance, 18*(5), 1–15.

Song, S.-H. (2006). Workplace Friendship and Employees' Productivity: LMX Theory and the Case of the Seoul City Government. *International Review of Public Administraton, 11*(1), 47–58. doi:10.1080/12294659.2006.10805077

Sprinkle, G. B., & Maines, L. A. (2010). The benefits and costs of corporate social responsibility. *Business Horizons, 53*(5), 445–453. doi:10.1016/j.bushor.2010.05.006

Stacchezzini, R., Melloni, G., & Lai, A. (2016). Sustainability management and reporting: the role of integrated reporting for communicating corporate sustainability management. *Journal of Cleaner Production, 136*(Part A), 102–110.

Stacchezzini, R., Mellon, G., & La, A. (2016). Sustainability management and reporting: The role of integrated reporting for communicating corporate sustainability management. *Journal of Cleaner Production, 136*, 102–110. doi:10.1016/j.jclepro.2016.01.109

Stam, E., Suddie, K., Hessels, S. J., & Van Stel, A. (2006). Los emprendedores con potencial de crecimiento y el desarrollo económico: Políticas públicas de apoyo a los emprendedores. *Ekonomiaz: Revista Vasca de Economía, 62*, 124–149.

Standardized Financial Statements (DFP). (2017). Retrieved from https://www.sicredi.com.br/html/conheca-o-sicredi/relatorios/

Stanga, K. G. (1976). Disclosure in published annual reports. *Financial Management, 5*(4), 42–52. doi:10.2307/3665456

Stanny, E., & Ely, K. (2008). *Corporate Environmental disclousures about the effects of climate change*. Rohnert Park, CA: Sonoma State University.

Steenkamp, N., Rahman, A., & Kashyap, V. (2010). *Recognition, measurement and disclosure of carbon emission allowances under the eu ets – an exploratory study*. School of Commerce and Law – CQUniversity.

Stites, J. P., & Michael, J. H. (2011). Organizational commitment in manufacturing employees: Relationships with corporate social performance. *Business & Society*, *50*(1), 50–70. doi:10.1177/0007650310394311

Stoeberl, P. A., & Sherony, B. C. (1985). Board efficiency and effectiveness. In E. Mattar & M. Ball (Eds.), Handbook for Corporate Directors. New York: McGraw-Hill.

Suchman, M. C. (1995). Managing legitimacy: Strategic and institutional approaches. *Academy of Management Review*, *20*(3), 571–610. doi:10.5465/amr.1995.9508080331

Suddaby, R. (2010). Challenges for institutional theory. *Journal of Management Inquiry*, *16*(1), 14–20. doi:10.1177/1056492609347564

Su, L., & Swanson, S. R. (2019). Perceived corporate social responsibility's impact on the well-being and supportive green behaviors of hotel employees: The mediating role of the employee-corporate relationship. *Tourism Management*, *72*, 437–450. doi:10.1016/j.tourman.2019.01.009

Sullivan, D. M., & Meek, W. R. (2012). Gender and entrepreneurship: A review and process model. *Journal of Managerial Psychology*, *27*(5), 429–452. doi:10.1108/02683941211235373

Sullivan, J. D. (2009). *The moral compass of companies: Business ethics and corporate governance as anti-corruption tools. (No. 7)*. Washington, DC: International Finance Corporation. Retrieved from http://hdl.handle.net/10986/23980

Supanti, D., Butcher, K., & Fredline, L. (2015). Enhancing the employer-employee relationship through corporate social responsibility (CSR) engagement. *International Journal of Contemporary Hospitality Management*, *27*(7), 1479–1498. doi:10.1108/IJCHM-07-2014-0319

Surroca, J., Tribo, J. A., & Waddock, S. (2010). Corporate Responsibility and Financial Performance: The Role of Intangible Resources. *Strategic Management Journal*, *31*(5), 463–490. doi:10.1002/smj.820

Suter, W. N., & Data, Q. (2011). *Introduction to Educational Research: A Critical Thinking Approach*. SAGE Publications.

Sweeney, L., & Coughlan, J. (2008). Do different industries report corporate social responsibility differently? An investigation through the lens of stakeholder theory. *Journal of Marketing Communications*, *14*(2), 113–124. doi:10.1080/13527260701856657

Tabachnick, B. G., & Fidell, L. S. (2001). *Using Multivariate Statistics*. New York, NY: Allyn and Bacon.

Tachizawa, T. (2011). *Gestão ambiental e responsabilidade social corporativa: estratégias de negócios focadas na realidade brasileira*. São Paulo: Atlas.

Tahri, W. & El khamlichi, A. (2019). Disclosure and Communication of the Corporate Social Responsibility (CSR) in Morocco: The Case of a Bank. In *ICT for a Better Life and a Better World* (pp. 247-261). Springer Nature.

Tahri, W., & El Khamlichi, A. (2019). Disclosure and Communication of the Corporate Social Responsibility (CSR) in Morocco: The Case of a Bank. In Y. Baghdadi & A. Harfouche (Eds.), ICT for a Better Life and a Better World: The Impact of Information and Communication Technologies on Organizations and Society (pp. 247-261). Springer International Publishing.

Tanggamani, V., Amran, A., & Ramayah, T. (2018). The Corporate Social Responsibility and Corporate Financial Performance Virtuous Loop: A Theoretical Framework. *Global Business and Management Research: An International Journal*, *10*(1), 331–344.

Tang, Z., Hull, C. E., & Rothenberg, S. (2012). How corporate social responsibility engagement strategy moderates the CSR–financial performance relationship. *Journal of Management Studies*, *49*(7), 1274–1303. doi:10.1111/j.1467-6486.2012.01068.x

Taoukif, F. E. Z. (2015). Analyse perceptuelle des déterminants de l'engagement sociétal des entreprises marocaines labellisées RSE: de la performance au développement durable - cas du maroc. Retrieved from https://tel.archives-ouvertes.fr/tel-01198977

Tenório, F. G. (Ed.). (2015). *Responsabilidade social empresarial: teoria e prática*. Rio de Janeiro: Editora FGV.

Teoh, H. Y., Pin, F. W., Joo, T. T., & Ling, Y. Y. (1998). Environmental disclosures-financial performance link: further evidence from industrialising economy perspective. In *Proceedings of the Second Asian Pacific Interdisciplinary Research in Accounting Conference* (APIRA). Academic Press.

The Economist Newspaper. (2017): The Safe Cities Index 2017. Retrieved from http://safecities.economist.com/safe-cities-index-2017

The portal for Sustainability Reporting (2017). *The GRI Standards: One year on*. Retrieved from https://www.sustainability-reports.com/the-gri-standards-one-year-on/

Thorne, L., Mahoney, L. S., Gregory, K., & Convery, S. (2017). A comparison of Canadian and US CSR strategic alliances, CSR reporting, and CSR performance: Insights into implicit–explicit CSR. *Journal of Business Ethics*, *143*(1), 85–98. doi:10.100710551-015-2799-6

Tian, J. J., & Lau, C. M. (2001). Board Composition, Leadership Structure and Performance in Chinese Shareholding Companies. *Asia Pacific Journal of Management*, *18*(2), 245–263. doi:10.1023/A:1010628209918

Tilling, M. V. (2004). Refinements to Legitimacy Theory in Social and Environmental Accounting.

Timmons, J. (2003). *Entrepreneurial thinking: can entrepreneurship be taught*? Coleman Chicago: Coleman Foundation.

Tinker, T., & Gray, R. (2003). Beyond a critique of pure reason: From policy to politics to praxis in environmental and social research. *Accounting, Auditing & Accountability Journal*, *16*(5), 727–761. doi:10.1108/09513570310505952

Tlemçani, A. (2009). Prise de conscience progressive des pouvoirs publics et des entreprises en matière de responsabilité sociale même si la confusion entre responsabilité sociale et responsabilité légale reste de mise. Retrieved from http://www.iteco.be/Responsabilitesociale-des-entreprises

Toumi, S. (2017). L'impact des mécanismes de gouvernance dans la gestion des risques bancaires et la performance des banques: Cas de la France, l'Allemagne et le Japon. Retrieved from https://tel.archives-ouvertes.fr/tel-01483783

Tranos, E., & Gertner, D. (2012). Smart networked cities? *Innovation (Abingdon)*, *25*(2), 175–190. doi:10.1080/13511610.2012.660327

Tresgallo, E. (2018a, February 6). El Ayuntamiento de Cayón duda de la legalidad de su radar solidario. *El Diario Montañés*. Retrieved from https://www.eldiariomontanes.es/region/valles-pasiegos/ayuntamiento-cayon-duda-20180206211807-ntvo.html

Tresgallo, E. (2018b, January 17). El radar solidario de Cayón recauda 18.000 euros que se destinan a familias necesitadas. *El Diario Montañés*. Retrieved from https://www.eldiariomontanes.es/region/valles-pasiegos/radar-solidario-cayon-20180117214925-ntvo.html

Tsai, Y. H., Joe, S. W., Lin, C. P., & Wang, R. T. (2014). Modeling job pursuit intention: Moderating mechanisms of socio-environmental consciousness. *Journal of Business Ethics*, *125*(2), 287–298. doi:10.100710551-013-1919-4

Tudor-Tiron, A., & Dragu, I. (2014). From sustainability to integrated reporting – the political perspective of institutional theory. *Studia Universitatis Babes-Bolyai*, *59*(2), 20–33.

Turker, D. (2009a). Measuring corporate social responsibility: A scale development study. *Journal of Business Ethics*, *85*(4), 411–427. doi:10.100710551-008-9780-6

Turker, D. (2009b). How corporate social responsibility influences organizational commitment. *Journal of Business Ethics*, *89*(2), 189–204. doi:10.100710551-008-9993-8

Turnbull, S. (2015). Defining and Achieving Good Governance. Retrieved from http://ssrn.com/abstract=2571724

Ullmann, A. (1985). Data in search for a theory: A critical examination of the relationship among Social Performance, Social Disclosure and economic performance. *Academy of Management Review*, *10*, 540–577.

UN Global Compact Network and GRI. (2018). Business Reporting the SDGs -Analysis of the Goals and Targets. Retrieved from https://www.globalreporting.org/resourcelibrary/GRI_UNGC_Business-Reporting-on-SDGs_Analysis-of-Goals-and-Targets.pdf

UN Global Compact Network and GRI. (2018). Integrating the Sustainable Development Goals into Corporate Reporting: A Practical Guide. Retrieved from http://globalcompact.pt/images/pdf/Practical_Guide_SDG_Reporting_08_2018.pdf

Valenzuela Fernández, L., Jara Bertín, M., & Villegas Pineaur, F. (2015). Prácticas de Responsabilidad Social, reputación corporativa y desempeño financiero. *RAE-Revista de Administração de Empresas*, *55*(3), 329–344. doi:10.1590/S0034-759020150308

Van Marrewijk, M. (2013). Concepts and definitions of CSR and corporate sustainability: between agency and communion. *Journal of Business Ethics*, 641–655.

Vance, S. C. (1975). Are socially responsible corporations good investment risks? *Management Review*, *64*, 18–24.

Varadarajan, P.R., & Menon, A. (1988). Cause-related marketing: A coalignment of marketing strategy and corporate philanthropy. *Journal of Marketing*, *52*(3), 58–74. doi:10.1177/002224298805200306

Varela, R., & Bedoya, O. (2006). Modelo conceptual de desarrollo empresarial basado en competencias. *Revista Estudios Generales*, *22*(100), 21–47.

Vázquez-Carrasco, R., & López-Pérez, M. E. (2013). Small & medium-sized enterprises and Corporate Social Responsibility: A systematic review of the literature. *Quality & Quantity*, *47*(6), 3205–3218. doi:10.100711135-012-9713-4

Veiga, J. E. (2009). Indicadores socioambientais: Evolução e perspectivas. *Revista de Economia Política*, *29*(4), 421–435. doi:10.1590/S0101-31572009000400007

Velte, P., & Stawinoga, M. (2017). Integrated reporting: The current state of empirical research, limitations and future research implications. *Journal of Management Control*, *28*(3), 275–320. doi:10.100700187-016-0235-4

Vialine. (2016). *Corporate information.* Retrieved from http://www.vialine.es

Villafañe, J. (2001). La reputación corporativa como factor de liderazgo. *Área Abierta*, (1), 4.

Vitola, F., Raimo, N., & Rubino, M. (2017). Appreciations, criticisms, determinants, and effects of integrated reporting: A systematic literature review. *Corporate Social Responsibility and Environmental Management*, *26*(2), 518–528. doi:10.1002/csr.1734

Viz-Blanco. M.J. (2016, April 13). *El radar solidario*. Retrieved from http://www.elcorreogallego.es

Votaw, D. (1972). Genius becomes rare: A comment on the doctrine of social responsibility pt. 1. *California Management Review*, *150*(2), 25–31. doi:10.2307/41164415

Waddock, S. A., & Graves, B. (1997). The corporate social performance-financial performance link'. *Strategic Management Journal*, *18*(4), 303–319. doi:10.1002/(SICI)1097-0266(199704)18:4<303::AID-SMJ869>3.0.CO;2-G

Waddock, S., & Graves, S. (1997). The corporate social performance-financial performance link. *Strategic Management Journal*, *18*(4), 303–319. doi:10.1002/(SICI)1097-0266(199704)18:4<303::AID-SMJ869>3.0.CO;2-G

Wagner, M. (2010). Corporate Social Performance and Innovation with High Social Benefits: A Quantitative Analysis. *Journal of Business Ethics*, *94*(4), 581–594. doi:10.100710551-009-0339-y

Wahba, H. (2014). Capital structure, managerial ownership and firm performance: Evidence from Egypt. *The Journal of Management and Governance*, *18*(4), 1041–1061. doi:10.100710997-013-9271-8

Waldman, D. A., De Luque, M. S., Washburn, N., House, R. J., Adetoun, B., Barrasa, A., ... Dorfman, P. (2006). Cultural and leadership predictors of corporate social responsibility values of top management: A GLOBE study of 15 countries. *Journal of International Business Studies*, *37*(6), 823–837. doi:10.1057/palgrave.jibs.8400230

Wang, Y., (2017). Taking Corporate Social Responsibility as Growth Strategy. doi:10.5772/intechopen.6902800

Wang, H., Tong, L., Takeuchi, R., & George, G. (2016). Corporate social responsibility: An overview and new research directions: Thematic issue on corporate social responsibility. *Academy of Management Journal*, *59*(2), 534–544. doi:10.5465/amj.2016.5001

Wang, M. (2017). The relationship between firm characteristics and the disclosure of sustainability reporting. *Sustainability*, *9*(4), 624. doi:10.3390u9040624

Wang, Q., Dou, J., & Jia, S. (2016). A Meta-Analytic Review of Corporate Social Responsibility and Corporate Financial Performance. *Business & Society*, *55*(8), 1083–1121. doi:10.1177/0007650315584317

Wang, R., Zhou, S., & Wang, T. (2019). Corporate Governance, Integrated Reporting and the Use of Credibility-enhancing Mechanisms on Integrated Reports. *European Accounting Review*, 1–33. doi:10.1080/09638180.2019.1668281

Wang, S., & Gao, Y. (2016). What do we know about corporate social responsibility research? a content analysis. *Irish Journal of Management*, *35*(1), 1–16. doi:10.1515/ijm-2016-0001

Wang, Z., Hsieh, T. S., & Sarkis, J. (2018). CSR Performance and the Readability of CSR Reports: Too Good to be True? *Corporate Social Responsibility and Environmental Management*, *25*(1), 66–79. doi:10.1002/csr.1440

Wang, Z., & Sarkis, J. (2017). Corporate social responsibility governance, outcomes, and financial performance. *Journal of Cleaner Production*, *162*, 1607–1616. doi:10.1016/j.jclepro.2017.06.142

Watson, S. (2011). Conflict diamonds, legitimacy and media agenda: An examination of annual report disclosures. *Meditari Accountancy Research*, *19*(1), 94–111. doi:10.1108/10222521111178655

Weber, O. (2017). Corporate sustainability and financial performance of Chinese banks. *Sustainability. Accounting. Management and Policy Journal*, *8*(3), 358–385.

Wei, Z., Shen, Zhou, H. & Li, J.J. (2017). How does environmental corporate social responsibility matter in a dysfunctional institutional environment? Evidence from China. *Journal of Business Ethics, 140*(2), 209-223.

Wen, Y. (2015). Money, liquidity and welfare. *European Economic Review, 76*, 1–24. doi:10.1016/j.euroecorev.2015.01.012

Wheeler, C., Colbert, B., & Freeman, R. E. (2003). Focusing on value: Reconciling corporate social responsibility, sustainability and a stakeholder approach in a network world. *Journal of General Management, 28*(3), 1–28. doi:10.1177/030630700302800301

Wigmore-Álvarez, A., & Ruiz-Lozano, M. (2014). The United Nations Global Compact Progress Reports as Management Control Instruments for Social Responsibility at Spanish Universities. *SAGE Open*, (April-June): 2–12.

Williamson, D., & Lynch-Wood, G. (2008). Social and environmental reporting in UK company law and the issue of legitimacy. *Corporate Governance: The International Journal of Business in Society, 8*(2), 128–140. doi:10.1108/14720700810863760

Williamson, D., Lynch-Wood, G., & Ramsay, J. (2006). Drivers of Environmental Behavior in Manufacturing SME and the Implications for CSR. *Journal of Business Ethics, 67*(3), 317–330. doi:10.100710551-006-9187-1

Wilmshurst, T. D., & Frost, G. R. (2000). Corporate environmental reporting. a test of Legitimacy Theory. *Accounting, Auditing & Accountability Journal, 13*(1), 10–26. doi:10.1108/09513570010316126

Windsor, D. (2001). The future of corporate social responsibility. *The International Journal of Organizational Analysis, 9*(3), 225–256. doi:10.1108/eb028934

Witchkonska, J. (2016). Corporate Social Responsibility: Selected Theoretical and Empirical Aspects. *Comparative Economic Research, 19*(1), 28–43.

Wong, K., Meng, T. W., Kiat, Y. B. A., & Gledhill, L.L.P. (2018). *Practical Law*. Thomson Reuters. Retrieved from https://uk.practicallaw.thomsonreuters.com/7-637-5107?transitionType=Default&contextData=(sc.Default)&firstPage=true&comp=pluk&bhcp=1#co_anchor_a734811

Wong, C. A., & Laschinger, H. K. S. (2013). Authentic leadership, performance, and job satisfaction: The mediating role of empowerment. *Journal of Advanced Nursing, 69*(4), 947–959. doi:10.1111/j.1365-2648.2012.06089.x PMID:22764828

Wood, D. J. (1991). Corporate Social Performance Revisited. *Academy of Management Review, 16*(4), 691–718. doi:10.5465/amr.1991.4279616

World Business Council for Sustainable Development. Corporate Social Responsibility: meeting changing expectations. WBCSD Publications, 2001. Retrieved from http://old.wbcsd.org/pages/edocument/edocumentdetails.aspx?id=82&nosearchcontextkey=true

Wu, W., Liu, Y., Chin, T., & Zhu, W. (2018). Will Green CSR Enhance Innovation? A Perspective of Public Visibility and Firm Transparency. *International Journal of Environmental Research and Public Health, 15*(2), 268. doi:10.3390/ijerph15020268 PMID:29401714

Yang, T., & Zhao, S. (2014). CEO duality and Firm performance: Evidence from an exogenous shock to the competitive environment. *Journal of Banking & Finance, 49*, 534–552. doi:10.1016/j.jbankfin.2014.04.008

Yasser, Q. R., Mamun, A. A., & Suriya, A. R. (2014). CEO duality structure and firm performance in Pakistan. *Asian Journal of Accounting and Governance, 5*(1), 57–68. doi:10.17576/AJAG-2014-5-05

Yassine, A., & Ibenrissoul, A. (2018). Pratiques de la Responsabilité Sociale dans les entreprises marocaines cotées: analyse du modèle quadridimensionnel de Carroll (1991) et application au cas marocain. Retrieved from https://hal.archives-ouvertes.fr/hal-01728603v2

Yeoh, J. (2005). Compliance with mandatory disclosure requirements by New Zealand listed companies. *Advances in International Accounting*, *18*, 245–262. doi:10.1016/S0897-3660(05)18012-X

Yermack, D. (1996). Higher market valuation of companies with a small board of directors. *Journal of Financial Economics*, *40*(2), 185–211. doi:10.1016/0304-405X(95)00844-5

Yin, R. K. (2010). Estudo de caso: planejamento e métodos (4th ed.). Porto Alegre: Bookman.

Yin, R. K. (2009). *Case Study Research - Design and Methods* (4th ed.). Thousand Oaks, CA: Sage.

Yoon, B., & Chung, Y. S. (2018). The effects of corporate social responsibility on firm performance: A stakeholder approach. *Journal of Hospitality and Tourism Management*, *37*, 89–96. doi:10.1016/j.jhtm.2018.10.005

Yuriev, A., Boiral, O., Francoeur, V., & Paillé, P. (2018). Overcoming the barriers to proenvironmental behaviors in the workplace: A systematic review. *Journal of Cleaner Production*, *182*, 379–394. doi:10.1016/j.jclepro.2018.02.041

Yusoff, H., Othman, R., & Yatim, N. (2014). Culture and accountants' perceptions of environmental reporting practice. *Business Strategy and the Environment*, *23*(7), 433–446. doi:10.1002/bse.1793

Zahra, S. A., Hayton, J. C., Neubaum, D. O., Dibrell, C., & Craig, J. (2008). Culture of family commitment and strategic flexibility: The moderating effect of stewardship. *Entrepreneurship Theory and Practice*, *32*(6), 1035–1054. doi:10.1111/j.1540-6520.2008.00271.x

Zeitun, R., & Tian, G. G. (2007). Capital structure and corporate performance: Evidence from Jordan. *Australasian Accounting. Business and Finance Journal*, *1*(4), 41–61.

Zeng, S., Xu, X., Dong, Z., & Tamb, V. (2010). Towards corporate environmental disclosure: An empirical study in China. *Journal of Cleaner Production*, *18*(12), 1142–1148. doi:10.1016/j.jclepro.2010.04.005

Zhang, Q., Oo, B. L., & Lim, B. T. H. (2019). Drivers, motivations, and barriers to the implementation of corporate social responsibility practices by construction enterprises: A review. *Journal of Cleaner Production*, *210*, 563–584. doi:10.1016/j.jclepro.2018.11.050

Zhou, S., Simnett, R., & Green, W. (2017). Does integrated reporting matter to the capital market? *Abacus*, *53*(1), 94–132. doi:10.1111/abac.12104

Zhou, Z., Luo, B. N., & Tang, T. L. P. (2018). Corporate social responsibility excites 'exponential' positive employee engagement: The matthew effect in CSR and sustainable policy. *Corporate Social Responsibility and Environmental Management*, *25*(4), 339–354. doi:10.1002/csr.1464

Zhou, Z., Zhou, H., Peng, D., Chen, X., & Li, S. (2018). Carbon disclosure, financial transparency, and agency cost: Evidence form Chinese manufacturing listed companies. *Emerging Markets Finance & Trade*, *54*(12), 2669–2686. doi:10.1080/1540496X.2018.1428796

Zorio-Grima, A., Sierra-García, L., & Garcia-Benau, M. A. (2018). Sustainability reporting experience by universities: A causal configuration approach. *International Journal of Sustainability in Higher Education*, *19*(2), 337–352. doi:10.1108/IJSHE-07-2016-0142

Zubeltzu-Jaka, E., Andicoechea-Arondo, L., & Alvarez Etxeberria, I. (2018). Corporate social responsibility and corporate governance and corporate financial performance: Bridging concepts for a more ethical business model. *Business Strategy & Development*, *1*(3), 214–222. doi:10.1002/bsd2.29

About the Contributors

Inna Sousa Paiva, PhD in Accounting, is an Assistant Professor in the Instituto Univeritário de Lisboa (ISCTE-IUL) and Vice Dean of ISCTE Business School. She has considerable academic experience in programs in financial accounting area. Her research interests are the implementation of international financial reporting standards and accounting quality and family firms. Researcher at Business Research Unit (BRU-IUL), she is the author of several publications in national and international journals, books and book chapters.

Luísa Carvalho has a PhD in Management from the University of Évora – Portugal. Professor of Management on Department of Economics and Management, Institute Polytecnic of Setubal, Portugal. Guest professor in international universities teaches in courses of master and PhDs programs. Researcher at CEFAGE (Center for Advanced Studies in Management and Economics) University of Evora, Portugal. Author of several publications in national and international journals, books, and book chapters.

* * *

Rodrigo Almeida has a Master's in Accounting (controller) (2018), graduated in Accounting (2015), Specialist in Administration (2011) and Graduate in Strategic Management of Organizations (2008). He has worked in Commercial, Industrial and Associations in the areas of controller, planning, budgeting, internal audit, suppliers and legal services (contracts). Participates in the NAF / UEM - Center for Accounting and Fiscal Support, an extension project. Short-term objectives: to act as a professor (accounting and administration) and in the corporate sphere in the area of sustainability (socioenvironmental accounting, sustainability reports and integrated reporting). Interests in research are on corporate social responsibility, integrated reporting, reference form, information asymmetry, legitimacy theory, stakeholder theory, credit unions and cooperatives, innovation, accounting for external users, controller, and managerial accounting.

Sandra Alves has a PhD in Accounting from the University of Aveiro, and a MSc in Accounting and Finance from Aberta University. She is an Adjunct Professor in the University of Aveiro, at the Higher Institute of Accounting and Administration. She lectures subjects of corporate accounting and financial accounting and reporting, in undergraduate and graduate courses of accounting.

Graça Azevedo holds a PhD in Management with a specialization in Accounting from the Higher Institute of Labor and Business Sciences - ISCTE (2006). She was Director of the Master's Degree in Accounting (2007-2015) and member of the Scientific Committee of the PhD in Accounting (2006 to 2009 and 2012 to 2015). She is Coordinating Professor at ISCA-UA where she has taught several curricular units, such as Accounting Regulation, Research Methodologies, Dissertation I, Advanced Accounting, Advanced Financial Accounting, Professional Project, Accounting Theory, Financial Accounting and Accounting Topics. In addition to teaching, he has also supervised master's dissertations and doctoral theses in the area of Financial Accounting. She has published several academic books and articles in national and international journals, such as the International Journal of Academic Research in Accounting, Finance and Management Sciences, Agricultural Finance Review, Academic Journal of Economic Studies, Journal of Business & Economic Policy and Revista Iberoamericana de Management Accounting. She is a member of the Editorial Board of the Accounting and Finance Research magazine and of the Scientific Committee Board of the Academic Journal of Economic Studies. She is an integrated member of the Accounting and Tax Research Center. Her research interests include: Accounting standardization; Financial Information Disclosure; Social responsibility; Integrated Reporting; Financial reports; Impression Management; Corporate Governance; Intellectual capital.

Rui Bertuzi da Silva holds a PhD in Business Sciences - Specialization in Management. The PhD thesis had been developed in the Corporate Social Responsibility field. He currently holds a position as an Invited Senior Lecturer at the same institution, lecturing on General Accounting, Financial Accounting, Sectoral Accounting, Corporate Social Responsibility, Financial Instruments Accounting, Fundamentals of Economics and Accounting, and others. In the field of research, he has supervised and been a jury in several Master's viva voce examinations and has been involved in lifelong learning projects regarding business related topics (business transfer, intercultural innovation, entrepreneurship, etc.). In addition, he is the author and co-author of scientific papers published in national and international journals, presented papers at national and international conferences and has been part of scientific committees in some international conferences. His main research interests are social responsibility, disclosure, and accounting.

Maria Braz graduated in Management and Master's in Accounting, both from the ISCTE Business School. Developing professional skills as risk analyst in a prestigious financial institution. Experience in talks in professional and scientific events.

Valéria Bressan is an Associate Professor in the Department of Accounting and Current Coordinator of the Center for Postgraduate Studies and Research in Controller and Accounting (CEPCON) at FACE / UFMG. Graduated in Administration with a degree in Cooperatives (1995-1999) from the UFV, a master's degree (2000-2002), a doctore (2006-2009) and a Ph.D. (2010) in Applied Economics from the Federal University of Viçosa. She was a full member of the education, Research and Extension Board (CEPE) of UFMG and member of the Research Chamber of UFMG (2016-2019). In addition to being a member of the Minas Gerais's Observatory of Cooperativism and the Brazilian Network of Cooperative Researchers. She is a reviewer of several scientific journals and coordinator of two CNPq research groups. She was president of the Advisory Committee on Applied Social Sciences at UFMG (05/2016- 04/2018), member of the Advisory Committee of Applied Social Sciences of UFMG from 01/2015 to 05/2018, and was coordinator of the undergraduate course in Accounting Sciences of FACE / UFMG (12/2014 to 12/2016). Constantly develops research projects with funding from development agencies, with specialization in the area of cooperativism. First winner of the ABDE-IDB Award in the area of Credit Development and Cooperativism in 2017 and 2018. She has experience in Credit Unions, working mainly on the following topics: Efficiency, Performance, Economic and Social Impacts, Corporate Governance, Evaluation Financial Analysis, Financial Statement Analysis, Results Management, Controller and Finance and Quantitative Methods Applied to Accounting and Finance.

Juan de la Cruz Sánchez Domínguez has a double degree in Business Administration and Economics, and a Master's Degree of Research in Economics, Management, and International Trade. He also has knowledge of English, German, Portuguese, and French. He is now doing his PhD thesis in corporate social responsibility.

M. Mercedes Galán-Ladero is an Associate Professor (Prof. Contratado Doctor) in the Department of Business Management & Sociology, at the University of Extremadura (Spain), where she teaches Marketing courses. She is currently engaged in innovative research in the areas of cause-related marketing and CSR, as well as social marketing and non-profit marketing; ethnocentrism, local food products and their internationalization, manufacturer brands and private labels.

Clementina Galera-Casquet is an Associate Professor (Prof. Titular de Universidad) in the Department of Business Management & Sociology, at the University of Extremadura (Spain), where she teaches Marketing courses (Master and Doctoral levels). She is currently engaged in innovative research in the areas of cause-related marketing and CSR, as well as non-profit marketing.

Dolores Gallardo Vazquez is a Lecturer and researcher in the Department of Financial Economy and Accounting at the Faculty of Economics Sciences and Business Administration at the University of Extremadura. She is an Economist specialized in Financial Accounting, Intellectual Capital and Corporate Social Responsibility, Expert in Implementation of International Accounting Standards, MSc in Training as university teaching in the European Higher Education, MSc in Management of Higher Education Institutions; Fellowship at Cranfield University based on a competitive aid from Spanish Government. She has managed the orientation and teacher training service at the university for four years. Now, she is managing the university social responsibility office. Her research interests range across several key areas within intellectual capital, corporate social responsibility, corporate volunteering, university social responsibility, social entrepreneurship, and social innovation. She has published in various peer reviewed journals, books, international conferences proceedings and monographs. She has also held lectureships at a wide variety of academic institutions.

Irina Gavancha is a manager of a portfolio of corporate clients, non-real estate sector and characterized as non-performing loans, at Caixa Geral de Depósitos, Portugal, with a degree in business management from the Instituto Politécnico de Santarém, Portugal, master's degree in accounting and taxation of the Universidade Lusófona de Humanidades e Tecnologia de Lisboa, Portugal, and PhD student in management with specialization in accounting at Instituto Universitário de Lisboa (ISCTE-IUL). She has authored a per-reviewed paper on credit risk analysis in mortgage lending, chapters on determinants of sustainability reporting in midsize companies, and disclosure of corporate social responsibility is associated with company performance. Key interests include credit risk analysis, financial reporting, and the relationship between accounting and sustainability.

Souhaila Kammoun is an assistant-Professor at IHEC of Sfax and researcher at CODECI, University of Sfax, Tunisia. She got her Phd in Economics at the University of Social Sciences of Toulouse 1, France. She has taught Economics at the University of Social Sciences of Toulouse as a Temporary Lecturer and Research Assistant. She has also taught Economics in several university institutions in Tunisia namely Microeconomics, Macroeconomics, Management and Economy of Innovation, Immaterial Economy, Digital Economy. Her research interests focus on Innovation, Dynamic Capabilities, Corporate Social Responsibility, Foreign Direct Investment and Fintechs. She has published a number of research articles in international journals and collective books. She is also the author of a book entitled: Innovation et compétences pour innover des firmes: Modélisation du comportement innovant dans l'industrie française (Editions Universitaires Européennes, 2015). She is currently an active member of the executive board of the Association Université-Environnement, at the University of Sfax. She was a member of the PAQ-ES project committee, director of the Master's degree in Entrepreneurship and International Development (Tempus Project funded by the European Union) and member of the scientific council at IHEC of Sfax. She was also president of the teachers' association at IHEC. She has held the positions of Head of the Department of Economics, Director of Studies and Vice-Director. She was also Director of IHEC of Sfax, Tunisia.

Kátia Lemos has a PhD in Accounting (University of Santiago de Compostela), Master's in Accounting and Auditing (University of Minho). Adjunct Professor of the School of Management (ESG) of the Polytechnic Institute of Cávado and Ave (IPCA) in the area of Financial Accounting. She is director of the Accounting and Taxation Department of the School of Management.

Ana Lopes has a Doctor in Management, with specialization in Accounting. Assistant Professor at ISCTE-IUL, Lisbon, Portugal. Professor and Researcher, she has vast experience in executive education. Director of the Master in Accounting and of the Post-graduate in Advanced Financial Accounting. Experienced in talks in seminars and other professional and scientific events, she is the author of a book on accounting, and author or co-author of papers published in prestigious journals (e.g., Australian Journal of Management, Accounting Education, European Business Review, Meditari Accountancy Research).

Maria Carolina Martins Rodrigues, International PhD in Management, University of Extremadura, Spain. Post-graduate in Knowledge management, University of Belgrano, Buenos Aires, Argentina, and a research fellow of CIEO (Algarve University). Her research interests currently are tourism; sustainability, economia circular, green knowledge, green intellectual capital, innovation, knowledge management, entrepreneurship, social responsibility, business models, business intelligence, business incubators, and Smart Cities. She is co-authored over 20 articles and book chapters and published in several scientific journals. She has also organised the Iberian Conference on Entrepreneurship and international Conferences of Sustainability and Innovation. Founder member and vice-president of the direction of Empreend - Portuguese Association for Entrepreneurship. Member of the direction of ARPIAC – Retirees, Pensioners and Elderly Association of Agualva-Cacém. She was Teacher in University Aberta (UAb), and University Moderna. In TAX Administration was Tax Administration Technician Advisor acting as coordinator in the International Relations Services Directorate (DSRI) and was Head of the Tax Service.

Albertina Paula Monteiro is an assistant professor of Porto Accounting and Business School. Her main areas of research are accounting, entrepreneurship, strategic management, and internationalization. She has published at international conferences and in the Baltic Journal of Management, the Euromed Journal of Business, the Journal of International Business and Entrepreneurship Development, and the Journal of Innovation & Knowledge.

Sónia Monteiro has a PhD in Accounting (University of Santiago de Compostela), Master in Accounting and Auditing (University of Minho). Professor Coordinator of the School of Management (ESG) of the Polytechnic Institute of Cávado and Ave (IPCA) in the area of Accounting, and coordinator of the disciplinary area of Financial Accounting and director of the Master's in Accounting and Finance. Director of the IPCA's Center for Research in Accounting and Taxation, and coordinator in the research line of Accounting and Social Responsibility.

Marguit Neumann graduated in Accounting (2003), Specialist in Management Accounting (2006), Master's in Development (2007). Doctorate at Development Economics from the Federal University of Rio Grande do Sul (UFRGS) and Sciences Economics from the University of Grenoble / France (2011). She is currently an effective professor at the State University of Maringá (UEM) in the Department of Accounting Sciences.

Verónica Ribeiro has a PhD in Accounting (University of Santiago de Compostela) and Master in Accounting and Administration (University of Minho). Professor Coordinator of the School of Management (ESG) of the Polytechnic Institute of Cávado and Ave (IPCA) in the area of Accounting and coordinator of the disciplinary area of Analitical and Management Accounting. Member of the IPCA's Center for Research in Accounting and Taxation in the research line of Accounting and Social Responsibility.

Simone Sanches graduated in accounting from the State University of Maringá (2000), master's in Administration from State University of Maringá (2003) and doctorate at Administration from Federal University of Rio Grande do Sul (2013). She is currently professor adjunto at the State University of Maringá. Department of Accounting Sciences (DCC) and Post-Graduate Program in Accounting (PCO), State University of Maringá (UEM). Topics of interest: financial accounting, integrated reporting, small and medium enterprises, accounting information governance, accounting research paradigms, interdisciplinary studies between financial accounting, economics, and corporate finance.

Luis Valdez is a research professor in the faculty of economic and administrative sciences of the Technological Institute (ITSON) since 2008. He has a doctorate in Business Administration and Management. He is currently responsible for the research body Management and Business Development of ITSON Guaymas and responsible for the Northwest region of the FAEDPYME International Network and is an active member of the CUMEX research network. His research lines are: entrepreneurship and human capital, corporate social responsibility, and marketing. He has been reviewer of the journals of SCIENCEDOMAIN international, Journal Economics Management and Trade of the USA, Journal of Information and Knowledge Management of the USA, Journal FAEDPYME of Spain, Journal Cuadernos de Investigación of Colombia and Journal Conciencia UAT México.

José Vale is a professor at the Polytechnic of Porto, Portugal, where he teaches several courses related to management accounting. He is PhD in management – specialized in accounting and management control, and MSc in administration and management. Also, he holds an MBA in commercial operation management. He is also a member of the Porto Polytechnic's Centre for Organisational and Social Studies, and a member of the Portuguese Centre of Studies of the Population, Economy and Society. His research interests are focused in the areas of intellectual capital (namely regarding its disclosure), social responsibility, and accounting.

Index

T

U

W

www.ingramcontent.com/pod-product-compliance
Lightning Source LLC
LaVergne TN
LVHW060409300926
849162LV00006B/1378